Perry

Happy Birthday!
Best Wishes
Priscilla & Buma

# WALTER &
# ALBERTINA
# SISULU

## IN OUR LIFETIME

# WALTER & ALBERTINA
# SISULU

## IN OUR
## LIFETIME

To Perry Calderwood
Best wishes for 2003
Elinor Sisulu
24/12/2002

*Foreword by*
NELSON MANDELA

DAVID PHILIP
PUBLISHERS

ELINOR SISULU

First published in 2002 in southern Africa
by David Philip Publishers,
an imprint of New Africa Books (Pty) Ltd,
99 Garfield Road, Claremont 7700,
South Africa

ISBN 0-86486-323-3

PRINCIPAL EDITOR: Helen Moffett
MANAGING EDITOR: Sean Fraser
CONSULTING EDITORS: Barry Feinberg,
Joyce Sikhakhane-Rankin and Luli Callinicos
DESIGN: Peter Bosman
BIBLIOGRAPHER: Ethel Kriger
PROOFREADER: Tessa Kennedy
PROOFREADER (XHOSA): Malusi M Mpulwana
INDEXER: Mary Lennox
REPRODUCTION BY Virtual Colour, Cape Town
PRINTED AND BOUND BY ABC Press

PHOTOGRAPHY
COVER: Peter Maltbie (centre); Bailey's African History Archives
(top left); Bailey's African History Archives (top right); Sisulu Family
Collection (spine); Jürgen Schadeberg (back flap)
PRELIMINARY PAGES: Mayibuye Centre (endpapers);
Private Collection: Rica Hodgson (title page)
PART OPENERS: Part 1 Peter Magubane; Part 2 Eli Weinberg;
Part 3 Mayibuye Centre; Part 4 International Defence and Aid Fund;
Part 5 Rica Hodgson
PHOTOGRAPHIC PORTFOLIO: As individually credited

# CONTENTS

# FOREWORD

If we as a liberation movement and a nation were to be given the choice of one life story to be told, that story would have to be Walter Sisulu's. In his life and the work of his life are captured and demonstrated the best, the noblest, the most heroic, the most deeply humane that our movement and our country represent and seek to represent.

It is universally agreed that our liberation struggle was one of the great moral struggles of the 20th century. For 90 years it has been fighting uncompromisingly for the liberation of our country and the emancipation of its people. Great freedom fighters – men and women of exceptional courage and commitment – have played their roles in making our movement what it is. Among those, the name of Walter Sisulu stands supreme: a giant and cornerstone of our movement.

When we talk about how entirely Walter has given, we cannot for one moment forget Albertina, who was such an integral part of that giving. Their stories have become one in this history of the struggle. Theirs is a partnership of 58 years, a marriage in the service of the struggle. Albertina Sisulu is one of those women who suffered immensely and who struggled heroically without ever flinching. In the dark days after the Rivonia Trial, she was one of the key links between the internal and external movement, and kept the embers of resistance alive.

This book pays due tribute to the life of this couple of freedom fighters, whose consistency and faithfulness to the struggle for freedom and justice has been legendary. This book puts in proper historical perspective their places in the South African story.

Walter and Albertina Sisulu have lived through and witnessed the major events of the last century that shaped South Africa. What is more important is that he was a key participant in decisively shaping and making that history.

Often in addressing younger people, I make the point that what counts in life is not the mere fact that we have lived – it is what difference we have made to the lives of others that determines the significance of the life we lead. There can be no greater and more inspiring example in the history of our organisation, and hence of our country, than Walter and Albertina Sisulu: a couple whose every deed speaks of leadership that made the kind of difference that brought us to where we are today as a country and as a people.

There are those among us who, after the attainment of democracy, have held high positions in government and public life and who have received awards and accolades from across the world. Walter Sisulu never held a position as a Member of Parliament or in the executive branch of government, and relatively few international awards or prizes came his way; yet his greatness as leader and freedom fighter is beyond dispute or argument. He was so at one with the struggle he led and participated in that it required no awards or position to affirm it.

Of course, on a personal level I can tell of a relationship – a friendship and comradeship – that was profoundly formative in my life. The unstinting commitment to the common good and to the service of the people completely filled the life of Walter Sisulu and deeply touched those like ourselves.

There are so many examples I can quote of the wisdom and leadership qualities of Walter. In all of those instances, he demonstrated the ability to see the broader picture and to project himself beyond the immediate considerations on which we found ourselves focusing.

His home was the meeting place for that generation of young men whose fierce debates and arguments provided important impetus to the birth of the ANC Youth League. Walter was central to that circle: he was the magnet that drew us all together.

That was Walter's hallmark: an ability to attract and work together with highly competent and talented young people, a ready sounding board for ideas. He was a powerful influence who exuded respect for their talents; he was a born diplomat. He was courageous, too, and his quiet self-confidence and clarity of vision marked him as a leader among us. He never asked of others what he was not prepared to do himself. Walter and Albertina have unstintingly devoted their lives to the struggle and to the people.

Neither can their family be forgotten. The Sisulus count among the many families who have suffered severely and who gave most selflessly of themselves.

The telling of the story of Walter and Albertina is more than a record; it is a lodestar for our future. While the circumstances and the specific nature of the challenges in our country might have changed, the task of our organisation remains much the same: to lead the country in creating a better life for all our people, particularly the poor. The cardinal attributes of Walter and Albertina remain as important to emulate today as they ever were. The absolute selflessness with which they gave their lives to the struggle is especially important to remember and hold dear as new conditions create the temptations of self-interest and personal enrichment. Their discipline in service of the organisation and the people must serve as an abiding example.

It is time that this story of our nation be told.

*Mandela*

NELSON ROLIHLAHLA MANDELA

# ACKNOWLEDGEMENTS

This book has been nine years in the making, a journey of epic proportions and one which would not have been possible without the guidance, encouragement and support of numerous individuals and institutions along the way.

First of all, I would like to thank my husband Max, who made sure that I took the first step of the journey, and my brother-in-law Mlungisi and my sisters-in-law, Sheila Sisulu and Beryl Simelane, who pushed me forward when I hesitated.

Any journey, especially one this lengthy, requires a huge amount of preparation before the first step can be taken. With hindsight, I realise the preparation began in my childhood when my mother, Betty Quinche, instilled in me a love of family history and genealogy. I am also deeply grateful to her for the struggles she waged to ensure that I received the best possible education. I am indebted to all the people, too numerous to mention here, whose input at some stage of my formative years helped to equip me for this mammoth task. In particular, I would like to acknowledge Ibbo Mandaza, Thandika Mkandawire and Zenebeworke Tadesse, who had a profound influence on me at a crucial stage in my intellectual development. I am also deeply grateful to Grace Robinson, whose unshakeable confidence in me pushed me to pick up the pen and write.

I would like to acknowledge the Ford Foundation for the book grant that enabled me to embark on this project. Special mention must be made of John Gerhart, the first director of the Ford Foundation office in South Africa, for his personal commitment to this project. Thanks to his efforts, I was privileged to spend six months as the 1993 Radcliffe International Visitor to the Mary Ingraham Bunting Institute in Cambridge, Massachussets. It was here that I was able to start substantive work on this project. I will be forever grateful to Florence Ladd, then the Director of the Bunting Institute, for her wisdom, guidance and hospitality during my stay. She made my time at the Bunting a magical experience. I benefited immensely from the time spent with a group of creative and dedicated women. To my "sister fellows" of 1993, especially Shanti Singham, Kiana Davenport, Linda Stout and Ellen Rothenberg – thank you for your love and support.

My work and stay in the United States was made easier by my dear friend Mary Tiseo in Boston, who assisted me in so many ways, and Ntsiki Langford in New York, who mobilised material support when I experienced financial difficulties. I am grateful for the hospitality and encouragement of Bob, Anne and Katha Seidman, Tom Levensen, Vukani Magubane, Tony and Mary Earls, Pamela and Wellington Nyangoni, Heeten Kalan, Emma Rothschild and Susan Dranoff, in Massachussets; Karen Brown at the Poynter Institute in Tampa, Florida; Dr Juel Smith at the Centre for Black Life at the University of South Florida; Nel Gibson and the Union of Black Episcopalians in New York; and Jennifer Davis, Rachel Kagan and the Africa Fund in New York. My thanks to John Taylor Williams, and to Lane Zachary for her encouragement and interest in this project in its earliest stages.

Throughout the research and writing of this book I have enjoyed the support and encouragement of friends both here and abroad. Space does not allow me to mention them all; they know who are they, and I sincerely hope that they also know how much their contributions have meant to me. I must acknowledge, however, the contribution of those who, sadly, are not here to celebrate the completion of this book: Gwen McMaster, Kate Truscott, Zine Chitepo, Esi Honono and Sue Sparks.

In 1998, I had the benefit of a three-month stint as an associate at the African Gender Institute (AGI) at the University of Cape Town. Lynne Rhode, Desiree Lewis and Zimitri Erasmus helped to make my associateship a useful and enjoyable one. I am also indebted to the staff of the African Studies Library at UCT. I continued to benefit from the support of the AGI when I spent several months at All Africa House at UCT in 2001. I am grateful to the AGI staff and the director, Professor Amina Mama. My thanks again to Desiree Lewis, Elaine Salo, Ginny Volbrecht and Cheryl Anne Michaels for making my stay in Cape Town a pleasant one. I am also thankful to the staff of All Africa House, especially Latchme Basson, for their assistance.

One of the difficulties of writing a book over a long period of time is finding "a room of one's own". I am grateful to Gail Gerhart for recognising this and organising office space for me at the University of the Witwatersrand. Gail also directed me to some valuable sources and did me the great favour of putting me in touch with Robert Edgar, who has been a constant source of help and inspiration. I thank them both for their sterling contribution to the preservation of South Africa's struggle history. I have also benefited from discussions with fellow writers and biographers, including Anthony Sampson, Jon Hyslop, Mark Gevisser and Ronald Suresh Roberts. My profound gratitude to my friends Nuruddin Farah, Amina Mama and Willie Kgositsile for confidence-building exercises, practical advice and moral support.

In Pretoria, Yvonne Muthien went out of her way to arrange for a space for me at the South African Development Education Trust (SADET), where I benefited from interaction with Professor Bernard Magubane, Greg Houston and Sifiso Ndlovu. I also appreciate the inputs of other members of the SADET network, especially Professor Jabulani Sithole and Nhlanhla Ndebele. I am also grateful to Professor Phil Bonner and the South African History Project, as well as the Institute for Global Dialogue, for hosting my 90th-birthday lecture on Walter Sisulu. My thanks to Riana Niemand, and Bob and Gill Tucker for practical help and logistical support.

I am indebted to the archivists at the Mayibuye Archives at the University of the Western Cape and the staff of what was then the Mayibuye Centre. My thanks also to the Robben Island Museum, especially its former director André Odendaal and researcher Noel Solani. I am especially grateful to George Houser and Herbert Shore for their valuable oral history of Walter Sisulu and their support of this project.

Mike Berning of the Cory Library in Grahamstown was incredibly prompt and helpful in his response to my research queries, and I thank him for putting me in touch with Sandy Rowoldt Shell, who worked diligently on the Sisulu, Thethiwe and Mnyila family trees. I also appreciate the advice and assistance of Omar Badsha of South African History Online and Iqbal Jazbhai of UNISA. My thanks to Xolelwa Kashe Katiya for her assistance with library research and Winnie Nkuma for assembling a fine collection of newspaper cuttings on the Sisulu family. My friend Carol Bloch did me a great favour by introducing me to her mother Una Bloch, who patiently and meticulously translated several thick files bursting with security police and Ministry of Justice reports from Afrikaans into English. It was a mammoth task that constituted a major contribution to the preparation of my manuscript. I am also thankful to translators Margaret Pretorius (Afrikaans into English) and Pamela Maseko and Lulu Mazamisa for their translations of letters and interviews from Xhosa into English. I must also thank Reverend Bongani Ntisane of Loveday Press for permission to use "Mthandi Wesizwe", the poem by John Solilo, and Ntombi Dwane for the translation. Thank you too, to Thulane Simelane and Dennis Brutus for their kind permission to reproduce their poems in this work, as well as Helena Dolny, for allowing us to reproduce Joe Slovo's poem.

The extended families, friends and contemporaries of Walter and Albertina Sisulu have been extremely supportive. I commend Nanziwe Thethiwe for her sterling research on the Thethiwe and Mnyila families. I am grateful to Uncle Stanford Thethiwe, my aunts Miriam Thethiwe and Gcotyelwa in Cape Town, as well as MaRadebe in Qutubeni. I would like to extend my thanks to all family members who were interviewed. As their names are mentioned in the text, I will not repeat them here.

I am also deeply indebted to the Titus family, especially Daisy Mase Titus, Walter's aunt and teacher, for patiently enduring our probing interviews. Many thanks to Mkhumbuzi and Kuku Titus and Sanele and Zingi Titus for their hospitality and logistical support during the research in the Transkei. Special thanks, too, to Stella Titus for her dedicated support, both in the Transkei and in Pretoria. My research for this biography was facilitated by moral and practical support from the African National Congress. I would like to express my appreciation to President Thabo Mbeki for his encouragement. I was spurred on by the question he constantly asked: "When are we getting our book?"

I am grateful to the Secretary-General Kgalema Motlante and his office, his deputy Thenjiwe Mtintso, the Treasurer-General's office and ANC spokesperson Smuts Ngonyama. I would also like to thank those who worked in Walter Sisulu's office when he was ANC Deputy President, especially Rica Hodgson, whose meticulous record-keeping was of immense value to me. My deepest appreciation goes to all the ANC leaders and activists who availed themselves for interviews and I would like to thank all those ANC members mentioned in the bibliography and the text. Thanks also to the Office of the Chief Whip in Parliament, especially Michelle McMaster. I would also like to acknowledge the contribution of members of the South African Communist Party and COSATU. I have greatly appreciated the input of Walter Sisulu's Robben Island comrades, who have been extremely helpful.

There is a group of people whose involvement in this project I can only attribute to divine intervention. Two who immediately come to mind are Joyce Sikhakhane-Rankin and Omar Motani, who in their different ways helped revive this project when it was in limbo. I cannot thank them enough for their friendship, support and encouragement.

Without my publishers, there would be no book and my gratitude to David Philip Publishers is immeasurable. I am especially thankful to Marie and David Philip and Russell Martin, for undertaking to publish this work. I deeply appreciate their patience and understanding during the long years of research. It is one of my regrets that I was not able to deliver this book to them much earlier.

The quality of this book has been enhanced by the excellent photographs, and I am thankful to Peter Maltbie and Tessa Frootko Gordon, and Jürgen and Claudia Schadeberg for their assistance. Thank you to Rita Potenza of South Photos, and to Reedwaan Vally and STE Publishers, and Marie Human, for their diligent photo research, and Lorna Bishop for her assistance with photo research and reproduction and distribution of the draft manuscript. My thanks also to Barbara Ludman and Siwela Mohale of *The Mail & Guardian*. I am grateful to Amina Cachalia for trusting me with precious photographs and for her support and encouragement.

In the final stages of this project, I have felt like one of those runners in the Comrades Marathon, whose legs are giving way as they approach the finishing line, seconds before the cut-off time. It looks as if they will not make it until other runners take hold of them and literally drag them across the finishing line. I am indebted to Brian Wafawarova and Jeremy Boraine, first for establishing the cut-off time and then doing everything possible to ensure that I cross the finishing line.

I am most thankful to Ethel Kriger for undertaking the mammoth chore of compiling the bibliography and Abdul Bermath for cross-checking it. I am grateful to my fellow-biographer Luli

Callinicos and consulting editors, Barry Feinberg and Joyce Sikhakhane-Rankin, for being part of the team that kept me on my feet when I was on the verge of collapse. I am immeasurably indebted to my principal editor, Helen Moffett, not only for her meticulous and painstaking work, but also for doubling up as a psychologist to a demented writer. I have spoken about divine intervention, and in this regard I have been thankful for the appearance of Malusi Mpulwana and Jan Marsh, who made invaluable inputs at a crucial stage of the writing process. In the same vein, I make special mention of Sean Fraser, who went way beyond the call of duty to pull everything together. I have been deeply moved by his commitment and dedication. And, of course, I am eternally grateful to Brenda Brickman, who dealt so patiently and capably with all the last minute crises. Thanks also to Pat Hopking and Nolene Goosen for typing up final drafts and to Pete Bosman for his exquisite cover and overall design.

My thanks, too, to former President Nelson Mandela, Ahmed Kathrada, Mac Maharaj, Mike Dingake and Fikile Bam for their comments on sections of the manuscript. I am grateful for Nelson Mandela's wonderful Foreword, and thankful for his autobiography, *Long Walk to Freedom*, to which I have referred extensively in this narrative.

I sincerely appreciate the assistance of members of my family throughout the process of researching and writing this book. I am thankful to Ntsiki Sisulu for her au pair services and typing services at the start of the project. My son, Mlungisi Jnr, assisted in the research process in the Transkei, while Shaka has provided valuable IT support. I am grateful to my nieces Pam and Zama Simelane, Ntsiki Sisulu and Maseeiso Sisulu for their help with transcribing interviews and typing documents. Palesa Mazamisa doubled up as a child minder and interview transcriber in the final stages. My thanks also to my sister Lucia Batezat for the mountain of documents and interviews she transcribed. I cannot overestimate the value of her contribution. I also appreciate the logistical support received from Linda (Ginyi) Sisulu, Thulane Simelane and Vuyelwa.

I would like to express my appreciation to Rok Ajulu for his contribution to the research process and his incisive critique of sections of the manuscript. I am also grateful to Leonard Simelane for being my first reader, and to Zodwa and Mamkhulu for their moral support. I am thankful to Zwelakhe, Jongumzi, Lindi, Beryl, Nkuli, Mlungisi Snr and Gerald for accommodating my frequent requests for interviews. Mlungisi's wealth of knowledge on the Sisulu family history has been of enormous value to this project and I will always be thankful to him for being just a phone call away whenever I needed some urgent information. I am thankful to Lindi, Nkuli and Beryl for their insights and ability to clarify problematic areas.

I take this opportunity to thank my family in Zimbabwe, especially my parents Betty and Maurice Quinche, my siblings Irene Stuhardt, Trevor and Jeremy Batezat and their families. Their moral support and good-natured tolerance of my neglect of family matters while working on this project is much appreciated. I also tender apologies to my Max, my long-suffering husband, for whose unstinting love, encouragement and support I will be forever grateful. To my children, Vuyisile, Duma and Sandile, I hope in time that your enjoyment of this book will make up for having had to cope with a writing mother.

Finally, there are no words to express my appreciation to Walter and Albertina Sisulu, firstly for trusting me with their story; and secondly, for respecting me as a writer and loving me as a daughter.

ELINOR SISULU

# PROLOGUE

The first time I met Walter Sisulu, I wept for a full 30 minutes. I was mortified. This first meeting with my future father-in-law had been eagerly anticipated on both sides. I had travelled from Harare via Johannesburg to Cape Town for the visit. Within the 40 minutes allocated by the prison authorities, I had to give him news of his exiled son Max, whom he had not seen for over 20 years. He also wanted to know more about this woman from Zimbabwe who was marrying his eldest son, the plans for our pending marriage, as well as hear news of friends and political associates in Lusaka whom he had not seen for decades. I was conscious of all this as I sat in that cold, cement-grey room in Pollsmoor Prison, yet try as I might I could not stem the flow of tears. I was saved from complete humiliation by the sympathetic presence of my future sister-in-law Nonkululeko, who calmly conversed with her father while I struggled to get a grip on my emotions.

I had not known what to expect as we were shepherded by prison warders through the labyrinthine corridors of the prison to the visiting room, a windowless box divided by a waist-high counter topped by a thick glass pane that reached the ceiling. Perched before the counter on high wooden stools, a warder positioned behind us, we waited for the prisoner. After a few minutes, a door on the opposite section of the room opened and a short energetic white-haired man dressed in greenish khaki prison uniform entered, accompanied by two warders. It would not be an exaggeration to say that he was bursting with joy. Despite the glass separating us, I felt as if I had been enveloped in an affectionate embrace. When I had entered Pollsmoor Prison on that morning in March 1986, Walter Sisulu was to me a legendary leader, one of the great fathers of African nationalism who had been in prison since 1964, when I was a mere six years old. Perhaps I had expected someone solemn and serious; instead I was overwhelmed by Walter's joyful exuberance, which seemed so incongruous given the bleak surroundings. I felt as if I had received a lesson in the triumph of the human spirit.

I had experienced the same warm welcome from Albertina Sisulu when I had arrived in Johannesburg the previous week. There was no weighing up or assessment of this future daughter-in-law, just complete acceptance and welcome to a new member of the family. By the end of my visit a powerful bond had developed between myself and my future parents-in-law, a bond that increased during my subsequent visits to South Africa in 1987 and 1988.

Shortly after our marriage in September 1986, Max introduced me to Valentin Gorodnov, a leading Soviet specialist in African history. Among his many books, Gorodnov had produced a substantive history of Soweto, and he was planning to write a biography on Walter and Albertina Sisulu. I found it fascinating that someone could write so authoritatively about a distant place that he had never visited. When he interviewed me about Walter and Albertina Sisulu, I was impressed by his knowledge of their lives and the passion with which he spoke about them, as if they were close friends with whom he had spent a lot of time. Unfortunately for Gorodnov, the dramatic changes that led to the collapse of the Soviet Union forced him to abandon his plans for a Sisulu biography.

My first conscious thought about writing the biography of Walter and Albertina myself surfaced during my visit to South Africa in 1987, when I told them about my interview with Gorodnov. It turned out that one or two writers had approached them for permission to write their life stories. Their response was cautious, mostly because they were concerned about the invasion of privacy that such an exercise would involve. Also, as major players in the turbulent drama of the late 1980s, the writing of their own life stories was not exactly a priority. I thought about how the lives of activists and political leaders like Walter and Albertina Sisulu were dictated by the exigencies of the moment. Rarely did they have the time or resources to reflect and record.

At that time I was working for the Ministry of Labour in Zimbabwe, researching and writing about women's work. Through my work, I had become increasingly conscious of the dichotomy between paid work in the public realm and unpaid and undervalued work in the private realm, and the gendered nature of this dichotomy. I belived that in African communities, this dichotomy extended to intellectual work – on one hand, there is knowledge that is validated through academic discourse, preserved by the written word and measured through the acquisition of academic distinctions; and on the other hand, we find the unwritten and undervalued knowledge within our families and communities, which is passed on through oral traditions in an increasingly haphazard way.

The value of family history was brought home to me by two contrasting events in 1989 that caused considerable emotional turmoil in my life. On 15 October 1989, my father-in-law, Walter Sisulu, was released after 26 years in prison. As he was welcomed to his Orlando West home in Soweto with scenes of wild jubilation, my father, Francis Batezat, was in hospital in Harare, Zimbabwe, terminally ill with cancer. My father died two weeks later, on 29 October 1998. These two incidents, one which brought a new beginning and the other which marked closure, had a profound effect on me.

My father had a typical African funeral. Hundreds of relatives, friends and acquaintances converged on his home in the days leading up to the burial. Their presence provided a unique occasion for reminiscence. The recollections of aunts, uncles and various other relatives made me realise how little I knew about my father. During the funeral service, I felt so frustrated by his sketchy obituary that I felt I should have written it myself – but then I realised that I could not have written anything more substantive.

I knew my father as a parent; I did not know enough about him as a person. I became conscious of the fact that my father had never recounted his personal history in the same way my mother did. For the first time, I appreciated the value of the stories and anecdotes that my mother, Betty Stuhardt, had always recounted during my childhood. Through my mother's recollections, I had learned not only of her own personal history but also that of my grandparents. Through her, I had learned the family genealogy. Through her, I knew of long-forgotten family quarrels that continued to impact on present-day relationships. Though I was not conscious of it at the time, my mother's recounting of family history was a legacy that helped me negotiate my identity in a colonial and patriarchal society.

At the time of his death, my father had four grandchildren – my two sons and the two daughters of my brother Trevor, all under the age of four. I felt a double sense of loss at my father's death – both for myself and for my sons and my nieces who would never know this grandfather. Just as my children were too young to understand this loss, they were also too young to appreciate the historical significance of the release from prison of their paternal grandfather. I felt it was my responsibility to pass this knowledge on to them. This feeling reinforced my concern about the lack of documentation of the social history of black communities, the history that lies outside the bounds of official historical discourse, and the need to write this history. Where better to start than with the lives of Walter and Albertina Sisulu? Theirs is a story of persecution, bitter struggle and painful separation. It is also one of patience, hope, enduring love and ultimate triumph. It is an epic saga of two people who rose from humble beginnings to become two of the most influential South Africans of the twentieth century – in short, a biographer's dream.

In telling this story, I have relied on the diverse tools of oral history, archival research and sociological and empirical data from a wide variety of sources. In addition to extensive interviews with the subjects themselves, the sections on Walter Sisulu's childhood and early political life are based on his unpublished prison memoir narrated to Michael Dingake and Lalloo Chiba. For Albertina Sisulu's family history and childhood, I have relied heavily on the oral history of the Thethiwe/Mnyila family prepared by Albertina's niece Nanziwe Thethiwe, as well as a narrative on Albertina's formative years by Joyce Sikhakhane-Rankin.

As far as secondary sources are concerned, I am indebted to excellent biographies of major figures like Nelson Mandela and Bram Fischer, studies of the major political movements of the period and accounts of the main political trials. Interviews with family members, friends, political activists and associates of Walter and Albertina Sisulu provided a rich source of information. I am even thankful to apartheid's bureaucrats for their obsession with documentation. Walter Sisulu's prison correspondence was preserved in its entirety, providing a valuable window into the inner life of my subjects. Police and justice department documents have been important in providing an insight into the oppressor's view of the protagonists. Because of the capacity of the human mind to deal with trauma by suppressing memory, it was sometimes difficult to elicit details of torture, detention and imprisonment from my subjects, and the police and prison documents, notwithstanding their fabrications and distortions, were helpful in this regard.

In writing this book, I have sought to do more than just to portray two political icons. I have tried to examine how these two people managed to bring up their children in an environment as inimical to successful parenthood as you will find. I have sought to show how they have come to be regarded as archetypal parents, both in the political and the familial sense, and how their all-embracing sense of family has informed their politics.

Biography is by definition an intrusive process, especially the genre of biography that seeks to interweave the personal and the political. I have been fortunate to have two subjects who accepted that this intrusion is part of the process of telling their stories and who responded with a frankness and openness that sometimes surprised me. They provided guidance and encouragement throughout the process, and not once did they close the door on any avenue of enquiry. My task was made easier by their recognition of the value of their story as a legacy for future generations. They have regarded the telling of their story as part of a continuing commitment to the youth who hold the future in their hands. It is a commitment best expressed in the words of Albertina Sisulu: "We are each required to walk our own road ... and then stop, assess what we have learned and share it with others," she tells us. "It is only in this way that the next generation can learn from those who have walked before them, so that they can take the journey forward after we can no longer continue. We can do no more than tell them our story – it is then up to them to make of it what they will."

# Part One

*1912–1939*

*Beginnings*

# UNIVERSITY OF LIFE

Knowledge is birth
1912 as we know it today
Through the confines of brazen lands
Blessed with a combination of new and old worlds
A calling in a time of disturbed morals
Of mankind far away

Knowledge is birth
As is the 1929 sight of poverty
As real as enforced labour
And hatred from the brotherhood of mankind
To sink this soul into deep abyss
And this nation you find on its knees
Waiting for salvation to dawn

The birth of the knowledge you share
To groom the leaders in your path
From 1964 trials of underground cadets
To island inmates

Your knowledge is birth
A fountain of inspiration
For graduates and freedom fighters
To scholars in the streets of '76
And the pain of gunfire
Culminating in a realisation
Of the fight of our fathers
And our fathers before them
So strong is this seed passed on
This fight for freedom
This fight for livelihood
This fight that lives forever
In hearts and minds
So strong this right
Passed on you pass
Passed on every slogan that passes
Passed on unwritten books
Passed on every fallen soldier passes
On past footprints of this soil
And the children of this soil
That you educated
With only the spoken word

THULANE SIMELANE

*Walter's grandson*

*o n e*

The village of Qutubeni lies on the slopes that rise from the deep valley of Amaqwathi in the east up to the Gilindoda Mountains in the west. Clusters of thatched mud huts nestle against the verdant undulating hillsides, while the Xuka River meanders through the valley below in a picture of pastoral beauty so characteristic of much of the Transkei countryside. Qutubeni was even more pleasing to the eye in 1912 when a young Xhosa woman, Alice Manse Sisulu, returned home to give birth to her first child. Then the hills were not scarred by huge dongas – the result of decades of erosion – and the landscape was not denuded as it is today. The pathway leading up to the collection of huts that made up the main homestead was lined with blue-gum trees and encircled by wattle trees. The carefully tended garden boasted an orchard with a variety of fruit trees. It was called the "Great Place" – a homestead befitting of the status of Vanqa Dyantyi Hlakula, the family patriarch who was also the headman of Qutubeni village and a lay preacher in the Anglican Church. The term "Great Place" traditionally referred to the home of the king or a chief, so it was somewhat of an exaggeration given that Dyantyi was only a headman, but the people in the area looked up to him as a chief nevertheless.

As a result of his exalted position in the family, community and the church, Dyantyi's home attracted many visitors. Dyantyi was close friends with the resident missionary, Canon Waters, the warden of All Saints Mission, situated a few miles from Qutubeni. Both Canon Waters and the local magistrate were frequent visitors. Any visitor to the mission was also taken to Dyantyi's home. These included magistrates and court officials and visiting missionaries. The "Great Place" was a kind of showpiece to visitors, some from as far afield as Europe.

Two generations down the line it is difficult to pull back the curtains of time to gauge how Alice felt during her confinement or how her family reacted to her condition. We can only surmise that it was a difficult time for her. Having a child out of wedlock was frowned upon in her traditional culture, and it was taboo for someone of her Christian upbringing. The fact that the father of the baby was a white man was an added shock. Interracial unions were not unknown in the Transkei, but they were not common. One of the few living people who can testify to what transpired in those years is Daisy Titus, nee Mase, whose uncle married Alice's sister Nora. Mrs Titus, who reached the grand age of 101 years in August 2002, was 11 years old at the time. She agrees that there was something of a scandal about Alice's condition, but resists being drawn into further discussion of such a delicate matter. She emphasises that Alice was highly respected and loved by her community. Clearly the love affairs of an ancestor are not an appropriate topic of discussion, especially where inquisitive descendants are concerned (Interviews, Daisy Titus, 1996 and 2000).

By all accounts, Alice was an unusual woman, strong enough to withstand whatever social sanctions came her way. She had been brave enough to venture out of her sheltered environment to seek domestic work in white households and hotels around the Transkei at a time when it was rare for young African women to engage in wage labour. In most indigenous societies in the southern African subregion, women were primarily responsible for the day-to-day activities of food production, processing and preparation. Since indigenous peasant households were heavily dependent on the agricultural labour of women for subsistence production, there were strong patriarchal constraints that prevented them from leaving to work outside the household; it was men rather than women who migrated to work in the colonial economy. Women of Alice's age – 28 – would have been long married and working in the fields, with several children in tow. To be a childless woman was a fate that could not be wished upon one's worst enemy. Children were cherished, and the general consensus was that it was better to have a child out of wedlock than to have no child at all.

Alice had her baby on 18 May 1912, a boy named Walter Max Ulyate. He was baptised at All Saints Mission in his mother's surname, Sisulu. The little we know about the boy's father is that he was Albert Victor Dickinson, born 9 July 1886, the son of Albert Edward Dickinson of Port Elizabeth. He worked in the Railway Department of the Cape Colony from 1903 to 1909, and in the Native Affairs Department from 1909 onwards, after being transferred to the Office of the Chief Magistrate at Umtata. In 1910, he was made a clerk on probation (*South African Who's Who*, 1950; *The Cape of Good Hope Civil Service List*, 1910). Mrs Titus recalls that there were conflicting reports as to whether he was a road supervisor or a magistrate. According to information from the Sisulu family, he was an Assistant Magistrate. It is possible that the road supervisor version emanates from his days on the railways, and that after joining the magistrate's office, he worked his way up from clerk to Assistant Magistrate.

In most Nguni traditions, when a man impregnates a woman before marriage, members of her family confront him to get him to acknowledge paternity and compensate for the "damage" he has caused. He has to pay what is referred to as *iinkomo zesisu* (cattle for the pregnancy). He may also choose to request to marry the woman, in which case there is a further negotiation that involves payment of more animals in the tradition of *ukulobola* (dowry). The Hlakula/Sisulu family delegated Alice's brother Clifford and another male relative to confront Dickinson. As he was a white man, they were apprehensive that they might meet with a hostile reception, but they were surprisingly well received. Dickinson acknowledged paternity, and some payment was made. The relationship between Victor Dickinson and Alice was acknowledged on both sides and continued for some time; four years later they had another child together, a daughter named Rosabella.

Walter grew up knowing that his mother and family had a high regard for his biological father. In their view, Victor Dickinson had done all that ought to have been done under the circumstances for Walter and Rosabella, except to marry Alice (for reasons best known to himself). Walter has vague memories of being shown photographs of his father and his father's sisters. It was said that, at some stage, Dickinson's sisters wanted to take Walter, but that the Sisulus refused to part with him. His father remained on the periphery of Walter's consciousness, however, and played no part in his upbringing. Dyantyi Hlakula was the main father figure in his life (his grandfather Abraham Moyikwa had died before he was born). Walter identified completely with the Hlakula/Sisulu family, and it was their philosophical outlook and way of life that shaped his worldview.

Walter would grow up knowing that he came from a clan that was part of the powerful Thembu chiefdom, which could trace its genealogy back 20 generations to King Zwide. The oral history of the Thembu traces their expansion from the foothills of the Drakensberg mountains towards the southeastern Cape coast (Mandela, 4; Gish, 6). The Thembu were one of several Southern Nguni chiefdoms that occupied the area between Natal and the Eastern Cape from at least the 16th century onwards. The major chiefdoms of the Southern Nguni, the Xhosa, Mpondo, Mpondomise and others, shared the Xhosa language and culture, and collectively they became known as the Xhosa nation (Peires, 86; Davenport, 62).

Like other chiefdoms that comprised the Xhosa nation, the Thembu were made up of a number of clans that had accepted allegiance to one royal clan. The Thembu royal clan were the Hala, and other major clans included the Vundla, the Gcina and the Qwathi. Walter was taught to identify himself as part of the Gcina clan, and from an early age was able to recite the clan praises: *Tyhopho, Myirha, Nokwindla* and *Malamb'endl'adlinyam'enyamakazi*. These referred to important ancestors, memorable actions by them and places of significance to the family.

The other important component of Xhosa identity was that of lineage. The clan has been described as "a group of lineages who did not quite understand how they were related to each other, but who believed through their common clan name and clan praises that they shared a common ancestor" (Peires, 5). Walter learned to trace his lineage to his earliest known ancestor, his great-grandfather Sisulu, who was born in the late 1700s in the Glen Grey District near Queenstown. Sisulu was a relatively prosperous livestock farmer who had three sons, Hlakula, Mlungwana and Abraham Moyikwa. Hlakula Sisulu was much older than his youngest brother, Abraham Moyikwa Sisulu, so much so that by the time Abraham Moyikwa was born, Hlakula already had three sons. Hlakula's eldest son, Vanqa Dyantyi Hlakula, born of the Great House in 1837, was in fact 20 years older than his Uncle Abraham. Dyantyi was followed by two younger sons of the Right Hand House – Stulumane Hlakula and Nyangwe Hlakula. It is not clear when the family converted to Christianity, but judging from Abraham Moyikwa's name, this possibly occurred in the period between Dyantyi's birth and that of Abraham Moyikwa, sometime in the 1950s.

Sometime in the 1860s, Hlakula Sisulu's three sons, Dyantyi, Stulumane and Nyangwe Hlakula, together with their uncle, Abraham Moyikwa, migrated from the Glen Grey District (which had been annexed to the Cape Colony in 1852) to the village of Qutubeni in the Engcobo District, which was then known as Thembuland Proper. They were part of a migration of the Thembu east-wards across the Indwe River. The reasons for the migration were complex, but essentially they arose from tensions following the annexation of Glen Grey in 1852, the subjugation of anticolo-nial chiefs, the growing demand by frontier whites for more land in the wake of the Eighth Frontier War, and the displacement of chiefdoms as a result of the cattle killings of 1856/7 (Bouch; Wagenaar; Davenport, 137).

Over a period of a hundred years, the Xhosa fought the European invaders in nine wars of dis-possession, dubbed Frontier or Kaffir Wars by the colonialists. They scored some spectacular suc-cesses, but they could not hold back the inexorable advance of the colonising forces. The Xhosa were driven steadily eastwards and the area later known as Ciskei was incorporated into the Cape Colony as British Kaffraria. Their cause was not helped by the disastrous cattle-killing episode of 1856/7 in response to the apocalyptic vision of a young female "prophet", Nongqause, which was conveyed by her uncle, the prophet and seer Mhlakaza. According to this vision, if the Xhosa people killed all their cattle, burned their grain and ceased cultivating the land, on an appointed day millions of cattle would appear, the granaries would be miraculously filled with corn, and their dead warriors would arise and drive the white people into the sea (Roux 1964, 40–41).

Nongqause's prophecy divided the people into believers and nonbelievers. Tragically, the major-ity of the Xhosa, frustrated by their territorial reversals, were desperate to believe anything. By the time it became clear that the prophecy was a false one, hundreds of thousands of head of cattle had been slaughtered, and the Xhosa were suffering the worst famine in their history. An estimated 40 000 people died of starvation and tens of thousands had no option but to cross the frontier and to beg for work on the white farms (Sparks 1990, 108; Roux 1964, 36–40; Welsh, 218–19). The cattle-killing episode broke the back of Xhosa resistance to colonial subjugation and settler pene-tration. Commander George Grey exploited the situation to the full and in 1858 drove the Gcaleka and their chief Sarili from their ancestral land, forcing them eastwards across the Mbashe River. The northern part of their territory was allocated to the Mfengu (Welsh, 221), and many of the Thembu chiefs from Glen Grey were coerced by the colonial administration to move into Gcaleka territory, which constitutes the present-day Tsomo, Cofimvaba and parts of Cala. The Hlakula/Sisulu fam-ily was among those Thembu who migrated further east into Thembuland Proper.

By the time Alice was born in 1884, the members of the Hlakula/Sisulu family were well estab-lished in Qutubeni. Each had their own homestead, although they shared a common cattle kraal and a common sheep and goat pen. The homesteads were separated by grassy fields where the ani-mals grazed. The village was divided into four wards – each with a ward-head. Dyantyi, together with the ward-heads, formed the village council, with Abraham Moyikwa as his chief adviser and right-hand man. Abraham Moyikwa married a woman named Mangwanya who had two children from a previous marriage – a daughter called Agnes and a son, Kubalo. Together, Abraham Moyikwa and Mangwanya had six children, three girls – Nora, Alice Manse and Nongalephi – and three boys – Clifford, Wetu and Theophilus.

Dyantyi Hlakula, Abraham Moyikwa and their kinsmen continued with livestock and subsistence farming as their ancestors had done before them, and their homes looked much the same as they had appeared in the days of their ancestors. In reality, the Arcadian appearance of their settlements obscured the extraordinary upheavals of the 19th century. The lives of the indigenous people in the whole southern African subregion were irrevocably transformed by European colonial conquest, and the Xhosa were no exception.

The colonial expansion eastwards continued, and by 1894 the annexation of Pondoland completed the process of annexation of the Transkeian Territories (Gish, 8). Christianity and commerce preceded formal political control in the reshaping of the world of the Xhosa. Throughout the 19th century, missionary influence spread rapidly across the southeastern tip of Africa. Thembuland seemed to be a particular target of missionary activity, and by 1893 the Wesleyan Methodists had established a dozen mission stations in the area (Gish, 11). The Anglicans and Presbyterians were also active in the area, and in 1855 the Anglicans established St Mark's Mission on the banks of the Kei in what was then Gcaleka territory under their king Sarili. In 1859, Qwathi Chief Fubu granted Anglican missionaries land to start a mission at Engcobo. Since permission was granted on the first day of November, All Saints Day, the mission was given that name (Coulter).

Missionary influence changed the consumption patterns of indigenous communities, opening the way for new markets. Missionary insistence on modest dress created a market for European clothing. In 1879, Henry Waters, the first missionary at St Mark's, likened it to an "English village with well-supplied shops, a wagon-making establishment and a shoe maker" (Wagenaar, 1988). By 1883, 17 white traders had established themselves between All Saints and Engcobo, as well as two African traders, Simon Mbalali and Pambani Ntombi (Wagenaar; Ajulu).

By the 1860s, the development of Queenstown in the Glen Grey District fostered the emergence of a commercial and agricultural class, involved mostly in the development of the wool trade. Peasant farmers responded to the new opportunities, and in the 1870s the production of wool rose dramatically. Engcobo was at first a little removed from the theatre of economic opportunities, but this changed after Engcobo was established as a magistracy in 1876. The old wagon route (now a major modern road) laid out in the second half of the 19th century connected Queenstown, Glen Grey's thriving commercial and administrative centre, to St Mark's, Cofimvaba, Tsomo, Engcobo and Umtata. The discovery of diamonds in Kimberley in 1867 and gold on the Witwatersrand in 1886 opened up opportunities for peasant farmers to supply agricultural produce to the new industrial workforce (Ajulu; Gish, 7). Dyantyi Hlakula's household was one of those that took advantage of the new opportunities and was able to produce enough food for sale as well as for own consumption.

While some households prospered, others became increasingly impoverished as they lost their independent means of subsistence. By the 1880s a process of social differentiation had taken root. Land alienation and the imposition of hut tax that came with the consolidation of colonial rule placed increasing pressure on households. A government edict of the 1880s ruled that hut tax had to be paid in cash and not in kind, thus gradually leading to the exodus of men to look for jobs outside the district (Gish, 12). The drought of 1895/6 resulted in dramatic livestock losses. A decade later, the region was once again devastated by rinderpest; it is estimated that the disease killed 85 per cent of the cattle in Engcobo. Even more than taxation, these disasters forced thousands of peasants to turn to wage labour for their livelihood, and by the turn of the century male labour migration, mainly to the mines on the Witwatersrand and to the farms and manufacturing sectors of the Cape Colony, had become an established pattern (Wagenaar; Ajulu).

The successful households were not those that remained tenaciously bonded to the pre-capitalist economy, but rather those that took advantage of the opportunities presented by the new order. The Christian households were generally more prosperous. Christianity created a new cleavage in Xhosa societies, one between the mission-educated "school" people and the *amaqaba* (also known as the "red-blanketed" people) who clung to their traditional ways. Their name became the verb *ukuqaba*, meaning to smear, because they refused to abandon their practice of smearing red ochre onto their blankets. They were not literate, and often highly suspicious of the "civilising" influences introduced by whites. Many of them were contemptuous of those who converted to Christianity, referring to them as *amagqobhoka*, meaning "the penetrable ones", those who had been "penetrated" by European ideas and values. There were nevertheless clear economic and social advantages to converting and, not surprisingly, numbers of Christian converts increased significantly with the establishment of colonial control. However, Christians remained a minority in the Transkei and, by 1891, only about 10 per cent of the local population had converted to Christianity (Gish, 8).

The economic subjugation of the African people was coupled with the whittling away of what little political rights they had enjoyed in pre-Union South Africa. When the British granted representative government to the Cape in 1853, it granted the vote to all male subjects of the Crown who were property owners and met minimal income qualifications. The few Africans who met these qualifications for the franchise were the small elite group of Christian Western-educated Africans produced by the Eastern Cape mission schools (Gish, 8; Mbeki 1984, 23). Among these often outstanding individuals was Henry Poswayo, who hailed from Manzana in Engcobo. One of the first African attorneys in the country, he studied at Zonnebloem in Cape Town, then proceeded to Northern Wales and London, where he qualified as a barrister-in-law in the early 1900s (Walter Sisulu, Notes for Prison Memoir).

By the 1880s, the Cape Colony had over 12 000 Africans on the common voters' roll and African voters represented a significant force in some constituencies. When the proportion of African voters increased from 14 per cent of the electorate in 1882 to 47 per cent in 1887 as a result of the annexation of the Ciskei and Transkei, the Cape Parliament decided to shift the goalposts by disqualifying all those who had become voters by virtue of their occupation of tribal land. This measure reduced African voting strength by 30 000 (Mbeki 1984, 23). This was to set a pattern: each time African voting strength increased, the franchise qualifications were raised. Nevertheless, Africans valued the Cape franchise, which was different from the situation in Natal; here Mbeki noted, "the registration procedure for Africans was so complicated that only three Africans ever acquired the vote there." In the Boer republics of the Orange Free State and the Transvaal, the question of franchise or political rights for Africans was never even a consideration (Walshe, 6; Mbeki 1984, 24).

After the Anglo-Boer War of 1899–1902, Africans hoped that the British victory would signal the extension of the Cape franchise to the defeated Boer republics. Instead, the opposite happened with the signing of the Treaty of Vereeniging. Britain's Colonial Secretary Chamberlain correctly noted that there was no "parallel in history" for the extraordinarily generous conditions granted by the victor to the vanquished (Bernard Magubane, 282). The question of franchise for Africans was sacrificed in the interests of white supremacy, and the South African Act of 1909 became law in May 1910. Magubane notes caustically: "Under the sovereign guidance of the 'Almighty God', the settlers of the four colonies were united into one legislative union. The act disenfranchised all so-called non-Europeans, except those in the Cape. The flagrant negation of democracy would define the South African state" (Bernard Magubane, 294). Sparks called it "an act of unprecedented betrayal of the black South Africans. For it was the first and only time an imperial power had given sovereign independence to a racial minority" (Sparks 1990, 130).

As was to be expected, Africans were deeply disturbed by the exclusion of any African voice from the incorporation of the colonies into the Union, as well as by the plans for a constitution based on racial division. In 1902, the South African Native Congress – the ANC's progenitor – had been founded in the Eastern Cape, partly in response to concern about issues of political rights and land by the educated black elite. In the same year, Dr Abdullah Abdurahman founded the African Political (later People's) Organisation in Cape Town, to represent the interests of the coloured community. The Natal Indian Congress had been formed under Mohandas Gandhi eight years earlier, in the same year Natal Indians were denied the franchise. African Vigilance associations were formed all over South Africa to explore ways to safeguard their rights. Intense discussions around the country culminated in the holding of a South African Native Congress in Bloemfontein in 1909, and a deputation was sent to appeal (unsuccessfully) to the British Parliament.

A national consciousness that transcended ethnic and regional divisions was beginning to develop among the educated elite, and opposition to the new political formulation created a unity of purpose. Christian education promoted the notion of a wider community embracing all Africans. The growing national consciousness was further fuelled by the influence of African graduates who had studied in Europe and the United States. From the mid-1890s to around 1914, as least 150 black South Africans pursued higher education in the United States. They were influenced, among others, by African-American luminaries Booker T Washington and WEB du Bois (Gish, 22; Walshe, 6; Karis and Gerhart, 8). One of these scholars was Pixley ka Isaka Seme, who graduated from Columbia and Oxford. From his undergraduate days in New York, he was fired by the dream of a nationwide congress of representatives of all the African people of South Africa. The harsh discrimination he experienced when he returned home in 1910 strengthened his resolve to make this vision a reality. Seme presented his idea to three fellow lawyers, also graduates of overseas institutions, Alfred Mangena, D Montsioa and RW Msimang. They agreed that the unity of the African people was essential, and supported the idea of a permanent nationwide Congress of African leaders. It was an idea whose time had come, and it was backed by prominent individuals such as the writer Sol Plaatje, as well as the various regional organisations that had been formed to protest against the discriminatory articles in the Act of Union.

Accordingly, they convened a conference of chiefs and prominent educated Africans on 8 January 1912 in Bloemfontein. In his keynote address to the gathering, Pixley ka Isaka Seme announced:

Chiefs of royal blood and gentlemen of our race, we have gathered together to consider and discuss a scheme which my colleagues and I have decided to place before you. We have discovered that in the land of their birth, Africans are treated as hewers of wood and drawers of water. The white people of this country have formed what is known as the Union of South Africa – a union in which we have no voice in the making of the laws and no part in the administration. We have called you, therefore, to this conference so that we can together devise ways and means of forming our national union for the purpose of creating national unity and defending our rights and privileges (Rive and Couzens).

The conference was a unique gathering. Writing about it many years later, politician and newspaper editor RV Selope Thema invoked the spirits of legendary African heroes: "It was a gathering of tribes that had never met before except on the battlefields ... It was a gathering of educated Africans who had never exchanged views before. It was a gathering ... of the departed spirits of the African race, among whom were such men as Sandile, Tshaka, Moshoeshoe, Cetywayo, Moroka, Khama, Sekhukhune, Soshangana and Ramapulana" (*Drum* 1953). Seme's motion proposing the formation of a national Congress was put to a vote and passed unanimously, to a standing ovation by cheering delegates. The South African Native National Congress (SANNC), later renamed the African National Congress (ANC), came into being. It was by all accounts an emotional moment and its participants had a strong sense of history in the making (Willan, 152–3).

As Alice Sisulu and the extended Hlakula/Sisulu family celebrated the birth of Walter on 18 May 1912, they were scarcely aware of the dramatic developments in distant Bloemfontein. They could not have imagined that the destiny of their newest baby boy would be inextricably intertwined with that of the new organisation.

# t w o

Walter Sisulu's earliest memories were not of his mother and their home in Qutubeni, but of her older sister Agnes, who lived in Cofimvaba, about 30 miles from Qutubeni. Alice had to go back to work and she decided Agnes would be the best person to take care of her baby. Walter also had a problem with his eyes, and Alice thought a change of environment might improve his condition. Agnes had no sons, so she and her daughters doted on the young Walter, who would later recall: "She considered me not only as company for her daughters but as a comfort to herself." Walter returned her affection: "She was a very powerful person whom I admired. She looked after the livestock. She was in charge. She milked the cows" (Houser and Shore Interviews, 1).

As Walter grew up, he took on the usual duties of a village boy – tending his aunt's cattle, sheep and goats. Though he had no recollection of his mother, Walter grew increasingly aware that he had a home elsewhere. He was also conscious of having a mother somewhere else because he addressed his Aunt Agnes as *Mamkhulu* (senior mother). One afternoon, when he was five years old, his Mamkhulu called him into the garden where he saw a woman with apron pockets full of fruit and a bundle of clothes, which he discovered later were for him. He was overwhelmed with happiness when Mamkhulu told him that this person was his mother.

About a year later, his mother visited again with a little girl whom he learned was his sister Rosabella. He was enchanted by the toddler. Walter was very happy with Agnes and her daughters, but after his mother's visits he longed to go home, a longing that was only fulfilled when he was eight years old. In 1920, Clifford Sisulu, his mother's younger brother, and Clifford's brother-in-law (wife's brother) Molteno arrived at Cofimvaba to take him back to Qutubeni. Walter had mixed feelings about leaving Cofimvaba – sadness at leaving his Mamkhulu and her daughters, and joy at the prospect of joining his mother and sister. Clifford and Molteno had come on horseback, bringing an additional horse they assumed Walter would ride. Walter had not yet learned to ride, so on the journey to Engcobo he had to ride alternately with each of the uncles, while the third horse was taken back on a lead. Walter considered this bumpy trip on horseback the most unpleasant experience of his childhood!

They stopped at Molteno's home at Manzana, probably because the journey was too long for Walter. Clifford left Walter in Manzana and returned to fetch him a week later. This time, they progressed to a village called Dungunyeni, about eight miles from Engcobo, where Clifford lived. Nora, Clifford and Alice's elder sister also lived at Dungunyeni with her husband, Albert Mase. Walter stayed there for two weeks, until his mother came to take him to Qutubeni. Upon his arrival at Qutubeni, Walter was immediately taken to Dyantyi's home, where he was reunited with his sister Rosabella, now four years old and known to everyone by her nickname, Barbie. There were a lot of people at the homestead on the day of his arrival; Walter was not sure whether this was because Dyantyi's home was always a meeting point for people, or whether they were there to welcome him.

Like all other boys in the village, Walter continued his apprenticeship as a herd boy. The boys had to get up before sunrise and proceed to the cattle kraal and sheep and goat pens. The main kraal and pens were at the home of Dyantyi's son, Job Hlakula, so Walter and some of the herd boys often slept at Job's place. The younger boys tended the sheep and goats, while the older boys attended to the milking of the cows. Dyantyi possessed the largest amount of land in the area for cultivation and grazing purposes. His livestock consisted of about 50 cattle, 150 goats, 80 sheep and a few horses. He was relatively well off by rural standards, but not as prosperous as his nephew Joel Hlakula, who owned 75 head of cattle, 150 goats, 1 000 sheep and about a dozen horses.

The boys spent the days in the fields attending to the animals. There was an abundance of wild fruit in the area and the boys often spent their summer days picking wild figs, wild berries (*manuqube*), wild carrots (*magontsi*), a grape-like fruit called *mnqabaza*, a fruit resembling black wild olives called *isiphingo*, and an oblong fruit known as *ingwenye*. Legend has it that the *ingwenye* fruit tree was the favourite haunt of leopards (*ingwe*). The village boys were fascinated by rock paintings that abounded in the caves of Qutubeni, amd spent hours examining and analysing them. They reproduced these paintings on adjacent rocks as well as in their school books. Walter remembers a huge cave full of rock paintings at Qutubeni. He and his companions used to shelter in the cave when they milked goats in the rainy season. The cave was so large that there were several wild fig trees growing inside. Walter later learned that the rock paintings in Qutubeni and surrounding areas had been carbon dated to thousands of years before, and provided evidence that the *Abathwa* (San) people were the earliest inhabitants of the area.

The cattle were driven to the kraals just before sunset. The boys then joined everyone for supper. Food was prepared in three-legged pots on open fires by the women of the family. Children usually gathered around the fireside chatting loudly and exchanging anecdotes.

In winter, the boys had to let the cattle loose into the fields after harvesting had taken place. Most of the fields were situated about two kilometres away from the homestead on the nearer side of the banks of the Xuka River. Before letting the cattle in, the boys gleaned whatever crops remained. The most common crops were maize and sorghum. The boys looked forward to this because they often managed to collect enough maize to sell to the village store in exchange for prized possessions such as whistles and mouth organs.

Apart from herding animals, Walter also learned how to ride. By the time he was 10 years old he could ride young calves in rodeo fashion and once broke his arm in the process. In 1925 he spent some time at the home of his mother's brother, Theophilus, who loved horses and bought them purely for the pleasure of owning them. Here Walter became proficient in riding and training horses.

He also became adept at the traditional sport of stick-fighting (*ukubetha iintonga*). The training grounds for stick-fighting were the *eqaqeni* (plateau on the mountain) and in the fields. Each fighter had a stick in each hand. The one in the left hand was for parrying the opponent's blows, and the hand was bandaged with strips of cloth from blankets and old rugs and bandages. The stick in the right hand was for attacking the opponent. The aim was to disarm the opponent or to lay him out flat on the ground.

Boys were initiated into stick-fighting immediately upon assuming herd-boy duties and the training process lasted until initiation rites at the ages of between 16 and 20. The fighters initially took on their peers and were promoted to the ranks of senior fighters as they gained experience. A boy's status depended on his stick-fighting abilities. Stick-fighting (which probably started as part of military training for protection against invaders) was a skill that was passed on from generation to generation. It was a form of entertainment at public functions such as weddings, initiation ceremonies and when cattle slaughtering took place. The greater a boy's ability in the sport, the greater his social standing within the community and his popularity among the girls and women.

There were often inter-village battles, which took place when boys of one village would challenge those of another village on the slightest pretext. In these fights, boys generally tried to hold the flanks in order to control the battle. If the flanks broke up deliberately, a retreat would be ordered and a counterattack launched. Walter participated in village battles in which only sticks were used, but witnessed some fights involving assegais. Only once did he see a serious injury.

Archie Khayingane never forgot how Walter "masterminded the defence" against a group of thugs from neighbouring villages, and Sindiswa Ndita, another of Walter's contemporaries, remembered him as a champion stick-fighter who fought honourably and was always generous in victory.

Dabulamanzi Gcanga, another old playmate, claimed that Walter was very stubborn and would not easily accept defeat. On one occasion, Walter fought with and defeated a boy who was two years older than him. By the time he got home, everyone had heard about his victory. His cousin Joubert Hlakula, the grandson of Dyantyi, was thrilled at the news. He complimented Walter and oiled and polished his sticks as a mark of tribute. There was general agreement that the Xhosa saying, *umdengentonga* (he may be short, but he becomes tall when holding a stick), applied to Walter (Interviews, Archie Khayingane, Sindiswa Ndita and Dabulamanzi Gcanga, December 1992).

Every village boy owned his own sticks, not only for fighting, but also for tending herds and defence against snakes and other such minor dangers. The sticks were taken from the forest in the Gilindoda Mountains. The forest was Crown land and was guarded by police, but this did not stop groups of boys from stealing into the forest and returning with big bundles of sticks. Each boy would then select his stick for straightness and hardness, shape it to his own requirements and oil it or polish it. They even carried the sticks to school, concealing them behind the classrooms. During school breaks, they would go to check whether the sticks were still safe.

Walter's first brush with the law took place as a result of a stick-stealing expedition in the forest. Ten-year-old Walter and two other senior herd boys were arrested and charged for stealing sticks. Dyantyi had to pay a 30-shilling admission of guilt fine for their misdeed. Walter felt he had done nothing wrong and that it was unreasonable for his family to be angry with him and not the white people who had arrested him. He became resentful when he felt that white people were patronising him, and was once rebuked by one of his aunts when she felt he had not been respectful enough to some of Dyantyi's white visitors. "You will never be *allowed* to work for a white man," she told him. Walter's reputation as someone who was not easily controlled was reflected in a praise name given to him by a neighbour: "Magqab' akadliwa nazibokwe." Literally, this meant "He is like green leaves so bitter that even goats [generally likely to eat anything] will not eat them." Figuratively, it suggested a person who could not be contained.

In 1923, Dyantyi Hlakula, who was already in his mid-80s, retired as village headman. His retirement was marked by the biggest ever gathering at the Hlakula home. Many dignitaries were present, including Dalasile, a senior Thembu chief and head of the Amaqwathi region. Dyantyi had conducted village affairs with great foresight and understanding – so much so that by the time Walter was an adult with his own family, he had not heard of anyone who had attained the degree of popularity that Dyantyi enjoyed during his headmanship of Qutubeni. Dyantyi's son, Patrick, became the acting headman. He would have been installed as headman but for an incident that raised questions about his integrity. A stray sheep had joined Patrick's flock, and with the passage of time came to be regarded as part of his own flock. When it was slaughtered, the question of its ownership was raised, Patrick got into difficulties, and was no longer deemed eligible for headmanship. Walter cites this as evidence of how upright leaders in the community had to be. The acting headmanship was passed onto Stulumane Hlakula'a son, Joel. Joel regarded his work as a teacher and church catechist as more important than being a headman. He continued acting as headman until someone else from the line of Qwathi chiefs was elected.

While Walter was at Cofimvaba he had attended the school near his Aunt Agnes's home, but only occasionally as a visitor. When he was formally enrolled at school for the first time on his return to Qutubeni, his sister Rosabella had already started school. Throughout his school career, Walter was an average student. He did not shine academically, but neither did he fail. Old school friends and teachers say he was very popular with fellow students and developed several lasting friendships. His old schoolmate Sindiswa Ndita recalled: "Walter was one character who could not be ignored – he was no troublemaker but his personality was that you could not help but notice him. Both him and his sister were generous and kind people."

Walter was strongly influenced by two of his teachers, S Mdaka and William Macozoma. He also considered himself fortunate to have Daisy Mase as one of his teachers. She was the sister-in-law of his Aunt Nora. She remembered Walter as a strong personality, very kind and considerate, especially solicitous towards his sibling Rosabella. She felt that although he was a highly intelligent boy, he never distinguished himself as a scholar. He had difficulty learning to write, and his handwriting was impossible to read. Also in the same class as Walter was Sam Mase, whose father was the brother of Daisy and Albert Mase. Because of the connection with Aunt Nora, Daisy and Sam treated him as a relative and he developed a firm and lifelong friendship with Sam.

His schooling was disturbed when, shortly after Dyantyi's retirement, Alice decided to send Walter and Rosabella to stay with Clifford's brother-in-law, Molteno, in Manzana. For a short while Walter and his sister went to school at Manzana, where his teacher was Diana Xuma. Diana's father was a Wesleyan minister, and her brother Alfred Bitini Xuma was a brilliant scholar who had left to study in the US the year after Walter was born.

Around 1924, Alice decided to build a house of her own at her brother Clifford's place at Dungunyeni. Believing that she now had her very own permanent home, she moved Walter and Rosabella to the school at All Saints Mission, which was midway between Dungunyeni and Qutubeni. Unfortunately Clifford and Alice quarrelled because Clifford's wife Nosimanga felt that her own status was being undermined by Alice's presence. At the time of the quarrel, the walls of the house were already up to roof level. In anger, Clifford had the walls pulled down. Alice lost heavily financially and had to leave Dungunyeni. According to Walter, his Uncle Clifford was not a cruel or unpleasant person, so it is difficult to understand his extreme action. One can only conclude that in a patriarchal society in which women were perpetual minors, always subject to male authority and control, Clifford felt threatened by his strong and independent sister.

Characteristically, Walter bore no grudges. He stayed on with his Uncle Clifford until he completed Standard Two and part of Standard Three. He returned to Qutubeni in 1926 and walked the two miles to All Saints daily, where he completed Standard Four and part of Standard Five. He was frequently late for school because he had to attend to the cattle first. He was often caned on the palms of his hands, given garden duty, or kept in during recess as punishment for his lack of punctuality and he "accepted it naturally like the other boys" (Houser and Shore Interviews, 12). He enjoyed school although he felt irritated by one of the white missionaries who, he felt, paid special attention to him because of his light complexion.

At Qutubeni, Walter stayed at the homestead of Dyantyi's son, Job Hlakula, while Rosabella lived at the Great Place with Dyantyi and his wife Nosisa. Job was one of the African soldiers who had fought and died in the First World War, and his home was taken over by his son Joubert Hlakula and Job's widow Lizzie Gxowa. Later, the household would be joined by Joubert's wife Florence. Both women were surrogate mothers to Walter. Joubert was much older than Walter, but his sister Violet, like Walter, was born in 1912 and she bore a remarkable resemblance to Alice Manse. In later life, Walter would describe the kind of family life they had and the deep affection he felt for Violet and her mother Lizzie in a letter to Violet's son Lungephi:

> She will forever remain a picture of what I consider to be the embodiment of humanity itself. She was deeply religious, full of love and understanding of people. I was and still am happy to have grown under her tender care ... Though we lived in two homesteads, it was to all intents and purposes one household. We also had our meals during the day with the old people [Dyantyi and his wife], sometimes even morning prayers. We conducted our own prayers at night reading a Bible prayer book and hymns. Your mother took full charge whereas I led the singing regularly. This was the best period of my childhood life. My mother was working in hotels and boarding places in various parts of the Transkei. Yet we did not miss her. We had all the motherly love (20/1/86).

Walter loved singing and sang tenor and alto in the school choir. He also participated in singing competitions with other choirs. At All Saints, Christmas, Pentecost and the annual confirmation were the important occasions of the year. The children would hold regular meetings from September or October to plan the programme for Christmas Day. They collected funds to buy sheep and other requirements for the Christmas feast to which all the parents were invited. The feast was well organised, with the students taking on the tasks of cooks and waiters. After the Christmas church service at All Saints, everyone would return to the village for the great occasion.

All Saints students were expected to attend church services regularly and answer a verbal test on the sermon. Walter took a keen interest in the sermons. He loved the stories of Daniel in the lion's den, Abednego, Shadrach and Meshack, and of Moses crossing the Red Sea. Walter was most interested in David because "here was a small person who defeated a great enemy because he was able to plan. He killed a giant with a sling, the same kind of sling that we small boys would use to kill birds in the forest. I was usually the youngest and smallest boy in my group so I could identify with David." He loved to climb up to the top of the mountains behind his home and stand "looking at the four corners of the world and thinking about the things I read in the Bible".

Interested as he was in Bible stories, Walter was not religious and he read the Bible "in a critical way". From an early age he questioned the contradictions in the Bible. When he was 10 years old, he asked his guardian Dyantyi, "Who made God?" The question angered Dyantyi and Walter was slapped for what was perceived as impudence. He was told in no uncertain terms that it was not his business to probe into such questions. Walter was, however, involved in an unusual religious episode with his friend Sam Mase. Around 1926, the youth of Qutubeni were suddenly seized with religious fervour. Sam Mase called it a "spiritual revival" and believed that it was prompted by the sermons of a Reverend Titus, a relative of McDonald Titus, the man who later married Daisy Mase. The adults in the village were amazed when adolescents suddenly started to organise and conduct religious services at which they would get on the podium themselves and, in Sam Mase's words, "preach the whole blessed night". News of this revivalist phenomenon spread far and wide, and people from other villages would flock to attend the services. Walter enjoyed the drama of the whole affair, but was not carried away by the spirit of religious fervour in the same way as Sam Mase, who would remain deeply religious for the rest of his life.

Apart from Bible studies, Walter's favourite subjects were history and English. He and his friends loved reading about the legendary African heroes of the past. They admired the Zulu king Shaka's military prowess and rejected the portrayal of Shaka as a brutal murderer. They admired the wily tactics of the Sotho king Moshoeshoe who secured the safety of his people in the fortress of his mountain kingdom, Lesotho. "To us this was absolutely wonderful," he recalled, "but the most remarkable to all the boys was Makana, who sent a message to the military commander in Grahamstown to say 'I will have breakfast with you tomorrow morning'. By that he meant he was going to invade Grahamstown."

The story of Makana, the renowned Xhosa prophet and military general of Chief Ndlambe, was seared into the collective consciousness of the Xhosa people. Makana or Nxele (the left-handed) was defeated after his attack in 1819 on the colonial forces at Grahamstown and sent to Robben Island. In 1820, he was one of a group of prisoners who stole a boat and escaped from the Island. The story of how the boat shattered on the rocks and how Makana, clinging to the rocks, shouted encouragement to his fellow escapees before the waves closed over him, is the stuff of legend (Deacon, 56). Walter and his age-mates knew about *Esiqithini*, the island a few miles from Cape Town, that the British colonisers, like the Dutch before them, used as a place of imprisonment and banishment. They knew that other Xhosa leaders and chiefs – Maqoma, Siyolo and others – were sent to *Esiqithini* to languish with the lepers, chronically sick and mentally ill, for the role they played in the wars of dispossession. The most influential Xhosa chiefs who had participated in the cattle killings, as well as the hapless Nongqause, were also despatched to the Island (Smith, 53).

Walter had heard Dyantyi speak of Nongqause and the cattle killings. Dyantyi's good friend Canon Waters, who had been appointed warden of All Saints in 1886, was a linguist who spoke fluent Xhosa. He was the son of Reverend Henry Waters who had established St Mark's Mission in

1855, when the area was still part of Chief Sarili's territory. When the cattle killings were raging a year later, some of the nonbelievers who were being persecuted for refusing to kill their cattle, found refuge at St Mark's. Reverend Waters also provided for some of the Gcalekas who had to flee their homes when George Grey's commando came to drive Sarili and his people across the Mbashe River (Interview, Jeff Peires, 23/9/2002). Walter always had a strong emotional reaction to the saga of cattle killings, he was convinced that Nongqause was somehow used as a pawn in a Machiavellian plot by white colonialists to solve the labour problems of the white settlers.

The recent history of militant struggles in Engcobo fed into Walter's sense of being part of an oppressed people. He grew up hearing the story of how the Qwathi were moved from the fertile lands near Elliot to make way for white farmers. Adults would point out the large tracts of land owned by one or two people, while black people were crowded onto smaller, less fertile plots and forced to cut down on the sheep, goats and cattle they owned – and even prevented from picking up sticks in the forest. The Qwathi chief Dalasile was one of the most militant of the Thembu chiefs and many of the older family members had witnessed the Qwathi rebellion in 1880 when the white town of Engcobo came under attack and the magistrate's court, church and mission were burnt down, forcing the whites to flee to Umtata until peace had been restored (Coulter, 1988; Walter Sisulu, Notes for Prison Memoir).

Walter was even influenced indirectly, although he did not know it at the time, by Marcus Garvey's gospel of Pan-African liberation. From its inception in 1914, the influence of Garvey's Universal Negro Improvement Association (UNIA) spread rapidly through the West Indies, the Americas and Africa. By 1919, it was well on its way to becoming the largest Pan-African movement of its kind in history, and by the 1920s, Garvey's philosophy was beginning to have an impact in South Africa. Prominent figures like Sol Plaatje, the Secretary-General of the African National Congress, and the journalist Selope Thema were interacting with Garvey's movement, and UNIA branches had been established in Cape Town, East London and Pretoria. James Thaele, the ANC's Western Cape leader in the 1920s and '30s, edited an ANC newspaper *The African World,* which in 1925 published Garvey's famous essay on "African Fundamentalism" in an African language. The *Sunday Times* summed up the views of South Africa's white press when it raged: "A more treacherous, inflammatory, deluded and deluding publication it is difficult to imagine" (Martin, 140).

Walter was exposed to a warped version of Garvey's philosophy by one Wellington Buthelezi, who arrived in Qutubeni with his lieutenant, Reverend Twala, in the early 1920s. Buthelezi was a Zulu from Natal, but in Engcobo District he posed as a black American who had graduated from Oxford and Cambridge (Sampson, *Treason Cage,* 156). He and Twala held meetings at which, Walter recalled, "They talked about freedom for the black man and condemned the whites for their injustice and repression." Buthelezi preached that the Americans, who were all Negroes, were coming in aeroplanes to liberate them. There was enormous excitement in the village. "Although we knew very little about oppression, it was a welcome idea that black people who had got power were coming" (Houser and Shore Interviews, 17). Soon afterwards an aeroplane did fly over the village and Walter was convinced that the American liberators had arrived.

Buthelezi told them the education they were getting was that of a white man and they needed to get a black man's education. He set up schools around Engcobo run by Africans to educate people for the struggle against the white man. One of Walter's cousins left the school where she was working to teach at one of Buthelezi's schools. A number of the Qutubeni children, including Walter, also moved to the new school, but the whole scheme fell apart when they could not afford the half-crown fees that Buthelezi demanded. They returned to their old schools and life returned to normal. Eventually, the local people came to see Wellington Buthelezi for what he was, a con man who had succeeded in collecting thousands of half-crowns from people in the district. Nevertheless, Walter felt no resentment because the germ of an exciting idea had been planted.

Walter's passion for stick-fighting led to the premature end to his schooling just after he had started Standard Five. The teachers frowned upon stick-fighting and those who took part were punished. After being involved in a stick-fight, Walter skipped school to avoid punishment, going to work on the family farm instead. Dodging school for a week led to dodging school for a month, until he dropped out completely and worked full-time on the farm. Everyone was extremely impressed by his work on the farm, and it seems he was not encouraged to go back to school. When one takes into account Walter's later passion for education and his insistence that young people persist in it, the reasons for him dropping out of school seem quite flimsy. It could be that he had a learning disability like dyslexia, or that his was the kind of intelligence that could not find expression in formal academic education.

After working on the family fields for about a year, Walter made up his mind to go to Johannesburg. By this time (1928), his mother Alice had left Qutubeni for East London in search of work. More significantly, the paterfamilias, Dyantyi Hlakula, who, more than anyone else, had provided Walter with a sense of identity and stability, had died. After Dyantyi's death, Walter felt that there was nothing to keep him in Qutubeni.

By 1928, labour migration was a permanent feature of existence in Engcobo, as it was in the rest of the subcontinent. The 1913 Land Act, that iniquitous piece of legislation that institutionalised territorial segregation between black and white, restricting the share of land allocated to Africans to a paltry 7.3 per cent of the total land area of South Africa, did more than any other piece of legislation to transform independent African producers into wage labourers. The immediate impact of the Act was not as dramatic in the Transkei as in other parts of the country such as the Orange Free State, where sharecroppers on white farms became aliens in the land of their birth overnight. Because the Transkei had been designated a "native" territory ruled indirectly through local traditional authorities, it did not experience the same degree of land expropriation as other parts of the country (Gish, 6). Nevertheless by 1928, the effects of the Act were apparent and land hunger and its corollary, ever-increasing poverty, had made the Transkei region a significant exporter of labour.

For peasant youths like Walter, a stint in the gold mines of the Witwatersrand had become a rite of passage. Every year, more and more young men made the pilgrimage to the mines. Returning migrants boasted about the glitter and bright lights of distant cities and proudly displayed their clothing, watches, radios and other items bought from the towns to the awe and admiration of their listeners, among whom was Walter. Like other village boys, Walter longed for the opportunity to own such prized items and to experience for himself the exciting life of the towns. He discussed his decision to leave with Joubert's wife, Florence, who had by then become the matriarch of the family; next, he set about making arrangements for his departure.

At the age of 16, Walter was too young to enter into a contract as a mine labourer and the officer at the recruiting office at the Employment Bureau of Africa in Engcobo rejected his application, telling him to come back when he was 18. Walter then borrowed tax receipts from a cousin called Mino Masimini Hlakula, which indicated that he was a poll-tax payer and therefore old enough to be recruited. The receipts were submitted to the recruiting officer and Walter was issued with a contract in his cousin's name. This meant that his first journey out into the wide world was under an assumed identity – "Mino Masimini Hlakula".

On the appointed day, Walter travelled to Engcobo with two other young men from Qutubeni who were returning to the mines. At the recruiting office, they found about 50 other migrants. They were all issued with rations of bread and sugar for the journey before they were loaded onto a truck headed for Cala Road about 35 kilometres away, where they would board the train. Brimming with the exuberance and optimism of youth, Walter could not wait to start this new stage in his life's journey.

# *three*

One of Walter's most vivid childhood memories was of the influenza pandemic that struck the Transkei in September 1918, when he was still living with his Aunt Agnes in Cofimvaba. One day, work was suspended, the school was closed and everyone in the surrounding villages went to the town of Cofimvaba for inoculation against the flu. His child's mind could not grasp the gravity of the situation. He could only appreciate the novelty of going to town. Only later did he become aware of the havoc wreaked by the epidemic.

The Spanish Flu, the particular strain of the influenza virus that caused the 1918 epidemic, killed an estimated 40 million people worldwide. The second wave of the epidemic hit South African shores in September 1918, and spread with the speed of a deadly veld fire, leaving a quarter of a million dead in its wake. It was the worst natural disaster in the country's history (Phillips, XV). Migrant workers returning from the badly affected coastal cities like Cape Town and Port Elizabeth carried the disease into the heart of the Transkei, where it killed more than 30 000 people out of a population of one million (Phillips, 88). Well-known Zulu composer RT Caluza recorded the impact in his song *Influenza 1918:* "Yaziqeda izihlobo esizitandayo/abomama, nabobaba, noSisi, nobhuti/kweminy'imizi kwaqotula akwasala muntu" (It finished off our loved ones, our mothers and fathers, sisters and brothers. In some homesteads it finished off everyone, no one was left).

*Umbathalala*, as the flu was called in Xhosa, was particularly lethal to pregnant women and small babies. In the village of Camama, just a few miles from Cofimvaba, Bonilizwe Thethiwe was consumed by worry about his heavily pregnant wife Monica, who had been laid low with the dreadful contagion. Monica's mother, Nosenti Mnyila, also hovered by anxiously. In addition to their concern about Monica's condition, the adults in the household feared that the baby would be infected *in utero*. They were overjoyed when, on 21 October 1918, Monica gave birth to a healthy baby girl. A jubilant Bonilizwe praised God for the safe delivery of his daughter, and named her Nontsikelelo. Catholic missionary nurses (the only source of medical attention for the majority of sufferers in the Transkei) were in attendance at the birth, and to avoid infection of the infant, they insisted that Nosenti take her granddaughter literally at the moment of birth. As was the practice with infants who could not be fed by their mothers, Nosenti fed the baby with the juice of a root vegetable (*inembe*) as well as boiled cow's milk and *amasi* (sour milk). The Thethiwe and Mnyila families had reason to be thankful. Born at the zenith of the epidemic in a month that would be remembered as "Black October", Baby Nontsikelelo proved from the out- set that she was a survivor.

Nontsikelelo was the second child of Bonilizwe and Monica. Their eldest was a boy named Mcengi, born in 1913, and Nontsikelelo was followed by two brothers, Velaphi Elliot and Qudalele Stanford, born in 1921 and 1923 respectively, and a sister, Nomyaleko Florence, born in 1929.

For six months of the year, Bonilizwe was a peasant farmer who ploughed his fields, planted and harvested crops and tended to his cattle, sheep and goats. He was fortunate to have large fields at his disposal. For the remaining six months, he was a migrant worker on the gold mines of the Rand.

Bonilizwe Thethiwe, his brother and his two sisters were all born in Camama. They were of the Dlangiswa clan, part of the Mfengu people. Refugees from the Zulu kingdom who arrived in Xhosa territory in the 1820s came from the Bhele, Zizi, Hlubi, Bhaca, Xesibe and Ntlangwini peoples. These groups were all incorporated into the Xhosa nation, and by 1830 they collectively became known as Mfengu (from the verb *ukumfenguza* – to wander about seeking service) (Peires, 62).

Bonilizwe and his siblings could trace their genealogy back four generations to their great-grandfather Mahlasela, who lived in Qoboqobo, in the region of present-day Keiskammashoek. It was said that Mahlasela had risen to become one of the *amaphakati* (counsellors to the chief or king) in the Ngqika kingdom, even though he was an Mfengu and not a Ngqika by birth. At the time, the Qoboqobo people were plagued by *inqqawa*, a kind of wild cat that was killing sheep and goats, and Mahlasela and his son Mbolambi succeeded in killing the predator. Their subsequent popularity with the chief caused envy among the other councillors, and the chief warned Mahlasela that there was a plot afoot to kill him. Mahlasela and Mbolambi subsequently fled eastwards across the Kei River to Nqamakwe, where they settled at Ngculu location. They then moved on to Camama where they were given land at Ngxingweni by the local Thembu chief. Mbolambi's son, Thethiwe, and his brother then moved to a place in Camama that became known as kwaNdlangisa after their clan. Thethiwe was the father of Bonilizwe (Nanziwe Thethiwe, Unpublished manuscript, 2001).

Monica, Nontsikelelo's mother, was the daughter of Qingqiwe Mnyila and his wife Nosenti. The Mnyilas were also of the Mfengu people. Qingqiwe was a wealthy man and, as headman of Xolobe village, he was very highly respected. By all accounts, Monica was a very beautiful woman and, as the daughter of a headman, the *lobola* that Bonilizwe had to pay was higher than usual.

Monica survived her bout of influenza, but continued to be plagued by ill health. She suffered from arthritis or some similar ailment. Sometimes her joints were so stiff that she could not turn her neck or lift her hands. Bonilizwe was distressed by his wife's condition, especially when he had to leave for his six-month stints on the mines. They decided that when he was away in Johannesburg, Monica and the children should go to her parents in Xolobe. Consequently, Nontsikelelo spent more time in Xolobe than in Camama and when she was old enough to go to school, the family decided that it would be better for her to start school in Xolobe. When she was enrolled in the local primary school that was run by Presbyterian missionaries, the young Nontsikelelo was given a list of Christian names from which to choose. "The name Albertina was attractive to me. I was then baptised in my new name" (Joyce Sikhakhane-Rankin, Interview). Her family called her Ntsiki but to the missionaries and teachers, she was Albertina, and this was the name by which she became known in the wider world.

Albertina had happy memories of her early childhood years with her grandparents. She enjoyed the company of a host of cousins, many of whom lived at her grandparents' place or in nearby homesteads. Qingqiwe and Nosenti had three sons, three daughters and 32 grandchildren. A sign of Qingqiwe's prosperity was that his home was not the traditional set of huts, but a big square brick house with a corrugated-iron roof. The girls had one room, and the boys another. Qingqiwe had built huge tanks to store water from the summer rains, so they were spared the task of trudging long distances to draw water, one of the most tedious chores for rural girls and women.

When they were not at school, Albertina and her girl cousins helped the women of the family in the fields, where they cultivated vegetables, mainly potatoes, pumpkin and beans, as well as wheat, sorghum, oats and barley. The girls were allowed to have their own patch, and were permitted to sell the produce they grew on it. Albertina relished growing things, and this was the beginning of her life-long passion for gardening, which was to be a great comfort in times of stress. Qingqiwe also employed *amaqaba*, red-blanketed youths, to help in the fields. It was the responsibility of the young girls to look for wood. The Xolobe area boasts rolling grassy hills, but not many trees, and the girls would have to walk long distances to get wood. They would gather and cut wood, tie it into bundles and walk home balancing the bundles on their heads.

Within the extended family group, Albertina was the eldest of eight girls. As the eldest granddaughter, she was expected to take care of the younger girls. She showed strong maternal instincts and honed her mothering skills from an early age. She was about five years old when her Uncle Orpen's daughter Gcotyelwa was born. To her delight, the baby was brought to the Mnyila home to be raised by the grandmother. Albertina took charge, carrying the baby on her back, seeing to her meals and generally taking full responsibility for her welfare. Decades later, her face still glows with pleasure at the memory: "She was my baby and she was so beautiful, I loved her so much!"

Qingqiwe was one of those peasant farmers who had taken advantage of the thriving wool trade in the Cofimvaba, Xalanga and Tsomo areas, and was a significant producer of angora wool for the market. Albertina enjoyed the buzz of activity at sheep-shearing time. People from far and wide would come and work for her grandfather during this period. The wool would be transported to the market by a sleigh dragged by oxen. Later her grandfather bought a horse-drawn cart, and she and her cousins would ride on the cart among the bales of wool to the trading store where the wool would be sold. "Our grandfather would give each of us grandchildren our very own bag of wool which we would sell and keep the money ourselves." She loved the feeling of riding on the cart holding on to her very own bale of wool.

Qingqiwe also raised horses and Albertina learned to ride from an early age. By the time she was a teenager she was an expert rider, so much so that she was often chosen as an *umkhapi*, the maid of honour who, on horseback, led the bridal entourage at weddings. This was an exciting role and the young girls would prepare for days for the event. The *umkhapi* would wear an *isikhakha*, a short traditional skirt, and *amatikiti*, an assortment of different coloured beads around the neck. She would carry a white flag and on approaching a bend she would fling it out in a circular movement while turning the horse in the opposite direction. Weddings were big occasions attended by everyone for miles around, so there would be a huge audience to witness her *umkhapi* skills. On either side of the procession, ululating guests would throw flowers at the horses and the maidens.

There were always many visitors at the Mnyila homestead as Qingqiwe was a headman and also a member of the Bunga, the Transkeian council made up of elected and nominated members. The Bunga (the word means "council") was established through an Act introduced by Cecil Rhodes. Supposedly a form of local government suited to the tribal system, it was also supposed to aid the integration of Africans into the mining and industrial economy, as well as curbing the power of the chiefs. Albertina and her cousins learned from an early age to cook for large numbers of people and she saw something of the workings of the Bunga when she had to serve food to its members.

Qingqiwe and Nosenti had a strong commitment to serving the community. They would arrange assistance for the aged and infirm and would allocate groups of young men to plough and plant the fields of women who had been widowed. The Presbyterian missionaries also used to bring clothes for Qingqiwe to distribute to the converts.

Qingqiwe himself was not a Christian and he continued to wear the red ochre blanket of the *amaqaba*, but he got on well with the missionaries and he appreciated their efforts to establish schools in the district. He attached a lot of importance to education and at one stage he called an *imbizo* or meeting of all the villagers. He said it had been brought to his attention that many children were not going to school and he instructed every man in the area to collect the children and make sure they went to school. Years later when Qingqiwe died, and his son Campbell succeeded him as headman, he continued his father's practice of sending men on horseback to raid homesteads suspected of keeping children from school. He also stopped the practice of hiring the *amaqaba* children during sheep-shearing season because he believed every child should go to school.

Albertina and all the Mnyila cousins attended the local mission school, Middle Xolobe Primary, a 45-minute walk from their home. It was a pleasant school in a scenic setting at the confluence of the Ngubemhlope and Jonny rivers. It was co-educational, and catered for about 500 pupils, including a number of white pupils – the children of local missionaries and shopkeepers. The white children were completely integrated into the school community; they all spoke Xhosa fluently, and the only discernable difference in their treatment was that they were promoted faster.

Albertina was a bright pupil who was liked and respected by both teachers and pupils. She was a keen netball player and also sang in the school choir. The Mnyila family had a strong choral tradition, and like her cousins Albertina sang in the church choir as well. A former Middle Xolobe student, Miriam Matsha, who would later marry Albertina's brother Elliot, remembered Albertina as "a very responsible elder sister who always took the lead. She was a disciplinarian and was very serious minded. She was like a mother to the younger girls." She remembered how Albertina used to scold them for laughing at the red-blanketed people. "She used to tell us that we should never laugh at people who were not fortunate enough to have the benefit of education" (Interview, Miriam Matsha Thethiwe, 20/3/96). Her cousin Gcotyelwa, who was several years behind Albertina in school, recalled: "It was difficult following in Ntsiki's footsteps. Just because you came from the Mnyila family the teachers expected you to be like her" (Interview, Temperance Gcotyelwa Mnyila, 20/3/96).

There was a teacher, Mrs Mkoyana, who Albertina admired to the point of hero worship. "She was a lady teacher who I looked up to. She was professional and smartly dressed. I would look at her and think 'I want to be like that'." The teacher was a devout Christian, who constantly reminded her young charges that their behaviour had to be exemplary. Albertina never forgot one of her strongest messages: "Your behaviour is the best teacher. It is more powerful than anything you say."

Albertina's childhood happiness came to an abrupt end in 1929 when her mother was expecting her fifth child. It was a difficult pregnancy and Monica's condition had deteriorated. When Bonilizwe had to go to the mines, he took Monica and their two younger sons, six-year-old Qudalele Stanford and eight-year-old Velaphi Elliot to Xolobe. Since he expected that Monica would have to remain in Xolobe for a long time after the birth of the baby, Bonilizwe also transferred half his livestock – cattle, sheep, goats and even chickens – to the home of his parents-in-law. His eldest son Mcengi remained in Camama to take care of the homestead and the rest of the livestock. Bonilizwe was grieved to have to leave his wife in such a condition and when they parted he said: "Ndiyalekile" (I am afflicted by misfortune).

Monica and her children had not been long in Xolobe when they received a message that they should return to Camama because Bonilizwe was seriously ill. By that time Monica was heavily pregnant and virtually bedridden so that Nontsikelelo, Qudalele and Velaphi had to return with an older relative. On their journey they were caught in a ferocious storm. Almost deafened by thunder, with large hailstorms pelting down, they managed to find shelter in a thicket. They reined in the terrified horses and huddled together under a large sheet of buckskin, which Qudalele had had the presence of mind to carry, and waited out the storm. They felt that the storm was a harbinger of some terrible happening, and indeed they were right. They finally arrived in Camama to find their father on his deathbed (Nanziwe Thethiwe Interview, Qudalele Stanford Thethiwe).

Years later Albertina would realise that her father must have been suffering from some form of pneumoconiosis, a chronic disease of the lungs and bronchial tubes caused by the inhalation of metallic or mineral particles. Pneumoconiosis was an occupational hazard for miners and the number of black miners who died of the disease, uncared for and uncompensated by the Chamber of Mines, will never be known. No money could have compensated for the pain Bonilizwe must have felt at saying goodbye to his children, knowing that their ailing mother was in no condition to take care of herself, let alone five fatherless children. He turned to Albertina and asked her to promise to take care of her three younger siblings, saying, "I know you are strong." It was an extraordinary request. It was completely unheard of for a Xhosa father to place such a responsibility on his second-eldest child and a girl at that. Bonilizwe was flying in the face of the tradition that dictated that such a responsibility should fall to the eldest son. Moreover, Mcengi was five years older than Albertina, who was only 11 at the time. It was a defining moment in Albertina's life: "It could not have been easy for my elder brother who was standing next to me, but I resolved that day that I would honour my father's trust in me."

After the burial of their father, Albertina and her two younger brothers returned to Xolobe, this time permanently. Mcengi stayed for a while with the Thethiwes, but the paternal uncles laid claim to Bonilizwe's land and property and did not give Mcengi anything. Qingqiwe was upset when he heard this and sent for his grandson. Mcengi eventually went to work on the mines in Johannesburg.

Soon after her husband's death, Monica gave birth to her last born, Nomyaleko – the afflicted one. Albertina helped her grandmother to nurse Monica, whose condition was distressing, both to herself and those taking care of her: "Sometimes her joints were so painful that she would be unable to lie down," recalled Albertina. "She would walk around crying and we would bandage her with warm cloths, but she would have no relief. She did not respond to the traditional herbal treatments and at that time there was no hospital to take her to" (Joyce Sikhakhane-Rankin, Interview).

Albertina's desolation at her father's death was compounded by the fact that she had to withdraw from school for a while to take care of the new baby. She virtually became a surrogate mother to Nomyaleko or Flora, as the child came to be called. She also continued to look after her little cousin Gcotyelwa. Fortunately, the missionaries established a nursery school because they were anxious for people in the area to send their children to school. They knew that older children, especially young girls, were often kept back from school to care for babies and toddlers while their mothers and grandmothers were working in the fields. Albertina benefited from the new arrangement and was able to leave the two children there before going to school. Because the nursery was close to the school, she was able to dash out and check on the little ones during the school break.

Albertina loved swimming with her age-mates in the rivers near the school. They would enjoy diving from the high rocks. They were often joined by the *amaqaba* girls who they would envy because they could remove their clothes and swim wearing nothing but the wire bands they wore around their waists while the Christian girls had to swim in their petticoats and long bloomers. In a gesture of friendship, the *amaqaba* girls gave them each a waistband, which the Christian girls took to wearing under their clothes. Unfortunately, the rough wire snagged their petticoats, and when their aunts noticed this and discovered that they were wearing the waistbands of the *amaqaba*, they were thoroughly beaten, probably the only time Albertina ever received a beating. Another swimming expedition almost ended in disaster when Flora fell into the river and Albertina had to dive in to save her little sister. She suffered from terrible shock at the thought of what she would have said to the people at home if anything had happened to the child.

As they approached puberty the elderly women kept a close watch on the young girls. "They could tell when a girl started to menstruate, just by looking at her." If, horror of horrors, one of the young girls became pregnant, they would know even before the girl herself knew about her condition. The older girls were expected to monitor and guide the younger ones. "If you fall in love the older girls would talk to you and teach you how to behave. You were told that you must never be seen walking with a boy and that you must respect yourself," Albertina recalled (Joyce Sikhakhane-Rankin, Interview). Teenage pregnancy was rare and if it did happen, all the girls in that particular age group became the target of adult anger and would be castigated. "There was strong peer-group pressure among the girls to take care of their bodies. If one girl in the age group got pregnant, the whole group mourned by taking off their earrings for a few months." The boy who was responsible for the pregnancy would be circumcised immediately because it would be considered that he regarded himself as a man. His family would have to send *lobola* to the girl's parents. Unmarried mothers usually found sanctuary at the mission station, where they would have to repent for their sins. The Church had an interest in providing shelter to unwed mothers because it wanted as many converts as possible.

Tradition and Christianity combined to exert strong control over the sexuality of young girls. Grandmothers, aunts and older sisters periodically inspected adolescent girls to see if they were virgins. From a 21st-century point of view, it is difficult to see anything positive in such a practice, but Albertina and her peers did not object to the virginity inspections. They felt that these "instilled ownership and respect of one's body" and they were quite accustomed to the *ukuhlolwa* practice. A woman's last virginity inspection took place on the eve of her wedding. A kitchen tea would be held for the bride at which the guests would present gifts. These would include a range of household utensils including pots, crockery and traditional homemade artefacts such as woven grass mats and beads. If the bride failed the inspection and was found not to be a virgin, the guests would take back their gifts in disgust.

Albertina herself never entertained even the slightest suggestion of flirtation or improper behaviour. She was already thinking about becoming a nun and she devoted herself to her school work. After Standard Four, Albertina was promoted to the upper Xolobe Primary School where she did Standard Five. She was a prefect in school and in her final year she became head girl. She was a diligent student who was always top of her class. She had big dreams for the future, but there was another cloud on the horizon where her schooling was concerned.

As time passed, Albertina and her family realised that Flora was afflicted by some mysterious ailment. She started having fits, and was taken to the mission doctor who diagnosed her as epileptic. One day, when Albertina was away at school and her grandmother Nosenti was in the fields, Flora fell into a fire. Her mother, too weak and ill to move, was unable to get to the child to pull her from the fire. By the time help came in response to Monica's frantic calls, Flora's right hand was so badly burned that she had to have two fingers amputated. Once again, Albertina had to leave school to take care of her young sibling. Consequently, she was two years older than the rest of her class in her last year of primary school education, a disadvantage that cost her a scholarship to high school.

The Bunga ran a competition for primary school pupils across the Transkei. The prize was a four-year bursary to high school for the student who scored the highest marks in a test. Albertina wrote the test and came top, much to the delight of her family and the whole Xolobe village. The Bunga bursary was a prestigious award, and the names of the winners were published in the Xhosa newspaper *Imvo Zabantsundu*. Albertina's joy was short-lived, however. When the award panel learned that she was two years older than the rest of her classmates, she was disqualified on grounds of her age. She was bitterly disappointed because there had been no mention of an age criteria when she wrote the test. The bursary had been the answer to her dream of going to high school without having to burden her grandparents, who were already doing so much for her, with having to pay school fees. Knowing Albertina's background and understanding why she had missed two years of school, her teachers were angry about what they saw as unfair treatment of their star pupil. Because the Bunga awards were published in the newspaper *Imvo Zabantsundu*, there was a second article about the winner being disqualified on grounds of age.

Fate stepped in and, for a change, it was in Albertina's favour. The priests at the local Roman Catholic Mission read the story in *Imvo* and felt that there had been a miscarriage of justice. They communicated with Father Bernard Huss at Mariazell, who arranged for a four-year scholarship for the girl from Xolobe village. Albertina was overwhelmed by the news that she would be going to the prestigious Mariazell College.

The Mnyila family were thrown into a frenzy of preparations. Qingqiwe threw a huge party for his granddaughter and mountains of *mngqusho* (the traditional dish of samp and beans) and meat were prepared. "The whole village was there. You would have thought it was a wedding," recalled Albertina. She was overwhelmed when people turned up with all manner of gifts: "Their generosity was so touching. I was not expecting any gifts." Her grandparents gave her the kind of large tin trunk that was standard issue for students going away to boarding school.

On the appointed day in 1936, a nervous and excited Albertina, dressed in a navy-blue school uniform (called a gym dress), and armed with her provision basket and tin trunk, bade farewell to her family. Parting from her mother and Flora was difficult, but she had the assurances of her grandparents that they would be well taken care of. The leave-taking from her siblings and cousins was more boisterous. Escorted by Uncle Campbell and Mcengi, she left on horseback for Cofimvaba, the first leg of the journey. They spent the night in Cofimvaba, and went on to Camama the following morning. Before returning from a journey or going away, it was customary to visit the graveyard and inform the ancestors, so they visited the graves of Bonilizwe and other members of the extended Dlangisa clan. Albertina tidied the *izivivane*, the piles of stones on each grave. After paying homage to the ancestors, Campbell and Mcengi saw Albertina off on the next stage of her journey, a bus trip that would take her through Qamata to Sterkstroom, where she boarded a train to Mariazell College, in the town of Matatiele, situated at the foot of the Drakensberg mountains at the meeting place of the borders of the present-day Eastern Cape, KwaZulu-Natal and Lesotho.

Despite her nervousness about the strangeness of her surroundings, Albertina was made to feel immediately welcome by Emcy Mzinyathi, a home girl from Xolobe, who was a prefect at the school. Albertina appreciated having a "big sister" to look up to for a change. She was also pleased to discover that one of the male teachers was a Ndlangisa. He treated Albertina as a relative and took a keen interest in her academic performance and development.

She loved boarding school and settled very quickly into the Mariazell routine. The school day began at 4am when the students had to wash, dress and clean their dormitories. They then proceeded to the chapel for prayers. They had prayers twice daily, in the morning and the evening. They studied English, Xhosa, maths, history and geography. They also did domestic science and were taught to sew. "We were generally trained to be orderly and organised." Father Huss, who treated her as his protégé, arranged that during her free time she be given in-service training at the school's administration office. She would sort out correspondence, stationery, books and newspapers, tidy the office and play the role of messenger for members of staff.

Albertina was one of the students who did not go home for holidays because they benefited from free board and lodging. They had to pay for their keep by spending their holidays ploughing in the fields and working in the laundry and ironing room. They only went home for the December holidays. Though she missed her home, Albertina did not object to the arrangement. She was only too glad to have the opportunity to be at school.

She enjoyed the sports facilities at the school. The girls used to play netball and the boys football. For the first time in her life, she had access to a swimming pool. The pupils used to swim in long-sleeved ankle-length dungarees. "We changed in cubicles and you had to make sure your body was not seen by other girls."

The teachers were very strict and discipline was tight. Students were allowed to write and receive letters from home, but before outgoing letters were sealed, they were read by the teachers. Girls were not allowed to receive letters from anyone outside their immediate family unit. Although theirs was a co-ed school, they were strictly forbidden to mix with the boys. They were not even allowed to talk to the boys in class and when taking walks during break periods. But the boys and girls would always find means to communicate. The boys would open the taps of the huge tanks situated at the corners of the hostel buildings. The water would flood the irrigation furrows that passed the girls' dormitories. They would then "post" their letters on the flowing water to be picked up by the interested parties in the girls' dormitory. Albertina was bemused by this reckless behaviour. Discipline was strict and the punishment was immediate expulsion. She could not understand how people could take such foolish risks with their education.

Mariazell was not left untouched by the start of the Second World War in 1939. The German nuns were recalled to Germany, and the pupils and staff had to pray day and night for the war to end. The school bell would ring at midday, a signal for everyone to stop whatever they were doing and say the Hail Mary. The pupils did not know much about the war apart from what they were told by the teachers, who provided very little explanation. They were not allowed to read newspapers because "we were told that newspapers were for politicians".

Towards the end of 1938, Albertina had to make decisions about her future, as her stint in Mariazell was drawing to a close. By 1939, she would be in Form Four preparing to write her Junior Certificate at the end of the year. Some of her fellow students had plans to go to Lovedale and Fort Hare. The idea of university never occurred to Albertina because of her responsibilities.

Albertina initially wanted to follow in the footsteps of her favourite teacher at Middle Xolobe and become a teacher. She resolved not to marry, but to become a professional person so that she could provide for her mother and siblings. Her sense of obligation to them had increased with the death of her grandfather Qingqiwe in 1937/8. Qingqiwe's son Campbell had taken over as head of the family and headman of the village, and while he had always shown the greatest consideration to Monica and her children, Albertina could not help feeling that they should try as far as possible not to be a burden to him.

When she arrived home for the December holidays at the end of 1938, she was dismayed to learn that her Uncle Campbell had arranged a marriage for her. The young man was a law graduate from a very respectable family and he was considered a good match. Albertina rejected the idea: "I had my own plan."

While in Mariazell under the spiritual guidance of Father Huss, Albertina had converted to Catholicism. She admired the dedication of the nuns who taught them, and as she had resolved never to marry, she decided to become a nun. When she discussed her plan with Father Huss, he told her that nuns did not receive salaries. He also warned her that if she entered a convent, she would have to sever links with her extended family: "When you become a nun, you marry the Church. You will not be able to take care of your siblings." Father Huss suggested that the best way for her to get a career and support her family at the same time was to take up nursing, because she would be paid while she was training. It was a practical solution and Albertina took his advice. Under his guidance, she began applying to various training hospitals and by the time she left Mariazell at the end of 1939, she had been accepted as a trainee nurse at Johannesburg Non-European Hospital.

As she celebrated Christmas with her family at Xolobe, Albertina was overcome by a feeling of nostalgia. She missed her grandfather and knew that life would never be the same. She worried about going so far away from her ailing mother, but she knew that there was much more she could do for her family as a trained professional. She also knew that Monica was in the loving care of Nosenti. Albertina was encouraged by the progress of her siblings. At 10 years old, Flora was able to make herself useful around the household and, within the limitations of her illness, to take care of herself. Qudalele was doing well at boarding school and Elliot was proving to be an exceptional student. In January 1940, satisfied that all was as well as it could be at home, Albertina boarded the train to Johannesburg.

# *f o u r*

Walter was unnerved by his first sight of a train. He had heard about these fantastic machines, capable of carrying hundreds of people at a time and with the capacity to travel endlessly, and had tried to form a picture in his mind, but the reality far outstripped his imagination. The train whistle momentarily alarmed him, but the excitement of a dream come true and the presence of his companions quelled his anxiety.

The train, used exclusively for transporting recruits from the rural areas to the mines, was known as *Mbombela*. On its journey of about 1 000 kilometres, it would stop at countless small country sidings to load the human cargo destined for the mines. Conditions on the train during the two-day journey were, however, deplorable. Walter stowed his meagre luggage on the top bunk that served as both seating and sleeping accommodation for the duration of the long trip. The recruits had been given some rations and a small amount of pocket money for the journey. This would eventually be deducted from their pay-packets. But none of this could dampen Walter's spirits, as he looked forward to what lay ahead.

The three Qutubeni recruits were bound for Rose Deep Mine, situated between Germiston and Primrose, two small mining centres in the greater Johannesburg area. After disembarking at Germiston station, they walked to the mine compound. Walter's companions, who were acquainted with the various procedures, took Walter to the dormitories. The mine management had a policy of housing labourers from the same area in the same dormitory, so Walter and his companions joined 30 to 40 young men and some older men from Qutubeni and other places in the Engcobo District. As was the practice with recent arrivals, they were welcomed with coffee, tea and bread, and then bombarded with questions about the state of affairs at home.

The following morning, Walter was taken to the Compound Manager's office. The chief clerk, a man named Katangana, was living with one of Walter's relatives, so he welcomed Walter as family. Katangana felt that Walter was too young for underground work, so he took it upon himself to discuss the matter with the manager, who then arranged for Walter to work for the dairy farmer who delivered milk to the mine. Walter was released from his contract after his relative Joel Hlakula repaid the cost of Walter's train fare, rations and pocket money at Engcobo's recruitment office.

Walter was then collected by his new employer, a farmer called Muller, and taken to his farm on the outskirts of Germiston. His new job was tedious and exhausting. He had to wake at 2am to wash the bottles, fill them with milk, seal them and pack them into crates for delivery, the first of which had to be completed by 6am. Walter delivered the milk by horse and cart. He then returned for a short rest before preparing for the afternoon delivery. He worked seven days a week and up to 12 hours a day, for which he was paid one pound per month, including board and lodging.

Walter never received any post from home, nor did he write to his family. His only contact with his family was through Katangana, the chief clerk. The other five employees at the farm were not Xhosa-speaking, so he felt lonely and homesick. After working at the dairy farm for eight months, he quarrelled with the dairy farmer and his wife. Muller whipped Walter with a *sjambok* (a heavy whip or flexible stick) to the point of bleeding, and an outraged Walter decided to report the matter to the police. After many enquiries and a long trek on foot, he finally reached the police station, only to be cursed and clouted across the face by a policeman. In addition to handing out verbal and physical abuse, the policeman detained him and sent a message to his employer to collect him. Walter had received his first lesson in South African justice.

Walter had no alternative but to go back to work, but he soon left again after another minor quarrel. This time he went to the pass office to find out what the procedures were for leaving his place of employment. The official at the pass office turned out to be a friend of Walter's employer. He asked Walter to return to the farm, but this time Walter was adamant. Mrs Muller also tried to persuade him to come back, but to no avail.

Walter was able to get his papers in order, and with the help of another acquaintance from Qutubeni, he got a job as a domestic worker for Captain Todd, a senior official at Rose Deep Mine. Not long afterwards, Todd accused Walter of stealing and eating the dog's meat. They quarrelled and Walter was dismissed. Todd was decent enough to arrange for Walter to work as a sweeper (*Matshanyela*), whose task was to clean and sweep the mine dormitories. For this, he was paid two pounds and ten shillings a month.

Like the other young workers, Walter handed over his pay to the older miners, who acted as guardians to the young men. He retained about ten shillings for personal expenses such as tobacco (he had taken to smoking a pipe). All personal matters and expenditures, such as weekend plans or the buying of clothes, had to be referred to the guardians. The latter were highly respected as men of integrity who never abused their position. Walter soon learned the wisdom of consulting them before spending any money.

The workers looked forward to Sunday, the only day when they could visit family and friends and receive visits from workers from other mines. These social gatherings relieved the monotony of mine life. Adjoining the mine complex were a host of shebeens and gambling dens where confidence tricksters operated. One Sunday, Walter saw a crowd surrounding a man who had laid three bottle tops on the ground. Under one of the tops was a pea. Spectators were laying bets as to which bottle top the pea was under. The trickster enticed Walter by allowing him to play without placing a bet, then encouraging him to bet. Walter bet five shillings (one fifth of his monthly wage) and lost. Anxious to win his money back, he bet a further five shillings, then his watch, then his hat. When he had nothing else to bet, he tried, without success, to argue that he had been cheated. Dejected, he returned to the mine, where he was thoroughly scolded by his elders and told he would never be allowed to go out alone with money again. This was the first and the last time in Walter's life that he gambled.

Despite his youthful follies, Walter was seen as "educated" and would be asked to write letters for the older men who could not read or write. Some of the letters to their wives and children that they dictated were very moving. Evenings were the best part of the day, when a host of stories was told, especially by the older miners. Spellbound, Walter would listen until late at night. On Friday evenings, the miners were treated to film shows in an "open-air cinema". The silent films would be projected onto a wall outside. Walter's enjoyment of the evenings was marred when he learned about the practice of sodomy taking place in the dormitories. Walter was shocked and disturbed to learn that this was not uncommon among miners, especially those on long contracts. He found the idea repugnant, but understood it as an inevitable consequence of the labour migration system in which men were deprived of a stable family life.

In the rural areas, those who had worked in the mines and cities would boast of their ability to speak languages other than Xhosa. Walter used to be very impressed when they showed off by using "exotic" idioms and proverbs, mostly in Sotho. He therefore went out of his way to develop friendships with the Sotho miners in order to learn their language. Some firm friendships resulted, and the Sotho miners became very fond of him.

Walter often visited his mother who, at the time, was living in the inner-city ghetto of George Goch, where she earned a living by doing washing for several families. He was unhappy about his mother living in what was called a "location" because of prevailing attitudes that to do so was "not respectable". The stigma derived from the fact that apart from beer-brewing, prostitution and laundry, there were almost no employment options for black women in the urban areas. Alice meanwhile tried to persuade her son to return to school. She was keen for him to get into St Peter's College in Rosettenville, but Walter had had enough of city life and was hankering to return to Qutubeni. He worked on the mine for eight months and returned home when his contract expired towards the end of 1929.

Walter arrived at Qutubeni loaded with gifts of sweets, tobacco, tea, coffee, sugar and other food-stuffs that the villagers expected to receive from any returning migrant. Just before going home, he had gone to Germiston and bought himself a new suit, hat and shoes. On arrival, he reimbursed his cousin Joel for the amount he had paid for the cessation of Walter's contract. He then handed the balance of his earnings to Joubert and Florence Hlakula, who had by that time assumed over-all responsibility for the wellbeing of the family in Qutubeni. His reunion with his sister Rosabella was particularly joyous. There was a large gathering to welcome him, with all the festivities and excitement that usually accompanied the return of migrants.

At the beginning of 1930, Walter, together with four other village boys aged between 17 and 21, made preparations for their circumcision ceremony, which would mark their coming of age. They attended initiation school – a temporary structure consisting of a thatched roof and grass walls – situated about half a mile outside the village boundaries. For three to four months, special attend-ants (usually relatives) cared for the boys. During this period, the *abakhwetha*, as the initiates were called, had to smear their bodies with white ochre, wear only blankets and sleep on the floor. This was considered to be a period of self-development, a time for leading an upright and monastic life, cultivating self-discipline and preparing for the assumption of greater responsibilities in life. At the end of the designated period, the initiates had to wash their bodies in a river, not a stream. Qutubeni initiates always washed in the Xuka River, about two miles from the initiation school. After a thorough wash, they were given blankets to wear, and only upon their return to their homes were they permitted to wear ordinary clothing.

The end of the initiation period was marked by a huge celebration attended by family, friends and relatives. Any guest was at liberty to say a few words and the initiates were subjected to a number of long and serious lectures on their future responsibilities. In Walter's case, both Joubert, as head of the household, and Joel Hlakula made the main speeches. The gist of their messages was that his boyhood life had ended and that he was now a man. As such, he was expected to leave the carefree ways of young boys and become a serious adult who had a contribution to make to the public life of the village by participating in the village council or *Nkundla*. The giving of presents followed the speeches. After this ceremony, the newly acquired status of the young men was acknowledged by all. For a further period of about two months, the "new" young men (*ikrwala*) were expected to bathe in the river every morning and evening. This symbolised the washing away of the last rem-nants of their boyhood.

Around this time, Walter first started taking a romantic interest in girls. He was attracted to a vil-lage girl called Nondingo, who was two years his senior. She was feared by the local young men and exercised a strong influence over other girls. He also liked Nozinboyi Dlwati, a girl from an-other village who stayed at All Saints. Despite his budding feelings, nothing materialised in the way of a concrete relationship.

Walter returned to Johannesburg in mid-1930 to go back to work. As a young man, he had to pay taxes and help support his family. His main responsibility was to pay school fees for Rosabella, who was a student at All Saints and who would soon be completing Standard Six. As he was now of age, Walter had no problems entering into a contract in his own name, and he returned to Rose Deep Mine accompanied by a fellow initiate and friend.

On being told that he was to work underground, Walter protested to no avail. He then went to the Witwatersrand Native Labour Association (WNLA), which cooperated closely with the Native Recruiting Office, to make a complaint and demand a refund of recruitment costs for himself and his friend. Such behaviour was unheard of, and he was threatened by the *indunas* (boss-boys) at the Native Recruiting Office, informed that he had to complete the contract, and chased away.

Mine officials usually took advantage of raw recruits and forced them to work underground unless they were declared medically unfit to do so. Their working day was strenuous and exhausting, and lasted about nine hours. Walter worked underground loading cocopans with ore. The rock was dynamited last thing in the evening, and the ore was loaded into cocopans and cleared away the next day. He was also the personal teaboy (*picannin*) of the white foreman, who was fond of him because of his youth and his ability to speak English. It was also the *picannin's* job to light the fuse when the rock was dynamited.

One day, the mineshaft in which Walter usually worked caved in, and several miners were killed. Fortunately, he was not in the shaft at the time. Shaken and depressed by the accident, Walter and three other boys from Engcobo decided not to go underground any more. Walter approached the compound manager, who agreed to transfer them above ground. Their case was helped by the fact that some of the senior clerks were "home-boys" from Engcobo, who were able to intercede on their behalf. Walter was transferred to where the ore was processed with cyanide, but his salary was reduced from three pounds a month to two pounds and ten shillings.

"Boss-boys" drove the miners mercilessly and did not allow them to stand upright. While they were popular with the white miners, the "boss-boys" were feared and hated by the black miners, especially because they were reluctant to assist in any way unless they were bribed with gifts. Miners would also often have to do their washing or clean their quarters. Complaints about the "boss-boys" were rare, as these led to beatings at the hands of those against whom the complaints had been made.

The frustrations of compound life often led to petty quarrels between individuals, quarrels that could sometimes spark off faction fights. During his stint at Rose Deep, Walter often heard of faction fights, but he never witnessed any.

High levels of frustration and aggression were not surprising, considering the abysmal conditions in the mining compounds. The overcrowded, poorly lit and badly ventilated dormitories consisted of concrete bunks set into the walls. The miners had to provide their own bedding, and the heavy smoking of most miners aggravated the stuffy conditions. Washing and bathing facilities were generally inadequate and miners had to queue for long periods for the few showers that were available. Toilets were provided by the bucket system, and the daily removal, emptying, cleaning and replacing of the buckets was the responsibility of a special group of workers.

The thing that irked Walter most about life in the dormitories was the complete lack of privacy. The suffering of other miners also disturbed him. The disease "miner's phthisis" (a form of tuberculosis) was very common. Sick miners were treated at a hospital situated on mine property, just outside the mine complex. It was a shared facility for miners from Rose Deep and Glen Deep mines. Walter felt that it was very unfair that sick miners were not paid. Their contracts were suspended for the period they were hospitalised and reinstated only when they were discharged and back at work. Miners were also subjected to the practice of "deferred pay". This was when wages were banked by the mine management and paid to the worker without interest at the end of a specific period.

The poor quality and meagre quantity of food was a constant source of dissatisfaction among the miners. One weekend, they held a meeting at which they resolved to take up the matter with the mine authorities. Walter was excited about this, the first meeting attended by such a large number of miners. He was impressed by the determination and boldness with which the speakers addressed the meeting.

An ultimatum was presented to the authorities – that unless the general manager met with a deputation from the miners, the entire compound would stop work on Monday. Furthermore, if the demands of the workers were not met, the miners would march to the Johannesburg offices of WNLA. The manager agreed to meet the deputation, and after hearing their grievance, he immediately agreed to an improvement in the preparation of the food.

It was Walter's first experience of organised industrial action and he enjoyed the thrill of victory. As an 18-year-old rural migrant, he had no knowledge of previous struggles by the miners. It was only later that he would learn that theirs was not the first protest at Rose Deep Mine. In November 1919, 300 mineworkers from Rose Deep had marched to Johannesburg to protest against their miserable diet. He also learned that unhappiness about low wages and rising prices had resulted in a number of strikes by black miners between 1917 and 1920, culminating in the November 1920 strike in which 71 000 black workers forced the closure of 21 mines. Cordons were thrown round each compound and the army was rushed in to brutally suppress what was then the largest strike in the history of the South African mining industry (Callinicos 1994, 94).

Years later, Walter would develop a deep interest in the "Rand Revolt", the 1922 strike by white miners in response to the decision by the Chamber of Mines to cut the cost of white labour by reducing the proportion of white to black workers, transferring some semi-skilled jobs to black workers at lower rates of pay. Jan Smuts, the Prime Minister of the Union, declared martial law in response to the strike. In three months of bloody clashes, he used the full force of the army against the white working-classes of the Witwatersrand (Lerumo, 45).

Walter continued working for some time after his 120-day contract expired before returning to Qutubeni in mid-1931. By that time, he had made up his mind never to return to the mines.

As a young adult, Walter participated actively in the social life of the village, attending weddings, funerals and church meetings. He used part of his earnings to buy a horse (for seven pounds) and a saddle (for five pounds). He especially enjoyed attending weddings, which were important social occasions. Preparations started about a fortnight before the wedding. These included the practising of songs and dances, bush parties where the bride and groom practised singing, and the training and preparation of horses for the wedding procession. Trotters and other horses were decorated with bells and balloons. Like Albertina, Walter enjoyed these opportunities to display his horsemanship, preparing and training his own horse for such occasions. Walter was also privileged to conduct the village choir, an honour that was usually reserved for more senior men in the community.

Walter also participated in listening to petty complaints by villagers. He was part of the "prosecution", but the accused could be found guilty only by the village "jury". Young girls often attended these village court cases, and Walter admits to showing off for their benefit.

A large meeting at Engcobo, where the magistrate and Bunga members were giving a report to those assembled, made a lasting impression on Walter. The magistrate announced that people would have to cull their stock, especially the goats, which were destroying the trees and depleting the soil. A red-blanketed man stood up and caused a sensation by saying that the magistrate as a white man thought himself superior, and that what he had just stated was a declaration of war. He asked why black people were being asked to limit their stock while each white farmer in Elliot (Elliotdale) had huge herds of livestock. He asked why the magistrate did not tell the white farmers to cull their stock, and concluded that the remedy was to remove the white farmer.

The red-blanketed man's statement sent shock waves around the meeting. The chiefs asked him to withdraw his statement. He refused. All he would say was that the magistrate was there only to convey the instructions of his superiors and that people should sleep on the matter, which should certainly be sent to the Paramount Chief for a final decision. Walter was most impressed by the defiance of the red-blanketed man, and would often recall the incident in later life.

When he had first returned home to Qutubeni, Walter had learned that a cooperative society had been established in the village to provide for loans and assistance in times of bereavement. He had decided to join, and paid the registration fee of two pounds ten shillings. Towards the end of 1931, he borrowed money from the society to go to East London to look for work.

Walter knew nothing about the 1929 Wall Street crash and the Great Depression, but he, like millions of his compatriots, suffered the consequences. In East London, he joined the thousands of people trudging the streets looking for work. A crippling drought, overpopulation in the reserves, and the enforced culling of livestock had combined to force thousands of peasants off the land and into the towns. The wealth of rural people was measured by their livestock, and for many households, being forced to reduce the numbers of animals they kept was a recipe for even greater poverty. Meanwhile, the permit system was vigorously applied to try to limit the number of rural migrants flocking to the towns to seek work. Walter hated the constant police raids, in which those without Lodger's Permits were forced to flee into the forests to avoid arrest.

Walter's arrival in East London also coincided with the end of a strike that had been organised by the Industrial Commercial Union (ICU). Employers were angry about the strike and often turned job-seekers away with the sarcastic remark: "Go to Kadalie, he will give you a job." Puzzled by this remark, Walter was curious to know who this figure was, and joined the crowds who gathered every Sunday at a large sportsground to hear Kadalie speak. Clements Kadalie was originally from Nyasaland (modern-day Malawi) and, like many of his compatriots, had migrated southwards. He arrived in the Cape in 1918 and soon became the moving spirit behind the formation of the millenarian trade union movement, the Industrial and Commercial Workers Union (which was to become the ICU). The ICU quickly grew into a mass-based organisation that spread through the country with the speed of a veld fire, reaching its zenith in 1928, when it claimed a membership of over 100 000. Even if this claim was exaggerated, as some have argued, there can be no doubt that by the mid-1920s, the ICU was a challenge to the ANC's position as the most significant African political organisation (Karis and Carter, 155–6). By 1926, Kadalie "had become a power in the land so that newspapers accorded him as much publicity as they gave to any cabinet minister" (Roux 1964, 162). Kadalie amassed a large following in the rural areas by implying that through the ICU, the people would be able to get back their land.

As was to be expected, the ICU became the target of state repression and the spate of strikes it inspired often resulted in bloodshed. In 1920, police and angry white civilians fired on ICU members as they demonstrated for the release of their leader Masabalala, and 23 people were killed (Lekota, 86).

By 1928, it had become quite clear that the ICU had run too far, too fast, and its organisational weaknesses were catching up with it. Communists within the ICU accused Kadalie of being dictatorial. They demanded better financial management and a more militant policy of struggle. Stung by this criticism and urged on by white liberal sympathisers, Kadalie purged the organisation of communist influences. Well-known communists like James La Guma, Ernest Khaile and John Gomas, who were all part of the ICU's National Council, were expelled (Roux 1964, 164). The ICU was further wracked by a power struggle between Kadalie and his powerful lieutenant AWG Champion, who had built up the largest and wealthiest branch of the ICU in Natal. The rivalry culminated in the secession of the Natal ICU, which became the ICU (Natal), under Champion's leadership (Roux 1964, 176).

The combination of internal division and lack of a clear policy and programme, together with state repression, ended the dream run of the ICU. When Walter heard him speak in the early 1930s, Kadalie could still draw the crowds with his speeches about the grievances of the African people, but by then, the ICU was a spent force. Walter found Kadalie "a powerful speaker and an impressive personality" but he was a man "who spoke more about himself. He conveyed the impression that he was in a position to do anything for his own welfare but was sacrificing his time for the benefit of his people".

Walter also attended meetings addressed by RH Godlo. A journalist and protégé of the ANC Secretary-General Sol Plaatje, Godlo was the editor of the Xhosa monthly paper, *Umlindi we Nyanga*. He was also the founder and president of the South African Congress of Advisory Boards (Karis and Gerhart, 4). Walter had been encouraged by some young ladies to join the popular temperance organisation, the Independent Order of True Templars (IOTT), better known by its nickname "I Only Take Tea". He met Godlo, who held a senior position in the IOTT, at one of their functions. Walter's impression of Godlo was that he was articulate and dignified, and that his oratory skills were superior to those of Kadalie.

Walter had heard a lot about Walter Rubusana, a founder member of the ANC. Consequently, he was keen to meet the man who had acquired legendary status when he became the first and last African ever to be elected to the Cape Provincial Council upon winning the seat for the Thembuland constituency in 1910. One of Walter's favourite books was Rubusana's classic work, *Zemk'iinkomo Magwalandini* (figuratively translated as "Defend your Heritage"), an anthology of traditional epic poetry, didactic Christian essays and Church history. Walter, however, was interested only in the oral poetry. A minister of the Congregational Church, a writer who had helped found the Xhosa newspaper *Izwi Labantu* in 1898, and a politician, Rubusana was a man of many talents. He was part of the 1909 delegation of African and coloured leaders who went to London to present grievances to the British government. The delegation had failed in its objective of reversing the "colour bar" clauses in the draft Union constitution, but it did succeed in preventing the absorption of the three British High Commission territories of Botswana, Lesotho and Swaziland into the Union of South Africa. Rubusana was one of the founder members of the ANC and was elected its Vice-President at its inaugural conference in 1912.

By the time Walter tried to visit him in East London, Rubusana was 72 and had long retired from active politics. Unfortunately, when friends took Walter to Rubusana's home, the veteran politician was not there. Walter always regretted not meeting him.

In East London Walter stayed with Joel Hlakula's brother-in-law, and often visited his mother's younger brother, Theophilus. Though he did not have to pay rent, the months of unemployment ate into his meagre reserves, and he had to sell his clothes to survive. He managed to find work in a dairy, but this spell of employment lasted only two weeks.

Walter finally managed to secure an interview for a position as a domestic worker with a garage owner named Barnes. Barnes wrote to All Saints to verify details about Walter, received a favourable reply and hired him. Walter went to live in a well-furnished room in the backyard of the Barnes's big double-storey house. Working under a white housekeeper called Maggie, Walter cleaned the house, served as a waiter and carried out general domestic duties. His wages were one pound and ten shillings a month, with free food and lodging. For the first time in his working life, Walter was happy with his job. He got on well with the Barnes family, and became firm friends with the Barnes's teenage daughters, Yvonne and Molly, who often visited him in his room. He got on well with Maggie, the housekeeper, who treated him as an ally, and confided in him about household affairs and her dissatisfaction with the family. In comparison with most other white people, Walter found Mr and Mrs Barnes very liberal, and he and Maggie were treated equally well. However, there were limits to Mr Barnes's egalitarianism. When Maggie fussed about things that made her unhappy in the house, such as Mr Barnes's habit of pouring hot water over live crabs, he would tell her, "Even in heaven I will sit upstairs and you will sit downstairs."

It was during this period in his life that Walter read the book *Up From Slavery* by Booker T Washington. He was particularly struck by the ways in which Washington dealt with his poverty, including the detail that he owned only one set of clothes – which he washed daily. (Walter told his mother this story, and thereafter she referred to anyone who had only one set of clothing as a "Booker T Washington".) "It was interesting ... how he was determined to go on improving himself, developing himself, ... go[ing] ahead with what he wanted to do" (Houser and Shore Interviews, 216). Walter also read the writings of WEB du Bois; he felt that he was culturally influenced by Washington's, but that Du Bois was more of a political influence.

Although he was satisfied with his job, Walter decided to return to Qutubeni at the end of 1932. Before leaving for home, Walter remembered that not long after his arrival in East London, he had met a white woman who had asked him, in Xhosa, where he came from. When he told her he was from Qutubeni, she told him she had a son who ran a chemist's shop in Engcobo. She asked Walter to let her know when he returned home, so he went to see her before leaving for Qutubeni. She asked him to take some canned fruit to her son, but when he delivered the parcel, he received a frosty reception from the son, who was aloof and cold. Walter found this to be typical of the general attitude of whites in the Transkei.

Walter returned to Johannesburg in 1933, where he went to stay in Doornfontein with his mother. He was somewhat taken aback to discover that he now had a stepfather, a Mr Handile. They shared one yard with about 10 families of various races, who made up a microcommunity of their own. The address was 23 Van Wyk Street, close to what is now the Ellis Park sports complex. Doornfontein was one of Johannesburg's inner-city slum areas in which people of diverse racial and ethnic origins lived side by side. Walter would find out many years later that one of his neighbours in nearby Beit Street was a young Jewish boy, Joe Slovo, who was to describe Doornfontein as "the lowest rung in the Jewish residential ladder" (Slovo, 14).

Walter managed to get a job with Premier Biscuits, a subsidiary of Premier Milling Company, in Siemert Road in Doornfontein. His job was to take empty tins to the white women who packed the biscuits. He then had to load the packed biscuits onto the lift. He also helped in the baking department. The day shift started at 8.10am and lasted till 5pm.

Alice, meanwhile, was still working as a washerwoman. Walter helped her out over weekends by delivering washing to Yeoville, Bertrams and Bezuidenhout Valley. He also attended night school at the Bantu Men's Social Club (BMSC) in Eloff Street Extension, and then at the Swedish Mission School. He took driving lessons from a taxi-owner, got his temporary driver's licence and became acquainted with the city. He failed his first driving test and never went back for another one.

In 1934 Walter, his mother and stepfather were among thousands of black inner-city residents who became victims of the Johannesburg City Council's "slum clearance" policy. These areas had always been looked upon with disfavour by the Council, partly because of the squalid conditions and their tendency to breed crime, but mainly because of their interracial character. "Slum clearance" was considered the solution to the problem, and in 1904 an outbreak of bubonic plague provided the Council with a cast-iron excuse to remove the African residents of the so-called "Coolie Location" in Braamfontein to a newly established location at Klipspruit, 13 kilometres outside of the city proper. Klipspruit was to become the heart of present-day Soweto (Bonner and Segal, 13). In the 1930s, Johannesburg was hit by an influx of thousands of destitute white farmers, casualties of the collapse of white agriculture in the wake of the Great Depression. They had to be accommodated somewhere, and to avert further interracial residential mixing, the city fathers decided to embark on another round of clearances. The urban municipalities secured changes to the Urban Areas Act, which freed the Johannesburg City Council from any obligation to provide alternative accommodation for black residents evicted from inner-city slums. The Slum Clearance Act of 1934 also facilitated the forced removal of people (Bonner and Segal, 15).

To make way for segregated housing, thousands of black families from the inner city areas like Doornfontein were forced to move from their homes during the 1930s. Most of them were moved to the new African township of Orlando, 15 kilometres southwest of Johannesburg and adjacent to the main road to Potchefstroom (Bonner and Segal, 16). When work on the new township began in 1931, the Council declared that they were building "the biggest and finest township in the Union of South Africa". A report in *The Star* newspaper claimed that "Each house has a neat veranda and either two or three airy apartments, such as many Europeans would not despise" (Bonner and Segal, 17).

In 1934, Walter, his mother and stepfather were among the many families forced to move to the new township of Orlando where they discovered that the rosy picture painted by the Council was a complete illusion. They found a four-roomed house with a roof and not much else. There were no floors, simply bare earth. There was no electricity or running water inside the house. Drinking water had to be fetched from communal taps, and latrines operated on the bucket system. After moving to Orlando, Walter stopped going to night school because of transport difficulties. He was always short of money because a substantial part of his wages had to cover the train fare from Orlando to Johannesburg, whereas when he lived in Doornfontein, he had simply walked to work.

Walter and his stepfather did not get on, mainly because of the amount of money that Walter spent on Rosabella's education. "My stepfather could not understand this question of educating girls." His stepfather, who was a heavy drinker, felt that Walter should contribute that money to the household expenses instead. The friction between them worsened, and after constant quarrels, Walter moved out and stayed with friends. Shortly thereafter, his mother and stepfather separated. His stepfather moved out of the house and because a woman could not rent a house in her own name, the lease was made out in Walter's name.

At Premier Milling Company, Walter began to have discussions with one of the older workers, a man called Mgadi. Mgadi had connections with the trade union movement and introduced Walter to a number of trade unionists. He also introduced Walter to a white couple who lived in Village Main. It was the first time Walter had met whites who wanted to be addressed by their Christian names rather than being called "Baas" or "Madam".

At the beginning of 1936, Walter initiated a strike at Premier Milling to demand higher wages – an increase of two shillings and sixpence a week and an allocation of bread. Walter presented the demands of the workers to Mr Fischer, the manager, who simply ignored him. All the workers from the biscuit department agreed to report to work, but not to start working. It was agreed that they would wear their best clothes; according to Walter, "We reasoned that if the men were wearing their best suits they would not be easily persuaded to soil their clothes by going into the factory." Unfortunately, he was to be proved wrong.

The workers assembled at 9.30am at the corner of Market and End streets, about one block away from Premier Milling and marched to the factory. The manager confronted them as they entered the factory premises. As their spokesman, Walter repeated their demands. The manager's response was simply to ask the workers one by one whether or not they wanted to work; if so, they should stand to one side. At the end of this exercise, Walter and three other workers were left standing alone. Seeing that they were outnumbered by those who had agreed to go back to work, the three remaining workers caved in and joined the others, leaving Walter isolated. Under the circumstances, he decided that he would rather leave the job than return to work: "I was not fired. I was asked, 'Do you want to work?' I did not answer. I just took my things and left. In fact, my testimonial said: 'He left on his own.'"

Walter heard later that some of the workers had suggested that he should be given one shilling a month for his maintenance, but others had opposed this move, saying that Walter had been given a chance to return to work and had not taken it.

Walter then got a temporary job with the newspaper *Bantu World*, a newspaper owned by two white businessmen jointly with a company controlled by the Chamber of Mines. The editor, Robert Victor Selope Thema, had left his job as superintendent of the Bantu Men's Social Centre to run *Bantu World* when it was established in 1932 (Basner, 69). Selope Thema was one of the founder members of the ANC and had been the editor of the defunct ANC newspaper *Abantu-Batho*. He was recognised as one of the finest journalists of his time, and Walter had great admiration for him: "Thema was a dignified and impressive person who spoke with great authority, even when he spoke to whites." Walter also admired the journalists who worked at *Bantu World*, especially HIE and RRR Dhlomo, two brothers who were to become renowned for their poetry, novels and plays (Luli Callinicos, Interview, 10/6/90).

At the time, *Bantu World* was conducting a campaign to get a bigger share of the market, especially in advertisements, so it employed a number of young men as advertising agents. Walter became an agent for *Bantu World*; he also wrote several articles on current events for the paper. One of his pieces described police harassment of those brewing and selling native beer, and argued that it was essential for people to drink naturally brewed beer – interesting given that he himself never drank alcohol! He never had a byline nor was he paid for these articles because they were placed in the local columns or under "Letters to the Editor".

Shortly after starting work at *Bantu World*, Walter decided to become a distribution agent. He managed to acquire an agency for a number of papers: *Bantu World* (later *Naledi*), *Ilanga lase Natal*, *Imvo Zabantsundu*, *Mocho Chonono*, and the Rhodesian newspaper, *Bantu Mirror*. At first Walter did well from the commission he received. He then got some schoolboys to help him sell the papers. Unfortunately, most of them sold the papers but did not hand the money over to Walter, who was hopeless at chasing up debts. He operated as an agent for three years, but was rendered bankrupt by 1938/9, mainly because of money misappropriated by the schoolchildren.

In addition to his agency, Walter continued to look for full-time work. Not long after leaving Premier Milling, he got a job with Herbert Evans & Company in Doornfontein. He worked there for about a year and then went to work for L Suzman & Co in Sauer Street, where his Uncle Clifford worked. His job was to perform clerical work in the despatch department and help make out orders. One day, he was instructed to help load a truck. He refused, arguing that loading trucks was not part of his job, and was dismissed as a result.

In 1936, a population census, supervised by the Johannesburg municipality, was carried out, and Walter was appointed one of the enumerators. He was paid five pounds for interviewing 500 households in Orlando and filling in the census forms. As a result of police raids for pass laws and liquor permits, people were suspicious of any official enquiry into places of birth, work and other personal details. Not surprisingly, Walter received a hostile reception when he went about his work – he was often chased away and on one occasion even beaten. He sometimes had to enlist the help of the municipal police to carry out his duties.

In 1938, Walter was employed by the Union Bank of South Africa as a marketing agent. His job was to persuade potential customers to open a bank account. He would then dispense complimentary money-boxes to new customers to encourage saving. He enjoyed this because "I was working on my own. I was not controlled by anybody". Occasionally, he worked as a teller in the non-white section of the bank, as a stand-in for tellers who were on leave. His work for the bank put him in contact with a wide variety of people; for example, he visited factories where he spoke to workers. Students at St Peter's in Rosettenville were an important target audience, as were clerks in the civil service (Luli Callinicos, Interview, 10/6/90).

It was during this period of his life that Walter was learning that being a black person in South Africa meant being constantly on the wrong side of the law. While job-hunting after his departure from Premier Biscuits, he was arrested and taken to Hillbrow Police Station on the grounds that "something was wrong with his pass book". He had to pay a ten-shilling admission of guilt fine, a hefty amount for someone in his circumstances. What he found even more disturbing were the assaults he witnessed at the police station. He was shocked and angered to see police assaulting some prisoners with the butts of their guns.

Walter hated the pass laws with a passion and would always maintain that his abhorrence of the pass law system was the main reason he embarked on a path of political activism. Because of his light skin, Walter was not arrested as often as his peers were. He could easily have escaped the trauma of pass arrests altogether if he had chosen to take on a coloured identity, as coloureds were not required to carry passes. Some friends and family members suggested this to him, but he found the idea absolutely abhorrent. "I am a black man, I am an African, I am subject to all the laws that affect my people," was his response. He was determined never to use his outward appearance to his advantage, "because I never wanted to see my colour determine my race. I was an African in every sense of the word. No less, no more" (Houser and Shore Interviews, 37). He believed that there was no point in running away from an oppressive system. "I would rather suffer under the system, until I had defeated it."

While distributing leaflets for *Bantu World*, he had another brush with the law when he intervened on behalf of a young girl who was being harassed by a ticket examiner on the train to Orlando. When Walter tried to find out why the girl was crying, the conductor pushed Walter aside. Walter grabbed his collar and hung on until the conductor's shirt tore. Instead of sympathising with Walter, the other passengers made disparaging remarks.

When the train pulled in at New Canada Station, Walter was handed over to the police and taken to the Orlando Police Station, where he says he saw "hell itself". Walter was taken to an isolation cell (*khulukutu*, in South African prison jargon), where he found that some of the prisoners were Mpondo miners who had been involved in a spate of murders using bicycle spokes as weapons. The place was crawling with lice and bugs, and the blankets were filthy. Prisoners were regularly assaulted. Walter was detained for three days, charged with assault and found guilty. His family paid the three-pound fine.

His mother later told him that the bail money had been obtained from his father, Victor Dickinson, who was by then a Crown Prosecutor in Johannesburg. Walter was uncomfortable discussing the matter with his mother. He harboured a degree of resentment towards the father who had not seen fit to have a relationship with his children. He did not approve of his mother's "friendly attitude" towards this absent father and his position created an awkwardness between them. Consequently, he never asked his mother for any details of her continued contact with Dickinson, or the support she got from him. Some commentators have argued that as a result of his relationship (or rather lack of it) with his father, Walter grew up harbouring bitter resentment towards whites (Holland, 30). All those who know him well maintain that bitterness is not part of Walter's emotional make-up. He himself feels that bitterness is too strong a word: "Irritation, yes, but never bitterness." He has always maintained that whatever resentment he may have felt towards whites arose from his experience of growing up in a racially oppressive society, and not from his attitude to his father. Whatever hostility Walter felt towards his biological father was tempered by the fact that he never felt that he had missed out on anything as a result of his father's neglect. Having grown up in the warm embrace of his extended family guided by the powerful paternal figure of Dyantyi Hlakula, who he worshipped, Walter was stable and secure in his identity.

Despite his display of disinterest to his mother, Walter was curious about Victor Dickinson, and towards the end of the 1930s he went to court a couple of times "to witness him in action". Walter even engineered a meeting with him in the early 1940s. He had heard that Dickinson was the chairman of Equity Building Society, so he made an appointment to see him ostensibly to discuss a loan. At the time, Walter was in the process of setting up an estate agency, so he outlined his business plan to Dickinson and another director of the company. They listened politely and gave him some advice, but did not grant the loan. Walter's real motive for setting up the meeting was "to see if he remembered he had a son". Although he was perfectly polite and correct, "a real gentleman",

Dickinson gave no sign of any such recollection, and Walter was too proud to raise the matter. Father and son therefore did not acknowledge each other in any way at this, their first and last meeting. Curiosity satisfied, Walter dismissed Dickinson from his mind completely.

Despite the hazards of urban township life, the move to Orlando constituted a break from the past for Walter, and "home" became Orlando and not Qutubeni. This shift came about partly because during the 1930s, many of his extended family members moved to Johannesburg. They were among the many who moved from the rural areas to the towns to escape the overcrowding and poverty in the reserves. At any one time there were at least 10 or more family members staying in their four-roomed house. Rosabella completed her education at All Saints and went to teach in Springs for a while before joining Walter and their mother in Orlando in 1934. Alice's brother Clifford, who had been staying in Bellevue near the city centre, brought his wife and two children from the Transkei, and moved in with Walter and Alice. Other family members who stayed with the Sisulus were Caleb Mase (the son of Alice's sister, Nora), his daughter Nancy, and his cousin and Walter's old school friend and age-mate, Samuel Mase. Evelyn Mase, Sam's younger sister, also joined the household to continue her education at Orlando High after she had completed Standard Four at All Saints.

Walter took an active part in the social life of Orlando and began to emerge as a public figure. He was a founder member of a choir of about a dozen men and women who performed in the Johannesburg townships. The choir did not survive long because it was not financially viable. It performed on the basis of bidding from members of the audience; songs requested by the highest bidder were sung. The choir suffered from lack of promotion, and its performances were irregular. Eventually, it was absorbed into the Orlando Musical Association (OMA), which was much more sophisticated and even had its own fund-raising campaign. The OMA was auditioned by the South African Broadcasting Corporation (SABC), and its performances were occasionally broadcast. Walter became its chairman, which he considered a great honour.

One of the members of the choir Walter had helped set up was Nomaledi Xuma, a teacher in Sophiatown. She was the younger sister of Dr Alfred Bitini Xuma, a medical doctor and up-and-coming politician. Nomaledi introduced her brother to Walter in 1936. There was an instant connection because the Xumas were from Manzana in Engcobo, and their sister Diana had been Walter's teachers in the days when he attended primary school in Manzana. Dr Xuma was very strict, and would allow Nomaledi to attend choir practice only if Walter fetched her from the Xuma home in Sophiatown. Walter greatly admired the highly educated doctor, who had been trained in the United States and Scotland. Xuma in turn treated Walter like a younger brother, and became the Sisulu family's doctor.

Under Dr Xuma's influence, Walter became a member of the Bantu Men's Social Centre in Eloff Street Extension near Faraday Station. It had been established in 1932 by the missionary Dr Ray Phillips of the American Board Mission – he would later become the principal of the Jan Hofmeyr School at the BMSC – and was "designed to 'moralise the leisure time' of the growing black middle class by sponsoring a vast array of educational, recreational and Christian-related activities … Thriving under the patronage of the city's leading white liberals, the BMSC became the focus of all the social and cultural activities for educated Africans in Johannesburg for over 30 years" (Gish, 66). The Centre boasted a library, an auditorium, a refreshment area, meeting rooms, recreational facilities and classrooms. It was a major venue for social events such as wedding receptions, public functions such as lectures on race relations, and musical and dramatic productions. Members played indoor games such as billiards and tennis and took part in the weekly debates of the Gamma Sigma Club. In about 1938/9, Walter joined the Gamma Sigma Club, a debating society for the Witwatersrand area, organised by Ray Phillips. The club discussed the political problems facing the

African people. At the time, Walter was not aware that Phillips had been subsidised by the Chamber of Commerce and had been specifically assigned the task of gauging African opinion. At the Gamma Sigma Club, he met Ashby Peter (AP) Mda, a teacher who was very active in the Orlando Branch of the Transvaal Teachers' Association.

Walter had become a rugby fan in East London, where he had been a frequent visitor to the sports ground to watch rugby matches. In Orlando, he also became a regular at rugby matches, and he became chairman of the Orlando Occidental Rugby Club.

Walter's interest in African history led to his membership of the Orlando Brotherly Society (OBS), a cultural organisation that was formed in 1935. The Society met on Sundays and had an annual meeting to which the public was invited. The annual meeting was usually opened by veteran politician and businessman, Meshack Pelem, one of the four founding vice-presidents of the ANC (Luli Callinicos, Interview, 10/6/90). Elections were held for the positions of President and Secretary, and they even had a chaplain, Reverend Mayaba. Soon after Walter joined the Society, Mr Kongoma was made President and Walter was elected Secretary. Women also attended meetings and participated in some of the discussions, but Walter admits that "The question of women holding positions was not a matter we paid much attention to in those days". They discussed issues that affected them economically and politically, and were interested in historical events, especially Xhosa history. They would read and discuss classic Xhosa works such as Rubusana's *Zemk'iinkomo Mgawalandini* and *Ityala laMawele* by the highly acclaimed Xhosa writer and poet SEK Mqhayi.

Walter used to furnish reports of the Society's discussions to *Bantu World*, which would publish them in the form of articles. The Society was also committed to community upliftment schemes, and its members often visited the Diepkloof Reformatory for Juvenile Delinquents to talk to the boys there. The latter spoke frankly about the offences they had committed. Walter believed their plight to be the result of the poverty and miserable conditions of the African people.

Through the Society, Walter came into contact with the leading figures in the township. Because most of its membership hailed from the Eastern Cape, some claimed that the Society was a tribal organisation, an allegation that Walter vehemently rejected. The presence of Herbert Mdingi and his brothers Frank and David in the Orlando Brotherly Society probably contributed to perceptions that it was a Xhosa organisation. The Mdingis were originally from Centane in the Transkei. They were direct descendants (great-grandsons) of the great Xhosa chief, Hintsa of the Royal House of the Gcaleka. Herbert often spoke with vehemence and hostility about the cruel manner in which the British murdered Hintsa. (Hintsa's ears were cut off as keepsakes and his teeth were dug out with bayonets.) All three Mdingi brothers were prominent in public life, partly due to their illustrious ancestry, but also because they were striking personalities, good sportsmen and accomplished orators. Herbert Mdingi was 20 years older than Walter, but despite this age difference, the two men became firm friends. Walter acknowledges that Mdingi played an important role in shaping his political outlook, especially concerning resistance to white domination.

Herbert Mdingi was also a moving spirit behind the Orlando Vigilance Association (OVA). Most members of the Orlando Brotherly Association were also members of the OVA, and Walter joined in 1934. The OVA tried to address the grievances of Orlando residents, the main ones being the permit system and the constant police raids for liquor and passes. Depending on the issue, the OVA worked either in cooperation with or in opposition to the Native Advisory Boards (NABs), with whom they were sometimes in competition. Whether the Advisory Boards should report directly to the OVA (which maintained that it was the organ of the people) or directly to the people was a source of constant friction. However, on the matter of permits, the two bodies presented a common front.

The Advisory Boards had been set up in terms of the Native Urban Areas Act of 1935 to counter the impact of the ANC, which was by then recognised as the body that officially represented the people. The NABs were statutory bodies, with some elected and some nominated members.

In 1936, the Transvaal Vigilance Association (TVA) was set up, with the OVA as a founder member. Its main function was to protest against the pass and liquor raids, and to articulate the grievances of urban Africans. The TVA held its first conference in Germiston in 1936. Delegates came from all over the Witwatersrand – from the East and West Rand, Benoni, Boksburg and Germiston. At this conference, Walter met Gaur Radebe, who was elected secretary of the TVA. Radebe was a member of the ANC and the Communist Party, and the delegate for the Native Western Township. As it turned out, he had been one of the protestors who had demonstrated against the census in which Walter had acted as an enumerator – a coincidence that amused the two men.

Through his social and business activities, Walter's network of friends and acquaintances was increasing exponentially. In 1936, the Orlando Brotherly Society's work with disturbed juveniles took him to the home of Charlotte Manye Maxeke, who in the 1930s had been appointed probation officer for African juvenile delinquents (Karis and Gerhart, 4: 81–2). Maxeke had a long political career dating back to the 1913 protests against the pass laws, when hundreds of followers of the Bantu Women's League (which she had helped to establish) were imprisoned. In 1918, as president of the League, she had led a deputation to General Botha, which contributed to his decision not to impose passes. Despite her achievements in the League, she was barred from becoming a full member of the ANC. The Congress constitution of 1919 did not accept women as members, only as associates in the form of the Bantu Women's League. "They needed us to help by making tea," was Maxeke's comment (Basner, 23). It was clear to Walter that such a woman could never be consigned to making tea. The first black woman graduate in South Africa, Maxeke had studied in Tusgekee University in the United States, and had been a student of the great African-American intellectual, WEB du Bois, the founder of the National Association for the Advancement of Colored Peoples (NAACP). She and her husband had founded the Wilberforce Institute, which became one of the Transvaal's major secondary schools for Africans. She was described by one of her colleagues as a "virtual treasure house of knowledge about the history of African political movements" (Basner, 23). Walter was in complete awe of this powerful woman and did not talk much in her presence "because I was too young then to know much about anything". She made a deep impression on Walter and helped shape his consciousness about what women could achieve in a political movement.

Though he felt that he did not know much at the time, Walter's political horizons were expanding rapidly. His interaction with *Bantu World* editor Selope Thema gave him an insight into the African political scene. Selope Thema, who had acted as Secretary-General of the ANC while Sol Plaatje was in Europe during the First World War, was one of the founder members of the Johannesburg Joint Council, a movement that comprised Africans and whites. The Joint Councils had been established in 1921 in the wake of a visit to South Africa by the Ghanaian-born educator, Reverend James Aggrey. In the mould of Booker T Washington, Aggrey preached the gospel of racial appeasement through dialogue between blacks and whites, and tried wherever he could to counter the spread of Marcus Garvey's more radical philosophy of black liberation. Fired by Aggrey's vision of inter-racial dialogue, South African liberal JD Rheinallt Jones set up the Johannesburg Joint Council as a discussion group to promote cooperation between blacks and whites. Joint Councils of "Europeans" and "Natives" were started in a number of towns throughout the 1920s. In 1929, the Joint Councils played an important role in creating the South African Institute of Race Relations, which was to conduct research in the interests of promoting good race relations (Basner, 68; Gish, 62–3; Karis and Carter, 4: 150).

Though three leaders he admired (Selope Thema, Dr Xuma and Charlotte Maxeke) were all involved in the Joint Councils, Walter was never attracted to these councils, and did not believe that they could address the burning issues affecting black people. He was more interested when Selope Thema and Dr Xuma called for a national convention of all Africans to coordinate opposition to the Hertzog Bills, which had been produced by the coalition of the ruling Afrikaner National Party under General Hertzog and the opposition South Africa Party under General Smuts.

The All African Convention held in Bloemfontein in December 1935 was an impressive assembly of political heavyweights such as had not been seen since the 1912 founding of the ANC. All shades of political opinion among black South Africans, from the radical left to the most deeply conservative, were represented. Delegates from across the political spectrum were unanimous in their condemnation of the nefarious Bills being mooted: the Native Representation Act, which sought to remove the remaining African voters in the Cape from the common voters' roll; and the Native Land and Trust Act, which would complete the process of alienating Africans from their land begun by the enactment of the Native Land Act of 1913.

Unfortunately, the eloquence of the views expressed concerning the destruction of the last vestige of African political rights was not matched by any brilliance in devising strategies to confront the threat. The august assembly could come up with no better plan than a deputation to the Prime Minister, General Hertzog. The deputation met the same fate as previous similar deputations to the British government and Crown to call attention to the rights of native peoples. Hertzog listened politely to the delegation, which was headed by luminaries such as Professor Jabavu, the first African professor in South Africa, Dr Xuma and Dr Moroka, a distinguished physician from an aristocratic Tswana family in Thaba Nchu – then sent them on their way. He subsequently rammed a compromise down their throats in the form of an amended Bill that would place Africans on a separate voters' roll that would allow them to elect three white representatives to parliament and a Native Representative Council (NRC), a body that would advise the government on African affairs (Gish, 86; Lerumo, 67; Basner, 61; Karis and Carter, 2: 6). Despite calls for the boycott of the NRC, especially by the left-wing theoreticians of the Cape, several leading figures in the All African Convention stood for election to the new body. Among those elected were RH Godlo and Selope Thema.

Walter followed these events because of his interest in the individuals he knew rather than the organisations involved. However, one of the things that impressed him about the Convention was its condemnation of the Italian attack on Abyssinia (Ethiopia), in a resolution condemning European imperialism on the African continent. The resolution, which also supported a continental and worldwide liaison among people of African descent, appealed to Walter's anti-imperialist sentiments (Karis and Carter, 2: 9). In the mid-1930s, Walter met JB Marks, the prominent trade unionist. A leader in both the Communist Party of South Africa (CPSA) and the ANC, by the late 1930s he had helped revive the flagging fortunes of the ANC in the Transvaal. During the Abyssinian War of 1935/6, Walter attended public meetings addressed by Marks in Orlando: "The manner, determination and conviction with which JB spoke made a tremendous impact on me."

By 1938, Walter's cousin Samuel Mase had introduced him to literature from the Left Book Club. One day, Sam was passing a small shop around Kerk Street in central Johannesburg when a pamphlet in the window display caught his eye. Sam had dreams of starting his own business, so he entered the shop to buy the pamphlet entitled "How to get more money". Sam discovered that the title of the pamphlet was somewhat misleading. It turned out to be a pamphlet written by Communist Party member Rusty Bernstein urging workers to join their trade union if they wanted to earn more money! (Interview, Sam Mase; Bernstein, 58) The shop turned out to be the People's Book Shop, which carried titles of the Left Book Club. Sam immediately became a member, and like a good Communist, he shared his literature with Walter. The very first piece of left literature Walter read was Stalin's 1913 article on the National Question.

One of the books Sam introduced him to was *The Making of the Transkei* by Govan Mbeki. Walter was therefore delighted when one day in 1938, Sam brought Govan Mbeki home to visit the family. Mbeki was a student at Fort Hare who would come to Johannesburg during holidays to work for a chain of stationery shops, selling newspapers. He and Walter became good friends and would on occasion visit the Bantu Men's Social Centre. Mbeki did not, however, share Walter's enthusiasm for the place: "We used to go there and listen to the sophisticated people of Johannesburg. They wore suits and spoke their high-flown English. I never learned anything from them. Sometimes I despised them because they were not in the struggle for the liberation of their people." Unlike Walter, Mbeki was not impressed by Xuma and Selope Thema, and the two young men agreed to disagree about their attitudes to these individuals. Much later, Mbeki would comment that one of Walter's most remarkable attributes was that he had had little formal education, yet he was able to hold his own among the most formidable intellects of the time (Interview, Govan Mbeki, 1995).

Around 1938, Walter met Kaizer Matanzima, the Thembu chief who was related to the Mdingis. Walter felt most honoured when George Mdingi asked him to take Matanzima, who was visiting from the Transkei, on a tour of Johannesburg, and even introduced him to the director of the Union Bank. "I was the first person to bring Matanzima right into the township. At that stage I was proud of [him] because here was an educated chief who could now play a very important part in the affairs of the people" (Interview, Wolfie Kodesh, 20/9/95).

When it had become obvious by 1938 that war in Europe was inevitable, Walter was convinced that black men should not take part. He was impressed by the rise of Japan because he felt solidarity with a non-European power. His anti-war feeling was so strong that it placed great strain on his friendship with Herbert Mdingi. When Mdingi joined the Civil Guard and Walter witnessed his erstwhile friend in uniform, the rupture was complete. Walter saw the Civil Guard as part and parcel of the war effort and did not believe it was for the protection of the population. He lost all confidence in Mdingi and dismissed him as a sell-out and a yes-man. In 1939, he read about the anti-war stance of the Indian Congress leader, Dr Yusuf Dadoo. Passionate about cooperation between Africans, Indians and Coloureds, Dadoo formed the Non-European Front in 1939. Walter was so impressed that he went to Dadoo for a medical consultation.

Other leading ANC members and trade unionists Walter came to know at this time included Zephaniah Mothopeng, who taught at the same school as his sister Rosabella, and who would later become a leader of the Pan-Africanist Congress, RG Baloyi, a businessman who became Treasurer-General of the ANC in 1941, and Barney Ngakane, an ANC member in Orlando. Although he did not realise it at the time, Walter was gravitating slowly but surely towards his new political home.

# Part Two

## 1940–1964

## The Forging: Marriage and Politics

I do not want my house to be walled
in on all sides and my windows to be
stuffed. I want the cultures of all
lands to be blown about my house as
freely as possible. But I refuse to be
blown off my feet by any. I refuse to
live in other people's houses as an
interloper, a beggar or a slave.

MAHATMA GANDHI

The year 1940 marked the beginning of a decade of rapid economic and political change in South Africa. In contrast to the Depression of the early 1930s, the war years resulted in an economic boom. The war created new opportunities for the manufacture of goods previously imported from Europe and for the manufacture of munitions and military equipment. By 1943, manufacturing had outstripped the contribution of mining to the gross national product. This phenomenal growth resulted in a huge demand for labour, especially on the Witwatersrand. African workers accounted for most of the increase in the labour force. The African urban population almost doubled between 1939 and 1952, and many of the new migrants were women.

For the first time, large numbers of black women were drawn into wage labour in the manufacturing sector and the proportion of women to men in the urban African population increased (Lodge, 11). A small proportion of the new female migrants were young women moving to the cities in pursuit of higher education, in the fields of nursing, teaching or social work. Albertina Thethiwe was among this number.

Albertina's two-day journey to Johannesburg was in the relative comfort of a second-class coach in a regular passenger train, a far cry from the crowded, slow-moving *mbombela* that had ferried her father to the mines when she was a child. Trepidation vied with excitement as her train pulled into Johannesburg's Park Station in January 1940. Egoli (the City of Gold) had the reputation of being a bewildering and dangerous place, a Sodom and Gomorrah, where *tsotsis* hid around every corner and where life could end with the quick flash of a knife. It was natural for a young country girl from a sheltered background to feel intimidated and a bit frightened. Egoli certainly lived up to its reputation for the new arrival from Xolobe. She had barely lugged her heavy suitcase off the train when she and Adelaide Tselang, the senior nurse who had come to meet her, were startled by a commotion on the platform. Barely a few feet from them, a terrified white man was running for his life with a knife-wielding black man in hot pursuit. Moments later, several burly railway policemen had seized and overpowered the would-be attacker. Albertina shuddered to think of the fate that awaited the offender.

Albertina had barely regained her composure when she was confronted by another unexpected sight just outside the entrance of the station – a queue of extravagantly decorated rickshaws. The human-drawn carts were festooned with enormous feathers and painted in every colour of the rainbow. This spectacle was made even stranger by the exaggerated gyrations of the rickshaw pullers as they tried to outdo each other to attract customers. Albertina was thankful for her knowledgeable and streetwise escort, who quickly identified the sturdiest driver. In no time, their human taxi was moving at a brisk pace towards the Johannesburg Non-European Hospital, in the general direction of what is now Hillbrow.

Albertina took to nursing like a duck to water. Her upbringing, which had inculcated high standards of cleanliness, discipline and a strong work ethic, stood her in good stead. Her compassionate and empathetic nature made it easy for her to relate to patients. Caring for her mother and Flora had provided her with years of practical experience, albeit unrecognised. She enjoyed the lectures at the nursing college and the elementary clinical work on the wards. She took great pride in her starched white uniform, nylon stockings and brown shoes polished to a high shine. Her only disappointment was that on the wage she earned she was not able to send home as much money as she had anticipated. After paying for compulsory items such as nylon stocking, books and stationery, she had very little to spare. Because of her frugal lifestyle, she was able to save enough to buy clothes for her siblings from time to time.

Some nurses railed against the strict rules about receiving visitors or going out, but for someone who had prepared herself psychologically to be a nun, the restrictions were not a problem. Moreover, Albertina's fear of venturing out into the city was greater than her desire to explore. Her first impression at Park Station was reinforced by stories of *amalaita*, street-wise young thugs who harassed young girls in the streets, and gangs of *tsotsis* who robbed and sometimes beat people. Then there were the deadly murderers who could use a sharpened bicycle spoke to inflict a fatal wound on their unfortunate victim in a flash. The numbers of patients admitted to hospital with stab wounds and bicycle-spoke punctures bore testimony to the violence out on the streets, and Albertina wanted no part of it.

Soon after her arrival in Johannesburg, Albertina received a message that Father Huss had informed the priests at St Peter's diocese in Rosettenville of her presence at Johannesburg General. There was an expectation that she would go to St Peter's for mass, but she preferred to attend the interdenominational chapel on the hospital premises.

Some of the nurses tried to tempt her with invitations to the Bantu Men's Social Centre, to attend dances, plays and musical recitals and no doubt meet eligible young men, but Albertina resisted until they gave up and left the reserved country girl alone. She barely left the nurses' home until the end of the year, when she managed to buy her own ticket home for the holidays.

Albertina's enjoyment of her nursing training was marred by the racial segregation practised at the hospital. Decades earlier, the Transvaal Provincial Administration had contracted Catholic nuns to run the section of the hospital catering to black patients. As increasing numbers of Afrikaner working-class women entered the nursing profession, they gradually replaced the Catholic nuns. Albertina and her cohorts found themselves in an environment where the white nurses were always in authority. A black nursing sister, no matter how senior, could never have authority over white nurses, while even junior white nurses could give orders to black sisters. White nurses occupied all the senior positions in the wards and the nursing colleges. It was Albertina's first experience of racism and it was a shock to her system. In Xolobe, the missionaries and local traders had never made her feel inferior. They had treated her grandfather with the deference due to him as a chief and when he called meetings they would attend like anyone else in the community. At Mariazell, the missionaries had been strict, even harsh, but Albertina always felt that this discipline was for the good of the pupils, and she had never felt discriminated against.

Although the racist practices at the hospital rankled, Albertina tried to tolerate the situation as par for the course in a segregated society, but an incident six months into her training demonstrated to her that racism could have fatal consequences. A horrific accident at Park Station resulted in a number of deaths and injuries to dozens of patients. The emergency wards of the non-white section of the hospital were swamped with critically injured patients. The extent of their injuries reminded Albertina of stories she had heard about the horrors of war and soldiers dying on the battlefield.

To cope with the crisis, all medical staff, including those on leave, were summoned, and worked nonstop to cope with the unprecedented number of emergency cases. Because there were not enough beds, even seriously injured patients had to sleep on the floor. Meanwhile, beds in the "European'" section of the hospital were empty, as only a few of those injured in the accident were white. Senior black medical staff appealed to the hospital authorities to allow black patients into the white section, as an emergency measure. Their pleas fell on deaf ears. This incident had a profound effect on Albertina. To deny patients the best possible medical care because of the colour of their skin, in her eyes, was a violation of the sacred duty of the medical practitioner to do everything possible to preserve life.

In her second year of training, Albertina began to feel more relaxed. She bought a racquet and started playing tennis at the courts on the hospital grounds. She felt quite daring, decked out in her pleated knee-length skirt and short-sleeved shirt. She also began to make new friends. Among the new intake of nurses, she became friendly with Rose Mtshula, a young woman who originally came from Queenstown, as well as Rosabella (Barbie) Sisulu and Evelyn Mase. One of her cousins, Jumba, a migrant worker who lived in Alexandra Township, made contact and started to visit her regularly. He took her out shopping until she felt confident enough to venture into the city herself.

However, Albertina's sense of wellbeing was shaken by the death of her mother, Monica, in early 1941. Given her mother's long years of illness, her death was not too much of a shock, and Albertina might have coped well with her loss if she had been allowed time to go home for the funeral and mourn with the rest of her family. Nevertheless, her application for compassionate leave was turned down, and the hospital authorities were completely unsympathetic. The matron asked why she needed to go home. "She asked me 'What are you going to do? Are you going to wake her up?'" The priests at Rosettenville tried to intercede, but the matron refused to budge and made it clear that Albertina would not be able to get any time off. She had to go on duty as if nothing had happened. "It was as if a dog had died," Albertina recalls bitterly. She felt desolate that she had been unable to observe the funeral rituals that marked what was for her the end of an era.

The opening years of the new decade also marked a period of dramatic change in the life of Walter Sisulu. In the space of two years he moved house, started a new business, joined the political party to which he would dedicate the rest of his life and formed three relationships that would redefine his life's trajectory.

In 1940 Walter was fortunate enough to secure a permit for a house just across the Klipspruit River in the township of Phomolong in the new area of Orlando West. The new four-roomed house was a huge improvement on the Orlando East house. It had two bedrooms, a kitchen and a small room, which, though it had no bathtub, they called a bathroom because it had a shower enclosure. Unlike the old house, where they had access to only a communal tap, the Phomolong house had a tap in the backyard. The new house also had cement floors and a ceiling. The house was just a stone's throw from Phefeni Station, so from the early hours of the morning they were subjected to the thundering roar of passing trains. However, given the critical shortage of housing for black people, this was a minor inconvenience.

Walter, Barbie and Alice Manse moved to No. 7372 Magang Street in 1940, leaving Sam and Caleb to take over the Orlando East home. Clifford and his children Boysie, Nokuzola and Kenneth also managed to secure their own house in Orlando. Walter and his mother liked their new home. Because so many people from Orlando East had moved to Phomolong at the same time and therefore knew each other, a sense of community emerged almost immediately. Two landmarks of Orlando West were the imposing Holy Cross Church, the largest Anglican Church in Soweto, and Uncle Tom's Community Hall diagonally opposite on the busy thoroughfare running from Klipspruit Road to Dube No. 7372 was a stone's throw from Uncle Tom's, tucked just behind the Holy Cross Church. Alice enjoyed living almost in the backyard of the church and became very involved in church affairs. Meanwhile, Barbie had decided that she had had enough of teaching and wanted to become a nurse. Evelyn Mase had also decided to take up nursing, so the two young women both became trainees at Johannesburg General.

By 1939, it had become clear to Walter that there were no prospects for his advancement with the Union Bank. The headquarters of the bank had moved to Pretoria, and only one person was retained in the non-white department. Walter decided to start an estate agency. Through his participation in the Transvaal Vigilance Association, he had come to know people involved in civic affairs in Alexandra and Sophiatown. Alexandra Township, located about 20 kilometres north of the Johannesburg city centre, was (and still is) an anomaly among Johannesburg's affluent northern suburbs. Poor, overcrowded and crime-ridden, Alexandra was nevertheless seen as an urban

Promised Land by its inhabitants because it was "one of the few areas in the country where Africans could run their own affairs, where people did not have to kowtow to the tyranny of white municipal authorities" (Mandela, 70).

The other freehold area, Sophiatown, a place that would inspire poets, writers, politicians, musicians and priests, was even more loved by its inhabitants. Situated six kilometres west of the city centre, next to Western Native Township and the suburbs of Martindale and Newclare, Sophiatown was a cultural melting pot, a unique blend of all South Africa's black communities. Indians, Africans, people of mixed race and even Chinese lived together in chaotic harmony. It was a place where the educated elite – journalists, doctors and teachers – rubbed shoulders with gangsters whose philosophy was to "live fast, die young and make a good-looking corpse in a glamorous coffin". Walter loved Sophiatown. It was a place that appealed to his sociable nature and his disregard for class and status. With his extensive network of friends and acquaintances in these areas, Walter was well placed to launch his business.

He took out a broker's licence and, in partnership with a man called Msimang, opened the Non-European United Estate Agency. From 1940 onwards, Walter was in increasing contact with the Indian communities of Fordsburg, Vrededorp and the city centre. He was particularly friendly with the Vandeyar brothers and Goolam Pahad and had already established business contacts with the Akalwayas from Fordsburg. They had concluded a verbal agreement whereby Walter was to act as their agent in acquiring properties in Sophiatown and Western Native Township. The partnership with Msimang ended when Walter discovered that Msimang had undermined him by making a private deal with Akalwaya involving a number of properties. Walter then agreed to act as a sub-agent of an estate agent called Lipschitz, whose offices he shared. While Walter was out one day, Lipschitz received 100 pounds from one of Walter's clients, a Mr Wadee, and issued a receipt on Walter's behalf. Walter knew nothing of this until Wadee's lawyers issued a summons against his agency. Lipschitz admitted to Walter that he had taken the money and was unable to pay it back. Walter took the matter to court, but was unable to get anything and had to pay legal costs. Some time later, an acquaintance told Walter that he had read in the *Government Gazette* that there was some money due to him. Walter did not attach any importance to the matter and did not pursue it. Only later did he realise that the money was from Lipschitz's estate!

After parting from Lipschitz, Walter formed a new company with four others: Willie Thabethe, Mr Dinelane (who had been Chief Induna at Rose Deep Mine where Walter had worked in the 1920s), Mr Nyokana and Dr Mbere. The name of the company, Sitha Investments and Trust Co. (Pty) Ltd, was derived from the first syllables of Sisulu and Thabethe. Walter and Thabethe were joint managing directors, and Dinelane the chairman of the company. Julius Mali and Joe Matlou were also involved in the company, although it is not clear in what capacity.

The office of Sitha Investments was at 35 West Street on the corner of Commissioner Street, off Diagonal Street. It was extremely difficult for black people to rent offices in the city centre, and it had taken Walter the better part of a year to obtain the necessary permission. Only after several letters to the relevant authorities and a petition to the Governor General of Johannesburg did he succeed (Luli Callinicos, Interview, 5/2/93). Number 35 was conveniently located in the west end of the city, a vibrant colourful corner adjacent to KwaDabulamanzi, an Indian factory that specialised in selling hats. The area was peopled by pavement hawkers and traditional herbalists selling their wares on the pavements in front of Indian shops packed with all manner of goods at bargain prices. Music blared from the many record shops to attract potential customers from among the ceaseless flow of commuters and shoppers hurrying to and fro (Callinicos 2001, 69; Joyce Sikhakhane-Rankin, Interview, Juliette Mogale 6/10/2002).

Walter had maintained contact with the ubiquitous Gaur Radebe, his acquaintance from the Vigilance Association. As well as being a member of the Communist Party and the ANC, Gaur Radebe became one of the founder members of the African Mineworkers' Union, which was formed in 1941. He also worked as a clerk, interpreter and messenger for Witkin, Sidelsky and

Eidelman, a law firm that had a large African client base. Radebe's boss, Lazar Sidelsky, worked with a German businessman, Hans Müller, who used to lend money to people who wanted to build their own houses in Alexandra. As security, Müller would get the borrower to register a bond in favour of Müller Small Loans. Although he charged higher interest rates than the building societies, Alexandra residents had no choice but to go this route. This was because the building societies would not lend to them, as the area was seen as a bad risk. Müller did very well in his business and Sidelsky handled the registration of the bonds in his favour.

As an estate agent working with clients from Alexandra, Walter encountered Müller in the course of his work. Müller introduced him to Sidelsky, and soon they had an arrangement whereby Walter would take clients to Sidelsky to register their bonds and would receive a small commission in return. Sidelsky had great respect for Walter, whom he described as astute and intelligent. Walter, meanwhile, knew that Sidelsky was decent enough not to take advantage of vulnerable clients. "Our firm restrained itself from taking advantage," maintained Sidelsky very firmly. "We never made enemies out of our customers." Walter also appreciated the fact that the firm Witkin, Sidelsky and Eidelman had employed Gaur Radebe. In the view of most white employers, Gaur would have been considered the quintessential "cheeky native", a Communist "agitator" and rabble-rouser. Walter also got on well with the young Communist lawyer, Nat Bregman, a cousin of Sidelsky, who also worked for his firm (Interview, Lazar Sidelsky).

Walter also recruited Juliette Mogale, a young trainee teacher who worked as a part-time rent collector for Witkin, Sidelsky and Eidelman. She also worked part-time for the Swazi Mercantile office in Alexandra, where Swazi nationals working on the Rand paid their dues or taxes to King Sobhuza. Walter told her he wanted her to work for him because of her "work experience and good understanding of ANC politics and discipline". He had found it difficult to admonish his previous secretaries because they were older than him. Juliette was overjoyed when he arranged for her to have typing and bookkeeping lessons at the Left Book Club (Joyce Sikhakhane-Rankin, Interview, Juliette Mogale 6/10/2002).

While the agency was always busy, as a commercial venture Sitha Investments was ultimately doomed to failure. This was because the kind-hearted Walter behaved more like a social worker than a hard-headed businessman. His agency was well known as a place where help could be sought, and "troubled widows from as far afield as the West Rand consulted the agency about removals and other threats" (*Sunday Times*, 8/10/1989). At the very least, Walter could refer those who approached him to his lawyer friends.

In 1940, Walter was formally recruited into the ANC by trade unionist Alfred Mbele. Although busy with his estate agency, Walter became increasingly preoccupied with ANC work. He considered the period immediately after joining the ANC as the most important of his life: "I was struggling before, you know, directionless. When I got to the ANC I began to change, even though the ANC at that time did not properly formulate its policies."

Not long after he became a member, Walter was elected treasurer of the Orlando Branch of the ANC. Membership of this branch fluctuated between 100 and 200 in the early 1940s, but its influence was significant out of all proportion. The main activity of the branch was addressing local grievances such as pass law arrests and liquor raids.

On a national level, the ANC was emerging from its political slumber of the 1930s and undergoing a period of revitalisation under the leadership of Dr Alfred Xuma. After his return from London in 1938, Xuma had become increasingly critical of white liberal paternalism, and convinced of the need for a stronger assertion of African political rights by Africans themselves. He regarded the 1936 Hertzog Bills as "a betrayal of all the Christian, liberal principles that he and his educated African colleagues held most dear". He had also been influenced by the spirit of Pan-Africanism he had encountered in London among other African and West Indian nationalists engaged in their own struggles against European domination. He was also unhappy with the inadequate and ineffective response of the All African Convention (AAC) to the Hertzog Bills (Gish, 100–101). After his election as President-General of the ANC in December 1940, Xuma threw himself into the rejuvenation of the ANC's organisational machinery.

He worked tirelessly at improving the financial situation of the ANC, reviving and streamlining provincial and branch organisations and exerting discipline over the provinces. During his presidency, the ANC was transformed from "a loosely bound federal movement whose major activity was its annual conference into a more tightly functioning and centralised national organisation" (Karis and Carter, 2: 71). Xuma was supported in his efforts by his dedicated Secretary-General, Reverend James Calata, an Anglican clergyman from Cradock in the Eastern Cape. Xuma also spread enthusiasm for the ANC among prominent intellectuals like Fort Hare's Professor ZK Matthews, his brother-in-law, Dr Roseberry Bokwe, and Dr Silas Molema (Gish, 114).

Xuma also made a contribution to the development of a clear policy for the ANC, overseeing the modernisation of the ANC's outdated 1919 constitution. Together with Calata and Matthews, and assisted by a left-wing Afrikaner lawyer, Bram Fischer, and former Wits history professor, William MacMillan, he drafted the African Claims in South Africa. This important document was an interpretation of the Atlantic Charter "from the point of view of the African people". It included a Bill of Rights that demanded the removal of discriminatory legislation, and in a departure from previous policy statements, it called for unqualified universal franchise. The African Claims statement was adopted by the annual ANC conference in December 1943, and became the basic policy statement upon which later ANC documents were based.

Xuma wisely acknowledged the history and tradition of the ANC by inviting former ANC presidents John Dube, SM Makgatho, ZR Mahabane and Josiah Gumede to serve as honorary life presidents in recognition of their past leadership. This gave them the privilege of participating in meetings of the ANC executive (Gish, 116). Even as he honoured the old guard, Xuma was acutely conscious of the ANC's need for an infusion of new blood.

In one of their many discussions, Xuma spoke to Walter about the spirit of the 1940 conference at which he had been elected President. He spoke of a demand at the conference by a group of left-inclined youth for a new spirit and a new order. (This group had included Moses Kotane, a prominent Communist Party member.) Xuma expressed his concern about the gulf between the older and younger generations. Walter shared these concerns and took it upon himself to look out for new talent to recruit to the ANC. When a young man called Nelson Mandela walked into his office one day in 1941, Walter immediately recognised his potential. "I knew that he was someone who would go far and should be encouraged. He was the kind of young man we needed to develop our organisation."

The office of Sitha Investments was a hive of activity. People were constantly dropping in, not necessarily for business, but more often than not for political meetings or, in the case of people from the Transkei, for help in finding their feet in the city. One such person was Nelson Mandela. In 1941, Mandela and his cousin Justice had run away from their home in Mqhekezweni in the Transkei to Johannesburg to escape arranged marriages. These had been planned for them by Justice's father and Mandela's guardian, Chief Jongintaba Dalindyebo, the Acting Regent of the Thembu people. The two young men had great difficulty in settling in Johannesburg. As soon as people in the Thembu community heard of their escapade, they would have nothing more to do with them. Mandela had stayed for a short while at the home of one of his cousins, Garlick Mbekeni. When he told Garlick that he wished to study law, Garlick, who came from Engcobo, said he would take him to "one of our best people in Johannesburg, my homeboy who knows these issues".

On arrival at Walter's office in Barclay Arcade, a receptionist asked the two young men to sit and wait for her boss, who was in a meeting with a client. Mandela had never seen an African woman typist before and he watched fascinated as she rapidly typed a letter. The only typists he had seen in the offices of Umtata and Fort Hare were white males who typed "using two fingers to peck out their letters". Mandela describes the meeting with Walter thus: "She soon ushered us into the inner office, where I was introduced to a man who looked to be in his late twenties, with an intelligent and kindly face, light in complexion, and dressed in a double-breasted suit. Despite his youth, he seemed to be an experienced man of the world. He was from the Transkei, but spoke English with a rapid urban fluency. To judge from his well-populated waiting room and his desk piled high with papers, he was a busy and successful man. But he did not rush us and seemed genuinely interested in our errand" (Mandela, 79).

Mandela was highly impressed by Walter:

> This was 1941 and I had never seen a black man in an office, let alone running an estate agency. I did not even know what an estate agency was. I later asked my cousin what degree Sisulu had. Garlick thought he had only passed Standard Six. I found this difficult to believe but it was confirmed by someone else. "But how can this be?" I asked. "With such fluency in English and with such offices?" The reply was that "He has knowledge and skills from the University of life and Johannesburg is a good place to learn" (Interview, Nelson Mandela 11/8/93).

Walter listened carefully as Mandela explained how he had been studying for a BA degree at Fort Hare in 1940, but had left before completing it as a result of a protest action. Walter felt that Mandela should be assisted in his ambition to study law, so he took the new arrival off to Witkin, Sidelsky and Eidelman, and asked Sidelsky to article Mandela. "They did not give me the impression that they were very keen but he [Walter] was one of their important clients who brought them business" (Interview, Nelson Mandela 11/8/93).

Sidelsky was unable to article Mandela immediately, but agreed to take him on as a clerk while he completed his BA degree by correspondence. Shortly after Mandela's visit, Walter received a message from Dr Xuma warning Walter not to accommodate Mandela and Justice or make any arrangements for them. Walter decided to ignore this instruction.

Nelson Mandela was not the only casualty of the Fort Hare expulsions who found his way to Walter's office. Oliver Tambo, a serious and thoughtful young man from Bizana in the Transkei, was another. Born to poor parents who could not afford to send him to school, Tambo's intellectual prowess earned him the sponsorship of the Anglican Church, and he was able to board at Holy Cross Mission and attend St Peter's Secondary School. After achieving an outstanding academic record at St Peter's, he had been awarded a Transkeian Bunga scholarship to study for a BSc degree at Fort Hare. His studies were cut short when he was expelled after the 1941 strike, and he returned to Johannesburg at the beginning of 1942 to teach at his former school, St Peter's. Tambo visited Sitha Investments with Congress Mbatha, an ANC member and teacher at St Peter's, and Lancelot Gama, the brother of Lymon Gama, one of Walter's business associates who kept his books and did his tax returns (Callinicos, Unpublished manuscript, 13).

Walter was impressed by Tambo's intelligence and serious nature, and the two men developed a close personal relationship on the basis of a shared political outlook. The friendship between Walter and Mandela also grew from strength to strength, and shortly after they met, Mandela moved to the Sisulu home for a few months.

Mandela has warm memories of Walter's mother's hospitality: "We had a lovely time at No. 7372. The old lady treated us as her children, though she would sometimes find it difficult to provide enough food because we were so many and they were not a wealthy family. I was struggling, so I was not paying anything and they looked after me very well. I have nothing but praise for her" (Interview, Nelson Mandela 11/8/93).

Mandela admired Alice's enquiring mind: "She liked to investigate things. For example, she was very interested in what I was studying. I had to explain in detail what it meant to be studying law. For a person of her generation, she was very sharp. She passed on those qualities to Walter and his sister" (Interview, Nelson Mandela 11/8/93).

Tambo also became a regular visitor to the Sisulu home. Alice Manse grew to love him like a son and he would accompany her to church on Sunday mornings. When Tambo took up part-time law studies in the late 1940s, Walter helped him to get articled to the Johannesburg law firm, Kawalsky and Tuch. Walter later told Oliver Tambo's biographer, Luli Callinicos, that whenever he came across a bright young man, he would encourage him to take up law because knowledge of the law was an important weapon in the struggle (Luli Callinicos, Interview, Walter Sisulu 27/6/90).

Just after he met Mandela in 1941, Walter had the most significant encounter of his life. He was visiting his sister Barbie and Evelyn Mase at Johannesburg General Hospital when he bumped into an acquaintance, Jumba, who was visiting his cousin, Albertina Thethiwe. Jumba introduced Walter to his cousin, and Walter was instantly captivated. "She appealed to me right from the beginning. I at once made efforts to take her out." Albertina was hesitant at first. She related to Walter as the brother of Barbie and cousin of Evelyn. In the hierarchical environment of the nursing home, she was their senior and they related to her as an older sister. Albertina was nevertheless sufficiently impressed by the "very handsome" young man who, even though he came from a place close to her own home, was schooled in urban ways and appeared to be very sophisticated in her eyes.

Walter was fond of going to the "bioscope", so he invited Albertina to watch a film and the relationship developed from there. He soon took Albertina home to meet his mother and she became a regular visitor at No. 7372. Here she became accustomed to the buzz of political discussion among the young men who visited the house. So close were Walter and Mandela that she assumed they were related to one another. Coming from a sheltered background as she did, Albertina was not politically conscious. Her interest in politics developed during her courtship with Walter, and the couple spent much of their time together discussing political issues and attending meetings. Politics had by then become Walter's consuming passion. At that time, the burning issue for him was the formation of a Youth League.

Walter was the only delegate elected by the Orlando Branch to attend the ANC's annual conference in December 1942. Although the branch had 200 members and was therefore entitled to send up to 10 delegates, it was only able to send one delegate, due to a lack of funds. On the train journey to Bloemfontein, Walter met Pixley ka Isaka Seme, one of the founding members of the ANC and its president from 1930–37. Seme spoke at length about the importance of chiefs. Walter was struck by his conservative nature and understood why the ANC had gone into decline after he took over the presidency from the more radical Josiah Gumede in 1930.

By contrast, Walter was highly impressed by Moses Kotane, whom he met at the same conference. He had heard a lot about Moses and their first meeting had a great impact on Walter: "I admired his down-to-earth manner and the calm, logical and reasoned way in which he presented his arguments."

It was customary at the time for ANC conferences to be opened by an official of some government department. The 1942 conference was opened by an official of the Non-European Affairs Department, who wished the conference the best of luck in its deliberations and emphasised the cooperation between whites and "natives", and the need to be reasonable and exercise patience. Walter noticed the presence of other top officials from government departments: these included the Chief of Police and the Manager of the Native Affairs Department. In his first address to an ANC conference, Walter spoke about the intended removals from Sophiatown, the atmosphere of uncertainty this issue was causing and the lack of freehold rights for Africans. (Walter had also been asked to represent the Sophiatown Ratepayers Association at the conference.)

Walter also attended the 1943 ANC conference, which he thought was "one of the most important and busiest conferences in the history of the ANC". The conference dealt with the new constitution of the ANC, which effectively modernised the organisation. It abolished the House of Chiefs provided for in the 1912 constitution; it elevated the branch, which became the basic unit of the organisation; and it centralised authority by creating a working committee of five executive members living within 50 miles of the President (Lodge, 25). One of the most important changes in the new constitution was the according of full equality to women members. (Prior to this, women could only be associate members.) The ANC women's section was formed under the leadership of Madie Hall Xuma, the wife of Dr Xuma.

The ANC and AAC were holding their annual conferences in Bloemfontein at the same time but at different venues. There was an overlap of membership between the two organisations – many senior members of the ANC were also members of the national executive of the Convention. This led to a division of loyalties. Both conferences moved that discussions be held between the two organisations with a view to bringing about a single organisation that would be the mouthpiece of the African people, and a Joint Committee composed of nine members from each organisation was set up. The Joint Committee proposed that the AAC be the mouthpiece and the ANC be its affiliate. Nine voted in favour of the motion, six against and three abstained. This motion was, however, completely rejected by the ANC conference "which was well attended by enthusiastic young people whose loyalty to the ANC was undivided" (Interview, Walter Sisulu). The ANC conference subsequently passed a resolution to the effect that the ANC was the mouthpiece of the African people; that the AAC was controlled by the Non-European Unity Movement, and to that extent it was no longer an African organisation, but that common purpose between the two organisations must be sought. The decision at the conclusion of the two separate conferences was that a joint session be held under the joint chairmanship of Xuma and Jabavu. This session could not come to any definite agreement and the matter was referred to the respective incoming executive committees.

The emergence of the African Democratic Party (ADP), a new party started in 1943, was also discussed at the 1943 conference. This party was formed by Paul Mosaka, a Fort Hare graduate and the youngest elected member of the Native Representative Council. Mosaka was assisted by Senator Hymie Basner, a former Communist and the most radical of the white members of parliament elected by Africans (Karis and Carter, 2: 72). Mosaka had been an ANC member and had even helped to draft the African Claims statement, but had decided to set up a new party because he was unhappy with what the ADP manifesto described as the "disorganisation, political stagnation and general inaction" in the ranks of the ANC.

The ADP was represented at the 1943 ANC conference, where it stated that its aim was to become a party within the ANC. However, a change in the constitution, which made the ANC a unitary organisation, precluded this. Xuma was hostile to the ADP and dismissed it as a "divisive force". The ANC Orlando Branch was at the core of the opposition to the ADP, and at the conference Walter spoke out against it, stressing the necessity of the ANC asserting itself as the leading organisation in South Africa.

At the 1942 conference, Lancelot Gama had drawn attention to the unrest among the youth at educational institutions around the country, especially Fort Hare, where there was a student strike at the time. He argued that this unrest was a manifestation of the mood and militancy of the youth, and hence it was necessary to galvanise and direct it along proper political channels. At the end of the conference, the executive was authorised to institute an ANC youth league, which would include students at Fort Hare (Meli, 108).

International events such as the Italian invasion of Ethiopia, the expectation of a new deal after the Second World War, and the growth in size and militancy of the African trade unions were powerful political stimuli for the students and graduates of elite educational institutions such as Lovedale, Healdtown, Adams and Fort Hare. It was a period of political ferment in which young intellectuals and professionals gravitated towards each other, seeking answers to the political predicament of the African people, answers that they did not believe established organisations such as the ANC were able to provide (Karis and Carter, 2: 99).

Although he was from a working class rather than an academic background, Walter Sisulu was comfortable in these circles, and played a key role in bringing together influential thinkers to realise the desire to form a youth league.

In 1943, AP Mda often met with Anton Lembede, a brilliant young lawyer who had come to Johannesburg to serve articles with the law firm of Dr Seme. Lembede, who was to become the leading theoretician of the Youth League, was born in Natal in 1914 to a desperately poor peasant family. First he trained as a teacher at Adams College, then while teaching, he studied for his BA LLB degree through correspondence with the University of South Africa. In 1945 he became one of the first Africans in South Africa to attain an MA in philosophy. In 1946, he became Dr Seme's law partner.

Lembede introduced Mda to Jordan Ngubane, a friend whom he had met when they both attended Adams College. An accomplished journalist, Ngubane was working for the *Bantu World* under Selope Thema. The three friends often engaged in long political discussions. One evening in 1943, Lembede and Ngubane accompanied Mda to the Sisulu home in Orlando West, where they were introduced to Nelson Mandela and Oliver Tambo.

Lembede made a strong impression on Walter and Mandela. "From the moment I heard Lembede speak, I knew I was seeing a magnetic personality who thought in original and often startling ways" (Mandela, 110). Walter was impressed by Lembede's towering intellect and the fact that he had "not only a national but also a continental outlook".

This small but dynamic group was highly critical of the conservatism of the ANC leadership and believed that the time was ripe for more radical action based on the mass mobilisation of the African people, especially the urban working class. The young men parted after agreeing to extend discussions of the formation of a youth league to an ever-widening circle of young activists.

Walter exerted a strong influence on Mandela's decision to join the Youth League and its parent body, the ANC: "... more and more I had come under the wise tutelage of Walter Sisulu. Walter was strong, reasonable, practical and dedicated. He never lost his head in a crisis; he was often silent when others were shouting. He believed that the African National Congress was the means to effect change in South Africa, the repository of black hopes and aspirations. Sometimes one can judge an organisation by the people who belong to it, and I knew that I would be proud to belong to any organisation of which Walter was a member" (Mandela, 110).

"I didn't know the name of the ANC until I was at Fort Hare, but even then I did not identify myself with the ANC until Comrade Walter recruited me. I tended to follow what he was doing because he was a man who made a tremendous impression on my thinking. He recruited me to the Youth League and I automatically became a member of the ANC" (Interview, Nelson Mandela 11/8/93).

One of the clerks in Walter's estate agency was the brother of Peter Raboroko, an ANC member and president of the Transvaal African Students' Association. Walter met with Peter Raboroko and they agreed on the need to hold a meeting of those who considered themselves part of a youth movement. In October 1943, Raboroko convened a meeting at the Domestic and Cultural Workers Club Hall in Diagonal Street to plan the formation of a youth league. Before the December 1943 annual conference of the ANC, discussions were held with Dr Xuma to ensure his support for plans to form a youth league (Karis and Carter, 2: 100).

At the 1943 ANC conference, in his presidential address, Dr Xuma issued a call to the youth, despite a prophetic warning from the veteran trade unionist, AWG Champion, that a youth league would bring about his [Xuma's] downfall. At the conference, the formation of a youth league was duly authorised.

Meanwhile, Walter met with Lionel Majombozi and Willie Nkomo, who were prominent members of a group of medical students at the University of the Witwatersrand participating in discussions on the formation of the Youth League. Walter, Majombozi and Nkomo had lengthy discussions on the practical steps needed to set up the Youth League. A Provisional Committee was established at the beginning of 1944, with Walter and Congress Mbatha as joint convenors. Like Oliver Tambo, Mbatha was an alumnus of St Peter's Secondary School and Fort Hare. He also taught at St Peter's in the 1940s, was secretary of the Transvaal African Teachers' Association, and in 1943 was on the committee that drew up the African Claims document. Willie Nkomo was elected chairman of the Provisional Committee, with Lembede, Mda, Ngubane, Mandela, Tambo and Walter making up the rest of the committee. Operating as a subcommittee of the Provisional Committee, Lembede, Ngubane and Mda drafted the Congress Youth League manifesto and constitution (Walshe, 352).

In February 1944, a delegation of several Youth League members, including Walter, Ngubane, Mda and Nkomo, visited Dr Xuma at his home in Sophiatown, and presented him with the draft manifesto and constitution of the Youth League. Xuma was very disturbed by the steps that had been taken, and felt that the young activists had usurped the position of the National Executive. He said that when the resolution to form a youth league had been adopted, he had assumed that it was the President-General who would take the initiative on the matter.

"Xuma upbraided us with long philosophical words," says Walter. "He referred sarcastically to the Youth League manifesto as 'your high learned manifesto' (Walter Sisulu, Notes for prison memoir, 45). Xuma felt that the draft manifesto indicated that the Youth League constituted a different organisation, when at best they should be no more than a pressure group. Although Xuma had been approached alone, it was clear that his position reflected that of the entire ANC National Executive.

The delegation tried to allay Xuma's anxiety by pointing out that, within the framework of the ANC constitution, the Youth League could only be an auxiliary body, not a separate organisation. This argument carried no weight with Xuma. They contrasted the Youth League to the African Democratic Party, pointing out that far from wanting to be a separate organisation, the Youth League wanted to work within and strengthen the ANC. They obtained Xuma's grudging acceptance of the Youth League constitution and manifesto by emphasising that one could not become a member of the Youth League without being a member of the ANC, and that all members of the Youth League over the age of 17 would have to pay subscription fees that covered membership of the ANC, and would have to act in all matters in keeping with the policy and activities of the ANC.

The blessing of the mother body obtained, albeit reluctantly, the inaugural conference of the ANC Youth League was held on Easter Sunday, 1944, at the Bantu Men's Social Club. About 200 people attended. The conference was opened by Selope Thema, the speaker of the ANC, and Anton Lembede gave a talk on the history of nations. Lembede was elected President, Victor Mbobo vice-president, Tambo secretary and Walter treasurer. Other executive members were Mda, Peter Burman, A Nxumalo, J Mokwena, Congress Mbatha and David Bopape. With all the energy and confidence of youth, they had no doubts of their ability to realise their aim of steering the ANC to a more militant course of action.

# t w o

Albertina Thethiwe was the only woman present at the inaugural meeting of the Congress Youth League. It was not the first such meeting she had attended. Since they had started courting, she accompanied Walter regularly to his meetings. She did so in a supportive capacity, and did not consider becoming a member herself, as the Youth League was very much a young men's organisation. Surviving Youth League activists find it difficult to explain why this was so. They certainly had no objections to the involvement of women and Albertina was never made to feel unwelcome at their meetings. Ellen Kuzwayo, the only woman who did become active in the Youth League, later wrote in her autobiography: "I wish I could say why there seemed to be no outstanding women in the ranks of the ANC Movement at that time. If they were present, for some reason or other I missed them." She remembered Albertina "as the smiling and pleasant wife of Walter Sisulu, a kind hostess who served the committee members of the Congress with tea after long and intense meetings" (Kuzwayo, 139, 245).

In later years, Walter would remind Albertina of her presence at that historic Easter Sunday meeting in 1944. "Admit it, my dear," he would tease, "you only had eyes for your boyfriend." By that time the happy couple had already decided on the date for their wedding. The story of their proposal is an endearing one. One day while they were strolling in the streets of Johannesburg, Albertina dressed to the nines, complete with hat, gloves and handbag, Walter took her hand, looked into her eyes and asked the all-important question. He recalls with amusement her unexpected response: "I was so taken with her from the moment we met that in a short space of time the question of marriage came up. She replied that before we considered marriage there was something she had to tell me about herself. She went on to say 'I have children'. We were holding hands when she said this. I was so shocked and flabbergasted, I dropped her hand. 'How many?' I asked. 'Three,' she replied. My mind was racing ahead – getting married to a woman with children was regarded as a social stigma." Walter timidly asked how old the children were. She hesitated and he was in complete confusion. She then smilingly explained that she had assumed responsibility for her younger siblings when her father had died, and that she had vowed to make a home for them. Walter was impressed by her sense of responsibility and said he would gladly share that responsibility with her when they married. He wasted no time in living up to his promise, and promptly arranged for Albertina's brother Elliot (Velaphi) to come to Orlando East to complete his high-school education. Elliot got on well with Walter's mother, who was very fond of the studious young man who wanted to become a minister in the Presbyterian Church.

When Albertina had an operation to remove her appendix in 1942, Walter arranged for her to recuperate at the home of Samuel and Caleb Mase in Orlando East. After she recovered, they went to the Transkei together. Albertina had indicated to her family that she would be bringing a visitor home. Walter was well received and a sheep was slaughtered to welcome him. Albertina's family suspected the purpose of his visit, but there was no talk of marriage on that occasion. Walter met Albertina's aged grandmother Nosenti and her uncle and guardian Campbell Mnyila, without whose permission she would not be able to get married. Fortunately, Campbell, who had studied at Fort Hare and worked for a firm of attorneys in East London, was favourably disposed towards the ANC and was therefore very pleased to meet Walter. Gcotyelwa, the young cousin whom Albertina had looked after as a young girl, and Campbell's daughter, Phumla, were in a flurry of excitement about the visitor. Before the visit, Albertina had warned them not to say anything about this "white man", as he could speak Xhosa very well. Gcotyelwa recalls that someone had circulated a newspaper cutting that featured a picture of Walter Sisulu, the Director of Sitha Investments. The young girls promptly nicknamed him "Director".

After the Xolobe visit, Walter proceeded to Qutubeni, where it was arranged that his Uncle Mbuti Kwambi would make a formal proposal to Albertina's family. Kwambi, who knew Albertina's uncle fairly well, duly went to Tsomo to make the proposal, which was accepted. This was followed up by another visit by Walter, accompanied by Kwambi, Caleb Mase and Selwyn Ngcali, another of Walter's uncles. *Lobola* was discussed and agreed upon, and Walter and Albertina returned to Johannesburg.

While Walter and Albertina were making marriage arrangements, a whirlwind courtship had been taking place between Nelson Mandela and Evelyn Mase. The couple had met at the Sisulu homee and had married in January 1944. AP Mda, Walter's Youth League colleague, had also fallen in love with Albertina's nursing friend, Rose Mtshulu. Rose maintained that it was Walter who encouraged the romance and their subsequent marriage (Interview, Rose Mda). Soon after these events, Walter and Albertina made a second trip to the Transkei to finalise their own wedding arrangements. Walter was accompanied to Tsomo by his uncle Ngcali. This time, discussions did not proceed as smoothly as before. An argument arose over where the marriage was to take place. Walter wanted to get married in Johannesburg and Albertina's uncle, Campbell Mnyila, insisted that the wedding take place in the Transkei. In the heat of the argument, Walter found himself talking in English, making Ngcali uncomfortable – it was not the done thing to talk English in discussions of that nature. He tried to urge Walter to talk Xhosa, but Campbell said, "Leave him, let him go on." Campbell then asked Walter in English: "Have you ever been married?" When Walter said no, Campbell replied "If you have never got married, how can you know anything about it? You have to learn from us." Walter capitulated. "It was a powerful argument. I had no response."

Although their wedding banns had already been read in Johannesburg, they had to change their plans and make arrangements to be married by the magistrate in Cofimvaba. Campbell Mnyila was attending a sitting of the Bunga at the time, so he was not able to attend the civil ceremony at the court. He wrote a long letter to the magistrate instead, introducing Albertina and confirming that he had given his consent for the young couple to marry.

The ceremony took place on 15 July 1944. Ngcali, who was the headman at Cofimvaba, told Walter that it was the accepted practice to salute the magistrate. To Ngcali's embarrassment, Walter refused, saying he would greet the magistrate, but he was not prepared to salute him. The magistrate noticed the exchange between Walter and Ngcali, but did not take offence. Instead, he remarked that it was a pity that Albertina was being taken away from the Transkei where her nursing skills were badly needed.

After the legal ceremony, a wedding reception was held at Albertina's home in Tsomo. The newlyweds then returned to Johannesburg, where they had another reception at the Bantu Men's Social Club on 17 July. It was a glittering social occasion with a popular jazz band, the Merry Blackbirds, providing the musical entertainment. Mandela was best man and Evelyn one of the bridesmaids. Dr Xuma and Anton Lembede were among those who made speeches, as was Solomon Kowalsky, Walter's lawyer. Walter had invited his old friend, Herbert Mdingi, to speak but to his disappointment, Mdingi was not prepared to forgive their earlier quarrel, and refused to attend the reception. Walter bitterly regretted their rift and wished he had not been so harsh in his judgement of Mdingi. However, he was not short of distinguished people to speak at his wedding. In his speech, Lembede warned Albertina that she was marrying a man who was already married to the nation.

As soon as they were married, Walter and Albertina keenly anticipated having their first child. So eager were they to become parents that when there was no sign of a pregnancy after three months of marriage, they consulted a doctor. Unsurprisingly, he advised them to go home and be patient. Before the year was out, there was a baby in the family, but from an entirely unexpected quarter.

While Walter and Albertina had been absorbed in courting and wedding arrangements, his sister Barbie had also fallen in love with a young man called Thomas (Tilly) Lockman. Walter knew Lockman, who had also worked for the Union Bank, but did not approve of the relationship. He felt that Lockman was a superficial character, who was not the right person for Barbie. However, he realised that his interference would not end the relationship and took the view that his sister was an adult who had to make up her own mind. Walter and his mother were very disappointed when Barbie had to abandon her last year of training because she was expecting a baby. Nevertheless, they put their disappointment aside and celebrated the birth of Barbie's son Gerald in December 1944. When Gerald was eight months' old, Albertina insisted that Barbie leave the baby with them and go back to complete her training.

By then, Walter and Albertina had their own baby. Their first son, Max Vuyisile, was born on 23 August 1945. It was the era of home deliveries and Max was born at No. 7372 with a midwife, Rachel Nkosi, in attendance. Rachel Nkosi did more than assist with the delivery; she also advised Albertina to apply for a transfer from Johannesburg General to Orlando Clinic, which was short of nurses. Albertina was grateful for this suggestion, as working in Orlando meant she would be able to return home to breastfeed her baby during the day. It was a wrench leaving her baby behind at home after a few months, but she counted herself fortunate that Alice was only too happy to take care of another baby. Anxious not to overburden her mother-in-law, Albertina would get up before dawn, light the coal stove, heat the water for washing, prepare the breakfast and do the laundry. She was proud of the fact that by the time she left for work at seven, the babies' napkins would all be washed and hanging on the line.

Walter and Albertina were deliriously happy in their marriage and loved their babies to distraction. Albertina got on well with her mother-in-law, who respected the rights of her *makoti* (daughter-in-law). "She took me as her own daughter and refused to follow the tradition that as a *makoti* I should be given a new name by which I would be addressed in my new family. She said no, she is not a cow that can be given another name. She must have the name she is born with and I will continue to call her Ntsiki." She encouraged Albertina to go back to work and devoted herself to looking after her grandchildren. The only difference they had was over the religion of the children. Walter and Albertina had married in the Catholic Church. Walter had said that he would not convert to Catholicism, but that he would allow the children to be Catholic. However, when her grandchildren started arriving, Alice refused to allow them to be raised as Catholics. Albertina gave in to her and even started attending Anglican church services herself.

In November 1948, Albertina and Walter had their second son, Mlungisi. Barbie had by then completed her training and was working at the clinic in Noordgesig, the working-class coloured area adjacent to Orlando East. She had married Tilly Lockman, and in March 1949 gave birth to her second child, a daughter they named Beryl. When Barbie's maternity leave was over, Gerald and Beryl were taken daily to their grandmother in Orlando.

Walter and Albertina had other additions to their household too. After her grandmother Nosenti died in 1944, Albertina could not stop thinking of her sister Flora (Nomyaleko), who was still living at Uncle Campbell's home. "According to tradition, Uncle Campbell was her official guardian but after my grandmother died, I had a dream in which my mother came to me and said: 'Nomyaleko is ill. Why did you leave her? You know you have to look after her.' I immediately woke Walter and told him about the dream. He said, 'Tomorrow we will send money for her to come here.' We sent the train fare and asked Uncle Campbell to send Flora. He refused. This went on for some time until we virtually 'stole' Flora away. One of our relatives who was coming to Johannesburg brought Flora, as if for a short visit. The short visit became a long visit and eventually it was accepted that Flora would not go back to Xolobe."

By that time, Albertina's brother Stanford had completed school and begun working in the clerical department of a Cape Town company. Like Albertina, he had a yearning to be financially independent and to build his own home. Her other brother, Elliot, had completed high school and

Walter had helped him to secure financial assistance to study theology at Fort Hare. After his graduation, he returned to Orlando East, where he married Miriam Matsha in 1948.

Miriam moved into No. 7372 as well. Albertina was delighted with her new sister-in-law. Miriam was their home girl from Xolobe, and she had been one of the junior girls who had looked up to Albertina when they were at Middle Xolobe School. The young bride was amazed at the numbers of people who visited the Sisulu home, many of them staying overnight. "Never in my life did I meet so many people in such a short time." She learned that many of them were prominent political figures. "The best political education I had was living at No. 7372." Like many young married couples, Elliot and Miriam Thethiwe struggled to find a place of their own. Fortunately, Elliot succeeded in his ambition to become a Presbyterian minister, and in 1952 he was allocated a church house in Orlando East.

Decades of neglect of African housing by the government, together with rapid urbanisation during the war, had created a housing crisis of enormous proportions. During the war years the Johannesburg municipality had done nothing to address the housing shortage or provide any infrastructure for this swelling working class. In Orlando, virtually every outhouse and backyard was packed with desperate tenants. Even then the backyard shacks became too crowded; the sewerage buckets overflowed, the communal taps ran dry. Yet the Johannesburg Council seemed to be immune to the problem. Into this crisis stepped James Mpanza, a highly shrewd and charismatic figure. He had once killed a man, but had had his death sentence commuted. Subsequently he converted to Christianity, convinced that his life had been spared for a purpose. After he was released from prison, Mpanza came to Orlando where he was soon elected to the local advisory board. Walter first met Mpanza when his cousin Caleb Mase was arrested for a pass offence. Mpanza took up the matter in his capacity as a member of the advisory board and Caleb was released.

For years, Mpanza wrote letter after letter to the Minister of Native Affairs about the housing crisis, but his appeals fell on deaf ears. He had attended the ANC's annual conference in 1943 where he motivated for the ANC to warn the government about the serious social consequences of lack of accommodation for Africans. One day in 1944, Walter attended a mass meeting where Mpanza called him aside and told him that he was planning to lead some people to settle on a vacant municipal plot in Orlando West. Walter did not grasp the significance of what he was planning until the following week when, on a Saturday afternoon, Mpanza led the people (as he said) "across the River Jordan to the promised land". Followers in their thousands, desperate for a roof over their heads, put up shelters, under his supervision, with any material at hand – hessian, cardboard and even dry corncobs. Township residents called the place "Masakeni" after the hessian sacks that covered the makeshift shelters. Mpanza's ragtag army was fiercely loyal to him and resistant to the Council's attempts to remove them. Mpanza's middle name "Sofasonke" (we will die together) took on a literal meaning and became the name of this new movement.

There followed a series of struggles in which the Council tried to deport Mpanza, eject the "squatters", tear down their shelters, and deport the unemployed or those without passes to the rural areas. In one confrontation with the police, two people died. In the ensuing court case, the judge ruled that Johannesburg was obliged to provide homeless people with shelter. The following year, the Council provided extremely basic "site and service" facilities in the new location of Jabavu. In November 1944, the government passed new legislation to prevent squatting, and by 1945 all the people of Shantytown had been forcibly removed (Bonner and Segal, 25).

Despite the destruction of his Shantytown, Mpanza had succeeded in forcing the Council to provide shelters, no matter how rudimentary, to the homeless. He was determined to pursue his messianic mission. One day in 1946, Walter was on his way home from work when he learned that violence had broken out near the Orlando Community Hall, where hessian shelters had been erected. A fight between the occupants of the shelters and the municipal police who were trying to demolish them had resulted in two deaths and several wounded. The municipal police had been forced to flee into the Community Hall, where they were besieged by the angry squatters. Walter quickly contacted Lembede and they rushed to the scene. By that time, police reinforcements had arrived and were ready to attack the squatters, who were clearly intent on defending themselves. Walter, Lembede and Paul Mosaka, who they met at the scene, immediately began negotiating with the police brigadier not to order an attack on the angry crowd. The brigadier replied that he just wanted to liberate the municipal police. Walter and his colleagues suggested they wait until morning, by which time tempers would have subsided. With some difficulty, they got the police to agree, provided the wounded municipal police were removed. They then persuaded the squatters to free the wounded. The remaining police were freed the next morning, and Walter felt that a bloodbath had been averted.

Walter was fascinated and excited by this bold grass-roots initiative to claim the land, and those members of the Youth League who lived in Orlando decided to assist in any way they could. Walter, Nelson Mandela and Anton Lembede contacted Mpanza and offered their services. Mpanza had developed a convincing legal argument: the Johannesburg Council was responsible for black workers, who were prohibited from owning land because they were black. He quickly grasped the value of Youth League support. Nelson and Anton gave their legal services at no cost. Xuma gave his blessing to the project and even donated 25 pounds to the cause on behalf of the ANC. As the informal settlement grew, it soon became clear that the shelters were not adequate to keep out the cold and wet. Together, Mpanza, Walter, Nelson and Anton Lembede developed a strategy to compel the City Council to take responsibility.

"Mpanza spoke to me and Nelson," Walter recalled. "[He] said, let's pass a resolution at the Orlando Residents Association. It must be moved by Nelson and seconded by me in which, he says, that on 29 January, we the residents of Orlando shall evict the subtenants. That resolution was moved; and *that* strategy moved the City Council" (Luli Callinicos, Interview, 23/6/90).

Walter called this a "genius approach". Mpanza convened the meeting at Orlando Community Hall and the resolution was passed. The resolution was followed by a march of 1 000 families in the city streets, demanding housing. The Council was alarmed by the warning that should it fail to take action, the subtenants would make their own arrangements (meaning that they would invade vacant land). A meeting was set for the following Sunday and the city councillors turned out in full force. At the time, the Labour Party controlled the Johannesburg City Council. Walter knew the councillor for the Hillbrow ward, Hilda Bernstein, the only Communist ever to be elected to public office in South Africa by an all-white electorate (Karis and Gerhart, 4: 6). In her tenure as a councillor, she campaigned tirelessly for improvements in African housing. At the meeting, the Council promised to do everything in its power to relieve the situation – after declaring that it would not have its hand forced by lawlessness. Finally, the Council made a vacant lot available at Jabavu, four miles away from Orlando, where the homeless were allowed to put up temporary shelters.

The intense struggles of the grass-roots Sofasonke Movement in pushing for houses and their remarkable achievement, partial though it was, opened people's eyes to the potential for action. Mpanza had inspired a squatters' movement throughout the Witwatersrand, and new camps mushroomed everywhere. Members of the Springbok Legion started a camp of their own in Orlando, which they called Tobruk, and Reverend Michael Scott, the first and only white squatter, joined them, an act of solidarity that caused shock and consternation in white church circles and drew admiration from Walter and other members of the Youth League.

This episode confirmed for Walter and his comrades the importance of working with the mass base. In contrast, ANC and Communist Party stalwarts had convinced the Communist Party (SACP) not to support Mpanza. Later, Rusty Bernstein wrote: "Our judgement had been wrong. The Party, which always aimed to lead in mass action, had been out-flanked and by-passed" (Rusty Bernstein, 104).

For the black opposition, and for Walter in particular, 1946 was the year that dispelled any illusions about the liberalism of the Smuts government. Smuts had aroused hopes when he had hinted that there would be an easing of segregation after the war, and Xuma had sent Smuts a copy of the African Claims statement, the ANC's interpretation of the Atlantic Charter. This received a cold response from Smuts, who dismissed it as a "propagandistic document" and refused to accept that the Charter's assertion on human rights was applicable to the situation of black South Africans (Callinicos, Unpublished manuscript). Walter, however, believed that the African Claims statement was one of Xuma's greatest achievements. Through the African Claims, Walter believed that the ANC was asserting its rights, not only as a mouthpiece of the African people in South Africa, but also as an organisation that had a say in world affairs.

Two further acts of popular resistance in 1946 were the African mineworkers' strike and the Indian Passive Resistance campaign. The impact of these events was not always immediately apparent, but in years to come, Walter acknowledged the profound, long-term influence they had on the Youth League, the ANC and on him personally.

Walter had read about Mahatma Gandhi's campaigns in South African and India, and the Indian struggle for independence from the British. He was also familiar with the history of the Indian Congresses in South Africa, and Yusuf Dadoo was one of his heroes, so he followed closely the progress of the Passive Resistance campaign against Smuts's Asiatic Land Tenure and Indian Representation Bill of June 1946. The "Ghetto Bill" – as it came to be called – restricted the freedom of movement of Indians, circumscribed the areas where they could live and trade and severely restricted their right to buy property. In return for this objectionable law, the Indians were to be given a token representation by whites in Parliament (Mandela, 97; Bunting 1998, 135). Walter was impressed by the efficiency and organisation of the Passive Resistance campaign. The Transvaal Indian Congress (TIC) headquarters were situated opposite Walter's offices, so he was able to witness all the hustle and bustle going on at the time of the campaign. When he visited the TIC offices, he was particularly impressed by the women involved in the campaign, among them Amina Pahad, the wife of his friend Goolam. He felt inspired by these Indian women, whom he had once assumed to be conservative and unwilling to involve themselves in public life. He also admired students like Zainub Asvat and the young Ahmed Kathrada, who suspended their studies to devote themselves full-time to the campaign.

Walter also received regular updates on the campaign from Mandela, who was studying at the University of the Witwatersrand at the time. Mandela was close to two fellow students, JN Singh and Ismail Meer, who were leaders in the campaign. Walter was profoundly moved by the determination and commitment of the Passive Resistance volunteers, whose campaign lasted two years. During this time, over 2 000 people went to prison, including Drs Dadoo and Naicker.

Although the Passive Resistance campaign was confined to the Indian community, the ANC and Youth League expressed solidarity with their cause. A leading ANC official from Germiston, Joshua Makue, and Reverend Michael Scott both participated in the Passive Resistance campaign. The campaigners also lent their support to the mineworkers' strike in the same year, and protested against its ruthless suppression. The outcome was a sense of a common, wider cause.

The miners' strike was one of the outcomes of the impact of the Second World War on the economy of South Africa. While the cost of living rose steadily in the early 1940s, miners' wages remained the same. An average mineworker's wage in 1946 was the same as it had been in 1943, which in real terms represented a 15 per cent drop in earnings. Mine owners stuck to their old argument – that black mineworkers were migrants, so their families were supported by the land, and their wages were merely extra income, and thus not crucial to their families' survival. Effectively, the mines relied on the unpaid labour of the women in the rural areas to subsidise their cheap labour system.

In 1941, the African Mineworkers' Union (AMWU) undertook to organise the miners – a difficult task because they were housed in closed compounds, under tightly controlled conditions. But by holding regular Sunday meetings at key places such as the Market Square in Newtown, membership slowly grew. By 1943, the union was ready to challenge the mines on the issue of wages. Black trade unions in the manufacturing and service sectors had managed to win significant wage gains through struggles and strikes, but under War Measure 145, the mines (themselves experiencing a profit squeeze) fell under a specially protected category. The government then stepped in and commissioned an enquiry, the Landsdowne Commission, thus delaying union action; while the war was on, it hesitated to alienate its black working force (Lerumo, 76; Simons and Simons, 570–8).

Walter was keenly aware of these developments, particularly as Gaur Radebe and JB Marks, both Communist Party and senior ANC members, were involved. The commission dragged its feet, fobbing off increasingly urgent enquiries for the duration of the war. Finally, after the war had ended, the government announced its decision to raise wages by a wholly inadequate amount, below even the commission's recommendations. To cap it all, the food rations in the compounds had deteriorated and portions were smaller. Thoroughly aggrieved, at a meeting on Market Square in Newtown, union members called loudly and unanimously for an immediate strike (Lerumo, 76; Simons and Simons, 570–8).

The Youth League decided to actively support the strike, which started on 12 August 1946. Walter and his League colleagues supported the Council of Non-European Trade Unions' (CNETU) decision to call for a general strike in sympathy with the mineworkers. Lembede, Self Mampuru, Paul Mosaka and Barney Ngakane of the Transvaal ANC executive approached Walter with a daring proposal: they felt that for a general strike to be successful, it would be necessary to sabotage the railway line between Soweto and New Canada Stations. They asked Walter if he would be prepared to undertake such a task, and discussed the dangers and implications. They mentioned that there was a real possibility that he could lose his life and assured him that should something go wrong, Albertina and his baby son could depend on the goodwill of the organisation (this was a little idealistic, given that this action was being planned without the approval of the notoriously cash-strapped ANC).

Walter was aware that there would be strongly divided opinions in the ANC on such a matter, but he felt there was a strong need for concrete action in a crisis situation, so he accepted the commission without consideration for his personal safety. The group decided to approach Hymie Basner, the most radical white representative for natives in the South African Senate, to ask for help in securing dynamite and detonators. Walter was among a carload of young men who went to Basner's house, where they made their unusual request. Basner was shocked, but agreed to acquire the explosives. He left them waiting while he went in search of explosives, and returned in the early hours of the morning to say that he had been unsuccessful. The plan was abandoned, and in later years, Walter marvelled at how he could have entertained such an incredibly reckless, harebrained scheme.

The general strike was violently crushed because it was simply not possible for its leaders to develop a coherent plan in the face of widespread arrests and intimidation. Walter later reflected that it was far too ambitious to organise a general strike at such short notice. In five days of brutality, the police beat the workers back into their compounds, and then, stope by stope, underground. The strike of 70 000 workers, the largest in South African history so far, was over. The ANC received reports that 11 miners had been killed and hundreds badly injured. Fifty-two leaders of the Mineworkers' Union and the Communist Party were charged under War Measure 145, which made it a criminal offence for Africans to strike. Walter attended the court case in which several of the accused (including Moses Kotane, JB Marks, Yusuf Dadoo and Rusty Bernstein) were found guilty or fined (Sampson 1958, 78; Lerumo, 78). Dr Xuma sent a cable to Smuts and the Minister of Native Affairs, expressing shock at the use of force against the mineworkers, and proposed that the Native Representative Council (NRC) sitting on 14/15 August be adjourned in protest against the brutal treatment of the miners. The NRC members accepted his proposal, and even the most conservative members agreed that, under the circumstances, the NRC was no more than a "toy telephone".

Walter and his Youth League colleagues were happy to hear of the adjournment of the NRC, which they had long dismissed as a dummy institution that should be boycotted. The Youth League attended the NRC debates, taking the opportunity to lobby its councillors to abandon the idea of working in dummy institutions.

Like most of his Youth League colleagues, Walter was becoming impatient with Xuma's cautious approach and distaste for any form of mass action. He did, however, admire Xuma's grasp of international affairs and followed closely his trip to the US in 1946 to lobby at the first General Assembly of the United Nations against the South African government's proposal to incorporate South West Africa (Namibia) into the Union of South Africa. HA Naidoo and Sorabjee Rustomjee of the TIC and NIC also went to the United Nations to present the case of the treatment of South African Indians. Hymie Basner added his voice, describing the iniquities of the gold-mining industry and Smuts's role in breaking the mineworkers' strike (Bunting 1998, 136; Basner, 188; Gish, 148).

Walter noted with interest the welcome the South African team received from the Council of African Affairs, run by Paul Robeson, the acclaimed African American singer and political activist, and Max Yergan, an African American activist who had spent several years working in South Africa. Walter was amused by the story of how Smuts had bumped into Xuma at a New York reception, and had asked what he was doing in New York. Xuma responded: "I have come to be near my Prime Minister. I have had to fly 10 000 miles to meet my Prime Minister. He talks about us, but he won't talk to us" (Gish, 148).

Xuma returned home to a hero's welcome after the UN General Assembly rejected South Africa's plan for incorporating South West Africa on 14 December 1946. The basis had been laid for UN condemnation of South Africa's policies, and Walter saw the episode as a lesson on the value of international lobbying.

Through shared struggles, such as the collaboration between the ANC and the Passive Resistance campaign organisers during the miners' strike, as well as racial discrimination experienced by the wider black community, Xuma, Naicker and Dadoo agreed that their organisations should work together in future in their common quest for social justice. This took the form of the Dadoo-Xuma-Naicker Pact in March 1947, a six-point agreement between the presidents of the ANC, the TIC and the Natal Indian Congress (NIC) to work together for a universal franchise and the abolition of all forms of racial discrimination (Vadi, 46). After the signing of the "Doctors' Pact" – as it came to be known – a mass meeting was held at Market Square to celebrate.

Walter was not at this meeting, but he heard all about it from an enthusiastic Lembede, who told him that Youth Leaguers "should accept to work with other non-Europeans on the basis of equality and independence on matters of common interest". Walter was rather surprised, as Lembede headed those in the Youth League who emphasised African nationalism and the independence of the ANC, and was very suspicious of other groups he suspected of wanting to be dominant in any political relationship. It had been Lembede who had sponsored a motion (supported by Walter and Oliver Tambo) to exclude Communists from membership of the Transvaal ANC unless they first resigned from the Communist Party (Karis and Gerhart, 4: 56). Xuma and the ANC NEC (National Executive Council) had rejected the motion; although Xuma was no supporter of Communism, he felt that the ANC should accommodate all shades of opinion (Gish, 133). But the Youth League firebrands were concerned that the Communists might want to control the ANC under the guise of joint action, and opposed the idea of joint programmes. Mandela recalls that they even went so far as to storm the stage at some Communist Party meetings, tearing up posters and capturing the microphone (Mandela, 101). Walter would later be very embarrassed to admit that on a few occasions, he had also been involved in the breaking up of Communist Party meetings.

Walter was never to know whether Lembede's comment on the Doctors' Pact meeting was a one-off comment, or whether it represented a shift in his position on working with Communists or the Indian Congress. When he walked into Lembede's office on 27 July 1947, he found him writhing in agony. Joined by Nelson Mandela, they called Dr Silas Molema, who had a practice nearby. Molema immediately sent Lembede to Coronation Hospital, where he died on 29 July. The cause of death was "cardiac failure" with "intestinal obstruction" a contributory factor. "There are blows from which it is possible to recover quickly; there are others which leave a gaping wound in one's soul for a lifetime." So wrote journalist and Congress Youth League member Jordan Ngubane in tribute to his friend Anton Lembede (Edgar and ka Msumza, 30). Ngubane's words summed up the feelings of Lembede's friends and colleagues, not least Walter Sisulu, who was beside himself with grief.

On the eve of the white elections in May 1948, Dr Dadoo and the Communist Party organised a mass nonracial "Votes for All" campaign to challenge the concept of "whites-only" elections and to campaign for the extension of the franchise to all the people of South Africa. The ANC was invited, together with the trade unions and the Indian Congresses, to sponsor the event. It was to be a regional campaign confined to the Orange Free State and Transvaal. Mandela, who had by then been elected to the ANC's Transvaal Executive, presided over a press conference at which Dr Xuma announced the campaign. However, when they learned that the ANC would not be leading the campaign, the Transvaal Executive decided to withdraw. They felt that the campaign would be a Communist-controlled affair and that they should only participate in campaigns led by the ANC. They were also concerned that the campaign might be an attempt to set up a permanent organisation that would rival the ANC (Mandela, 103; Bunting 1998, 157–8; Rusty Bernstein, 109).

Indian Congress leaders JN Singh, Maulvi Cachalia and Ismail Meer proposed a joint session with the Transvaal Executive to discuss the matter. Walter, Tambo and Mandela were mandated by the Transvaal Executive to convey its opposition. At this meeting, the Indian Congress leaders tried to reassure them that there was no plan to turn the campaign into a permanent organisation. They argued so eloquently that they persuaded Walter that they had no ulterior motives, and he said he saw no reason for the ANC not to support the campaign.

Tambo and Mandela were so angry with Walter for abandoning their mandate that when they left the meeting, they refused to walk with him and would not speak to him for two days. Mandela finally sarcastically told Walter that he had been persuaded when Ismail Meer had praised him as a wise man (Callinicos, Unpublished manuscript).

The controversy continued when the President of the Transvaal Executive, Constantine Ramahanoe, was persuaded by Ismail Meer to issue a statement of support and a call to ANC members to support the campaign. This time, Walter supported Tambo and Mandela in their condemnation of Ramahanoe's defiance of the decision of the Transvaal Executive. He felt that it was wrong for Ismail to persuade Ramahanoe to defy his executive, and that this behaviour smacked of the kind of manipulation that made the Youth League suspicious of joint programmes with the Communists and the Indian Congress.

The Votes for All affair meanwhile caused deep divisions within the Transvaal Executive. Walter supported Mandela when he moved for a vote of no confidence in Ramahanoe. Other executive members supported Ramahanoe, and the meeting broke up in disarray. Lionel Ngakane, the chairman of the Orlando Branch of the Youth League, and its secretary, Victor Mbobo, were also drawn into the fray. They were summoned by the Transvaal Executive and taken to task for their support of the Votes for All campaign. Mbobo was suspended and Lionel was expelled from his position of chairman (Interview, Lionel Ngakane 5/11/97). The furore in the Transvaal ANC notwithstanding, 300 to 400 delegates attended the highly successful Votes for All Assembly at Gandhi Hall in

Fordsburg. Lionel Ngakane defiantly attended the conference as a representative of the Federation of Progressive Students, and announced: "I feel very sore about the resolution of the Transvaal African National Congress which condemns the Assembly. It means our Congress is a stumbling block. Which will come first: our rights or our leaders?" (Bunting 1998, 158).

The 1948 election victory of the National Party completely dashed any hopes of democracy and a better deal for black people. Instead, Africans were facing an unprecedented white backlash. Even the more moderate ANC leaders were beginning to see the need for new ways of responding to increasing injustice and oppression. As Professor ZK Matthews pointed out in response to the National Party victory:

> What further measures of repression were in store and what should their reaction be? Gradually the idea emerged that the time had come for a more militant policy. For years African organisations had pinned their faith on moderation: on petitions and deputations, on mild requests for this or that concession, on what they called constitutional methods of struggle. They had met every deprivation of their rights with the hope that it was only temporary and that they would eventually earn rights of citizenship by their loyalty and the recognition of their contribution to the country. Surely reason would prevail over unreason? Now they began to realize that the country was being set on a different course which meant permanent denial of any stake in the country for them (Matthews, 157).

The Youth League had long recognised the need for the adoption of a more positive line of action than the deputations and petitions of the past. Since Lembede's death in 1947, a document had been circulating among ANC leadership at various levels (Lodge, 26). This document, a proposal for a detailed programme of action, was drafted by the National Executive of the Youth League (consisting of Sisulu, Mandela, Mda, Tambo, Njongwe and David Bopape). Their proposal was presented at and adopted by the Transvaal provincial conference of the ANC and thereafter discussed at the ANC annual conference in 1948 (Karis and Carter, 2: 104).

At the 1948 conference, the chairman, AWG Champion, took advantage of Dr Xuma's temporary absence and tried to sabotage the resolution to adopt the Programme of Action by closing the conference early. This was resisted by both Josias Madzunya, an ardent proponent of African nationalism, and Elias Motsoaledi, a Communist Party member. Both Africanists and Communist Party members saw the need for the resolution. At that point, Xuma arrived and agreed that there was no time to discuss the resolution. It was settled that the resolution should be referred back to the branch and provincial levels, and then referred once more to the 1949 annual conference.

The Programme of Action was a radical departure from the ANC's standard policy of operating within the bounds of the law. It asserted the Youth League commitment to African nationalism, freedom from white domination and the attainment of political independence. It advocated a campaign of mass mobilisation through boycotts, strikes, civil disobedience and noncooperation (Karis and Carter, 2: 337–8).

During this period, the Youth League was considerably strengthened through the efforts of AP Mda, the main author of both the Programme of Action and the Basic Policy of the Congress Youth League. Mda had become president of the Youth League after Lembede's death, and he worked tirelessly to extend the influence of the Youth League nationally. By 1948, the Youth League had established a presence in Natal and parts of the Cape. In the same year, Mda encouraged Godfrey Pitje, a young anthropology lecturer at Fort Hare, to start a Youth League branch at that university (Karis and Gerhart, 4: 85). The Fort Hare branch of the Youth League brought a new generation of radical young men into the fold, most notably the brilliant intellectual Robert Sobukwe, Joe Matthews (the son of Professor ZK Matthews) and Nthato Motlana (Pogrund, 29).

Throughout 1949, the Programme of Action was debated within the ANC at branch and provincial levels. In November 1949, Walter, Mandela and Tambo visited Dr Xuma at his home in

Sophiatown to solicit his support for the Programme of Action. They acknowledged all that Xuma had done for the ANC, then went on to inform him that they believed the time had come for the President to be supported on the basis of his policies. "We told him that gone were the days when the choice of leader depended on his status as a doctor or lawyer. It now depended on whether he could muster the support of the masses of the people" (Interview, Nelson Mandela 1993). They said the matter of the Programme of Action would be coming up at the conference, and they believed it would be adopted. Next, they informed Xuma that they would accept his presidency if he accepted the Programme of Action. They told him the time had come to open a new chapter, and argued that this could only be done by embarking on mass action and courting arrest. They cited examples of Gandhi and Nehru, who built their organisation by embarking on mass action and going to jail.

This greatly angered Xuma. "What do you know about Gandhi and Nehru?" he said. "You come to lecture me here!" (Interview, Nelson Mandela 1993). Xuma said he had no intention of jeopardizing his prosperous medical practice by going to prison. He did not fundamentally disagree with the Programme of Action, but he was convinced that the priority should be to focus on the building of the ANC as an organisation before embarking on such radical action. The argument went on until late into the night. Xuma felt that the young men were arrogant and disrespectful, and insisted that he was not going to be bribed or blackmailed – he would not support their Programme and they could keep their votes. He virtually pushed them out of his house and closed the gate behind him. At 11pm there was no public transport to Orlando, so they stayed overnight at the home of Les Gama, who lived nearby.

In 1949, arrangements were made for the annual conference of the Youth League to be held in Bloemfontein just before the annual ANC conference. It was the most well-attended Youth League conference ever. The strategy of the Youth League was discussed and candidates for the incoming executive decided upon. It was agreed that the Youth League would only support those candidates who supported the Programme of Action.

The Youth Leaguers approached Professor ZK Matthews to stand as President-General, as it was felt they needed someone of his stature to stand against Xuma in the election. Professor Matthews declined to stand. He felt that the Programme of Action was too radical and that the Youth Leaguers were "naive firebrands who would mellow with age" (Mandela, 131). The Youth League was also turned down by Logan K Ntlabati, a prominent member of the ANC executive, whom they approached to stand for the position of Secretary-General. He declined, says Walter, "probably because he realised that the Programme of Action was a militant programme which he could not possibly undertake without jeopardising his position as a teacher" (Interview, Walter Sisulu 1993).

The Youth League found an alternative candidate in Dr James Moroka. The great-grandson of the Tswana chief Moroka who gave military protection to the Voortrekkers in the 1830s, Moroka was a wealthy businessman in his hometown of Thaba Nchu in the Orange Free State. Like Xuma, he was a successful and highly respected medical doctor who had trained abroad. He was also a popular political figure, a member of the AAC who was elected to the Native Representative Council in 1942 (Karis and Carter, 4: 97–8). Moroka was an unlikely candidate in that he was not a member of the ANC; in fact, he knew so little about the organisation when he was approached that he kept referring to it as the African National "Council" (Mandela, 131). However, he had a reputation for militancy, he supported the Programme of Action, and he was the only person of the stature of Xuma who was willing to stand.

At the ANC annual conference in December 1947, the Programme of Action was analysed paragraph by paragraph before it was adopted unanimously with minor amendments (Meli, 118). Among those who spoke about the Programme were Moroka, Sobukwe, Mda, Njongwe and Walter. It was proposed that only those who were willing to implement the Programme of Action should be elected to the new executive. In an electoral coup for the Youth League, Dr Moroka was elected President-General and Walter was elected Secretary-General, defeating the Communist

Party candidate, Dan Tloome. The Youth League's plan had been for Walter to stand for the post of Treasurer-General, and he had had no intention of standing for the position of Secretary-General, but at election time, Dr Gama, supported by Nxumalo (one of the Wits medical students), proposed Walter's name.

Although surprised at his election, Walter was ready to take up the challenge and do everything in his power to implement the Programme of Action. He knew that it had to be a full-time commitment: "I knew when I was elected ... that the whole burden of mobilising the movement was on my shoulders and it was something I would not be able to do if I had other interests" (Interview, Walter Sisulu 1993). He decided to give up Sitha Investments and devote himself full-time to ANC work. This was really a formality as, since the formation of the Youth League, Sitha Investments was more of an ANC office than an estate agency, and business was so bad that the company had gone into receivership in 1947.

Walter discussed the matter with Albertina, who fully supported his decision and was more than happy to take over entirely as breadwinner of the family. She even subsidised the ANC by paying for Walter's monthly railway ticket. He thus became the first full-time Secretary-General of the ANC, with a salary of five pounds a month. "It was five pounds by word of mouth," says Walter. "In reality I never received it, because the movement was always short of money." He jokes about how the executive once decided to increase his salary to 10 pounds, until Xuma pointed out that it would be ridiculous to do so when he was not even receiving the five pounds! (Interview, Walter Sisulu 1993.)

Professor ZK Matthews was highly critical of Walter's decision. "Walter, this is irresponsible," he said. "How do you aspire to lead the nation if you cannot even provide for your own family?" (Interview, Walter Sisulu 1993.) Walter replied that he had no alternative. As one of the principal architects of the Programme of Action, he was duty-bound to ensure its implementation.

The next decade saw a new era in resistance politics, as the ANC set about implementing the Programme of Action, which would transform it from an ineffectual protest movement to a mass organisation that would change the history of South Africa. Walter Sisulu would be a central figure in that transformation.

*t h r e e*

When Walter Sisulu moved into the modest ANC headquarters in New Court Chambers in Commissioner Street, around the corner from his old offices in West Street, he was acutely conscious of the burden of responsibility that his new position entailed. On the eve of the 1949 ANC conference, he had been arrested for nonpossession of a pass. He had been so incensed by the way the police had treated him that he had gone to the conference intending to propose a plan of physical retaliation against the police. When he was elected Secretary-General, he dropped the idea because "I felt I had to conduct myself differently".

Walter said he knew that his election meant he "was starting a new chapter altogether". Many years later, his friend and political comrade Ruth First would talk about how Walter's leadership represented a new era in the life of the ANC:

> This is the period when Walter Sisulu, night and day, became the centre of the organisational drive of the ANC. And this is the start of a new history in the life struggle of the ANC. And from this time on, largely under the leadership of Sisulu, though not exclusively, we have an ANC in direct and continuing contact with the masses, leading political strikes and mass disobedience campaigns. We have the reconstitution of the ANC with a system of branch and cell organisations which prepared it for the period when the ANC was forced underground and we have a policy of unity in action in the ANC ... which policy was in fact initiated in this period under the secretaryship of Walter Sisulu (Speech, Walter Sisulu's 70th birthday, 1982).

One of the first things Walter did after his election was to inform Yusuf Cachalia of the TIC that the ANC was ready to cooperate on any issue. Walter had become convinced of the need for Africans and Indians to work more closely together after the Durban riots of January 1949. He had been utterly appalled by the violence sparked off when simmering tensions between the two communities exploded into a full-scale confrontation after an Indian trader beat an African youth for shoplifting. Indian shops and homes were burned, 50 Indians and 87 Africans were killed, and thousands were left homeless.

Walter believed that whatever the tensions between Africans and Indians, it was the racial propaganda of the Nationalists that had aggravated the situation. He believed that Malan's government had a direct interest in fanning the flames of Zulu/Indian hostility, especially in view of India's independence in 1947 and that country's challenge to South Africa at the United Nations.

Walter and Tambo were among the African and Indian leaders who rushed to Durban to resolve the crisis at the height of the riots. Joe Matthews, one of the young Fort Hare Youth Leaguers, was at the home of Natal ANC president AWG Champion when Walter walked in, having arrived in Durban that morning. Champion, the playwright HIE Dhlomo and his brother RR Dhlomo who were also visiting Champion, teased Walter mercilessly about how an important man like Sisulu could move around carrying nothing more than a briefcase (Interview, Joe Matthews 20/12/2001).

Walter sensed that Champion was not entirely convinced about cooperation between Africans and Indians, but he accepted the NEC's stance, and he and Ismail Meer of the NIC toured the riot area in an open loudspeaker van to appeal for calm (Callinicos, Unpublished manuscript).

Walter supported Xuma's call for a conference between Indian and African leaders. This conference, which took place on 6 February 1949, resulted in a joint declaration of ANC and SAIC leaders calling on their people to devise ways of future cooperation (Bunting 1998, 169; Gish, 152). Walter had been horrified to see two oppressed peoples at each other's throats and was convinced that the only way to prevent future such occurrences was through joint action. He was becoming increasingly convinced that the only way to counter the neo-Nazi ideology of the Nationalist Party was through a policy of principled nonracialism.

Walter's first priority and driving ambition as Secretary-General was to see that the Programme of Action was implemented. It was not an easy task. When he took over the ANC national office, he inherited 400 pounds, a clerk and one full-time typist. He had to contend not only with meagre resources, but also with different ideological strands within the ANC, all of which were represented on the NEC.

The liberal old guard was represented by veterans who had been part of Dr Xuma's NEC in the 1940s: Dr Xuma himself; Rev. James Calata, the former Secretary-General who, in Walter's view, had made a sterling contribution to the revival of the ANC in the 1940s; Dr Roseberry Bokwe; Logan Ntlabati, the school principal known for his talent in drafting resolutions and memoranda; and Dr Silas Molema, whose criticism of the administrative failings and financial disorder of the ANC probably led to his election as Treasurer-General in 1949. Also part of the Xuma era was the former Treasurer-General Richard Baloyi, a wealthy Alexandra businessman who owned an estate agency and a bus company. (PUTCO Bus Company was originally Baloyi's bus company.) Baloyi had also been part of the committee that drafted the African Claims document. Walter had become quite friendly with Baloyi during his days of agency work in Alexandra. Reverend Skomolo, Anglican clergyman in the Eastern Cape, who on occasion served as ANC chaplain, had also been elected to the 1949 NEC. Like Calata, Skomolo tried to serve as a moderating influence on what were seen as extremist tendencies.

The Youth League was represented on the NEC by Walter, Oliver Tambo, Godfrey Pitje (who had been elected president of the Youth League when AP Mda was forced to resign due to ill-health), James Njongwe (who would in 1954 succeed ZK Matthews as President of the ANC in the Cape), Victor Mbobo and Fort Hare lecturer, Joseph Mokoena. Neither Mokoena nor Mbobo would ever really be active on the NEC. Moses Kotane and Dan Tloome, who had been narrowly defeated by Walter in the contest for Secretary-General, were the two Communist Party members on the NEC. Not quite fitting into any of the above categories was Dr Moroka himself, somewhat of an outsider to the ANC. Gaur Radebe was also difficult to categorise. The veteran trade unionist had been expelled from the Communist Party in 1942 for money-lending activities, but remained a great admirer of Stalin and according to Walter, "even bought himself a coat like Stalin, all buttoned up." Radebe had briefly flirted with Paul Mosaka's African Democratic Party in 1943, before rising to prominence in the Alexandra Branch of the ANC.

The various ideological camps within the ANC were, however, never cast in stone. As one historian pointed out: "While liberals and communists borrowed the language of orthodox nationalism, orthodox nationalists professed a vague socialism; communists employed the Christian idiom of liberalism and here and there a liberal might be found praising the colour-blindness of communists. Among politically conscious activists looking for theoretical moorings, there was a tendency to drift in and out of ideological camps as first one set of perspectives and then another seemed best to illuminate the perplexities of the African predicament" (Gerhart, 88).

The new NEC had its first meeting in January 1950 to discuss administration in general and the implementation of the Programme of Action in particular. They also discussed the riots that had taken place around Johannesburg in 1949 in response to the tightening of liquor laws and pass laws. They agreed that it was necessary to find ways to harness the popular anger against increased police raids into organised political activity. But before the NEC could take any action,

Walter was faced with his first crisis as Secretary-General. Still smarting from his election defeat, Xuma commented to Walter that "now that Moroka was President-General, all the affairs of the ANC would be known to the police". Walter was shocked at the insinuation that Moroka was a police agent, and he asked Xuma if he had evidence to back up this serious allegation. Xuma was not able to provide such evidence, but made the same accusation in a letter to the NEC, which was read out at an NEC meeting in the presence of both Moroka and Xuma. The rest of the NEC condemned the letter, especially Oliver Tambo, who said: "This dirty letter must be removed from the records of the ANC." It was an extremely painful confrontation, according to Walter: "Oliver had been one of his [Xuma's] favourites so for Oliver to respond in that manner was very humiliating for Xuma."

Xuma abruptly resigned from the NEC. In a public statement to *Bantu World*, published on 18 March 1950, Xuma cited the "bribery and corruption" of the Youth League's election tactics as the main reason for his resignation. He wrote that he would rather resign than carry out a policy he did not support. Walter, Tambo and Mandela in turn publicly accused Xuma of mis-representing the issues surrounding his failure to be re-elected (Letter to *Bantu World*, 1/4/50, quoted in Gish, 166). Selope Thema weighed in in an editorial, condemning the Youth League's conduct towards Xuma, and the debate raged for months in the pages of *Bantu World* (Gish, 166). Walter felt that the NEC had been correct to reprimand Xuma, who had allowed his vision to be clouded by bitterness and envy.

Walter was deeply pained by the fallout with Xuma. In later years, he was to say, "we should have exercised more patience with him, and we could have been kinder." He felt that Xuma "was not radical enough to take the struggle to another stage, so he had to go, but it could have been done in a better way. At the time we lacked complete appreciation of the work he had done for the ANC. Sometimes people criticised him unfairly when they said he liked money. He was more dedicated to the cause than to making money. He would use his own money to pay ANC salaries. That part is often forgotten".

Although he had overstepped the mark by accusing Moroka of being a police spy, subsequent events would reveal that Xuma had been correct in his assessment that Moroka was not an appropriate choice for the post of President-General of the ANC.

Meanwhile, Walter suggested that Mandela be co-opted onto the NEC in place of Xuma, because he was extremely hardworking. With Mandela on the NEC, Walter, Tambo and Mandela became closer than ever and the three of them together became a familiar sight. Ellen Kuzwayo, who worked closely with Mandela and Walter in those years, commented on their contrasting sartorial styles:

> I remember the glamorous Nelson Mandela of those years. The beautiful white silk scarf he wore round his neck stands out in my mind to this day. Walter Max Sisulu on the other hand, was a hardy, down-to-earth man with practical clothing – typically a heavy coat and stout boots. Looking back, the third member of their trio, Oliver Tambo, acted as something of a balance with his middle-of-the-road clothes (Kuzwayo, 139).

As close as they were, the three friends had powerful disagreements, mainly over the ANC's relationship with the Indian Congress and the Communist Party. Mandela and Tambo continued to be suspicious of these groups. They clashed over the Defend Free Speech Convention, convened by the Transvaal ANC in cooperation with the Johannesburg District of the Communist Party, the TIC and the provincial branch of the African People's Organisation (APO). (The Convention had been organised in response to the banning of Sam Kahn, a popular white Communist and lawyer who had been elected as a "Native Representative" in Parliament.)

In February, Gaur Radebe, who was also on the executive of ANC's Transvaal Provincial Congress, presented Walter with a typed report based on his personal observations of the conduct of the Transvaal Executive and the ANC. The essence of the report was that the Communists, some of whom were members of the ANC's Transvaal Executive, were trying to undermine the Programme of Action.

Walter felt the report was highly exaggerated and the result of Radebe's personal hostility towards the Communist Party. He persuaded Radebe not to submit the report to the NEC "because it was a bad report and likely to create unnecessary misunderstanding".

When the Transvaal Executive made its plans for the Defend Free Speech Convention known, there was much hostility in Youth League circles, and sentiments similar to those of Radebe were expressed. Much of the hostility was directed at David Bopape, who was secretary of the Transvaal ANC and a member of the Communist Party. Walter had a great respect for Bopape, and could not believe the accusations directed against him.

Dr Moroka agreed to preside over the Defend Free Speech Convention, and at the request of the organisers, Walter wrote a message of encouragement. On the eve of the Convention, Walter was confronted by Mandela and other members of the Youth League. Mandela argued that Walter's conduct was encouraging the undermining of the Programme of Action, and that his presence at the Convention would make matters worse. Walter also came under fire at a Youth League meeting held at his house. Zeph Mothopeng was one of the angry Youth Leaguers who maintained that Walter had no right to send a message to the Convention. They also attacked Dr Moroka's decision to attend the Convention without consulting the NEC. As a result of this opposition and criticism, Walter decided not to attend the Convention. He was not convinced that by so doing he had made the correct decision, but he felt he owed loyalty to his colleagues. He therefore left town to attend an unavoidable prior appointment in Brits on 26 March, the day of the Convention.

The Convention was a tremendous success, and Moroka arrived at Johannesburg Station to a grand welcome. He was transported in a flower-bedecked carriage to Market Square, where he delivered his first public address as ANC President-General to over 10 000 people (Bunting 1998, 174). The Convention took a decision to stage a one-day strike on 1 May, as a protest against restrictions on speaking at meetings (and particularly against the restrictions on Sam Khan, JB Marks and Yusuf Dadoo) and in support of higher wages and other worker demands (Karis and Carter, 2: 406).

The Youth Leaguers opposed the strike because the ANC had not initiated the campaign. They saw the decision to hold a May Day strike as further evidence that the Communists and the Indian Congress wanted to undermine the Programme of Action and steal the thunder of the ANC. The ANC NEC was divided on the matter.

Moroka and Walter came under heavy criticism for their part in the Convention, and they were accused of causing confusion in the minds of the people. Walter argued that the ANC's Transvaal NEC, which was one of the organisations that called for the May Day strike, had the right to initiate campaigns at a provincial level. As a result of Youth League hostility, the ANC NEC was forced to disassociate itself from the proposed May Day strike, but it did not veto it either. Communist Party members Kotane and Dan Tloome obviously supported the strike. The Youth League, on the other hand, actively campaigned against the mobilisation of support for the strike (Karis and Carter, 2: 406).

Mandela was one of those who opposed the May Day strike and argued with Walter that the ANC should concentrate on its own campaign (Mandela, 109). He joined other Youth Leaguers in heckling pro-strike speakers and disrupting public meetings. At one meeting, Rusty Bernstein, who was one of the Communist Party organisers, noted that Mandela "appeared to be heckler and disrupter-in-chief" (Rusty Bernstein, 116).

At a meeting in Newclare, Mandela and another Youth League member physically removed Yusuf Cachalia from the stage. Mandela was annoyed when the young TIC activist Ahmed Kathrada challenged him in Commissioner Street about his stance on the May Day strike.

Kathrada, whom Mandela described as "barely 21, and like all youths eager to flex his muscles", told Mandela that the African masses supported the strike (Mandela, 109).

There was indeed substantial support for the strike, and it was estimated that half the African workforce on the Witwatersrand heeded the call to stay at home on 1 May 1950. Much of the success could be attributed to the tireless efforts of seasoned Communists and trade unionist organisers like JB Marks, David Bopape and Dan Tloome (Lodge, 34).

A heavy police contingent was deployed on the Witwatersrand, and meetings and gatherings were banned for the day. On the evening of the strike, 19 people were killed and over 30 injured in clashes with the police. Walter and Mandela almost found themselves on the casualty list. They were watching some protestors marching in Orlando West when a group of policemen fired in their direction. They flung themselves to the ground as mounted police galloped into the crowd, lashing out with batons. Walter and Mandela made their way to a nearby nurses' dormitory, where they took cover while police bullets smashed into the walls around them (Mandela, 109). When the shooting finally stopped, they emerged to survey the damage and ferry some of the wounded to hospital.

The following Sunday, Dr Moroka fiercely criticised the brutality of the police when he addressed the funeral held for some of the victims in Alexandra. Huge crowds attended the funerals, and afterwards some angry mourners stoned buses and police cars. Walter's personal experience of the May Day strike demonstrated to him the value of thinking carefully through strategy and tactics before embarking on militant action.

Shortly after the May Day tragedy, Dan Tloome and David Bopape asked Walter what the leadership intended doing about the shooting. They also discussed the Unlawful Organisations Bill, which, if passed through Parliament, would outlaw the Communist Party. They wanted to know if Walter had anything in mind by way of a response. Walter suggested an emergency session of the Working Committee with a view to calling a conference of national organisations.

The National Working Committee (NWC) had been formed at the suggestion of Dr Xuma and he had presided over it until his resignation from the NEC. The NWC was appointed by the NEC and was made up of NEC members who lived within a 50-mile radius of the ANC's national headquarters in Johannesburg. The NWC had a much greater degree of independence under the Moroka presidency than under Xuma. Busy with his practice in Bloemfontein, Moroka was a poor correspondent and was content to leave matters to Walter and the NWC (Karis and Carter, 2: 407). It was Walter who kept up with members through letters and personal visits. This meant that far more power was concentrated in the hands of the Secretary-General than had previously been the case.

When Walter consulted AP Mda and Mandela, he found that they were not keen on a conference of organisations if it meant working with Communists. They still suspected the Communists of wanting to dominate. According to Walter, "Nelson and Mda placed themselves as guardians of the Youth League on this issue." Walter, however, felt the Communists were genuine and would not try to dominate. He was also confident that those in the ANC would not allow themselves to be dominated (Interview, Anthony Sampson, November 1995).

In response to Mandela's argument that the ANC should take action in its own right, Walter maintained that once the ANC had taken the initiative, that was good enough. He was adamant that the response to the threat posed by the Unlawful Organisations Bill was so important that it was necessary to bring all sectors of the national liberation movement together. He wanted to go as far as including the advisory boards, but his Youth League colleagues drew the line at this. They reluctantly agreed that Walter should call an emergency conference of other national organisations on 14 May 1950.

Because of the urgency of the matter, invitations were extended by telegram to the ANC Youth League, the South African Indian Congress, the Communist Party, the African People's

Organisation, the Non-European Unity Movement and the Transvaal Council of Non-European Trade Unions. The Women's League was not invited, because it was felt that they were covered by ANC representation. The Youth League was specifically invited because of their opposition. All the organisations accepted the invitation except for the Unity Movement, which declined on the grounds that it believed in "principled unity", and not in "ad hoc committees".

Dr Moroka presided over the Emergency Conference, which was also attended by Dr Naicker, the President of the South African Indian Congress. Representatives of all the organisations present were united in their opposition to the dreadful Bill and their understanding of the grave consequences of such an Act, not only for the Communists, but for all their organisations. The proposed Act would outlaw the Communist Party of South Africa and make it a crime, punishable by a maximum of 10 years' imprisonment, to be a member of the Party or to further the aims of Communism. According to the Bill, the definition of Communism was so broad that it defined anyone seeking social change as a Communist. The definition of Communism also included encouraging feelings of hostility between black and white. The Bill was thus a weapon that the government could use to proscribe any organisation or restrict any individual who opposed the government (Rusty Bernstein, 116; Mandela, 110; Roux 1964, 380).

Yusuf Dadoo argued for a united front against the government and Mandela agreed with him. "It was at that meeting," recalled Mandela, "that Oliver [Tambo] uttered prophetic words: 'Today it is our Communist Party, tomorrow it will be our trade unions, our Indian Congress, … our African National Congress'" (Mandela, 110). The press statement released by Walter stated that the Conference was "of the emphatic opinion that this [the Unlawful Organisations Bill] is the most serious threat to civil liberties of the 11 million people of the country" (Unlawful Organisations Bill: Press Statement issued by the Secretary-General of the African National Congress, 14/5/50).

In his personal memoir, *Memory Against Forgetting*, Rusty Bernstein analysed the significance of that 14 May 1950 assembly convened by Walter Sisulu: "At the meeting hatchets were buried including that between the Youth League and those who had convened the stay-at-home. A unified council of war was set up to run a joint campaign – something the movement had been previously unable to do. The government had created the first all-inclusive alliance against its own policies. There is little reference to that meeting in the histories, yet there – unnoticed – the foundation stone was laid for the ANC coalition that would come to dominate the next decades of South African liberation politics" (Rusty Bernstein, 116).

The following week, the ANC NEC held an emergency meeting at Dr Moroka's home in Thaba Nchu on 21 May 1950. Walter was deeply moved by Moses Kotane's "tearful and special appeal" that in the face of a dire threat, they should drop all their past differences and fight as a united people. He directed the appeal especially to the Youth League. Godfrey Pitje, then president of the Youth League, AP Mda and Oliver Tambo were present at the meeting. Walter considered Kotane's appeal to be a turning point that cemented unity between the leftists and the nationalists. It was decided to call a national day of protest. On 11 June, Dr Moroka announced that 26 June 1950 would be a National Day of Protest and Mourning (Karis and Carter, 2: 408). The date of 26 June was chosen so that the protest could take place before the Bill became law. It was legal to protest a Bill before it actually became law, but not after it was passed (Callinicos, Comments on the text).

Despite Walter's optimism about unity, there was still some strong opposition to the idea. NEC member Rev. JJ Skomolo wrote a private letter to Prof. Matthews complaining that people had lost lives, properties and jobs in the May Day strike and before those wounds were healed, the NEC wanted another strike. "The nation is not ready. If we are to be at the mercy of the Communist Party, take it from me, the Congress hasn't got another year to live. The engine and brain of the Congress cannot be the Communist influence" (Karis and Carter, 2: 447).

In the meantime, members of the Communist Party faced the traumatic task of closing up shop. Sam Kahn, the Communist lawyer who was Native Representative in the House of Assembly made an announcement to Parliament on 20 June 1950: "Recognising that on the day the Suppression of Communism Bill becomes law, every one of our members, merely by virtue of their membership, may be liable to be imprisoned, without the option of a fine, for a maximum period of ten years, the Central Committee of the Communist Party has decided to dissolve the Party as from today" (Clingman, 86). Moses Kotane addressed the last general meeting of Johannesburg Party members, who listened in stunned silence as he announced the Central Committee's decision to dissolve the Party formally on the last day of parliamentary debate on the Act (Rusty Bernstein, 121).

In terms of the Suppression of Communism Act, a "Liquidator" had been appointed to compile a list of former members or supporters of the Communist Party. "Listed" persons were liable to any number of administrative actions without recourse to law. As Rusty Bernstein pointed out, "Listing" sounded innocuous, but could be the gateway to multiple forms of repression. Without trial or hearing, the Minister could prohibit "listed" people from any place, communicating with any other "listed" people, taking part in teaching, writing or publishing anything, attending any gathering or belonging to any organisation (Rusty Bernstein 126; Lerumo, 81). Over 50 Johannesburg Party members had already been informed by the Liquidator that their names would be included on the official lists of Communists unless they could provide evidence to convince him otherwise (Rusty Bernstein 126). The Liquidator's dragnet would be spread wider and wider in subsequent decades, resulting in even the most avowedly anti-Communist individuals being listed as Communists.

After the meeting in Thaba Nchu, Walter threw himself into frenzied preparations for the 26 June strike. He had been appointed organiser and joint secretary with Yusuf Cachalia of the National Day of Protest Co-ordinating Committee. Because he had to travel around the country to mobilise support for the campaign, he asked Mandela to manage the campaign headquarters in Johannesburg. Walter appreciated the fact that once the NEC had made the decision to embark on a joint campaign, Mandela put aside his earlier reservations and worked flat out to implement the decision: "Nelson did a tremendous amount of work on that campaign and I was able to fully rely on him."

Walter's first stop was Durban, where he met the Zulu Paramount Chief at the home of AWG Champion, who had been at the helm of Congress politics in Natal since 1945. Although Walter got on well enough with him, he always felt that Champion was a politically divisive character. In the late 1930s, the Natal ANC had operated in separate factions, one led by founding father John Dube and the other by Champion, who finally wrested control from Dube, becoming president of ANC Natal in 1945 (Gish, 114). When Walter raised the matter of the Day of Protest, Champion condescendingly remarked that as far as Congress was concerned, he was a borrowed man because at heart, he was really an ICU man. He also told the Paramount Chief that the latter was only king of the Zulus while he, Champion, was "Izwelonke", the universal leader. Walter felt that this remark typified Champion's approach.

Walter proceeded next to Port Elizabeth, where he found that the local activists were highly organised. He addressed a crowd of 15 000 people, at that time the largest gathering for a political meeting in Port Elizabeth. He then took a flight to East London, his first time on a plane. The flight had been organised by his friend and fellow NEC member James Njongwe, who, Walter remembers, "liked to do things on a grand scale". He was met at the airport by Dr Apavoo, a local Indian doctor who set up his meetings for him. Walter stayed at the home of a high-school teacher, Mr Kwinana, the secretary of the East London ANC branch, where he held meetings with local ANC leaders until the early hours of the morning. The ANC Executive in East London appeared hesitant and afraid. They argued that there was no point in going on with the strike, as time was too short and people would not respond. Walter replied that he had just addressed 15 000 people in Port Elizabeth. Walter also met Clements Kadalie, and asked for his support.

An energetic and enterprising young journalist called Jantjie organised a public meeting to mobilise support for the strike. After Walter addressed the crowded meeting, two members of the local executive proposed a motion against the strike, saying that while they supported the action, there was not enough time to make the strike a success. They said they hoped Walter would come back another time, when they would be ready for him. At that stage, the meeting became rowdy, with clear disagreement from sections of the audience. Walter later learned that the people had been subjected to intensive anti-strike propaganda from the City of East London.

Walter returned to Johannesburg to find arrangements for the strike in full swing. The national leadership had assembled at the strike headquarters in Nugget Street in Doornfontein to assess incoming information on 25 and 26 June. Kotane, JB Marks, Dadoo, Yusuf and Maulvi Cachalia, and James Phillips, the APO leader, were among those who were there. Walter felt that it was significant that, for the first time, this group of mainly ANC and SAIC members were meeting not at a conference, but in a social atmosphere of friendliness and solidarity. The dominant feeling was that this moment marked the unfolding of a militant campaign against oppression.

There was a bit of a rumpus when Gaur Radebe, who had been put in charge of the campaign in the Orange Free State, gave a highly dramatised report on how he had mastered the situation. "His mind was full of revolution, he was imagining the revolution was on," recalled Walter. They were all thrilled by the report, except for JJ Mtwesi, who had actively supported the May Day strike, but had been opposed to the 26 June strike. He could not understand why the Youth League had opposed one and yet supported the other. Irritated by Radebe's exaggerated report, he picked an argument with Solly Makgogo, the secretary of the Transvaal Council of Non-European Trade Unions, and a fight broke out. Walter and Mandela were indignant that such an incident should occur in an ANC office. Walter grabbed Mtwesi by his jacket lapels, and told him to "stop his nonsense".

With the exception of Port Elizabeth, where there was a huge mass stay-away, the strike was not a major success. It had been too soon after the May Day strike, and its critics were correct – there had not been enough time to organise it properly. There was a partial stay-away in the centre of Johannesburg, Evaton and Alexandra. In Bethal, ANC activist Gert Sibande (who later became Transvaal president of the ANC) led a demonstration of 5 000 people that made headlines around the country (Mandela, 111). In Natal, there was greater support among the Indian working-class than among African workers (Vadi, 52). The SAIC and ANC found themselves in a sticky situation when the Durban City Council fired those Indians who had stayed away and replaced them with Africans. Walter was not surprised at the success of the campaign in Port Elizabeth, which he attributed to the high level of trade union organisation.

Walter felt that while the strike had not been successful, neither was it a failure. In his report on the National Day of Protest, he wrote that "as a political strike, held after only two weeks notice and, in the face of intensive and relentless police intimidation, 26 June was an outstanding success" (Karis and Carter, 2: 410). He agreed with the assessment that it marked a milestone in the development of "unity in action" of the national liberation movements: "June 26 was the creation of what you call today the Alliance. For the first time we were joined in national action by decision and agreement" (Luli Callinicos, Interview, 27/6/90). The National Day of Protest also marked the birth of the concept of 26 June as Freedom Day (Lerumo, 86).

After the National Day of Protest, Walter went on a trip to the Eastern Cape, mainly to fundraise in order to cover expenses that had been incurred during the strike. He spent three months there doing organisational work, mainly the consolidating of branches, holding branch meetings and raising money. It was Walter's first experience of fundraising and he was fortunate to be accompanied by Naran Naidoo, a Johannesburg trade unionist respected within the Indian community because his father, Tambi Naidoo, had been Gandhi's right-hand man in the 1913 Passive Resistance campaign. Both Naran and Maulvi Cachalia were active supporters of Gandhi, and both were experts in collecting money, according to Walter. He found it interesting that the Indian community in East London was organised into smaller communities, each with its own spokesman. For example, the Gujeratis had their own spokesman and so did the Tamils. Walter learned that when collecting funds it was necessary always to meet first with these spokesmen.

Walter and Naran were accompanied on their fundraising rounds by James Njongwe and the local Indian Congress leader SR Naidoo. They toured Port Elizabeth and East London, and the whole trip netted them the handsome sum of 1 100 pounds. In East London they met a wealthy businessman who stated categorically that he was not prepared to support any organisation in which Dadoo and Naicker were leaders because, according to him, they were the people who were causing all the trouble the Indians were experiencing. Walter thought his comment was a sad reflection on how the oppressed sometimes blamed their leaders rather than the repressive laws of the government.

Walter also visited local coloured and Indian trade union officials, as well as the local townships. He then paid a quick visit to Albertina's family in Xolobe. He was driven there by Moosa Bulahi, and there was some concern when the family saw Bulahi, because they thought he was a white man and wondered how they would accommodate them. Walter had to reassure them that there would not be a problem. Walter returned to Johannesburg shortly afterwards, glad to see his family after a long absence. By that time, Max was five years old and Lungi was three. Albertina was also expecting their third baby.

The tension between the ANC's Africanists and the Communists raised its head again when JB Marks decided to stand against Ramahanoe for the presidency of the Transvaal ANC at the provincial conference in October 1950. Walter recalled that "some people were frightened by JB's move, and felt that this would bring down the wrath of the government on the ANC because JB was a known Communist Party man". Walter's position was that the ANC should not shun anyone because of the Suppression of Communism Act, given that this legislation was also aimed at the ANC. At the conference, there were strong objections to JB's candidature. The result was that Selope Thema attempted to stand as well, but the conference broke down into such disorderliness and rowdiness that the chairperson was forced to close down the meeting. The matter was referred to the national conference in December, which decided that the NEC should convene another meeting to be presided over by the President-General to carry out elections in terms of the Constitution and in a proper fashion. Moroka presided over the conference held in March 1950, and JB Marks was duly and formally elected as President of the Transvaal ANC.

In response, Selope Thema, Mtwesi and Josias Madzunya formed a "Nationalist-Minded Bloc" within the ANC to oppose the growing influence of Communists and Indians in the Congress. Although appearing at first to be an internal pressure group, the Bloc printed its own membership cards in 1951.

The NEC took the difficult decision to expel Thema and Mtwesi for trying to form an organisation within the organisation. They found it very painful to expel an old veteran whom they all respected. Walter told Thema that he had been a great inspiration to him, and that he was grieved by the line Thema had taken. He asked Thema to reconsider his views and decisions. Thema declared that he would not change his mind, but Walter felt that the old veteran was embarrassed and uneasy about the stand he had taken. The Nationalist-Minded Bloc quickly faded away, but the Africanist challenge would come up again and again in the coming years.

The events of 1950 had strengthened Walter's commitment to joint action with like-minded liberation organisations. Once the basic principle was accepted – that in all campaigns the ANC had to lead the struggle – Mandela and Tambo were much more amenable to working in alliance with other opposition organisations. One commentator notes that "Their shift can be explained by their personal experiences of close cooperation and their reassessment of their need for allies in the face of threats to all opponents of apartheid. In 1950 at any rate, the shift of leading Youth Leaguers appeared to be due more to a growing self assurance than to ideological reorientation" (Karis and Carter 2: 409).

Walter was certainly convinced that they had gained sufficient confidence as a national group not to be unnecessarily sensitive about cooperating with other groups (Meredith, 84). His personal contacts with major Communist Party and Indian Congress leaders, Moses Kotane, JB Marks and Yusuf Dadoo in particular, also influenced his outlook.

Walter had always admired JB Marks, and their friendship, which had started in the early 1940s, grew from strength to strength. He regarded JB as a charming and approachable man with a sharp wit. A dynamic politician and dedicated trade unionist, JB had a knack for establishing friendships with many young people, and he was popularly known as "Uncle JB", Walter remembers that even Lembede, with all his hostility towards Communism, had a great personal liking for JB Marks. Walter once told JB that the national struggle was of primary importance and the class struggle was secondary. Therefore, Walter argued, there was no need for the Communist Party of South Africa. JB replied: "You will learn, my boy, of the necessity of the CP."

Moses Kotane and Yusuf Dadoo played a fundamental role in Walter's political development, and he quickly identified them as giants of the struggle. He was always struck by the originality of their thinking and the fact that "neither of them quoted famous works". He felt that they always provided satisfactory explanations to his political questions. Walter would often comment that Moses Kotane commanded the respect of everyone in the liberation movement because he did not have a dogmatic approach. Mandela also found his antipathy towards Communism receding as a result of all-night debates with Kotane.

Another Communist Party member whom Walter admired was Ruth First. Back in 1945, he had attended a meeting at the Bantu Men's Social Centre at which Ruth gave a report on the inaugural meeting of the World Federation of Democratic Youth (WFDY) that had just taken place in London, and at which she had been a delegate. The intelligent young girl who addressed her audience with such confidence and eloquence made a tremendous impression on Walter. He also remembers a meeting at his house where Josie Mpama, one of the first African women in the Communist Party, took on the Youth Leaguers who were attacking the Communist Party. "She turned down her mouth and said: 'Who are these youth who are so old?'" In Walter's view, these formidable women enhanced the stature and prestige of the Communist Party.

Walter had also developed good working relationships with Indian Congress leaders Yusuf and Maulvi Cachalia and Communists Elias Motsoaledi, David Bopape, Dan Tloome and Michael Harmel. He also had a deep respect for Bram Fischer, whose integrity and sincerity of intent were, in his view, beyond question. His personal contacts with his political colleagues had a greater impact on Walter than any ideological formulation.

This was true of some of the other leaders as well, as Bram Fischer's biographer, Stephen Clingman, has pointed out:

The personal contacts, in other words, made a difference, and a general readiness to work across racial boundaries in the liberation movement was deepened. These people did not only represent political parties and ideological tendencies, but, through their connections and constant interplay, their increasingly tactile knowledge of one another, were becoming something of a family network, with all the personal loyalties such a relationship entailed. These were relationships, loyalties and connections that were to have long-lasting political and historical effects (Clingman, 191).

The ANC's annual conference from 15 to 17 December 1950 was a departure from previous conferences. The Secretary-General's report was no longer a presentation of his personal opinion, but had to reflect the views and opinions of the NEC as a whole. The same applied to the President-General's address. A new system had been instituted whereby the President-General's address was drawn up by a Secretariat, and had to include an analysis of national and international issues, as well as indications for the future direction and development of the struggle. This new emphasis on the accountability of leadership and collective decision-making was very much in keeping with Walter's views.

On the last day of the conference, Walter received news that Albertina had given birth to their third son. He rushed home to a family celebration to welcome the new baby, whom they named Zwelakhe. What had been a hectic and action-packed year for Walter ended on a joyful note, but he could not help wondering what kind of future was in store for a black child born at a time when the Nationalist government had embarked on a mission to destroy any vestiges of rights enjoyed by black people in South Africa with a ferocity that would make previous governments seem benign.

"South Africa belongs to us once more," DF Malan had declared in his victory speech in 1948 (quoted in *Long Walk to Freedom*, Mandela 104) and as soon as he assumed power, his Nationalist government rushed through a plethora of laws to promote its declared aim of officially applying strict and overt racial segregation (as opposed to the more tacit customs of segregation). Racially discriminatory laws had of course been a feature of South African life for half a century, and the lives of black people were circumscribed by the pass laws, exclusion from direct franchise, curfew regulations, the 1913 and 1936 Land Acts, job reservation for whites, the refusal to recognise black trade unions, liquor prohibitions and many other forms of oppression. These laws and regulations were now being tightened and extended in order to secure and maintain the preservation of social, economic and political power in white Afrikaner hands. The policy of "total apartheid as the ultimate goal of a natural process of separate development" meant that blacks would not be included in the whites-only welfare state (Simons and Simons, 604). In his study, *The Rise of the South African Reich*, Brian Bunting wrote that the Nationalist government planned to "unmix what has already been mixed, to separate one section from the other, to enforce isolation and difference, to establish a rigid caste system backed with all the force of the law" (Bunting 1986, 158). Apartheid laws made blacks even more vulnerable to further economic exploitation with the formalising of migrant labour through the planned creation of Bantustans, and paved the way for Afrikaner hegemony through systemic and violent oppression of black South Africans. As Nelson Mandela would later write: "The often haphazard segregation of the past 300 years was to be codified in a monolithic system that was diabolical in its detail, inescapable in its reach and overwhelming in its power" (Mandela, 104).

In the very first session of Parliament after coming to power, the Nationalist government attacked the already limited franchise of Asians and coloureds. The Asiatic Laws Amendment Act withdrew representation of Indians from Parliament (1949), and the Electoral Laws Amendment Act (1949) made the conditions for registering coloured voters so strict that it was virtually impossible for any coloured to register. This was followed up by the Separate Registration of Voters Bill (1951), which removed coloureds from the common voters roll and placed them on a separate roll, as had been done to the Africans in 1936 (Bunting 1986, 135;

Karis and Carter, 2: 411). The Prohibition of Mixed Marriages Act of 1949 outlawed marriage across "races". If a South African resident entered into a mixed marriage outside the country, the marriage was void in South Africa.

The 1950 Parliamentary session had seen the passing of both the Immorality Act Amendment (which outlawed sexual contact between people of different races) and the Population Registration Act, the cornerstone of apartheid legislation, which provided for the classification of all South Africans into one of four racial groups.

In the same session, the Group Areas Act provided for enforced compulsory residential segregation of different racial groups; to achieve the racial separation envisaged by the Act, hundreds of thousands of people would have to give up their homes and move to the appropriate area for their racial group. The government also began the process of identifying "black spots" – black neighbourhoods surrounded by white areas. Plans were soon under way for the removal of these "black spots" under the pretext of "slum clearance": Sophiatown and the neighbouring areas of St Martins and Newclare were first on the list (Bunting 1986, 135; Gish 170).

Other new discriminatory laws included the Unemployment Insurance Act (1949), which excluded from insurance benefits those earning below a certain amount and all migrant workers, irrespective of their earnings; the Railways and Harbours Amendment Act (1949), which enforced racial segregation on the trains; the Race Classification Act and the Native Building Workers Act (1951), which prohibited Africans from performing skilled work in urban areas except in the townships. The Separate Amenities Act of 1951 extended segregation to post offices, municipal swimming pools, beaches and other public government facilities. Segregation was later extended to all public places, including restaurants, cinemas and even factory assembly lines. And there were many other restrictions in the pipeline (Callinicos, Comments on text).

The Natives' Representation Council (NRC) was to be abolished by the Bantu Authorities Act, 1951. The passing of the NRC went unmourned by Walter and his colleagues. At best, it had been an ineffectual talkshop, at worst it had been a source of much division in the ANC, with perpetual disagreements over whether or not it should be boycotted. However, this indicated that the Nationalist regime was not interested in preserving even a semblance of representation for Africans. Under the Bantu Authorities Act, the NRC was replaced with something much worse – the Bantu Authorities, who were not popularly elected but were appointed (and dismissed) by the Minister of Bantu Administration and Development. The Bantu Authorities Act provided for the establishment of tribal, regional and territorial Bantu Authorities in the reserves, and aimed to establish tribally based or ethnic states, thus dividing the African population into smaller entities called Bantustans.

In the opening months of 1951, the focus of protest was the Separate Registration of Voters Bill, the legislation to remove coloureds from the common voters' role. Coloured people had been hard hit by the new apartheid laws, and there had been protests in 1948 against the racial segregation on trains in Cape Town. The system of racial classification under the Population Registration Act was particularly humiliating for coloured people, involving as it did tests for specific racial characteristics (Lodge, 39–40).

According to Walter, there was a feeling among the leadership of various organisations that something had to be done. It was agreed that at the very least, a campaign should be launched to arouse the indignation of the coloured people. As a result, Yusuf Dadoo went to Cape Town, where he worked with Sam Kahn and the radical coloured trade unionist, John Gomas. In February, a conference in Cape Town brought together representatives of the African People's Organisation (APO), the SAIC, the ANC and local community groups and trade unions. The outcome of the meeting was the forming of a Franchise Action Committee (FRAC), which has been described as a "curious alliance involving both left-wing trade unionists and some of the most accomodationist coloured politicians, including supporters of the state-sponsored Coloured Advisory Council" (Lodge, 40).

On 11 March, 15 000 coloured protestors marched through Cape Town in a political strike organised by FRAC. Protests were also held in Port Elizabeth in May (Karis and Carter, 2: 411).

Walter was invited to Cape Town to open the FRAC meeting in March. He found that there was some controversy over whether FRAC should be a purely coloured body, or whether it should be open to everyone. Dadoo, trade unionist and Communist Party leader Ray Alexander, and Sam Kahn were already members. Khan argued that it should be open to all, while Gomas and others opposed him. Walter agreed with Gomas's view that because of the historical conditions in the country, a purely coloured body would be more effective in mobilising coloured people than a nonracial structure. Walter put his views strongly to Dadoo, Alexander and Kahn, but in the end bowed to their argument that there was a tradition in the Cape for organisations to be nonracial. Gomas was angered by the Communist Party's insistence on a nonracial body and later complained to JB Marks. Marks told Walter that he was sympathetic to Gomas's view and he regretted that the experience marked the beginning of Gomas's anti-white views, which would become permanent.

After the FRAC meeting, Walter stayed in Cape Town for three weeks addressing branch meetings and holding discussions with the local leadership. He stressed that the movement was entering a new era, hence there was need for a new approach. While in Cape Town he met Frances Thaele, sister-in-law of the late James Thaele, who had been the Western Cape ANC president in the 1930s (Karis and Gerhart, 4: 154). Walter had always been interested in the flamboyant leader, a self-proclaimed "Professor" who was a strong proponent of Marcus Garvey's philosophy. Frances Thaele showed Walter a black, green, gold and red flag. She said her brother-in-law had told her it was the original ANC flag, and it was his idea that the ANC flag should have those four colours.

Around April/May 1951, Walter made two visits to Natal. One of the people he met on his first visit was Albert Luthuli, the respected leader who had been Chief of the Groutville Reserve since 1935 and a member of the Native Representative Council in the 1940s. When AWG Champion had become president of the Natal ANC in 1945, Luthuli had been elected to the Executive Committee (Luthuli, 90). By the time Walter met him, Luthuli had resigned from the Executive in protest against Champion, who had reverted to an early Congress practice of choosing his own Executive, a practice which Luthuli found "retrograde, undemocratic and unconstitutional" (Luthuli, 101).

During his meeting with Walter, Luthuli asked why the ANC's annual conference only lasted two or three days, and pointed out that this did not allow sufficient time to discuss matters of great national importance. He also complained that most people only took an interest in the ANC at conference time. Walter agreed that Luthuli had a good point, but explained that most of those attending the conference had jobs, and could not easily take off for as long as a week. He was nevertheless impressed that Luthuli, who was not even an office-bearer at the time, was showing such a keen interest in the wellbeing of the organisation: "Here was a man who concerned himself with matters of national importance."

On his second visit to Natal, Walter had to mediate in a long-standing dispute between Champion and Msimang, the secretary of the Natal ANC. Walter had received many complaints over the years concerning the fact that Champion and Msimang were the only delegates to the annual conference and that they decided on policy and generally considered leadership to be vested in themselves alone. Champion, against whom these criticisms were principally directed, was also contemptuous of the Youth League, and exerted a powerful conservative influence in Natal. Msimang, who had served on the committee that had drawn up the Programme of Action, clashed with Champion over the latter's hostility to the Youth League (Karis and Gerhart, 4: 18, 105). Walter was on reasonably good terms with both men, and managed to smooth out the difficulties between them.

Walter then travelled to the Natal village of Nqutu, accompanied by the provincial secretary of the Natal Youth League, MB Yengwa, and the poet, HIE Dhlomo, who was also a reporter for *Ilanga Lase Natal*. They received an enthusiastic response from the villagers and a sheep was slaughtered in their honour. They learned that the meeting was the biggest ever held in the area and tribesmen had travelled from afar to attend it. The burning issue was opposition to the "rehabilitation schemes" that the government had been setting up in the Native Reserves. Put in place supposedly to "rehabilitate the land" to save the overcrowded reserves from ecological disaster, the schemes involved an increased range of controls over the use of land for grazing and cultivation, stock limitation, restriction on the collection of firewood and other measures (Lodge, 265). Rural people were resisting the rehabilitation schemes because of the threat to their livelihood. In November 1950 disputes over land and stock led to a rebellion in Witsieshoek Reserve in the Orange Free State. Fourteen peasants and two policemen were killed. Mass arrests followed and Paulus Mopeli, the local chief and other leaders were imprisoned or banished. (Mbeki 1984, 111). Walter signed a statement on behalf of the ANC that strongly condemned government action in Witsieshoek, and ended with the defiant words: "We demand land, not bullets. We demand freedom, not serfdom!" (Police Files.) The Witsieshoek rebellion was to be the first of a series of uprisings in a decade of resistance to the Bantu Authorities Act in rural areas around the country.

Walter spoke about the ANC Programme of Action and encouraged the people to mobilise in order to resist the government's rehabilitations schemes. He was later told that his speech had made a lasting impression, and that an ANC branch had been established at Nqutu.

The Natal ANC decided to make use of the Secretary-General's visit by organising a huge meeting at Cato Manor, which Walter addressed together with Chief Luthuli. Walter took the opportunity to stress the need for unity between Africans and Indians, and draw attention to the government's role in pitting the two groups against each other. He had been dismayed by the attitudes he had encountered in his discussions with ANC branches in Natal. He was disturbed to find that some took pride in the 1949 riots, and was amazed by the view held by some that because whites had defeated the Africans, there was some justification in accepting ill-treatment at their hands. On the other hand, because Indians had never defeated Africans, they had no right to look down on them. Because of views like these, Walter felt it was imperative to emphasise unity. Luthuli backed Walter's call for unity in his speech, even though he had privately complained to Walter that the selfish attitude of the Indian traders had been responsible for the clashes of 1949.

Meanwhile, the truce that Walter had engineered between Champion and Msimang was short-lived. Champion continued to passively resist the implementation of the Programme of Action. He never gave feedback on meetings at ANC headquarters to the provincial congress, and ran the province like his personal fiefdom. Consequently, the Natal membership was kept in the dark about what was happening in the rest of the country. The Youth League responded to Champion's hostility to the Programme of Action by approaching Chief Luthuli to stand for president at the 1951 annual provincial congress. Luthuli agreed to stand and in May 1951 was elected to the post of President of ANC in Natal. It was a result that Walter welcomed. The removal of Champion was a positive development. His replacement by someone of the calibre of Chief Luthuli was an added bonus.

When Pixley ka Isaka Seme, one of the founding fathers of the ANC, died in June 1951, ANC leaders, young and old, congregated in Johannesburg for his funeral. The NEC met after the funeral to discuss the next steps in implementing the Programme of Action. Walter had already raised the idea of a national civil disobedience campaign in an informal discussion with Mandela and others. According to his plan, selected volunteers from all racial groups would deliberately invite imprisonment by defying certain laws. Mandela was enthusiastic about the idea, but still had reservations about joint action with the Indian Congress. In his capacity as the recently elected president of the Youth League, Mandela argued that the campaign should be exclusively African (Mandela, 115). When Walter outlined his plan to the NEC, Dr Molema asked whether Walter expected people to go to jail and risk contracting tuberculosis. Dr Moroka responded sharply by asking whether he was afraid.

The NEC decided to call a joint conference of the national executives of the SAIC and the APO, and to invite observers from the Franchise Action Council (Karis and Carter, 2: 412). The meeting of the joint executives on 29 July 1951 approved the idea of a systematic and organised campaign of civil disobedience based on the principles of peaceful resistance.

To implement its decision, the meeting appointed a Joint Planning Council made up of Dr Moroka as chairman, Walter Sisulu and JB Marks from the ANC NEC, and Yusuf Dadoo and Yusuf Cachalia from the SAIC. After the meeting, Walter, Kotane and JB Marks held discussions with Bram Fischer, Rusty Bernstein and the brilliant lawyer Vernon Berrange, who was consulted on the legal implications of the plan. The Communist Party members had doubts about the viability of a civil disobedience campaign.

Within several months, the Joint Committee had produced a draft plan which Walter, Dadoo, Cachalia and JB Marks took to Thaba Nchu for Moroka to sign. They were accompanied by Mr Chari, the secretary of the Indian High Commissioner to South Africa, who wanted to meet Dr Moroka. From Thaba Nchu they took the opportunity to pay a quick visit to Lesotho. Next they proceeded to Durban to start canvassing for the proposed campaign.

Here they met the ANC and NIC separately. The NIC leaders JN Singh and Ismail Meer had reservations, as did Chief Luthuli, the new Natal ANC president. Neither side had recovered from the trauma of the 1949 riots. Luthuli's view was that the campaign was inadvisable, given the hostility between Africans and Indians. He suggested a postponement until a better and healthier relationship could be forged between the two groups. Walter argued that the matter should be viewed from the standpoint that both groups were victims of white oppression, and that bonds could be forged only through joint struggle. His argument prevailed, and both the Natal ANC and the NIC accepted the plan in principle.

From Durban, they proceeded to the Transkei, where they met with the Bunga. The arrival of JB Marks caused great excitement among the Pondos in the Bunga, as JB hailed from Pondoland. They were happy that he had "come home", and insisted that his trip should extend beyond Umtata. Chief Nelson Sigcau invited all the campaigners to Pondoland, saying there would be "women, beer and dagga" to entertain them. Time constraints prevented them from accepting this rather extravagant invitation. Walter was not impressed by the inducements on offer, but with the benefit of hindsight, he felt that they should have accepted the invitation because of the support they would have garnered for their campaign.

The Bunga members seemed to be in awe of Walter and his colleagues, and impressed by the plan they outlined. They promised their full support and were still in the midst of discussions when police officers from the Special Branch arrived. Walter suspected that the owner of the Umtata boarding house where they had spent the night had informed the Special Branch of their presence. The officers asked Dadoo and Cachalia for their permits to enter the Transkei, and asked Cachalia what his nationality was. When he responded that he was South African, they persisted with the same question until he replied that he was a South African of Indian origin. After the police left, it was clear that the members of the Bunga were thoroughly intimidated, and their enthusiasm quenched.

Walter and his colleagues decided to leave Umtata. On their way to Idutwya, about 30 miles from Umtata, they were once again accosted by the police and this time taken to the police station. Walter sent for Govan Mbeki (who was running a cooperative store in Idutwya), to be a witness in case the police detained them. When Mbeki arrived, the police took his particulars. Both Yusufs were asked to produce their permits to be in the Transkei.

When the police asked Walter for his permit, he told them that as one born and bred in the Transkei, he was more entitled to be there than they were. He was then asked for his tax receipts, which he could not supply, not having paid taxes for 15 years. The police took his particulars and let them go. They considered themselves fortunate not to have been detained.

They pushed on to Port Elizabeth, Cape Town and Kimberley, meeting with activists and trade unionists, with varying degrees of success. After their two-week trip, they returned home to discussions with their respective working committees, and drew up a report that contained a detailed plan of action for the campaign. There was no shortage of laws to choose to resist, but the list was narrowed down to six, chosen carefully to obtain the widest support, and based also on the experiences gained during the tour around the country. Like the Passive Resistance campaign, defiers were to register and to defy in groups for their own protection. Given the violent and provocative behaviour of the police on May Day 1950, as witnessed by Walter and Nelson, discipline and peaceful behaviour were emphasised. On a practical level, defiance involved breaking "petty" apartheid regulations – using white entrances to post offices and train stations, for example, or for non-Africans, entering black locations without permission (Callinicos, Comments on text).

The proposed Defiance Campaign was the main item on the agenda of the ANC's Annual Conference, held from 15–17 December 1952 in Bloemfontein. As well as the usual reports, the Defiance Campaign plans were distributed in booklet form to the delegates.

Among the observers was Manilal Gandhi, the son of Mahatma Gandhi, and editor of the *Indian Opinion*, a publication founded by his father in 1904. Walter presented the plans, and in the course of the ensuing discussion, Manilal Gandhi asked for permission to address the conference. Others objected, but Walter thought it proper that he be given the opportunity. Gandhi argued that satyagraha involved an understanding of certain principles, such as nonviolence and discipline. He thought that Africans were not ready for that, and advised the Defiance Campaign. His lengthy speech annoyed everybody.

Generally there was enthusiastic support for the campaign plan. Some Cape delegates, including ZK Matthews, said they had certain reservations, but they assured the Conference that once the plan was adopted and implemented, those in the Cape would not be found wanting. Mandela raised his old objections to a joint campaign with the Indian Congress (Mandela, 115). Eastern Cape leader James Njongwe was hesitant at first, so JB Marks asked Raymond Mhlaba, the Eastern Cape trade unionist, ANC and Communist Party leader, to secure Njongwe's support. This was Walter's first meeting with Mhlaba, and they struck up a friendship that would continue for years thereafter. Despite the objections, the plan was adopted enthusiastically.

Immediately after the ANC conference, the SAIC held its conference in Johannesburg and adopted the Defiance Campaign plan. In terms of the plan, Walter wrote a letter to Prime Minister DF Malan on behalf of the NEC, which both he and Moroka signed. Mandela helped to draft the letter and took it to Moroka in Thaba Nchu for his approval and signature. Moroka, whose great fear was that things were being done secretly by Communists, had taken a liking to Mandela, who was able to assure him that it was all the ANC's effort (Karis and Gerhardt, 2: 476).

The letter to the Prime Minister, dated 21 January 1952, called on the government to repeal repressive legislation not later than 29 February 1952, failing which the ANC would embark on a Defiance Campaign. The letter noted that the cumulative effect of the new laws was "to crush the national organizations of the oppressed people; to destroy the economic position of the people and to create a reservoir of cheap labour ...; to prevent the unity and the development of the African people to full nationhood" and to humiliate them in a host of ways (Karis and Carter, 2: 476).

The tone of the letter was carefully pitched to imply that its authors and the ANC were equal in status to the apartheid government, and it was this "impertinence" that so annoyed Malan that he refused to respond directly. When it came, the reply, signed by Malan's private secretary, categorically rejected the ANC's arguments and warned that the government would "deal adequately with those responsible for inciting any subversive activities whatsoever". It also scolded the authors for writing to the Prime Minister instead of to the Minister of Bantu Administration.

Walter and Moroka responded on 11 February: "The African National Congress has at no time accepted the position that the Native Affairs Department is the channel of communication between the African people and the State. In any event, the subject of our communication to you was ... one of such general importance and gravity affecting the fundamental principles of the policy practised by the Union government, and its effect on the relations between Black and White, that it was considered appropriate to bring these matters directly to the notice of the Prime Minister."

In response to the statement that there are "permanent and not man-made differences between Africans and Europeans which justify the maintenance of these laws", Walter and Moroka wrote: "The question at issue is not one of biological differences, but one of citizenship rights which are granted in full measure to one section of the population, and completely denied to the other by means of man-made laws artificially imposed, not to preserve the identity of Europeans as a separate community, but to perpetuate the systematic exploitation of the African people." The letter emphasised the intention to conduct the campaign in a peaceful manner, and noted that "any disturbances, if they should occur, will not be of our making" (Karis and Gerhart, 2: 481–2).

Walter and Moroka's letter was widely publicised and this in itself gave the Defiance Campaign considerable publicity and greater impetus. The stage was set for an exciting standoff.

*f o u r*

On 6 April 1952, white South Africa celebrated the tercentenary of Jan van Riebeeck's arrival at the Cape, while black South Africa held protests and demonstrations as a prelude to the Defiance Campaign. "To put it simply," wrote Chief Luthuli, "while they celebrated 300 years of white domination, we looked back over 300 years of black subjection" (Luthuli, 104). On that day, the ANC deployed various people to address mass meetings around the country. Dr Moroka addressed a crowd of over 5 000 people in Freedom Square in Fordsburg. In an inspiring address, Walter outlined the plan of the campaign and Mandela, Kotane, David Bopape and Dan Tloome also made speeches (Bunting 1998, 190). Mass rallies also took place in Durban, East London, Pretoria and other centres (Karis and Carter, 2: 416). Walter paid particular attention to the arrangements for the Port Elizabeth meeting because it was the largest, with Professor ZK Matthews, JB Marks and Ida Mntwana addressing a crowd of over 30 000. Marks and Mtwana were both very popular figures and their presence was a great attraction. Professor Matthews also thrilled the crowd with an uncharacteristically militant speech.

The ANC NEC and Joint Executives met in Port Elizabeth on 31 May and announced that the campaign would take place on 26 June. In the evening, a farewell banquet was held for Professor Matthews, who was going to spend a year in the United States as a visiting professor at Union Theological Seminary in New York City. The next day, the Joint Executives addressed a mass rally at which Dr Moroka called for 10 000 volunteers (Karis and Carter, 2: 416). Walter felt that both meetings were a tremendous success – morale was high and there was great enthusiasm for the Defiance Campaign.

A National Action Council was formed, as well as National Volunteer Boards for both the ANC and SAIC. Mandela was appointed National Volunteer-in-Chief of the ANC throughout the country. Maulvi Cachalia was his counterpart for the SAIC. Mandela also became the chairman of the Action Committee Joint Volunteer Board (Mandela, 119). This pattern was followed throughout the country at lower levels, so that even local branches had branch volunteers-in-chief.

In the run-up to the campaign, Walter was besieged by a stream of local and international visitors, some who came to offer support and encouragement, and others who tried to influence the course of events. A regular visitor was Manilal Gandhi, who continued to argue that the Defiance Campaign was inadvisable. Walter patiently spent hours trying to allay Manilal's fears that the ANC and the campaign were led by Communists, but he disagreed with Manilal's view of passive resistance as a quasi-religious tenet. The ANC leaders saw passive resistance as a tactic and not an inviolable principle, and differentiated between passive resistance and defiance. The aim of the latter, according to Walter, was to goad people into action, so that they would not fear imprisonment.

Walter also received an emissary from Swaziland's King Sobhuza, who expressed the King's concerns about the danger of potentially bloody clashes. The Swazi king, who had attended the ANC's inaugural meeting in 1912, wanted to use his influence to appeal to the ANC to find ways to avoid conflict. Walter said that the ANC appreciated the King's advice and concern for his own people, and carefully explained the strategy for the campaign. The representative was assured that violence would be avoided at all costs and at all times.

Another "royal" visitor who graced Walter's office was Prince Wani Yusuf of Abyssinia. The Prince was intelligent, articulate and knowledgeable. He was also a linguist, who spoke Yiddish, among other languages. Walter had met him during his estate agency days. Responding to an advertisement in the *Sunday Times* by a company that offered loans, Walter and his business partner Thabete had found themselves at the Maritime House offices of the Prince, where they were overawed by the luxurious offices manned by white employees. Told by a secretary to sit down and wait for the Prince, Walter and Thabete found themselves leaping to their feet when the Prince walked in, as if a judge had entered court. They had a friendly discussion, but Walter cannot recall whether they were granted a loan.

Just before the Defiance Campaign, the Prince, who had been referred to Walter by Yusuf Dadoo, came with a bold proposition. He proposed that the ANC send him to the USSR to obtain arms for conducting the revolution. His view was that the Defiance Campaign could not succeed, and that only an armed struggle would solve the problems of South Africa. On a subsequent occasion, he met with Walter, Dadoo, JB Marks and Dan Tloome. He spoke as if he was well acquainted with the Soviet Union, and when JB tried to test his knowledge, he gave an accurate description of the ships on which JB had travelled to the USSR. Walter, however, was not convinced that the Prince's offer was genuine. When he discovered that the Prince had previously been convicted of fraud, Walter accused him of planning to use the movement for his own ends. The Prince never forgave Walter for this, although he remained close to JB Marks.

Throughout the campaign, Walter's office was flooded with journalists from all over the world. He also received many distinguished international visitors, among them Lord Buxton and Christopher Mayhew, a cabinet minister in the Labour Government. These exchanges shaped Walter's skill in handling the press and giving interviews. He learned to "size up such people" and he believed the experience helped sharpen his intellect. He was proud that throughout his term of office as Secretary-General, he was never reprimanded or challenged by the ANC over his statements in the course of such interviews and press briefings.

Walter remained acutely conscious of the importance of the international community in the struggle against apartheid. In 1950, he had prompted members of the Executive to draft a memorandum to the United Nations. This caused quite a stir; it was subsequently published in booklet form under the title "South Africa Behind Bars" and circulated at the UN headquarters. In this way, Walter laid the foundation for the international solidarity campaign by being the first to place apartheid on the international peace agenda. Until then, the only South African issue to come before the United Nations had been the treatment of peoples of Indian origin in South Africa, and that had been brought by India (Interview, Joe Matthews 20/12/2001).

Early in 1952, Walter wrote to the Congress of Racial Equality in New York to request assistance in mobilising support for the Defiance Campaign. He received a response from George Houser, who pledged to raise some money. A regular correspondence ensued in which Houser kept Walter informed about his efforts to mobilise support in the United States, while Walter updated him about the progress of the campaign (Africa Fund archives). The ANC decided to make use of Professor ZK Matthews' presence in the US by making him an informal ambassador for the campaign. Walter put him in touch with Houser, who was able to make use of his presence for fundraising purposes. Houser was inspired by Walter to establish an organisation called Americans for South African Resistance, the forerunner of The American Committee on Africa and its sister organisation, the Africa Fund. Speaking many decades later on the 25th anniversary of the Africa Fund, Walter acknowledged that the significance of Americans for South African Resistance was "that it pioneered the idea of an organised lobby against apartheid outside South Africa and helped inscribe the issue of apartheid on United States foreign policy" ("Challenges to Africa", *The Africa Fund Lectures*, September 1991).

While mobilising support for the Defiance Campaign, Walter also established contact with, among many others, civil rights leader Reverend Martin Luther King and the famous African-American singer, actor and activist Paul Robeson, who was then chairman of the Council on African Affairs. Walter was a great admirer of both the music and the politics of Paul Robeson, and he greatly appreciated the work done by Robeson's Council on African Affairs. (Copies of Walter Sisulu's letters are in the Alphaeus Hunter Collection in the Schomberg Library, New York.)

The Defiance Campaign was to inspire activists throughout the world, from India to the Caribbean, from the Civil Rights Movement in the US to international Christian organisations. Walter recalls that Krishna Menon, then Minister of Defence of India, also wrote a pamphlet on the Defiance Campaign. The ANC also received letters of support and encouragement from hundreds of individuals from all corners of the globe.

Walter felt fortunate to have a strong team supporting him. He especially appreciated the energy and enthusiasm of Mandela who was at the ANC office every day, despite the fact that he had a full-time job as a lawyer. Walter also worked closely with Kotane, JB Marks, Oliver Tambo and Yusuf Dadoo. Their efforts were hampered somewhat when early in May, the government banned Kotane, Marks, David Bopape and Johnson Ngwevela, chairman of the Western Cape Regional Committee of the ANC. Under the Suppression of Communism Act, they were ordered to resign from their political organisations and stay away from all gatherings. The banned leaders immediately decided to become the "vanguard of defiers" by attending and addressing meetings and by the first week of June, Kotane, Bopape, Dadoo and Marks had all been arrested (Bunting 1998, 191; Karis and Carter, 2: 412). It was a clear signal to the rest of the leadership as to what was in store for them.

The organisational work of the ANC and the huge demands on his time meant that Walter saw little of his family. The Sisulu home continued to be a mecca for political activists, so even when he was at home, there was little opportunity for the luxury of a quiet, peaceful moment with his family. Walter never felt any sense of conflict, however. He strongly believed that the path he had taken was the only one that would ensure a decent future for his children. He was fortunate in having the total support of both his mother and his wife. They were enormously proud of Walter and they considered his long absences a small price to pay for the elimination of unjust and oppressive laws. The incongruously named Native Abolition of Passes and Co-ordination of Documents Act of 1952 (this provided for the replacement of previous passes, with a new reference book; it was mandatory for all Africans, both men and women, to carry this at all times) had created a groundswell of anger among African women. Women's resistance against passes had a long history in South Africa, but the Defiance Campaign provided the first coherent and organised form of protest (Wells, 103). Women's anger against this Draconian version of the hated pass law found expression in the Defiance Campaign, and the participation of women in organised political activity increased exponentially. Albertina could not be blamed for thinking that her husband, the originator of the campaign, was one of the most brilliant men on the planet.

Like thousands of other African women, Albertina eagerly anticipated becoming a volunteer but before doing so, she had to make a long-anticipated trip to the Transkei. It had been a number of years since she had visited, so in June 1952, she set out to Xolobe with seven-year-old Max, five-year-old Lungi and two-year-old Zwelakhe. Uncle Campbell and the Mnyila and Thethiwe clans were overjoyed to see them, especially the little *bazukulwana* (grandchildren). As is customary, a sheep was to be slaughtered in their honour, and Max and Lungi were taken to the kraal to select an animal. Confronted with the sight of so many sheep, they turned tail and ran to their mother, crying that the sheep were looking at them! On another occasion, Albertina went visiting at another homestead and left the children in the care of her relatives. When she returned, she found that Zwelakhe had been crying nonstop because he was hungry, and they had no idea what to feed him. When asked what the baby ate, Max and Lungi had responded: "Amazambani amashiweyo." No one knew what they were talking about because *amazambani* is a Zulu word for potatoes, not known in the Transkei, and *amashiweyo* is the adaptation of "mashed". Albertina said she had not realised until then what little urbanites her children were.

After a couple of weeks in the Transkei, Albertina received a telegram from Walter indicating that she should cut short her holiday because he was going to court arrest on the first day of the Defiance Campaign. Albertina and the children left immediately for Johannesburg.

The Transvaal campaign was to start at midday on 26 June, when a group of volunteers would court arrest by entering an African township near Boksburg without permission. The volunteers would be led by Nana Sita, president of the TIC and Rev. Tantsi, acting President of the Transvaal ANC. A well-known adherent of Gandhi's principles of nonviolence, Nana Sita was a highly respected veteran who had been one of the principal organisers of the Indian Passive Resistance campaign. Rev. Tantsi was equally respected in Christian political circles and had been the official Transvaal ANC chaplain since 1948. The campaign organisers felt that Nana Sita and Tantsi would make a very dignified duo who would enhance the stature of the campaign and, in Mandela's words, "show the authorities that we were not just a group of rabble rousers" (Mandela, 121).

Mandela, who was in the ANC office overseeing the day's demonstrations, became concerned when Rev. Tantsi had not arrived by mid-morning. His concern turned to dismay when Tantsi called to inform him that he was ill and his doctor had advised him against defying. (Tantsi later confessed to Walter he had not been ill, but was not in a position to go through with the planned act of defiance.) Mandela, faced with the task of finding a replacement at short notice, turned to Walter and said: "You must go." Walter was scheduled to lead a batch of volunteers in Johannesburg together with ANC activist Flag Boshielo, but he sympathised with Mandela's predicament. It was of vital importance to have senior leaders at the fore of the first event so that the leaders did not appear to be hanging back while the rank and file were courting arrest. Mandela decided that Walter's suit was "not practical dress for prison" and quickly arranged some old clothes for him (Mandela, 121).

There was a festive atmosphere as Walter, Nana Sita and the colourful and dramatic ANC leader Marupeng Seperepere led more than 50 singing volunteers towards the township. A huge crowd of supporters cheered them on, especially the elderly Nana Sita, who despite the pain in his arthritic limbs, walked up and down among the volunteers, encouraging them, and urging them to keep up their spirits. The procession was watched by a strong police contingent and dozens of journalists and photographers. There was a tense moment as they reached the locked township gates. The police were uncharacteristically restrained and there was speculation about whether they would wait until the journalists departed before attacking the volunteers. After about an hour, the police ordered the gates to be opened and the volunteers poured through like water through a burst dam. The shrill whistle of a police lieutenant signalled their arrest (Mandela, 121). They were loaded into police vans and taken to the local police station.

That evening, the group of volunteers that Walter had been supposed to lead proceeded as planned under the leadership of Flag Boshielo. They courted arrest by marching in the street after the eleven o'clock curfew (Interview, John Nkadimeng 28/8/2002). They had barely begun when they were arrested. Mandela and Yusuf Cachalia had just emerged from a meeting reviewing the day's events and planning for the week ahead when the police pounced on them. They could not very well argue that they were not scheduled to defy and be arrested until a later stage, so they were taken into custody with the other defiers (Mandela, 122).

The following day (27 June), the Sita batch of volunteers, as they came to be called, were taken to Boksburg Prison, where they were charged with conspiring to commit public violence. As they entered the prison, the volunteers sang *Nkosi Sikelel' iAfrika* with such deep feeling that, according to Walter, "the whole prison population was aroused". Some of the volunteers were brutally assaulted by the police, and four were put into isolation cells. When the superintendent of the prison arrived, Walter complained about the assault and isolation of the volunteers. Two policemen immediately grabbed him and dragged him to the punishment cells. One of the black warders assigned to guard him complimented him on his courage, and he and Walter became quite friendly.

Later, Walter was taken to work in the garden with his fellow defiers. The common-law prisoners working in the garden were encouraged by the warders to insult the volunteers. Walter spoke to them and, in his words, "defused the situation". (Among the prisoners they found Chief Paulus Mopeli, who was serving a six-month prison sentence for his role in the Witsieshoek rebellion.) Walter and Nana Sita were made to push wheelbarrows for the entire day until they were compelled to insist that Sita be excused on medical grounds. Walter continued labouring for a while, then decided that he had done his share and was not prepared to continue. The warders were so angry that Walter believes they would have assaulted him if it had not been for the volunteers, who made it very clear that if their leader was touched, there would be retaliation. Walter was taken to the superintendent who, although quite aggressive towards him, assured him that he would not be made to work too hard. After that, the warders adopted a more conciliatory attitude and allowed the prisoners to have rest breaks and smoke breaks. Walter had given up smoking, but he started again while in prison.

On 21 July, Walter, Sita and their group of volunteers were taken to court. The charges of public violence had been dropped. Instead, the Africans were convicted for not carrying passes and the Indians for "entering a Native location". Before sentencing, Walter delivered a short statement from the dock, which has been described as "a prototype of many other statements that were to be made from the dock in succeeding years" (Karis and Carter, 2: 419). It was a clear articulation of his commitment to the struggle against white supremacy:

> As an African and national secretary of the Congress I cannot stand aside on an issue which is a matter of life and death to my people. My duty is perfectly clear – it is to take the lead and to share with the humblest of my countrymen the crushing burden imposed on us because of the colour of our skins ... In conclusion, I wish to make this solemn vow in full appreciation of the consequences it entails. As long as I enjoy the confidence of my people, and as long as there is a spark of life and energy in me, I shall fight with courage and determination for the abolition of discriminatory laws and for the freedom of all South Africans, irrespective of colour or creed (Karis and Carter, 2: 484).

After their release, Nana Sita, Walter and their batch were welcomed by a huge reception at the Trades Hall, where the leaders all made speeches. Walter does not say much about his speech, but remembers the speeches of Sita and Seperepere as inspirational. Seperepere's speech was short and dramatic. Wearing a military-style khaki suit with epaulettes and gold buttons, clutching a baton under his arm, he declared: "I am tired of waiting for freedom. I want freedom now. I will meet Malan at the crossroads and I will show him what I want." Whereupon he banged his baton on the podium and sat down abruptly (Mandela, 126–7). He received the longest ovation.

Walter was heartened by the response to the campaign. Over the next four months, from Johannesburg to Cape Town, from Durban to East London, groups of volunteers from all walks of life entered African townships without permits, sat in railway carriages and on park benches reserved for "Europeans only", and broke curfews. Penalties for the minor offences generally involved a few nights in jail, often with the option of a small fine. The campaign spread to smaller towns and rural settlements, especially in the Eastern Cape (Rusty Bernstein, 135). Women were among the most enthusiastic supporters of the campaign. Thousands of women volunteered and there were even "women's days" when only women defied (Lodge, 141; Sampson 1958, 88; Mandela, 123). Shortly after she got back from the Transkei, Albertina presented herself at the ANC offices to volunteer. She was bitterly disappointed to be told, politely but firmly, that when one parent was already in jail after having defied, the remaining parent would not be allowed to volunteer.

As the Defiance Campaign gained momentum, white South Africa became alarmed. "Before the late Forties," wrote Chief Luthuli, "the whites were hardly aware (except at election time) of the nine or ten million Africans who surround them and carry them on their backs. Now they were forced to at least register our presence" (Luthuli, 106). The campaign signified a dramatically increased organisational capacity within the Congress organisations. As Anthony Sampson notes: "The springing up of volunteers in centres a thousand miles apart, controlled by a central organisation, was something altogether unexpected" (Sampson 1958, 88). On 30 July, the government responded with police raids on the homes and offices of ANC and SAIC leaders in 16 centres around the country. The Sisulu home was one of those targeted, the first of many such raids they would have to endure over the years. They were to learn to wait patiently while the police sifted through books and papers, collecting whatever they thought was relevant.

Two weeks later, Walter was among the first of those arrested in a group of 20 ANC and SAIC leaders. They included Dr Moroka, JB Marks, Mandela, Bopape, Tloome, James Phillips, Dadoo, Nana Sita, Ahmed Kathrada, and Maulvi and Yusuf Cachalia. They were charged for promoting Communism under the Suppression of Communism Act, and all released on £100 bail. Dr Moroka was arrested and charged in Thaba Nchu. Walter was accused Number One in the trial that followed. The Defiance Campaign trial, as it came to be known, attracted huge crowds with each court appearance. During their preparatory appearance on 26 August, thousands of people, among them ANC activists, Indian schoolchildren and white students from Wits, demonstrated their support outside the courtroom. As they sang and shouted, the chief magistrate had to ask Dr Moroka to appeal to the throngs of supporters to disperse. The crowd relocated to an empty field near the courtroom where they held meetings for the remainder of the day (Schadeberg 1990, 47). The case was remanded until November.

Not only the government showed an interest in ending the campaign. The Institute of Race Relations had also put out feelers regarding ending the campaign. In the early stages, Dr Xuma asked to see the ANC NEC to discuss the campaign. Walter suspected that Xuma's approach was connected with previous approaches by the Institute of Race Relations, but Xuma insisted that he was coming in his personal capacity. He asked Walter and Mandela to consider calling off the campaign, and said that he was sure that arrangements could be made for them to see the Prime Minister. Walter and Mandela replied that they were not interested in seeing the Prime Minister, they were interested in the repeal of the laws. That was their last contact with Xuma.

Around September, the United Party spoke to Walter about ending the campaign. They said that if it was made public that the United Party had persuaded the ANC to end the campaign, it would boost that party's chances of winning the 1953 elections. If they won, they said they would be willing to repeal all the laws the ANC was protesting against, with the exception of the pass laws. Repealing these would be difficult because they would be confronted by powerful mining interests. They were, however, open to negotiation on the matter. Walter conveyed their proposal to the National Action Council for the Defiance Campaign and the National Working Committee of the ANC. Their response was to ask what the United Party would do if it lost the election. The United Party had no answer, and the idea was thus rejected by the ANC.

By October 1952, the campaign had reached its zenith and over 5 000 people had been arrested. In that month, the campaign suffered a serious blow when riots broke out in Port Elizabeth. Walter hastened to Port Elizabeth to assess the situation. After discussions with the local leadership, he issued a public statement in which he criticised the police for provocative conduct and reaffirmed the principle of conducting the campaign on the basis of nonviolence. He called on the people to remain calm and not to allow themselves to be provoked, as violence would only work in the interests of the government and would discredit the Defiance Campaign.

While Walter was putting out fires in Port Elizabeth, at the beginning of November 1952, riots erupted in Johannesburg, Kimberley and East London. In confrontations between angry stone-throwing crowds and trigger-happy police, 40 died and hundreds were injured. Press headlines focused on the deaths of six white people, especially the murder and mutilation of a nun. The government tried to link the ANC with the riots, while the ANC leadership was adamant that government *agents provocateurs* were responsible (Karis and Gerhart, 2: 422). The ANC in Port Elizabeth was up in arms when the City Council imposed a curfew and a ban on political meetings for three months. An emergency regional conference decided on an indefinite strike. The provincial president James Njongwe was opposed to the idea and Walter agreed with his argument that a long strike was bound to collapse, which would do harm to the morale of the people. Raymond Mhlaba and the trade unionist, ANC and Communist Party activist, Gladstone Tshume, insisted on nothing less than a week-long strike. One evening, as this matter was being heatedly debated at the vestry of Gladstone's brother, Rev. Ben Tshume, the police burst in and proceeded to issue banning orders on six of the leaders at the meeting, among them Gladstone Tshume and Njongwe.

The banned leaders were forced to leave the meeting while their remaining colleagues continued the discussion. However, they were so shaken by the arrival of the police that the motion was put forward to abandon the idea of the strike. Walter prevailed on them to stage a one-day protest strike. The plan was announced at a mass meeting held later that night, and the one-day protest that was subsequently held was a great success.

The issue of cooperation with other races continued to be a controversial one during the Defiance Campaign. The nationalists within the Youth League supported the campaign, while Selope Thema and the nationalist-minded bloc remained implacably hostile to it. Selope Thema vented his hostility towards the campaign in the pages of *Bantu World*, destroying what little political credibility he had (Karis and Gerhart, 4: 157). Rather than declare an open rift within the ANC leadership, the Africanist camp within the Youth League organised themselves into an informal group called the "Bureau of African Nationalism". This group saw itself as a protector of Africanist principles within the ANC, and supported the campaign, but with an African nationalist interpretation. They sought to promote their views through the publication of a bulletin, which carried articles by AP Mda and other Cape-based Youth Leaguers like TT Letlaka (then provincial president of the Youth League in the Cape), JN Pokela, CJ Fazzie and Robert Sobukwe (Gerhart, 134–5).

Marupeng Seperepere, who had defied with Walter and Nana Sita, headed another group of mainly ex-Communists turned extreme nationalists who called themselves "Bafabegiya" (those who die dancing). They opposed Mandela's candidacy to the post of president of the Transvaal ANC (to fill the position that JB Marks had had to vacate when he was banned earlier in the year). Marupeng decided to stand against Mandela and lost, so Mandela became the new president of the Transvaal ANC in October 1952 (Mandela, 127).

While the Africanists sought to exclude the participation of whites, Walter and Oliver Tambo, on the other hand, were discussing their concern about the minimal participation of whites in the Defiance Campaign. They discussed the matter with Yusuf Cachalia, and decided to call a meeting of whites sympathetic to campaign ideals to explore the issue of white participation. In November 1952, Walter and Tambo told a gathering of about 200 sympathetic whites at Johannesburg's Darragh Hall that they were concerned about the lack of participation of white democrats in the campaign, and were afraid that this would create the view among black people that all whites approved the racial policies of the Malan government. The meeting was hailed as historic by many, leading as it did to the formation of the Congress of Democrats in October 1953 by a group of mainly Communist whites committed to the principles of nonracialism. It is likely that the meeting also influenced the formation of the Liberal Party in May 1953, by whites who were opposed to the opposition United Party's racial policies, but at the same time did not want to be identified with the Communists who would form the core of the Congress of Democrats (Lazerson, 68; Callinicos, Unpublished biography of Oliver Tambo).

At the end of November, Walter and his co-accused were back in court for the Defiance Campaign trial. The trial proved to be an eye-opener for the ANC, as they realised the extent to which the police had infiltrated spies and informers into their ranks. A number of policemen who had posed as defiers gave state evidence. One of them had regularly visited the ANC offices and had willingly run errands for Walter. Flag Boshielo had told Walter that he did not trust this individual, but Walter had dismissed Flag as overly suspicious. Paul Joseph had also warned Walter about a volunteer named Moreko, who also turned out to be a state witness.

But more disappointing than the infiltration by police and informers was the conduct of Dr Moroka. Firstly, he chose a separate defence, a clear signal that he was trying to distance himself from his co-accused. When Mandela tried to convince him of the political inadvisability of separating himself this way, Moroka complained that he had been excluded from the planning of the campaign (Mandela, 128).

It was true that as President-General he was part of the Working Committee and therefore should have been in constant contact with his executive, especially the Secretary-General, but is was he who had been content to leave matters to Walter. He was a poor correspondent, and it had been Walter who had made the effort to maintain contact. Walter had found Moroka easy to deal with but not really politically profound. He was content to remain a figurehead.

Moroka's lack of political depth became apparent on the witness stand. When his lawyers asked him who among the accused were Communists, Moroka began pointing out Walter, Yusuf Dadoo, and others, until the judge, Justice Rumpff, stopped him. His fellow accused cringed when Moroka stated that there could never be equality between blacks and whites in South Africa. Like his colleagues, Walter was angry and disappointed with Moroka's behaviour, but later he came to understand it. For someone who laid great store on his respectability and standing in his community, the police raids on Moroka's home and surgery, and his subsequent arrest, were unendurable.

Walter and his co-accused were found guilty and sentenced to nine months' imprisonment with hard labour, suspended for three years. Once convicted under the Suppression Act, they were considered statutory Communists and were placed on the Liquidators' List.

By December 1952, the Defiance Campaign had virtually petered out and the number of volunteers had dropped dramatically. The riots in October had been a major blow to the nonviolent image of the campaign. The last major and highly publicised act of defiance was led by Patrick Duncan, son of a former South African governor-general, and Manilal Gandhi, who had revised his stand on the campaign. Also with them were the veteran Afrikaner trade unionist Bessie du Toit and Dr Percy Cohen, a dentist and member of the Communist Party. Together they marched into a township in Germiston without a permit and were arrested.

The Public Safety Act and the Criminal Laws Amendment Act of December 1950 put the nail in the coffin of the campaign by providing for severe penalties against deliberate law-breakers. Under the new law, defiers risked flogging and sentences of up to three years in jail (Sampson 2000, 73). "It was impossible to imagine that people would continue with the Defiance Campaign inviting such heavy penalties," recalled Walter. "In the light of this, it was obvious that if the Defiance Campaign was not called off officially, there was a danger of the campaign dying out on its own."

There was no opposition when the campaign was called off in January 1953. Although the Defiance Campaign did not succeed in its stated objective of forcing the repeal of the unjust laws, Walter believed that it was a great success: "Nothing had raised the political consciousness of the masses so high up until that time. Nothing had been more effective in fostering a growing discipline and militancy. Volunteers looked upon themselves as a para-military force. Efficiency had increased within the movement, as well as determination. There was no longer the great fear of imprisonment and people were prepared to undergo such hardships; people were looking forward to greater things."

One of the most positive outcomes of the Defiance Campaign for the ANC was an increase in membership by leaps and bounds – from a few thousand to an estimated 100 000 in just six months. Some white people began to question the future of the country and the campaign led indirectly to the birth of the Congress of Democrats, the Liberal Party and, later, the Progressive Party. The campaign also drew world attention to the issue of racial oppression, and in December 1952, the General Assembly of the United Nations decided to set up a commission on the racial situation in South Africa.

After the excitement of the Defiance Campaign, there was countrywide enthusiasm for the ANC's annual conference in 1952, which assumed greater significance than previous ones. Preparations were extensive and the conference was held in Johannesburg for the first time ever, probably because many of the leaders who had been banned lived in that city. At about this stage, Mandela was banned for six months and, just before the Conference, Walter heard that police were looking for him in order to ban him. The Working Committee felt that Walter should go underground to avoid being banned, because it was very important that the Secretary-General be present at the conference. Walter therefore went underground while the police hunted everywhere for him. He did not even tell Albertina where he was hiding.

The NEC met at Walter's underground headquarters at Kliptown the day before the conference. It had become practice for the Secretary-General and the President-General to present their reports for approval by the NEC before they were presented to the conference. After Walter had presented his report, Moroka put forward his presidential address, in which he praised the King of England, the monarchy and the Commonwealth. The NEC was aghast and told Moroka that he had taken a line that was foreign to the ANC. He was told that the Executive disassociated itself from his report and he could present it in his personal capacity only, not as President-General.

The NEC also discussed the likelihood of the ANC being banned. There were indications that this was a possibility. In preparation for this, a resolution was drafted for presentation to the members, giving the NEC extraordinary powers, for example, while it could not alter the ANC's constitution, it could act as the National Conference.

The annual conference took place in the Trades Hall. It was agreed that in order to avoid the police, Walter should disguise himself by wearing a Muslim coufia (religious hat). Although the venue had been cordoned off, Walter was taken past the police without their recognising him. As soon as he had reached the stage in safety, the chairman announced his presence and called upon him to present the report of the Secretary-General. Walter did so, and was able to stay for the subsequent discussion. The police were obliged to wait outside, as they were barred from the conference itself, and Walter was able to slip away undetected.

When the time came for elections, it was clear that Moroka was no longer looked upon favourably and people were already casting around for a new President-General. Chief Luthuli was a very popular candidate. Just the previous month, the government had deposed him as Chief of Groutville when he had refused to resign from the ANC. His defiance of the government had increased his popularity. Both Njongwe and Moroka stood for the presidency, but Chief Luthuli won, and was elected President-General.

There were also some moves to remove Walter as Secretary-General. Regional politics came into play, with a contingent from Natal favouring MB Yengwa, the provincial secretary of the Natal Congress. The Eastern Cape Branch, which had played such an important role in the Defiance Campaign, also wanted to project its own position, and there were cliques from the Transvaal as well, which connived with these moves. Both Yengwa and Robert Matji contested the election for the post of Secretary-General, but Walter won the election comfortably.

The new NEC met on 17 December to discuss the future. It took advantage of new extraordinary powers of the NEC to create the positions of Deputy President-General and Deputy Secretary-General, Mandela and Diliza Mji being respectively elected to these posts.

After the intense and hectic months of the Defiance Campaign, there was a lull in Congress activities as the various political organisations regrouped and reflected on strategies and tactics. The police finally caught up with Walter and served him with a six-month banning order that prohibited him from attending gatherings and confined him to the magisterial district of Johannesburg. The only advantage of this restriction was that he was able to spend more time at home with his children. In May 1954, Walter and Albertina celebrated the birth of their fourth child, a daughter. Because they had waited so long for a girl, they named her Lindiwe (the one we have waited for). She was also named after Lindiwe Ngakane, the daughter of Walter's friend Barney Ngakane. Walter and Albertina were thrilled to have a daughter after three sons, and they threw a big celebration party. Lungi remembers all their political "uncles" attending the party – Mandela, Duma Nokwe, Ahmed Kathrada and Yusuf Dadoo, who brought each of the children a present.

The lull in ANC activities gave Walter some time to follow up an NEC resolution made in 1950 to the effect that the ANC should consider ways of convening a Pan-African Congress. Walter had therefore written to various organisations and governments in Africa. The gist of his letters was that the time had come for progressive movements to coordinate their activities, and for the oppressed people of the continent to take control over their destinies. He was encouraged by enthusiastic responses from Ethiopia, Liberia, Libya and Egypt, as well as from national organisations. He also received a letter from Fenner Brockway, the head of the Movement for Colonial Freedom, saying that it had come to his attention that there were plans afoot for a Pan-African Congress. He suggested that the matter be left to him and to his movement to manage. Walter replied that Pan-African Congresses had, in the past, been held in Europe, and that such a congress should take place in Africa.

Walter also decided to take the opportunity to pursue his international solidarity work when he and Duma Nokwe, who was by then the president of the Youth League, received an invitation to attend the 1953 Youth and Student Festival in Bucharest, Romania. Walter discussed the invitation with Moses Kotane, JB Marks and Mandela. Kotane was not in favour of the trip, although he did not openly oppose it. He felt that as Secretary-General of the ANC, Walter would open himself to all kinds of criticism by visiting a Communist country. Kotane may have had in mind Josiah Gumede, ANC President-General from 1927, who, after returning from a visit to the Soviet Union, declared: "I have been to the new Jerusalem." Gumede's positive attitude to a tactical alliance with the Communist Party had alarmed conservatives within the ANC, especially the Chiefs. As a result, he lost his presidency to Seme in 1930 (Bunting 1998, 201; *Sechaba*, December 1982).

Mandela reported on the plans for Walter's trip at an NEC meeting in Natal, which Walter did not attend. Chief Luthuli made no objections at the time, but he later denied having any knowledge of the trip and complained that he had not been informed. It was decided that Dan Tloome should act as Walter's deputy in his absence, as the Deputy Secretary-General, Diliza Mji, was banned at the time. Ahmed Kathrada, the leader of the Transvaal Indian Youth Congress, who had spent nine months working for the World Federation of Democratic Youth in Budapest in 1951, was responsible for practical arrangements for the trip. Walter and Duma were unable to get passports, so they had to make do with affidavits from lawyers confirming that they were South African citizens, and Kathrada managed to get them tickets for an El Al flight to Tel Aviv. The flight was delayed and they spent a nerve-wracking couple of hours at the airport hoping the security police would not turn up.

Eventually, they took off safely, but because of the delay they missed their connecting flight to London. They caused quite a stir at Tel Aviv airport when they could not produce passports and had to explain themselves to immigration officers who spoke little English. Walter and Duma kept their explanations to a minimum, repeating over and over the words, "South Africa Malan fascist". They were kept at the airport until the early hours of the morning. Eventually, an interpreter was brought in and they were able to explain who they were. They were then taken to the Ambassador Hotel in Tel Aviv. Because there was some difficulty in getting El Al connections for their onward journey, they were forced to remain in Israel for two weeks with expenses fully paid by the airline. They later felt that this delay was a blessing in disguise, because it afforded them an opportunity to see the country.

They had landed in Israel at a time when South Africa was very much in the news – DF Malan had just visited and the play *Cry the beloved country* was currently being performed. As soon as it became known that the two leaders were in Israel, Walter and Duma were taken to a performance and introduced to the audience, following which they expressed their thanks for the hospitality of the Israeli people. The cast (which was made up of Israeli actors who had painted themselves black), officials and stage-hands were ecstatic at meeting them.

A round of invitations followed. At one of the many parties they attended, their hosts asked them to sing some songs. Walter and Duma sang *Mayibuye* to the tune of *My Darling Clementine*. The Israelis were disappointed to hear a Western melody and demanded something indigenous. Walter and Duma obliged and felt they had learned a lesson about the importance of a people's culture. They also visited Jerusalem, a tremendous experience for men from a Christian back-ground. They crossed the River Jordan and went to the place where it was said that Jesus had had his Last Supper.

Wherever Walter and Duma went, they severely criticised the Israelis for having invited Malan to Israel – a man who had openly sympathised with the Nazis. The majority of the Israelis they spoke to agreed, and were themselves critical of the invitation, but some defended the action of Ben Gurion's government.

Walter and Duma also stayed overnight at a kibbutz of about 3 000 people. They were interested to see books on Marxism-Leninism and Stalin's works lining the walls. They were also introduced to Moshe Dayan, the so-called Hero of Haifa. Wherever Walter and Duma went, the Israelis related the story of their own struggle, but the South African vistors were disturbed by the hostility between the Israelis and the Arabs. Once, when Walter took a little boy's hand, the child, mistaking Walter for an Arab, pulled his hand away.

Walter spent another fortnight in Israel at the end of his trip. On his second visit, he managed to track down old friends of his – Naomi Shapiro and her husband Jack Barnett. Walter had met Naomi in South Africa when she had been a correspondent for the left-wing publication, *New Age*. The couple had been members of the Communist Party of South Africa and they were members of the Israeli Communist Party. Walter learned from Naomi and Jack that the Communist Party was very active in Israel and that it published journals and six newspapers in different languages. The Party had seven members in the Knesset (the Israeli Parliament), four of whom were Arabs. Its members did not share the enthusiasm of much of the Jewish population for the new state of Israel, and were critical of the discriminatory practices against the Arabs. Naomi and Jack showed Walter the slums where the majority of Arabs lived, and informed Walter that while all Israelis were obliged to carry ID cards, the papers of the Arabs held a distinctive mark identifying them as objects for closer scrutiny and interrogation.

It was a bit too close to home for Walter. He did have a certain admiration for the Israelis and their enthusiasm, but he did not sympathise with them. He was not particularly impressed by those who had left the Soviet Union to settle in Israel, nor did he approve of the Israeli government call-ing on Jews throughout the world, including the socialist countries, to settle in Israel. He felt that the Communist Party should have been in power in Israel as it was the only party in a position to bring about harmonious relationships between the Jews and the Arabs.

From Israel, Walter and Duma flew to London via Athens, Rome and Paris. Because they had no passports, the Italian police escorted them directly from one plane to another. When they arrived in London, they were cross-examined and thoroughly searched. Although their documents were not in order, the immigration officials said that they could not prevent Walter and Duma from entering Britain as they were citizens of the Commonwealth. At the same time, they wanted to be sure that the two South Africans had contacts in London who would be responsible for them during their stay. Walter mentioned Christopher Mayhew, who was a cabinet minister in the Labour Party, and Lord Buxton, both of whom he had met in South Africa.

Immigration officials rang Buxton, but he was not in – he had gone fishing. Walter then mentioned Michael Scott, and this proved sufficient. While they were being interviewed, two people approached Walter and Duma. One of them was the South African Communist Party member, Dave Kitson, who made the mistake of greeting Walter in Zulu. Walter, who did not know Dave, immediately suspected that he was from the South African police, and completely ignored him until he explained that he had been sent to meet them by the committee responsible for the South African contingent to the Festival!

Walter and Duma ended up staying with Dave Kitson. He introduced them to a number of South Africans in London, among them Vella Pillay and his wife Patsy. Walter was shocked when Vella suggested they meet in a pub. Not realising that the pub is an important social institution in England, he could not believe that a meeting could take place in one. Dave also introduced Walter to Desmond Buckle, a Ghanaian journalist, who became Walter's closest companion in England.

Walter met several important leaders of the British Communist Party, including R Palme Dutt and Idris Cox, chairman of the international section of the British Communist Party, and chairman of its African affairs department respectively. Walter had a long argument with Palme Dutt and Cox about the Pan-African Congress that he had proposed. Palme Dutt and Cox tried to discourage him from pursuing the idea. Walter pointed out that Britain was the centre of the colonial world, and expressed surprise that the Party did not focus more on colonial affairs. He cited the example of the Council for Africa in the US, headed by Paul Robeson, and pointed out that the Council for Africa helped publicise and raise money for African campaigns while the British Communist Party did nothing. Palme Dutt sarcastically replied that their members were not like Fenner Brockway, who was a Member of Parliament. Walter maintained that the struggle had to be broadened, that Pan-Africanism was a popular movement, and that the British Communist Party needed to pay attention to it.

Walter was also able to meet with Simon Zukas, who had been the Vice-President of the African National Congress in Zambia, with Kenneth Kaunda serving as secretary under him.

The South African Festival Committee responsible for arranging the trip to Romania was made up of Communist Party members Harold Wolpe, Lionel Foreman and Ismail Bhoola. Lionel Foreman was on the executive of the WFDY, a position Walter considered to be very significant and important for South Africans.

The committee chartered a plane for the South African contingent to travel from London to Romania. Duma Nokwe headed the delegation of 25 South Africans, which included Communist Party members Arthur and Hazel Goldreich, Harold and Anne-Marie Wolpe, Ben Turok, Dave Kitson and Frank Marcus, ANC members Henry "Squire" Makgothi, Alfred Hutchinson, Lindi Ngakane, Greenwood Ngotyane (secretary of the Railway Workers' Union) and Frank Marquard (President of the Food and Canning Workers' Union).

Also on the plane were the British contingent to the Festival and Senator William Morrow from Australia, at one time the President of the Peace Council of Australia, whom Walter befriended.

After an overnight stop in Czechoslovakia, they entrained for Romania. On arrival in Bucharest, they received a huge welcome on the station platform. The people were genuinely excited to see them, and they were treated to a display of traditional Romanian circle-dancing and singing, with the throwing of handkerchiefs and much pulling, pushing and kissing. The Romanians were thrilled at meeting Lindi Ngakane. She was the first black woman they had seen, and they looked at her in wonder and touched her skin and her hair. Someone asked her, "Are you a kaffir?" Lindi explained that "kaffir" was an extremely derogatory word, which should not be used. The person concerned was very ashamed and apologised profusely.

The organisers divided the new arrivals into general groups and honoured guests. Walter and Senator Morrow shared a chauffeur and an interpreter – a beautiful young doctor who had survived being incarcerated in a Nazi concentration camp at the age of 11. She remained Walter's interpreter throughout the festival, and he was amused at the way she pronounced his name: "Vaalta". She in turn embarrassed him when she asked him to spell the word "negotiation". Spelling was never his strong point!

Here, too, Walter found himself playing his usual role of mediator and peacemaker. A constant stream of people showed up at his hotel. The South African delegates came with daily complaints about their accommodation and quarrels among themselves to be sorted out. Delegates from elsewhere in Africa also complained to Walter that the South African whites were contemptuous, and they could not gain access to Lindi because the whites were monopolising her. Walter spent a lot of time attending to problems arising from the hostility towards the whites present. He was also visited by journalists from various parts of the world, as well as African delegates who wanted to discuss the ANC's proposal for a Pan-African Congress. It was agreed that the matter of the Pan-African Congress would be discussed once they reached Poland. Walter met the entire Executive of the Women's Federation and struck up friendships with many women who were deeply interested in the position of women in South Africa. Walter also met the country's leader, President Petro Groza, and other cabinet ministers, as well as the general secretary of the Communist Party. He was shown state farms, factories and various development projects, where he was impressed to see women engineers at work. He also met peasants in the countryside and learned that they were still finding collectivisation problematic.

The festival itself was an impressive and exciting affair, and Walter was thrilled by the music and the folk culture of the Romanians. When the South Africans were asked to present an item, they obliged with "Daar kom die Alabama". Throughout their six weeks in Romania, they were treated to delicious five-course dinners.

From Romania, almost the entire South African contingent proceeded to Poland to attend the conference of the International Union of Students. It was the first international conference that Walter had attended, and he was impressed by the simultaneous translation system. The highlight for the South African delegation was when Lindi Ngakane was called to the rostrum to speak. Walter felt that she "put the South African situation very clearly and beautifully and she captured the hearts of many delegates".

The meeting to follow up on Walter's motivation for a Pan-African Congress took place in Warsaw between representatives of various countries. It was agreed that the Egyptian and Ghanaian delegates would discuss arranging such a congress with their respective governments. Walter and Ben Turok, who were staying in the same accommodation, had the opportunity to address the workers at a factory. They complimented them on their achievements, especially the rebuilding of Warsaw, which had been razed to the ground during the Second World War.

At this point, Walter found himself dealing with a delicate situation. Lindi Ngakane had fallen in love with a young Czech student who wanted her to remain with him in Czechoslovakia. Knowing that she would never be able to return home with her husband because mixed marriages were illegal, Walter had to assert his authority; he could not allow her to stay. He also felt responsible to Lindi's father, Barney Ngakane, the Transvaal ANC leader and his good friend. Walter decided that Lindi should return to South Africa with the delegation, and then find her own way back if she still wanted to marry the Czech student.

The Soviet Union was next on Walter's itinerary. Together with Duma and Ismail Bhoola, he began the two-day train journey to Moscow. Walter had a moment of anxiety when Duma disappeared on the train. After a long search, he found him having a rip-roaring time in the company of two Russian generals. The generals invited the famously abstemious Walter to join the party and offered him a drink. When he refused, they complained that he was a reactionary.

Upon arrival, they were booked into a hotel facing Red Square and given two interpreters. During their few days in Moscow, Duma addressed the Komsomol (Young Communist League).

The interpreters were very disappointed when he delivered his address in English, as they had hoped it would be delivered in Xhosa. Apart from wanting to show off their knowledge of Xhosa, the interpreters believed that speaking in English reflected an acceptance of white domination.

Next, the trio embarked on the 12-day journey from Moscow to Peking on the Trans-Siberian Railway. They spent a night in Manchuria while a fault in the train was repaired, then proceeded to Peking. They travelled on a special official train to Peking. During their six weeks in China, they toured 15 of China's 30 provinces, visiting major tourist attractions and attending a variety of official functions. Walter was introduced to people as the Secretary-General of the ANC, the national movement. Translated into Chinese, this was "Kuomin tang", which led to some embarrassing misunderstandings, as this was the name of Chiang Kai-shek's Nationalist Movement, which had recently been defeated after a long and bloody civil war.

Walter found the trip fascinating. Even with the language barriers, he found the Chinese people warm and friendly. The only thing that Walter did not like was the food, much to the embarrassment of Duma Nokwe, who cringed whenever Walter asked for English food. The Chinese thought that Walter was very backward in his culinary tastes. He did, perhaps, have an excuse; during their unscheduled stop in Manchuria, arrangements were made with the locals to kill and cook a sheep for their visitors. By some sleight of hand, the villagers enjoyed the sheep, while Walter and his comrades ate a most peculiar meal. Later, they found out that they had dined on camel! (Helen Moffett, Interview, Ismail Bhoola, May 2002.)

Walter was fascinated by the elaborate parades in celebration of the national day on 1 October. On that day, he and Duma attended a banquet at which they were introduced to the Chinese leader, Chou en Lai. Walter thought he had a magnetic personality. During the course of the evening, Chou en Lai made endless toasts, but he showed tremendous stamina and stayed sober throughout.

Before Walter had left South Africa, Mandela had asked him to discuss the possibility of armed struggle with the Chinese. "Though we believed in the policy of nonviolence, we knew in our hearts it wasn't going to be a satisfactory answer," Walter recalls (Houser and Shore, 89). When Walter raised the issue with his Chinese hosts, they warned him that revolution was a very serious affair, not to be embarked on lightly. The leaders of the Central Committee told him that they should not be misled by slogans and should analyse the situation carefully before reaching a decision (Houser and Shore, 89).

Walter was also asked to broadcast a radio message to the Chinese people. He spoke of the experiences at the festival and the historical significance of the revolutions of 1917 and 1949, as well as the future that was unfolding both in the USSR and China. He made a similar broadcast in Moscow a few weeks later.

While in Peking, Walter met with the Indian Ambassador, who invited him to India. However, time was running out, and they had to fly back to Moscow.

From Moscow, Walter and Duma went to Azerbaijan for three weeks. Walter found the people there very warm and talkative, in contrast to the inhabitants of Moscow. On the whole, Walter was less impressed with the Soviet Union than he was with China. However, he was amazed by the amount of construction going on in Moscow, especially the building of the university and the Metro underground. He also visited Red Square, the Kremlin and Moscow's state library with its millions of books. They were treated to an evening at the impressive Bolshoi Theatre, where they saw a performance of the ballet *Swan Lake*.

Before beginning the return trip to South Africa, Walter spent a few more days in London. He addressed a meeting at Holborn Hall together with former South African trade unionist Solly Sachs. Here he emphasised that the English had an obligation to the people of South Africa because of the colonial relationship and the manner in which South Africa had been handed over to the whites by the British government. Walter also gave an account of the situation in South Africa to a group of British MPs at a meeting arranged by Fenner Brockway. Together with Lionel Ngakane, Walter also visited Seretse and Ruth Khama, who were living in a suburb on the outskirts of London. Seretse was especially impressive in his understanding of the South African situation and Walter raised the question of reviving political activity in the Protectorates.

During his stay in London, Walter met many veterans of the Pan-Africanist Movement. One of them was Wallace from Sierra Leone, who had worked with both Kenyan nationalist Jomo Kenyatta and George Padmore of the Pan-Africanist Movement. Wallace told Walter that Nkrumah was interested in forming regional Pan-African organisations. Walter also communicated with Kenneth Kaunda of the African National Congress of Zambia and Mbio Koinage, the brother-in-law of Jomo Kenyatta. Walter proposed some form of Africa-wide movement calling for the release of Jomo Kenyatta. Also from London, Walter wrote to Nkrumah suggesting that the matter of Kenyatta's release be taken up at the United Nations. He even sent him a draft of a suggested resolution.

Throughout his trip Walter had been in constant touch with South African writer Peter Abrahams, and he eventually met him in London. He also met Colin Legum, a former member of the Labour Party in South Africa, and a senior reporter for *The Observer*. In a telephone interview with *The Observer*, Walter had been asked about his impressions of his trip, and had responded that he was very impressed by the Chinese. *The Observer* then published the interview with a twist, saying that Walter was not impressed by the European Communist Movement. Walter was very annoyed. He protested to the editor about the misrepresentation of his statement and demanded that the paper publish a correction. When *Observer* reporter Anthony Sampson subsequently came to South Africa, he appealed to Walter not to hold the unfortunate incident against him.

Colin Legum, who had just returned from South Africa, was deeply interested in the reaction of the African people back home to Walter's visit to the socialist countries. He informed Walter that there was such great hostility to his trip that he did not believe that Walter would be able to retain his position in the ANC. Walter told Legum that his impressions were mistaken, and that although he accepted that there would be hostility against him, it would only be from a few intellectuals.

Walter then returned to Israel for two weeks before flying back to South African via Nairobi. On his return to Johannesburg on 14 December 1953, he was thoroughly searched and questioned for several hours by the immigration authorities, who were reluctant to let him into the country because they suspected him of being a prohibited immigrant. He was finally released and given three days in which to prove that he was a South African citizen, failing which he would be sent back to Israel. From the airport he was taken to Park Station, where he managed to get the last train to Orlando and his surprised family. Nobody was expecting him because the papers had carried a report to the effect that Walter had been seen in London on that very day. One story, which made the rounds, was that Walter had gone to Churchill and demanded transport to South Africa. Walter grabbed a few hours' sleep; early the next morning, before he could even greet his children, he had to leave for the ANC's annual conference in Queenstown, where he would learn of the reaction to his trip.

Walter arrived in Queenstown in the Eastern Cape to the most well-attended annual conference in the ANC's history. He was praised by some and vilified by others for his actions. He attempted to give a report to the NEC, but some members refused to accept it as the NEC had not sanctioned Walter's trip. Walter pointed out that Chief Luthuli was aware of the trip, having been informed about it by Mandela. Unfortunately for Walter, Chief Luthuli had no recollection of the discussion with Mandela, who was not at the conference to back up Walter's story.

Duma Nokwe was also present at the conference, having returned to South Africa two weeks before Walter. He was also rebuked by the anti-Left delegates, who wanted to know who had funded the trip. Allegations were made that Mandela had used funds from an Indian government donation to the Defiance Campaign to finance the trip. In response to these unfounded rumours, Walter asked Duma Nokwe to present a report on how they came to be invited, and how the trip was financed by WFDY. He also reported on the festival itself, the International Union of Students' Congress, and impressions of life in the socialist countries in general. There was still dissatisfaction. While Walter was away, speculation had been rife that he would arrange to procure weapons for an armed struggle in South Africa. Those who supported the trip were critical that he had not done enough in this regard. The anti-Left group tabled a motion of no confidence, but this was defeated, and it turned out that many people at the conference were indeed happy about the trip. Kotane's biographer Brian Bunting noted that in contrast to Josiah Gumede, who was deposed from the post of President-General in the wake of his trip to the Soviet Union, Walter and Duma Nokwe "were consolidated in their positions of leadership" (Bunting 1998, 201).

Asked by a reporter from the left-wing weekly *Advance* whether his experiences overseas had affected his views about the future of South Africa, Sisulu replied: "The immediate task of the people of South Africa is to win the right to determine what sort of society they are going to live in. When democratic rights have been won, we can discuss what type of social system we are going to have. Meanwhile democrats of all shades must unite to win political equality." Asked whether his trip may have antagonized supporters of Congress, Sisulu said: "As far as non-whites are concerned, certainly not. They look upon these countries as their friends who have unreservedly supported their case at the United Nations Organisation. My visit was a goodwill visit on behalf of democratic South Africa, both black and white. South Africa needs friends both in the East and the West" (Bunting 1998, 202).

After the conference, Walter had to rush back to Johannesburg and present himself at the immigration office to prove that he was a South African citizen. His mother accompanied him and signed a document confirming that he was her son. The customs officials had, meanwhile, confiscated all Walter's souvenirs – including books by Mao and a photograph of the head of the International Section of the Youth Organisation in China.

Over the next few months, Walter was amazed at the excitement and continued interest in his trip. There were numerous articles in the press and he was highly amused by one of the headlines: "Six Natives go to Moscow." He wrote a couple of articles himself, including one entitled "I Saw China" (published in *Liberation* in February 1963). He attended a series of meetings on the Witwatersrand organised by local branches of the ANC in a Chinese-style suit, and received very enthusiastic receptions. Early in February, he addressed an ANC meeting in Durban and the South African Society for Peace and Friendship with the Soviet Union in Johannesburg. During this meeting, members of the Special Branch entered the hall and asked everyone to remain where they were. Colonel Prinsloo went up to the platform and announced that he was investigating the question of treason. "This was the first time that the word 'treason' had been used," noted Walter. The police took away documents belonging to the speakers and inspected literature on a table in the hall. After the speeches had ended and the audience had asked questions, the police told them that in accordance with the Suppression of Communism Act, the names and addresses of all those present would be taken.

On 19 February, Walter's friends Bram and Molly Fischer held a cocktail party in his honour. Walter spoke to the mostly Communist gathering, about the powerful impact the trip abroad had had on him. He spoke of how impressed he had been by what he saw in China and the Soviet Union, although he felt that in the latter "there was a bit too much of Stalin in everything". A few days later, he addressed a meeting on Colonial Youth Day (which fell on the anniversary of the Indian student and military demonstrations of 1946), speaking enthusiastically about the significance of the role of the youth in the national liberation movement.

While Walter and his colleagues had won many admirers as a result of their trip, they also had to contend with bitter opposition from the Africanist bloc within the ANC. In March 1954, Potlako Leballo, one of the most passionate adherents of exclusive African nationalism, was elected chairman of the Orlando Branch of the Youth League. He attacked the ANC members who had gone on the trip as "Eastern functionaries" and he nicknamed Walter "Mao Tse Tung" (Karis and Gerhart, 3: 21). Leballo and his group were also highly critical of the ANC's increasing cooperation with the South African Coloured People's Organisation (SACPO) and the Congress of Democrats (COD), formed in September and October 1953 respectively. Leballo's increasing hostility led to his expulsion from the Youth League, an action that resulted in a protracted dispute between the Orlando Branch and the Transvaal Provincial Executive of the Youth League. In November 1954, Leballo began issuing a journal called the *Africanist*, which became the mouthpiece for the Africanist viewpoint within the ANC (Gerhart, 141.) With the launch of the *Africanist* and the agitation of Leballo and his associates, the fault lines in the ANC were fast widening into an unbridgeable chasm.

Walter's trip had become something of an urban legend, and he became even more popular than ever before with members of the media. Doc Bikitsha, who was a young up-and-coming journalist in the early 1950s, recalled that Walter, Mandela and Tambo used to frequent Kapitans Oriental Restaurant in Kort Street. When Walter was having a meal there "he did not appear to mind us young and rowdy reporters who used to peep into the bottle too often. But we tended to avoid Mr Mandela, a fan of Mr Madanjit Kapitan's curried chicken, because he did not take kindly to our bohemian antics. If we chanced on Mr Tambo at this popular inn, we preferred to 'take a U-turn' because he was blunt about his dislike of excessive drinking" ("Memories of Nelson and Walter are still served at Kapitans", *Sunday Times* 8/10/89).

In the 1940s and 1950s, only a handful of good restaurants were open to blacks in Johannesburg. Apart from Morotsele's and Kapitans, there was the Blue Lagoon in Princess Street run by the mother of Juliet Mogale, one of Walter's secretaries. In the backyard of the Blue Lagoon were rooms that the ANC used to hire for people who came to consult with headquarters. "Mr Sisulu frequented all these eateries and you couldn't miss him in a Diagonal Street crowd wearing his conical Basotho straw hat," recalled Bikitsha. "Sometimes the late photographer Bob Gosani, the late journalist Can Themba and I met him at Lenvic House, where we would discuss the day's politics in the offices of the pioneer trade unionist, Mr JB Marks. After the indaba, Mr Sisulu would vanish to Macosa House and dear JB would treat us to a bottle of brandy, which was a luxury to us in those days of prohibition" ("Memories of Nelson and Walter are still served at Kapitans", *Sunday Times* 8/10/89).

More often than not, Walter could not afford to eat out. The mid-1950s were difficult years for the ANC financially, and there were many months when Walter did not receive his five pound paycheck. Bertha Gxowa remembered how the ANC treasurer could only allocate sixpence for a plate of pap, chips or bread for each volunteer or staff member who worked there. "Once uTata would get his half-a-loaf of bread, he would break it into pieces and share it with any one who had no food." The offices themselves were bare: "there were no chairs made of leather. There would be just a solitary narrow rickety bench" (Joyce Sikhakhane-Rankin, Interview, Bertha Gxowa). Mendi Msimang, a member of the Youth League who worked as Walter's secretary on a voluntary basis, also remembers sharing the lunchtime packet of chips with Walter (Callinicos, Unpublished biography of Oliver Tambo).

When times were really hard, Walter and Mendi could always go to Kathrada's flat at 13 Kholvad House in Market Street for a plate of curry. This flat had been a central meeting point for leaders when Ismail Meer occupied it during his student days. The tradition continued when Kathrada took over the flat in the 1950s. Goolam and Amina Pahad at Orient House also provided a home away from home in the City Centre.

In 1952, Tambo and Mandela had opened a law practice at Chancellor House in Fox Street, just across from the Magistrates' Court. News of the only black law firm in the city spread quickly, and in no time Tambo and Mandela were besieged with clients. As Tambo's biographer Luli Callinicos has pointed out: "The 1950s saw increasing hardship for blacks in the metropolis. As apartheid's social engineering began to be applied with growing determination, removals from multi-racial residential suburbs, pass law offences, prosecutions based on racist legislation, the imprisonment of trade unionists, 'loiterers' or 'cheeky natives' crammed the law courts and stretched the firm of Tambo and Mandela to its limits" (Callinicos 2001, 135).

During the Defiance Campaign Tambo and Mandela both struggled to cope with the sheer volume of their political work on the campaign and the legal defence of numerous volunteers. Visiting their offices one day, Walter was taken aback to find their waiting-room bursting at the seams with clients seeking legal help for friends or relatives who had been arrested for defying. Concerned about the weight on their shoulders, Walter went out and literally plucked Mendi Msimang from a queue in which he was waiting to defy. He told Msimang that he would better contribute to the campaign by assisting Tambo. Msimang was duly articled to the firm (Callinicos, Unpublished Biography of Oliver Tambo).

As the work of the ANC piled up, Walter was always on the lookout for young talent to relieve the burdens of the senior leadership. Henry Makgothi recalled how in 1951, soon after he had graduated from Fort Hare, he bumped into Walter and Mandela walking along, deeply engrossed in conversation. Mandela introduced Makgothi to Walter, who immediately asked where he stood in relation to the struggle "after all that big talk at Fort Hare". Mandela laughed and said that Makgothi's apparent isolation was "the calm before the storm" (Wolfie Kodesh, Interview, Henry Makgothi 1991). Makgothi went on to become very active in the Defiance Campaign and was one of the ANC members who attended the WFDY festival in Romania. Makgothi recalled that during the Defiance Campaign, he became more closely involved with the organisational machinery of the ANC, and learned about its inherent weaknesses and strengths. In the Transvaal, branches were poorly organised and operated virtually independently:

> Subscriptions were not properly collected, membership was loose ... If any one person can take credit for having seriously attempted to solve these and other problems – and I don't belittle the enormous sacrifices of comrades such as John Motshabi, Philip Mathole, Alfred Nzo, Thomas Nkobi, etc. – that person is Walter Sisulu ... he neither spared himself nor complained about the privations he suffered. On the contrary, he would see to it that those of us who worked for nothing for the organisation had something to eat, shoes, or even a shirt. His devotion became proverbial and made us feel small and ashamed of complaining" (Wolfie Kodesh, Interview, Henry Makgothi 1991).

After the Defiance Campaign, there was much discussion in the ANC about future activities. One such discussion took place at the dinner table of Professor ZK Matthews, at his home in the small town of Alice in the Eastern Cape, not long after his return from the US in May 1953. Professor Matthews, his wife Frieda, his son Joe, Dr James Njongwe, and Robert Matji, the provincial secretary of the ANC in the Cape, discussed the need for a campaign that would "capture the imagination of the people". The idea that appealed most was Joe's suggestion for a "Congress of the People" to draw up a "Freedom Charter" (Karis and Carter, 2: 57). Joe was so excited about the idea that he immediately wrote to Walter about it. Walter was therefore not surprised when he learned that Professor Matthews had made a public call for a Congress of the People at the Provincial Congress of the ANC in the Cape in 1953. The proposal was put to the ANC's 1953 annual conference, and the result was a resolution to prepare for a Congress of the People to work out a Freedom Charter for all groups in the country. The conference instructed the ANC NEC to make immediate preparations for the campaign, which was to become one of the most significant ever in the history of the struggle (Vadi, 68).

On 1 March 1954, acting on this resolution, Walter invited the national executive committees of the ANC, the SAIC, the SACPO and the COD to a joint conference to discuss the idea of a Congress of the People (Vadi, 68). The conference was held on 20–21 March in Tongati, Natal, in a dusty classroom in a rural school for Indian children. The venue was chosen because it was near Stanger, to which district Chief Luthuli had been confined by a banning order.

Professor Matthews made a presentation based on a memorandum he had drawn up for a Congress of the People. He explained that such a Congress would be a giant step forward. It would draw up a Freedom Charter as a blueprint constitution for a democratic, nonracial and unified South Africa. "It was an exciting vision, even when set out in an unemotional professorial tone," Bernstein recalled. "It seemed to have just the sweep of vision which we needed to break out of the quietus, and to inspire the movement with new enthusiasm. It felt like an idea whose time had come" (Rusty Bernstein, 141–2).

The conference concluded with the appointment of a National Action Council to organise the campaign. The Secretariat of the National Action Council (NAC) was made up of Walter, Yusuf Cachalia, Lionel Bernstein and Stanley Lollan. Chief Luthuli, Elias Moretsele, Oliver Tambo, Robert Resha, Enoch Tshunungwa, Joe Slovo, Rica Hodgson, Piet Beyleveld, George Peake and Ahmed Kathrada were also on the NAC. Ismail Vadi has noted that "the composition of the National Action Council was significant in that it served as the first truly nonracial forum for the planning of joint political work for the Congresses. In this sense it can be seen as the forerunner of the Congress Alliance that emerged after the Congress of the People itself" (Vadi, 74; Karis and Gerhart, 3: 19).

Immediately after the meeting in Natal, Walter proceeded to the Eastern Cape to attend to ANC organisational matters and to canvass for the Congress of the People. He received an enthusiastic welcome and was asked to relate his experiences on his overseas tour. He then reported on the plans for the Congress of the People campaign and was encouraged by the tremendous support for the idea. Walter was overwhelmed by requests for visits by individual branches. He had so many invitations that he spent two weeks in the Port Elizabeth area alone. The women of the area also held a huge reception for him.

In spite of all the political work that had been done in the Transkei, Walter was concerned that there were no well-organised ANC branches in that area. He therefore travelled to the Transkei, where he brought together a few activists to form a nucleus for a subregion. He also made arrangements for a conference in Umtata, which Chief Luthuli was scheduled to address. After two months in the Eastern Cape, Walter finally returned to Johannesburg.

At the end of June, Walter headed back west to the Eastern Cape to attend the annual conference of the Cape Province ANC in Uitenhage. The conference kicked off with a huge mass meeting addressed by Walter, Chief Luthuli (who was able to attend, as his one-year ban had just expired) and Ida Mntwana. They were given a tumultuous welcome by thousands of people. Dozens of security police attended the meeting, taking notes of all the speeches. Professor Matthews welcomed the police with the wry comment that they were "the main link between the African people and the government" (Karis and Carter, 3: 21). Professor Matthews later noted with satisfaction that while the police were concentrating their attention on the hall where the reception was being held, the delegates slipped out to another venue, where the real business of the conference was dealt with in an all-night discussion (ZK Matthews, 177).

The National Conference of the ANC Youth League was also held in Uitenhage at the same time and Walter delivered the opening address. He praised the Youth League's alliance with anti-colonial movements around the world and criticised the "isolationism" of the Africanists, whom he accused of misinterpreting the politics of Lembede and Mda (Karis and Gerhart, 3: 21). This was an allusion to the ongoing conflict between the Orlando Youth League Branch and the Transvaal Province Youth League. Joe Matthews was re-elected President-General of the Youth League and Duma Nokwe Secretary-General (Karis and Gerhart, 3: 21).

Professor ZK Matthews introduced Walter to the delegates at the Uitenhage conference:

> As for the General Secretary, it is hardly necessary for me to welcome him here. He is a son of the Cape Province ... During his recent Cape tour he was instrumental in taking the ANC to the heart of the Transkei, that area that is supposed to be surrounded with an Iron Curtain. During his brief sojourn there, they sought him here, they sought him there, they sought him everywhere, and when he had already returned to headquarters, they were still seeking. He will soon have to be known as Mr Walter 'Scarlet Pimpernel' Sisulu, the ubiquitous General Secretary of the ANC (Karis and Carter, 3: 128).

Walter did not only seem to be everywhere during his stint as ANC Secretary-General; he also seemed to know everyone. He interacted with all the major political activists of the time, young and old, conservative and radical. He could count among his friends leaders and members of the ANC, the Communist Party of South Africa, the trade unions and even members of the Non-European Unity Movement, which was implacably hostile to the ANC. His capacity to establish deep and lasting friendships across barriers of race, class, ethnicity, religion, gender and age facilitated his political work and considerably strengthened the ANC.

Professor Matthews and Walter were much more than political colleagues. They had become close friends, despite the difference in their ages and their political outlooks (Matthews was associated with the liberal Centre in ANC politics, while Walter was associated with the Left). Joe Matthews testifies to how much his father liked Walter, and the feeling was mutual. The friendship with the elder Matthews extended to his son Joe, who became especially close to Walter when he moved to Johannesburg to study law at Wits after graduating from Fort Hare. Joe, who became National President of the Youth League in 1953, used to often visit Walter at his offices in Newcourt Chambers, then later at Macosa House. "Walter would take me out to lunch. We would often go to Mr Moretsele's restaurant for pap and *mogudu* (tripe) and there we would have long conversations. I just loved being with Walter." Joe Matthews believed that Walter's ability to relate to and work with people of different generations was crucial to the development of the ANC: "He respected youth. He did not look down on their ideas and reject their experience ... He could also relate to older people like my father, Chief Luthuli and that generation. Everybody loved Walter. He could work with anybody. He was in contact with all branches and provinces of the ANC. He was a man with many ideas. He was a diplomat who could solve problems and conflicts. Walter was the centre of ANC activities. I believe that he was the real architect of our freedom." Matthews is amused, however, at the characterisation of Walter as the "quiet engine of the ANC". "He may have been the engine, but he certainly was not quiet. He could shout and bang the table with his fists when he was angry" (Interview, Joe Matthews 20/12/2001).

There are many others who testify to the same qualities in Walter. Wilton Mkwayi, the Eastern Cape trade unionist and one of the leaders of the Defiance Campaign, describes Walter as a true collective leader who consulted widely and ensured that everyone's opinion was taken into account. "U'Xhamela wawuthunga lombutho we ANC." ("Xhamela pulled together [literally, "sewed together"] this organisation, the ANC.")

It was not only his colleagues in the liberation movement who recognized Walter's central role in the ANC. From 1950 onwards, the Security Branch began to keep him under close surveillance and to record his every movement. In his study entitled "The Individual, Biography and Resistance in South African Public History", Ciraj Rasool comments:

> The police file on Walter Sisulu contains much more than merely a collection of records documenting his encounters with the apartheid state's security machinery. It is also a testament to surveillance of political activists by the state ... Indeed more than merely a documentary source on political activity or policing, the security police dossier can be seen as a species of biography, an instance of biographical attention to an individual, as a mode of surveillance, regulation and terror.

A Security Branch memorandum that constitutes a record of Walter's meetings and activities notes that Walter Sisulu "had a good domestic and Christian upbringing ... He however lost his way when he became secretary of the 'Orlando Brotherly Society'. This union made him eager to create better economic conditions for the Bantu". Another of Walter's crimes, according to the security police, was that he "has inculcated into the non-whites that they are oppressed and he encourages them to fight for their freedom" (Walter Sisulu, Ministry of Justice Files).

In October 1953, the government began preparing a notice to ban Walter from participation in the ANC and numerous other organisations sympathetic to the ANC. On 28 October, the Deputy Commissioner of the South African Police wrote to inform the Secretary of Justice that Walter was overseas, and that the notice of his banning would be served on him on his return. In January 1954, the Commissioner of Police wrote again to the Secretary of Justice: "I have the honour to inform you that the abovementioned native is back in the union and this notice can now be served on him" (Ministry of Justice documents).

In a memorandum dated 22/1/54, the Commissioner wrote: "Sisulu is regarded as one of the most dangerous agitators in the country. He recently returned home from an extended tour through Eastern Europe and Communist China and it is known that he also spent time in Moscow as guest of the Communists. He undoubtedly, while there, received instruction in Communist propaganda methods and it is regarded as necessary that his activities be stopped in order to prevent him from spreading his undermining views here." The police motivated that he be prevented from attending any meeting anywhere in the Union of South Africa for two years and that he be confined to the magisterial district of Johannesburg.

Another Compol memorandum of June 1954 stated that Walter Sisulu "has definitely, directly and indirectly encouraged a spirit of enmity between the white and non-white races of the Union, thus aiming at the realisation of communism in the Union." The memorandum described his rise in the ANC until he became Secretary-General in 1949:

> After that there was no holding him. In that position he travelled all over the Union with intensive organising of the African National Congress. Not satisfied with the borders of the Union, he also started going abroad.
>
> While doing this organising work he also continually addressed other leftist organisations and in his speeches he did not mince his words. He is one of the most outspoken Communists of the time.

He is exceptionally well-spoken, and thus in a position to captivate his audience, and then to exploit the feeling that he has brought about which he managed to do thoroughly. He admits to having received the greatest hospitality from all the countries behind the Iron Curtain, to such a degree that in China and Russia special trains were put at his disposal, and that he even inspected the Russian army and that he made speeches on Peking radio. He admits to depicting the South African picture there and it is more than clear that this is the same picture, if not a worse one, than that which he usually paints here. As a result of the overseas visits, he has also been promised support by foreign powers in his struggle in South Africa, the struggle which he on numerous occasions depicted in unequivocal terms, as the struggle against white domination of the non-white races, and that his objectives [are] a government of the proletariat ... His general behaviour was such that he was charged on 2/12/52 for contravention of Section 11 (b) of Act 44 of 1950, as amended, but even this conviction had no effect on his above behaviour.

In a letter dated 13 September 1954, the Deputy Permanent-Representative of South Africa's Permanent Delegation to the United Nations informed the secretary of External Affairs in Pretoria that "Mr Sizulu [sic], secretary of the ANC, had approached a large number of respectable and other organisations in the US to solicit funds for what he calls 'campaign plan'".

On 22 July 1954, Walter was ordered, in terms of Section 5 of the Suppression of Communism Act, to resign as a member, official or office-bearer of the ANC and any of the Congress-related organisations. In terms of Section 9 of the same Act, he was prohibited from attending any gatherings for over two years. Anthony Sampson, the editor of *Drum* at the time, was with Walter at No. 7372 when the banning order was served:

He was talking with his usual analytical detachment about bannings and detentions, when two Afrikaner detectives walked in. They were surprisingly friendly: "Ah! We've found you at last! Two letters from the Minister of Justice for you!" "I've been expecting you," Sisulu answered. "Only two? It won't make any difference you know. The struggle will go on." The detective smiled: "Cheerio then – Afrika!" (Sampson, 2000, 92.)

Walter subsequently issued a statement to inform members of the ANC that he had been ordered by the Minister of Justice to resign from the ANC, and consequently to give up his position as Secretary-General:

I was elected to this position by you in 1949, since when I have endeavoured to the utmost of my ability to serve my people and to be worthy of the confidence you placed in me.

I am now forced to resign from the organisation but I wish to assure you that I shall be entirely at your disposal and will not hesitate to answer any call that may be made by the ANC.

His statement also outlined the crippling effects of the bans on the leaders of the liberation movement: "The people's leaders have been forbidden from attending any gatherings whatsoever, they are being removed from their places of employment, some have been exiled. Almost the entire National Executive of the African National Congress has been removed from office." He urged people to continue with the work of organisation building: "Honesty, selflessness, vigour, determination, initiative and faith are some of the qualities you require. The Government has already been shaken, the time has passed when they could rule the country as if we, the people, did not exist. The time is against them, the world is against them. We, on the other hand, are encouraged by the great spirit of the people of South Africa, by the growth of the national liberatory movement, the unprecedented political consciousness and by the fact that the truth is with us, we enjoy the confidence of the entire world in this noble, just task for which we are pledged to fight until the dawn of freedom" (Message by Walter Sisulu, Secretary-General of the ANC, Treason Trial record).

When he received the banning order, Walter had been making arrangements to attend an NEC meeting in the Orange Free State. Walter's ban from gatherings was effective immediately, but he was given seven days in which to resign from all the organisations listed in the banning order. He decided to take advantage of this brief hiatus by going to the NEC meeting on 24 July, held in Botshabelo Location at Bethlehem High School. The principal of the school, LK Mtlabathi, was the ANC provincial president of the Orange Free State. He organised lunch for the six NEC members, so that in event of a police raid, they could innocently claim to be having lunch. The ploy did not quite work out, as the police did storm the meeting and arrest Walter, refusing to listen to the lunch story. Because the arrest took place late on Friday afternoon, Walter had to spend the weekend in jail before a bail hearing could be arranged.

The next Monday, Walter was able to return home after being given bail of £100. He had to return to the Orange Free State for the trial, which was held in the Regional Court in Kroonstad. Joe Slovo represented Walter, who was sentenced to three months in prison with compulsory labour for a crime unique in history, namely: "Attending a gathering in order to partake of, or be present whilst others partake of, refreshment (in the nature of tea and/or edibles and/or a meal)" (Bunting 1998, 208). Walter was allowed bail pending appeal, and another defence team, this time headed by Bram Fischer, managed to win the case on appeal on 24 November 1955.

In his statement on being banned, Walter commented on the rash of banning orders on ANC and SAIC leaders: "They will remain your leaders because they still belong to our liberation struggle and they will still find a way to make their contribution. They have not been rejected by us, but forcibly thrown out by our enemies" (Schadeberg 1990, 77). Oliver Tambo took over as acting Secretary-General in Walter's place, and was formally elected to the post in 1955. Tambo was a very busy lawyer and could not manage the full-time organisational work, so Walter continued to work in a full-time capacity underground, with Tambo having the power to veto anything he did. Walter continued to deal with the ANC's correspondence and preparation of reports, in effect remaining the de facto Secretary-General.

Since virtually the entire ANC NEC was banned, including Chief Luthuli, Mandela, JB Marks, Kotane, Njongwe, David Bopape and Dan Tloome, the leadership in Transvaal came to the decision that people must continue with their work, as far as possible.

The Security Branch noted that: "After Sisulu was restricted, his public activities decreased to such an extent that he no longer came into the limelight ... However he has dug himself in (established his position) and there is plenty of evidence from utterly reliable and delicate sources that he is, in secret and behind the scenes, as busy as before with advice and guidance and instigation among the non-whites" (Walter Sisulu, Ministry of Justice files).

By the time Walter was banned, he was a familiar and much loved figure far beyond Congress circles. In his stint as an openly active Secretary-General he had achieved a great deal, and ANC members continued to regard him as their Secretary-General. As Professor Matthews pointed out: "It is of course impossible for any Minister to ban anyone from the ANC. As far as the ANC is concerned, these sons of Africa are still members of our organization with their names written indelibly not on paper, but in the hearts of our people, where they are beyond the reach of governmental interference" (Karis and Gerhart, 3: 169–170).

After its dissolution in 1950, members of the Communist Party of South Africa slowly and carefully regrouped. By 1953, they were in a position to formally reconstitute the Party underground in the form of the South African Communist Party (SACP). Soon after his trip abroad, Walter started attending Communist Party political education classes. He was impressed by the discipline, training and methodology of the Communists. During 1954, he attended a properly organised Marxist study group. Michael Harmel, whom Walter considered a brilliant theoretician, was given the task of running the group. Walter ultimately joined the SACP in 1955, just before the Congress of the People. In the same year, he attended the SACP conference in Johannesburg, and in 1956, he became a member of the Central Committee of the SACP.

His experiences in Eastern Europe and China were a significant factor in his decision to join the SACP, but even before the trip, Walter had become part of a distinct Left group within the ANC. He was also attracted by the intellectual appeal of Marxism. It provided a coherent theory of society that made increasing sense in the light of the crude economic exploitation of black men and women in South Africa. Where the Youth League had found Marxist theory to be Euro-centric, Walter was interested in the fact that black Communists, particularly Marks and Kotane, were forging an African Communism. The CPSA's sympathetic approach to African nationalism (and their slogan prioritising a "black republic") he gauged to be sincere and not manipulative, despite their reputation. It is significant that he managed to persuade even Christian intellectuals such as Tambo, who was no pushover, of the value of working with such experienced and shrewd allies. In addition, Walter had the ability to be both organisationally disciplined (a trait emphasised by both the Youth League and the Communist Party) and flexible in his ability to think through strategies and tactics, as illustrated in the Defiance Campaign. His sincerity and tendency to trust others unless they proved themselves to be otherwise tended to bring out the best in people.

The most powerful factor in his decision to become a Communist was the influence of individuals he knew well and admired. He was impressed by the unswerving dedication and commitment of people like Rusty and Hilda Bernstein, and Jack Hodgson, as well as Michael Harmel, whom he saw as an outstanding theoretician. He was strongly influenced by JB Marks, Yusuf Dadoo and Moses Kotane, as well as Brian Bunting, who articulated clearly the things Walter admired most about Kotane:

> Kotane clearly saw the need for a Communist party and also for a national organisation for the African people, and it was largely as a result of his work that the two organisations never came to loggerheads. Kotane never regarded the ANC as a rival to the Communist Party ... For he understood clearly the distinct roles of national organisation and a party of the working class guided by the philosophy of Marxism-Leninism, and never allowed the two to get mixed up, either in his own mind or in the practical work of organising the people. It was because they recognised the quality of his work that the leaders of the ANC, including its Youth League, were always able to accept Kotane as one of themselves, and eventually also to accept the Communist Party as an ally in the struggle (Bunting 1998, 181).

Bunting may as well have been writing about Walter when he described Kotane's appeal: "But in addition to the political factor, there was also the personal element which also won the confidence of those who worked with him, and that was his integrity, his solidity as an individual, his stubbornness in fighting for what he believed to be right. In a way this was also an expression of his national pride, his desire to demonstrate that as an African he could be both a good communist and a patriot" (Bunting 1998, 181).

In the conditions of illegality and persecution in the wake of the Suppression of Communism Act, membership of the reconstituted SACP had to be a closely guarded secret. Walter had even greater reason to guard the secret of his membership. Confirmation that the ANC Secretary-General was a Communist would have been devastatingly divisive. As it was, the ANC had to respond constantly to allegations that it was a Communist-controlled organisation. As late as 1955, questions were still being asked about Walter's trip to Eastern Europe. In an interview with *Drum* in January 1955, Chief Luthuli responded:

> As far as Mr Sisulu's visit to Moscow is concerned, it was a personal invitation, not an invitation to the Congress; his visit was not in any way an official Congress visit. Professor Matthews also accepted

a private invitation to go to America. Both Mr Sisulu and Professor Matthews gave semi-official reports to the Congress on their visits, but this does not mean that the Congress was influenced either by America or Russia. So as far as I know, the Congress lays no bars to its leaders, duly invited, going to any country in the world (Schadeberg 1990, 78).

Like Kotane, Walter saw himself as an African who could be a good Communist and a patriot, and his primary loyalty always lay with the ANC.

The year 1955 was dominated by three major campaigns: the Congress of the People; the campaign against Bantu Education; and the Western Areas removals campaign. If anything demonstrated the grim and ruthless logic of apartheid laws, it was the mass removal of black people from Sophiatown, Newclare and St Martins. In 1951, the government announced its plan to remove the black residents of Johannesburg's western townships and resettle them in Meadowlands, near the township of Orlando.

From early 1954 onwards, huge crowds attended ANC-organised protest meetings on Wednesdays and Sundays in Sophiatown's Freedom Square. Fiery speeches were matched by defiant slogans. "We are not moving", "Over our dead bodies", could be heard on the lips of even the youngest citizens of Sophiatown (Resha, 57). One of these meetings was to have been addressed by Chief Luthuli, whose earlier ban had expired. He was received at Johannesburg airport with another banning order. Chief Luthuli had to watch from a house near the square while Walter addressed the meeting in his stead. The photographer Eli Weinberg, a good friend of Walter's, took some memorable photographs of the mass gathering of thousands who had come from all over the Witwatersrand.

Walter, Mandela and Tambo worked closely with Robert Resha, a key organiser of the protest campaign, who had organised 500 "Freedom Volunteers" to mobilise resistance to the removals. Towards the end of January 1955, the government announced that the removals of 152 families would take place on 12 February. People did not know what to do. Walter recalls a meeting of the joint executives of the ANC, SAIC and COD at which COD members Jack Hodgson and Cecil Williams advocated meeting force with force. Others suggested setting up barricades. When these ideas were dismissed as unrealistic "tempers flared and personal insults of cowardice were thrown around," recalls Walter. The meeting decided that alternative accommodation with pro-ANC families would be arranged for the families targeted for removal.

Residents expressed their shock and anger at a huge protest meeting in Freedom Square, where among others, Robert Resha delivered an emotional address. The youth were very angry and demanded action. They took the slogan "Over our dead bodies" literally, and were prepared to engage in a physical confrontation with the police. Joe Modise, one of Sophiatown's ANC leaders courageously told the 500 youthful activists that they were not in a position to take on the army and the police. The young activists were very resentful and felt betrayed by their leaders. Walter and other ANC leaders realised just how dangerous the slogan "Over our dead bodies" was. "It meant that we would be prepared to fight when we really were not in a position to do so." Walter would forever afterwards have a dislike of inflammatory slogans.

On 9 February, three days before the scheduled removals, thousands of police and soldiers descended on Sophiatown. They cordoned off the area, threw belongings into the street and loaded families onto the trucks that would transport them to Meadowlands (Mandela, 154). Over the next two years, the forced removal of the people of Sophiatown continued relentlessly and, by 1957, only a handful of property owners remained in the crumbling, dying neighbourhood (Gish, 176). Dr Xuma was one of the property owners who clung on to the last, but eventually even he had to leave his elegant house in Toby Street.

Walter felt that peaceful methods of protest had had little effect in the face of a ruthless and determined regime, so insensitive to the feelings of black people that after the rubble of Sophiatown was bulldozed, it erected a new whites-only suburb called Triomf (Afrikaans for Triumph). Although he had never lived in Sophiatown, he had strong connections with that community from his estate agent days, and he shared the sadness and heartbreak of people who had a deep and abiding love for the place.

On 26 June 1955, Walter and Mandela drove to a dusty field in the township of Kliptown, not far from their homes in Orlando West, to witness the historic Congress of the People. Both of them were banned and could only observe the process from the fringes of the 7 000-strong audience. Walter remembers watching the proceedings from the roof of the shop of Jada, one of his friends in Kliptown. It was deeply gratifying for them to watch the culmination of a two-year long process in which "Freedom Volunteers" had invited people throughout the country to formulate their demands on the way in which they wanted to be governed.

Walter had worked closely with Rusty Bernstein, Joe Slovo and Yusuf Cachalia on the committee processing the demands that poured in from all over the country. Rusty Bernstein produced the first draft of the Freedom Charter, which was passed on to Walter and other leaders a few days before the Congress of the People.

At the Kliptown gathering, the Freedom Charter was presented section by section to the 2 884 delegates from all walks of life, who had travelled from all corners of the country to attend. Chief Luthuli called it "perhaps the first really representative gathering in the Union's history" (Karis and Gerhart, 3: 61).

Proceedings on the second day were interrupted by a dramatic police invasion. Armed police and plain-clothes detectives confiscated thousands of copies of the draft charter and other papers and documents. The process of reading out the Freedom Charter, clause by clause, nevertheless continued even as police searched, photographed and recorded the names of people.

Walter shared the view of many that the Congress of the People was the most highly organised campaign the movement had ever undertaken. It had sealed the Congress Alliance consisting of the ANC, SAIC, SACPO, COD and newly formed South African Congress of Trade Unions (SACTU), and produced a common political programme that would survive the test of time.

One group that greatly enjoyed the festive atmosphere and excitement of the Congress of the People were the ANC children who were organised into *masupatsela* (pathfinders), and who marched proudly through the crowd to parade on the stage in Congress colours. Gerald, Max and Lungi revelled in the excitement of the rehearsals before the big day, and the novelty of being picked up in a truck that transported all the children to Kliptown. While perhaps not quite grasping the political meaning of the Congress, they understood that it was an important occasion to do with the struggle against white domination.

Like many other children with parents in the Congress Alliance, the Sisulu children grew up seeing their parents interact constantly with people of all races. Their home was a nonracial island in a segregated society, and they mixed freely on equal terms with children of other races. The children of many of the Congress of Democrats (COD) leaders also grew up with the sense that a segregated society was abnormal. They had organised themselves as the Young Democrats, which Ilse Fischer called "a kind of baby COD". They attracted police attention from an early age. On one occasion, when the police questioned them at a meeting, they asked nine-year-old Sheila Weinberg if she was the daughter of Eli Weinberg. She responded: "I only have to give you my name. I don't have to tell you anything else."

In September 1955, the South African police staged the most sweeping political raid in the country's history. Books, documents, typewriters and other items were seized from homes and offices of

Congress leaders, the offices of the left-wing publication *New Age,* and Father Huddleston's priory in Sophiatown. Even the Central Indian High School, where Harmel and Hutchinson's futuristic play had been staged, was not spared the attentions of the police. The head of the Special Branch declared that the raids were undertaken to investigate high treason and sedition (Sampson 1958, 111; Karis and Gerhart, 3: 67).

Walter was among the 500 people raided at home. From then on, police raids would become a permanent feature in the life of the Sisulu family. Policemen banging on the door as if they intended smashing it down, stamping around the house ferreting for documents like a pack of hungry dogs digging for bones, shining torches into startled sleepy faces, trampling their mother's well-tended garden with their heavy boots – these images remain deeply etched in the memories of the Sisulu children.

Lungi has never forgotten his father's reaction to the pre-dawn raids. "On some cold winter mornings we used to be woken up by some white cops searching the house. There would be these black cops standing shivering in the passage and Tata would say to Mama: 'You're going to have to make coffee for these people. They're cold'" (Green, 1991). Walter was calm about the raids and indicated to Albertina that this was merely a sign of worse things to come. "He told me that one day he would be going to jail for a long time and I must prepare for it."

When Anton Lembede had warned Albertina on her wedding day that she was marrying a man who was already married to the nation, he probably did not foresee that she would soon develop a commitment to national liberation as unshakeable as that of her husband. During the 1940s, Albertina's involvement in politics had been in a supportive capacity. Her salary was the main and often only source of income for the family. Though she often attended political meetings with Walter, she did not actively participate in ANC structures until the 1950s.

The ANC Women's League, formed in 1943 under the leadership of Madie Hall Xuma, the African-American educationist, social worker and wife of Dr Xuma, did not have a separate programme from the mother body. It operated in a supportive capacity in activities such as catering and fundraising for the ANC. It was only after the Defiance Campaign that the Women's League became really active, and a whole new generation of women leaders emerged.

The ANC Women's League received a boost when, on 17 April 1954, the Federation of South African Women (FEDSAW) was launched at a national conference held at the Trades Hall in Johannesburg. One hundred and fifty women from all over South Africa attended the conference, which adopted a special Women's Charter (Wells, 107). This Charter stated FEDSAW's aims: both to fight apartheid's unjust laws and to emancipate women from the special disabilities they suffered in society. FEDSAW, with the ANC Women's League as its largest and most dominant affiliate, mirrored the Congress Alliance in terms of its representation of women from all the Congress organisations, as well as the trade unions. Albertina quietly combined her home visits to patients with the political work of distributing leaflets about the Congress of the People, and exhorting women to join the new Federation. She threw herself into the other great campaign of 1955, the boycott in protest against the Bantu education system.

"My womb is shaken when they speak of Bantu Education." When she uttered these words, Lilian Ngoyi articulated the feelings of black women throughout South Africa. Albertina Sisulu certainly felt anger and revulsion to the depths of her being at the idea of a system of education deliberately designed to emphasise ethnic differences among black children, and to train them to occupy an inferior position in life. No other piece of legislation, not even the Pass Laws, ignited as much anger and outrage in black communities as the Bantu Education Act of 1953. In terms of the Act, control of all education of Africans was transferred to the Bantu Education Department on 1 April 1955.

As 1 April approached, there were fierce debates within the ANC on how to respond to the pernicious legislation. The NEC eventually decided on a week-long boycott beginning on 1 April. Delegates at the 1954 conference rejected this decision in favour of a permanent boycott.

According to Nelson Mandela, "The Conference was the supreme authority, even greater than the Executive and we found ourselves saddled with a boycott that would be impossible to effect" (Mandela, 156).

Walter recalls that there was tremendous popular support for the boycott in Orlando. The ANC Women's League and FEDSAW played a key role in the boycott campaign by organising alternative schools for children. Many teachers resigned in protest against Bantu Education and some of them successfully ran the alternative Congress-organised schools (Mandela, 157). Albertina actively participated in the campaign, and the Sisulu home became the venue of one of the alternative schools. The Sisulu children were among those who were withdrawn from school, attending the school run from their own home instead.

When the government made it illegal to run unregistered schools, the alternative schools were referred to as "cultural clubs". These were not sustainable in the long term, however, especially in the face of police harassment, and eventually they withered away. When the government announced that boycotting schools would be closed permanently, and that children not back at school by a particular date would not be readmitted, parents faced the terrible choice of Bantu Education or no education at all. Reluctantly, parents sent their children back to school and the boycott collapsed (Mandela, 157).

Some of the churches closed down their schools rather than hand over their control to the government. Others gave their schools over to the Bantu Education Department rather than close their doors. The Catholics, the Seventh Day Adventists and the United Jewish Reformed Congregation decided to continue as private schools without state subsidies. Albertina and Walter decided to send their children to the Seventh Day Adventist schools, even though this meant considerable financial sacrifice as the fees were necessarily much higher.

At the end of 1955, the ANC Women's League had held its first national conference in Johannesburg. Shortly thereafter, the ANC Women's League and FEDSAW set up a joint working committee to coordinate the women's anti-pass campaign. Over the next few months, women organised networks and held regular weekend meetings in the townships (Wells, 111). The depth of popular resentment towards passes convinced the joint working committee that it could organise a gigantic protest at the Union Buildings involving tens of thousands of women from all over the country. ANC Women's League and FEDSAW member Ruth Mompati, who was working in the offices of Mandela and Tambo at the time, recalled that some of the men in the ANC were not impressed by their plans:

> They thought we were being too ambitious and that it would be impossible to organise such a huge protest. Because we were part of the ANC we had to keep the NEC informed about what we were planning. When it was discussed at the NEC we heard that there was resistance to the idea but Walter Sisulu said no, let us see what the women can do. I can tell you, that made him very popular with the women! (Interview, Ruth Mompati, November 2001.)

Walter's faith in the women was vindicated and, in a feat of remarkable organising, thousands of women from all over the country converged on Pretoria on 9 August 1956. Women made enormous sacrifices to make the trip, many of them travelling at their own expense. Seventy delegates from Port Elizabeth raised 700 pounds to charter an entire railway coach. It was reported that some women even sold their furniture to raise money for the journey (Lodge, 144; Interview, Ruth Mompati, November 2000). In Soweto, organisers of the march received information that the police were planning to stop women in groups of more than 10 from travelling to Pretoria. Albertina Sisulu was one of the leaders who had to ensure that the message was quickly passed through the ANC Women's League networks, so that the women could find ways to circumvent the ruling. It would have been very easy to stop groups of people travelling by bus, so most women decided to take the train to Pretoria. At 2am on the morning of 9 August, Albertina was at Phefeni Station buying tickets to distribute to women leaving from that station. The train was filled to capacity and she never forgot the electrifying atmosphere as they approached Pretoria (Joyce Sikhakhane-Rankin, Interview, Bertha Gxowa 9/8/2002).

Present on that historic day, Albertina proudly watched Lilian Ngoyi, Rahima Moosa, Sophie Williams (later De Bruyn) and Helen Joseph deposit the petitions in front of the empty office of the Minister of Native Affairs. For a full 30 minutes, 20 000 women stood in silence in the fore-court of the Union Buildings before they sang in unison: "Strydom, you have tampered with the women, you have struck a rock!" They then dispersed quietly and went home to ponder on an event that was to inspire women for generations to come.

# six

"We are investigating charges of high treason." This was a familiar refrain by the police when they raided Congress meetings, confiscating papers, leaflets and other paraphernalia during the mid-1950s. Ever since the Defiance Campaign and the Congress of the People, the charge of high treason had become a big stick that the apartheid government waved over the head of the ANC and its alliance partners. The threat had been about for so long, however, that Congress activists did not take it seriously. Even when the Minister of Justice announced in April 1956 that he was investigating a case of high treason, and about 200 people would be arrested, there was no great alarm in Congress circles.

The stick finally came down in dramatic fashion in the early hours of 5 December 1956, when the South African security police carried out their largest and most dramatic raid ever. In dawn swoops around the country, police arrested 140 people. Those from outlying areas such as Natal and the Eastern Cape were flown to Johannesburg by three special military Dakota aircraft. They were all taken to the Old Fort, Johannesburg's forbidding hilltop prison.

Those arrested were a motley collection of doctors, lawyers, priests, journalists, trade unionists, clerical workers, factory workers and even a Member of Parliament. They included Chief Luthuli and Professor ZK Matthews, who was then the Acting-Principal of Fort Hare, and his son Joe. Almost the entire national executive of the ANC had been arrested, as well as leaders of the other Congress organisations. Women's organisations had not been spared and prominent leaders such as Lilian Ngoyi, Helen Joseph and Ida Mntwana were among those arrested. The list read like a who's who of Congress politics with a few notable exceptions – one of whom was Walter Sisulu.

Walter was as surprised as anyone else at his exclusion from the august company at the Fort. He had been alerted as soon as the 5 December raids had started, and had immediately left home. He was surprised to find on his return that the police had not been by to collect him. So wide had the dragnet been cast that any senior leader who had not been arrested was regarded with some suspicion. A man called Mankazana challenged Walter about why he had not been arrested. Walter's reply was that he thought it might be because he had been banned from political activity during the past two years. "Have you abandoned your principles because you are banned?" was Mankazana's response. It was enough to make Walter regret that he had not been arrested!

Walter decided to visit the prisoners at the Fort. He found them in high spirits. Old friends had been reunited, and new friendships were being forged as activists and leaders who had heard of, but never met one another, came together, courtesy of the apartheid government. He was especially impressed by the fortitude of Oliver Tambo, who was due to get married to a young nurse by the name of Adelaide Tsukudu later that month. Tambo was determined to go ahead with the wedding, even if it meant bringing the minister and the bride to the Fort! (Callinicos, Unpublished biography of Oliver Tambo.) If Walter felt left out of the camaraderie at the Fort, he did not have to wait long to join his comrades. On 12 December, he and Albertina were awakened by the distinctive hammering on the door. Walter shouted from the bedroom: "Have you arrived?" Soon he was on his way to the Fort in the custody of two white policemen.

Walter was among 16 people arrested on that day, bringing the total number of treason arrestees to 156. Ahmed Kathrada and Jack Hodgson, were arrested in the same swoop. Rusty Bernstein, whose wife Hilda was still in the maternity home, having just given birth to a son, was also picked up. Joe Slovo, who had already become part of the defence team for the treason accused, became an accused himself when he and his wife Ruth First were arrested in the early hours of the same morning (Slovo, 94). Joe, Rusty and Jack joined the 20 or so white men in their section of the Fort, while Ruth was taken to join the other white women.

Walter found that his colleagues had been divided into two groups, each occupying a large communal cell. He was placed with other senior leaders. The prisoners had already organised themselves into political committees. Luthuli likened it to a "Joint Executive of the Congresses" and Mandela called it "the largest and longest unbanned meeting of the Congress Alliance in years" (Luthuli, 148; Mandela, 187). Their programme of activities also included physical training, debates, indoor games and talks on a variety of subjects, including the history of the ANC and the SAIC, and religious services as well. They had also formed the Accused Male Voices choir, the star of which was the Eastern Cape trade unionist Vuyisile Mini, who entertained them with his extraordinary bass voice.

Walter was encouraged to learn that the Bishop of Johannesburg, Ambrose Reeves, was organising a fund to cover their legal costs. On receiving news of the arrests, Canon John Collins, the founder of the London-based organisation, Christian Action, had immediately guaranteed legal costs and support for the 156 accused and their families (Collins, 202; *Observer*, Review, 5/5/91). Walter had met Canon Collins during the latter's visit to South Africa in 1954. He had great respect and admiration for the man who had raised money for the legal expenses of volunteers during the Defiance Campaign. Canon Collins rose to the occasion once again, and the Treason Trial Defence Fund ensured the setting up of a defence team that included some of the greatest lawyers to grace South African courts – the likes of Israel Maisels, Sidney Kentridge, Vernon Berrange, Harold Nicholas, Bram Fischer and Joe Slovo, who defended himself.

The accused made their first appearance in court on 19 December 1956 for the start of the preparatory examination that would determine whether the charges were sufficient to commit them to trial. Because there was no existing court large enough to accommodate 156 accused, the old army Drill Hall in downtown Johannesburg's Twist Street was hastily transformed into a makeshift courtroom. As they were driven to the courtroom in the police *kwela* vans, the accused could hear the cheers of hundreds of supporters who had lined the streets to the Drill Hall. There had been a huge response to the treason arrests, and "We Stand by Our Leaders" committees had sprung up all over the country. Outside the Drill Hall, thousands of placard-carrying supporters had started arriving at the crack of dawn in a huge show of support for the arrested leaders.

The scene in the improvised courtroom was chaotic, as the accused were united with delighted family members and friends. Once everyone was seated and the proceedings finally got under way, no one could hear what the magistrate was saying; there were no loudspeakers and the acoustics in the cavernous Drill Hall were disastrous. The proceedings became even more farcical the next day, when the accused arrived in court to the extraordinary spectacle of a huge wire cage that had been constructed to accommodate them. The defence lawyers were furious, and objected in the strongest possible terms to their clients being "caged like wild beasts". They threatened to walk out if the cage was not removed forthwith. To add to the drama, proceedings were brought to a halt by the sound of gunfire outside, as police clashed with supporters, resulting in 22 people being injured. The next day, over 500 police surrounded the Drill Hall.

The cage was dismantled over the next few days as the 18 000-word indictment was read out. The accused were charged with conspiracy to overthrow the state by violence and establish a Communist state in its place. The high treason charge was based on statements and speeches made since the Defiance Campaign up till the Congress of the People. The Freedom Charter was cited as both proof of their Communist intentions and evidence of their plot to overthrow the government (Mandela, 190; Sampson 2000, 105). The Treason Trial Fund covered the costs of bail, which was granted on 21 December. With typical apartheid logic, bail was racially differentiated, being fixed at £250 for Europeans, £100 for Indians and £50 for Africans and coloureds.

The accused were nevertheless able to go home, relieved that they would be spending Christmas with their families. Rusty Bernstein was able to go and bond with his baby son Keith, the "Treason Trial" baby. Oliver Tambo arrived home just in time for his wedding. Sadly, Nelson Mandela returned to an empty home. His marriage to Evelyn, which had been strained for some time, had finally ended in separation. Evelyn had confided her troubles to Albertina, who tried to console her as best she could. Walter tried to talk to his friend, but in Mandela's words: "I was very short with him, telling him it was none of his business. I regretted the tone I took because Walter had always been a brother to me and his friendship and support had never faltered" (Mandela, 193). Walter and Albertina were grieved by the breakdown of the marriage of two people whom they cared for deeply.

On 9 January 1957, the Treason Trial accused were back in court for the preparatory examination, which would enable the magistrate to establish whether there was a sufficient case for the trial to go to the Supreme Court (Sampson 2000, 106). Rusty Bernstein likened the atmosphere to "that of a return to boarding school after a vacation – a sinking feeling of depression, mixed with pleasure at seeing the same old gang again" (Rusty Bernstein, 171). The camaraderie among the accused would continue to grow in the many months they would spend together. Joe Slovo pointed out the irony of the situation: "… there sat shoulder to shoulder in alphabetical order, 156 African, coloured, Indian and white political activists (a scene never before witnessed in South Africa's history) charged among other things, with the crime of creating hostility between black and white races in South Africa!" (Slovo, 94.)

"Inter-racial trust and cooperation is a difficult plant to cultivate in the poisoned soil outside," noted Rusty Bernstein. "It is somewhat easier here where racial discrimination and privileges have been set aside and the leaders of all ethnic factions of the movement are together and explore each other's doubts and reservations, and speak about them without constraint. Co-existence in the Drill Hall deepens and re-creates their relationships" (Rusty Bernstein, 179). Walter agreed that the Treason Trial created greater understanding between the different components of the Congress Alliance. He noted that their two weeks at the Fort together had cemented the beginnings of firm bonds of friendship between Chief Luthuli and the Indian Congress leaders, especially Monty Naicker.

The trial also allowed for more interaction between those with different ideological outlooks. Walter noticed that during the course of the trial, the Chief and Moses Kotane had become very close. Walter was surprised when the Chief confessed to him one day: "I am not a Communist, but if Kotane ever asked me to join the party, I wonder what I would do" (Bunting 1998, 239). Walter also believed that the trial fostered inter-generational cooperation by bringing together such a large number of activists of all ages. Walter, who was 45 at the time, added a great deal to what he already knew about ANC history through his interaction with veterans like Rev. Calata.

The forcible bringing together of the Congress Alliance leadership had another great advantage. Walter's view was that: "the government wanted to immobilise us and put us out of action. Instead, in some ways, we were able to do more political work than before when we had to worry about problems of communication. We were all in one place and were able to plan strategy and tactics together." Because they were concentrated in one place, the leaders also became more accessible to ordinary members. As Rusty Bernstein noted: "The quality of leadership is transformed. Soon everyone inside and outside the movement knows how and where to contact them without any protocol. Delegations and individuals make the journey to the Drill Hall in search of advice and assistance" (Rusty Bernstein, 178).

Among those who came to the Drill Hall looking for advice and assistance were ANC people involved in the Alexandra bus boycott. This had begun in January 1957 in protest against a one-penny increase in the bus fare to the Johannesburg city centre. It was a spontaneous mass-based movement, in which over 50 000 commuters decided they would rather walk 20 miles a day than accept yet another demand on their already meagre incomes. Local groups came together to form an Alexandra People's Transport Committee. Alfred Nzo, the ANC chairman for Alexandra, and Thomas Nkobi were part of the committee. Nzo and Nkobi regularly briefed the ANC leadership at the Drill Hall about the progress of the boycott, which soon spread to Pretoria, Port Elizabeth, East London, Uitenhage and other centres. Beyond all expectations, the Alexandra bus boycott continued for over three months, and newspapers were filled with compelling images of people trudging their daily 20 miles, while sympathetic white motorists braved police intimidation to provide lifts to the weary walkers (Sampson 1958, 210; Karis and Gerhart, 3: 276; Gish, 186). The boycott finally ended in mid-April; six weeks later, the government introduced a new Bill in Parliament, the Native Services Levy Act of 1957, which provided for a subsidy for bus fares. Anthony Sampson noted that "It was the first act of parliament in the 47 years of the union to be passed directly as a result of African pressure" (Sampson 1958, 214).

While media attention was focused on the bus boycott, a virtual war was raging, largely unnoticed, in the countryside, as government mobile units tried to impose reference books on the female population in the farming towns of the Transvaal and Orange Free State. Angry women resisted in Potchefstroom, Driefontein, Nelspruit, Bethlehem, Lichtenburg, Balfour, Wakkerstroom, Standerton and countless rural *dorps*. Protesting women were arrested and sometimes even shot and killed (Wells, 116).

In the Bafurutse reserve in the Marico District, adjoining the border with Bechuanaland (Botswana), women's protests fused with strong resistance to the Bantu Authorities Act. Chief Abraham Moiloa, already in the Native Department's bad books for refusing to sign the Bantu Authorities Act in 1956, was deposed after women in his district resisted taking out passbooks. Crowds of women, furious about the deposition of their chief, seized passbooks from the few women who had taken them out, and burned them. The government responded by unleashing a reign of terror in the area, forcing Chief Moiloa and many of the Bafurutse to flee into Bechuanaland. Father Charles Hooper, who was based in Zeerust at the time, provided a moving account of the struggles of the Bafurutse people in his book *Brief Authority* (Mbeki 1984, 114).

Rural resistance to the Bantu Authorities Act was a feature of the closing years of the 1950s. Resistance in Sekhukhuniland, Zululand and the Transkei resulted in massive state reprisals, especially where the murder of government quislings was involved. Many peasant leaders were deported, had their homes burned down, or suffered long spells of imprisonment. Some of the Treason Trialists, Gert Sibande and John Nkadimeng in particular, were in touch with the peasant organisations. A leader among farm-workers in the Eastern Transvaal, Sibande was known as the "Lion of the East". Nkadimeng has never forgotten how distressed Walter was when 11 peasants from Sekhukhuniland, including Chieftainess Madinoge Morwamoele, were sentenced to death for their part in the uprising in that area: "He said we must organise a committee to organise a good defence so that they can successfully appeal against their sentences. We used to strategise on this issue in our tea and lunch breaks during the Treason Trial" (Interview, John Nkadimeng, August 2002). The appeal was successful and the sentences of the 11 leaders were commuted to life imprisonment. Walter always regretted that the ANC did not do more to support the struggles of peasants in the rural areas.

While the ongoing drama of resistance and revolt was being played out outside the courtroom, the Treason Trial accused were sitting month after dreary month through the preparatory examination. The first few months were taken up by the incredibly monotonous process of recording 12 000 documents and entering them as evidence. This was followed by a succession of police detectives giving evidence on the Congress meetings they attended. Many of the police could barely speak English, yet they claimed to have taken notes of political speeches by Congress leaders. The results were often nonsensical. One detective, for example, quoted a Congress leader as having said in his speech: "Van Riebeeck came to South Africa with a gang of vegetables" (Sampson 1958, 23).

Some of the witnesses spun the most fantastic tales. One Solomon Ngubase, playing on white fears of the Mau Mau uprising, claimed that the ANC had started the Mau Mau movement in South Africa in 1951 before it broke out in Kenya! The same witness claimed that Walter and David Bopape had gone to Russia to get ammunition and "a certain kind of gas powder to be thrown at European areas". Vernon Berrange had no trouble exposing the witness as a thief and a fraudster in cross-examination (Sampson 1958, 33).

About four months into the preparatory examination, the State trotted out its "expert" on Communism, Professor Andrew Murray, head of the Department of Political Science at the University of Cape Town. His performance under cross-examination was laughable; defence lawyer Berrange read passages from books and then asked Murray to label them Communist in spirit or origin or not. One of the passages Murray labelled as Communist turned out to have been written by Abraham Lincoln; another which Murray described as "straight from the shoulder communism" turned out to have been written in the 1930s by Murray himself (Mandela, 197).

As the proceedings dragged on with no end in sight, the accused began to feel the strain, especially those who came from outside Johannesburg. They had to endure enforced periods of separation from their families. At one stage, Joe Slovo complained: "We could be here ... for the rest of our lives" (Sampson 1958, 34). Finally, on 11 September, the prosecutor announced that the State's case in the preparatory examination had been completed. The magistrate gave the defence four months to prepare its case, involving sifting through 12 000 documents and 8 000 pages of typed evidence, and the court adjourned until January 1958 (Mandela, 198).

The adjournment came just in time for Walter, because on 9 October 1957, he and Albertina celebrated the birth of another daughter. They named her Nonkululeko (Mother of Freedom). Since she was born in the year that the Russians launched Sputnik, the first human-made satellite to orbit the earth, Walter also gave the new baby the nickname Sputnik.

During the adjournment, the Attorney-General announced that charges would be dropped against 65 of the accused. Chief Luthuli and Oliver Tambo were among those against whom charges were dropped.

In January 1958, the remaining 91 treason accused were back in court and the preparatory examination finally ended on 10 January. The State signalled how seriously it was taking the case when the pro-Nazi, anti-Communist Oswald Pirow was brought out of semi-retirement to head the prosecution. Pirow, a known admirer of Adolf Hitler, was better known as former Minister of Justice in the Hertzog government than as a lawyer (Karis and Gerhart, 3: 365; Rusty Bernstein, 183). Unlike some of his co-accused, who were deeply concerned about Pirow's appointment, Walter was not too concerned. He felt that the State was making little headway, and it was too late for Pirow to salvage the situation.

After 13 months of preparatory examination, the magistrate found that he had sufficient reason for putting the accused on trial in the Transvaal Supreme Court for high treason (Mandela, 198). The court adjourned in the same month and the accused went home to pick up the threads of their lives and gird themselves for the next round of the battle.

During this period, Walter appreciated more than ever before the moral and material support he received from Albertina and his mother, Alice Manse or Gogo as everyone now called her. He had witnessed the havoc the protracted trial had caused in the personal lives of many of his co-accused, and he valued the harmony in his household. He counted himself especially fortunate that his wife and his mother got on so well and were completely united in their unstinting support for his political work.

The only cloud on Walter's domestic horizon was the situation of his sister Barbie, who had enjoyed professional success, and was highly respected by the community of Noordgesig, where she was in charge of the clinic. However, Barbie had not experienced the marital harmony that her brother so enjoyed. Her marriage to Tilly Lockman had ended when Beryl was barely two years' old. Her second marriage to Lester Smith was equally unhappy, and a source of much pain to those closest to her. Beryl recalled that "Tata [Walter] and my mother had a very close relationship, but I saw even as a child that he and Mama [Albertina] were very much against this marriage of hers, and felt sad that she was going through so much suffering" (Interview, Beryl Simelane 1998). As a result of the unhappiness in their mother's home, Gerald and Beryl were very much part of the Sisulu household, and spent more time at No. 7372 Orlando West than they did at Noordgesig.

Since Walter was banned and could not attend gatherings, he had to stay at home during the Treason Trial adjournments. This was a bonus for the children, who loved having their father at home. His children remember him as a nurturing father who would bath and dress them. Albertina was extremely strict about the children taking responsibility for household chores, regardless of gender, and Walter supported her to the hilt in this regard. Lungi remembers his father saying to them: "You children, hurry up and clean the house before your mother comes home." Max recalls that it was Walter who taught them how to polish floors to a high shine.

Lungi particularly enjoyed reading the newspapers to his father: "When he came home very tired, he would say 'Just read to me please'. I would then go through the paper. When there were words I pronounced wrongly, he would correct me. My reading improved tremendously. He also helped my general knowledge. For example, I knew all about the happenings in the rest of Africa because Tata followed those events closely" (Interview, Mlungisi Sisulu, November 1998).

One weekend during a Treason Trial adjournment, Albertina and the younger children went to pay a family visit, Gogo was in Noordgesig with Barbie, and unusually for the Sisulu home, there were no relatives or friends staying over. Max was very pleased, as it was a rare treat to have his father all to himself. One day they agreed that Walter would go out to buy some meat and Max would do the cooking. "I waited and waited and he didn't come back. Eventually Duma Nokwe came to tell me that he was arrested. So there I was alone, with no meat and no Tata" (Interview, Max Sisulu, April 1995). Walter had been arrested for a pass offence, but all ended well when Duma secured his release the next day. Max, however, would always begrudge the police the time lost with his father, especially in future years.

August 1958 marked the start of the Treason Trial proper. To the great dismay of the accused, the case was shifted to Pretoria, no doubt to remove the accused from their support base in Johannesburg. The shift to Pretoria was a huge inconvenience to the accused. None of them lived in Pretoria, and few had their own means of transport. This meant they had to get up extremely early each morning to catch the rickety old bus that the government had provided to transport them to and from Pretoria. Walter, Duma Nokwe and others had to make the two-and-a-half hour trek from Orlando West to Pretoria for the duration.

The change in venue was especially difficult for Mandela, who had been desperately trying to address the backlog in his joint law practice with Oliver Tambo. The absence of both Mandela and Tambo had been disastrous for the once-thriving practice. After his acquittal Oliver Tambo worked hard to revive the practice, but the damage had been done and they were suffering severe financial difficulties (Mandela, 201). The daily trips to Pretoria were a burden for Mandela for personal reasons as well. In June 1958, he married Nomzamo Winnifred Madikizela, a young social worker at Baragwanath Hospital. Winnie was an extraordinarily beautiful and vivacious young woman from Bizana in Pondoland, adjacent to Mandela's home area in the Transkei (Mandela, 199). At their wedding in Bizana, which Walter was unable to attend because of his banning orders, Winnie's father warned her in his speech that she was marrying a man who was already married to the struggle (Mandela, 201).

In Pretoria, the trial was held in the Old Synagogue, a disused synagogue that had been converted into a Special Criminal Court. "Appropriately enough," wrote Joe Slovo, "the judges [Rumpff, Bekker and Kennedy] sat where the Torah [law scrolls] would have been kept and the accused faced them as they would have done had they been taking part in a religious service" (Slovo, 102).

The defence team was augmented by the brilliant Israel Maisels and Bram Fischer. Maisels immediately argued for the judges to recuse themselves. Justice Ludorf, who had been assigned to the case originally, agreed with the defence position and recused himself, but Justice Rumpff declined to do so. Walter was quite satisfied with the outcome. He remembered Judge Rumpff from their Defiance Campaign case in 1952, and thought he was about as fair a judge as they would get in the apartheid judicial system. Mandela believed that Judge Rumpff wanted a conviction but was "too brilliant a judge to commit a disgrace" (Sampson 2000, 122).

After a long legal argument by the defence attacking the vaguely worded indictment, the prosecution suddenly withdrew the indictment in October 1958, and replaced it a month later. The new shorter indictment left 61 of the accused to be tried at a later date and was directed at 30 people who were considered guilty of particularly revolutionary or violent incitement (Sampson 2000, 123). Walter and Mandela were among the 30 "first liners". The decision on whether to try the other 61 would depend on whether the first 30 were convicted or acquitted.

The actual trial of the 30 remaining accused finally commenced at the Old Synagogue in August 1959. They were formally arraigned and pleaded not guilty. The prosecution argued that the essence of the crime of high treason was "hostile intent". Such intent was evident in the demands of the accused for complete equality. To achieve the demands of the Freedom Charter in their lifetime would inevitably result in a violent collision with the state (Meredith, 169).

During the next two months, the Crown entered some 2 000 documents into the record and called more than 200 witnesses, most of them from the Special Branch. Once again, the defence team exposed the unreliable nature of their evidence. The state case suffered a severe setback when the chief prosecutor, Oswald Pirow, died of a stroke on 11 October 1959 (Mandela, 220). In the same month, the accused mourned the death of one of their number, Lionel Foreman, the brilliant young lawyer and journalist who had been one of the 61 whose indictment had been withdrawn. He had provided an account of the arrests and the preparatory stages of the trial in a book co-authored with ES Sachs entitled *The South African Treason Trial*. In March 1960, they would lose another fellow accused, Ida Mntwana, the veteran women's leader and first national president of FEDSAW.

After Pirow's death, Professor Murray was brought out once again as an expert witness on Communism. He was no more successful than on the previous occasion, when Berrange had humiliated him. Maisel's ruthless cross-examination forced him to concede that the Freedom Charter was not a "Communist document", but a response by black people to the injustices of white supremacy (Meredith, 171–2).

The prospects for the accused seemed brighter after Murray's evidence, but in January 1960, the prosecution produced a speech by Robert Resha, secretly recorded by the security police, made to a group of Freedom Volunteers during the Congress of the People campaign in 1956. In his speech, Resha had urged the volunteers to do as they were told by the organisation. If the organisation told them not to be violent, then they were to obey, but if they were called on to be violent, then "you must be absolutely violent, you must murder! Murder! That is all." The damage seemed considerable, but through cross-examination of its witnesses, the defence managed to show that Resha's speech was taken out of context and did not represent ANC policy (Mandela, 221). However, by the time this occurred, the trial would be completely overtaken by external events.

By mid-1958, the government mobile units issuing reference books, which had invoked such resistance in the rural areas, were approaching Johannesburg. Black nurses were already seething with rage at a new directive to the South African Nursing Council demanding identity numbers for all nurses and student nurses. The directive was communicated to hospitals throughout the country by the Nursing Council in Pretoria. Nurses immediately realised that these identity numbers were linked to passbooks, and organised a demonstration at Baragwanath Hospital. The delegation met with the hospital authorities and pointed out that the "identity number" that the Nursing Council had asked them to demand from nurses meant that nurses would have to carry passes. They warned that forcing nurses to carry passes would have a disastrous effect on the whole administration of hospitals and clinics. Soon thereafter, the Nursing Council dropped this demand (Resha, 120).

On 21 October, Maggie Resha, who was part of the nurses' protest, led a demonstration of over 1 000 women from Freedom Square in Sophiatown to protest against the ongoing removals from Sophiatown. Hundreds of women were arrested. Women in Alexandra also demonstrated against passes. After three days of demonstrations at the Central Pass office, there were over 2 000 women in jail. Among them were Albertina Sisulu and Winnie Mandela, who had been part of a demonstration organised by the ANC Women's League in Orlando.

Albertina, Winnie, June Mlangeni, Greta Ncapayi and others from Orlando were among the 1 200 women who were taken to the Fort, where they found women crammed like sardines in filthy cells. As she tried to find some space to sit down, Albertina noticed Winnie kneeling on the cold cement floor, her head in her hands. She appeared to be in some distress. Albertina asked her what was wrong and Winnie responded that she thought she was miscarrying. Albertina's midwifing instincts took over, and she immediately got the other women to make enough space to enable Winnie to lie down. She took off her overcoat, covered Winnie and tried to nurse her as best she could. The miscarriage was averted and the baby saved, although Winnie had to endure two miserable weeks in prison (Harrison, 65).

So intense was the resistance to passes that many women were prepared to stay in jail without paying any bail or fine. FEDSAW leaders Helen Joseph and Lilian Ngoyi found themselves at odds with men in the ANC on this issue. In Helen Joseph's words:

> Women were determined to serve their full sentences but their husbands wanted them to come out because of the care of their homes and their children. The ANC did not believe the women could sustain a period in jail because they were not trained for it, but the Women's League and Fedsaw had confidence in the women, despite the spontaneous nature of the protests. However, the ANC asserted its authority at a special meeting with Lilian and me and we had to obey. We were disappointed and a little angry at first but we were a part of the whole liberation struggle. There was no room for any rebellious spirit on our parts and there was none. Bail and fines were paid and the women returned to their homes (Joseph 1986, 69–70).

Mandela gives a different account of the disagreement. He maintained that he asked Lilian to consult the women on the matter. After taking a poll of the prisoners, they found that many women "were desperate to be bailed out and had not been adequately prepared for what would await them in prison". As a compromise, Mandela suggested that the women spend a fortnight in jail, after which he would bail them out. Lilian accepted this arrangement (Mandela, 208).

Albertina felt that while some women might have been eager to get bail, their particular group was quite prepared to remain in jail. So great was her outrage against the imposition of passes that she had left one-year-old Nkuli at home. Walter was proud of her, although he was very worried about the conditions in the overcrowded prison. He made a point of taking food to the Fort every day. Mandela and Tambo had a busy few weeks arranging for bail for the women, but eventually they were all released.

The women's protests earned them increased respect within the ANC. According to Maggie Resha, there were increased demands at branch, regional and provincial gatherings for men to get rid of their passes in order to link up to the campaign by the women. "These demands led to the National Conference of the ANC in 1959, unanimously adopting a resolution to that effect. The date set by the conference was 31 March 1960" (Resha, 134).

While the Treason Trial had cemented the Congress Alliance, it had widened the rift between the Africanists and the ANC leadership. The Africanist voice in the ANC had become more strident each year, especially in the Transvaal.

After years of bitter conflict and acrimony, matters finally came to a head at a special conference held to elect a new executive in November 1958. Prevented from entering the conference, the Africanists decided to branch out on their own. In April 1959, the Pan Africanist Congress (PAC) declared its existence to the world at a three-day inaugural conference in Orlando. Former ANC Youth League member Robert Sobukwe was elected president and Potlako Leballo was elected national secretary.

As much as he valued unity within the ANC, Walter felt that the break was inevitable. In an article entitled "Congress and the Africanists" in *Africa South* (July–September 1959), Walter analysed the split:

> In recent months much has been published in the South African press about the 'Africanists' and their attempt to capture the leadership of the African National Congress. The struggle reached a climax at the Transvaal Provincial Conference of the ANC ... on 1st and 2nd November 1958. The Africanists attempted to 'pack' the conference, but most of their supporters failed to qualify as delegates. They then tried to break up the conference by force, and when this attempt was defeated, they withdrew, announcing that they were leaving Congress and intended forming a new organisation.

Walter argued that the whole affair had been much exaggerated by the press and that in reality, the Africanists enjoyed neither significant support nor influence in the ANC. He believed their departure had strengthened, not weakened the ANC. "Their departure has greatly pleased the great majority of Congressmen, who regarded them as a noisy and disruptive clique, and who consider the talk of a 'major split' in Congress as absurd." Prophetically he predicted, "It is unlikely that the Africanists will make much progress or maintain much cohesion among themselves now that they have left Congress."

He went on to explain the difference between the Africanist outlook and that of the ANC:

> Even though the Africanists have not evolved any definite programme and policy, the general trend of their ideas is manifest: it lies in a crude appeal to African racialism as a reply to White arrogance and oppression. The principal target of their attacks is the broad humanism of the African National Congress, which claims equality but not domination for the African people, and regards South Africa as being big enough and rich enough to sustain all its people, of whatever origin, in friendship and peace.
>
> In their letter of secession from the ANC, they declare that 'the Kliptown Charter' is 'in irreconcilable conflict' with the 1949 Congress 'Programme of Action', seeing that it [the Freedom Charter] claims that the land no longer belongs to the African people but is 'auctioned for sale to all who belong to this country'. Leaving aside the inflated polemical language of this statement ..., the intention is clear: it is a denial that any section of the population other than the descendants of indigenous Africans have any rights in the country whatsoever.

Referring to the statement "In 1949 we got the African people to accept the nation-building pro-gramme of that year", Walter responded by invoking a bit of history: "Actually the 1949 Programme of Action was a regular Congress document, adopted at a national conference on the initiative of the Congress leadership and issued under the signature of the present writer. Only one or two of the Africanists had any hand in it."

Walter defended the Freedom Charter as being in a direct line of succession to the 1949 Programme of Action and the African Claims of 1943 and "many statements of Congress policy and principle over the years". He argued that "while ANC policy has naturally evolved down the years, in changing circumstances at home and abroad, becoming more detailed and clearer in for-mulation, it has retained throughout a fundamental continuity and consistency which is striking and remarkable". The ANC he said, repudiated the idea of "driving the White man into the sea" as futile and reactionary and it had "consistently sought the cooperation of other political groups and other races, of religious, liberal and leftist groups and organisations, in its struggle for free-dom and equality."

Walter argued that the Congress policy of anti-racialism enjoyed the support of the over-whelming majority of Congress membership and gave the ANC the moral high ground in its struggle against white domination:

> Nothing has brought greater credit to the ANC in the eyes of Africa and the world than its stead-fast refusal to respond to the vicious persecution of the Nationalists and their predecessors in the Union Government by a blind and irrational 'anti-Whiteism'. It has shown the African people to be larger-minded than, and morally superior to their oppressors; it strikingly refutes the ri-diculous claims of 'White South Africa' about alleged African 'immaturity' and 'unreadiness for self-government'.

Walter then referred to the decision that had been taken at the National Workers' Conference in 1958 – that the ANC and other Congresses hold an anti-election strike against the whites-only general elections. He had been particularly annoyed by the Africanist leaders Madzunya and Leballo, who had campaigned against the strike. By doing so, he felt that they had sided with the forces of oppression against the ANC. "Congress is a broad and tolerant organisation, firmly wedded to democratic principle and refusing to impose any single ideology on its members. But, at the same time, the ANC is not merely a debating society, and cannot tolerate open sabotage of its struggle. The National Executive promptly expelled Madzunya and Leballo for their treach-erous activities and it is notable that this action was warmly applauded by branches throughout the country."

He ended on a cautionary note:

> In a country like South Africa, where the Whites dominate everything, and where ruthless laws are ruthlessly administered and enforced, the natural tendency is one of growing hostility against Europeans. In fact most Africans come into political activity because of their indignation against Whites, and it is only through their education in Congress and their experience of the genuine com-radeship in the struggle of such organisations as the Congress of Democrats that they rise to the broad, non-racial humanism of our Congress movement.
>
> With a state policy of increasingly barbaric repression of the African people; with the deliberate destruction of every form of normal human contact between people from different population-groups; and with the systematic banning and isolation of the convinced and fervent anti-racialists among the Africans from political activity, there is no knowing what the future will hold.
>
> The Africanists have thus far failed, but their mere appearance is an urgent warning to all demo-cratic South Africans. The Africans have set a wonderful example of political wisdom and maturity to the rest of the country, but they are not perfect, any more that any other community of men

and women sorely beset. In certain circumstances, an emotional mass-appeal to destructive and exclusive nationalism can be a dynamic and irresistible force in history. We have seen in our own country how, decade after decade the Afrikaner people have followed yet more extreme and reactionary leaders. It would be foolish to imagine that a wave of black chauvinism, provoked by the savagery of the Nationalist Party may not some day sweep through our country. And if it does, the agony will know no colour-bar at all.

*The winds of change are sweeping across the African continent ... Oh yeah, oh yeah! Viva Africa!* The words of the bouncy Namibian freedom song by SWAPO guerrilla Jackson Kaujewa were inspired by British Prime Minister Harold McMillan's famous "wind of change" speech before the South African Parliament on 3 February 1960. In that watershed year, the winds of change were indeed blowing across the continent. Seventeen African countries were set to attain independence in 1960, which had been declared Africa Year by the United Nations.

In South Africa, the new decade had opened with riots in Cato Manor near Durban; and in Pondoland, resistance against the imposition of Bantu authorities broke out into open rebellion in February (Karis and Carter, 3: 330). Increasingly fierce resistance to apartheid and the heady progress of decolonisation in the rest of Africa fuelled the optimistic sense that freedom was just around the corner. Such a dream seemed not inconceivable at that heady moment. The PAC trumpeted its anti-pass campaign as the first step towards freedom and independence by 1963.

It was not to be. The Sharpeville massacre and the brutal repression in its aftermath cruelly demonstrated the unrealistic nature of such hopes. The very first day of the PAC's anti-pass campaign – 21 March 1960 – ended in tragedy when police fired on thousands of anti-pass demonstrators, killing 69 people and wounding 186. The chain of events that followed the shootings was to alter South Africa's political landscape irrevocably. The winds of change had indeed blown in South Africa; but they had blown backwards.

The day began quietly enough. In Orlando West, the trundling Treason Bus had just picked up Walter and his fellow trialists for the journey to Pretoria, when they saw Sobukwe and a small group of followers making their way towards Orlando Police Station to present themselves for arrest. Walter could not help feeling a flash of irritation. The ANC had been annoyed by Sobukwe's announcement that the PAC campaign would begin on 21 March. Walter felt that this was an opportunistic attempt to steal the thunder from the ANC campaign scheduled for the end of March. The PAC's eleventh-hour invitation to the ANC to join forces with them had been declined by Duma Nokwe, who wrote that the ANC was "unwilling to support action which had not been properly prepared for and which had no reasonable chance of success" (Karis and Carter, 3: 331–2).

At the trial, Chief Luthuli was in the witness box, giving evidence for the defence on the ANC's commitment to nonviolence (Mandela, 222). During proceedings, the disturbing news of a massacre began to trickle in and the alarmed trialists felt the first intimations of the grief and outrage that would shake the nation.

That evening, in the funereal atmosphere that prevailed in Soweto, Walter and Albertina discussed the tragedy. Albertina had heard details of the casualties through her nursing contacts. Those who had seen the dead and tended to the wounded were horrified by the extent of their injuries. The fact that the wounded in hospital were placed under arrest added to the general sense of outrage. Albertina was stunned. "For people to be massacred in a peaceful protest, for women and children to be shot in their backs, was just too much to bear."

Despite his frustration at the PAC's ill-planned and ill-fated campaign, Walter could not fail to be stirred by the emotional song "Vukani Mawethu", which Johannes Nkosi played over and over again on Msakazo Radio to mark the tragedy. The song exhorted black people to wake up and unite, "the fault is with us because we are not united."

Nkosi was fired from the state-controlled radio for suspending all programmes to play the dirge-like song, but his actions were applauded by his community. Walter recalls: "The effect was powerful. I was deeply moved."

Later that night, Walter met with Mandela, Duma Nokwe and Joe Slovo to work out a response to the tragedy. They decided on a countrywide strike, after which they consulted Chief Luthuli, who agreed with their proposal (Mandela, 226). On 24th March, Chief Luthuli declared that Monday, 28 March would be a day of protest and mourning marked by a nation-wide stay-at-home. The PAC came out in support of his call.

The killings precipitated an unprecedented outpouring of grief and defiance, with the most dramatic response in Cape Town. Beatings and harassment by the police failed to prevent striking workers from bringing the cities' key industries to a standstill. To contain the situation, the government announced a temporary relaxation of the pass laws, and Chief Luthuli publicly burnt his pass on 27th March. Walter, Nelson Mandela and Duma Nokwe were among the thousands who followed his example when they burnt their passes in Orlando West.

The National Day of Mourning on 28th March turned out to be the biggest strike in the country's history. Shaken by the scale of the protest, the government had already announced that it would legislate to ban the ANC and PAC if the need arose (Pogrund, 139). The ANC had long decided that in event of a ban, a senior member of the organisation should be sent to represent the country abroad. Walter had suggested Oliver Tambo as the ideal candidate. Immediately after the government announced its intentions, Tambo hastily left Cape Town, where he was attending a meeting. The next day, he crossed the border to Bechuanaland, thus beginning his 32 years in exile.

On the Day of Mourning, the Unlawful Organisations Bill was introduced to enable the government to ban the ANC and PAC. On 29 March, Walter attended a NEC meeting where it was decided that if the ANC was banned, the organisation should issue a statement saying that it would go underground. Govan Mbeki was especially summoned to attend the meeting and asked to undertake the organisation of the ANC in the Eastern Cape.

On 30 March, virtually all known activists were arrested in pre-dawn swoops around the country. Some of those arrested had not been politically active for many years. In total, nearly 2 000 people were arrested under section 4 of the Emergency Regulations.

Walter was one of those arrested and taken to Newlands Police Station in Johannesburg. Mandela, Duma Nokwe and most of the other trialists were also taken to Newlands. They were held all day, with no food or water, in filthy, bug-infested cells. That evening they were called one by one to the front yard of the police station, where they were "released" for a few seconds, then re-arrested under new Emergency regulations. This was when they first learned that the government had declared a State of Emergency.

In Cape Town, on the same day, PAC leaders were arrested when police descended on Nyanga and Langa in the early hours of the morning. In Langa, workers in a migrant labour hostel were dragged from their beds and assaulted by police. Albertina's brother, Reverend Elliot Thethiwe, who was the minister of the Langa Presbyterian Church, rushed to open the doors of the church to enable those fleeing to seek refuge.

News of the police invasion spread like wildfire and groups of workers marched the 10-kilometre route to the city centre, their numbers swelling to 30 000 by the time they reached Caledon Square. Leading the march was Philip Kgosana, the young PAC regional secretary. In a dramatic moment, unparalleled in the history of the country, the young leader, clad in schoolboy shorts and backed by a crowd of tens of thousands, confronted the police in the heart of the white city.

The police promised Kgosana that the Minister of Justice would meet him later that day, on condition he asked the crowd to disperse. If any single event demonstrated the nonviolent nature of black resistance, it was that one. On Kgosana's orders, "the 30 000 demonstrators turned as one and made their way home" (*Drum*, March 1961). When Kgosana and his delegation returned later that afternoon, they were told the Minister would not see them, and were promptly arrested under Emergency regulations.

The next day, police, army and navy units cordoned off Nyanga and Langa, and proceeded to beat and arrest people in house-to-house searches. This pattern of police action was repeated in townships across the country, until resistance finally began to peter out in the second week of April, by which time 21 000 people had been detained (Schadeberg 1990, 150).

On 8 April, the PAC and ANC were both banned under the newly passed Unlawful Organisations Act.

South Africa's international standing had been irrevocably damaged by the Sharpeville massacre and its aftermath. The Johannesburg stock market crashed, and there was a massive outflow of capital. Property prices plummeted as panicky whites emigrated in droves. The day after the Sharpeville tragedy, the US State Department had taken the unprecedented step of reprimanding South Africa for the deaths. On 1 April, the UN Security Council intervened in the South African situation for the first time by voting for a resolution blaming the government for the tragedy and calling on it to change its policy (Karis and Carter, 3: 336). International condemnation of the nationalist government's racist policies reached a crescendo, and international isolation became a reality. The Afrikaans newspaper *Die Burger* commented gloomily: "South Africa has become the polecat of the world."

The Treason Trial had entered its hundredth day during the tempestuous month of March 1960. The occasion was marked with a special "birthday" cake made by Mrs Thayanagee Pillay, who had provided lunches and teas for the accused throughout the trial. The prosecution finally closed its case on 10 March.

The defence began by arguing that the terms of the Emergency regulations were so broad that there was a danger that statements made by defence witnesses while giving evidence might be deemed subversive. Justice Rumpff agreed that witnesses would not be able to give evidence freely under the State of Emergency, and the trial was adjourned until Tuesday, 19 April.

Walter and his fellow accused were taken to prison in Pretoria, where they were held for the duration of their detention. They realised that the trial was now taking place under vastly different political circumstances. On the eve of the banning of the ANC and the PAC, Duma Nokwe had commented bitterly to Helen Joseph: "This trial is out of date." His words echoed the sentiments of most of the accused. After Sharpeville, the trial had become a relic from a past era in a struggle that had been completely overtaken by events outside the courtroom (Joseph 1963, 21; Hilda Bernstein 1989, 20). Walter and his comrades also realised that they faced a long spell in jail. They would certainly not be at home for Easter.

In prison, the detainees encountered gross racial discrimination in their living conditions. The black prisoners' quarters were grim in the extreme, while the whites felt pain that they were held, according to Joe Slovo, in "our white men's prison palace with … all the mod cons usually advertised in the 'To Let' columns" (Slovo, 139). The detainees fought a running battle with the authorities over the poor conditions. These improved slightly when they threatened to take their complaints to court (Mandela, 289).

The detention of the accused had a detrimental impact on the progress of the trial. The Johannesburg lawyers sometimes drove all the way to Pretoria, only to be denied access to their clients. Consultations that were permitted were hurried and unsatisfactory. On 25 April, the defence team proposed that they withdraw from the case in protest against the Emergency, a plan the accused supported (Mandela, 296). In court the next day, Duma Nokwe described the practical difficulties in consultation that had arisen as a result of the Emergency regulations. He then made the dramatic announcement that the accused were instructing the defence counsel to withdraw. The visibly shocked judge warned the accused of the dangers of conducting their own defence, but they remained adamant. From then on, Duma Nokwe and Nelson Mandela conducted the defence.

They had worked out a strategy to drag out the case until the Emergency was lifted and the defence team could return. This entailed each of the accused conducting their own defence and calling on all 28 co-accused as witnesses. After lengthy negotiations, the prison authorities conceded to their request to be allowed to have consultations to prepare their defence. This request had presented the authorities with a quandary, because prison regulations forbade contact between prisoners of different races and gender. In a major concession, the authorities allowed Helen Joseph, Lilian Ngoyi, Leon Levy and Bertha Mashaba to be transported to the African men's prison for consultation.

The efforts to maintain apartheid in the same room resulted in the ludicrous situation described by Nelson Mandela: "The authorities erected an iron grille to separate Helen and Leon (as whites) from us and a second partition to separate them from Lilian and Bertha (as African women) ... Even a master architect would have had trouble designing such a structure" (Mandela, 293).

The accused, who found it laughable to be elaborately separated from one another in prison while they were allowed to mingle freely in court, remedied the situation by removing the metal barrier. The ensuing consultations were very important for their morale. Helen Joseph described the experience of preparing the evidence with Farid Adams, Mandela, Duma Nokwe and Walter: "They helped me to clarify things and although they often suggested variations in the emphasis, they always left the final decision to me, for it had to be my own statement. It was a unique, bizarre way to learn political history, but who ever had such illustrious tutors?"

In May, Walter and his co-accused in the men's section, heard from Helen Joseph that the group of 21 left-wing white women who had been detained under the Emergency wanted to go on a hunger strike. The men were not in favour of this, as they felt the main purpose of a hunger strike was to get publicity, which would not be possible under the Emergency conditions. Despite their reservations, it was decided to show solidarity with the women by staging a three-day hunger strike. The women meanwhile voted for an indefinite strike and held out for eight days, relenting only when a medical specialist warned them that they risked permanent injury. Walter admired the courage of these women, and felt that their militancy had put the menfolk to shame.

The husbands of seven of the women had also been detained, leaving 19 children without parents. Among them were Toni Bernstein, Barbara Harmel, Ilse Fischer and Mark Weinberg, who mobilised the rest to protest against the detentions. In the tradition of their parents, the children, together with 12-year-old Lungi Sisulu and 11-year-old Beryl, demonstrated on the steps of Johannesburg City Hall, carrying placards demanding the release of their parents. They were arrested and taken to Marshall Square. After several hours, Ilse telephoned her father Bram, who came to their rescue. He told Ilse that they should have stuck it out a little longer to see how the police would have handled the matter. Lungi and Beryl went home after their first taste of police custody, very proud of the many newspaper reports on the incident (Interview, Toni Strasburg 1992; Interview, Ilse Fischer 2002).

On 31 May, the government began releasing detainees, leading to speculation that the Emergency was about to end. The Treason Trialists accused recalled their defence, believing that their release was imminent, but they remained in prison for months.

On 5 August, they wrote to the Minister of Justice, pointing out that no formal charge had been laid against them during their four months in detention, and demanding their immediate and unconditional release (Joseph 163, 107).

There was no response to their letter and the trialists were among the 400 detainees who were not released until the end of the Emergency on 31 August. That day, the trialists were able to walk out of court and make their way home amid much celebration. The next day they returned to court, still glowing from the joy of homecoming, only to learn that the Crown had ordered their re-arrest on a technical matter regarding bail. The defence lawyers angrily opposed this and won, and the trialists resumed their daily journey between court and home.

Walter recalls that after their release from prison, people were extremely jittery. "At one of our meetings, the guards who were keeping watch noticed police in the vicinity. There was a panic, as people started jumping fences, probably to the great astonishment of the passers-by. JB Marks and I toppled over a fence. Ben Turok moved so fast he was not seen again! Bram and JB were conspicuous fleeing in their white shirts! But Moses [Kotane] was cool and calm. He never ran, neither did Ruth. This was the effect of having just been released from prison. We did not want to go back!"

During their five months in prison, the ANC leaders devoted considerable time to the question of how the organisation should continue the struggle underground. "Our discussions usually centred on the question of armed struggle," recalls Walter. "We were divided on this issue. Some people felt that since they were in jail anyway, for nonviolent protest, they might as well go to prison for something more tangible" (Walter Sisulu, Notes for prison memoir, 123).

Once the Emergency had been lifted, the NEC met secretly in September to begin the reorganisation of the ANC.

On coming out of prison, Walter had been surprised to learn that ANC and PAC leaders in exile had agreed to cooperate in a South African United Front. He was not comfortable with the idea because he did not see how unity between the ANC and PAC could be achieved abroad when there was no unity at home. His assessment turned out to be correct. By the end of 1961, the United Front had ceased to exist in practical terms and it was formally disbanded in March 1962.

However, during its brief existence, the United Front did score one important victory. Before and during the Commonwealth Prime Ministers' Conference in March 1961, its members lobbied successfully for the exclusion of South Africa from the Commonwealth because of the policy of apartheid. Confronted with opposition to apartheid from the majority of Commonwealth leaders, Verwoerd withdrew South Africa's request for membership.

The Treason Trial defence had closed on 7 October, after which the case was adjourned for a month. Walter and Albertina decided to use the time to take a rare holiday with their two youngest children, Lindi and Nkuli.

They spent a night in Pietermaritzburg at the home of Dr Chota Motala, a close friend of Walter's, en route to the Transkei. In Umtata, they spent the night at one of the boarding houses known as "Amakhaya". Here Walter realised that he had forgotten his hat at Dr Motala's home. He knew that if he did not wear a hat, he would be regarded as *irumsha*, an urbanite. He therefore had to fork out to buy a new hat. "We only had 15 pounds for expenses. For people visiting the Transkei, that was nothing." They then bumped into Enoch Tshunungwa, a former ANC organiser, who offered them a lift to Engcobo. After a few miles, he asked for petrol money. Walter asked Albertina for the purse, but to their horror they realised that they had left the purse back at the "Amakhaya". They rushed back to find the room already occupied and no trace of the purse.

Without a penny on them, they somehow managed to get to Walter's home village in Qutubeni. Walter was dismayed to find the Hlakula home completely impoverished. The plantation, the garden and the fruit trees were all gone. Joubert Hlakula had long since passed away, but his wife Florence was still living there. The suffering and illness they found made the fact that they had arrived penniless especially humiliating. Rural people generally believed that city folk had plenty of money, and could not believe that Walter had no money on him. Tradition also required that they buy presents and slaughter a sheep. Walter got a sheep on credit, then took a bus to Tsolo, where he borrowed money from a distant relative.

By now they were anxious to return to Johannesburg. They managed to get a lift to the home of Albertina's uncle, Campbell Mnyila, in Tsomo. As headman of the village and a member of the Bunga, Campbell was relatively well off and able to help them. They felt they had finally shaken off the ill fortune that had dogged them throughout the holiday.

One of the issues that had been raised during the prison discussions was Verwoerd's intention to hold a whites-only referendum on whether or not South Africa should break its nominal ties with Britain and become a republic. The ANC was opposed to the type of republic proposed by the government, on the basis that all people should partake in the shaping of a new constitution based on racial equality (Meli, 140). In the referendum, held on 5 October 1960, a narrow majority voted in favour of a republic, and the government decided on 31 May 1961 as the date for the proclamation of the republic.

In response, senior ANC leaders, after consultations with other political parties, resolved that there should be an "all-in" African Conference in March 1961, in Pietermaritzburg, to urge other communities in the country to support the demand that the government convene a national convention before the date of the proclamation of the republic.

As part of the preparation for the conference, Walter toured the country with Ameen Cajee, an ANC colleague. Because of Walter's ban, he could not address public meetings, so they organised small house meetings instead. Walter, Nelson and Monty Berman also travelled to Lesotho to meet Ntsu Mokhetle, leader of the Basutoland Congress Party and one of the first members of the Youth League when it was inaugurated at Fort Hare. Monty hired a car and posed as a member of the German Embassy. According to Walter, "His whole demeanour was that of a diplomat." While travelling though the Orange Free State, the car developed engine trouble. As they worked on it, some students came by. They looked at the spectacle of the black man (Mandela) standing with his hands in his pockets while the white "master" (Monty) fiddled with the car, and one of them remarked, "There are a lot of funny things going on here."

On the eve of the All-In Conference, 13 members of the organising committee were arrested and charged with publishing documents for a conference "to further the aims of the ANC". Despite the arrests, the conference went ahead as planned. Even the discovery of a bugging device in the hall where the meeting was to take place did not deter the 1 400 delegates. They simply marched through the rain to an alternative venue.

The unexpected appearance of Nelson Mandela at the conference generated intense excitement. By some oversight, his recently expired ban had not been renewed, giving him the opportunity to stand on a public platform for the first time in years. Mandela's speech and the conference resolutions called on the government to hold a truly representative national convention to work out a new nonracial democratic constitution. If the government did not meet this demand, the conference resolved to stage countrywide demonstrations on the eve of the proclamation of the republic (Karis and Carter, 3: 359; Schadeberg 1990, 163; Mandela, 306).

Three days after the Pietermaritzburg conference, the Treason Trial finally came to a close. After closing arguments, the judges asked for a six-day adjournment to study the matter, an optimistic sign for the accused. They were indeed acquitted, and the verdict sparked off jubilation and celebration around the country. Members of the defence team were carried shoulder-high out of the courtroom. Soweto was at the heart of the celebrations, where it was said that "there was a party in every home on the night of 29 March" (Joseph 1986, 101).

Walter and Albertina celebrated at a party at the home of Ruth First and Joe Slovo, but the joy of the trialists was however marred by sadness that the verdict had come too late for one of them, Elias Moretsele, the veteran ANC leader who had died suddenly on March 13.

It was ironic that the court had come to the conclusion that nonviolence was the policy of the ANC at the very time that the ANC leadership was questioning its effectiveness. At a secret meeting the day after the court adjourned, the decision was taken that if he was acquitted, Nelson Mandela would go underground (Mandela, 302).

While others celebrated the end of the trial, Mandela went into hiding in a safe house before embarking on a trip around the country to organise the anti-Republic strike. Shortly afterwards, Walter also went underground for the duration of the strike. When he was not visiting different parts of the country, he stayed in the Johannesburg apartment of Wolfie Kodesh, a member of the Congress of Democrats who worked as a reporter for *New Age*. Mandela was also hiding out at Wolfie's place, so they had the opportunity to discuss and plan all aspects of the strike.

The government's response was a massive show of intimidation, with the country placed virtually on a war footing. A new law gave the police the power to arrest and detain anyone without charge for 12 days. Almost all meetings were banned and over 10 000 people were arrested. Most alarming for township dwellers in the Witwatersrand was the invasion of military trucks carrying armed police and helicopters hovering menacingly overhead. Verwoerd warned that anyone advocating a multiracial convention would be "playing with fire" (Karis and Carter, 3: 363).

Early reports on the anti-Republic strike were not encouraging. The SABC reported that more people were going to work than staying at home. Disheartened, Mandela called off the strike. However, while the stay-at-home had not been as successful as had been expected, it certainly was not a failure. Reports from the railways and bus companies in the Witwatersrand indicated a stay-away of 60 per cent and foreign correspondents contradicted local reports of failure (Benson 1990, 128; Karis and Carter 3: 363). Taking into account the unparalleled levels of state intimidation and difficulty of organising a strike underground, Walter felt that the strike had been successful.

# *eight*

The May 1961 strike brought to a head the debate that had been raging in the ANC on the question of the armed struggle. Walter had felt for some time that revolutionary violence was the only remaining course of action for the ANC.

Walter and Nelson had discussed the possibility of armed struggle as far back as 1952. After May 1961, they were both convinced that the time had come for the ANC to adopt a policy of revolutionary violence. Apart from the fact that the ever-increasing brutality of the State made lawful political activity virtually impossible, Walter's belief that the ANC should abandon its policy of nonviolence was influenced by a number of considerations – international liberation struggles and guerrilla warfare elsewhere, the peasant revolt in the Transkei and the fact that other organisations were on the verge of embarking on armed struggle. There was a certain romanticism about guerrilla warfare at the time, when, as Allister Sparks put it: "a whiff of guerrilla action seemed all that was needed to roll back the forces of imperialism" (Sparks 1990, 269).

The ANC was by no means the first organisation to opt for violence. The SACP had already made this decision, and Ameen Cajee and Monty Berman both told Walter that they were joining the National Committee for Liberation (NCL). This was a small group of mainly white, middle-class activists who, impatient with the Liberal Party's commitment to nonviolent protest, embarked on a sabotage campaign in September 1961 (Lewin, 15).

Walter and Nelson decided that Mandela should propose the idea of an armed struggle at a Working Committee meeting in June 1961. Moses Kotane shot down Mandela's proposal, arguing that an armed struggle would expose innocent people to enemy fire. Mandela backed down and afterwards upbraided Walter for remaining silent instead of supporting his argument. "He [Walter] laughed and said it would have been as foolish as attempting to fight a pride of angry lions" (Mandela, 34). Walter cannily arranged for Mandela and Kotane to meet privately to thrash out the matter, after which Kotane suggested that Mandela raise the matter at the next Working Committee meeting. "This time, Moses was silent and the general consensus was that I should make the proposal to the National Executive in Durban. Walter simply smiled" (Mandela, 321).

At the NEC meeting in Durban, Mandela argued that as violence was inevitable, whether the ANC wanted it or not, the ANC should take the initiative in setting principles of attacking symbols of oppression, not people. Chief Luthuli hated the idea of violence and it took a whole night of discussion to get him to even consider it. Finally, the Chief suggested a compromise. It was agreed that it would not be correct for the leadership to embark on violence when the masses had joined the ANC on the understanding that its policy was one of nonviolence. Thus, the ANC would not oppose the formation of a military organisation, but it would not endorse it either. In other words, such a military organisation, although linked to the ANC and under ANC discipline and overall control, would be autonomous (Mandela, 322).

Even after this exhaustive discussion, Chief Luthuli was not entirely convinced. The next day, at the Joint Executive meeting of the Congress Alliance, instead of putting forward the agreement of the previous night, the Chief said the matter was such a serious one that it should be discussed afresh (Mandela, 323). They were back to square one, and once again the debate raged all night.

Finally they reached a resolution, and, in a historic decision that was to alter all their lives dramatically, Mandela was given the mandate to form a new military organisation that would not be under the direct control of the ANC, which was to maintain its policy of nonviolence (Mandela, 323).

The new organisation, Umkhonto we Sizwe (Spear of the Nation) (MK) was formed, with Mandela as chairman and Walter as political commissar. Govan Mbeki, Joe Slovo, Andrew Mlangeni and Raymond Mhlaba were also recruited to the original High Command. Walter was involved in laying down the basic organisational framework of MK, which consisted of the National High Command, Regional Commands, Local Commands and cells.

On 23 October 1961, it was announced that Chief Luthuli had been awarded the Nobel Peace Prize. This was not only a great honour to the Chief; it was also a diplomatic coup for the ANC and a slap in the face of the Verwoerd regime. Duma Nokwe and Walter enlisted the aid of Mary Benson to help the Chief deal with the throngs of journalists and the deluge of mail which he had received from all over the world (Benson 1990, 132). The Chief gave his Nobel Peace Prize address in Stockholm on December 11.

Umkhonto we Sizwe was launched on 16 December, the anniversary of the Battle of Blood River in 1838, when a handful of Boers had defeated a horde of Zulu warriors. The timing was significant. This was the Day of the Covenant, when the Afrikaners celebrated white supremacy. That MK attacks took place on this day was a direct challenge to that supremacy. Nevertheless, there were complaints that it was inappropriate for MK to emerge just after Chief Luthuli had received the Nobel award. Through discussion and persuasion, Walter managed to prevail upon those who objected.

On the appointed day, a series of explosions went off at electric power stations and government offices in Port Elizabeth and Johannesburg. Posters and pamphlets announced the existence of MK, and noted that the national liberation movement had consistently followed a policy of nonviolence in the face of persecution by the government.

White South Africa responded to the announcement of MK's sabotage campaign with horror, and the government made clear its intention to smash the new organisation. The general response within the ANC circles was one of jubilation, especially among the youth.

However, Ben Ramotse had been seriously injured and Petrus Molefe killed when a bomb they were trying to detonate exploded prematurely, news that deeply disturbed Walter. At a meeting to review the launch of MK, Chief Luthuli was clearly embarrassed about the timing and unhappy about the apparent recklessness that led to the casualties.

Another leader was even more critical, and depicted Walter as wild and unsuited to the responsibilities he was shouldering. The suggestion was made that the Joint Executives of the Congress Alliance should control MK activities, but the MK leadership felt that the organisation needed to have independence of action. Eventually, it was agreed that the Communist Party and the ANC were to assume joint authority of MK.

Organisational problems in MK were to be expected. The leadership was operating under the most trying of circumstances, as police surveillance and harassment of political leaders intensified. While Walter was underground, police raided the Sisulu home several times and police spies were placed to watch the house around the clock.

The raids continued after Walter returned home. "The police were a regular feature at home," recalls Max. "They used to come every day ... Tata would ask Mama to make tea for them. While they were having their tea, Tata would slip me some documents to take to the neighbour's yard. Eventually in anticipation of raids, we put some documents in plastic bags and buried them." For as long as the Sisulu children could remember, their father was in and out of jail, but at least during the 1950s he had been able to spend some time with them at home. But by 1961, "We saw less and less of Tata and the police [took more and more]," according to Max.

Apart from the raids, the Special Branch followed Walter everywhere, especially Sergeant Dirker, who hovered around Walter like some malevolent spirit. Dirker took every opportunity he could to harass and humiliate Walter. One day, Walter bumped into Michael Harmel outside the office of

*New Age*. As they stood talking, Dirker and another detective appeared, and demanded to see Walter's pass. Dirker then insisted on seeing the contents of an envelope Harmel was carrying. Harmel asked him if he had a search warrant, and was told, "I don't need a warrant. I am looking for Communism." Dirker then confiscated the envelope and ordered the other detective to search Harmel. Walter was arrested, detained overnight, and served with a five-year banning order. He was also fined for not having a reference book.

Harmel later decided to sue Dirker, with Walter as the defence's main witness. In a rare judgment against the police, Dirker was ordered to pay 200 pounds damages to Harmel. The judge remarked that Dirker was a consistently evasive witness, while Harmel and Sisulu were both highly intelligent, calm and collected witnesses (*Spark*, 7 March 1963).

A few days after this brush with Dirker, Walter accompanied Alfred Nzo to a fundraising party at Lillian Ngoyi's home. Within minutes of their arrival, the police appeared and arrested Walter, Alfred and Lillian for breaking their bans. Charges against them were dropped, but not before they had spent three days in jail.

During 1962, Walter had the dubious distinction of being probably the most arrested political leader in the country. On returning from one of his trips around the country to consult and organise, Walter was arrested by Dirker and taken to the Johannesburg Fort, where he was put in a communal cell with about 150 other prisoners. Walter's defiance generated a lot of interest, and some long-term prisoners approached him to discuss the miserable conditions in the cell. Before he had a chance to take matters further with them, he was moved to the hospital section.

His new cell was luxurious by comparison; it was clean and there was even fresh linen on the bed. The police colonel in charge of the prison came to see Walter. "He appeared to be a decent chap … but he immediately changed his attitude when I complained that I did not want to be treated differently from the other prisoners and that I wanted to go back to the communal cell. He became sharp and told me that he had orders that I should be kept in the hospital section."

The colonel informed Walter that Ben Ramotse (the MK soldier who had been injured on December 16) was also in the hospital section. The next day, Walter met Ben in the Colonel's presence, and they were told that they could sit in a particular place and chat in privacy. Walter interpreted this as a crude attempt to eavesdrop. The Colonel made one remark that Walter found very strange: "You may be in prison today, but tomorrow you will be in the government. I am merely a servant."

That evening, someone approached Walter's door and greeted him warmly. Speaking from outside the cell, the mystery visitor told Walter that his name was Makena and that he had been working in Pretoria prison, where he had befriended both blacks and whites who had been detained under Emergency laws. When he asked after Joe Slovo, it became clear to Walter that the Special Branch, which was trying to link Walter and Joe Slovo to the recent acts of sabotage, had planted Makena there.

Makena told Walter that he could organise liquor if Walter wanted it, and even suggested that Walter could drink through the keyhole using a straw! Walter politely told him that he did not drink alcohol. Next, Walter overheard Makena talking to Ben Ramotse, encouraging him to write to his lawyer and slip the note under the door so that Makena could deliver it.

Walter was surprised and touched when Molly Fischer arrived with food for him. He had no idea how she managed to persuade the prison authorities to let her in. The next day, he was taken to a doctor and asked to complete a form giving his medical history. The following day, the doctor told him the form had been mislaid and asked him to fill in another. This form was later to be produced in court as evidence of Walter's handwriting!

After several days, Walter was taken to Marshall Square where he found himself face to face with Dirker, who told him his arrest was for a pass offence. Walter was furious. "You are a very small man to do this," he told Dirker. "I will never rest until I break your neck!" Dirker replied. A huge row ensued, to the amazement of everyone in Marshall Square. It was almost unheard of for a prisoner to quarrel with a member of the Special Branch. Walter was taken back to the Fort, and appeared in court on a charge of fraud for forging his pass. Walter used the opportunity to denounce the pass laws. On 31 January, he was found not guilty. In his judgment, the magistrate said that the court should not be influenced against Sisulu because he disliked pass laws.

By 1962, the external mission of the ANC was well established with offices in London, Ghana and Dar-es-Salaam. Early in 1961, the ANC had received a message from Oliver Tambo asking for more people to assist with the ever-increasing volume of work. It was part of Walter's brief to decide who should serve on the external mission, and he was responsible for sending Frene Ginwala, Ruth Mompati, Robert Resha and others abroad.

Mandela also led an ANC delegation to a conference for the Pan-African Freedom for East, Central and Southern Africa (PAFMECSA) in Addis Ababa in February 1962. PAFMECSA, the predecessor of the Organisation of African Unity (OAU), was committed to providing support for liberation movements in Africa. In 1962, the first batch of MK men left for military training outside the country, including Mandela.

The MK manifesto had expressed the hope that the first acts of sabotage would "awaken everyone to the realisation of a disastrous situation to which the Nationalist policy is heading". But by 1962, it was clear that far from serving as a wake-up call to white South Africans, the sabotage campaign was driving them more firmly into the Nationalist laager. White attitudes were hardened by the murderous campaign of *Poqo*, a spontaneous grass-roots movement with tenuous links to the PAC. In 1962 and 1963 *Poqo* was responsible for the brutal murders of seven white people in the Cape and Transkei (Karis and Carter, 3: 669). Verwoerd had shrewdly called an election in October 1961 to consolidate his power, which turned out to be the greatest victory for the Nationalists since coming into power in 1948 (Karis and Carter, 3: 56). With the white electorate firmly behind it, the government launched its counter-offensive.

New legislation, commonly called the Sabotage Act, was passed on 27 June 1962. The law provided for the house arrest of banned persons (who could leave only to go to and from work) and a minimum sentence of five years and a maximum of death for sabotage.

The new legislation was immediately put to use, with devastating effect. On 30 July 1962, the government listed 102 persons (52 whites, 35 Africans, 9 coloureds and 6 Indians) as having been banned. These included Chief Luthuli and Oliver Tambo. Those banned could no longer make any public statements because the new Act proscribed the reproduction of any statement by people who were banned from gatherings. A banned person was also forbidden to communicate with other banned people or receive visitors (Karis and Carter, 3: 664).

Anti-apartheid activist and writer Hilda Bernstein described the Act as the "foundation stone of the repression, imprisonment without trial, torture and murder that was to follow." It defined the term "gathering" so loosely as to make it virtually illegal for a banned person to go to a cinema or have a cup of tea with a friend (Hilda Bernstein 1989, 28).

On June 28, the day after the Sabotage Act was passed, Walter was arrested and charged under the Unlawful Organisations Act. He was released on bail and ordered to report to the police station twice a week. On 10 July he presented himself at the Johannesburg Magistrate's Court to face the charge, this time with Harold Wolpe representing him. By this stage, the impact of the Sabotage Act was becoming apparent.

Hilda Bernstein described the scene: "On one day, the Johannesburg Magistrate's court resembled a conference of the liberation movement, when about 20 members of the congress organisations appeared on various charges; nine members of the Congress of Democrats charged with 'acts calculated to further the objects of an unlawful organisation' (they had put up posters supporting the ANC); several Africans, members of the Women's Federation and others, charged with 'creating a disturbance' on the City Hall steps during the protests; ... and Walter Sisulu arrested and charged under the Suppression of Communism Act" (Hilda Bernstein 1989, 30).

Walter's next arrest was the result of unwanted assistance from a Good Samaritan. While Nelson Mandela was out of the country, the external mission of the ANC had requested the history of the ANC. This was written up in a document entitled "The Sword and the Shield". Walter and Duma Nokwe were taking it to Joe Matthews, whose task it was to send it out of the country. En route, the ubiquitous Sergeant Dirker and another detective arrested Walter, who promptly slipped the document onto the pavement. Unfortunately, a bystander saw something dropping from Walter's hand and, in a misguided attempt to be helpful, he picked it up, ran after Walter and said, "Here, you dropped this." Needless to say, the police pounced on the document. Walter was taken to Marshall Square and charged with promoting the activities of an illegal organisation.

In October 1961, the movement secretly purchased Lilliesleaf Farm, a smallholding in Rivonia, one of Johannesburg's white northern suburbs. Arthur and Hazel Goldreich, a Johannesburg couple, posed as the affluent new owners. The reality was that the large farmhouse, shielded by trees, was a safe house for activists involved in underground work. The black man living in the domestic worker's cottage was none other than Nelson Mandela.

After his trip abroad, Mandela returned to Lilliesleaf on 20 July. The next day, members of the Working Committee – Walter, Duma Nokwe, Moses Kotane, Govan Mbeki, Dan Tloome and JB Marks – converged on the farm for a secret meeting. Mandela reported back on his trip, during which he had met major African leaders and heads of state. He had also visited London, where he had met leaders of the Labour and Liberal parties. He explained that the concerns of the African leaders (about the ANC's affiliation with the Communist Party) had to be taken into account, as they would be the ones who would be financing and training MK. This necessitated reshaping the Alliance so that the ANC would take on a more prominent role, and appear more independent (Mandela, 361).

The committee felt that such a serious departure from policy merited the consultation of the entire leadership. They all agreed that Mandela should go to Durban to brief Chief Luthuli, except for Mbeki, who felt that this was too dangerous. Govan's argument was overruled, but he was to be proved right.

Mandela left for Durban the next day, where he met Monty Naicker and Ismail Meer. They were disturbed by the suggestion that the ANC needed to take more of the lead within the Congress Alliance. Chief Luthuli also expressed disquiet; he felt that the ANC should not be dictated to by foreign politicians. Mandela then went on to brief the MK Regional Command in Durban about the offers of training and support they had been promised. He explained that MK's tactics were currently limited to sabotage, but if this was not effective, they would have to embark on guerrilla warfare (Mandela, 371).

The leader of the Durban Regional Command was Bruno Mtolo, a charming young man whose skills as a handyman and electrician were useful to MK. Mandela had never met him before, but subsequent events would ensure that his was a name he would not forget.

On 5 August, Nelson Mandela was arrested en route back to Johannesburg. The police were elated. After 17 months, they had finally captured the "Black Pimpernel".

Two days later, Walter was arrested while walking down Commissioner Street and taken to Marshall Square. He was sitting in contemplation in his cell when he heard a familiar voice. Mandela, who was in the cell next door, had recognised Walter's cough and had called out to him.

Disappointed to find that the other had been arrested, but at the same time happy to be together, they spent the rest of the night talking.

Mandela was charged with inciting workers to strike during the May 1961 stay-at-home and with leaving the country illegally. Walter was held for 12 days before he was charged with incitement, also arising from the stayaway. He was then transferred to Pretoria prison, where Mandela was also being held. Although they were isolated from each other, Walter and Nelson managed to communicate about the tactical question of Walter's bail. According to Mandela:

> Walter had applied for bail – a decision I fully supported. Bail had long been a sensitive issue within the ANC. There were those who believed that we should always reject bail ... I ... believed we should examine the issue on a case-by-case basis. Ever since Walter had become the secretary-general of the ANC, I had felt that every effort should be made to bail him out of prison. He was simply too vital to the organisation to be allowed to languish in jail. In his case, bail was a practical not a theoretical issue. It was different with me. I had been underground; Walter had not. I had become a public symbol of rebellion and struggle; Walter operated behind the scenes (Mandela, 380).

Walter was duly released on R1 000 bail and ordered to report twice weekly to the police.

On 15 October 1962, Mandela appeared in the Regional Court in Pretoria on an incitement charge, while Walter appeared in the Johannesburg Regional Court. The days before the trial had been marked by demonstrations by thousands of supporters in the main centres of the country.

In Johannesburg, the African benches of the Regional Court were filled long before Walter's appearance. Supporters filled the corridors, with the crowd spilling out onto the pavement. Walter was greeted with cries of "Afrika" when he emerged from the court. He was grabbed by chanting supporters and carried shoulder-high into the street.

A few days later, all gatherings held to protest the arrest or trial of anyone for any offence were banned. The Minister of Justice also issued house-arrest orders for Ahmed Kathrada and Walter, making them second and third persons in South Africa to be placed under arrest. (Helen Joseph had the distinction of being the first.) In terms of the order, Walter was not allowed to be away from his home between 2pm on Saturday and 7am on Monday morning, and before 7am and after 6pm on weekdays. He had to remain within the magisterial district of Johannesburg, and was also not allowed to be in any "location, native hostel or native village" other than Orlando West. He was forbidden to communicate with other banned persons and could not receive any visitors except for a medical practitioner.

The house-arrest order could not be served on Walter because he was attending an ANC conference in Lobatse in Botswana, the main purpose of which was to address the enormous organisational problems that had confronted the ANC since its banning in 1960. As one of the main organisers of the conference, Walter travelled to Lobatse a few days early to finalise preparations. He addressed the first arrivals on the eve of the conference, and then rushed back home. Newspaper reports had announced that he was to be placed under house arrest, and he knew he had to return before the Special Branch pinned the notice on his door, as his absence would make him liable for a jail sentence of up to three years. The day after his return, 27 October, Security Branch detectives served him with the original copy of the banning order.

As the political repression mounted, Albertina and Walter knew that it was just a matter of time before the lengthy jail sentence they had long anticipated became a reality. For political activists, the Draconian new laws translated into daily persecution and torment that took its toll on family life. The police became more aggressive by the day and their raids caused much anger and frustration. During the course of one raid, the police, not satisfied with turning the house upside down, demanded that Walter stand up and empty his pockets. This infuriated Walter to the extent that his mother had to restrain him.

Walter worried about the impact of constant police raids and harassment on their children, and he and Albertina made arrangements to send the children to school in Swaziland. They were also eager to get the children out of the deliberately inferior Bantu education system. Max, who had spent three years at a boarding school in Bethel in the Transkei, completed his junior certificate in 1960. Albertina wanted him to go to Swaziland with his younger siblings, but he decided to enrol at a private college in Johannesburg.

While they had prepared themselves psychologically for intensified political persecution, nothing prepared Walter and Albertina for the bereavement they experienced in the closing months of 1962. Gogo, who had been a very healthy old lady, suddenly became ill. She became hypertensive – a condition that was no doubt exacerbated by the constant police harassment of her son – and developed heart trouble. Her condition deteriorated rapidly and she died on 5 November 1962 at the age of 78. Gogo had been an institution in Orlando West. As one of the first residents of the township and one of the most active members of the Anglican Church, everyone in the community knew her. Family members, neighbours and friends converged on the Sisulu home to mourn her passing. As people were paying their respects, six black policemen arrived and tried to force themselves through the front entrance. Walter pushed them out and told them to use the back door. The police left, only to return later that night. They announced that the mourners constituted a "gathering", arrested Walter and took him to Marshall Square for the night.

Gogo was buried at Nancefield cemetery on the 11 November. Walter had to apply to the Department of Justice for permission to greet the mourners and attend his mother's funeral.

Gogo's death seemed to mark the unravelling of the family. A few weeks after the funeral, Gerald decided to join MK and to go into exile. He left for Botswana in December 1962, and early in 1963 he was flown to Dar-es-Salaam with Duma Nokwe, Moses Kotane and other ANC leaders who had gone into exile.

Not long after Gogo's passing, Barbie became ill. Plagued by constant headaches, she was admitted to hospital in February 1963, where she was told she had to have surgery. Although she seemed to be optimistic, she must have had a premonition. "She was quite cheerful and happy," recalled Max, who visited her in hospital. "She jokingly asked me if I would look after Beryl if she died." The day before the operation, Barbie said to Albertina, "If anything happens to me, you will be left with the children. I do not have to ask you to care for them because you have mothered them even while I was alive." She then asked Albertina to come to the hospital at 3 the next afternoon. When she arrived, she was met with the news that Barbie had died on the operating table at 3pm Albertina was devastated, not just emotionally, but at the implications: "Barbie's death really left me all alone. With my mother-in-law gone and Walter in and out of jail, I knew that I would have to bring up all the children alone."

It was a traumatic time for Walter, one that he prefers not to talk about. A message had to be sent through the ANC underground to Gerald, and Beryl was brought back from boarding school to attend the funeral. One small mercy was that there was no police interference this time, and Walter was able to attend the funeral. He was touched by the response of the Noordgesig Community, particularly one of Barbie's supervisors who spoke movingly of Barbie's work and dedication to the community.

At the time of his sister's death, Walter's trial was coming to an end. He was charged on four counts: being a member of the ANC; taking part in ANC activities; furthering an aim of the ANC by advocating a national convention; and incitement to strike in that he conspired with Nelson Mandela and others to call the May 1961 strike.

A large number of witnesses gave evidence on Walter's numerous arrests, including the time he had surreptitiously dropped a document in the street. This "Sword and the Shield" document, which had been retrieved by the well-meaning passer-by, became a crucial piece of evidence. On 4 March 1963 Walter was found guilty on two of the four counts and sentenced to three years on each count. In a controversial move, the magistrate, Mr EL van Zyl, refused to grant bail pending appeal. Joe Slovo challenged this, referring to the Supreme Court ruling that a magistrate had no discretion over bail whatsoever.

The tussle that followed would have been amusing if it had not been so serious. The magistrate stated that he did not agree with the Supreme Court decision on bail. An increasingly incredulous Slovo pointed out that the magistrate was bound by the order regardless of whether or not he agreed with it, and noted that any application to the Supreme Court would involve the magistrate in costs.

Walter was meanwhile hustled down into the cells where he was allowed to say a brief goodbye to Albertina before being driven off to Pretoria jail under a heavy police escort. Meanwhile, the lawyers locked horns over the issue of his bail. The Supreme Court ordered the magistrate to follow their ruling, so he had no choice but to grant bail. The next bone of contention was the amount. Eventually, bail was set at R6 000 and Walter was released from Pretoria Prison on 9 March (*Spark*, 14 March 1963).

On 3 April 1963, Walter was placed under 24-hour house arrest. The order stipulated that he could not communicate "in any manner whatsoever" with anyone other than his immediate family, a magistrate, policeman or doctor. Beryl, who had come to live with the family following the death of her mother, was not on the list of people with whom he could communicate, and an application had to be made to the Chief Magistrate to allow her to stay in the house.

Realising that prison was inevitable, Walter decided to take leave of his family to go underground as a full-time leader of MK. On 19 April 1963, he said goodbye to his children, promising them that he would not leave the country and he would stay in touch. In an effort to inject some humour into a grim and distressing moment, Max reminded them of the R6 000 bail with the wry remark, "There goes the people's money!" People had been posted around the house to check for the police. Once the coast was clear, Walter stepped out of the house and disappeared into the night.

When she returned from work on the following day, Albertina found Special Branch detectives waiting for her. They had already interrogated Beryl, and now it was her turn. Albertina had no idea where Walter was. An intensive search by police had failed to reveal any trace of him. There was speculation in the press reports that he had taken the "secret escape route" to Botswana, bound for Tanzania. Other reports claimed that he had been seen in Lourenço Marques in Mozambique. In reality Walter was underground, inside the country.

Walter's bail was discussed in the Senate on 29 April. The Minister of Justice was disturbed by the fact that when an accused was found guilty, a magistrate had no right to refuse bail if the matter went to appeal. On the matter of Walter's absconding while on bail, the Minister remarked: "If I could only sell all of them for R6 000."

The government intensified repression with the passing of the General Laws Amendment Act on 1 May 1963, which allowed the State to hold suspects for 90 days without charging them. The only dissenting voice in Parliament was that of Helen Suzman, the lone Progressive Party member, who stood up to the bullying of the Nationalist Party in condemning the Bill. The "90-day Act", as it became known, marked the virtual abrogation of *habeas corpus* (a prisoner's right to be charged with a specific crime or released), and it was used on political activists with devastating effect.

Albertina became the first female victim of the notorious law when Special Branch detectives arrested her on 19 June 1963 while she was treating patients. She asked for permission to go home to change out of her uniform and pack a suitcase. It was a heart-wrenching moment for her because the children had just returned home for the holidays: "When I came home, I found the children's suitcases in the passage." Nkuli, who was attending a local primary school, came home just in time to kiss her mother goodbye. "So the dogs have come to take her," she remarked bitterly to Beryl, as she watched her mother leave.

A few days later, police made another 90-day arrest, just three streets away from the Sisulu home. The latest detainee was the widowed Rose Mbele, a colleague and close friend of Albertina. The two women had worked together since the foundation of FEDSAW in the 1950s and later in the ANC Women's League. Mrs Mbele's three children were left to fend for themselves. In the words of Albertina's friend and colleague Maggie Resha, "An eagle's nest on top of a precipice is more secure than a black woman's home."

The day after Rose Mbele's arrest, Max became the next 90-day victim when he was arrested and detained at Marshall Square. Max, who was studying for examinations at the time, knew that the police would come for him, and tried to evade them by going to stay with his friend Maye. He only went home to eat, change and check on the other children. Spies posted around the house alerted the police, who picked him up. His siblings watched yet another member of the family being taken away. "The bravest was six-year-old Nkuli," recalls Max. "She was visibly upset but she tried hard not to cry."

Albertina, who was held incommunicado during her detention, had no idea that Max had been arrested. Walter, on the other hand, was well aware of Max's detention but was powerless to act. An article on Albertina's arrest in the *Post* of 23 June 1963 aggravated his anxiety about the children, carrying as it did a picture of a woebegone Beryl, Lindi and Zwelakhe. *Drum* also highlighted the plight of the Sisulu and Mbele children, "the 90-day orphans", and wrote scathingly of the inhumanity of a detention law that "harm[ed] those who are least able to fend for themselves – the children of detained people".

The plight of the children prompted an outpouring of public sympathy. Mrs Leslie Minford, wife of the Deputy Consul-General of the British High Commission, was among those who sent food parcels to the children. A businessman from Coronationville was so concerned that he offered to care for them all. The neighbours, particularly Elizabeth Makhubu (known as MaMtshali) and Albertina's cousin, Vuyiswa Dubasi, insisted that the children remain in their own homes. They maintained that it was their responsibility to take care of the children in the absence of their parents, although they were happy to entrust Nkuli to the care of Albertina's brother Elliot in Cape Town. However, when Elliot arrived in Johannesburg, government social workers would not allow him to take Nkuli.

Lungi remembers that the interference of these social workers was bitterly resented, and their suggestion that the children be taken into care was regarded with great suspicion. "The social welfare department for the black community fell under the Native Affairs Department. We could not trust them. They could only have sinister motives for making such an offer and we objected strongly to being removed from our home."

Desperate to track down Walter, the security police tried their utmost to extract information from Albertina. She was taken to Langlaagte police station where she was locked up in a small, bare room. Three mattresses piled up on top of each other served as a bed. For the first week of her detention, she was fed rice, meat and vegetables with hot coffee twice a day – a luxurious diet by prison standards. When it became apparent that she was not prepared to talk about Walter's whereabouts, she was put onto spare rations of porridge and pap only.

In an interview, Albertina described her detention as a curious mixture of loneliness and exposure. She had no contact with other prisoners, yet she felt that she had no privacy. "Every time I wanted to wash, I had to cover the window with a small piece of cloth." The loneliness was unbearable: "There was nothing to read, nothing to do, nothing to occupy my mind – nothing except to think of what was happening to my children at home." The police played on her anxiety cruelly. "Security Branch men threatened that my children would be taken over by the State. I nearly lost hope" (*Drum*, August 1963).

The police asked Albertina the same questions over and over. Late one night, a police officer came to her cell and told her that Nkuli was in intensive care at Baragwanath Hospital, very ill with pneumonia. He told her that she would be free to go if she told them where her husband was. Shattered as she was, she told the policeman that for the sake of both her husband and her child, she could not betray the struggle.

His eyes were hard. "Then you will die in this cell and rot in the ground," he said. "You will not see either your husband or your children again." I … found myself saying, "I was born of the soil. I can only become part of it again"… I prayed that God would give me the strength to do what I knew was right and not to allow that policeman to know my inner fear" (Charles Villa-Vicencio, Interview, Albertina Sisulu).

While his mother was experiencing her private hell, Max at least had the company of other prisoners at Marshall Square. At first he was placed in a common cell with other ANC members, then moved to another cell that normally served as a holding place for awaiting trial prisoners. He shared this cell with two men, one of whom had been arrested for stealing. The other, a mean-looking giant of a man, had been arrested for murder, so Max tried to make himself as inconspicuous as possible. Fortunately he was later moved to another cell where the older prisoners were very supportive.

At the age of 17, Max was the youngest detainee. This caused something of a stir. Even the most hardened warders were shocked that a young boy could be arrested for no other reason than that the police were looking for his father, and some brought him books to read and extra food. From time to time, the security police would interrogate him on Walter's whereabouts, and he would tell them he did not know where his father was.

Walter agonised about the fate of his family but he had to push his anxiety about them to the back of his mind as he grappled with the perils of underground work. Because so many activists had been banned, placed under house arrest or forced to flee the country, the underground machinery had been thrown out of gear. Consequently, there was an enormous amount of work to do.

On 26 June, Walter made a 15-minute radio broadcast from underground. It was referred to as "a typical Sisulu message – direct, forceful and down to earth" (Pamphlet, Southern Africa – The Imprisoned Society, May 1982). Walter began with the following assurances: "Sons and daughters of Africa: I speak to you from somewhere in South Africa. I have not left the country. I do not plan to leave." He explained that their leaders continued to work underground, and then bluntly summed up the state of the nation:

Our house is on fire … There is no time to stand and watch. Thousands are in jail including our dynamic Nelson Mandela … Robben Island is a giant concentration camp for political prisoners. Men and women, including my wife, rot in cells under Vorster's vicious laws to imprison without trial …

South Africa is in a permanent state of emergency … We, the African National Congress, will lead with new methods of struggle … We say: the hour has come for us to stand together. This is the only way to freedom. We warn the government that drastic laws will not stop our struggle for liberation. Throughout the ages men have sacrificed – they have given their lives for their ideals. And we are also determined to surrender our lives for our freedom.

In the face of violence, men struggling for freedom have had to meet violence with violence. How can it be otherwise in South Africa? Changes must come. Changes for the better, but not without sacrifice …

We face tremendous odds … But our unity, our determination, our sacrifice, our organisation are our weapons. We must succeed! We will succeed! Amandla! (Pamphlet, Southern Africa – The Imprisoned Society, May 1982)

There was increasing concern among the underground leadership about the safety of Rivonia. Too many people in detention knew about the farm, so it was decided to vacate it. A meeting on 6 July was to have been the last one held there. At that meeting, it became apparent that another meeting had to be held to discuss "Operation Mayibuye" on 11 July. The question arose as to where this meeting should take place. Walter made the fateful suggestion that they use Rivonia as a venue one last time.

On Thursday 11 July, Walter had an appointment to see a dentist at Lilliesleaf Farm just before the meeting. Walter was late for the appointment, and the increasingly nervous dentist eventually said he could not wait any longer. At that moment, Walter arrived with Govan Mbeki and Raymond Mhlaba. While he attended to Walter, the dentist asked if there would be bloodshed in South Africa.

As soon as the dentist had left, the meeting began. Walter, Govan Mbeki, Kathrada, Raymond Mhlaba, Rusty Bernstein, Dennis Goldberg and Bob Hepple were all present. About 15 minutes later, they noticed a dry-cleaning van drive into the yard. At first the group assumed it was delivering goods to the homestead. Then the back doors of the van opened and armed police and dogs sprang out. In a vain attempt to escape, Walter, Kathrada and Mbeki climbed through a back window. As Walter landed on the ground, he stared straight into the jaws of a growling police dog. As he was being handcuffed, he asked: "How are my wife and my son?" One of the officers sneered, "You ask about your wife and son now. You should have thought about them before you started all this!" Walter's old enemy, Lieutenant Dirker, was one of the policemen present. He was placed in charge of the document search and set to work with relish. He could barely contain his joy and boasted to Walter, "This will set you back 20 years."

Everyone on the property was rounded up – the caretaker, the Goldreich's domestic worker and all the other workers. Meanwhile, the unsuspecting Arthur Goldreich drove straight into the police dragnet. Hazel was the next one arrested when she arrived at the house, followed by the hapless dentist when he arrived at the property later that evening.

The 17 people arrested in the raid were detained under the 90-day law. In the 10 days following the raid, the police searched the house and grounds minutely, removing carloads of documents.

The Rivonia arrests were the culmination of weeks of painstaking searching for Walter by the security police. According to Jimmy Kantor, who probably got the information from police sources, a 90-day detainee agreed to tell the police where Sisulu was hiding in return for R5 000. The police negotiated the amount down to R3 000 and learned that Walter was in the Rivonia area (Kantor, 39).

At the beginning of July, the police were combing the roads and lanes of Rivonia looking for Walter's hideout, when they received a second piece of information which enabled them to home in on Lilliesleaf Farm (Hilda Bernstein 1989, 55).

By the morning of 11 July, all was ready for the raid. To ensure secrecy, a search warrant had not been arranged. At the last minute, the head of the security police insisted on a warrant. Because this had to be obtained from a magistrate, the raid had to be postponed until the afternoon. The delay was a stroke of luck for the police. If the raid had taken place in the morning as planned, the police would not have found Walter and his colleagues.

The raid was a sensational coup for the police and they launched into an orgy of self-praise and congratulation. The police believed they had dealt a deathblow to black resistance and all that remained was "a mopping-up operation". John Vorster, the then Minister of Justice, said, "... the wealth of information that was captured in the Rivonia raid will considerably ease the task of the police in running to ground all internal subversive organisations."

The Rivonia arrests were a shattering blow to the liberation movement and a tragedy for the families of those arrested. Walter's family did not feel the impact of his arrest immediately. The younger children were back at boarding school in Swaziland where they were somewhat cushioned from the shock. At Marshall Square, Max heard the news through the prison grapevine and it was confirmed when some white warders came in grinning broadly to tell him his father had been arrested. He was released a week later, but Albertina was not so lucky.

With no contact with anyone except security police officers, Albertina could hear the news only when they chose to tell her. Almost three weeks after the raid, on 30 July, security police entered her cell carrying a newspaper with the headlines about the Rivonia raid blazoned across the front page. They tried to persuade her to make a statement on the grounds that, as her husband had already been arrested, she could not betray him. She refused, which cost her another week in detention. On 6 August, a policeman took her fingerprints and told her she could go. "I was flabbergasted. I thought I was going to be transferred to another jail. I was given no warning. I hadn't a cent on me, so I walked down the street ..., hoping to meet someone I knew. I did – and got a lift home" (*Rand Daily Mail*, 7 August, 1963).

Albertina found Nkuli and Max at home. Nkuli was so overjoyed at her mother's unexpected appearance that she was still jumping up and down hours later. The joy of Albertina's reunion with her children was marred by the grim situation at home. Before she could even begin to consider the implications of Walter's incarceration, she had to confront the fact that the police were once again hounding Max. She was afraid that it was just a matter of time before he would be arrested again, and painfully concluded that his only option was to leave the country. When the ANC suggested Max go into exile, she strongly supported the idea. She had been home for only a few days when Max left on the first stage of his journey into exile. Albertina's face is drawn in pain at the memory: "I stood by the window and watched him go across the field to Phefeni station to catch the train. He was wearing a white shirt and it was a windy day. I stood there praying ... I just wanted him to get out safely."

Max was part of a small group who travelled to Zeerust by train. Here they were picked up and taken to the Botswana border. They waited until night before crossing and making their way to Lobatse. From there they were taken to a refugee camp in Francistown that housed mostly ANC and SWAPO refugees awaiting further transportation to other destinations, mainly Tanzania.

Among the people most affected by the news of the Rivonia raid was Harold Wolpe, Walter's friend and lawyer. Since he had become a partner in the law firm of his brother-in-law Jimmy Kantor, Harold Wolpe had taken on a number of political trials, usually without charging fees. Unknown to Jimmy, Wolpe's involvement in politics extended much further than defending political activists. It was only a matter of time before police investigations would reveal that Wolpe had handled the legal purchase of Lilliesleaf Farm (Wolpe, 88). Knowing that his arrest was imminent, Wolpe went into hiding.

Six days after the Rivonia arrests, Wolpe was arrested near the border. He was taken to Marshall Square where he met up with his friend, Arthur Goldreich, as well as Mosie Moolla and Abdulhai Jassat, two 90-day detainees he had recently defended. The four men bribed a young warder, Johannes Greef, and managed to escape. Goldreich and Wolpe managed to slip into Swaziland, where they laid low at Father Hooper's mission.

Vernon Berrange, one of the defence lawyers in the Treason Trial, was enlisted to charter a plane for the two fugitives, who flew to Lobatse disguised as priests. The East African Airways Dakota that was to take them to Dar-es-Salaam landed in Francistown on 28 August in readiness to leave early the next morning.

Wolpe and Goldreich were not the only ones who rejoiced at the prospect of escape. Max was part of the group scheduled to leave on that flight. He had his mind set on military training, and was anxious to move on. He had no idea that the inclusion of the two fugitives would jeopardise their departure. The would-be travellers were all disappointed when they learned that the aircraft had been destroyed by a mysterious fire during the night.

It was obvious that Goldreich and Wolpe were the targets of a sabotage attempt. Arrangements were made for a replacement plane from Dar-es-Salaam, but the airline decided it was too risky to transport South Africa's most wanted men and recalled their aircraft. The next plane that was chartered crashed at the border town of Mbeya en route to pick up the passengers.

Eventually Goldreich and Wolpe were flown out in a small aircraft that, for security reasons, took off about 100 miles north of Francistown, and flew to Dar-es-Salaam via the Congo. The other refugees, including Max, were flown out in separate planes. Max landed in Dar-es-Salaam, where he stayed until he was sent to the Soviet Union.

The successful escape of Goldreich and Wolpe was a serious embarrassment to the South African government, at a time when government ministers and police generals were boasting about how they had smashed all subversive elements. In typically racist fashion, they saw Goldreich as the mastermind of the Rivonia conspiracy, the "communist agitator" influencing the otherwise content natives. Vorster described his escape as a great setback and remarked that a trial without Goldreich would be "like producing Hamlet without the Prince" (Joffe, 7).

*nine*

Immediately after her release from detention, Albertina had turned to Bram Fischer to discuss Walter's legal defence. Bram and Molly were a tower of strength, just as they had been in the days of the Treason Trial. Bram was already assembling a defence team for the Rivonia men, and had enlisted the assistance of Arthur Chaskalson and George Bizos.

Bram advised Albertina to approach Joel Joffe to act as the instructing attorney. Albertina did not know Joel, but she had faith in Bram's recommendation that he was a highly principled man and a competent lawyer. When she met Joel, she liked his quiet manner and was also impressed that he had postponed emigrating to Australia to take on a case on the vaguest of briefs, from people who did not even have the means to pay him.

Joel Joffe was firmly opposed to apartheid, but he knew little about black politics. When the Rivonia arrests were reported, Walter Sisulu was the only name that was familiar to him: "I was aware vaguely that he was a figure of considerable importance amongst non-white people. But apart from this I knew nothing either of the people involved or their cause" (Joffe, 1).

On 7 October, Joel Joffe heard through the legal grapevine that the Rivonia prisoners were to appear in court the following day. When he phoned Percy Yutar, the prosecutor, to check whether this was correct, Yutar confirmed the rumour and advised Joffe to be at the Supreme Court in Pretoria next morning. The next day, Joffe, Bizos and Chaskalson arrived at the court only to find that they had driven from Johannesburg in vain. There was no sign of the Rivonia men. When they contacted Yutar, who offered no apology, he told them the case would begin only the next day.

Joffe and his colleagues went to the local jail to meet their prospective clients for the first time, but the prison authorities refused to allow them to consult with the white prisoners and the black prisoners at the same time, on the grounds that mixing between prisoners of different races was forbidden. After much argument and an appeal to higher authorities, permission was finally given for the consultation.

After their arrest, all the Rivonia prisoners were put in solitary confinement and interrogated by members of the Special Branch. During Walter's interrogations, the security police told him that he was facing a very grave charge, and that if convicted, he would be sentenced to death. However, he could escape the death penalty if he was prepared to give evidence or to give information "confidentially". They also told him that some of his white comrades had already given information implicating him. Walter emphatically rejected their offer, saying that the other prisoners could talk if they wanted to, but he would never give information about his colleagues.

On 7 October, after 88 days in solitary confinement, Walter was taken from his cell, fingerprinted and charged with offences under three Acts (Joffe, 23). The next day he discovered that his co-accused included those arrested with him at Rivonia, as well as Elias Motsoaledi and Andrew Mlangeni, both of whom had been arrested a few weeks earlier. Also among their number was Nelson Mandela, who had been brought from Robben Island, where he had already served nine months of his five-year sentence.

Because the men had been held incommunicado for so long, the gathering turned out to be more of a reunion than a legal consultation. In Joffe's words: "They were drunk with speech, with human communication and contact, with being able to talk, to meet with and touch other people, too involved in all these new sensations, too intoxicated ... to consider serious problems of law ... They seemed to have little interest in what we were discussing, and to be only really interested in news of their families and their welfare" (Joffe, 23, 25).

George Bizos then explained that the outlook was bleak. The charges against them were serious, probably high treason or sabotage, the penalty of which could be anything from five years imprisonment to the death sentence. Neither Walter nor his colleagues were shocked by Bizos's sombre assessment. He had simply confirmed what they already suspected.

Early on the morning of 9 October, the Rivonia prisoners were handcuffed and put into a Black Maria especially constructed for the trial. Inside the vehicle, a steel partition separated the white prisoners from their black colleagues. The prisoners' vehicle was at the centre of a convoy headed by a limousine carrying the colonel in charge of Pretoria prison and other high-ranking police officials. Traffic was held up for the convoy as it travelled the mile-long journey from the jail to the Supreme Court. As the convoy entered the backyard of the court, the huge iron gates at the entrance clanged shut behind them. The prisoners were hustled into a small cell in the basement of the court building.

After the accused were seated, Mr Quartus de Wet, Judge-President of the Transvaal, took the bench. Percy Yutar handed copies of the indictment to the court and to the defence. The indictment alleged that the accused had committed 222 acts of sabotage between August 1961 and July 1963 in preparation for guerrilla warfare. Bram Fischer immediately argued for a six-week adjournment on the grounds that the defence needed more time to prepare its case. He said the State had had three months to prepare, while the defence had only just been handed a copy of the indictment. He pointed out that "the accused in this case are people who carry the deep respect of a very large section of the population, and for this reason alone justice should be seen to be done" (Joffe, 28). Yutar argued that some witnesses had to be called before the end of the month because he feared for their safety. The judge, eager to get on with the case, said an adjournment of three weeks would be sufficient.

Their first court appearance, brief though it was, gave some indication to the defence and the accused of what they were up against. Quartus de Wet was one of the last judges appointed by the United Party in the pre-apartheid era, so he was not considered a puppet of the Nationalist government. While they were cautiously optimistic about the judge, they had no expectations of fair play from the prosecution. In typically euphemistic fashion, Walter described Yutar as "an unpleasant man". Dubbed "Percy-Cutor" by opponents and colleagues alike, Yutar's main ambition was to become the first Jewish Attorney-General in South Africa. He was mortified that all the white people involved in the Rivonia conspiracy were Jewish. He specifically asked to be assigned to the Rivonia Trial "to vindicate the Jewish community in South Africa and prove that not all Jews are communists" (Kantor, 161–4).

From the outset, Yutar displayed an almost fanatical hatred of the accused and everything they stood for. He made things as difficult as possible for the defence by holding back information. Before the first hearing, he refused to give the defence a copy of the indictment, yet he had given advance copies to the press. The first time the defence saw the indictment was in court; yet on the same day the *Rand Daily Mail* featured an article on the charges accompanied by a carefully posed photograph of Yutar holding a bound copy of the indictment.

The accused and their legal team spent the three-week adjournment preparing their defence. After they won the battle for black and white accused to be allowed to consult together, the prison authorities allocated a special office for this purpose. Because they suspected that the room was bugged, the group devised a system of coded communication. When dealing with sensitive issues, they took to writing notes, which were passed around and then burned. They had to be careful not to be seen by the police who hovered around the doorway.

There *were* lighter moments; on one occasion, Lieutenant Swanepoel, a burly, red-faced Special Branch officer, noticed the prisoners furtively passing a note around. He pounced on it just as

ABOVE: *Walter and Albertina, wedding reception, Johannesburg,*
*17 July 1944.* (Sisulu Family Collection)

ABOVE: *Walter and Albertina, wedding party, Bantu Men's Social Centre, Johannesburg,*
*17 July 1944. Among the guests were Nelson Mandela (far left), Evelyn Mase (flanking the groom)*
*and Anton Lembede (flanking the bride). In the back row, between the bride and groom,*
*is Walter's sister Rosabella.* (Sisulu Family Collection)

TOP: *Walter's mother, Alice Manse Sisulu, and Orpah Nokwe, mother of Duma Nokwe, at Father Huddleston's feeding scheme, Orlando West, circa 1950s.* (Sisulu Family Collection)

ABOVE LEFT: *Gerald and Jasu Lockman, holding young Walden, Kitwe, Zambia.* (Sisulu Family Collection)

ABOVE: *Ahmed Kathrada stands on the roof of Kholvad House, 27 Market Street, Johannesburg, where he had an apartment.*
(Courtesy Ahmed Kathrada)

LEFT: *Elinor Sisulu with her two children, Vuyisile (9 years) and Duma (7 years), 1995.* (Peter Maltbie)

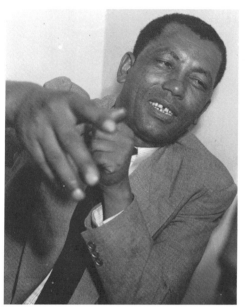

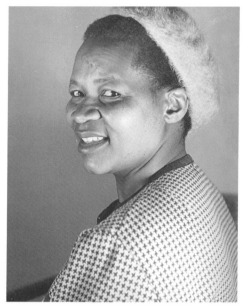

ABOVE: *Walter Sisulu, 1952.*
(Jürgen Schadeberg)

ABOVE: *Albertina Sisulu, circa 1950s.*
(Eli Weinberg)

ABOVE: *Robert Resha, Walter and Yusuf Cachalia, Human Rights Day, 1952.*
(Eli Weinberg, Mayibuye Centre)

ABOVE AND LEFT: *Albertina celebrating with friends after her release from 90-day detention in 1963.* (Bailey's African History Archives)

ABOVE: *Walter (second from right), China, 1953.* (Unknown)

ABOVE: *Walter (far right) and Oliver Tambo (flanking Walter) at the ANC's 41st annual congress in Queenstown, December 1953.* (Bob Gosani)

TOP: *Walter chats to comrades outside the courtroom during the Defiance Campaign, 1952. In the background are JB Marks (left), Yusuf Dadoo (centre) and Ruth First (right).* (Jürgen Schadeberg)

ABOVE: *Police photo of Walter in disguise, taken after Rivonia arrest, 11 July 1964.* (Prison Files, Department of Prisons).

LEFT: *Walter burns his pass book, March 1960.* (Mayibuye Centre)

ABOVE: *Albertina and June Mlangeni arrive at the Palace of Justice for the Rivonia Trial, 1964.* (Times Media)

TOP RIGHT: *Walter disembarks from the "Treason Bus", followed by Rusty Bernstein, 1958.* (Peter Magubane)

RIGHT: *Max Sisulu, Moscow, 1968.* (Sisulu Family Collection)

ABOVE: *Beryl, Lindi and Zwelakhe, August 1963.* (Sisulu Family Collection)

RIGHT: *Walter, prison photograph, circa 1970s – the only existing photograph of Walter during the 1970s.* (Prison Files, Department of Prisons)

ABOVE: *Thabo Mbeki, Max Sisulu and Lindiwe Sisulu with friends, Swaziland, 1974.* (Sisulu Family Collection)

Kathrada was about to burn it, only to be thoroughly embarrassed by the message: "Isn't Swanepoel a fine-looking chap?"

The main focus of their discussions was the indictment, which was, by all accounts, a bizarre document. It should have been a clear statement of the charges against the accused. Instead, according to Joel Joffe, "it was a shoddy and imprecise document". When the defence asked for more details, the prosecution's standard response was that "these facts are within the knowledge of the accused. The defence lawyers decided to apply to have the indictment quashed. They also asked Vernon Berrange to join their team.

On 29 October, the accused were once again escorted to court amid heavy security measures. At the main entrance, scores of gun-toting police strutted around. Albertina was among the crowds of relatives and friends of the accused who had assembled at the court entrance. The massive show of armed force was not only designed to reinforce the image of the Rivonia prisoners as evil and dangerous men; it was also aimed at intimidating their supporters. The State had also elected to hold the trial in Pretoria, where it would be easier to prevent large crowds of ANC supporters from gathering outside the court. At roadblocks leading into Pretoria, police demanded passes from all black people.

For Albertina and many other friends and relatives of the accused, determination to see their loved ones far outweighed any fear of police intimidation. Ignoring the hostile display, they filed into the building and filled the seats to capacity. Dozens of people stood against the wall and others squatted on the floor. Hundreds stood waiting outside the court, first in boiling heat and then in pouring rain. Albertina managed to get a seat and was pleased to see her old friend Hilda Bernstein coming over to greet her, but a policeman prevented Hilda from reaching her, saying: "You are not allowed on this side, it is for natives." Hilda later wrote: "I have to go back to the white benches ... We have known each other for years, worked together on the Women's Federation, and her husband sits next to mine, on trial for their lives, but I may not sit next to her" (Hilda Bernstein 1989, 121).

There was intense international interest in the trial, and the courtroom was besieged by numerous foreign television crews. Dozens of foreign journalists sat in the well of the court, while ambassadors and diplomatic representatives filled the VIP stand.

As family and friends waited in anticipation, the prisoners, each one flanked by two warders, were led from their basement cell up to the dock which had been especially constructed for the case (Bernstein, 107; Joffe, 27; Kantor, 158).

Bram Fischer proceeded to work through the indictment with a fine toothcomb, exposing its numerous defects and the absurdity of some of the allegations – such as the fact that many of the acts of sabotage in which Mandela was said to be involved took place while Mandela was in prison. Kantor's lawyer, George Lowan, followed with a thundering attack on the indictment in dramatic language, a complete contrast to Bram's deliberate and halting manner. Between the two of them, they tore the indictment to pieces, leaving Yutar squirming with embarrassment.

Unable to defend the indictment on grounds of law, Yutar attacked the motives of the defence and, close to tears, begged the judge not to "squash" the indictment in a high-pitched squeak (Joffe, 48; Bernstein, 126). Justice de Wet ignored Yutar's entreaties and pronounced the indictment defective. He said it was unheard of for the accused, when seeking further particulars of charges against them, to be told "this is a matter you know all about". Such an improper reply presupposed guilt of the accused.

Confusion broke out in the court because, technically speaking, the accused were now free. Captain Swanepoel rushed into the dock and thumped each of the accused on the shoulder with the announcement, "I arrest you on a charge of sabotage!" Security police and prison warders hastily pushed the prisoners down the stairs into the cells. The loud sobs of Toni Bernstein, Hilda and Rusty's teenage daughter, added to the drama.

Percy Yutar served his revised indictment at a court hearing on 12 November. Even this version was full of holes. The new indictment split the former sabotage charge into two parts. The first sabotage charge alleged that the accused recruited people for instruction in the manufacture and use of explosives and for military training inside and outside South Africa. Accused one to seven – Mandela, Sisulu, Goldberg, Mbeki, Kathrada, Bernstein and Mhlaba – were charged both in their personal capacities and as members of the National High Command of MK. The second sabotage count alleged further recruitment of people as well as conspiracy to commit acts of guerrilla warfare and violent revolution. The third charge alleged contravention of the Suppression of Communism Act and the soliciting and receiving of money from within and without South Africa to further the acts of subversion.

A total of 193 acts of sabotage were listed. Again there was no information on who committed which act of sabotage.

Bram Fischer complained that at the previous hearing, the State had promised to provide further particulars on the charges within seven days, but had failed to do so, making it impossible to formulate any defence.

The trial was finally set down to begin on 3 December. During the preceding week, the accused discussed at length how they should plead. According to the letter of the law, they were guilty. They belonged to banned organisations that were committed to overthrowing the government. But they did not consider themselves guilty because the laws they had broken were oppressive and unjust. On the other hand, they were not prepared to deny many of the State's allegations. The solution they arrived at was demonstrated at the formal opening of the trial on 3 December. When asked to plead, Mandela said, "The government should be in the dock, not me. I plead not guilty." The expressions on the faces of the police and court officials ranged from amazement to horror. Walter followed with his plea: "It is the government which is guilty, not me." The judge admonished him, but Walter calmly maintained: "It is the government which is responsible for what is happening in this country. I plead not guilty" (Joffe, 59; Bernstein, 141; Mandela, 422). The other accused all proceeded to plead in the same manner.

Yutar's opening address was largely based on the "Operation Mayibuye" document that had been found at Rivonia. He said the accused had embarked on a sabotage campaign as a preliminary step towards guerrilla warfare, and promised that the State would produce documents and witnesses to show that the accused, together with others, had planned the violent overthrow of the government in 1963 (Joffe, 60; Bernstein, 142).

The State kicked off with the testimony of the servants and farm labourers who had worked at Lilliesleaf Farm. These witnesses, some of whom were mothers of young children and some of whom had been physically abused, were thoroughly intimidated by the threat of remaining in detention indefinitely and would say anything to satisfy the security police.

Seventy-year-old Florence Ntombela had been detained twice for no other reason than that she had once heard Walter speak at a meeting. It was only during her second spell in detention, when she became so ill that two heart specialists had to be called in, that she remembered vaguely that Walter had said something about bombing. It was obvious to all that she was not sure what Walter had said, or even whether it was Walter who had spoken (Bernstein, 148).

Later in the trial, when he gave evidence for the defence, Walter pointed out that, at that date, there could have been no talk of bombings, as MK had not even been formed yet, adding that he had "no doubt that some suggestion was made to Mrs Ntombela to put certain evidence" (Walter Sisulu, Evidence, 55).

The farm workers knew little about politics and were not able to say much more than who lived at the Rivonia farm and who visited. Their evidence did not in any way strengthen the case of the prosecution. It seemed to the accused that Yutar was going to great lengths to prove what they were prepared to admit freely. While they were not too concerned about the evidence that placed them at Rivonia, the accused were worried about the incriminating documents stored there. Just before he was sentenced in 1962, Mandela asked Walter to make sure that all his books and notes were removed from the farm. In the first week of the trial, Yutar produced an escape note that Mandela had written when he was at Johannesburg Fort. It turned out that Walter and his colleagues had decided to preserve the note for historic reasons (Mandela, 424).

In the second week of the trial, Yutar, with much posturing, pulled out his trump card: Bruno Mtolo, of the Natal Regional Command of MK, who was happy to testify against his former colleagues. Yutar at first asked that the evidence of "Mr X" (as he referred to Mtolo) be given in camera, arguing that his witness was in "mortal danger". This was a ridiculous claim, because Mtolo was in detention and remained so throughout his evidence.

Mtolo spent several days describing MK sabotage operations in which he had been involved. He was the first witness to directly implicate Mandela in MK activities through his evidence on the meeting Mandela had held with the Natal Regional Command during his visit to Durban in August 1962. Mtolo had also visited Rivonia where he had met with Walter, Govan Mbeki and Kathrada.

Mtolo had little formal education, but he possessed a quick mind and a prodigious memory. He himself boasted that "Dr Yutar said that in all his years of practice he had never come across any person, not even a European, with a memory like mine" (Mtolo, 157). He described events that had taken place several years before with remarkable clarity and seemed to be able to quote entire conversations verbatim. His evidence was extremely damaging for the accused not only because of his information about MK, but also because of the skilful way he interwove fact and fiction.

Walter and his colleagues were devastated by Mtolo's evidence, not so much because of the information he possessed, but because he seemed to relish his role as an informer. Knowing as much as they did about police intimidation and torture, they understood how people could break down in detention and turn state witness. What they could not understand was how someone could happily accept that role, going out of his way to implicate as many people as possible, and volunteering information that the authorities had not even requested.

Mtolo justified his actions by blaming the leadership for betraying the ANC. He castigated those who had left the country, saying they had "run away"; in the same breath, he condemned those who had stayed behind "only for the money which was pouring into the country" (Mtolo, 154). He claimed that MK had not paid him, yet its leaders lived in comfort. He was particularly scathing about Walter, whom he claimed lived in a grand home with "posh furniture like a European".

Walter was certain that the security police prompted Mtolo's attack on him. Joel Joffe supported this view: "This was the first of a number of such attempted smearings of the accused … They were not designed to secure a conviction but rather to undermine the public standing and reputation of the accused and the organisation to which they belonged. The general tenor was that the leaders lived well while their followers suffered and sacrificed" (Joffe, 88). This certainly seemed to be a theme of Mtolo's biography, *The Road to the Left*, a piece of anti-ANC propaganda published after the Rivonia Trial. In it, Mtolo embellished his story about Walter's furniture: "His house looked like one of the showrooms in West Street, Durban. The carpet only showed the turn-ups of your trousers and it felt as if you were walking on cotton wool." He also took a dig at Walter's light skin: "I thought his complexion matched his beautiful furniture." He went on to describe a Walter Sisulu few people would recognise: "It is true that Sisulu had a big following among the rank and file, but one could not compare him to Luthuli or Mandela. As a leader … he lacked the quality of coming down to the level of his individual followers … he looked power drunk to me" (Mtolo, 73–4). He criticised Walter for sending other people's children and not his own son for military training – ironic, given Gerald and Max's exile.

Berrange's cross-examination exposed a number of inconsistencies in Mtolo's evidence and revealed that he had been a thief who had spent a number of years in jail. But the damage had been done. As Joel Joffe noted: "Any lawyer will know that the most difficult witness to attack is not the outright liar but the one who is telling 90% of the truth, but slipping in 10% of lies" (Mtolo, 77).

By the time Mtolo completed giving evidence, things looked grim for the accused. A guilty verdict seemed to be a certainty. The most that their legal team could do for them was to avert the death sentence.

Supporters faced considerable difficulties in travelling to and from Pretoria, as well as continual harassment. Security police took the name of each and every black spectator and photographed them as they left the court (Kantor, 232). Nevertheless, a die-hard group from the ANC Women's League attended every day. Because of her awkward working hours, Albertina battled with transport and often had to rely on friends for lifts. Eventually she arranged to be on permanent night duty so she could attend the trial and see Walter, who was allowed two visits a week.

When Beryl, Lungi, Zwelakhe and Lindi came home from Swaziland for the December holidays, she did not know what to tell them about their father's situation. "As a mother I did not want to scare them, but at the same time I did not want to give them false hope. After all, the lawyers had warned us to prepare for the worst." She regretted that they could not visit their father – prison regulations did not allow children under 16 to visit. She was particularly worried about the way Nkuli was pining for her father. "Although Walter's political work often took him away from home, when he was at home he attended to the children. Nkuli really missed all that attention and she would often complain 'Ever since Daddy left home, no one has given me a bath!' That was not true of course, but it was her way of expressing how she missed her father." Nkuli's complaints exacerbated Albertina's own feelings of isolation and loneliness. She missed Walter as never before. In the past, when he was away from home, she always had Gogo and Barbie to turn to and she could look forward to his return. This time she knew that once the trial ended, the separation would be permanent.

Albertina's problems were worsened by her shaky financial situation. The expense of sending four children to boarding school was beginning to tell. Many of those she would have turned to for help in the past had left the country or were under house arrest. "But there were people who were very supportive. Vuyiswa Dubasi and Elizabeth Mtshali and some of my neighbours were always there for me. Molly Fischer also helped me throughout the trial. Violet Weinberg would get second-hand clothes for me to sell and that helped earn a few extra pennies."

When she went to visit Walter, she never talked about the difficulties at home or her anxiety about the future. She felt that she had to be strong and show him that she was coping. Their half-hour visits were mostly spent talking about the children. Walter always wanted a detailed report on each one of them. They could not discuss Max openly because prison warders were present during all visits, but they found ways of making veiled reference to him. Walter was ecstatic when Albertina managed to convey that Max had arrived safely in Tanzania.

The Rivonia Trial re-opened in January 1964 with the continuation of the State's case. A succession of state witnesses gave evidence, little of which was relevant to the charges against the defendants. The judge chose to ignore the obvious browbeating of witnesses in 90-day detention. He also ignored clear evidence of coaching of witnesses, some of whom said one thing on Friday and a different thing when they returned to court on Monday.

An aspect of the case that Walter and his colleagues enjoyed was Vernon Berrange's devastating cross-examination of witnesses. Berrange had considerable success in exposing inconsistencies and outright lies in the testimony of many of the state witnesses. If the judge had been more impartial, Berrange's performance might have had more bearing on the outcome of the trial. His particularly ruthless exposure of one of Yutar's star witnesses took place on the day two prominent

American sociologists, Dr Gwendolen Carter and Professor Tom Karis, visited the court. As they sat in the VIP box, the entire court observed the varying expressions of disbelief, astonishment and amusement on the faces of the two distinguished guests.

An infuriated Yutar retaliated by ordering that VIPs should no longer be allowed to sit in the box. The next day, Dutch and American Embassy officials were turned away by court officials and were allowed back only after the judge overruled Yutar's instructions.

Yutar seemed to have infected the police with his anger. The following day, they took the names and addresses of all the spectators in the non-white gallery. On that day Albertina had brought her son Mlungisi to court with her. Children under 16 were not allowed in court, so 15-year-old Lungi should not have been there, but he was so anxious to get a glimpse of his father that Albertina did not have the heart to leave him behind.

During the tea interval, Dirker came up to Lungi and demanded to see his pass. Lungi explained that he did not have to carry a pass because he had not yet turned 16. Although Dirker was aware of Lungi's age, he promptly arrested Lungi. Albertina refused to be parted from him, so she had to watch as her son was locked up. "I was determined not to move from there without him. I sat outside his cell until late afternoon when he was released." Fortunately, as Lungi was taken from the courtroom, Albertina had been able to alert Joel Joffe, who threatened to sue the commanding officer of the prison with unlawful arrest and detention if Lungi was not released. Joffe was convinced that if he had not threatened legal action, Lungi would have spent the night in jail (Joffe, 109).

Later that evening Albertina was horrified to learn that Caroline Motsoaledi, the wife of one of the accused, Elias Motsoaledi, had also been arrested during the tea interval. Again Joffe had tried to intervene, but was told that she was being arrested under the 90-day Act. She was taken away crying: "What about my babies? They will be all alone!" Bram Fischer complained to the judge about the arrests, but Justice de Wet dismissed the complaint in an offhand way, and made no effort to find out what possible reason there could be to detain the mother of a six-month-old baby and six other children. He also did not bother to find out why Caroline Motsoaledi, who was no political activist, remained in detention for 156 days. By the time she was released, the Rivonia Trial was over and her husband far away on Robben Island.

Apart from Bruno Mtolo, the only other witness whose evidence really disturbed the accused was that of Patrick Mthembu, the only high-ranking ANC leader who had turned state witness. They felt terribly betrayed by Mthembu, who knew all of them personally. What they found most despicable was that Mthembu saved his own skin by laying much of the blame for his own activities in MK on Elias Motsoaledi. A few months later, at the trial of Wilton Mkwayi, he contradicted the evidence he gave at the Rivonia Trial. As a result of this testimony, Mkwayi was also sentenced to life imprisonment (Bernstein, 168).

After Mthembu's evidence, Walter felt so pessimistic that he wrote a letter to Max to try to prepare him for the worst. Unbeknown to Walter, Max had already left Tanzania for the Soviet Union. The letter was delivered to Gerald, by then undergoing military training in Czechoslovakia. He ensured that Walter's letter eventually reached Max.

My beloved son,
You cannot imagine how happy I was when I learned about your escape from South Africa with Wellington. I only hope that you chaps have reached your destination.

It is my desire that you should begin your studies in England, which is more or less a world centre today, and most suitable as a starting point for young men of your age.

In regard to our case, the state will close its case this week on Friday. Thereafter the case will at least take another month. We have no illusion about its outcome, whatever happens to us the history is on the side of the oppressed people.

I am suggesting that you may expect anything. The state has a very strong case. You can imagine when people like Mtembu and others who were members of the organisation have turned state witness against us. I am [indistinguishable] sorry that Nelson is involved. The spirit of chaps is however high.

This brings me to this — in view of this situation your brothers and sisters including Beryl will naturally look to you for guidance and assistance. That means great responsibility on your part. At present your mother manages well. After all we have many sympathetic friends in many parts of the world.

In spite of this grave position, we have not lost hope; the battle is never lost until it is won ...

I understand that all the kids have passed including our star, Nkuli.

I would very much like to hear about your position before the end of March as it may be difficult thereafter. There is nothing wrong with writing to your mother. There is no security risk involved since your escape has been well publicised. This applies to Thabo as well. Why is he not writing to his father? Can you find out?

Do not write to me. I am not supposed to write this letter. You may not refer to it directly. Just write to your mother and I will know that you have received my letter.

Your loving father, Walter

Sergeant Dirker was the last of the 173 state witnesses to testify. Characteristically, he lied throughout his testimony. He claimed that the "Operation Mayibuye" document was found lying open on the table in the room where Walter and his colleagues had been having a meeting when they were arrested. In reality, the document had been stashed away in an unused coal stove. The purpose of Dirker's lie was to give the impression that the document was under discussion at the time of the arrest, which would support the prosecution's allegation that all those in the room were members of the High Command (Bernstein, 155).

Because they all hated Dirker, the accused asked Berrange to be merciless in his cross-examination. After tying Dirker in knots with his incisive questions, Berrange referred to the case in which Michael Harmel had successfully sued Dirker, reminding him that the judge had described him as a "consistently evasive" witness. Berrange reduced Dirker to a stammering, stuttering mass. The accused were treated to a bizarre spectacle: the bullying Special Branch officer, who had made their lives a misery for so long, burst into tears (Kantor, 284).

In the opening stages of the trial Percy Yutar had declared, with characteristic melodrama, that never had he been presented "with a more powerful case against each and every accused than in this case" (Joffe, 46). As the trial progressed it became clear that Yutar's declaration was an exaggerated one. The evidence against Kathrada, Bernstein and Mhlaba was particularly weak. The defence felt that because there was a possibility of acquittal for these three, they should take the witness stand and the evidence against them be examined in detail.

The evidence against the rest of the accused was so overwhelming that there was no doubt they would be found guilty. What remained to be determined was whether or not they would get the death sentence. To avoid this, the defence would have to convince the judge that the accused had not decided on guerrilla warfare and that their policy of sabotage was one that avoided the taking of human life. The defence lawyers believed it was possible to prove this from documents. With the exception of George Bizos, they believed it would not help the case for their clients to take the witness stand.

The accused, however, were determined to take the stand. They saw the case as an opportunity to make a political statement. They wanted to show that, even if they were guilty in the legal sense, they had been morally justified in what they had done. Because the Rivonia Trial was the focus of international interest, the accused saw it as a unique platform to state their political beliefs.

They were also keen for Mandela to present their side of the story in a clear statement of their aims, beliefs and actions. They decided that the stop-start nature of the question-answer format of cross-examination would not allow for a lucid and coherent statement. Rather than give evidence in the witness box, Mandela opted to give a statement from the dock.

Their defence counsel warned them that such a statement would not hold the same legal weight as evidence that could be tested by cross-examination. This option might even have a negative impact, as the judge might interpret it as a tactic to avoid cross-examination (Bernstein, 188; Mandela, 430). The accused nevertheless decided that the advantages outweighed the disadvantages, and Mandela set about drafting his statement.

Once it had been decided that Mandela would not enter the witness box to testify, Walter became the key defence witness who would have to bear the brunt of Percy Yutar's cross-examination. His co-accused, who had the highest regard for Walter's abilities, did not see this as a problem. After all, Walter had played a major role throughout the trial in working out the defence strategy. Rusty Bernstein described him as "the senior strategist": "Everybody sought Walter's opinion, even Nelson" (Talent Consortium, Interview, Rusty Bernstein).

From an early stage, Joel Joffe had become aware of Walter's stature and influence: "Walter was … one of the most impressive personalities amongst the accused. He was a man of deliberation and careful judgement. At no time during the whole of that period did I ever hear Walter make a hasty decision, or venture an appraisal of anybody or anything without first weighing it carefully, deliberately, generally against his own immediate, instinctive reactions. On every issue, the other prisoners gave the greatest weight to Walter's opinions … neither Nelson nor anyone else made any decision without first seeking Walter's opinion. After a short time we on the defence team found ourselves behaving in the same way. Walter proved to have a judgement of situations and people that, in my experience, was seldom wrong" (Joffe, 3).

Despite his admiration for Walter, Joel Joffe confessed concern that Walter might not be able to cope with the role of key defence witness: "It was a difficult decision to place such tremendous responsibility … on Walter. It was not that we doubted his staunchness, but some of us … doubted his ability to cope with the formidable cross-examination which would be unleashed against him" (Joffe, 133). The major concern was Walter's low level of formal education compared to that of Yutar, whose BA LLB and Doctor of Law degrees made him the most highly qualified public prosecutor in the country. Walter's co-accused dismissed these doubts; they were confident that Walter would be a match for Yutar (Joffe 134; Bernstein, 199).

With the exception of George Bizos, the defence lawyers believed that Yutar would put Walter under a lot of pressure by focusing on technical legal points. They were certain that he would steer clear of politics: "We did not credit that any prosecutor anywhere would choose to tackle a witness like Sisulu on the one subject on which he was an expert, and the prosecutor was not" (Joffe, 134). Bizos, however, was prepared to bet that Yutar would stray into politics and find himself completely out of his depth.

Walter himself was not in the least intimidated by the prospect of being cross-examined by Yutar. He had spent a great deal of time in court the previous decade, and had seen the finest lawyers of that period in action. He did not rate Yutar highly. He calmly prepared his testimony and looked forward to crossing swords with the prosecutor.

Many of his friends could attest to Walter's prowess in courtrooms, including Wolfie Kodesh. As a journalist, he often reported on political cases and was once present when Walter, facing one of his many pass offences, found himself without a legal representative. The magistrate agreed to let Walter defend himself. Wolfie remembers Walter becoming "king of the court", giving a lesson on the operation and effect of the pass laws. The court personnel were transfixed. When the magistrate found some of his statements impermissible, Walter used a different form of words to have his argument accepted. Afterwards, the magistrate formally congratulated him on his performance (Barry Feinberg, Interview, Wolfie Kodesh 2002).

The defence case opened to a packed courtroom on Monday 20 April. Security police and pro-government supporters, among them a large number of students from the conservative Pretoria University, took up much of the space in the white section of the public gallery. Relatives, friends and supporters of the accused had turned up in full force. Among them were Albertina, who had come as part of a large contingent of ANC Women's Leaguers, and Winnie Mandela, accompanied by Nelson's mother who had travelled from the Transkei. The atmosphere was one of great excitement and anticipation. Albertina recalled that they felt that something momentous was about to happen.

The proceedings opened with Bram Fischer's outline of the defence case. He said some of the state evidence would be admitted by some of the accused, but some of it would be challenged. At the end of his summary, Bram Fischer announced that the defence case would begin with a state-ment from the dock by Nelson Mandela. The defence had gone to considerable lengths to con-ceal its strategy from the prosecution, so the announcement came as a complete surprise to Yutar. He had obviously prepared to cross-examine Mandela, and with his plan gone awry, he jumped up in panic: "My lord, I think you should warn the accused that what he says from the dock has far less weight than if he submitted himself to cross-examination!" The judge responded sarcastic-ally: "I think, Mr Yutar, that counsel for the defence have sufficient experience to be able to advise their clients without your assistance" (Mandela, 432; Bernstein, 192; Joffe, 130).

Mandela then proceeded to make his historic statement from the dock. Speaking in calm, meas-ured tones he traced his own political development, and outlined the long struggle of the ANC to secure the rights of the African people through nonviolent means. He described the reasons for turning to violence and the founding of Umkhonto we Sizwe. He explained the distinction between Umkhonto and the ANC, and Umkhonto's choice of sabotage as a method of struggle. He emphasised that sabotage had been chosen because it did not involve loss of life and would keep racial bitterness to a minimum. Mandela challenged allegations that the aims and objectives of the ANC were the same as those of the Communist Party, explaining that African nationalism had always been the creed of the ANC. He said that the close cooperation between the ANC and the Communist Party was merely proof of a common goal – the removal of white supremacy. He pointed out that no one would label the British or the Americans as Communists because they co-operated with the Soviet Union against Hitler.

His voice rising slightly, Mandela described the conditions under which Africans lived in South Africa, concluding "Africans want a just share in the whole of South Africa … Above all we want equal political rights, because without them our disabilities will be permanent … this then is what the ANC is fighting for. Their struggle is a truly national one. It is a struggle of the African people, inspired by their own suffering and their own experience. It is a struggle for the right to live." (Mandela, 438).

Mandela had spoken for five hours. The impact he had on the court was profound. Albertina recalls it as one of the most moving experiences in her life: "Outside it was a cloudy day with a fine drizzle coming down. It was dark inside the courtroom and completely quiet. I could not take my eyes off Nelson standing there. Walter was sitting next to him. After an hour, Walter passed him a glass of water. He went on describing our history and our struggle. By the time he had reached the end of his address we were moved beyond words. And the women! The women were all in tears. When he said 'I am prepared to die,' I did not realise that tears were pouring down my face."

When Mandela stopped speaking, there was complete silence for half a minute or more. His audience had just heard one of history's great political speeches.

Walter took the witness stand next, and Bram led his evidence, beginning with Walter's personal history and political development. Walter said his political views were inspired by the desire to achieve emancipation for the African people from European domination and oppression. The achievement of political rights for the African people was a fundamental necessity. He wanted the best of both socialism and capitalism and was influenced by socialism in his outlook. He then outlined the policy of the ANC and the historical circumstances that led to the formation of Umkhonto we Sizwe. The ANC, he said, welcomed all who strove for African freedom.

Bram then took him through his personal experience of the hardships suffered by the African people. Next, he spoke of his political development since joining the ANC in 1940, the attitude of the Youth League to the Communist Party, and his numerous arrests in the 1950s and 1960s. He described the change in ANC policy in 1949, the adoption of the Freedom Charter, the banning of the ANC in 1960 and the ANC's attitude to nonviolence. He said that the preaching of nonviolence had not been easy because the masses of oppressed people had always doubted the wisdom of this policy. "They have always felt it would never achieve anything, but the African National Congress ... argue[d] that political demonstrations, political strikes and boycotts could bring about change. They could force the rulers to negotiate ... but when the government decided to ban organisations, to ban leaders, to make it illegal to even conduct actions such as economic boycotts and meetings, then our argument could no longer hold" (Walter Sisulu, Evidence, 10). The suppression of all legal means of protest had brought about a situation which no self-respecting African could accept.

He said Sharpeville and the Pondoland massacres led some ANC leaders to question the policy on nonviolence. They were also influenced by events elsewhere in Africa: "They were aware that in Africa, one country after another [was] getting freedom and that the African National Congress, although it was one of the oldest organisations, was not coming anywhere near their cherished ideals. It did not surprise some of us that the people should now become impatient" (Walter Sisulu, Evidence, 10). He personally believed that unless the government changed its policy, civil war would eventually become inevitable. "I felt that in the interest of my own people, it would be better that we should bring about a state of affairs whereby such violence would be controlled" (Walter Sisulu, Evidence, 11).

He said he personally hated the destruction of property and hated the loss of life even more, "but I am a realist. I realise that the African people, like all oppressed people, have got a moral right to revolt against oppression" (Walter Sisulu, Evidence, 12). He went on to describe the ANC's policy on sabotage, the relationship between ANC and Umkhonto, and explained that he was at a meeting of the High Command when the Operation Mayibuye document was discussed. Some supported it and others did not. He himself felt that guerrilla warfare was not a feasible proposition at that stage. By the time of the Rivonia arrests, no decision had been taken on the issue of guerrilla warfare.

When asked if, looking back, he considered that he could or should have acted otherwise, Walter expressed no regrets: "I can't see how I could have done otherwise ... even if I myself did not play the role I did, the others would have done what I have done instead" (Walter Sisulu, Evidence, 57).

The accused had agreed that in giving evidence they would observe a clear principle of not exposing others in their organisation, or in any way threaten the operation or existence of their organisations (Joffe, 123). This was a departure from previous political trials in which the accused had tried to exonerate themselves by naming and implicating others (Bernstein, 204). Walter ended his evidence-in-chief by affirming this principle: "I would like to make my position clear, my lord, that I am prepared to testify in this case in regard to the part I have played and in regard to the part which my organisation played, and some of the people connected with this, but ... I certainly would find it difficult ... to answer questions which might lead to revealing the workings of my organisation and confidential matters ... I am aware that by so doing I might worsen my position, but I find that I cannot do otherwise" (Walter Sisulu, Evidence, 57).

On that note, Walter's evidence-in-chief ended and Percy Yutar began his cross-examination. Deprived of the opportunity to cross-examine Mandela, Yutar directed all his venom at Walter. He had given instructions to the police to have Walter isolated for the entire duration of his evidence. He was not allowed contact with his co-accused during lunch adjournments or recess and during exercise periods in jail. He was even driven to court in a different vehicle.

The other accused, who were busy preparing their own evidence, were greatly inconvenienced by this arrangement, because they needed to consult with Walter. As they did not want to give Yutar an excuse to claim that the witness was being coached, defence counsel decided not to protest unless Walter himself complained (Joffe, 144). Vernon Berrange went to speak to Walter during one of the recesses to find out whether he felt he was capable of withstanding the isolation, as his cross-examination was dragging on for so long. Walter told Vernon that he was coping well with the situation (Joffe, 155).

The contest between Walter Sisulu and Percy Yutar has been described as "one of the most remarkable ever seen in a South African court" in which "Sisulu proved his impeccable legal and political reflexes" (Clingman, 317). Yutar began the cross-examination with questions about injuries or death caused by sabotage.

Yutar: I'm a little intrigued about the professed feeling of the ANC and the Umkhonto We Sizwe, that in the acts of sabotage committed, there was no injury to life, no killing of persons.
Sisulu: That is absolutely correct!
Yutar: Did the ANC or the MK ever take the precautions to see that as a result of the commission of the various acts of sabotage, nobody was injured and nobody would be killed?
Sisulu: The manifesto itself of Umkhonto We Sizwe makes the position perfectly clear, the choice of targets makes the position perfectly clear that the intention was not to injure anybody at all.
(Walter Sisulu, Evidence, 58.)

Giving examples of acts of sabotage involving railway trucks, Yutar continue to press this point. Walter then pointed out that not all the acts of sabotage placed before the court were the acts of MK (Walter Sisulu, Evidence, 59). At that point, the judge interrupted to give an example of a bomb blast at Benoni Post Office in which a passer-by had been killed.

Justice de Wet: If you're going to start bombing buildings, is it possible to avoid that type of accident? If you start putting explosives next to buildings, can you ever be sure that you're avoiding killing or injuring people?
Sisulu: My lord, an accident is an accident ... if the intention of the plan itself and the method used, for instance, at night when the people are not there –
Justice de Wet: ... as long as you haven't got the intention of killing people, it doesn't matter if you kill people, is that your argument?
Sisulu: No sir, I am saying that the precautions are taken in order to avoid this type of thing ... I'm not saying that it can't happen, but I'm saying that the precautions are taken that it should not happen.
(Walter Sisulu, Evidence, 60.)

Defence counsel and the accused were surprised and disturbed by this intervention by the judge. There had been no suggestion that the accused had killed or injured anyone. On the contrary, a number of state witnesses, even the malicious Bruno Mtolo, had testified that the policy of MK was at all times to avoid the loss of life.

Questions of killing or injuring anyone were beyond the scope of the indictment. The defence lawyers felt that a more competent judge would have brought this line of questioning to a halt. Instead, encouraged by the judge's questions, Yutar continued to badger Walter with questions about sabotage acts and the threat to human life. The judge meanwhile intervened again to ask whether there was any concern about the possibility that some passer-by might be injured in a bomb blast.

Walter was clear in his response: "It did worry us! My lord, the very question of embarking on a question of this nature, sabotage, is a matter which exercised a great deal of thought in our minds. It was not a matter we easily arrived at. Our plans were that to the best of our ability, this must be avoided."

By the end of the first day of Walter's cross-examination, it seemed likely that George Bizos would win the bet with his colleagues. As he had predicted, Yutar was more concerned with attacking Walter's politics than with dealing with the facts of the case. For example, when referring to an ANC propaganda pamphlet, Yutar adopted a tone of righteous indignation, as if he was personally offended that the ANC had dared to challenge white supremacy. The pamphlet warned the whites of South Africa that if the government did not change its policy, political violence would become a way of life. Yutar seemed particularly incensed by a passage that said the white man faced a future of terror, uncertainty and steadily eroding power:

Yutar (quoting from pamphlet): "You will keep a gun on your side, not knowing who to trust, perhaps the street cleaner is a saboteur, perhaps the man who makes your tea at the office has a gun? You will never be safe and you'll never be sure" ... and that is what you were telling the white man!

Sisulu: It says the more they drift apart, the more likelihood there is of this situation.

Yutar: Then you end up "you will have launched a war you cannot win." You now accuse the white man of launching the war!

Sisulu: It is the white man, who is, instead of meeting the reasonable demands of the people, instead of discussing the demands of the people ... is ... preparing for war.

Yutar: And you are here contemplating that if the white man does not give into the demands of the black man, there will be a war which [the] white man can never win!

Sisulu: Inevitably it must lead to that situation!

Yutar: And that is your view, and that is the view of the African National Congress?

Sisulu: Yes, after 50 years of patience and of a reasonable approach.

(Walter Sisulu, Evidence, 71–7.)

Yutar then launched into a pattern of questioning that would become a feature of his cross-examinations. He would ask questions that had no bearing on the case with the aim of gathering information for the Security Branch (Joffe, 138). The accused nicknamed these sallies "fishing expeditions", and Walter consistently refused to take the bait. After a long wrangle in which Yutar tried to get Walter to divulge the address at which a certain meeting had taken place, Walter made his position clear:

Sisulu: I'm afraid my lord, I won't be able to implicate people. I won't answer that question!

Justice de Wet: You're not prepared to answer?

Sisulu: I'm not prepared to answer.

Justice de Wet: Yes, very well. (Walter Sisulu, Evidence, 86.)

Another "fishing expedition" involved the funding of the ANC. Here Yutar was hoping to trip Walter into saying something incriminating, and dangled the name of Canon Collins and Christian Aid in front of him, insinuating that they had sponsored acts of sabotage, but Walter patiently and doggedly refused to corroborate this:

Sisulu: I have told you I'm not answering questions dealing with money. You're not going to trap me by putting it that way!

Yutar: I'm not trapping you.

Sisulu: Well, I told you, I'm not answering anything about money!

(Walter Sisulu, Evidence, 230 –31.)

Walter's refusal to answer questions made Yutar extremely agitated: "You know Sisulu, if you want to take up this attitude, you might as well say 'now I'm not prepared to give any further evidence'!" Walter replied, "No, I have explained that matters ... which might involve prosecution of other people, I would not answer questions relating to that."

As well as trying to elicit information for the Security Branch, Yutar tried to use the cross-examination to smear ANC leaders, especially Chief Luthuli, whom he sarcastically referred to as "President Luthuli". He persistently tried to find out from Walter whether Chief Luthuli knew that the ANC had approved the new policy of violence. Walter remained obdurate: "You won't get anything from me about Chief Luthuli!" (Walter Sisulu, Evidence, 177).

Yutar's next strategy was to try to browbeat and confuse Walter by reading parts of documents, then by demanding an explanation and rephrasing the same questions over and over. He was not very successful. Walter insisted on taking his time to answer. He told Yutar he could not digest all the information at once and asked him to read documents and letters in their entirety. This annoyed Yutar so much, he snapped nastily: "Come, come Sisulu! Even though you've only passed Std 4, you've exhibited ... that you have a fairly good command of the English language, if I may say so!"

Referring to Mandela's report on his tour of Africa, Yutar asked how the ANC could profess to have a policy of cooperation between black and white when the countries that supported it were against cooperation between black and white. Walter said the ANC was prepared to stand by its policy and educate people in South Africa and abroad that the only solution in South Africa was for black and white to live together. At this point, both judge and prosecutor inadvertently displayed their own fears and prejudices.

> Justice de Wet: Living together, but doesn't that involve according to your ideas, control by the non-white element?
>
> Sisulu: My lord, we have always maintained that perhaps because of historical conditions in this country, that the mere fact that the African are in the majority would not mean black domination.
>
> Justice de Wet: No black control? Won't mean black control?
>
> Sisulu: Only in the sense that the majority of voters will be black.
>
> Justice de Wet: That necessarily means control, not so?
>
> Sisulu: Well it might be that control can be exercised by both races together, elected together.
>
> Justice de Wet: You would never agree to that, would you?
>
> Sisulu: Why not?
>
> Justice de Wet: You're being represented by a white person?
>
> Sisulu: ... my lord, we don't want to be represented, but we say if the people of South Africa elected Dr Verwoerd, by all means let him come to Parliament. He is elected by the whole lot. We are not fighting the issue on the basis of colour. We say that can never work.
>
> (Walter Sisulu, Evidence, 230.)

Throughout the cross-examination, Yutar tried to characterise the ANC leaders as reckless and irresponsible people who allowed ordinary people in the organisation to suffer while they remained safely in the background or fled the country. The question of whether the ANC leadership was cowardly or not was completely irrelevant to the case, yet the judge did not stop this line of questioning. Instead, he asked questions that revealed his own bias: "Isn't that rather typical of patriots, that they're always prepared to let the rank and file take the risk, and see that they don't put themselves in danger?"

Walter replied that this was not his interpretation. It was only in the case of war that the rank and file went forward while the generals were not exposed. Again, the judge interrupted: "But exactly the same things happen with people who are plotting a rebellion or a revolution. They look forward to being the government in due course, and they see to it that they preserve their own skin!"

Yutar also tried to paint a picture of the ANC fomenting dissatisfaction through propaganda, but Walter was more than a match for him: "It would be a strange thing that the Africans in South Africa are the only people who do not know they are oppressed! The people in Africa are getting freedom and the people in South Africa do not know that they are oppressed!"

Walter consistently refused to allow Yutar to put words in his mouth or twist his own statements, as is evident by his response to Yutar's cross-examination:

Yutar: Let's now come to "Operation Mayibuye". Our first submission is going to be that there was a conspiracy between the accused, the South African Communist Party, the African National Congress and the Umkhonto We Sizwe, to commit sabotage and wage guerrilla warfare together as a start to this armed struggle that you envisaged! Do you agree with that?

Sisulu: I have put the position in my own words, that we did discuss the preparation for a guerrilla warfare. That in the event of everything else failing, that guerrilla warfare would be resorted to.

Yutar: You are not prepared to accept the way I put it?

Sisulu: No, well you're putting it in your own way. I'm putting it in my own way.

(Walter Sisulu, Evidence, 246–8.)

Later Walter scored an important moral point concerning guerrilla warfare:

Sisulu: The National Executive of the ANC would not take a matter like this lightly. It is a serious matter, a serious matter of war.

Yutar: Of course it is, high treason!

Sisulu: I am not talking about legal liability; I am talking about the seriousness even to embark on a thing like this. That it requires serious consideration, it will involve the life of people.

(Walter Sisulu, Evidence, 291.)

Throughout the five days of cross-examination, Walter was the most unflappable witness. There were only two occasions when he became angry and responded emotionally. The first was when Yutar commented that the police did not arrest people indiscriminately:

Sisulu: They arrest many people indiscriminately. For no offence people have been arrested....They arrested my wife, they arrested my son. That is indiscriminate.

Yutar: As far as you are concerned!

Sisulu: ... If there is a man who has been persecuted, it's myself. In 1962 I was arrested six times. I know the position in this country!

Yutar: You do?

Sisulu: I wish you were in the position of an African! I wish you were an African and knew the position in this country! (Walter Sisulu, Evidence, 210.)

Yutar was later embarrassed to discover that 15-year-old Lungi had been illegally arrested as he sat in the gallery watching his father on trial for his life.

The second instance was when Yutar referred to Sharpeville and Langa as examples of places that had well-organised uprisings. Walter responded angrily: "Sharpeville! The massacre was done by the government. The world knows that! The unarmed innocent people were killed, not by the Africans!" (Walter Sisulu, Evidence, 349.)

After the marathon cross-examination, Walter was re-examined by Bram to refute the judge's suggestions that Walter and his co-accused remained safely in the background while their followers risked their lives in dangerous missions. Bram got Walter to recount the constant harassment and persecution he had experienced in the last few years of his political activity. Walter also told the court that during his interrogation, the police had told him he could save himself if he informed on his comrades. Bram asked, "So you did not accept any offer, though it may have saved you from the death penalty?" Walter responded "Yes".

Walter's performance in the witness box earned him much admiration. Kathrada expressed the views of his co-accused: "At the end of it all Walter emerged from the witness box as cool, as calm and unruffled as when he had entered it. Our lawyers … were amazed at his composure, his phenomenal memory and the masterly manner in which he acquitted himself. Only one phrase could describe his performance – absolutely brilliant" (Walter Sisulu, Notes for prison memoir, 135).

The defence lawyers had not been the only ones who had been concerned about Walter being the main witness. Kathrada recalled that after Bram Fischer informed the court that Walter would be the main witness, one of the court officials was so aghast, he approached the defence lawyers. "He had been following the case and had undoubtedly been privy to some talk among his fellow civil servants, including the prosecution and the Special Branch. He was undoubtedly influenced by prevailing notions in white society about the Rivonia saboteurs. However … he retained a sense of justice and fair play … He told the lawyer that it was irresponsible for the defence team to put such an unsuitable individual in the witness box." The official was afraid they were inviting the death sentence by placing such a huge responsibility on a man who was "not even dressed properly!" (At the time Walter had been wearing a carelessly knotted tie and an ill-fitting jacket that belonged to Max.) After Walter had given evidence, the same official came back – this time to express his astonishment and congratulations (Walter Sisulu, Notes for prison memoir, 135).

Joel Joffe thought Walter was one of the finest witnesses he had ever seen. "We felt that Walter in the witness box had been a triumph. The way he came through revealed his real qualities of stability, calmness and certainty that had made him a leader in his organisation … His colleagues who had persuaded us beforehand that he would be more than a match for Yutar had understood him well" (Joffe, 151). Joffe said he had never in his experience as a lawyer, seen a witness perform better under such extreme pressure:

> The whole court … had been impressed by this small man of meagre education but of tremendous sincerity, calm, conviction and certainty. It was difficult to say what the judge felt. His comments had been, in the main, snide if not sinister. He had betrayed a bitter prejudice against Sisulu … But at least we felt … the judge had come to understand that in Sisulu he was dealing with no run-of-the-mill criminal of the type he was accustomed to in his court. To sentence such a man to death would not be easy for any judge (Joffe, 151).

In April 1964, the British High Commission held a multiracial reception in Johannesburg to mark the birthday of Queen Elizabeth II. It was quite a radical thing to do at the time. Several white waitresses walked out when they discovered that they would have to wait on African and Indian guests (*Rand Daily Mail* 22/4/64). Albertina was one of the guests, and a photograph taken at the reception shows her, in her green and black Women's League uniform, talking to a concerned-looking Mrs Minford. Albertina had spent the day in court, listening to Walter in the witness box.

Albertina lived by the belief that one had to present a brave face to the world. Her smiling countenance effectively masked her inner turmoil. She was consumed with anxiety about the outcome of the trial. She suffered from insomnia and spent many nights agonising about the future. Albertina had always dealt with emotional trauma by immersing herself in practical action. She was the strong one and people relied on her. When her parents died, she had focused her energy on taking care of her siblings. When Barbie died, she focused on the practical arrangements for Beryl's future. During the trial, her lifeline was the Women's League. She may have spent her nights worrying, but during the day she had little time to reflect and agonise. She threw her energies into activities around the trial. There was the need to give moral and practical support to the families of the accused. When Caroline Motsoaledi was imprisoned, Women's League members took turns to visit the Motsoaledi home to see that the children, especially the baby, had food and were well looked after.

League members were also busy planning how best to demonstrate support and solidarity for their leaders, whatever the outcome of the trial. Albertina tried hard not to be pessimistic. The defence case had given her reason to be hopeful. She had been delighted by Walter's performance in the witness box: "I was so proud of him, the way he took it so easily. It was as if he was just conversing with Yutar." Mike Dingake remembers her response clearly: "Ntsiki was ready to marry Walter all over again. Every time she came back from court she was full of excitement as she regaled me with Tyhopo's extraordinary performance" (Letter to Elinor Sisulu, July 2002).

She believed all the accused had acquitted themselves well in the witness box and she had nothing but admiration for the defence counsel, but she knew that this was not a case that would be decided by legal argument. On the day before sentences were passed, she had her last visit with Walter at Pretoria Jail. She asked him to be strong and not to show any emotion if the death sentence was passed: "Please don't disgrace us."

On 11 June 1964, the Rivonia accused appeared before a crowded court. People had been gathering outside the courtroom since early morning. Some had spent the night outside the court building to ensure that they would get a seat. All the drama and show of power of the opening day of the trial were re-enacted. In the courtroom, Albertina listened with a sinking heart as the judge pronounced his verdict of guilty for all the accused, except Rusty Bernstein. She rejoiced for Hilda, but before anyone could respond, the security police pounced on Rusty and re-arrested him.

They left the court and assembled outside, where Albertina led the crowd in singing *Nkosi Sikelel' iAfrika*. They then moved to the back of the court just in time to see the convoy escorting the accused leaving for the prison. Inside their Black Maria, the prisoners heard the multitude of voices shout in chorus: "Amandla!" They pushed their hands through the iron bars in response: "Ngawethu!"

After the verdict had been passed, the defence lawyers went to see their clients, who were preoccupied with the question of how to conduct themselves in court if the death sentence should not be passed. The lawyers explained that beginning with the first accused, the judge would ask them if they could give any reason why the death sentence was passed. Mandela said he would have plenty to say. He would tell the court that his death would not mean the end of the liberation movement and that he was ready to die for his beliefs.

The lawyers pointed out that militant statements would not help their chances of a successful appeal. But to their shock, Nelson, Walter and Govan had already decided that they would not appeal against the death sentence.

As senior leaders of the liberation movement they felt that they should demonstrate that they were ready to die for their beliefs. Bram Fischer gave an account of this in a letter to a young exile: "I must tell you one important event ... Govan, Walter and Nelson came to an early morning consultation to tell us [that] if [the sentence] turned out to be capital punishment, they had made up their mind that in that event there was to be no appeal. Their line was that, should a death sentence be passed on them, the political campaign around such a sentence should not be hampered by any appeal for mercy ... or by raising vain hopes ... we lawyers were staggered at first, but soon realised the decision was politically unassailable. But I tell you this story not because of its political wisdom. I want you to know to what incredibly brave men you and others will have to be successors" (Meli, 158).

With heavy hearts their lawyers went off to prepare their pleas in mitigation of sentence, while the accused sat down to write what George Bizos referred to as "pleas in aggravation of sentence". Walter's statement was as follows:

Statement prepared and written by Walter Sisulu in the event of his receiving the death sentence.

I have dedicated all my life towards making a contribution to the best of my ability.

The destiny of my country and of my people has placed me in the position where I find myself today; namely to challenge the immoral laws of your government against my people and indeed against humanity.

I am to face the gallows simply because I have dedicated my life towards making my humble contribution to my fatherland and to the advancement of the aspirations of my people. I am condemned because I have dared to challenge the Apartheid Monster of the Vorster and Verwoerd clique.

All honest men have an obligation to smash oppression and tyranny wherever it exists and by whatever means. History is full of examples of the execution of those who stand for the truth.

I am quite confident that our blood will certainly water the Garden of Freedom!

The trial had caught the imagination of the international community, and the United Nations and apartheid groups around the world protested against the sentencing of the Rivonia men. In the UK, Joe Slovo, Yusuf Dadoo and the young Thabo Mbeki were among the thousands who demonstrated against the verdict.

That evening, the atmosphere in townships around the country was tense and solemn. In Orlando West, Women's League members had gathered at the Sisulu home to prepare banners to display outside court the next day. "We did not sleep on the night before D Day," recalled Albertina. "We spent the whole night writing those messages – 'We are proud of our leaders,' and 'You will not serve those sentences as long as we live.'" Armed with their banners, they left for Pretoria at the crack of dawn.

Their early departure stood them in good stead because Pretoria was like a city under siege. There were police roadblocks on all roads leading to Pretoria and throughout the Witwatersrand. Train and bus commuters were subjected to police checks and scores of people were arrested for pass offences.

Church Square was crowded with supporters and detractors of the convicted men. The detractors included a large party of students from the University of Pretoria. Albertina noticed a group of mainly white Wits University students who had come out in support of the Rivonia prisoners. In the jam-packed courtroom, people jostled for seats and the reporters filled the well of the courtroom and the doorways.

Harold Hanson led the defence argument in mitigation. He called on renowned author and Liberal Party leader Alan Paton to give evidence in mitigation. When first approached, Paton had asked if the lives of the accused were in danger. When he was told they were, he immediately agreed to give evidence. In his appeal for clemency, Paton said, "Aspirations can only be realised if people have political representation." He said he knew Mandela, Sisulu and Govan Mbeki personally: "There is no doubt about the sincerity of these men and their very deep devotion to their cause" (*The Star*, 12/06/1964). He said he wanted to ask for clemency for the future of the country.

Vindictive to the last, Percy Yutar rose to cross-examine Alan Paton. It is very rare for a witness in mitigation to be cross-examined because the accused have already been found guilty. Yutar admitted as much, but said he had to examine Paton to unmask him because he wanted to make political capital. With much sneering and innuendo, he tried to attack Paton's political credentials. Harold Hanson then rose to make his address in which he asked not for mercy, but "for the exercise of understanding, wisdom and compassion". The judge then pronounced the sentence: life imprisonment for the six accused.

The spectators had not heard the sentence. Albertina heard June Mlangeni shout "How long, how long?" "Life," answered Andrew. Albertina and her group rushed out of court and unfurled their banners. The stirring notes of *Nkosi Sikelele'* reverberated around Church Square as the 2 000-strong crowd sang. The women tried to form a guard of honour at the massive iron gates, but the convoy turned sharply left to avoid the crowd. They watched as it disappeared into the distance, carrying their husbands away.

# Part Three

## *1964–1977*

## *The Scattering: Detention and Exile*

## TO WALTER

I thought of you
standing soft-carpeted
watching Swans on the Spree
    I wonder why?
No sea gulls here
No salt-sprayed Quarry
The child I see is not a dream of ten years lost
She will laugh again tomorrow.

They honour me
sitting soft-cushioned
mouthing words of remembrance
    I wonder why?
I drain my glass,
a quick forgotten toast,
The hills I see don't hide the fields beyond
like the walls of your unchanging coast.

I tire of platitudes
and heraldic tears
to mark your years of trial
    Is this my life,
to wander the earth
in free and warm embraces?
At whim I choose the boundaries of my world
whilst yours are fixed in never-ending paces.

I tell myself
I am one of the mirrors of your courage,
suffering the good life for you.
But comfort's chains caress and soothe
corroding the will to prise them loose.

JOE SLOVO

*Berlin Gasthaus auf dem Spree 1973*

# *o n e*

A life sentence in apartheid South Africa meant exactly that – spending the rest of one's life in prison. There was no possibility of parole, and certainly not for Walter. Legally, he would be in prison even after his death – a previous sentence of six years had been added to his life sentence, so his charge sheet read "Life plus six years". This did not worry Walter. For him, a life sentence was a reprieve: "Once we did not get the death sentence, I had hope that we would see the freedom day." Alone in his cell in Pretoria that night, he felt calm and relaxed after the suspense of the trial.

At midnight Walter was woken by Colonel Aucamp and given 15 minutes to pack his things. A few minutes later he and all his co-accused, except for Dennis Goldberg who remained in Pretoria, were marched down the long corridors, the numerous prison gates clanging behind them. They were handcuffed, placed in leg-irons and chained to each other in pairs ("so when you went to the toilet, your partner had to go as well"). They were then driven under heavy police escort to a small military airport just outside Pretoria. Dirker and Lieutenant van Wyk accompanied them in the back of the police van. Dirker handed out sandwiches and drinks and the mood was jovial. Van Wyk assured them that they would not spend more than a few years in prison. They sang freedom songs and Walter and Kathrada joked about how strange it was to be given sandwiches by Dirker.

Political prisoners were normally taken by road or flown to Cape Town, then to Robben Island by boat, but in the case of the Rivonia prisoners, the regime did not want to take a chance. They were the first and only prisoners ever to be flown right onto the Island. The military transport plane that carried them landed at about five in the morning on the small landing strip usually used by government officials and top brass (Mandela, 454–5).

As he stepped onto the soil of Robben Island on that freezing June morning, Walter felt relaxed. After the confines of Pretoria Prison, which he had hated, he welcomed the sense of openness on the Island: "I could see the sky. This gave me a sense of relief." His attitude on his arrival was also the result of years of psychological conditioning. He had prepared himself for this fate, so there was a sense of acceptance: "I was not a passer-by."

Escorted by gun-toting guards, they chatted and joked during the 10-minute walk from the landing strip to the old prison, which served as a reception area. At the entrance of the building, they had to strip naked and change into the Robben Island prison uniform. Kathrada was given the "Indian and Coloured uniform" – long trousers, shoes and socks, while his comrades were issued with the "African uniform" – khaki shorts, a thin khaki jersey and a canvas jacket. Kathrada was mortified that he, the youngest in the group, was given better clothing than men who were his seniors, both in age and political status. In deference to their status they were all given shoes instead of the rubber sandals made of car tyres normally allocated to African prisoners (Mandela, 455).

Walter was registered as prisoner number 471/64, the four-hundred-and-seventy-first prisoner to be incarcerated on Robben Island in 1964.

The day after the Rivonia sentences had been passed, Tiny Nokwe, the wife of Duma, gave June Mlangeni a lift to Pretoria to visit Andrew. As they approached the prison they noticed someone on the upper floors of the building waving vigorously, as if to attract their attention. They could see no good reason why some strange man should be waving to them so they ignored him, until he dropped a piece of paper. They stopped and watched. The piece of paper fluttered down and landed right in front of them. It turned out to be a note informing them that the Rivonia men had been taken to Robben Island at three o'clock that morning (Interview, June Mlangeni, 1992). They passed the news to Albertina when she arrived later. Albertina and June were surprised and angered by the abrupt removal of their husbands. The police had indicated that the men would remain in Pretoria for a while to consult with their lawyers about the possibility of an appeal (Clingman, 11:24). Albertina and June returned home, sick with disappointment.

On that same Saturday, Molly and Bram Fischer set out on the long drive to Cape Town to have a few days' break after the trial and to celebrate their daughter Ilse's 21st birthday. Their journey ended tragically, with a car accident in which Molly was killed. Molly's death was a terrible blow to a family and community already traumatised by relentless police persecution. Stunned by the terrible news, Albertina joined the many friends and comrades who flocked to the Fischer home to sympathise with the family. As she reached the front gate, Bram came out to meet her. He gripped her hand tightly and said, "I am so glad you have come," over and over. Choked with emotion, Albertina stood silent, unable to find words of consolation.

Molly was cremated on the following Friday, a week after the Rivonia Trial ended. Three hundred people of all races attended the funeral, many of them under banning orders that prevented them from offering even a few words of comfort to each other. George Bizos and Bram had to persuade a distraught Hilda Bernstein not to defy her banning order by speaking at the funeral. After the burial, Ruth and Ilse presented Albertina with three suitcases, the clothes that their mother had packed for the fateful trip to Cape Town and which had been retrieved from the car after the accident. Ruth and Ilse laundered and repacked the clothes and decided to give them to Albertina "because she was so important to us". For Albertina, their gesture was symbolic: "Their mother was gone and this meant I was their mother." She pondered for a long time on the cruel irony of Molly's death. The life sentences of the Rivonia men and Molly's death – she would always link the two events.

A couple of days after Molly's funeral, Bram and Joel Joffe travelled to Robben Island to consult with their clients on whether they should appeal against their sentence. Cut off as they were from the outside world, the Rivonia prisoners had not heard about Molly's death. Overjoyed to see Bram again, Walter had greeted him eagerly and asked after Molly. Bram mumbled that she was all right, but it was clear from his demeanour that something was terribly wrong. Walter thought Bram's tone "was like someone who is destroyed inside" (Houser and Shore Interviews). Towards the end of the consultation, Mandela also asked how Molly was. Bram turned away abruptly, almost rudely, Walter felt, and they were puzzled because "Bram was not the type of person to be rude, not ever". After the departure of Bram and Joel, Major Visser, the prison official guarding them explained the reason for Bram's odd behaviour (Mandela, 461; Clingman, 11:30). They were devastated and moved beyond words that despite Bram's bereavement, he had taken the time to travel all the way to the Island to attend to them. Their distress would have been even more acute if they had known that it was the last time they would see Bram.

*Dit is die Eiland! Hier gaan julle vrek!* (This is the Island! Here you will die!) These were the words that greeted hundreds of political prisoners as they set foot on Robben Island in the early 1960s. The Rivonia prisoners were the latest additions to the ever-increasing numbers of political prisoners incarcerated on the Island in the wave of arrests and detentions that followed the passing of the Sabotage Act in 1962. In 1962, the prison population had consisted of a handful of prisoners, mostly hardened criminals. These were followed by a wave of PAC prisoners on short sentences of two to three years. In April 1963, the PAC leader Robert Sobukwe had been sent to Robben Island. He was detained under the infamous "Sobukwe clause", legislation especially passed to keep him imprisoned after he had served his sentence. Sobukwe was to remain on Robben Island for six years.

Once the original Robben Island building was filled to capacity, prisoners were accommodated in corrugated-iron sheds called the *zinktronk*. Prison labour was used to build a new maximum-security prison from stone that the prisoners excavated from the Island quarries. By the time the

Rivonia group arrived, the new prison housed over a thousand political and common-law prisoners in an H-shaped building in the complex, known as sections E and F, or the general section.

Robben Island in 1964 was a grim and wretched place. Mandela found that the prison had changed since his first stint: from what "seemed more like an experiment" in 1962 to "the harshest, most iron-fisted outpost in the South African penal system" (Mandela, 459). By 1964, the coloured warders who had smuggled food, cigarettes and newspapers to prisoners had been removed and replaced by white warders who could barely conceal their fear and loathing of black prisoners.

The psyche of the warders was shaped by white supremacist ideology and *swart gevaar* ("black danger"). The murders of whites in the *Poqo* campaign were still fresh in their minds and, politically ignorant as they were, they could not make a distinction between the PAC, the ANC or any other black African organisation. In the lexicon of warders, all political prisoners were *poqos* who had to be punished for daring to challenge white supremacy; and Robben Island was the place to exact retribution.

Prisoners in the general section were abused and assaulted on a daily basis. In the quarries they had to work like slaves to meet daily quotas. After work they had to strip naked and line up in front of the warders, who would search their clothes. The prisoners were then expected to do the humiliating *tausa*, a kind of dance in which the prisoners clicked their tongues (to show if there was anything in the mouth), leapt high into the air, twisted around, clapped their hands above their heads and landed with their legs apart, torsos bent forward and rectums exposed to the warder. Political prisoners, however, flatly refused to do the *tausa*.

From time to time prisoners were subjected to systematic assaults by warders. Medical care was virtually nonexistent in the early years and prisoners who went to the dispensary for treatment were often assaulted and told they were too lazy to work. Warders arbitrarily charged prisoners for not working. The most common punishment was withholding of meals. Prisoners found guilty of serious offences were sentenced to solitary confinement and "spare diet", which consisted of three days of nothing but the water from boiled mealie rice, followed by three days of boiled mealies. The "spare diet" punishment could go on for as long as 42 days. Sometimes prisoners would come out of the isolation section looking like skeletons.

The high-profile prisoners in the isolation section were generally spared the brutal physical assaults experienced by the general section prisoners. Prison authorities were more careful about the treatment of the Rivonia group, as its members remained the focus of a good deal of international attention. It was also known that their lawyers would not hesitate to expose any instances of torture.

From the outset, the prison authorities went to great lengths to prevent any contact between the Rivonia group and the rest of the prison population. On 24 July 1964, the Commanding Officer of Robben Island recommended to the Commissioner of Prisons in Pretoria that the Rivonia prisoners be kept in total isolation for an indefinite period because they were all leading figures in the ANC and held in high esteem by their supporters. "It is therefore extremely undesirable that above-mentioned seven prisoners come into contact with other prisoners, as they will definitely continue with their undermining activities which will cause endless trouble" (Walter Sisulu, Prison Files). The prison authorities believed the Rivonia men required extraordinary security measures, so they decided to build a special section within the new prison complex for them. Walter and his colleagues were transferred from the old jail, which had served as their temporary home, to the newly completed isolation section, referred to as *makhulukuthu*, a prison slang term for isolation cells in prisons throughout the country. The Robben Island *khulukuthu* section consisted of a quadrangle built around a cement courtyard. The quadrangle was made up of three double rows of cells with a corridor running through the middle. On the fourth side was a 20-foot wall topped by a walkway on which guards patrolled with Alsatian dogs. The Rivonia prisoners were placed in single cells in the easternmost row of the quadrangle. The cells were tiny, just seven-foot square. Each cell was marked with the prisoner's name and prison service number.

The winter of 1964 was one of the coldest ever recorded in South Africa. Buffeted by fierce southeasterly winds in the summer and northwesterly winds that bring drenching rain in the winter, Robben Island is completely exposed to the elements.

The new prisoners had to acclimatise to a harsh prison regime in bitterly cold weather. Their clothing and their bedding, which consisted of a sisal mat, a soft felt mat and three threadbare blankets, offered them little protection against the inclement weather. When Mandela complained about the damp oozing from the walls and floors of the cells, the Commanding Officer told him that the moisture would be absorbed by their bodies (Mandela, 456). Apart from a bottle of water and a sanitary bucket, the six-foot-square cells were bare. When Eddie Daniels, the only member of the Liberal Party to be imprisoned on the Island, started his sentence in November 1964, he likened the single-cells section to a death chamber: "There was total silence – everything around me was grey. There was a long corridor … it was cold, it was bleak, it was frightening!" (Schadeberg Interview, Eddie Daniels).

Neville Alexander, Fikile Bam, Leslie van der Heyden, Lionel Davies and Don Davis of the Yu Chi Chan (YCC) group joined the Rivonia men shortly after arriving on the Island. In the weeks that followed, more prisoners were transferred from the general section. They included the poet Dennis Brutus and PAC leaders Zeph Mothopeng and Clarence Makwethu (Meredith, 282; Mandela, 287). Over the years, the number of prisoners in the single-cells section would fluctuate as those with shorter sentences left and new prisoners came in. This section was known as the leadership section and, although many high-profile prisoners were kept there, the choice of who should be placed there was fairly arbitrary. Some rank-and-file prisoners, like the three peasants from the Transkei who had been jailed for plotting to assassinate Kaizer Matanzima, were put in the single-cells section, while leaders like the ANC's Harry Gwala and the PAC's Johnson Mlambo were kept in the general section. Prisoners were sometimes transferred from one section to another as a result of altercations with the warders or with other prisoners.

The daily routine in the isolation section began with the ringing of a wake-up bell at 5.30am. A second bell at 6.00am was the signal for prisoners to clean and tidy their cells. When the cells were unlocked, the prisoners would go to the bathroom to empty and clean their buckets and to wash. In the first few weeks, the Rivonia group was taken separately to the bathroom in the mornings, but this attempt to keep them isolated from the other prisoners in the segregation section did not work in practice. Waiting for the Rivonia men to wash first, taking them back to their cells and then letting the other prisoners out was a process that could take the whole morning. Mandela made things harder for the warders by deliberately taking his time about washing. If the warders tried to hurry him up, he moved even slower. Eventually, everyone in the section had to be let out at the same time (Interview, Fikile Bam).

After washing, they went back to their cells for breakfast. At first the common-law prisoners dished out the food, which would then be taken to each prisoner in his cell. Once again, this process took too long, so it was changed. The *khulukuthu* prisoners would collect their food as it was dished out, and then take it to their cells. Walter hated the daily diet of boiled mealies. He tried to relieve the monotony of the diet by making sour porridge, keeping a little porridge to make a culture. From time to time, the cells would be raided, and the warders would discover the sour porridge and throw it away. Walter was charged and punished several times for this transgression.

Hard labour was a central feature of life on the Island. The prison population was divided into work teams assigned to different tasks, which included digging for stone in the stone quarry or lime in the lime quarry, chopping wood, making or repairing roads, collecting seaweed, and cleaning the yards and cells. Most prisoners worked in the stone quarry. Political prisoners were generally allocated the most difficult jobs, while common-law prisoners were generally assigned the less strenuous "staff jobs" in the hospital, offices and kitchen (Alexander, 30; Buntman, 1994). Although they were treated slightly better than the general section prisoners, the men in the single cells were not spared the rigours of hard labour.

The day after their arrival in the isolation section, the Rivonia group had been put to work in the prison courtyard. Every morning the prison authorities dumped a large load of stones at the entrance of the yard. Using wheelbarrows, the prisoners had to move the stones to the middle of the yard. They then had to sit in rows, cross-legged on the ground and "knap stones". In prison parlance, this meant pounding stones with heavy hammers weighing anything from four to 16 pounds, until the stones were crushed to fine gravel (Mandela, 458; Meredith, 285). It was monotonous and back-breaking work, made even more tedious by grim warders constantly on watch to ensure that the prisoners did not talk to each other.

Their only break came at noon when lunch was served from a metal drum. They then continued work until 4pm, after which they washed themselves. Walter described the showers as brackish, with only a small towel about the size of a baby's napkin provided for drying. "It was one of the most horrible things – cold salt water early in the morning and in the evening" (Houser and Shore Interviews). They were allowed to shower twice a week, on Wednesday afternoons and Saturday mornings, and to change clothes once a week – on Saturday mornings.

At 4.30pm they had to collect their supper, which was dished out by common-law prisoners, and return to their cells to eat. By 6pm they were locked up for the night and ordered to sleep at 8pm (except for those who were later given permission to study). Warders prowled up and down the corridors continuously, often moving without shoes so the prisoners could not hear them approaching. The lights in their cells were never switched off, making it difficult to get enough sleep to face the next day's grinding routine. Mike Dingake remembers Walter adapting to this: "Tyhopo was quite comfortable with it, hinting that he might find it difficult to fall asleep in the dark when released. It must have been quite a job for [Albertina] to wean him from the habit!"

To the chagrin of the South African government, the Rivonia Trialists continued to be the focus of international attention. Press reports about inhumane conditions on the Island had also put the regime under pressure. In an effort to counter the allegations, the government allowed a trickle of carefully selected visitors to inspect the prison and meet the high-profile prisoners.

A few weeks after they had arrived on the Island, Walter and his colleagues were surprised when the warders took away the hammers they used to crush stones and gave them sacking to sit on and old pieces of linoleum to put at their feet. Each prisoner was given a needle and thread and a pile of old frayed prison jerseys, which they were told to mend. Rather bemused, they set about this task, wondering why the prison authorities were suddenly trying to make them more comfortable. The mystery was solved by the arrival of a reporter and photographer from a London newspaper, the *Daily Telegraph*. After watching them work for a while, the reporter interviewed Nelson Mandela. After the interview, Mandela agreed to be photographed, provided Walter joined him. While the photograph was being taken, Walter and Nelson discussed the visit. They believed the prison authorities had allowed the visit because the *Daily Telegraph* was a conservative newspaper, and that any article written about the visit would be used as government propaganda. Nevertheless they felt it was important to take the opportunity of stating their case to the reporter (Mandela, 454).

One day in January 1965, the *khulukuthu* prisoners were loaded onto a truck and driven to the lime quarry, a couple of kilometres away from the prison complex. The lime and stone quarries on Robben Island dated back to the mid-seventeenth century, when convicts incarcerated by the Dutch East India Company had to mine the Island's lime and blue slate for the nascent building industry on the Cape mainland (De Villiers, 26, 29). When the modern-day prisoners first saw the lime quarry, it looked as if a huge spoonful of earth had been scooped from the hillside, leaving bare its dazzling white innards.

After very basic instructions from the warders, the *khulukuthu* prisoners set to work with picks and shovels. Chipping at the layers of rock in order to get at the lime seams was gruelling work. By the time they were taken back to their cells, their hands were blistered, their bodies aching, and they were covered in lime dust from head to toe.

Other well-known political prisoners continued to join the single-cell prisoners. Among the new-comers were Wilton Mkwayi, Mac Maharaj, Billy Nair and Pascal Ngakane. Also added to their number were several common-law prisoners – hardened criminals from the gangs in the general section. The authorities had placed them there to spy on the political prisoners and generally to provoke them. According to Mandela, one of these unpleasant characters, known as Bogart because he projected a Humphrey Bogart-like macho image, would demand Walter's breakfast every morning (Mandela, 485). Walter remembered this differently, implying with a twinkle in his eye that he parted with his breakfast voluntarily: "I never liked the prison breakfast anyway. To call it breakfast was decorating it with a name it did not deserve. You could not regard it as real food. It was just something you took to survive."

While working in the quarry, the gang members began to sing songs mocking the political prisoners, such as "What did you want at Rivonia, did you think you would become the government?" The political prisoners responded by singing freedom songs. The singing contest went on for several weeks and gradually the political prisoners outsang their rivals. Eventually the authorities became concerned about the political content of the songs and banned all singing (Mandela, 484). Walter was angered by this and complained: "We must have been the only prisoners in the country who were not allowed to sing while working."

Work in the quarry was made more difficult by the attitude of the warders, who goaded the prisoners and were often very abusive for no particular reason. Every prisoner was singled out for abuse at some stage. Captain Kellerman, one of the prison officials working in the administrative offices, was hostile towards the prisoners whenever he had to inspect their work. During one of his inspections of the lime quarry, he unleashed a torrent of unspeakable abuse at Walter and Raymond Nyanda, the prisoner who was working next to him. For Walter, who never used profanities – even the word "damn" was too strong for him – this kind of verbal abuse was truly vexatious to the spirit.

The older men in the group could have asked to be exempted from work in the quarry on grounds of age or ill health. The prison authorities encouraged this, but Walter said they refused to even consider the idea: "We could never have taken a line like that. It would have isolated us from the rest of our comrades. Going to work was an advantage, not a disadvantage. It enabled you to communicate with your fellow prisoners." He enjoyed the short walk to the quarry – it was the only time he and his colleagues got to see anything of the Island. For Walter, time spent in the open air was infinitely preferable to remaining cooped up in the prison building. He hated the weekends when, except for half an hour's exercise in the morning and the evening, they were locked up in their cells with nothing to do other than sit in silence and reflect on their fate.

# t w o

Prisoners in South Africa were classified into four categories – A, B, C and D. The "A" group enjoyed privileges such as contact visits, radios and newspapers, unheard-of luxuries for "D" prisoners. First-time offenders were usually placed in the "B" group when they started serving their sentences, while habitual criminals were placed in the "D" group. All political prisoners were classified as "D" group prisoners, along with the most hardened criminals. It was extremely difficult for political prisoners to be upgraded, and this could only be after they had served a quarter of their sentences. "D" group prisoners were allowed to send one letter to and receive one letter from their families every six months. All letters to and from prisoners had to go through the prison censors. Any reference to politics or to persons other than family members was prohibited.

Walter wrote his first letter to Albertina a few days after his arrival on the Island. That took care of his quota for the first half of the year. He became rather distressed when he had not yet received a reply from Albertina after a month. He knew that she was not a great letter-writer, but had assumed that in the circumstances, she would respond promptly. He was especially anxious for news about his children, Max in particular. The South African government's propaganda machine always claimed that the ANC tricked young people into leaving the country by promising education abroad, and that once outside the country, the young recruits were forced into military training. The opposite was true. The attitude of the ANC leadership was that those young people who left the country with the intention of continuing their education should not be diverted to military training. It was often the young exiles themselves who decided to drop their schooling once they had left the country. According to Albertina, "Many of them were stubborn and wanted to go for military training because they were excited by the idea of becoming soldiers." During the Rivonia Trial, Walter and Albertina had been horrified to hear, through the ANC grapevine, that Max had opted to go for military training rather than to further his education. Walter had managed to smuggle messages to Ruth First, who was in London by then, asking her to find out why Max had not gone to school and to remind him that he could go into the military only after he completed his education. By the time he was taken to the Island, they had not yet had a response from Ruth.

He finally received Albertina's long-awaited reply in September.

11 August 1964

Darling Walter,

You cannot imagine how pleased everybody was to hear from you. I received your letter yesterday afternoon, the 10th August 1964, it was dated 12 July 1964. One wonders how quick the letters can be if they take a month to reach one. In any case darling it is not important.

We thought that after the sentence, they [would] keep you people in Pretoria for about one or two months, and would have enabled us to see you before leaving for the Island, but to add to the strain we had, when we took food to Pretoria the following day, we were told you had left for the Island. In any case darling we are very happy to hear from you.

Nkuli is doing very well at school ... Her daily song is that next year when she is in Std 1 she will write a letter to Daddy and tell him to come back home because we are longing for him. If Daddy refuses to come home she will go stay with him in prison. Lungi and Beryl are doing well ... In their last tests they did badly, but they have picked up wonderfully in their June tests. They both wrote wonderful letters after the sentence, saying that they were happy it was not the death sentence.

Your brave Lindi says "Mama, be brave. As long as they are not sentenced to death we will see them again." A person who took it bitterly was Zwelakhe. They say he cried the whole day at school until Father sent him to bed. He has not written since. I have written two letters to him. The only reply I got was that he wants to come back home. In any case, don't worry about that Darling I will manage him when he comes home in December.

I got all your clothing from Pretoria. I was pleased to learn that you are studying. I know you will make it. It is never too late to learn. I am going to tell your sons to study hard because it will be a disgrace if you can pass examinations and they fail. I have spoken to many people about Max and I am prepared to be firm about his schooling. I think I will succeed in getting him back to school.

Yes, Walter, we were all upset about Molly ... Darling I will be seeing you soon if all goes well. I am at present doing night duty so don't be surprised at seeing many mistakes. All are well at home. Greeting from all your kids.
Your loving Tinie.

It was obvious that Albertina had not yet received Walter's second letter, written in August. In a letter dated 9 September 1964, she wrote that it had been a pleasure to receive his second letter, but heart-breaking to learn that he had not yet received her letters: "I think the fault lies with the authorities because your letters take a month before they reach us."

Immediately after Walter's arrival on Robben Island, Albertina set about making arrangements to visit him. This proved more difficult than she had anticipated. First she had to wait for official confirmation that Walter had been taken to Robben Island prison. Next was a letter from the Commanding Officer of Prisons setting out the rules for visits. One of the requirements was the presentation of a passbook. Without a pass she could not possibly visit the Island, so after all the years of resistance she finally had to capitulate and apply for the hated document. It was a painful and humiliating process. The bureaucrats went out of their way to give her and other women in her position a difficult time. They would deliberately harass them and ask them where they were when other people were getting their reference books. They also created delays. However, with the help of Joel Joffe, Albertina finally managed to get the pass.

Her efforts to visit Walter were further complicated by a five-year banning order. At 9.30am on 5 August 1964, two security policemen turned up at her house to deliver it. Signed by BJ Vorster, the Minister of Justice at the time, the order was valid for five years – from 5 August 1964 to 31 July 1969. Albertina received the order with a sinking heart, but she was not surprised. The few political activists who were not in exile, banished or in prison had invariably been banned, so she had been expecting some kind of restriction. She was not aware, however, that if the Security Branch had had its way, she would have been banned in 1963.

In November 1963, they had written to the Ministry of Justice requesting that Albertina be placed under Group B restrictions. The Justice Department responded: "Sisulu has to date attended only those hearings involving her husband. If she is forbidden to do that now, some quarters will have the opportunity to kick up a fuss" (Letter from Captain Coots to the Secretary of Justice S.4/2704, Ministry of Justice files). To avoid adverse publicity, it was decided that "the restrictions must be postponed until after the Rivonia Trial when it can be submitted again". (Memo from Secretary for Justice to Commissioner of Police 10/12/63. Ministry of Justice files).

A month after the Rivonia Trial ended, the Security Branch once again urged that Group B restrictions be applied to Albertina and furnished a Supplementary Memorandum on Albertina's activities. The following were some of the many "activities" listed as justification for the banning:

- 14,15, 11/59. Subject attended the annual conference of the African National Congress (Women's League) in Johannesburg and said inter alia, "Let us not allow ourselves to be played about by the Boers."

- 28/1/60. Subject was amongst those who held placards in front of Baragwanath Hospital during the visit of Mr Harold McMillan [sic], prime minister of England.
- 15/12/61. Was noticed at Jan Smuts airport on the arrival of Luthuli from Oslo.
- 19–20/3/62. Helped with arrangements to murder Chief Kaizer Matanzima and to burn his house while in Pretoria.
- 3/1/63. According to documentary information subject's name appears on documents which come from a certain Maggie – presumably Maggie Resha from Dar es Salaam. In the document subject's deceased mother-in-law is praised as a "Freedom Fighter" and "a mother to a great leader."
- 15/2/63. Attended the trial of Walter Sisulu, her husband, in Johannesburg.
- 10/3/63. Mrs E. Armstrong from Victoria, Australia, wrote to the Minister of Justice to protest against the detention of subject.
- 19/1/64. Johannesburg – A meeting of FEDSAW under the chairmanship of the subject was convened. The subject expressed herself as follows: "The present government is oppressive ... The ninety-day detainees who are said to have hanged themselves in the cells were actually killed by the police".
  In February 1964 it [was] determined that subject is the active link between the ANC refugees outside the RSA and the chief executive of the subversive movement within the RSA.
- 21/4/64. Subject was present at a multi-racial reception held at the British Consulate.
- 24/1/64. A photo of subject which appeared in "World" shows her in cheerful conversation with the wife of the press attaché at a garden party at the United Kingdom Embassy, this was after her husband had been sentenced.

In a handwritten communication following the official letter of request to the Secretary for Justice, Major Burger of the security police wrote: "Lieutenant Coetzee phoned requesting that the restrictions of Sisulu and Nokwe [Tiny Nokwe, wife of Duma] should receive urgent preference. Compol has been informed ... if the above two are restricted, it would deal a heavy blow to the ANC" (File 3/50/484, Ministry of Justice files). In a memorandum to the Minister, the Secretary for Justice supported the Compol request: "Her activities without doubt further the objectives of communism and thus Compol's suggestion that Group C restrictions should be applied is important."

The Minister decided against Group C restrictions, which entailed 24-hour house arrest. Instead, Albertina was placed under the less severe Group B set of restrictions. This meant that she was confined to the magisterial district of Johannesburg. Even within the Johannesburg area, she was prohibited from visiting any location, hostel, village or compound where black people stayed, any factory, any newspaper or magazine office, any university, school, college, or educational institution, and any coloured or Asian area, except Orlando, where she lived. She was also prohibited from communicating in any way with any banned or listed person, except her husband. She was not allowed to be in any way involved with the preparing, compiling, printing, publishing or dissemination of any publication, or to give any educational instruction in any manner or form to any person other than her own children. She was also banned from attending any social or political gathering or any gathering of students. A "gathering" was defined as any gathering in any room, office, hall, house or any other place with more than three persons present and/or any number of persons of different races. She was also required to report to the Commanding Officer of Orlando Police Station every Wednesday.

Because she was confined to the Johannesburg area, when she finally received her permit to visit the Island, Albertina had to apply to the Chief Magistrate of Johannesburg for permission to leave the magisterial district. He in turn had to refer her request to the security police. After she received the permission from the police via the Chief Magistrate, she was able to make travel arrangements for mid-September. Before she left, she had to report to the nearest police station to inform the police that she was on her way to the station and the time her train was due to leave. In Cape Town, Albertina had to report her arrival to the police at Caledon Square. She had to show them her permit to visit Robben Island and tell them where she was staying in Cape Town. The police then followed her to her brother Elliot's home in Langa. A police vehicle was parked outside the house until she returned to Johannesburg. This set the pattern for all her subsequent visits.

Elliot took Albertina to the quay where she had to board the boat to the Island. She joined a queue in front of a small office. Most of the people in the queue were relatives of common-law prisoners. The boat was small and uncomfortable and the sea was rough. It was her first trip on a boat and she became very seasick. "I could not stand the smell of the boat. It upset me so much. I was miserable and nauseous on that first visit." On arriving on the Island, they were treated like prisoners. They were warned that they were only allowed to speak English or Afrikaans during the visit and they could only speak about their families. The police shouted orders at them about where to stand and they went forward when their names were called. "There was no place to see them properly. We were in the open veld. There was a fence right around and a table in the middle. A policeman was standing at the table. We were a group of about 20, all speaking at the same time. When the noise seemed to rise to a crescendo, the policeman banged the table. There was silence for a few minutes, then people would start to talk again, the noise level would rise until the policeman banged the table, and then we would start all over again."

A satisfactory conversation was impossible. Before she knew it, the 30-minute visit was over and they were on the boat, headed back to the mainland.

The impact of Walter's incarceration on Albertina was much greater than she cared to admit. She showed a brave face to those around her, but she missed Walter desperately and felt the absence of Gogo and Barbie more keenly than ever. She was the only adult in the house, and many of the friends who would have provided support and company were banned or in exile.

Her movements were drastically curtailed by her banning order, and friends who had rallied around to give her support found it increasingly difficult to visit. She suffered badly from insomnia and the months of strain and anxiety began to take their toll. In a letter to Walter, dated 22 October 1964, she wrote:

> This is just to inform you that I arrived safely on the 21st September and on the 22nd I was admitted at Bara Hospital with backache and I was discharged on the 19th October. I am still at home on sick leave and my back is still not quite well. I am sure you are wondering why I don't tell you how I travelled back home.
>
> Darling, I am very sorry to be so absent-minded, you asked me to buy a book on that piece of paper I had, but I can't find it now. I wonder if it can be possible for you to write and tell me the name of the book again. Sorry, Walter, I know how you would feel.

Apart from her anxiety about Walter spending his first Christmas on Robben Island, Albertina spent many sleepless nights worrying about how she would feed her children when they came home for the December holidays. "There was hardly anything to eat and I had to close the doors and windows to keep out the aroma of delicious food coming from the houses of our neighbours. We were so lonely. The people who we would normally spend the day with were not there. It was the worst Christmas we had ever had."

Albertina's financial woes continued during the next few years because she could not really afford to send her children to school in Swaziland. She spent every spare moment sewing *lishweshwe* dresses and knitting jerseys and baby clothes to try to make some extra money. She also bought eggs at wholesale prices and sold them at a small profit. What was not sold, the children had to eat. "Sometimes we would have eggs for supper for days on end," recalls Nkuli. "As a result, I hate eggs to this day." Albertina relied heavily on credit for clothes and food. Her worst times were when the children had to go back to Swaziland – because it was always a job to scrape together enough money to buy their supplies for school. Lungi recalls how she would send the children to

MaDumezweni or MaDlamini to "pick up the parcel". It was only when he was much older that he realised that "the parcel" was money his mother had had to borrow from the neighbours.

Some neighbours and friends continued to offer moral and material support at the most difficult times. Lungi recalls how supportive some of the neighbours were. "Bab'uMakhubu would pass by every evening without fail to see if we were all right. His wife MaMtshali virtually stayed at the house at the most difficult times to console Mama. Bab'uMncube from Number 7373 was also very supportive." Mr Sasekile who owned a grocery store in Killarney allowed Albertina to take groceries on credit and pay when she had the money. Although there was electricity in Soweto by the 1960s, the Sisulu family, like most other Soweto families, continued to rely on a coal stove for cooking and heating. Another neighbour, Bab'uZondo delivered five bags of coal a month, completely free of charge throughout the 1960s.

Albertina tried as far as possible to hide her anxiety from her children. Nkuli recalls that "Mama would never complain when she was worried. As I grew older, I noticed that if she was depressed she would simply say she wanted an early night and go off to her bedroom." One day, she felt truly desperate because the children were complaining about how hungry they were and she had not a cent on her. She told them not to worry, that she would go out in a while and buy something. She went to her bedroom and prayed. "I do not go to church, but I have always believed in my God and that He would provide when things got really bad." She was still praying when the children called her. She went out to find a neighbour at the door. The neighbour held out a R10 note and said "Mama, I thought you might need this" (Sparks Interview, 25/5/84). "Those were bad times," Albertina would later recall, "but the community did a lot to help me. The importance of community, of belonging and of caring for one another was again reinforced in me" (Villa-Vicencio, Interview).

Some of the Anglican priests who had become family friends over the years were an important part of Albertina's support network. Father Blake, who taught at St Peter's in Rosettenville, was always concerned about the wellbeing of her family and would look in on the children whenever he visited Holy Cross Church. He was fond of the children, especially Beryl, who used to confide in him when things were really desperate. He often came to Albertina's assistance, either by paying the rent or contributing to fares to send the children back to school.

In Swaziland, Father Charles Hooper provided invaluable support when Albertina was facing a losing battle to pay school fees. One day he sat Beryl down and explained to her that she needed to write to organisations in Norway for bursaries. Beryl wrote several letters which Father Hooper sent off to Norway. Their efforts were rewarded with bursaries that covered the school fees of Beryl, Lindi, Zwelakhe and Mlungisi.

As much as she missed the children, Albertina could only have them home once a year, partly because she could not afford to pay for them to come home every holiday. The other obstacle was the problem of travel documents. By the early 1960s, the days when people moved freely between South Africa and Swaziland were over. The South Africans introduced border controls and insisted on passports. After Lungi was accepted at St Christopher's in 1962, Joel Joffe had helped Albertina to apply to the Minister of Justice, for a passport for Lungi. The Minister denied this request, with the result that Lungi had to jump the border to go to school. Once in Swaziland, he could not risk going back to South Africa unless absolutely necessary, because of increased border controls. Military camps had been set up at Oshoek border post, the Sichunuza border post further south and Golela border post on the Natal side.

When Lindi, Beryl and Zwelakhe started school in Swaziland in 1964, Albertina got around the passport problem by arranging for them to travel with people who had children of a similar age. Since children could travel under the passports of their parents, the Sisulu children masqueraded as the children of adults with passports.

In 1965, a travel consultant promised Lungi that he could get him a passport. Because he was waiting for his passport, Lungi did not go back to St Christopher's at the beginning of the year. He also wanted to take the opportunity to apply for a pass. He had just turned 16, so he was now eligible to visit Walter on Robben Island, for which he needed a pass. He went to the township administrative office for a letter to confirm that he was on Albertina's house permit, then to the Labour Office for a stamp to indicate that he was a student. During the months of waiting for his documents, he was regularly visited by the security police. To avoid harassment, he often went to stay at Berry Matole's home in Pretoria. In July 1965, Lungi enrolled at Morris Isaacson School in Soweto. He found the work difficult because he had not studied Afrikaans in Swaziland and the maths syllabus was different. Despite these difficulties, he managed to pass the Junior Certificate examination in December.

By the beginning of 1966, it was clear that Lungi was not going to get his passport. He returned to St Christopher's where he found that he had to repeat a year because the Swazi syllabus was so different. By the time he completed matric and returned home (at the end of 1968), he had still not succeeded in getting a passport, so he continued to cross the border illegally. Other students in the same position joined him: "From Swaziland we used to sleep at the priest's house and jump the border in the early hours of the morning. We would then walk 30 miles to Piet Retief. Other students who had lost their passports later joined me. I often led groups of four to 10 people across the border. We would walk through the plantations or forests parallel to the road. I later became more daring and discovered other routes, such as the Amsterdam border post where security was not so tight."

By the time he left school, Lungi had become an expert in jumping the border, a skill that would serve him well in later years.

*t h r e e*

During an inspection of Robben Island prison in 1965, the Commissioner of Prisons asked Nelson Mandela: "Now what is it you want about things like studies, what is it you want?" Mandela responded: "You should let the atmosphere of a university prevail here on the Island" (Alexander, 81). Mandela's response highlighted one of the key survival strategies of Robben Island prisoners. Neville Alexander later described how they turned the Island "essentially into an informal university and as a result made it possible for people who otherwise may have found it really monotonous, tedious and soul-destroying to see being on the Island as a constructive experience". (Schadeberg Interview, Neville Alexander). At the time, Mandela and Walter were the only prisoners on the Island who had permission to study; but even before the rest of the prisoners were granted study privileges in 1966, they had already started an informal political education programme. They engaged in intense political discussions and even held seminars and tutorials while digging and shovelling in the quarry. If Robben Island was a university, then the lime quarry was the main lecture theatre.

Among the first structured political discussions held in the lime quarry was a series of lectures given by Walter on the history of the ANC. Mandela believed that Walter "was one of the greatest living historians of the ANC", whose lessons "were wise and full of understanding" (Mandela, 557). Ahmed Kathrada agreed that no one could equal Walter in knowledge of the history of the ANC, knowledge that he had gained through long years of membership and his natural curiosity, which led him to gather as much knowledge as possible from his seniors (Interview, Ahmed Kathrada). Michael Dingake referred to Walter as a walking history of the organisation: "Comrade Walter's memory was phenomenal. Not only did he remember events, and the names associated with them, but also the circumstances under which they occurred" (Dingake, 214).

It was not only ANC members who were impressed by Walter's lectures. According to Neville Alexander, the YCC group attended the lectures with great excitement "because we had never read about this ANC. As Unity Movement people we had been so indoctrinated that we did not know the history of the ANC. Walter gave those lectures in a very attractive, anecdotal and sometimes analytical way" (Interview, Neville Alexander). After one of the lectures, Leslie van der Heyden asked Walter how the ANC could justify point two of the Freedom Charter, which said, "All national groups shall have equal rights." The Unity Movement felt that this point explicitly recognised racial groups. Neville Alexander recalled that Walter "was humble and honest enough to say he could not give a satisfactory answer and we should direct our question to Nelson, which we did" (Interview, Neville Alexander). The result was a lengthy debate between Mandela and Neville Alexander on the national question.

The debates between the ANC and the Unity Movement were not only confined to ideological questions. There were heated arguments on how to respond to oppressive conditions in prison. Their attitude towards the study privilege and the racially differentiated diets and allocation of clothing exemplified the differences in approach between the two groups. Political prisoners placed a high premium on the opportunity to study. But while they welcomed the permission to study, they were angered by the conditions attached to this privilege. The most irksome restriction was the prohibition on sharing and exchange of books between students and the lending of books to non-students. Prisoners were also not allowed to have their studies funded by anyone other than their families.

These conditions made it impossible for those prisoners who could not afford to buy books or whose families could not afford their fees to study. For political prisoners deeply committed to an egalitarian society, this was an outrage and some members of the YCC argued that it would be untenable to accept the study privilege under such conditions. They argued passionately that it was a right and not a privilege to study. The ANC group agreed with this position, but rejected the argument that accepting the study privilege would compromise their integrity. Walter was surprised that anyone would want to refuse the study privilege. He was one of those who believed strongly that they would be playing into the hands of the authorities if they did so. He was convinced that the regime could easily misrepresent the facts and spread damaging propaganda along the lines that the prisoners had refused to take up the opportunity to study (Mandela, 489–90; Dingake, 172–3).

Walter had successfully applied to study during the Rivonia Trial. When he arrived on Robben Island, he had to reapply and was given permission to enrol for GCE O-levels and an Afrikaans beginner's course. He signed the form on study privileges with the proviso: "Signed strictly under protest without prejudice to any right which I might have in law."

Racial differentiation in food and clothing also sparked heated debates among the political prisoners. Coloured and Asian prisoners were on the 'D' diet scale, while African prisoners were on the 'F' diet scale. In practice, this meant that African prisoners received less meat, vegetables, oil, sugar and salt in their diet than did coloured and Asian prisoners (1970 *Survey of the Institute of Race Relations*). Coloured and Asian prisoners received a quarter of a loaf of bread a day while African prisoners received none. Instead they were given porridge twice a day, boiled mealies and a foul-tasting health drink made of maize-meal called *phuzamandla* (literally, "strength drink"). According to Dingake, Walter "acquired a taste for *phuzamandla* and made it known that it would be part of his diet outside". The prison authorities claimed that these differences were based on the traditional dietary tendencies of the various racial groups. Needless to say, these insulting explanations caused anger and outrage among the prisoners, especially among the recipients of the unwanted privileges.

The first instinct of the YCC prisoners was to reject their racially based privilege by boycotting the types of food that were denied their fellow prisoners. They also wanted to refuse the long trousers, jerseys and underwear issued to them unless these were also given to the African prisoners. They raised the matter with ANC members, who discussed it in their structures. The ANC response was that while they admired the YCC stance, they felt that the general political strategy should not be to accept less. Mandela and Sisulu argued strongly that any privileges, even if confined to a particular group, should not be given up. They should struggle instead for everyone to be upgraded to the same level of privilege. A couple of coloured prisoners did try to refuse the additional winter clothing. The prison authorities insisted that if they did not want long pants they would have to go bare, because according to regulations they could not be given the short pants allocated to the African prisoners. One of the prisoners complained in writing about the discrimination. The response of the authorities was that if he was so concerned, he should ask to be reclassified as a Bantu (Dingake, 204; Daniels, 148; Interviews, Neville Alexander and Ahmed Kathrada).

After much discussion, the *khulukuthu* prisoners eventually arrived at an understanding that as long as they did not get equal treatment, coloured and Asian prisoners would share their food with their comrades. Unfortunately they could not do the same with clothing, but they agreed that they would take every opportunity to agitate for better food and clothing for all, and for the scrapping of all forms of discrimination. The same debate took place in the general section and they arrived at much the same conclusion – that to voluntarily reject part of what they were given would weaken the claim of the others, so they should rather accept what was offered and demand improvements for all.

Both the ANC and the Unity Movement prisoners were conscious that the regime was determined to break their morale and destroy their interest in all they stood for. Although both groups were united in the belief that they were engaged in a struggle for survival on several levels –

physical, emotional and political – their ideological differences translated into marked differences in the tactics and strategies of resistance in prison. The radical young revolutionaries of the Unity Movement were defiant and aggressive towards the prison authorities and ready for confrontation at every turn. Neville Alexander believed that the leadership of the ANC was "if not collaborationist in the worst sense of the term, at the very least anti-revolutionary". As a result of their prejudice against the Congress Movement, "there was a lot of tension, distance and I would say even provocative action on the part of ourselves". After they had been together in the isolation section for about four or five months, a dialogue was established between the two groups.

Because of his personal connections with Nelson and Walter, Fikile Bam was instrumental in facilitating these discussions. Nelson and Walter impressed upon their YCC colleagues that confrontation for its own sake was self-defeating and that there was no point trying to win each and every little battle only to lose the war. Neville Alexander recalled that "impetuous, tempestuous young people" that they were, they were very defiant towards the prison authorities. Consequently, they were given a hard time by the warders. One day Walter and Nelson advised him that this confrontational attitude would ultimately be destructive. They emphasised that since they would be in prison for a very long time, there was no room for any illusions. They advised him that to survive in prison and make it liveable and possible for people to use prison to learn something, they would have to adopt a different strategy (Interview, Neville Alexander).

The ANC also differed with the PAC on the question of what attitude should be taken towards the prison authorities. The PAC prisoners saw any form of cooperation with the prison authorities as a betrayal. They were not even prepared to negotiate for better conditions. They took Sobukwe's approach that to fight for better conditions in prison was to recognise their right to have him there in the first place. The ANC in general, and Nelson and Walter in particular, had a more measured and long-term approach to political struggle in the prison situation. They were prepared to accord the prison authorities a certain degree of respect and abide by the regulations, as long as this did not entail compromising their dignity. Though they preferred to avoid confrontation, they did not hesitate to take on the authorities when necessary. When they were pressured to crush an ever-increasing quota of stones, they adopted a go-slow strategy (Mandela, 459).

Walter recalled that the first time they walked to the lime quarry, the warders shouted at them to hurry. "Now Nelson is a very stubborn chap. He responded to this by walking very, very slowly and of course we all walked slowly too. The warders had to beg him to cooperate and walk faster." After that, the segregation prisoners walked to the lime quarry at their own pace, unlike the prisoners in the main section, who had to run to the stone quarry with Alsatian dogs snapping at their heels.

The ANC prisoners believed that the struggle for better conditions in prison was an extension of the wider struggle. Walter recalled that "like the [Rivonia] Trial, we wanted to make of prison a stage of the struggle for the Movement and we developed strategies for that" (Houser and Shore Interviews). A cornerstone of this strategy was to create the political machinery to operate as the ANC within prison in defiance of prison rules that no prisoner was allowed to speak on behalf of other prisoners or air the grievances of other prisoners.

The ANC machinery set up for the single-cells section was the High Organ or the High Command, as it was sometimes called. Members of the High Organ were the four NEC (National Executive Council) members Mandela, Sisulu, Mbeki and Mhlaba. Mandela and Mhlaba acted as the secretariat of the High Organ, with Mandela as the overall leader. There were some who felt that Walter, as the former Secretary-General of the organisation, should assume the mantle of leadership; but for Walter, there was no question that Mandela was the automatic choice: "There was no way we would be competing … We agreed on almost everything and knew how to settle our differences. Nelson and I knew how to work together" (Houser and Shore Interviews).

To counter criticisms of Xhosa domination, a fifth member was co-opted on a rotational basis. When MD Naidoo was jailed in 1967, he served on the High Organ in this capacity. Later Kathrada and Isu Chiba held this position at various times. A cell system consisting of three members per cell was set up and each member of the High Organ served as a contact for each cell. The High Organ dealt with the daily concerns of prison life and the maintenance of internal discipline (Mandela, 525). The High Organ was not an executive structure, although its opinions carried a lot of weight. Decisions from the High Organ to the cells were discussed, debated and sometimes rejected. The High Organ operated only in the single cell section. ANC cadres in the general section had their own structure, the Disciplinary Committee, better known by its acronym, the DC. In his *Memoirs of a Saboteur*, MK veteran Natoo Babenia described the interaction between the two structures:

> They would send stuff down for us to discuss. It would come to the DC and they would notify the dormitory 'PRO' who would then inform the group leaders. From there it would come to us in our groups of four. Matters would be discussed; our small decisions then taken back to the group leaders and then higher upwards. There was the possibility of democracy in all these structures, but there was also the chance for top-down telephones. Sometimes we would talk back to the leadership and tell them they [were] talking nonsense. Or it could work the other way around (Babenia, 160).

The first major act of mass resistance on Robben Island started in the general section in July 1966. Communication between sections was dangerous and difficult, but prisoners devised ingenious methods for passing messages from one section to another. These were distributed mainly through the kitchen. Prisoners working in the kitchens smuggled messages wrapped in plastic into the drums of food, which were distributed to all the sections of the prison. It was through such a message that the single-cells prisoners learned that their comrades in the general section had embarked on a hunger strike. Though the message did not give reasons for the strike, the single-cells prisoners immediately went on a sympathy strike. The next day, they learned that the strike had been sparked off when food had run out before all the prisoners had been fed. After a hasty consultation among the representatives of the political organisations, the majority of general section prisoners decided to go on a hunger strike.

At first the authorities were contemptuous of the strikers, but as the week progressed they became more concerned. They tried to break the resolve of the strikers by serving the most appetising food ever seen in Robben Island prison, but the prisoners held out. By the end of the week, many of the strikers were in a bad way. Some of them collapsed in the stone quarry and had to be carted back to the prison in wheelbarrows. On the sixth day, the authorities finally relented and agreed to look into the demands of the strikers. The demands included better food, clothing, an end to harassment by warders, that they be recognised as political prisoners, and that the prisons department provide recreation facilities. When the warders told them the strike was over, the single-cells prisoners refused to believe them. Worried that the authorities would try to play one section against the other, they continued to refuse food until the message came through from the general section that the strike had indeed ended (Mandela, 501; Dingake, 140; Meredith, 298; Babenia, 156; Naidoo, 151).

For the first few days after the strike the prisoners enjoyed improved food, but not for long. The authorities exacted their revenge by adding six months to the sentences of the 16 prisoners who they believed were the ringleaders. However, the strike did have some far-reaching effects. Not only was it a psychological boost for the prisoners, it had an impact on the warders as well. Shortly after the prisoners' strike, the bachelor warders embarked on their own hunger strike in protest against their diet, which was inferior to that of the married warders and commissioned officers. The prison administration hastily agreed to the demands of the striking warders, who immediately enjoyed a dramatic improvement in their diet. Realising that they owed their victory to the prisoners' struggle, some of the warders began to treat the prisoners with more respect. The authorities realised they could no longer afford to ignore the grievances of the prisoners and the hunger strike thus marked the beginning of a gradual improvement in conditions.

One result was that tensions between warders and prisoners decreased considerably. This was most evident in the lime quarry where the warder in charge, nicknamed Mazithulele because he was so soft-spoken, allowed the prisoners to talk as much as they liked. When he arrived on Robben Island in July 1966 to serve a 15-year sentence, ANC activist Michael Dingake was transferred to *khulukuthu* after a few days in the general section. He spent his first morning in the lime quarry briefing Nelson and Walter on the situation outside prison: "Three of us had our right feet on our spades and conversed. Mazithulele sat under a bush and never interfered. I continued my 'state of struggle' message with other groups in the afternoon; Mazithulele maintained his sweetness. The lime quarry wasn't bad" (Dingake, 145).

Under Mazithulele's relaxed regime, the lime quarry became a hotbed of discussion and debate. The prisoners analysed anything and everything, from the relationship between the ANC and SACP to whether tigers existed in Africa. The debates aroused a great deal of passion and some of the arguments went on unendingly.

The relative freedom of the lime quarry was brought to an abrupt end by a dramatic event. On 6 September 1966, the architect of grand apartheid, Hendrik Verwoerd, was assassinated in Parliament. Despite the embargo on news, the prison grapevine was so efficient that the prisoners sometimes got wind of the latest happenings before the warders did. The news of Verwoerd's death spread like wildfire through the prison. While delivering food to the quarry, one of the general section prisoners whispered the news to the *khulukuthu* men. In low tones, they excitedly discussed the sensational news while the warders were still unaware of what had happened.

The prison staff were plunged into mourning by the death of their beloved Prime Minister, while the attitude of the inmates ranged from indifference to jubilation. Walter was shocked by the brutality of the event and shared the ANC leadership's distaste for assassination as a way of dealing with the enemy.

Demetrio Tsafendas, the parliamentary messenger who stabbed Verwoerd to death, was tried, declared insane and sent to Robben Island. He was placed in the punishment cells in the isolation section. Prisoners who were in solitary confinement in the cells next to him tried to establish communication with him, but beyond a hesitant greeting, Tsafendas was uncommunicative. Walter and his colleagues saw little of Tsafendas beyond a glimpse of him in the opposite yard during his daily exercise period. Tsafendas remained a mysterious figure until his transfer to a maximum-security prison in Pretoria a few days later. (It has been said that Tsafendas was the only white prisoner to be sent to Robben Island. According to George Bizos, whose mother knew Tsafendas's family, this is not quite true. He may have passed as white, but he was born in Mozambique of a Greek father and Mozambican mother. Ill-treatment at the hands of his father, who was ashamed of having a mixed-race child, may have contributed to Tsafendas's mental condition.)

It was clear to the prison authorities that Tsafendas had no political affiliation. Although it was obvious that his crime had been motivated by mental instability, the regime nevertheless vented its anger on the political prisoners. In addition to Verwoerd's assassination, the government was shaken by a series of guerrilla attacks by SWAPO. Neville Alexander noted "that the political prisoners were in some ways being treated as hostages who had to be made to pay for the activities of revolutionary organisations with which they were associated, and often of organisations and individuals entirely unrelated to them" (Alexander, 33).

Within a day of Verwoerd's death, the sympathetic Mazithulele was transferred from the lime quarry and a new warder was brought in to replace him. The new man, Van Rensburg, was a brutal slave driver whose reputation preceded him. A swastika tattooed on his forearm signified his political leanings. Van Rensburg, promptly nicknamed Suitcase by the prisoners because he arrived in their section carrying a mini-portmanteau, went out of his way to make their lives as miserable as possible (Dingake, 146). He treated them like animals, shouting and screaming racial abuse at them all day long. He put them to work in the most difficult parts of the quarry and drove them to the point of exhaustion. It was so difficult for the older men to keep up that those who were younger and stronger tried to cover up for them. Not a day went by without one or more of the prisoners being charged for malingering or insubordination (Mandela, 514; Dingake, 147; Alexander, 33). Walter was among those charged several times for not working hard enough. Prisoners on these charges had to appear before the Island's administrative court and were sentenced to punishments ranging from withholding of meals to several days in isolation on "spare diet". To defend themselves, prisoners formed a legal committee made up of Mandela, Mac Maharaj and Fikile Bam, who had all studied law. The legal committee adopted a strategy of demanding "further particulars" for each charge. Van Rensburg, who was not the most intelligent of human beings, had difficulty in compiling the "further particulars". While they could outwit him in court, the prisoners had little protection against his vindictiveness in the quarry and he continued to persecute them mercilessly.

One day, some of the men were engaged in the recurring debate on the existence of tigers in Africa. The argument centred on whether *Inkwe/ingwe* meant tiger or leopard. There were those who argued that the existence of the word *Inkwe/ingwe* in the indigenous languages proved that tigers did once live in Africa. Those who believed that tigers never existed in Africa argued that *Inkwe/ingwe* meant leopard and not tiger, and that colonial missionary translators had caused the confusion when they incorrectly translated it as "tiger". On that particular day, the debate became so heated that voices were raised and work was forgotten. The argument raged on and orders from the junior warders were ignored until Suitcase felt he had to intervene. "Get on with your work! You talk too many and work too few!" he shouted. His grammatical errors sent the prisoners into paroxysms of laughter. Humiliated, Suitcase radioed his superior who rushed to the scene and ordered that Mandela and Masondo be handcuffed and taken to the isolation section for solitary confinement (Mandela, 516; Dingake, 149).

Angry and offended by the insult against their leader, Michael Dingake and Mac Maharaj approached Walter for advice on whether they should down tools in protest. Walter responded calmly: "Know your enemy, know your strength." "This classical argument did not mean passivity," wrote Dingake. "It implied that our actions had to be carefully calculated. Counterproductive steps had to be restricted. Impetuous actions could not be totally avoided but they had to be pruned down as much as possible" (Dingake, 149).

Walter believed that whatever action they took had to be decided upon after careful discussion by the prisoners' committee. Since their arrival on the Island, the High Organ had functioned as the representative structure of the single-cells section. At the beginning of 1967, the High Organ drew up a petition demanding better treatment. Members of all political organisations signed the petition but Neville Alexander complained that the High Organ was neither representative nor democratic. The prisoners then agreed to form a prisoners' committee made up of representatives of all political organisations. Because other organisations like the PAC and the Unity Movement were concerned about ANC domination, it was decided that the committee would be purely for purposes of consultation. Fikile Bam was the first chairperson and the committee later had a rotating leadership. Mandela generally acted as spokesman for all the prisoners when dealing with the authorities or receiving visitors (Mandela, 526; Karis and Gerhart, 32).

One morning in February 1967, the *khulukuthu* men were lined up to go to the lime quarry when the warders informed them that Major Kellerman had sent an order that talking on the way to the quarry and while working in the quarry was prohibited with immediate effect. The prisoners would only be allowed to talk during the lunch hour. Walter expressed the sentiments of the prisoners when he exclaimed loudly: "Rubbish!" Afraid that this reaction might spark off a rebellion, Michael Dingake instinctively grabbed at Walter's jacket to restrain him (Dingake, 147). When the warder demanded to know who had protested, the prisoners remained silent. They walked to the quarry and worked in sullen silence until the lunch hour, when the newly elected prisoners' committee met in the lunch shed to plan a response to the outrageous order.

In the middle of their discussion, they were surprised by the sudden appearance of Major Kellerman. It was unheard of for such a high-ranking officer to enter the prisoners' shed. They were even more surprised when he announced that the order not to talk was withdrawn. They began to suspect that something was afoot when Suitcase announced that he was withdrawing all charges against them and actually treated them like human beings for the rest of the afternoon. The suspicion raised by the uncharacteristic behaviour of the warders was confirmed when they returned to their cells that evening. They found that Mandela had been moved from cell No. 4 (near the entrance to the section) to cell No. 18 near the end of the corridor. They deduced correctly that this move signalled the arrival of an important visitor or visitors. The authorities obviously did not want Mandela to speak on behalf of all the prisoners, and had moved him to the end of the corridor in the hope that by the time the visitor reached his cell, there would be little or no time to talk to him. The prisoners decided to counter this strategy with a plan of their own. They agreed that the occupants of the first few cells should not waste the visitor/s time by voicing their own complaints. Instead they would simply direct the visitor/s to Mandela's cell.

The visitor turned out to be Helen Suzman, the lone Progressive Party MP and only woman in Parliament. Helen Suzman was an extraordinarily courageous woman whose slight build belied her formidable personality. For years she stood up to the Nationalist MPs who dominated in Parliament, often providing the only voice of protest against the passage of unjust laws. Walter had met Helen Suzman a number of years previously through Bram Fischer. Although he did not agree with all her political views, he admired her razor-sharp intellect and her determination to stand up for her convictions, no matter what the cost. She had already acquired a reputation for being the only MP who stood up for the rights of prisoners, so her visit caused great excitement (Suzman, 152; Meredith, 304). Just as they had planned, the prisoners at the beginning of the corridor said very little to Mrs Suzman, and in no time she had proceeded down the passage to Mandela's cell. Mandela presented the grievances of the prisoners to the discomfort of General Steyn, the Commissioner of Prisons who was escorting Mrs Suzman on her tour of the prison. Though it was their policy to fight for general principles rather than to battle against individuals, the prisoners felt that Van Rensburg's sadistic behaviour warranted special mention. After complaining about the terrible food, the lack of study facilities and the ban on newspapers among other things, Mandela turned to their treatment at the hands of the warders. He singled out Van Rensburg and mentioned the swastika tattooed on his arm.

While Mandela was briefing Mrs Suzman, a frightened Van Rensburg was apologising to the other prisoners for the way he had treated them. He even asked Pascal Ngakane to help him explain in good English to Mrs Suzman that it was his father who had made him have a swastika tattoo. When Mrs Suzman left without interrogating him as he had feared, Van Rensburg relaxed. The next day, he reinstated the charges he had withdrawn.

On her return to the mainland, Helen Suzman told Piet Pelser, the then Minister of Justice, what she had seen on the Island, and threatened to raise the issue of the warder with the swastika tattoo in Parliament. Worried that her report would make headline news around the world, Pelser promised to have the warder removed, although he could not act immediately because it would look bad for discipline. Within a fortnight, Van Rensburg was transferred from the Island.

The South African regime did not allow Helen Suzman to visit Robben Island for another seven years, but it could not prevent the yearly visits of the International Committee of the Red Cross. Many prisoners were released in the 1965–8 period after serving two- to three-year sentences. Accounts of their experiences played a major role in ensuring that the human rights violations on Robben Island remained the focus of international attention. The 1967 testimony of Dennis Brutus to the UN Special Committee on Apartheid was widely publicised and used in various publications, especially those of the International Defence and Aid Fund (Fran Buntman). This negative publicity put considerable pressure on the South African regime. When the South African Commissioner of Prisons attended an international conference in Stockholm on standard minimum rules for prisoners, he was met by demonstrations and humiliated by journalists who knew more about the conditions on Robben Island than he did (Naidoo, 203).

By 1967 the struggles waged by the prisoners, combined with external pressure from Helen Suzman, the International Committee of the Red Cross and the anti-apartheid movement, began to have some impact, and there was a substantial improvement in conditions in Robben Island prison in that year. A new dining room was built for the general section prisoners so they no longer had to eat their food squatting in the open (Dingake, 141). The prison hospital was moved from the corrugated-iron building known as the *zinktronk* to a modern new building. However, the new hospital turned out to be more of a showpiece than anything else, and medical treatment on Robben Island still left a lot to be desired. Prisoners were given permission to smoke. Prisoners in the general section no longer had to strip before the warders and the degrading *tausa* dance was stopped (Babenia, 159). Visits and letters were increased from one every six months to one every three months and large numbers of prisoners were given official permission to study (Alexander, 34). The provision of clothing improved and by 1969 all prisoners were given long trousers (Mandela, 535).

The introduction of soccer on Saturday mornings for general section prisoners generated great excitement and some controversy. The ANC prisoners welcomed the opportunity to relieve the boredom of prison life by enjoying a game of soccer, while a few of the PAC prisoners opposed the idea. They felt that the introduction of recreation was a propaganda stunt by the enemy. After heated debates, the opposing groups resolved their differences and Robben Island prison soon boasted a thriving soccer league administered by the Makana Football Association. (The league was named after Makana, the Xhosa leader who drowned while trying to escape from Robben Island in 1820.) Soccer was taken very seriously and the matches and administration of the game were modelled along international rules. Prisoners in the general cells were soon enjoying rugby, boxing and table tennis as well. They organised themselves into clubs and ran competitions. All these activities were overseen by a General Recreation Committee elected by the prisoners (Odendaal, 4).

At that stage, prisoners in the single cells were denied the privilege of joining in, but they managed to watch the soccer matches and shout encouragement from their cell windows until the authorities put an end to this form of entertainment by painting the windowpanes black. Such petty and spiteful acts aside, the single-cell prisoners did enjoy more freedom of movement. They were no longer locked in their cells all weekend and could mingle in the courtyard and meet freely. It became easier for them to hold meetings of the High Organ and prisoners' committees. Ministers and priests from different denominations were brought to the Island to conduct church services every Sunday. At first, the prisoners were confined to their cells and the ministers had to deliver their sermons from the passage. Later, the services were held in the courtyard and everyone attended, even those who were not particularly religious. They were also allowed to play Scrabble, chess, draughts and bridge, and like their comrades in the general cells, they organised Christmas concerts and competitions. In the early years they stood in their cells and sang down the passage, but by 1967 they were allowed to perform in the courtyard on Christmas morning, with the warders as their audience (Mandela, 539).

One concession prisoners fought hard for but failed to achieve was the right to have access to newspapers. Despite pressure from the International Red Cross, Helen Suzman and the prisoners themselves, the authorities remained unyielding. Denying prisoners access to news and giving them the impression that the world had forgotten about them was a key element of control. Like all political prisoners, Walter hated the sense of being cut off from the outside world and longed for newspapers: "Not to have a newspaper was a punishment I cannot describe" (Schadeberg Interview). His comrades felt the same way, and newspapers became the most valued form of contraband for political prisoners. Indres Naidoo wrote: "Newspapers were our lifeblood. We ate, slept and drank news."

Kathrada was always amused by Walter's insatiable hunger for news. News that was passed on was always discussed in groups. "Tyhopo would never be satisfied to hear the news from just one group. He would go from group to group listening to the same news. Eventually he would get hold of Mac [Maharaj] because Mac has a photographic memory and could recall each and every little detail. The two of them would walk up and down the courtyard analysing all the news." As much as he loved getting hold of a newspaper, Walter was sometimes troubled by the methods they employed. On one occasion a certain Brother September was the visiting cleric for the Sunday service. During the service, Hennie Feris and Eddie Daniels stole a newspaper from the Brother's satchel while he was earnestly praying. Walter later commented to Kwedi Mkalipi: "Imagine doing this on the outside: stealing something from a priest!" (Pippa Green, *Cosmopolitan*, 1991).

Mac Maharaj hit a news jackpot when he was asked by one of the night warders to help him write an essay for a newspaper competition. When the warder was chosen as a finalist for the competition, he asked Mac to write another essay. Mac promised to write the essay in exchange for a pack of cigarettes. Mac told Walter and Nelson that as the warder's fingerprints were on the cigarette pack, he was in a position to blackmail the warder. Walter protested that this would be immoral, but Nelson wanted to know what he would blackmail him for: "'Newspapers', he said. Walter and I looked at each other. I think Walter was the only man on Robben Island who relished newspapers as much as I did. Mac had already discussed his plan with the communications committee, and although we both had reservations about Mac's technique, we did not stop him" (Mandela, 509). Mac's threat to report him to the Commanding Officer so frightened the old warder that he gave him a newspaper every day until transferring out of the section six months later.

Unfortunately the news from outside was, more often than not, very depressing. For much of the globe, the 1960s were turbulent years of radical change and social protest, the decade that saw the blossoming of a counter-culture that espoused libertarian values and challenged established ways of thinking. For southern Africa, it was a decade of grim reaction that marked the heyday of white supremacy and the nadir of black resistance.

The South African economy had recovered from the setbacks of Sharpeville and for the remainder of the decade, South Africa experienced an unprecedented economic boom. Western investment poured into the country, and the national economy enjoyed one of the highest rates of growth in the world. Britain, South Africa's major trading partner, persistently opposed economic sanctions, and the high returns on investment ensured that British opposition to sanctions was supported by the other Western powers. The economic boom spelt prosperity for white South Africa, especially the Afrikaner population, which benefited from the aggressive affirmative action policy for Afrikaners in commerce and industry and the civil service. South Africa in the 1960s was a "white man's paradise" and white immigrants, mainly from Europe, flocked into the country.

During this period news from outside gave little cause for celebration for the Robben Island men. In 1965 they learned of the execution of Vuyisile Mini, Wilton Khayinga and Zinakile Mkhaba on 6 November 1964. Walter felt a profound sense of loss, especially for Vuyisile Mini, the dedicated trade unionist and gifted composer whose singing and wonderfully sonorous bass voice had so moved Walter during the Treason Trial. One of Mini's compositions, *Thath'umthwalo Buti sigoduke/balindile omama nobaba basekhaya* ("Take your things, Brother and let us go. They are waiting, our mothers and fathers, at home") had a special resonance for him. Walter's admiration would have been even greater if he had known that Mini had been offered the chance to save himself from the gallows if he agreed to testify against Wilton Mkwayi, but had turned down the offer (Meli, 159, 183; Karis and Gerhart, 4: 89). On 1 April 1965, all prisoners in the lime quarry observed a minute's silence to honour John Harris, the Liberal Party and ARM leader executed on that day for planting a bomb at Johannesburg Station (Daniels, 186).

At the end of 1965, the Rivonia men learned that their friend and comrade Bram Fischer had been captured after an incredible 290 days underground. Bram had led the SACP's attempts to regroup after the Rivonia Trial, but he had been operating against overwhelming odds. With information from police spy Gerald Ludi, who had successfully infiltrated the SACP, and betrayal by a trusted comrade and SACP member, Piet Beyleveld, the writing was on the wall for Bram. In September 1964, he was arrested. With Eli Weinberg and 10 other Party members, he was charged under the Suppression of Communism Act. In January 1965, while the trial was in progress, he went underground until his capture in November 1965.

In March 1966, he was put on trial for a second time on charges of furthering the aims of communism and conspiring to violently overthrow the government. The main witnesses for the prosecution were Gerald Ludi, Piet Beyleveld and the ubiquitous Bartholomew Hlapane. Hlapane's evidence, like that of Bruno Mtolo in the Rivonia Trial, was a skilful blend of fact and fiction, concocted to convince the court that Bram was as guilty as the men he had defended in the Rivonia Trial. In another parallel with the Rivonia Trial, Bram gave a five-hour statement from the dock, a powerful and moving statement that ranks as one of the great political speeches in history. Bram was sentenced to life imprisonment and incarcerated in Pretoria Prison.

In one of those strange coincidences of history, Bram Fischer had been captured on 11 November 1965, the day the white settler government of Southern Rhodesia made its Unilateral Declaration of Independence. Both events had serious consequences for the South African liberation struggle. Bram's capture signified the virtual destruction of the SACP's underground structures inside the country, and like the ANC before it, leadership of the SACP shifted to its external structures (Shubin, 74). Meanwhile, Rhodesia's illegal independence fuelled the launch of the Zimbabwean liberation struggle in 1966 and strengthened white supremacy in the whole subregion.

The prosecution in Bram's trial tried hard to prove that the International Defence and Aid Fund was providing "money for subversion". The only piece of evidence was a letter from Canon John Collins written to Walter in 1963. Bram categorically denied that IDAF money was used for political purposes. Not surprisingly, IDAF was banned in March 1966, thus making it a criminal offence for anyone in South Africa to receive funds from the IDAF for the legal defence and welfare of political prisoners and their dependents (Collins, 323).

In July 1967, the Robben Island men joined millions of South Africans in mourning the death of Chief Albert Luthuli, who had died mysteriously in a train accident in Groutville. His funeral attracted over 7 000 supporters, who defiantly displayed ANC colours in a rare public affirmation of the ANC. Although her banning order prevented her from attending the funeral, Albertina was actively involved in organising FEDSAW's participation in memorial services held around the country. On the Island, the political prisoners held their own memorial service for Chief Luthuli. Although he had been removed from political life and effectively silenced by banning orders and restrictions, Luthuli had remained a powerful symbol of the ANC and they felt a deep sense of loss.

The following year, the ANC suffered the loss of another beloved leader, Professor ZK Matthews. After his departure from South Africa in 1962, Professor Matthews had continued his distinguished career as Area Director for Africa based at the World Council of Churches headquarters in Geneva. He then served as Botswana's first ambassador to the US and representative to the United Nations until his death of heart disease in May 1968. As tributes poured in from all over the world, US President Lyndon Johnson arranged for the body to be flown home in the Presidential aircraft. Walter paid tribute in a letter to ZK's eldest son Joe:

My dear Joe,

I have heard with great shock and sorrow about the death of your dad. To us ZK Matthews was a father, a brother, a colleague and a guiding light. Indeed he was one of the greatest sons of Africa. His academic achievements, his great qualities of leadership embracing the highest standards of diplomacy will ever remain a shining example in our own time and for future generations ... His wisdom made a deep impression on me. His death removes one of the greatest and ablest men of our country.

_f o u r_

The mid-Sixties were depressing years for political prisoners and their families, and the correspondence between Walter and Albertina sometimes reflected the mood of the times. In a letter to Walter shortly after she visited the Island towards the end of 1965, Albertina wrote:

> I must say we were not very happy when we came back because we did not see you people properly. We only heard your voices and saw your shadows.
> My dear, we were all hurt about your remarks, that you always think of our birthdays and wish us good luck, but we never think of you on your birthday and wish you Happy Birthday. Walter, we always think of you, but we never know what to do, whether you are allowed a postcard or not. Nkuli says, don't worry _wena Tata ngenye imini ndizakuthengela iBirthday Cake enkulu namakhandlela ayo_ (Daddy, one day I will buy you a big birthday cake with candles) (Letter, 15/11/65).

A year later she wrote: "Darling, your last letter was not a nice one. It looked as though you were worried or not well. There were a lot of incomplete sentences. What was the matter, were you not well? Please, when you are not well report to the authorities and get medical attention. Never go on with that headache of yours because I know how it can treat you" (Letter, 19/11/66).

Letters to and from prisoners on Robben Island were heavily censored, and any mention of politics was either blacked out or the prison authorities withheld the letters. Prisoners and their families did however find ways to communicate political information in coded language. A letter from Albertina to Walter dated 25 November 1965 contained the cryptic message: "Our gardens are not too good at all this year. The drought has been too much. The worms are so powerful that as soon as you put in plants they are destroyed instantly." After pondering over this message for a while, Walter realised that the "gardens" referred to the underground work of the ANC, the "drought" was the general political situation and the "worms" were the informers who were everywhere and made political work so difficult. The following year Albertina wrote to Walter again: "This has been a bad year to us, dear. We got nothing from our gardens, the drought was too much, but we hope the coming year will bring some rain" (Letter, 12/7/66).

It was a devastatingly gloomy period for political activists trying to reconstruct the underground structures of the liberation movements. They had to contend with a ruthless and vastly more efficient security apparatus, which was given almost unlimited power by increasingly repressive legislation. A sense of hopelessness pervaded black communities around the country, and people generally shied away from politics, even in previously militant areas like Soweto and the townships of the Eastern Cape (Shubin, 74). Some black people were drawn to the Liberal Party because it was the only legal party that supported universal franchise. By 1968 even this avenue of political activity was closed when the Liberal Party decided to close shop after the passing of the Prohibition of Improper Interference Act, which made multiracial political parties illegal (Frederickse, 93).

As one of the few activists inside the country struggling to keep the embers of resistance alive, Albertina worked under difficult conditions. As a leader of FEDSAW and the wife of Walter Sisulu, she was a special target of the security police. In a memorandum to the Commissioner of Police, the Secretary of Justice had written of Albertina: "When her activities are examined it appears that the activities of both her husband and herself are the same. As her husband has disappeared from the scene, she will probably have to fill his shoes for the next number of years. She enjoys great support amongst the Bantu and is a very good speaker and organiser" (Ministry of Justice files, 10/12/63).

The security police harassed Albertina in a number of ways. Whenever she travelled to Cape Town to visit Walter, she had a police escort to ensure that she did not talk to other passengers or take part in any gathering. Her escorts travelled second-class while she travelled third-class. She would watch from her window as officers changed shifts along the way, disembarking at stations and waving to their colleagues who boarded the train to take over the task of watching her. After a visit to the Island in March 1966, Albertina received a letter from the Commissioner of Police asking why she had disembarked at Krankuil en route to Cape Town and demanding to know how she had reached Cape Town. It was possible that the police officers had somehow lost track of her during the journey and rather than admit this, they chose to report that she had got off the train. Albertina was bewildered by this accusation and vehemently denied that she had broken her journey in Krankuil (Letter from Commissioner of Police to Secretary for Justice, 23/5/66, Ref. S.4/2704).

In July 1966, both Albertina and Walter received letters from the Liquidator informing them that there was evidence before him that they were active members of the Communist Party. Walter responded by asking the Liquidator for more details. The Liquidator responded that sworn evidence had been placed before him to show that Walter had been a member of the Communist Party of South Africa since 1960 and took part in its activities by attending conferences of the Party. Walter used the strategy that political prisoners would use again and again when charged by the powers that be – he asked for further particulars:

Robben Island Prison
15/8/66

Greetings

Re: Communist Party of S.A.

Your letter of the 27th July 1966 was given to me on 8/8/1966.
   In this connection I should be pleased if you would kindly furnish me with the following further particulars to your letter: –
   How many affidavits have been placed before you to show that I was a member of the Communist Party of South Africa since 1960, and that I took part in its activities inter alia by attending conferences of the said party?
By who, and where were these made? The exact date must be specified.
In what capacity is it alleged that I attended these conferences?
And 5. When and where were the conferences held? The exact place and date must be specified including time when the said conferences started and closed.
6. The names and addresses of all persons alleged to have attended the said conferences, who presided over the conferences and who recorded the proceedings.
7. What was the nature of the business discussions?
8. Who were the speakers and what were the decisions?
9. The exact copies of affidavits in your possession.
10. Is it alleged that I took part in the activities of the said party other than by attending the said conferences? (a) If so kindly give me further particulars and full details of the nature of such activities. (b) The place where and the date when such activities took place. The exact place and time must be specified.

Greetings
W.M. Sisulu

Walter received a response from the Liquidator in December 1966 informing him that his name would not be included on the list of office-bearers, members or active supporters of the Communist Party at that stage.

A similar exchange of letters took place between Albertina and the Liquidator. The Ministry of Justice file on Albertina clearly shows that the attempt to list Albertina as a communist was based on testimony of the infamous informer Bartholomew Hlapane to the security police. Hlapane had alleged that the aim of the Communist Party was to infiltrate and dominate mass organisations. According to Hlapane, FEDSAW was one of the organisations under "communistic domination and control". He alleged that the three FEDSAW leaders, Albertina, Eufemia Hlapane and Gertrude Shope, were confirmed communists and members of the SACP.

In July 1966, Albertina wrote to the Secretary of the Ministry of Justice denying that she had ever been a member of the Communist Party of South Africa. A week later, she received a response from DP Wilcocks, the Liquidator, informing her that he had sworn evidence that she had been a member of the Communist Party of South Africa since 1956 and took part in its activities by attending so-called study groups. Albertina wrote back to the Liquidator again denying the allegation.

On 31 August 1966, the Liquidator wrote to the Commissioner of Police asking for supporting evidence and/or documentary proof over and above the information contained in the statements of Beyleveld and Hlapane. One can only surmise that further proof or supporting evidence was not forthcoming, and on 15 December 1966, Albertina received a letter from the Liquidator informing her that "It has been decided not to include your name on the list of office-bearers, members or active supporters of the Communist Party at this stage."

Joyce Sikhakhane, an ANC activist who worked as a journalist in Johannesburg in the mid-1960s, noted that as part of its broad psychological offensive, the apartheid security apparatus singled out families of political prisoners as a means of breaking the resilience of political prisoners. Certain people would try to provoke criticism of the leadership by asking questions such as "Why are their children studying in boarding schools in Swaziland when ours are in township schools?" Gossip about wives of jailed political leaders was rife on trains and buses:

> For example, during train or bus journeys, a "preacher" thumbing a testament would spontaneously rise from a seat and start singing or preaching, "Bazalwane/Christians, let us pray for so and so's wife. She has taken away another woman's husband. God, is this what the communists wanted? They're in jail and so the husbands of other wives should now go and support their wives. African custom is against wives sharing husbands. That's why the communists have been jailed. Communists want to introduce foreign ideas in our country." This type of preaching would go on and on ... (Sikhakhane-Rankin, Unpublished notes).

Sikhakhane, who lived in the same neighbourhood as the Sisulus, recalled that at some stage there was talk that Albertina was having a relationship with a local grocer. "However, the rumour quickly died down. MaSisulu's stature and reputation was such that people in the township dismissed the talk as nonsense. Fortunately the people recognised that this type of talk was part of the clinically orchestrated smears aimed at driving a wedge between the families of political prisoners and the communities in which they lived" (Interview, Joyce Sikhakhane-Rankin).

During those repressive years, many people stayed away from the families of political prisoners, while other neighbours and friends were prepared to risk intimidation by the police. When Metty Hluphekile Kubheka moved into the house next door to Albertina in the mid-1960s, the security police told her not to associate with the Sisulus "because they were bad people". Initially she was afraid to challenge the police but as she got to know her neighbours, her attitude changed. Albertina and Metty (nicknamed Gogo Mantongomane by the Sisulu children because she sold peanuts) became good friends, "the kind of neighbours who could knock on each other's door at any time and borrow tea-leaves or sugar" (Interview, Metty Hluphekile Kubheka, 1996). Metty came to hate the security police raids on the Sisulu home: "At times they were very rude. When they searched the house, they threw books and clothes all over the place. They were very noisy and they shouted at passers-by who tried to see what was going on."

Like most houses in the area, the toilet of Albertina's house adjoined that of Metty's in one outside building at the end of the garden. The wall between the two toilets was so thin that one could easily conduct a conversation with the person next door. Albertina's colleagues from FEDSAW would pretend to visit Gogo Mantongomane. They would then go to the toilet and have a "meeting" with Albertina in the toilet next door. Gogo would keep a lookout for the security police while pretending to be busy in her garden.

During this period, Albertina struck an uneasy balance between keeping a low profile politically while at the same time working to construct some semblance of ANC underground machinery. One of the people with whom she worked closely in this regard was John Nkadimeng. Nkadimeng was one of Walter's long-time political associates who had joined the ANC in 1950. Flag Boshielo later recruited him to the Communist Party. Nkadimeng had participated in the 1952 Defiance Campaign and later became a leading light in SACTU. In 1964, Nkadimeng had been found guilty of furthering the aims of the ANC and sentenced to two years in prison in Kroonstad.

After his release in 1966, Nkadimeng was placed under a banning order that confined him to Orlando. He knew that he had to lie low for a while because the security police maintained strict surveillance over ex-political prisoners. After careful enquiries he managed to establish that Albertina was one of the few ANC leaders still active. He managed to contact her and they set up an underground cell. Another activist, John Mavuso, joined them. The three of them maintained contact with the ANC leadership in Botswana, working closely with Nathaniel Nkosibomvu, who used to act as a courier. Their main activity was to facilitate the passage of ANC members who wanted to leave the country for education or military training. Albertina and Nkadimeng made contact with Ramokgadi and Manci (Malume). Together they managed to develop a formal working committee that managed to operate, albeit with difficulty. They had to develop links with other provinces, a difficult task because they were unable to hold formal meetings (Interview, John Nkadimeng, 4/2/95).

Because they were both banned, it was illegal for Albertina and Nkadimeng to communicate with each other. However, they mastered the art of surreptitious meetings. Nkadimeng would visit Albertina at Shanty Clinic pretending to be her relative. She would then accompany him to the gate, supposedly chatting about family matters with her "relative". Other underground activists would go to the clinic as patients and while Albertina was taking their case histories, they would exchange political information.

The only other chance Albertina had for political work was between the time she knocked off work at 5pm and went to report to the police station at 7pm. In the intervening two hours she sometimes found the chance to rush to a meeting.

Albertina received help in her political work from an unexpected quarter. Lungi was eager to help. He had learned to drive at a very early age, and during school holidays he used to drive their 1950s Consul Limo. By the time he was 14 she was able to send him to pick up people, who he learned much later, were MK cadres. He also acted as a courier, carrying messages between Albertina and her fellow activists.

Lungi worked most closely with Nkadimeng and they developed their own methods of communicating. For example, Lungi would arrive at a prearranged meeting place and see Nkadimeng sitting on a stone. As soon as he saw Lungi, Nkadimeng would get up and walk away. Lungi would then sit on the same stone. After a while he would surreptitiously look under it and pick up the letter or message that Nkadimeng had left behind. The letters were mainly to people who were leaving the country and contained instructions on how to get out. Sometimes Lungi and Nkadimeng would arrange to meet in the city. Lungi would pass Nkadimeng as if he did not know him, then he would watch as Nkadimeng disappeared into a doorway. They would then move casually to their meeting place, where Lungi would deliver his message. Among family and friends, Lungi was legendary for his inability to be on time, but when it came to underground work he was amazingly punctual. "He was completely reliable," recalled Nkadimeng. "From the outset I told him the life of this thing depends on him being on time" (Interview, John Nkadimeng, 4/2/95).

Underground work was stressful and dangerous and Albertina was always conscious of the need to be extremely careful. She knew police informers lurked everywhere. They could be among the staff at the clinic or even among the people with whom she worked in the movement. Towards the end of 1967, Albertina became increasingly uncomfortable about working with John Mavuso. At first she had complete confidence in Mavuso. After all, he was a member of the National Executive and one of their main couriers. While Max was still in Botswana, he had sent a pair of shoes for Albertina back with him. Mavuso was their main contact with the ANC leadership in Lusaka and they thought he was very clever to be able to sneak in and out of the country without getting arrested. However, Albertina became suspicious about the way he would delay reporting back when he returned from Lusaka. She also heard that he had started a factory producing school uniforms. People in the community were asking questions about how Mavuso had suddenly come into so much money that he could be opening factories. Albertina expressed her concerns to Nkadimeng, who did some of his own investigating. He reported back to Albertina that she had good reason to be suspicious of Mavuso. They decided not to confront him, but simply froze him out of their activities.

Despite these setbacks, Albertina felt they were making some headway in rebuilding the underground structures of the movement. In September 1968 she wrote to Walter: "Though we have not got enough rain yet this year, our gardens are not as poor as all these other years. I think by next year we will have enough vegetables. So rest in peace in the Island. We are not going to starve long" (Letter, 17/9/69).

At the beginning of 1968, the sense of isolation that prisoners felt in their early years on Robben Island was greatly relieved by the increase in the number of letters D group prisoners were allowed to send and receive. Walter was thrilled at the opportunity for increased contact with his family, especially his children, but was disappointed when responses to his letters were not forthcoming. Mike Dingake wrote about their attitude to unanswered letters:

> To buoy our spirits Comrade Walter and I invented a mischievously insinuating slogan *abanakusenza nto* (they won't do us a thing). When comrades asked "who won't do you a thing" we replied "anybody who thinks he/she can break us by not writing to us, including the Boers who withhold our letters, *abanakusenza nto!*" Comrades would threaten to inform our wives that we were lumping them together with the enemy. But it was proper to try to make light of the wretched feeling of being unwanted and deserted. Letters were a mighty psychotherapy (Dingake, 165).

Walter became increasingly irritated by his unresponsive sons. Early in 1968 he complained to Albertina: "Wrote to Lungi and Lakhe at the beginning of December but there has been no reply yet despite the fact that I had earnestly requested them to reply."

He also expressed his disappointment to Beryl and Lindi: "You will no doubt remember that it was three years ago when I wrote to you and received your prompt reply to my letter. What a wonderful letter it was! I can now promise you more regular correspondence of at least twice a year, provided that you do not behave like your brothers. I have written several letters to them and what is more, I requested them to reply to my letters and yet they have not done so up to now" (February, 1968).

Walter was not the only one who was irritated. In March 1968 he heard from Albertina: "I am writing this letter wondering why you have decided to keep quiet … I would be very pleased to know what is happening. Look dear, I am not against you writing to anybody but I think my letter must be replied [to]" (Albertina to Walter, 15/3/68).

The prison censorship service created confusion between prisoners and their families because they caused lengthy delays in the delivery of letters. Both incoming and outgoing letters were censored, and between 1966 and 1969 there were only two censors to go through the mail of hundreds of prisoners (Dingake, 160). To make matters worse, the censors often sent letters for further vetting to security police headquarters in Pretoria. The security police would then advise whether the letter should be given to the prisoner or withheld. Warders were cruel enough to announce to a prisoner, "You have received a letter but you are not getting it." This type of censorship applied mainly to letters from active members of the liberation movements, even if they were members of the prisoner's family. As a result, Walter was not allowed to receive letters from Max. Several years elapsed before sympathetic warders would convey the contents of Max's letters to his father (Dingake, 166).

Walter responded in May 1968 to Albertina's "hot letter" as he called it: "Let me clarify matters concerning correspondence. Your January letter reached me at the end of February, and it was indeed wonderful. I replied to it on 1st March. Your next letter, 'the hot one', I received on the 13th April and I replied the same day. I no longer want to comment on correspondence between myself and your children" (Walter to Albertina, 5/68).

Walter's complaints finally bore fruit in the form of a long letter of apology from Lungi:

I am very, very sorry to have caused you so much trouble. I know I am to blame for everything. You know I had always sworn to myself that I would do anything to please you, but when we got your letter, I was disgusted and even surprised at myself. I had actually written to you when yours came but I had not yet finished writing it. The reason being that I had planned to write to you the longest letter ever, and that meant I had to write everyday. Unfortunately things did not turn out my way, the letter got lost, this that and the other thing (Lungi to Walter, 1/7/69).

Walter accepted the apology – and the excuses – graciously:

I was very pleased to receive your letter. It was really a great relief to me. I was worried and concerned that my own children would find it difficult even to drop me a line in spite of repeated requests. Tell Mummy that my high blood pressure has been considerably reduced as a result of your letters. My dear son, my only purpose was that I should be in contact with my children and that correspondence was the best possible method in the circumstances. Besides letter writing is something good for a student of any language. It is an art which must be developed. Through these letters we can understand each other. It is the only way I can hope to shape the character of my children.

Walter empathised with Lungi about his dread of examinations: "I suffer from the same disease. I however realise that it is an attitude which can be harmful. It can undermine one's confidence." He also tried hard to encourage the intellectual development of his children, writing: "Lungi, I am interested in your other cultural activities, e.g., sport, music, novel reading, newspapers and journal reading and theatre going. I am also interested to know about some of your friends" (Letter to Lungi, 1/7/69).

He expressed approval that Lindi was planning to take piano lessons and he encouraged them in their reading: "When you are at home ask Yusuf to loan you *Glimpses of World History* and read for Lindi, Nkuli, Alice, Thenji and even Mummy. Even if you read only 100 pages, it will be of interest." He told Lindi and Beryl that he had just finished writing an essay entitled "Women

Famous in History". "It really fascinated me. I began to reflect seriously on the role of women in public affairs. Gone are the days when science in its various forms and public affairs are the preserve of men. 'Knowledge is power'. This goes for women as well" (Letter to Lindi and Beryl, February 1968). Walter was delighted when he received a letter from Lindi declaring her ambition for him to see a newspaper headline one day saying: "Lindi Sisulu, the first African woman in space!"

By 1967 prisoners were also allowed to receive three photographs a month. Walter was thrilled to receive photographs of his family. Each time he got one he commented in detail on the faces in the image. He wrote to Lungi about one of his favourite photographs: "Make no mistake, none of you can surpass my wonderful wife ... The photo is an inspiration and comfort to me" (Letter to Lungi, 1/7/69).

Apart from his family, Walter also wrote to various relatives and friends, often doling out advice and encouragement to the younger ones. When his nephew Bungu was going through a difficult time, he responded: "I am rather sorry about your difficulties. But I am sure everything will come right. Greatness is in principles ... I have confidence my boy that you will develop into a full and responsible man" (Walter to Bungu, 2/7/69).

Walter was particularly excited to re-establish contact with his dear old friend Sam Mase in February 1968:

My dear Cousin,
I have been thinking about you and the family for some time now. You and I have grown up together, and what is more is that we have lived together for many years. Your parents and your brother Gordon and his wife were very fond of me. These are things which are not easy to forget. Among the people in the village of my birth, who I look up to is yourself. You have followed your religious course, I have followed politics, but I am sure we respect each other's views. As for myself, I have nothing to regret, because I am satisfied that my cause is just. Those who think otherwise will be judged by posterity. History will vindicate my stand.

I hope you will realise how much value we attach to any letter we write and that you will reply to my letter as soon as you get it. When you write do not exceed five pages but not less. Pardon me for jumping about in writing this letter. I do not know what to say and what to leave out.

In the same period Walter also wrote to his former teacher Sam Mdaka, much to the amusement of his prison colleagues. "We teased him about it, saying 'how can someone of your age still be writing to your teacher?'" recalled Kathrada. Walter was delighted by his old teacher's lively response. Mdaka informed Walter that he was teaching at an isolated place called Sinqumeni on the mountain tops near Ugie. He was supposed to be on pension, but because of the shortage of teachers he had been asked to continue teaching. He had news of people Walter had asked after – Macozoma who had since died, DB Mxutu who had become a postmaster at Ncora, Rev. HN Gcanga who was the preacher at All Saints and Dabula, the principal at Manzana. He also reported on the drought in the Transkei: "In my lifetime I do not think we have had such a drought as we have this year. People are starving. Cattle are dying. Labour centres are going to be flooded." He congratulated Walter on his studies: "I am so happy to learn you are still as keen on education as you were when you were my scholar. I wish you every success in your endeavours. A man is never too old to learn. Success always follows on the heels of hard labour." He brushed aside Walter's apology for his poor handwriting, saying it was similar to his own: "Like teacher like child. Your writing is not any worse than your teachers" (Letter, 1/7/68).

In the following year, Mdaka informed Walter that the drought had ended, but too late to save the mealies and the livestock. "To help poverty-stricken citizens, women are hired to make roads. There are no foremen to drive them. See them at work you would wonder how long they would take to do a stretch of a mile. Hang! They take their time." Walter was amused by Mdaka's comments on the Transkei parliament:

Oh, I dared not contest a seat in Parliament. I would never stand the heckling and the silly remarks. I understand one has to be thick-skinned to be a member of Parliament, as I see it does not fit serious minded and highly strung people. Such people would soon have stroke or heart failure! I think you would do well in that sphere, not me. Our Qwati young chief is very quiet. Why he is so quiet, I do not know. The boy has command of the English language and is not empty headed. Tshunungwa of St Marks is a front bencher. He distinguished himself in the "No confidence debate". He was so steamed up that he even quoted you, saying what he said was supported by men like you. He was in his very best form (Letter, 12/6/69).

Shortly after this, the security police visited Sam Mase in Engcobo. They suggested that his corresponding with Walter Sisulu could lead to suspicions that he was a member of the ANC. Sam was firm in his response: "Because of my religion and my knowledge of politics I was very brave and could face anybody. I told them I was related to Walter and he had every right to correspond with me about family affairs. Since politics teaches you to be brave, anything you say you should be prepared to stand for" (Interview, Sam Mase, 2001).

After Walter had been sentenced, the performance in school of all the children initially deteriorated and then picked up again, except for Zwelakhe, who seemed to be the most badly affected by his father's incarceration. Makgatho Mandela, who was also at St Christophers, and Zwelakhe became difficult and rebellious. On one occasion, they ran away from home and were found after a week. Father Hooper travelled all the way from Swaziland to discuss Zwelakhe's behaviour with Albertina. He told her he would try his very best to keep Zwelakhe in line. Meanwhile Zwelakhe moved from St Christophers to a Catholic school in Swaziland. At the end of one of the holidays, Albertina had borrowed money for the children to return to school. When it was time to go to the station, they discovered that Zwelakhe was missing. They had to hunt for him and they eventually found him in the township with friends.

Zwelakhe concedes that at the time his youthful mischief bordered on criminal activity. He began to carry a knife and got involved in some very rough fights in Soweto. On one occasion, he and his friends got hold of a gun. When he went home on holiday, he would be the tough guy from boarding school. When he returned to school, he was the tough guy from Soweto. "Either way I had a reputation to uphold."

Albertina was furious when Zwelakhe refused to go back to school and a clash of wills ensued between mother and son. Albertina would wake him up at the crack of dawn, "because people who are not in school should be working!" She was so strict that he eventually told one of the nurses who worked with her that life at home was such hell that he preferred school. Zwelakhe returned to Swaziland, but his problems continued and eventually he was expelled. In November 1966 Albertina wrote to Walter: "It has taken me a long time to write to you because I had certain problems I wanted to put straight before writing. First was Zwelakhe's expulsion from school and that took place after my return from Cape Town in September. I tried to get him a place in other schools, but I failed because it was too late to admit any student at that time of the year. I had to get him a private teacher. In short he is now going to another school at the end of the year."

At the height of her problems with Zwelakhe, Albertina received disturbing news about Max. The frantic messages that she and Walter had sent about Max's schooling filtered through the channels of the ANC in exile and finally reached Moscow at the end of 1965. By that time Max had already completed one year of military training, so when JB Marks summoned him to order him back to school, Max was quite happy to comply. Instead of returning to the camps in Tanzania with the rest of his unit, he enrolled at the Plekhanov Institute for Economics in Moscow at the beginning of 1966. His high-school sweetheart, Mercy Vutela, also enrolled at the same institute.

Mercy had left South Africa shortly after Max and was sent to study in the Soviet Union. In Moscow she was reunited with Max, and their relationship became more serious. By the second half of 1966, they were married and expecting a baby.

Albertina received the news with considerable concern. Max was only 20 – in her view, far too young to get married. To complicate matters, Mercy was the daughter of Greta Ncapayi, Albertina's friend and colleague who had worked with her in the ANC Women's League and the Rand Nurses Professional Club. Naturally, both mothers were frustrated that the objects of their anger were so far away, well out of reach of maternal scolding. Albertina tried to play down her feelings of disappointment and to focus on the positive when she conveyed the news to Walter: "We have been blessed with a son, born of the Sisulus by the name of Mlungisi. He was born on 20 August. That means he is sharing a birthday with his father. So my dear, you have a grandchild. You wanted to know what the mother is doing. They are in the same school ... I understand they are completing in 1969 ... They say we need not worry, the child will be well looked after and that it will not disturb their studies."

She went on to ask Walter to write to Greta because "that would release her from her worry. She is a bit disturbed about what the children did. So if you write and show her that it is not so important to cry over spilt milk ... I am sure she will be happy to receive a letter from *umkhozi wakhe*".

Albertina's fears that the couple were too young were not unfounded. She waited anxiously for further news from Max and in September 1967 she reported to Walter: "At last I received a photo [of] our little Lungi with a confusing letter, which I don't understand. In any case I will discuss it with you when we next meet" (Letter, 26/9/67). When she visited Walter on 25 December 1967, she informed him that their new grandson was doing well, but his parents were divorcing after just one year of marriage and that Max was taking care of Lungi. Both were distressed by the news. If it had been possible, Albertina would have gone to Moscow to collect her grandchild, but under the circumstances there was absolutely nothing she could do.

Albertina had travelled to Cape Town with Nkuli. Their return journey was a nightmare. The trains were packed, so the only bookings they could get were in third class. That meant sitting upright for over 36 hours. They were hot and uncomfortable, and little Nkuli drove her mother to distraction by asking repeatedly when they would get home.

Albertina and Nkuli arrived home to the news that Zwelakhe had been arrested on 23 December for failing to produce his reference book. He had spent Christmas in jail and was released on the 27th, a few hours after Albertina and Nkuli returned home. As if this was not enough, they found that Lungi had been assaulted by a group of men on Christmas Day. At the time, Lungi had been staying in Pretoria to avoid the security police. He had travelled from Pretoria to spend Christmas Day at home. As he arrived home, a stranger attacked him, right in front of the house. When he tried to fight back, three other men joined in and beat him severely. One of the men even drew a knife. The reason for the attack and the identity of the attackers remained a mystery, but the family suspected the security police. If they did not carry out the attack themselves, they certainly knew the identity of the attackers; official documents revealed later that they watched the house closely and recorded the number plates of every car that parked in the vicinity.

On Robben Island, Walter had been looking forward with great anticipation to a visit from Zwelakhe on 6 January, and was puzzled and disappointed when Zwelakhe did not turn up. "Darling, what happened to Zwelakhe's visit?" he wrote in his next letter to Albertina. "You can well imagine, I went to the usual place and waited for an hour and came back without knowing what had happened to my child. 'Mntakwethu, intliziyo ilulwandle'. To this day I do not know precisely what happened" (Letter, 6/1/68).

When he received Albertina's letter about the upheavals over the Christmas period, she explained that Zwelakhe had been unable to visit because he had lost his pass: "Now we have to start from the beginning again, trying to get another duplicate. You know what it is to get a pass. Now we will have to start applying again for June holidays because the March holidays are very short. You don't know how we were all upset about it. We were just imagining you thinking all sorts of things" (Letter, 31/1/68). She also informed Walter about the attack on Lungi. "Fortunately they did not stab him but he was badly assaulted. I found him in great pain, his face swollen but he recovered soon afterwards" (Letter, 31/1/68).

Zwelakhe finally did get to visit his father that June when he travelled to Cape Town with Makgatho. They stayed with Thembekile in the Cape Town suburb of Retreat and travelled to the Island together. Zwelakhe was excited to see his father after such a long period, but their conversation was rather stilted at first. Walter asked Zwelakhe if he had a girlfriend. "This made me feel awkward because you never speak to your father about girlfriends. After a while the conversation began to flow and I began to ask him about life in jail and some of the people in jail. Then it was his turn to feel awkward because the warders kept saying: 'Sisulu, you can't answer that.'"

Walter delighted in the visits of his children. Seeing them was an affirmation of the survival of the family in difficult circumstances. Beryl had been the first of the children to visit him in July 1967. She recalled how light-hearted he was: "His face would light up and he would say 'stand up and turn around,' or 'move back' or 'you have gained weight'. He would always ask 'How are you progressing?' His memory was remarkable and he would be interested in what was happening to each and every one in the family. One thing that struck me was that he never lost hope. He always let me leave with the impression that they would never die there. They were going to come back home. I remember how devoted he was to Mama. He would always say 'You children must look after your mother, you mustn't worry her" (Interview, Beryl Simelane, 28/12/93).

Walter's concern about the pressure on his wife shows in their correspondence. In 1968 he wrote: "I am rather worried about the heavy burden upon your shoulders. Indeed, I have a feeling you are undergoing a very strenuous time in all respects. Please, do write to me at any time you feel like doing so. Do not wait for my letters. The only way of you and I exchanging opinions is by correspondence. Tell me any problem which you may have."

Nkuli and Lindi could not visit Robben Island because they were under the age of 16, so Walter relied on Albertina's reports on their progress. In January 1968 she wrote: "Lindi is now a big girl of 14 years and she is busy counting that she is left with only one year before she can see you. She did very well, she got a first-class pass. She was 4th out of 74 students. She is now doing Form 2" (Letter, 1/1/68). In December 1968, Beryl, Lindi and Nkuli had a rare holiday in the Cape. Walter savoured Albertina's lively account of their adventures:

> They visited many important places like Table Mountain, Cango Caves and Fort Hare. In Cape Town they were taken to Table Mountain and went up in a lift ... Oh! dear you can imagine how they felt. At Table Mountain they bought postcards and your daughter wrote to her mother in English and the ending was your daughter, Tunku ... I forgot to mention Groote Schuur Hospital where they made an appointment with Chris Barnard, but unfortunately he had an emergency operation so they could not see him, but they were taken on rounds in and out of the Hospital. At Fort Hare they did the same but the most interesting place was the Cango Caves. There they had oral examinations and obtained certificates as Cavemen. This means that when they were asked to get down into the caves ... they were not afraid so they were called Cavemen because of their bravery (Letter, 8/5/69).

In September 1968, Albertina was excited to hear from Max after a long silence. "Bantu wrote us a nice long letter. He says he is graduating next year June. He is taking a Masters degree in Economics. Can you see we are old? We have graduates already" (Letter, 17/9/68). Walter was pleased to hear that even Zwelakhe had settled down and was studying hard: "Zwelakhe is at home attending school at Orlando High, and for his Latin lessons he is at Britzius College. He is doing well. He looks quite determined now. He is even thinking of going to Fort Hare for his degree" (Letter, 17/9/68).

Beryl and Lungi had left school in Swaziland after they had written their Cambridge O-level examination at the end of 1968. Earlier in the year, Albertina had written to Walter about Beryl's plans for her future: "Beryl is asking if she could be permitted to take up nursing as a career, after matric. I promised to raise this with you. Now we will wait on your decision. I personally have no objections if she feels that way. After all she is the one who should tell us what she wants" (Letter, 31/1/68). Albertina did, however, encourage Beryl to consider going to university.

When the 'O' results came out, Beryl had failed two subjects but had managed to achieve an 'A' in English in that year. Father Hooper had been so impressed by this that he had arranged a scholarship abroad for her. She was frustrated by the fact that she did not have a passport. She travelled to Swaziland in September 1969, crossing the border illegally to make arrangements for her trip overseas. After discussing the matter with Father Hooper, Beryl realised that taking up the scholarship would mean going into exile. When she thought of Max, who was so far away, and Gerald, who they had not heard from since his departure in 1962, she decided that she had no desire to leave home, not knowing when she would be able to return.

In any event a tragedy at home pushed all thoughts of travelling abroad out of her head.

She was stunned by the news that Thembekile Mandela had been killed on 28 September 1969 in a head-on collision with another car near Touwsrivier in the Cape. He had been travelling with Thoko Mhlanga, the mother of his two small daughters, and Thoko's sister-in-law, Irene Simelane. Thembi and Irene were killed instantly and Thoko sustained serious injuries. Beryl told Father Hooper she had to attend the funeral and returned home immediately.

Thembi's death was a shock to the Sisulu family. To Walter and Albertina, he had been a beloved nephew and the children had looked up to him as a big brother. Beryl was particularly affected because of her close relationship with Thembi. He had introduced her to Thoko while they were at school in Swaziland and the two had become firm friends.

Albertina felt deeply for Thembi's parents. She knew that Thembi had been a tower of strength to his mother, Evelyn, and his death was a cruel blow. Like Albertina, Evelyn had struggled to send her children to school in Swaziland. It was clear that as a Jehovah's Witness Evelyn was not involved in politics, but this had not stopped the apartheid regime from denying her a passport, forcing her to rely on other people to take her children to and from school. She had also battled to pay school fees until Thembi introduced her to the South African Institute of Race Relations. The SAIRR then assisted with school fees for Makaziwe and Makgatho.

When Mandela received the news on Robben Island, he was inconsolable. Walter was called by his fellow prisoners, who told him something was drastically wrong with Mandela. Walter entered his cell and knelt by his bed. Mandela handed him the telegram. There was nothing Walter could say. He took Mandela's hand and sat with him throughout the day until lock-up.

In Orlando West, the Madiba clan rallied around Evelyn. Tatu'Mdingi played the role of father and helped arrange the burial. Predictably, Mandela was denied permission to attend his son's funeral. He could only write a letter of condolence to Evelyn and try to come to terms with his son's death without the consolation and closure of the funeral ritual. It was a time of deep anguish and despair – when the burden of imprisonment weighed most heavily.

# *f i v e*

In May 1969 Walter celebrated his 57th birthday. It was his fifth year in jail. Albertina tried to send him an encouraging message, but she could not avoid expressing the pain of separation: "My wish is that your health be good till the lights of South Africa shine again and our demands are fulfilled. That your spirit remains the same for your goal is very near ... Needless to say how I feel about you Walter ... You know things like birthdays are breaking the hearts of mothers because they know what it means to bring a human being to this world. Let me therefore darling tell you we feel lost because we know that if you were here we would be celebrating with you but don't worry, it won't be long" (Letter, 5/1969).

Despite Albertina's attempt at optimism it was clear, as the decade drew to a close, that the repression of the 1960s was by no means over. If anything, the apartheid state had become even more ruthless and efficient. In response to increasing insurgency by SWAPO, the government had introduced the notorious Terrorism Act, which applied to both South Africa and Namibia. Section 6 of the Act allowed the police to arrest and hold detainees incommunicado indefinitely without charge. The Act was applied retrospectively back to 1962. Helen Suzman, the only MP who voted against the Terrorism Act when it was passed in Parliament in 1967, called it "the harshest of all the measures undermining the Rule of Law". "With these three acts – the Sabotage Act, the Ninety-day Detention Law and the Terrorism Act," wrote Suzman in her memoirs, "the Rule of Law was utterly destroyed in South Africa. The government had empowered itself to crush all resistance to its relentless extension and implementation of apartheid" (Suzman, 98–99).

On 31 July 1969, Albertina was informed that her banning order had been renewed for another five years, and she was placed under partial house arrest. The security police surveillance report used to justify the extension of Albertina's banning order was a mixture of fact, distortion and complete fabrication. The report correctly stated that Albertina had continued to be a member of the Executive Committee of FEDSAW and that she worked with Nkadimeng and Mavuso in what it referred to as the "secretariat of the ANC in Johannesburg". The report contained the usual allegations that Albertina was active in the SACP. She was also said to be planning to buy municipal houses for returning terrorists.

One of the wilder allegations in the report was that in March 1968 Nelson Mandela had given orders for Albertina to arrange a protest when an action to strike his name from the roll of attorneys was brought before the Transvaal Supreme Court in Pretoria. There had been a move to strike Mandela off the roll of attorneys, which he had contested. However, it was completely untrue that he had instructed Albertina to arrange a demonstration. Mandela was well aware that Albertina was banned and she would have courted certain arrest if she had arranged such an action. It would have also been completely out of character for Mandela to ask anyone to protest on his behalf.

Some of the allegations bordered on science fiction. When Beryl first visited Walter on Robben Island she had complained that Walter was wearing glasses without any frames. Albertina therefore bought Walter a new pair of glasses and presented them on her next visit. According to Compol "it was suspected that a secret message was hidden in the frame of the spectacles". Then there was the bizarre claim that a white man called Platz-Mills from London had given Albertina a secret writing apparatus that looked like a mirror and that Albertina used this apparatus to write messages to leaders abroad! (Ministry of Justice files, Compol report, 21/7/69.)

It is difficult to know whether the security police really believed their own allegations, or whether they were just cynical fabrications to convince the Ministry of Justice to impose further restrictions. The latter is more likely because if the police had had real evidence they were certainly empowered by repressive legislation to detain Albertina indefinitely.

The Compol memorandum also revealed the security police interest in fomenting divisions between Winnie Mandela and Albertina. It was alleged that, according to "information from a delicate source", Albertina had told Edith Sophazi and another person that she did not trust Winnie Mandela. Compol also alleged that Albertina was "competing with Winnie for leadership of FEDSAW". But since Winnie was not part of any FEDSAW structure, Albertina could hardly have competed with her in that area. Albertina was also extremely careful about what she said about colleagues, so the "delicate source" was also clearly an unreliable one. Albertina did, however, have serious misgivings about some of the people with whom Winnie associated and the way she operated.

Early in 1969 two young women, Joyce Sikhakhane and Rita Ndzanga, visited Albertina. They had come to deliver a message from Winnie Mandela inviting Albertina to join her in an underground initiative. Albertina had no hesitation in turning down this overture. She gently explained to the two emissaries that she did not think it wise for her and Winnie to work together because they were both banned and under strict police surveillance. The security police would pounce on the smallest bit of evidence that they were working together. While she liked and respected Joyce and Rita, she felt that they were not careful enough and too many people knew about their activities. She knew that, like herself, Winnie was a major target for security police infiltration. In their situation patience and caution were essential, and Albertina did not believe that caution and patience were Winnie's strong points.

Albertina warned the two young women not to take unnecessary risks, but according to Joyce: "Young radical activists that we were, we did not heed MaSisulu's words." Joyce and Rita proceeded to Lilian Ngoyi, where they delivered the same invitation from Winnie. Lilian was much more blunt than Albertina. "You, Joyce," she said, "when the security police give you electric shocks in your genitals, what will you do? Can you guarantee that you will not talk?"

She cautioned the two women against getting involved in reckless schemes. They later wished they had heeded the advice of the two veteran leaders when they were arrested and detained under Section 6 of the Terrorism Act in May 1969. They were part of a group of 22 activists who were arrested at that time and held without charge for several months. Among them was Winnie, who had been arrested in the middle of the night while her two young daughters looked on. During her detention Winnie was interrogated non-stop for five days and five nights.

Rita Ndzanga's husband, trade unionist Lawrence Ndzanga, was also detained. Rita was brutally beaten and almost all the detainees were tortured. They were held until October 1969, when they were finally charged with 21 offences under the Suppression of Communism Act. They remained in custody until their court case in December 1969, which came to be known as the "Trial of the 22". They were acquitted on 16 February 1970, but immediately redetained. In June 1970 they were taken back to court in an attempt to link them to the MK guerrilla Benjamin Ramotse, who had been captured in Botswana in 1968 and so badly tortured that he had barely survived. Ramotse had been kept in solitary confinement for two years before his trial. The State added the charges Ramotse was alleged to have committed to the original charges, and the indictment was changed to terrorism.

The lawyers successfully applied for separation of trials, although their clients were, in the interests of solidarity, prepared to stand trial with Ramotse. Once the trials were separated, the lawyers applied for discharge on the grounds the 22 accused could not be tried twice on the same charges. They were finally released on 14 September 1970. Benjamin Ramotse was found guilty and sentenced to 15 years on Robben Island.

Albertina had expressed her concerns about the 22 trialists to Walter in May 1970 in a round-about way, using Winnie's clan name: "Ngutyana and friends are still away and that is not treating us well at all." Walter managed to smuggle a letter of encouragement to Rita Ndzanga and she responded on 28 October 1970: "I was so happy to receive a letter from my leader. It is such an honour to both me and my husband. We never knew we meant so much to you. We are out as you already know. We are waiting for the results of the appeal lodged by the prosecution. We already know what to expect."

The security police were clearly aware that Albertina was politically active. However, they were not able to pin anything on her, although they did come close in the case of Amos Lungephi Lengisi, Walter's nephew, who was convicted for terrorism in March 1969. Lengisi was one of the few MK guerrillas who infiltrated the country in the late 1960s. He had undergone military training in Odessa and Moscow in 1965, after which he returned to Tanzania. In June 1968, Lengisi and another MK cadre had travelled to the Kenyan port of Mombasa where they convinced a crew member of a cargo ship headed for Cape Town to smuggle them aboard. Hiding in a cupboard for most of the journey, the two stowaways arrived in Cape Town and managed to disembark disguised as crew members. Wearing three sets of clothing and carrying a huge amount of cash, they went their separate ways. Lengisi went to Engcobo because he knew a lot of secret hiding places there, although he naturally avoided his mother's home. He recruited some young people and trained them to use firearms. He established a little branch of the ANC and travelled around the area.

Around July/August 1968, Lengisi visited Johannesburg disguised as a priest. Albertina was surprised when Lengisi turned up at her house. Conscious of the dangers of his presence, she immediately took him to another place and arranged that he meet Nkadimeng and Nkosibomvu. They advised him to keep away because of the danger of police infiltration. After his return to the Transkei, Lengisi was arrested on 26 September 1968. Lengisi's comrade with whom he had entered the country had been arrested in Durban the day before and revealed Lengisi's whereabouts when he broke down during interrogation.

When he was interrogated by the security police, Lengisi was asked if he had met Albertina Sisulu and John Nkadimeng during his visit to Johannesburg. He denied meeting them. They then asked him if Albertina was a member of MK. He said, "I don't know because I would never work with a woman on MK issues." The security police were well aware that he was related to Walter Sisulu and told him that he was where he was as a result of Sisulu's influence: "You drank the poison [of politics] at an early age."

Lengisi was tried in Pietermaritzburg in January 1969 with 12 other MK cadres. Matthews Ngcobo was the first accused and Lengisi the second accused. The witnesses were made up mostly of the people Lengisi had recruited and trained. Most gave evidence because they had been thoroughly intimidated but two of the witnesses seemed to relish giving evidence. Influenced by Nelson Mandela, Lengisi and his colleagues all made statements from the dock. All were convicted in March 1969 and given sentences ranging from 12 to 20 years. Lengisi received the highest sentence of 20 years. He was then despatched to Pretoria Maximum Prison. After 11 months in the death cells of Pretoria Maximum, he was content to be transferred to Robben Island.

When Amos Lengisi arrived in Robben Island in 1970, his hopes of seeing his famous uncle were dashed. He was one of a dozen ANC guerrillas who were placed with about 40 SWAPO guerrillas in the old *zinktronk*. They were confined to their yard even when working, with little opportunity to see other prisoners. The 30-odd prisoners in the single-cells section were taken to and from work in a closed lorry and a warder would clear the road as their lorry approached. They were taken separately to visits and to church. They wrote their exams separately and had separate leisure activities. By 1970, most of the *Poqo* prisoners (who had been on shorter sentences) had left, while new ANC prisoners continued to come in, making them the majority on the Island.

In a long letter smuggled out of prison sometime between 11 December 1970 and 9 January 1971 Kathrada described the conditions that prevailed at the time (Letter to Sylvia Neame, December 1970; *Letters from Robben Island*, 46–51). He described the relationship with warders as "cordial and with some decidedly warm". He felt that the political prisoners were a good influence on the warders who "have discussed most intimate matters and sought advice; a blind man listening to a tête-à-tête will find it hard to believe it is between a prisoner and warder".

When they started working in the lime quarry in 1964, the Commissioner of Prisons had promised the B section prisoners that if they worked hard, they would spend no more than six months in the quarry, after which they would be given less strenuous and more satisfying work. The promise was never kept and the prisoners worked in the quarry for over a decade. When the International Red Cross officials visited the Island in 1968, the prison authorities told them that there were no prisoners working in the lime quarry. For the duration of the visit, the prisoners were removed from the quarry and taken to work elsewhere (Interview, Ahmed Kathrada). The prisoners responded with a kind of permanent go-slow. "Our official work still remains the lime quarry and pick and shovels," wrote Kathrada in 1970. "But for the past few years we have not really worked. We have demanded creative work. They say they are unable to. So we just go to the quarry and do nothing" (Letter to Sylvia Neame, December 1970).

This state of affairs came to an abrupt end towards the end of 1970. In the same letter, Kathrada gave an account of the drastic change that came with the arrival, around Christmas, of a new Commanding Officer and a new team of head warders. "We are told they have come to 'clear up' this jail and to impose discipline, which they maintain has completely broken down."

The new reign of terror, which was clearly sanctioned at the highest level, was possibly in response to a letter of protest written by Mandela, on behalf of all prisoners, at the end of 1969. Mandela articulated the prisoners' unhappiness about the use of brute force, arbitrary assaults and monotonous and energy-sapping labour. He argued for meaningful and creative labour and urged the prisons department "to take appropriate measures to relieve the situation before matters get out of control". It is easy to imagine how the imperious tone of the letter, which Anthony Sampson described as reading "like an official report from the head of a department", would have annoyed the *verkrampte* elements in the prison department (Sampson 2000, 222).

If the prisons department wanted to do the opposite of what Mandela had recommended, they could not have chosen a more appropriate person to carry out their plan than Piet Badenhorst, the new Commanding Officer. Following in the tradition of brutal warders before him, like the Kleynhans brothers and Van Rensburg, Badenhorst (nicknamed Kid Ruction by the prisoners) was renowned for his uncouth behaviour and foul mouth. He did not hesitate to use his favourite expression *jou ma se moer* at every opportunity. He commanded a new set of crude and obnoxious young warders, all determined to outdo each other in their spiteful treatment of the prisoners.

From the outset, Badenhorst made it clear that he was not interested in any form of cooperation or peaceful coexistence with the prisoners. He ignored Mandela's request for an introductory meeting, the first Commanding Officer to do so. He suspended all legal procedures and processes of jail administration. There was a marked deterioration in the quality of the food and the arbitrary withdrawal of meals became a common occurrence. Prisoners were manhandled on the way to the quarry and banned from singing freedom songs while they worked. They were constantly subjected to intrusive body searches, and their cells were raided on a regular basis. Books and papers were confiscated, censorship increased and recreation facilities reduced. Visits were cancelled without explanation. Walter was devastated when a visit with Lungi was cut short when Lungi asked what he thought of being a citizen of the Ciskei.

Prisoners were continually subjected to trumped-up charges that landed them in solitary confinement (Mandela, 543–545; Meredith, 312; Sampson 2000, 223; Daniels, 151; Dingake, 178). "We were made to eat in the rain," wrote Michael Dingake. "Nozinja, Pollsmoor and Dictionary [nicknames of the warders] were assigned to our section with a mission to put us in our place by inflicting physical and mental pain. The relative deference previously accorded to our section was discarded in favour of unparalleled vindictiveness" (Dingake, 178).

Prisoners naturally reacted with horror at this dramatic reversal of their hard-won gains. They complained bitterly, but their protests were ignored. Some prisoners who demanded to see lawyers were thrown into solitary confinement. The new administration seemed to be bent on turning the clock back to the harshest years of the 1960s (Mandela, 543). "It seems," wrote Kathrada, "we have entered a period of intensive provocation and repression which will require tremendous patience, careful planning and bold action" (Kathrada, 53).

Shortly after he arrived on the Island, Badenhorst announced that he was punishing them for laziness by dropping their classification by one notch (Mandela, 544). The downgrading had a thoroughly demoralising effect on the prisoners because it meant automatic loss of certain privileges, the number of letters that they could write and visits they could receive. Worst of all, those who dropped from the C to D grade lost their studies because prisoners in the D grade were not entitled to the study privilege (Mandela, 150; Dingake, 178).

In May 1971, amid all the misery of Badenhorst's tyrannical rule, Walter had an unexpected and pleasant surprise. The group of Namibian prisoners who had been confined to the *zinktronk* were moved to the B section cells. Lengisi was moved with them. Walter was naturally elated by the appearance of his nephew and eager to hear all about what was happening outside. Lengisi regaled him with his adventures, and for two days they spent every free moment in each other's company. Their reunion was, however, interrupted by a shocking event.

Tension had been running high in the B section as a result of a hunger strike that the Namibians had started in protest against arbitrary denial of meals by the head warder. In solidarity the other prisoners in the section joined the strike. One night, a gang of warders carried out an unprecedented raid on the section, wreaking havoc from 1am to 4am. Prisoners had to stand naked with their legs apart and arms outstretched while warders rummaged through their cells. It was at the height of winter and Walter was suffering from a bad cold. "I felt so ill, I thought I would die. It was the one occasion in jail that I felt bitter, angry and bitter. I will never forget it."

While he stood shivering against the wall, Walter could hear the shouts and cursing of the warders and the screams of prisoners being beaten up. The fiery SWAPO leader Toivo ja Toivo retaliated when a warder punched him, and was so severely beaten for daring to fight back that his cell was spattered with blood. Japhta Masemola was beaten unconscious. Other prisoners had their testicles twisted. As a result, one of them urinated blood for days afterwards. Lengisi was one of the 28 prisoners who were brutally beaten. The raid finally came to an end when Govan Mbeki collapsed with severe chest pains. Fikile Bam was so incensed by Mbeki's collapse and distressed that he was powerless to protect the man whom he regarded as a father that he wept bitterly for the first and only time in his prison experience (Alexander, 23; Mandela, Daniels, 152; Interview, Fikile Bam).

The next morning the prisoners elected Walter to make a formal complaint about the assault. Unfortunately, Chief Warder Fourie, who had led the raid, was the officer who came on that particular day to attend to the complaints and requests of the prisoners. Walter could barely contain his anger when he confronted the unrepentant warder. "He and Walter had a stand-up slanging match, but it was the last time that an organised assault was launched against us," recalled Eddie Daniels. A week later Walter, Neville Alexander, Kwedi Mkalipi and Eddie Daniels represented the prisoners in an interview with Fourie and Van der Westhuizen, another of the chief warders. They spoke out strongly against the treatment they were receiving and the warders seemed to take them seriously (Daniels, 152). However, Badenhorst summoned them individually over the next few days and angrily admonished them for daring to speak on behalf of all the prisoners. He summarily dismissed their complaints and blocked all reports to lawyers.

The prisoners responded by smuggling out messages lobbying for Badenhorst's dismissal. Mandela and Walter led another delegation to meet with Badenhorst. They laid down their demands, threatening hunger strikes, go-slows and work stoppages if he did not restore their privileges and behave in a more humane and responsible way (Mandela, 547). A surprisingly chastened Badenhorst said he would consider their complaints. The final nail in Badenhorst's coffin came in the form of a visit to the Island by three senior judges, one of them Judge Corbett, head of the Cape Provincial Division of the Supreme Court.

General Steyn, the Commissioner of Prisons, who had escorted the judges, introduced Mandela as the prisoners' representative. Mandela declined the judges' offer of a private interview, and voiced his protest about the assaults of prisoners in the presence of the officials. When Badenhorst interrupted him with a threat, Mandela calmly pointed out to the judges: "If he can threaten me here in your presence, you can imagine what he does when you are not here." Judge Corbett concurred and Mandela continued with the prisoners' grievances. After the departure of the judges, the ill-treatment stopped and, within months, Badenhorst was transferred from Robben Island.

New prisoners were always welcomed with mixed feelings by the Robben Island men. The capture of political associates was not good news. On the other hand, new arrivals were welcomed for the information they brought, and their first days of incarceration were spent giving lengthy briefings to their fellow inmates. In 1968 they had heard that the ANC had forged an alliance with Joshua Nkomo's Zimbabwean African Peoples Union (ZAPU), and that the ANC and ZAPU had mounted a joint operation in Rhodesia. The arrival on the Island of MK guerrillas who had fought in Zimbabwe caused quite a stir and they were pumped for every bit of information they could provide (Sampson 2000, 213; Naidoo, 214–15).

Justice Mpanza, one of the commanders of the Luthuli Brigade, the first MK detachment to cross the Zambezi, was sent to the B section. Mpanza gave Walter, Mandela and colleagues a detailed account of the August/September 1967 clashes between the ANC/ZAPU forces and the Rhodesian forces, who had been assisted by South African paramilitary forces and aircraft. Some freedom fighters were killed, others captured and a large group, under the command of Chris Hani, retreated to Botswana where they were arrested. In a second incursion into the Sipolilo area of Zimbabwe in December 1967, more fighters were captured, while others retreated to Zambia. Nine of the captured MK cadres were tried and sentenced to death in Zimbabwe. Their sentences were later commuted to life imprisonment.

The Wankie campaign could not by any stretch of the imagination be called a success, but it boosted the morale of the ANC prisoners on Robben Island. "As commander-in-chief of MK, I was terribly proud of our soldiers," wrote Mandela (Mandela, 522). Ever the optimist, Walter did not see the campaign as a failure but as one step in the long and tortuous journey to freedom. From the isolation of Robben Island, it was easy to romanticise the campaign. The Wankie veterans were welcomed like heroes by prisoners in the general section, who sang about taking the country "the Castro way" (Sampson 2000, 213; Naidoo, 214–15).

A more sombre assessment of events was provided by James April, another Luthuli Brigade veteran, who landed on the Island in 1971. April had started his MK career at Dennis Goldberg's Malmesbury camp. He left South Africa in June 1961 for military training in Czechoslovakia and had been jailed in Botswana in the wake of the Wankie battles. They had been convicted of illegal possession of firearms and given sentences ranging from three to six years. The Botswana government subsequently bowed to pressure from the OAU and released them after about 18 months (Karis and Gerhart, 30). After April's release, he continued with his MK work and was re-infiltrated into South Africa in December 1970 as part of MK's strategy to open lines of communication into South Africa and train cadres inside the country. He was arrested in Durban, found guilty on three counts of contravening the Terrorism Act and sentenced to 15 years in jail.

The B section community welcomed April's arrival. For the first time, they were able to receive a first-hand account of the ANC consultative conference that had been held in Morogoro, Tanzania in April 1969. The conference, the first in the exile era, had been convened to iron out the organisational and strategic problems of the ANC. According to Kathrada, "We may have had second-hand reports but from James we had the authentic report of what happened at Morogoro. It was also the first time we heard a first-hand report of the Zimbabwe incursions. We had heard rumours based on propaganda from the regime and also exaggerated reports on our side about casualties inflicted on the enemy. Not surprisingly, his arrival generated a lot of excitement."

The main problem facing the ANC in exile was the lack of progress in the armed struggle. Through close cooperation with Rhodesia and Portuguese-controlled Angola and Mozambique, the tightening of control over South West Africa and the construction of a huge military base on the Caprivi Strip, South Africa had strengthened its borders, creating a strong buffer zone to prevent the infiltration of guerrilla forces. The independence of Botswana and Lesotho in 1966 and Swaziland in 1968 had done little to alter the situation. They were so economically dependent on South Africa that they were effectively part of that country's *cordon sanitaire* (Karis and Gerhart, 6, 7).

In the absence of established routes to enable them to return to South Africa and operate inside the country, it was impossible to infiltrate large numbers of guerrillas. The few who were returned, like Lengisi, were quickly arrested. The ANC tried to deal with the boredom and discontent of the hundreds of MK cadres sitting in the camps, waiting to go home and fight, by sending many of them for retraining. This was referred to as the "sharpening of the spear", until some complained that there was a danger that the ANC would continue sharpening the spear until there was no spear left! (Sibeko, 98.) It was not only the would-be soldiers who were concerned about the absence of action on the battlefront. The Tanzanian and Zambian governments and the OAU Liberation Committee were also applying pressure on the liberation movements to "get down to real fighting" (Karis and Gerhart, 28). The Wankie campaign was the ANC's response to this pressure. Unfortunately, the campaign did not succeed in its aim of establishing a base in Zimbabwe to service future incursions and ultimately infiltrate fighters into South Africa. Instead, its failure deepened the sense of malaise in the ANC camps. Those who had participated in the campaign were unhappy about the way they were treated on their return to Zambia, and complained about the lack of direction in the armed struggle.

Mounting criticism of the leadership was voiced in a memorandum by a group of MK commanders and commissars, listed under the signature of Chris Hani. This alleged that the leadership was out of touch with events in South Africa, and was scathing about the rift between the political leadership and the military rank and file. The memorandum caused a stir in the ANC, and its authors were suspended. However, similar complaints were echoed in other quarters of the ANC, and it became clear that the problems could not be swept under the carpet. Hence the Morogoro Conference.

A major preoccupation of the conference was how to further the armed struggle and ensure communication between the exile movement and the movement inside South Africa. A new body called the Revolutionary Council was created to integrate political and military strategy (Meli, 165). Another reform was an internal commission to address complaints and grievances (Lodge, 300).

The main outcome of the conference was a "Strategy and Tactics" document, the first major policy document of the ANC since the Freedom Charter. The Morogoro Conference also came to a decision on a long-standing debate in the external ANC – whether "non-Africans" should be allowed membership. It was decided to open the ANC to all members of the Congress Movement in exile. Only Africans could be members of the NEC, but the Revolutionary Council was open to non-Africans, and Yusuf Dadoo, Joe Slovo and Reg September were all duly elected to it.

The ANC leadership on Robben Island was naturally perturbed by accounts of bad management and low morale in MK camps. Mandela was so disturbed that he took the great risk of smuggling a letter to Tambo on the need for improvements in the MK camps (Mandela, 551).

The problems in the camps were not only a matter of political concern to Walter: the Sisulu family was to be more personally affected as well when the circumstances led to Gerald's defection from MK. After completing a two-and-a-half-year officers' course in Czechoslovakia, Gerald had been sent to Kongwa camp in Tanzania. Morale in the camp was very low because, recalled Gerald, "MK fighters had been languishing there for years and getting old. Some cadres had been there since 1961, from the time of Madiba's visit to Algeria. To make matters worse there were FRELIMO and ZAPU camps nearby that were really just transit points for fighters who would come from training and almost immediately be deployed to their countries. In the ANC camps people were going nowhere and people questioned whether they would ever go home."

Gerald's general unhappiness about the poor conditions and bad management at the camp were compounded by a power struggle between Ambrose Makiwane – who would later become a key figure in the breakaway Gang of Eight – and Joe Modise for the position of commander of the camp. Gerald supported Joe Modise because he felt that although Makiwane had been in the camp longer, Modise, having completed a full officers' course, was much better trained. Moreover, he knew Joe personally from the days when Joe sometimes used to drive Walter to Pretoria in the days of the Treason Trial.

Gerald somehow became embroiled in the conflict between the two men and felt resentful about getting dragged into the affair. He felt that the ANC leadership should have acted decisively and appointed a commander rather than "have two leaders fight it out in front of soldiers in the bush".

One of the main grievances in the camp, Gerald thought, was that there was not enough communication with the leadership and that MK fighters were not properly informed about what was going on. The last straw for him was the news that filtered to the camp about the alliance with ZAPU and the Wankie operation in Zimbabwe. "This was never properly explained to us. We just got everything through the grapevine. We were told that all the guys who were fighting there had been wiped out. This was very upsetting to me because one of the guys I trained with, one of my friends, had been killed." He felt that they had not been consulted about the issue and disagreed violently with the strategy of fighting in Zimbabwe. "I just could not see how South Africa should be liberated from the Zambezi and not the Limpopo. The whole plan was suicidal and I decided I wanted no part of it. I did not want to be used as cannon fodder, so I decided to leave."

Gerald went AWOL to Dar-es-Salaam where he was picked up by Tanzanian police and placed with a number of disaffected MK cadres in a remand prison. After some months, he went on a hunger strike. He was then released into the care of the ANC. From there he approached the PAC to ask for help to get out of Tanzania. "They told me there was no way they could accept me into their fold because of my relationship with Sisulu. I told them I was not planning to join them. I just wanted to get out of Tanzania." He travelled with a group of PAC cadres to one of their camps in Zambia, and then on to Lusaka.

In Lusaka, Gerald "gradually faded into Zambian society". One day he met some ANC people at a party, who locked him in a room. He managed to escape and reported the matter to the police. This incident made him decide to put some distance between himself and Lusaka. He headed for the Copperbelt region, where he settled down and lived quietly.

Although Gerald lost contact with his family for the next while, Max made efforts to see him on occasion. Ironically, the one person who knew the saga before anyone else was Walter. Kenneth Kaunda, who knew Walter personally, sent him a message on Robben Island letting him know that Gerald had left MK.

As the years progressed, Albertina became increasingly aware of the need to ensure that Walter did not lose touch with what was happening at home. She kept him informed about their extended family connections and sought his advice and opinions whenever she could. Towards the end of 1969, Albertina was proud and excited when Campbell Mnyila, the uncle who raised her, visited from the Transkei, accompanied by Walter's old teacher, Mdaka. She wrote to tell Walter of their two-week-long visit: "Oh! Dear we had a lovely time with the old men and do you know what my uncle did? He sent us R10. Is that not wonderful of him? Please write and thank him for that darling." The visit remained a cherished memory for Albertina because it was the last time she would see Uncle Campbell. The following year she had to write to Walter of her uncle's death (Letter, 12/8/70). She could not attend the funeral because of her banning order, so Flora and Lungi travelled to Xolobe in the Transkei to represent her. She also asked Walter to write a letter of condolence to Campbell's wife.

In 1968, Albertina wrote to Walter about her concern for Uncle Clifford's failing health. The following year, Uncle Clifford had to have his right leg amputated as a result of complications arising from diabetes. He was still staying at Number 1715, the old house they had shared in Orlando East. Albertina was worried that there would be no one to look after him after his discharge from hospital. Kenneth was dead and Nokuzola was not in a position to attend to her father. Albertina decided to take care of the old man herself, but because she was banned she had to make a special application to the Chief Magistrate for permission to take him into her house. The Chief Magistrate referred the application to the security police, who then had to make their recommendation to the Minister of Justice. The Secretary for Justice finally wrote back: "Kindly inform Sisulu that the Honourable Minister of Justice acceded to her request that her father-in-law may live with her" (Ministry of Justice file on Albertina Sisulu, No. 2/1/1297).

As always, the correspondence between Walter and Albertina was dominated by the children and their education. In May 1969, Albertina expressed her anxiety about the children's progress: "Day in and day out I am cracking my head trying to place each and everyone of them in a proper position" (Letter, 8/5/69). She was clearly under a lot of stress and in May 1970 she wrote: "… my health is failing, dear Walter. I have been on and off work, suffering from high blood pressure with dizziness. But don't worry about that, it is old age. You know when you are getting old, you become weak and sickly. I have been very well all these years. It's only 1970 that seems to treat me badly. But I am better now, Walter, gone back to work again."

Both Albertina and Walter were anxious for Lungi to go to university after he left school. Lungi was keen to study law because he felt that it was a way to address the injustices in the country. Both Lungi and Makgatho Mandela had applied to a number of universities and were discouraged on being turned down. One of the reasons given for these rejections was that Cambridge O-levels were not recognised in South Africa. Lungi managed to find a job as a clerk with a Johannesburg construction company and enrolled to study part-time for his A-levels.

Lungi continued to make trips to Swaziland despite the fact that he had no passport. Early in 1970, he was taking Nkuli and his girlfriend Sheila Mashile back to school when he was arrested at the Oshoek border post. Berry Matole, who had a passport, accompanied them. As they approached the border, Berry took the wheel while Lungi hid under the seat. Unfortunately for them, the car was searched and Lungi was hauled out. Berry and Lungi were taken to the local police station. When the police discovered that Lungi was a Sisulu, they placed him in solitary confinement.

Berry was soon released, but Lungi was detained for four months in nearby Carolina until the security police arrived to interrogate him. They tried to link him with the Trial of the 22, but they could not get anything out of him. He was then charged with attempting to leave the country without a passport. As soon as Albertina informed him of Lungi's arrest, Walter sent an urgent message to George Bizos, who then travelled to Carolina to defend him. Bizos managed to get Lungi off with a nine-month sentence suspended for three years.

Albertina also sought Walter's help in trying to persuade Beryl to continue with her education. After Thembi's funeral, Beryl had gone to Cape Town to stay with his widow Thoko to help her to recuperate. While she was nursing Thoko, she fell in love with Thoko's brother Leonard and decided to stay in Cape Town. She took up nursing at King Edward Hospital, but resigned in frustration in May 1970 because her certificates were not recognised. Albertina expressed her displeasure in a letter to Walter: "I have written to her advising her to go back to school. She may be lucky and get a space at Roma University next year. I don't know. Perhaps you have better advice, please help us … In fact I did not want her to take up nursing. I wanted her to take up medicine if she is interested in that line. You know what it is with our children, Walter, they always want their word to be final" (Letter, 22/5/70).

On a more pleasant note, Albertina was able to give Walter positive news about Zwelakhe's progress. After leaving Swaziland, Zwelakhe had attended Orlando High School. He recalls that around the age of 17, he felt as if a cloud had lifted and he began to read voraciously. "My life just turned around. I migrated from being almost a *tsotsi* to the life of an intellectual. I read everything I could and developed a deep love for art and culture." With other students at Orlando High, he began to become involved in serious political activity: "We began to have weekend meetings. We began to link up with old ANC people who were still around and have study groups."

In May 1970 Albertina proudly announced to Walter that Lindi had won first prize in a debating competition between all the schools in Swaziland. Lindi had just celebrated her 16th birthday, so she was able to visit the Island and receive her father's congratulations in person. She travelled to Cape Town by train and Beryl met her at the station. She had never been on a boat before and was bewildered by the half-hour trip to the Island. Her apprehension melted away when she set eyes on her father. Walter had been eagerly anticipating her visit and was so overjoyed to see her that he jumped up in excitement when she arrived. Lindi was upset by the reaction of the warder next to him: "As Tata stood up, the warder shouted at him and brought his stick down on the table. I felt bad that he was shouted at but he did not care. He tried to make me happy." Walter was filled with pride by the vivacious young woman before him. She could hardly hear what Walter was saying because all the other visitors were talking at the same time, but she settled down and chattered gaily about happenings at home. Walter was particularly interested in news of Lungi's girlfriend Sheila.

The following year, Albertina wrote to let Walter know that Lungi was getting married in December. There was much excitement, especially since it was the first wedding in the family home. By that time, Zwelakhe had left school and was working for a bakery, so he was able to contribute financially. Much was made of the fact that he bought his own suit. Theirs was a traditional African wedding with a ceremony at the bride's place on one day, followed by one at the groom's home. Because of Albertina's banning, it was not possible to have a large gathering at the house. Instead they had to hold the ceremony in the front yard of the newly built crèche opposite the house. Albertina applied for permission to attend the wedding, but received no response. She had to be content with watching the proceedings from her front garden. Sheila recalled going to embrace her at the front gate at the end of the ceremony: "It was a particularly painful and moving moment."

By the time she married into the Sisulu family, Sheila Mashile had some idea of the kind of harassment that came with the Sisulu name. Like Walter and Albertina, and indeed many African parents of the time, Sheila's parents had been determined not to let their children suffer the disadvantages of Bantu education. Sheila and her brother Lucas were therefore sent to school in Swaziland. Parents would take it in turns to transport children to school and on one of their trips to Swaziland, Zwelakhe Sisulu was one of the children who travelled with them. "He must have been about nine years old," Sheila recalled. "We were stopped by the police and this black policeman asked Zwelakhe what his name was. Quite calmly he gave a fictitious name. I marvelled at the composure of this boy who knew at such a young age that revealing his identity to the police would cause problems not only for himself, but for the rest of the group as well."

Much later, Sheila met Lungi through her friendship with Beryl at school. Their relationship blossomed and soon they were engaged. Sheila remembers with amusement the first night she spent at the Sisulu home. She and Lungi and Sheila had to attend a function in Orlando West. They knew it would end too late to return to Sheila's home in Rockville, so it was agreed that Sheila would spend the night at Number 7372. "When we arrived, we found Mama waiting for us. 'You must be tired, my baby,' she said. She gave me a nightdress and showed me my bed for the night – right next to hers in the same room. When it came to matters of decorum, MaSisulu was very firm."

After her marriage, Sheila saw the sterner side of her formidable mother-in-law. One day they were discussing the 1971 trial of the Anglican Dean of Johannesburg, Gonville ffrench Beytagh, who had been sentenced to five years for distributing IDAF money to dependants of banned individuals. The state had tried unsuccessfully to charge him under the Terrorism Act on the basis that he had allegedly tried to incite a group of Black Sash ladies to violence, a ridiculous accusation. At the time, they did not know that ffrench Beytagh's sentence would be overturned on appeal. Sheila lamented that five years was a long time and that at his age, ffrench Beytagh might die in jail. The thoughtless remark earned her a sharp reprimand from Albertina. "In this house," she said, "we do NOT talk about people dying in jail!"

Sheila's main observation about living with Albertina was how hard her mother-in-law worked: "She just never seemed to rest. She would spend her weekends doing laundry and constantly cleaning the house. She was fussy about cooking and cleaning and the feeding of people. The house had to be spotless and everyone who visited had to be served tea. At that time things were not easy financially, so the amount of food we cooked, especially meat, was just enough for the family. Then someone would come to visit, obviously about political business and MaSisulu would shout from the lounge, 'Aren't we eating?' and all of us in the kitchen would groan 'Oh no!' because there just was not enough to feed an extra mouth. When we would ask her later how she could put us in that position, she would say 'Awu, so the food was not enough? You should have told me, then I could have done without'."

Sheila arranged with Lungi, Beryl and Zwelakhe to put money together to buy Albertina a washing machine for her 54th birthday: "I felt so guilty about Mama doing laundry all the time and I was not about to spend my days helping her with the washing. At first she distrusted the machine and felt it did not wash the clothes properly, but after the first few washes she was so impressed that she named the machine 'MaSisulu'. When the washing machine was churning out load after load of laundry we would jokingly say 'MaSisulu is busy today!'"

Not long after Lungi and Sheila's wedding, Albertina had several additions to her household. In 1970, Walter's cousin Dwelisa Sisulu sent his eldest son Jongumzi (Jongi) to stay with Albertina. Eleven-year-old Jongumzi had seven younger brothers and sisters. In addition, Dwelisa was taking care of his sister's six children. He had been a driver for the railways, but was laid off after an injury sustained at work. Workmen's compensation for black people was minimal and alternative prospects of employment in the Transkei were virtually nonexistent, so Dwelisa's family was experiencing considerable financial distress. Like so many other rural parents, Dwelisa and his wife decided to send a child to relatives in the urban areas for better education and job prospects.

Albertina enrolled Jongi in a local school and he quickly settled down. He immediately warmed to Albertina: "She welcomed me and made me feel happy. She was a very strict mother who would always instil discipline in me. She always encouraged us to listen to the news and read newspapers." Jongi found life in Soweto infinitely more interesting than life in Engcobo. The only thing that disturbed him were the periodic police raids: "Life was not easy at 7372. There were many police raids and Mama was continually harassed. The police would jump over the wall and kick the doors. They would come in and search the house. They were particularly interested in books and would look through them and throw them all over the place. Mama would scold them and tell them they had no respect. She would demand to know who sent them and ask what they wanted. They would tell her that they were doing their job and did not have to answer her silly questions" (Interview, Jongi Sisulu, 30/4/97).

Not long after Jongi's arrival, Albertina received an astonishing message from Greta Ncapayi in Dube. Max's son Lungi had arrived in Soweto! Albertina was totally perplexed. She had no idea of the circumstances of Lungi's arrival and wondered why Max had not communicated with her. Her confusion turned to delight when four-year-old Lungi Sisulu Jnr descended on Number 7372 like a hurricane. Within minutes of his arrival, he had poured a 1lb packet of tea into the dog's dish.

He then took one of Uncle Clifford's crutches and raced off into the street with it. To top it all, he locked himself in one of the bedrooms and the handle had to be broken to let him out. He seemed oblivious to any scolding and simply jabbered on in Russian. A few weeks later, Albertina received a letter from Max that had been intended to reach her before Lungi's arrival.

After he had graduated from the Plekhanov Institute in 1969, Max had done a one-year officers' training programme at Segonye. The ANC then sent him to Tanzania. Because he was not sure where he would be staying in Tanzania and under what conditions, he had to leave little Lungi in the Soviet Union with the family of Sizakele Sigxashe, an MK colleague. Once he was in Tanzania, he arranged for Lungi to join him. However, by the time Lungi arrived in Tanzania, it was clear that Max would be travelling constantly and the nature of his work would make it very difficult for him to take care of Lungi. He decided it would be best to send Lungi to Albertina in Soweto. Lungi stayed in Dar es Salaam with Alfred and Regina Nzo while Max tried to find a way of sending him to South Africa. Max asked his ex-wife Mercy, who had remarried and was living in Lusaka at the time, to help get Lungi home to Albertina. Mercy had an aunt in South Africa who had a child of around the same age as Lungi registered on her passport. She arranged for her aunt to travel to Botswana to collect Lungi and take him into South Africa as her own child. Max wrote to Albertina about the arrangement and Mercy took Lungi to Botswana and handed him over to her aunt. Unfortunately for the Sisulus, the arrangements did not go according to plan and Mercy's aunt took Lungi to his maternal grandmother instead.

The Sisulus were most upset at what had transpired. Lindi wrote to Max saying: "Bhut'Vuyi, not that I'm trying to create hostility but could you please make it clear to them that the child is ours and WE WANT HIM!" Lindi and Nkuli were ready to march to Greta's house in Dube and collect Lungi. Albertina, fearing a row, stopped them and promised to settle the matter with Greta. An unspoken tug-of-war ensued between the two grandmothers. Albertina tried all methods of persuasion to get Greta to hand Lungi over, but to no avail. At that time, it would have been impossible to embark on a legal custody battle for a Russian-speaking child, born in the Soviet Union and brought illegally into the country. Above all, Albertina felt that an acrimonious battle between the two families would have a harmful effect on the child. So Lungi remained with Mam'Greta, and for years the question of his custody remained a sore point between the two women. Ironically, Greta continued to correspond amicably with Walter and in later years Lungi's two half-brothers on his mother's side would join him when he visited his grandfather on Robben Island.

On 21 October 1972, Albertina celebrated her 54th birthday with the best possible present Lungi and Sheila could have given her – a new grandson named Linda Zizwe (Wait for the Nations) by his grandfather. Albertina was in a more militant mood. She nicknamed him Ginyibhulu (Swallow the Boers). When Ginyi was three weeks old, Sheila had to return to the University of Lesotho where she was studying. A couple of months later, Beryl arrived with her son Thulani, who had been born in May that year. Because Beryl was working full-time in Cape Town, it was agreed that Thulani should stay with Albertina. She boasted to Walter that she now had to take care of twins. By then, Albertina's sister Flora had married and had two sons (Sipho and Elliot, both under five), so she really had a full house. Albertina solved the space problem by building extra rooms in the backyard, "backrooms" in Soweto jargon. She always made a point of describing to Walter every change she made to the house so that "he would not fail to recognise the place when he comes back home".

# *s i x*

For political prisoners, there was nothing better than academic achievement to raise their morale and make them feel their prison years were not wasted. Education was a major preoccupation of the Robben Islanders at a collective and an individual level. Former prisoners speak proudly of wiping out illiteracy on the Island. The appellation "University of Robben Island" was well deserved – many prisoners arrived there with no tertiary education, and left with one or more degrees to their name.

The prison correspondence of Walter and Albertina reflects this preoccupation with education. In the first few lonely years after Walter's incarceration, Albertina decided to study herself and passed her matric in 1969 through an adult education course. She constantly encouraged Walter in his own endeavours. "Darling, please don't be discouraged with the examination fever," she wrote in 1967. "Carry on, Walter, don't leave off your studies. I wish you were not far from me darling because I would help you."

Walter persevered with his O-levels, albeit at a very slow pace, since he was allowed to write only one examination a year. He passed commerce in June 1966, economics in June 1967, history in June 1968 and geography in January 1969. He started studying Afrikaans as well, but did not make much progress. Kathrada said that Walter seemed to have a psychological block where Afrikaans was concerned, but one of the few phrases he mastered was "Vandag is vandag". Kathrada recalled with amusement: "Whenever MaSisulu was visiting him he would repeat it over and over again."

Political prisoners generally agree that one of the greatest frustrations of studying in prison was the obstructionist attitude of the authorities. Some warders resented the fact that prisoners were allowed to study. Because they controlled all incoming and outgoing mail, it was a simple matter to sabotage the prisoners' efforts by deliberately delaying the sending of registration, tuition or examination fees. Walter was not spared these frustrations and his prison files reveal the numerous letters he sent urging warders to send fees, forms or assignments before the closing dates. Although he was studying through the Rapid Results College, the University of London was the examining body. Walter therefore paid his examination fees to and communicated with the University of London through the Cultural Attaché of the British Embassy in Pretoria.

By 1970, Walter was eagerly looking forward to completing one more subject to obtain his full certificate when he received a letter from the British Embassy stating that prison authorities had informed them that he was no longer permitted to study with an overseas institution. Walter took the matter up with the warder in charge of studies. When he received a negative response, he wrote a long letter of complaint to the Commanding Officer, who agreed that he could continue his studies on condition that all his correspondence go through the Rapid Results College and not the British Embassy.

Walter happily agreed to this and continued with his studies until the next stumbling block. In March 1971, the chief warder instructed raids on several cells in the B section. A warder seized five exercise books from Walter's cell. Walter had copied some letters into these books, an action that was in contravention of the rule that study material be used exclusively for studies. In his report to the Commanding Officer, the head warder wrote: "I am sure that if the prisoner's studies are returned to him, he will not hesitate to again use them for unauthorised purposes. He will also first have to appear before the Prisons' Board before his studies will be returned to him" (Prison Files of Walter Sisulu).

When Walter appeared before the Prisons' Board in March 1973, he applied to continue with his studies. The Commanding Officer Brigadier Aucamp approved Walter's application, but one of the warders took it upon himself to overturn the decision. Walter did not take kindly to this and wrote once more to the Commanding Officer: "This is my third letter to you on the subject of my GCE studies. The second letter, however, may not have reached you. Chief Warder Nortje tells me they are unable to trace it. The whole issue of my GCE studies has a long history that is not possible to deal with adequately in this letter. I hope, therefore, that you will be able to give me an interview so that I can place all the facts before you."

Walter did not get the interview with the Commanding Officer, but his application was reconsidered and approved with the comment from the chief warder to his underlings: "Apparently we are obliged to allow the prisoner to sit for the examination." Walter successfully sat for the O-level examination in English literature in January 1975.

Walter had another running battle with his jailers when he was refused permission in 1976 to continue studying for his diploma in local government (known as the IAC Diploma). The study officer reported that since he had enrolled for the course in 1973, Walter had written only one examination and that he was not serious about his studies: "No illness or acceptable excuses can be offered as reason for him not writing exams." Once again, Walter bombarded the prison management with long missives in which he pointed out that on one occasion, he had been unable to write the examination because the study officer had failed to forward his examination forms. In another instance, the money he supplied for his examination fees was not sent. When his appeal to the Commanding Officer was unsuccessful, he wrote to the Commissioner of Prisons. The Robben Island authorities refused to forward the letter and Walter finally had to abandon the IAC course, to his great disappointment, especially as he had spent a considerable sum of money on the course.

Walter then enrolled for a BA with UNISA. Apart from the obstacles put in his way by the prison authorities, Walter had to deal with his own handicaps. He had problems with his eyesight, and his handwriting was so bad that UNISA would sometimes send back his assignments. Walter's prison colleagues generally agree with Kathrada's assessment that Walter was a brilliant man but that this was not reflected in his academic studies: "He was always curious to know more and more. He was an intellectual but not in the sense of academic or formal training" (Interview, Ahmed Kathrada).

Though not very highly educated in the formal sense, Walter was respected for his intellectual capability and his understanding of politics and South African history, especially the history of the ANC. Mac Maharaj best describes the anomaly between Walter's reading capacity and his intellectual understanding:

He would plough through many books on his own, but for speed he would say "Just read this chapter and tell me what it says". He'd help you understand the chapter through his questions. He would cut through a problem by always getting to its essence whereas many of us who came from an academic background wanted to work around a problem, mulling over every phrase, every sentence and forgetting what is the main content. It is supposed to be basic to any good education to summarise a chapter in ten sentences. Many of us chaps never succeeded in doing that. We write a summary that is even longer than the chapter itself.

I remember reading a book on Historical and Dialectical Materialism. It was one of the books that we smuggled into prison – a highly philosophical book. I go back to work and Walter asks me to explain what this book is about. There were other prisoners – I'd rather not name them – who saw themselves as intellectuals, who had read the book too. We discussed it with Walter. He asked us questions about the book. His questions showed that his grasp of those philosophical problems was such that it was beyond the level of we who had read the books. I overheard one of those "intellectual" prisoners discussing with a fellow prisoner saying, "This man Walter. He's a bloody intellectual giant!" And the "intellectual prisoner" was someone from another political school who often despised people because they didn't have the necessary education.

Within a year of knowing Walter, even this particular individual was going to Walter for guidance on theoretical problems (Talent Consortium Interview, Mac Maharaj).

Over the years, Walter's informal lectures on the ANC had evolved into a fully fledged course of study known as Syllabus A. The syllabus, devised by the High Organ, consisted of two years of lectures on the ANC and the liberation struggle, a course on the history of the Indian Struggle by Kathrada, a history of the coloured people and a course on Marxism by Mac Maharaj. Nelson Mandela acknowledged Walter's contribution to Syllabus A:

It was Walter's course that was at the heart of all our education. Many of the young ANC members who came to the island had no idea that the organization had even been in existence in the 1920s and 1930s, through to the present day. For many of these young men, it was the only political education they ever received (Mandela, 557).

Nelson Mandela was much sought after by his fellow prisoners for his political and legal advice. General section prisoners of all political persuasions would consult him through smuggled notes between the sections. He spent so much time preparing judicial appeals for prisoners that his work amounted to an informal legal practice, and he joked about hanging a nameplate outside his cell (Mandela, 557). Govan Mbeki was the theoretician, who was admired for his intellectual prowess and much in demand as a teacher. Walter was often sought after for different reasons. "He is always concerned about the welfare and wellbeing of others, his fellow prisoners as well as the folks outside," recalled Kathrada. "Hence many of us would discuss our letters and visits with him in great detail, not omitting private affairs." Mac Maharaj described him as a father confessor to whom they went for emotional support and advice on family problems:

All of us went to him not necessarily because we expected answers, but because he was a person who was ready to give time to hear you out and listen to you with understanding. I personally found that I could discuss any personal problem, no matter how private, with him with great ease. I could discuss political questions with Comrade Mandela, but I never had a relationship with him where I felt so easy and comfortable as I did with Walter.

When Maharaj made a special request for a contact visit with his wife who was leaving the country on an exit visa, the Commanding Officer took the opportunity to humiliate him. Maharaj went to pour his heart out to Walter: "He gave me a hearing and asked me questions that enabled me to get a good grip on myself, to ask myself what were the limits that I could go to and what positions I should take in the future. I was then able to confront the Commanding Officer on the following day. I knew how to handle him" (Talent Consortium Interview, Mac Maharaj).

Ahmed Kathrada believed that prison life brought out the best in Walter:

Outside prison you would never come to know your fellow colleagues. You don't have time. It is in prison really where you come to know your colleagues in times of adversity and in times of relaxation. This is where some of the best and some of the worst comes out in human beings. Because it is a situation of severe deprivation of basic necessities, a prison situation is tailor-made for all kinds of tension. That is where a person like Walter just shines out (Talent Consortium Interview, Ahmed Kathrada).

Fellow prisoners found Walter self-effacing, a man who never sought credit for himself, who was slow to act, but courageous and decisive when he did take action. Maharaj describes a confrontation between warders and prisoners in the courtyard of the B section, when it became clear that the warders were about to assault the prisoners. Maharaj felt that as a member of the prisoners' committee, he should intervene. When he failed to defuse the situation, he called to Walter: "Tyhopo, there's a fight coming up here. Come and help." Walter continued playing draughts with Don Davis at the opposite end of the courtyard. Maharaj became angry and shouted: "Tyhopo, stop being insensitive." Walter responded: "No, let me finish this game of draughts." "Draughts!" cried a frantic Maharaj. "To hell with you, we are going to get killed here!" Maharaj rushed back to the fray, but when the warders started the assault, he retreated behind the other prisoners. To his surprise he saw Walter in front of him, face to face with the warders. "This incident had a tremendous impact on the way I saw myself. I actually went back to my cell feeling ashamed of myself," recalled Maharaj. "Here's me the heated revolutionary getting ready to take cover and here's the old man Sisulu coming unnoticed from behind to defuse the situation and having done so, not seeking any credit. He just went back to his game of draughts."

Walter was also famous, or sometimes infamous, for his extraordinary generosity. Kathrada maintains that Walter had no sense of private property:

Under prison conditions, the temptation is ever present to collect and hoard. But with Walter there is nothing he will not readily give away ... It used to be said that Laloo Chiba was the most generous person because he gave everything away. Sisulu was the only person more generous than Chiba because he also gave other people's things away.

We were isolated from the rest of the prison population, but prisoners being what they are, would manage every now and then to slip into our section. Invariably the bulk of the prisoners were from poor backgrounds and did not have any funds so at any opportunity they got, they would go mainly to Walter and say "Tata, I am short of toothpaste. Tata, I need a textbook or some such thing." With Tata, there was never a problem. He would simply walk into his cell and give away what he had. If he did not have it he would walk into one of the other cells, especially my cell, which was opposite his, take what was needed and give it away. I was once given a beautiful Schaeffer pen. Because I already had a good Parker pen, I gave the Schaeffer to Walter. The next thing I see another prisoner using the pen. Their response – "Tata gave it to me." I was very brutal – I took it back.

In his prison memoir, Michael Dingake wrote with affection about how Walter would gatecrash the "exclusive" tea club that he, Kathrada and Mkwayi had formed together.

I would miss Walter "Tyhopo" Sisulu, the incorrigible "scrounger" and "parasite" at our tea club sessions. "Tyhopo" was always unwelcome and welcome. "Tyhopo! Who invited you here?" the three of us would pretend to harass Tyhopo. "I invited myself!" Tyhopo would reply, smiling affectionately and sitting down to enjoy the tea with us. Our tea could never have been sweeter without Tyhopo. He is the sweetest man alive.

To sweeten the tea more, our uninvited guest usually proceeded without our permission to invite passers-by in the corridor: "Madiba! Zizi, don't you want some tea?" That was Tyhopo. Generous to a fault (Dingake, 230).

Walter was also renowned for his sunny disposition and his ability to laugh at himself. George Mbele, who served a four-year sentence on the Island from 1964–68, said, "Men like Walter Sisulu were always jovial. I never saw him without a smiling face ... We felt ashamed that we should feel the pinch of prison in his presence." Mac Maharaj had a similar recollection:

In the 12 years that I was in that prison I have never known a day when he was without a smile. Not one single day. I can recall months when I was moody and fighting with all my fellow prisoners because of this whole claustrophobic and closed atmosphere. He is the only individual I know who 1 can joke about in his presence and he takes it without you ever getting under his skin. So he was the butt of our jokes.

Cde Kathrada would always tease Walter about his driving, about how before he got to prison he had acquired a laundry service car or van. "He is driving at 10 km thinking he is breaking the speed limit for the world championship when a dog runs across the road. Walter drives off the road, gets out of the car to go and tell the dog to get out of the way and then proceeds to drive off." That was a standard joke. It virtually had a number to it.

He was also very patient. Some of us young people would question him about MaSisulu. How did he meet her? How did he propose to her? We questioned him in detail (Talent Consortium Interview, Mac Maharaj).

Kathrada agrees that "Walter was forever smiling. He hardly ever lost his temper. But he was absolutely firm in his principles. He was very flexible and pragmatic, but you would not get him to shift on matters of principle."

Fikile Bam never forgets how he was once a target of a rare outburst of anger from Walter. Fikile was a 23-year-old bachelor who was on the verge of becoming engaged to a young woman when he was imprisoned in 1964. The relationship ended when she went abroad while he was in jail. After some time, he started corresponding with someone else. That relationship also ended when she left the country. In a fit of frustration and disillusionment, Fikile blurted out to Walter that he would no longer bother with "this love nonsense". He declared that when he left prison he would simply propose to the daughter of a certain wealthy businessman. Walter was horrified by the cynical remark.

He looked at me in a way 1 had never seen before. He was shaking all over. His mouth was moving but he was so angry that the words wouldn't come out. Finally he said "You surprise me! 1 thought 1 knew who you were! How can you think of selling yourself, selling your soul!" He upbraided me about daring to think 1 could play around with a young woman's feelings. For the rest of the day he gave me a hard time. 1 really regretted that remark.

One of the qualities for which Walter was most admired was his capacity to reach out to people and make them feel part of a team. This gave him the ability to transcend political differences between fellow prisoners. PAC member Kwedi Mkalipi recalls that when he arrived on Robben Island, he was treated very badly by the prison staff and was thrown into *khulukuthu* naked. "There came Sisulu from nowhere and said 'I am Walter Sisulu, I come from your area.' My main reaction was 'What the hell, why do you come to me!' He addressed me by my clan name: 'Come here, Dlamini, let us converse. I want to ask you about the Transkei.'" Walter insisted that they talk to each other despite their political differences, and they became firm friends (Talent Consortium Interview, Kwedi Mkalipi).

Walter had maintained his old friendship with Zeph Mothopeng. He also got on well with Clarence Makwethu and even Japhta Masemola, who did not get on with most people, not even his fellow PAC members. Unfortunately, the friendly relations Walter had with PAC members and leaders on a personal level never translated into cooperation at an organisational level. Walter shared Mandela's conviction that their incarceration together on Robben Island presented ANC and PAC leaders with an opportunity to forge unity between the two organisations. They made some progress in unity talks with Selby Ngendane and Clarence Makwethu, but they got no further after the release of Makwethu and the arrival of John Nyati Pokela (Mandela, 524).

Walter was a great advocate of unity and he abhorred tensions and divisions within his beloved organisation. He was therefore unhappy when friction developed between Mandela and Mbeki over the ANC's attitude to separate development institutions such as the Labour Party, the Indian Council and the Bantustans. Mandela felt that the issue should be debated, while Govan Mbeki resolutely stuck to the 1962 Lobatsi Conference resolution that advocated a boycott of apartheid institutions (Buntman 30; Odendaal, 8). Walter shared Mandela's view, while Mhlaba supported Mbeki's stand. A memorandum describing the conflict was smuggled out of the Island and landed in Dr Yusuf Dadoo's papers. The document describes a personality clash and political impasse between Mandela and Mbeki that lasted from the late 1960s to the mid-1970s that was allegedly so severe that Mandela's leadership was called into question. According to this document, the crisis was resolved when the High Organ, which had changed membership since a new rotational system had been introduced in 1973, had had a candid discussion with the four leaders, and issued a report criticising them and making a number of recommendations to promote organisational discipline. Mandela's leadership was reaffirmed and the four leaders were reinstated on the High Organ (Buntman, 30; Odendaal, 8).

While he concedes that there was a personality clash between Mandela and Mbeki, Walter argues that the whole affair was exaggerated: "In a prison situation, there is bound to be disagreement on issues and people easily get irritated with each other. Madiba and Govan are both strong characters who are not easily swayed in any argument, but that does not mean there is a crisis." Mhlaba wrote in his memoirs that they had many disagreements, some of which were acrimonious, but they did their best to control the tensions (Mhlaba, 140).

Kathrada dismisses the memorandum as written by someone who did not know the true situation. He agrees with Walter and Mhlaba that at no time was the unity of the ANC threatened or the leadership of Mandela called into question. Govan Mbeki supported Walter's view that there were differences of view but these never led to hostility and bitterness, as was alleged. Walter himself admired Govan for his great intellect, but the two men did not see eye to eye on many issues. They argued for years about whether the High Command had approved the Mayibuye Plan, with Govan maintaining that it had and Walter insisting that it had not. Walter often recalled with affectionate amusement how they would walk in the courtyard arguing about some issue or the other. "Govan would then go to Mhlaba's cell, sit down, breathing heavily and complain, 'Man, Walter is stubborn.' In the meantime I would be in my cell thinking, 'Man, Govan is stubborn.'" but the arguments never affected the strong bonds of friendship and affection between the two men.

News of a bitter dispute within the ANC in exile reached Robben Island through letters to Wilton Mkwayi. The letters from former ANC NEC members ferociously attacked some of the ANC leaders, especially Moses Mabhida and Joe Modise. The prison authorities allowed Mkwayi to receive the letters uncensored, probably in the hope that his reply would encourage divisions within the ANC. After consulting his colleagues, Mkwayi wrote back condemning the dissidents.

The attacks stemmed from a conflict that had been brewing since the mid-1960s and which had not been resolved by the Morogoro Conference. Tennyson Makiwane and his cousin Ambrose, Themba Mqota, Pascal Ngakane, Jonas Matlou, OK Setlapelo, Thami Bonga and George Mbele were at the forefront of ANC members who vehemently opposed the decision to open membership to whites, coloureds and Indians (Lodge, 303; Shubin, 134; Ellis and Sechaba, 64; Karis and Gerhart, 5: 33; Sampson 2000, 266).

The rift between the Group of Eight (as they came to be called) and the ANC NEC widened and became increasingly acrimonious. Tambo's attempts to heal the rift were unsuccessful and he himself came under personal attack. Robert Resha never openly identified with the group, but was said to sympathise with them. He found himself increasingly at odds with the ANC leadership, and by the time of his death in 1973, he had been sidelined in the organisation he had so passionately supported. Matters finally came to a head at the unveiling of Resha's tombstone in London in 1975. Ambrose Makiwane, who gave the main tribute, used the occasion to publicly attack the ANC leadership, alleging that a small clique had hijacked the organisation. The diatribe against the ANC leadership was widely reported, both internationally and within South Africa. The reaction of the NEC was swift. It issued a blistering condemnation of the action, and the group was expelled in October 1975.

The group tried to set up a rival ANC, claiming Mandela as its leader. Through a smuggled message, Mandela made it clear that his loyalty lay with Oliver Tambo. The position of the Robben Islanders was unequivocal. They could in no way support the actions of the rebels. For Walter, their arguments echoed those that had led to the Africanist breakaway and the formation of the PAC in 1959, and he was shocked at Makiwane's statement, "Africans hate the domination of the Communist Party." He was saddened by the whole episode because among the eight were people he had known for many years, and whom he liked and respected. Jonas Matlou, Tennyson Makiwane and Themba Mqota were all Treason Trialists. Both Pascal Ngakane and George Mbele had been on Robben Island in the late 1960s. The Ngakanes had lived in Orlando, so Walter had known Pascal since his youth. Pascal was the son-in-law of Chief Luthuli and had been active in the ANC's underground in Natal during the 1960s. Walter was unhappy about the expulsions, but accepted the NEC's action: "My general idea was to be cautious about taking such drastic action, but I was satisfied that the NEC would not have done it without good reason."

The disaffected group failed in their efforts to set up an alternative ANC and, after several years, most of them returned to the fold. With hindsight, the Group of Eight saga turned out to be a storm in a teacup when compared to developments inside South Africa, where a new political generation was emerging, one that would change the course of South African history.

*s e v e n*

One of the quirks of apartheid bureaucracy was its penchant for giving innocuous and euphemistic names to the most heinous legislation. Sometimes the name given suggested the exact opposite of the legislation's aim. Thus the Extension of University Education Act of 1959 virtually excluded blacks from white universities by making it illegal for the latter to enrol black students without government approval. Black students were channelled to four new ethnically created universities, and the once proud Fort Hare was reduced to the level of a bush college for Xhosa-speaking students. For black students, the only alternatives to the tribal colleges were the government-run correspondence institution, the University of South Africa (UNISA), and the "Non-European" medical school run by the University of Natal (Karis and Gerhart, 5: 90; Beinart, 218).

Little did the architects of apartheid education imagine that from these institutions, designed to train blacks for subservience, a leader like Steve Biko would emerge, who would come to inspire a whole generation. They could not have imagined that these institutions would produce a core of assertive young people, confident and courageous exponents of ideas about the psychological and cultural liberation of black people that would cohere into the ideology of Black Consciousness (BC).

The rise of Black Consciousness started in the late 1960s. With the construction of four new ethnic universities, enrolment of black students increased fourfold between 1960 and 1971. However, the increase in numbers of black students was not matched by increased representation on an ethos of the National Union of South African Students (NUSAS). Black students became increasingly disenchanted, and matters came to a head at the NUSAS congress at Rhodes University when the university authorities barred black delegates from accommodation on the campus. The delegates voted against Steve Biko's motion for adjournment until a nonracial venue could be found, and settled for a motion merely to censure the university. The incident confirmed the sentiment of many black students – that their interests could never be adequately represented by a predominantly white liberal organisation such as NUSAS. After intensive consultation, an exclusively black student's body, the South African Students' Organisation (SASO), was formed in December 1968. Steve Biko was elected president of SASO at its inaugural conference at the University of the North, popularly known as Turfloop, in July 1969. In 1970, SASO withdrew its recognition of NUSAS, arguing that since it did not represent black students, it could no longer be considered a "national union".

SASO grew from strength to strength as it established itself on black university campuses and at teacher-training colleges and theological seminaries across the country. In 1972, SASO initiated the formation of the Black People's Convention (BPC), an umbrella body of a number of black consciousness organisations set up to "unite South African blacks into a black political movement which [sought] to realise their emancipation from both psychological and physical oppression" (Bonner and Segal, 73). Meanwhile, the African Students' Movement (ASM), which had been formed in 1968 "to voice student grievances and challenge the conservative nature of church youth clubs in Soweto" relaunched itself under the Black Consciousness umbrella in 1972 (Bonner and Segal, 73). The organisation, renamed the South African Students' Movement (SASM), aspired to become a national movement for all high-school students.

At first the government did not pay much attention to SASO and its related organisations, partly because Black Consciousness ideas and principles were more successfully propagated in the cultural arena than they were through direct methods of political mobilisation. It took some time for the government to realise that the cultural renaissance sweeping through the black townships was inspired by Black Consciousness and in turn provided a means of political mobilisation for that movement. The government was also lulled into believing that SASO's emphasis on black separatism was in keeping with its own separate development paradigm (Karis and Gerhart, 100). However, developments in 1972–3 soon changed the official attitude of benign neglect to one of direct confrontation.

The first danger signal for the government was the student unrest sparked off by the expulsion of Onkgopotse Ramothibi Tiro, 1970–71 president of the Students Representative Council at the University of the North. Tiro caused a sensation at Turfloop's 1972 graduation ceremony when he launched a stinging attack on Bantu education, white control of black universities and indeed the entire apartheid system. When he concluded with the message that times were changing and no amount of force could halt the drive towards human freedom, students cheered wildly while the startled white dignitaries and faculty sat red-faced with embarrassment and anger. To the dismay of the government, the boycott and demonstration by Turfloop students spread to other campuses (including the white universities of the Witwatersrand and Cape Town), as well as to high school students (Mbeki 1996, 25; Karis and Gerhart, 5: 120, 126; Maharaj, 32). These protests did not succeed in getting Tiro reinstated and a number of other students were also expelled. What the protests did demonstrate was that in the few years since its formation, SASO had become the most significant black political organisation in the country. OR Tiro became a hero to a whole generation of high-school students, and by the end of 1972, SASO's popularity was at its zenith (Gerhart, 296). In 1972, the SASO newsletter had a print run of 4 000 with a high pass-on rate that would make the readership at least three times that number. High-school students were avid readers of the SASO newsletter and 1972–3 saw young people establishing a plethora of youth organisations throughout the country (Gerhart, 297). Students were also increasingly exposed to banned literature from abroad that was filtering into the country. Historians Tom Karis and Gail Gerhart noted that "foreign writing, critically sifted for their most relevant ideas, enriched the language and analytical content of BC thinking, adding greatly to its broader impact. Never had black South African intellectuals made such a deliberate and thoroughgoing attempt to borrow and selectively adapt foreign ideas in order to influence mass thinking, and never had efforts to shape mass thinking met with such success in so short a period" (Karis and Gerhart, 5: 102).

Lindi Sisulu was one of the high-school students whose anger against apartheid found its home in the Black Consciousness movement. Lindi completed her O-levels at St Michael's in 1971, then went to Waterford College in Swaziland for A-levels. During school holidays she would attend meetings at Uncle Tom's Hall, just around the corner from the Sisulu home. The angry rhetoric of the young people addressing these meetings appealed to her and she began to associate with local Black Consciousness activists. From 1971 to 1973, she became active in the Black People's Convention (BPC): "I attended meetings and worked at one of the offices making newspaper cuttings and generally trying to make myself useful."

In 1974 Lindi was admitted to the University of Botswana, Lesotho and Swaziland (UBLS), where she studied political science. Like many young adherents of Black Consciousness, she became familiar with "struggle literature" – writings on Che Guevara and the Cuban struggle, the writings of Frantz Fanon, Paolo Freire, the black power activists Angela Davis, Stokely Carmichael and Eldridge Cleaver, and African nationalists like Kwame Nkrumah and Amilcar Cabral.

Albertina viewed Lindi's involvement in the BPC with caution. Lindi felt that her mother was proud of her political awareness, but concerned by her immaturity. She expressed this when Lindi attended the case of a man on trial for BPC activities. At the trial a young BPC woman gave evidence for the State; her colleagues saw nothing wrong with this, because it involved spreading the BPC message from the dock. Albertina was shocked and pointed out that it was unacceptable to give evidence for the State, but Lindi was so impressed by the glamour of the event and that the woman was putting the BPC message across that she did not agree with her mother's criticism.

Albertina was also alarmed by how young people like Lindi were interpreting Black Consciousness philosophy, especially with regard to the role of whites. While the Black Consciousness ideologues eschewed the involvement of white people in the struggle, at no point did they suggest that whites would have no place in a liberated South Africa. Steve Biko wrote in 1971 that the white man had come into the African house as a guest and had taken it over. Ultimately blacks "wanted to remove him from our table, strip the table of all trappings put on it by him, decorate it in true African style, settle down and then ask him to join us on our own terms if he liked" (Karis and Gerhart, 5: 100). However, anger against whites was so strong in his youthful constituency that some supported the notion that after freedom all whites should be driven into the sea.

This bothered Lindi. One day, while travelling to town with a Black Consciousness movement (BCM) activist, they passed a huge construction site. Lindi asked what would happen to such construction projects if white people were to be driven out after freedom. The activist responded that if a state could be created for the Israelis, then a state could be created for the whites. Lindi then asked what would happen to the infrastructure if there was a sudden and dramatic loss of white skills and black people were not skilled enough to maintain it. The activist castigated her, saying: "At heart you are a Canadian tourist, you come here for three weeks and you know nothing about the country." When Lindi got home she asked Albertina what would happen when white people were driven into the sea. Albertina asked, "Why in the first place would you want to drive them into the sea?" She went on, "Sisi, ask these comrades of yours how they will liberate the country." Lindi replied "It is a big secret." "Exactly," responded Albertina. "It is such a secret, they do not know."

Despite Albertina's concerns about the BCM, she was supportive of Lindi's involvement. Lindi appreciated the fact that her mother did not patronise her during their political discussions: "She did not say her way was better. She took all the time to discuss and explain. She had more time for me then than ever before. In a way I was her conduit for what was happening out there. She was not hostile to Black Consciousness, but she was aware of its limitations and she associated it with the radicalism of the youth." Lindi meanwhile knew that her mother was politically active but did not think much about what she was doing: "I felt that Mama, Nkadimeng and company were just concerned with setting up structures. They were not involved in any action. Their lack of activity confirmed my idea of a dead organisation."

Lindi felt her brothers encouraged her activism rather indulgently, but Lungi had reservations about the Black Consciousness movement. He himself worked closely with Stanley Mabizela, an underground ANC activist teaching in Swaziland. Mabizela had enlisted Lungi to collect information on members of the police who might be sympathetic to their cause and to provide him with updates on what was happening in the labour movement. Lungi frequently travelled to Swaziland to report to Mabizela and to take people out of the country. The illegal crossing routes he had learned while travelling to and from school came in handy, and he was an expert at spiriting people out of the country. "I would take high-profile people one at a time and students in groups of 10." Lungi shared the feeling in the ANC underground that there was a danger that the Black Consciousness movement might try to position itself as a replacement of the ANC. This anxiety was further fuelled by the attitude in Black Consciousness circles that the ANC was a conservative and apathetic organisation whose non-racial politics were inimical to the liberation of black people. Lungi conveyed these concerns to his father, but Walter had a different view: "We in the ANC did not regard the emergence of the Black Consciousness movement as hostile. We regarded it as part and parcel of the struggle and we welcomed it as a progressive idea" (Houser and Shore Interviews).

He would later write about the emergence of Black Consciousness as championed by SASO and BPC as a positive development in the liberation struggle:

That these organisations, the majority of whose members are African, have reached out and made Black Consciousness an idea which draws in all black people – Africans, Coloureds and Indians – is a measure of self-confidence and increasing maturity of the awakening forces in our country. That most activists are students, products of the education in racially and tribally organised government schools and universities, shows how repugnant apartheid is to our people and how all the power of the enemy cannot overcome the long-term objective forces that have been and are shaping our people as one people, and our country as one country (Maharaj, 83).

Walter also did not see Black Consciousness ideology as something new. After all, in the early 1940s Anton Lembede had urged Africans to become self-reliant, shed their feelings of inferiority and redefine their self-image (Edgar and ka Msumza, 1). Walter therefore saw parallels between the militant black nationalism of the Youth Leaguers in the 1940s and the Black Consciousness generation of the 1970s. He regarded black consciousness as a stage one had to go through before arriving at the "mature" position of nonracism:

Racism and the maintenance of the privileges the whites enjoy have become so hopelessly intermeshed in the life and thoughts of the whites that a reactive anti-whitism as a phase in the development of the political consciousness of individual blacks is almost unavoidable. The fact that non-racialism is a *leitmotif* in the programmes of almost all the forces in the struggle becomes an outstanding testimony of the maturity of their political and philosophical outlook and also points to deeper economic factors that are at play, and which rise above and beyond the constraints of racism (Maharaj, 83).

The different attitudes to Black Consciousness within the Sisulu family reflected the ANC's ambivalence about the new kid on the block. A veteran ANC member described SASO as "a baby organisation of confused people", but the ANC as a whole took Black Consciousness organisations and structures seriously and saw the need to seek active cooperation with it (Mbeki 1996, 35). The BCM also saw the need for cooperation and Biko made approaches to both the PAC and ANC to explore possibilities of unity between all the organisations (Karis and Gerhart, 140).

The student unrest in 1972 and developments in the labour movement at the beginning of 1973 removed any complacency that the government had had about the Black Consciousness movement. The wave of strikes that rocked Durban from January to March 1973, involving more than 60 000 workers, set the tone for a new era in South Africa's labour history and forced the government to reassess its labour legislation and policies (Kalan).

Although the Black Consciousness movement played no direct role in fomenting the labour unrest, the government banned Steve Biko and other key leaders of SASO and BPC in March 1973. By the end of 1973, the entire top tier of BPC leadership was banned. BPC leader Mosibudi Mangena was tried and convicted on a fabricated charge under the Terrorism Act in October 1973. He was sent to Robben Island in 1974, the first Black Consciousness leader to be incarcerated there.

This heightened repression forced a number of Black Consciousness leaders to flee into exile in Botswana, including OR Tiro who left in September 1973, becoming the SASM leader in Botswana (Karis and Gerhart, 5: 140). In his famous address at Turfloop, Tiro had stated that "The price of freedom is blood, sweat and tears" (Marks, 53). Tiro paid the ultimate price when he was assassinated by a parcel bomb on 1 February 1974.

Shortly after OR Tiro was assassinated, the security police visited Albertina. "They came boasting like peacocks," she recalled. "They said sarcastically, 'Have you heard the latest? Your son has been killed in a letter-bomb explosion. Who wrote to him? Was it you? Was it one of your family? Are you going to bury him?'" Albertina steeled herself to respond calmly. "Oh, so you managed to kill him at last?" she said. After they left, she quickly established through her underground contacts that Max had indeed been involved in a bomb blast at the ANC headquarters at the Liberation Centre in Lusaka. ANC Deputy-Chief Representative and prominent MK commander John Dube was killed instantly when he opened the parcel bomb. Max and another comrade were badly injured.

As a result of the bomb blast, Max suffered a permanent injury to his eardrum and his colleague was badly burned. Because they required specialised treatment that was not available in Zambia, Oliver Tambo arranged for them to go for treatment to the Burdenko Military Hospital in Moscow.

The first few months of 1974 had not been encouraging ones for those engaged in the liberation struggle, but a completely unforeseen event 5 000 miles away brought renewed hopes of eventual victory. On 25 April 1974, the Portuguese army, fatigued by fighting interminable colonial wars in Mozambique, Angola, Guinea Bissau and Cape Verde, toppled the Caetano dictatorship. The Portuguese coup had a profound impact on the liberation struggle in southern Africa. The overnight independence of Mozambique and Angola opened the rebel Rhodesian regime to guerrilla attack from three fronts and brought black Africa right to Pretoria's doorstep. White South Africa had to deal with its worst nightmare – no buffer zone to protect it against guerrilla infiltration, and two hostile Marxist states on its eastern and western flanks (Sparks 1990, 300).

Black South Africans were jubilant about the unexpected turn of events. On Robben Island, Walter and his colleagues greeted the news with quiet satisfaction. Samora Machel was hailed as a hero in black townships. To young black militants, freedom seemed to be just around the corner. SASO tried to tap into popular sentiment by organising pro-Frelimo rallies on the eve of Mozambican independence on 25 September 1974. The rallies were banned, but young militants celebrated anyway. Violent clashes ensued between police and youth, followed by countrywide raids and arrests of BPC and SASO leaders. Nine SASO leaders were tried on terrorism charges in a dramatic 17-month long trial. By the time they were convicted and sentenced to imprisonment on Robben Island in December 1976, the face of South African politics had been irrevocably transformed (Maharaj, 33; Gerhart, 299).

The geo-political realignment of the southern African subcontinent in the wake of Mozambican and Angolan independence, combined with economic recession, resulted in a reformulation of foreign policy by the Pretoria regime. South Africa needed new friends, especially in Africa, to counter pressure from hostile neighbours. South African businesses also needed new markets. In October 1974, Vorster launched his new 'détente' initiative. The brainchild of the infamous Bureau of State Security (BOSS), the détente strategy aimed to establish friendly relations with conservative African states and entice neighbouring countries into an economic alliance with South Africa. A flurry of shady deals and secret diplomatic contacts led to trips to Ivory Coast and Liberia for Vorster, while at home he tried to impress the world by making cosmetic changes to apartheid (Sampson 2000, 265; Greg Houston, Unpublished notes, 101; Sparks 1990, 303).

Vorster's Foreign Minister Pik Botha announced proudly to the United Nations that South Africa was on the road to reform, but his country's conduct in Angola demonstrated that South Africa was more interested in covert conflict than in having good relations with its neighbours. Launched under a cloak of great secrecy in September 1975, South Africa's invasion of Angola was carried out with the support and encouragement of the CIA. However, the refusal by US Congress to finance the operation, coupled with the fierce resistance of the MPLA and Cuban forces, gave South Africa no option but to withdraw in March 1976. The invasion did not succeed in preventing MPLA from coming to power, but it enabled South Africa to flex its military muscle, encouraging its securocrats to plan along the lines of further covert military operations in the region. Allister Sparks describes the excitement of the episode for the Pretoria regime: "CIA agents had flown in and out of Waterkloof air base at the dead of the night; there had been clandestine meetings in Washington and Paris, secret contacts in African capitals. It was all very exciting and engendered for these international pariahs a sense of belonging in the underworld of *Realpolitik* beneath the public world of anti-apartheid rhetoric and exclusion" (Sparks 1990, 307).

Meanwhile, the ANC was exploiting the new opportunities that had opened up in the region. It strengthened its ties with the MPLA and decided to make Angola the major training base for MK. The ANC had to tread more carefully in Mozambique, as the South African government was closely monitoring the ANC presence in neighbouring countries. FRELIMO was essentially a transitional government, so it was nervous about allowing the ANC to operate freely in Mozambique. However, the ANC did establish a semi-legal presence there, which facilitated contact with ANC veterans in Swaziland (Shubin, 161; Mbeki 1996, 37).

In November 1974, Thabo Mbeki and Max Sisulu went to Swaziland to attend an OAU conference and to set up an office in the tiny kingdom. This was no easy task. Although the Swazi king Sobhuza II liked the ANC, and even considered himself a member because his uncle and regent had taken part in the Inaugural Conference of the ANC in 1912, Swazi officials were generally hostile to members of MK. The only thing that prevented them from deporting Max and Thabo was the fact that King Sobhuza had received them as emissaries of Oliver Tambo.

Lindi Sisulu, who was studying at the Swaziland campus of UBLS, was absolutely thrilled by the arrival of Max and Thabo. It was the first time she had seen Max since he had gone into exile in 1963. Lindi was dazzled by Max and Thabo. She found they had all the answers to her political questions, and felt that she had found a home in the ANC. "Then I knew what I wanted ... With BCM I always had the feeling of being not quite accepted because I was from an ANC family, and also because I had gone to a private school. Max and Thabo made me feel comfortable and confident. The day Thabo said to me, 'Max is very proud of you,' I walked on air for some time." Lindi was excited about the prospect of running errands for them and providing a link with people in South Africa.

Thabo and Max used this opportunity to communicate directly with SASO leaders from Durban, who travelled up to Swaziland to meet them. During the course of their discussions, it became clear why SASO had not been responsive to previous approaches from the ANC. The BCM representative in Botswana had misrepresented the ANC, giving the false impression that the ANC would only cooperate with SASO if the latter agreed to become a junior wing of the ANC. The misunderstanding was cleared up and a working relationship between the two organisations was established, giving the ANC an opening into the most significant legal political organisation in South Africa (Mbeki 1996, 37).

Max's presence in Swaziland generated enormous excitement in the Sisulu family and provided the opportunity for a much longed-for family reunion. When Max had gone into exile in 1963, his siblings were still in school, so it was quite an experience for him to meet Lungi as an adult, accompanied by his wife Sheila with two-year-old Linda (Ginyi) and their baby daughter Nontsikelelo (Ntsiki), named after Albertina. Beryl had also travelled to Swaziland with her husband Leonard Simelane and their son Thulani. Included in the "delegation" were Zwelakhe, by then a cadet reporter for the *Rand Daily Mail*, Nkuli, who was in high school in Soweto, and Lungi Junior, who was beside himself with excitement at the prospect of seeing the father he remembered only vaguely. Max was fascinated by his new nephews and nieces and the highlight, of course, was the reunion with his son. Lungi had transformed from the four-year-old Russian-speaking child he was when they parted in 1967 to a nine-year-old Zulu-speaking Sowetan. Beryl and Zwelakhe did not have passports, so they were dropped off near the border, which they crossed by hiking through the forest both ways.

The reunion was a joyous occasion that enabled them to catch up with over a decade of family news. Naturally Max was interested in hearing about the wellbeing of his parents. Since he had first written to her in 1972, Lindi had kept him up to date with family news. In her first letter to him, she teased him about his attachment to his mother: "You're dying to hear about your mama, aren't you? Mama's big baby! Shame on you. You must be missing her and how you envy us! Well, she's up and kicking. She still does her scolding – lots of it too. When she starts she never stops and she can even remember that the other year you did this that and the other and she'll do the same thing the day after that and it gets a bit boring and annoying. But beneath it all she's soft. Nkuli and I have a way with her now when she gets into her scolding tantrums. We kiss her as soon as she starts and that goes a long way to dampening her anger."

As much as she would have loved to, Albertina was not able to travel to Swaziland to see Max. In July 1974 she had been issued with a third set of banning orders for a further five years – from 31 July 1974 to 31 July 1979. According to the new restrictions, she had to report to Orlando police station every Wednesday and she could not travel out of Orlando. If she wanted to attend work-related lectures in different townships, she had to apply for a permit from the Chief Magistrate of Johannesburg. These permits stipulated that she not enter the township where the lecture was to be given more than half an hour before the lecture started, and that she leave immediately afterwards (Ministry of Justice files).

Albertina was tremendously relieved to hear from her children, on their return from Swaziland, that Max had fully recovered from the effects of the bomb blast. She was also delighted by reports of the work he was doing in the ANC and looked forward to conveying this news to Walter. She felt that the family reunion had been a great success and had done much to soothe the pain of separation caused by exile.

Albertina was also relieved to hear that Max was in touch with Gerald. Once he had made his way to Lusaka after defecting from MK in Tanzania, Gerald had met Jasoda (Jasu) Bawa, a young Zimbabwean girl of Indian origin. She eloped with him, and they moved to the eastern part of the country. Here Gerald worked on the mines in the Copperbelt and eventually landed up running a garage in Kitwe. Although Gerald lost touch with his family at this point, Max visited him around 1971 and asked him to return to the ANC. Gerald refused. After this, Max visited Gerald and Jasu a few times to see their children, Walden (born 1970) and Beryl (born 1972).

Albertina had been dismayed when she first heard that Gerald had left the ANC, but she was relieved to hear he was married, had children and was successfully managing his own business. She felt this signified a level of maturity and responsibility.

On her next visit to Robben Island, Walter was delighted by her account of all the news from Max. It seemed that the chasm between home and exile was slowly closing.

# *eight*

In some respects, 1975 was a good year for the Robben Islanders. After years of deprivation they were allowed music for the first time. Through a rediffusion radio service broadcast between 5pm and 8pm over speakers in the corridors, they could listen to the likes of Nat King Cole, Miriam Makeba, Joan Baez and Nancy Ames. Kathrada wrote to Sonia Bunting about looking forward to hearing Harry Belafonte sing about "Silvie", who brought him "a little coffee and a little tea. She brought me nearly every damned thing but she didn't bring me the jailhouse key." They also had about 250 long-playing records that were circulated within the prison community. Paul Robeson was a great favourite and they had to wait weeks to get hold of one of his records (Letter to Sonia Bunting, 16/2/75).

Kathrada wrote about other improvements: "This year, for the first time in 12 years, we've been provided with hot showers; twice we have eaten guavas; Isu has been promoted to A group, which enables him to buy some chocolates, coffee, sugar, cocoa, etc, each month; small things all, but they make a big difference. Then we've seen some good films: *The Godfather, The Great Escape, Lion in Winter*, etc; we've been thrilled to be able to get a glimpse of Mohammed Ali ..." (Letter to Lilian and Raman, 20/9/75). In the same year, Mandela was given a bed for the first time because he suffered from backache. Over the course of the next few years, all the prisoners traded their sisal mats for beds.

The quality of life on the Island had been steadily improving over the years. From 1973, the B section prisoners gradually spent less and less time working in the quarry. They would be taken to saw and chop wood and sometimes to collect seaweed from the shore. They would line the strands of seaweed in rows on the beach to be dried, then exported to Japan. Walter enjoyed their days by the sea. In his autobiography, Mandela also evoked an almost idyllic image of their days by the seashore. The fresh sea air, the beautiful view of Table Bay harbour and Cape Town, and the sight of ships sailing by more than compensated for the discomfort of the cuts and grazes they sustained while trying to pull the seaweed from the sharp rocks near the shore. They would also collect clams, mussels, crayfish and perlemoen (abalone) which Wilton Mkwayi, their "cook", would make into a stew in a drum. The warders would sometimes sit down and join them in a picnic lunch on the beach (Mandela, 553).

The absence of bread in their diets was one of the persistent complaints of prisoners. Govan Mbeki complained that the prison authorities were the type of people who professed to be Christians and prayed, "Give us our daily bread", yet they thought nothing of depriving prisoners of their daily bread (Schadeberg Interview, Govan Mbeki). After the prisoners protested to a group of visiting parliamentarians, the prison authorities finally relented in 1971 and provided prisoners with bread rations on Wednesdays, Saturdays and Sundays.

In 1973, two new arrivals on Robben Island, Sonny Venkatrathnam and Kader Hassim, from the Unity Movement organisation APDUSA (African People's Democratic Union of South Africa), petitioned the prison authorities with a range of complaints about prison conditions. They were thrown into solitary confinement as a result, but they managed to smuggle out letters to their lawyers, who in turn got prisoners' wives to bring urgent court applications to the Supreme Court. In a judgment that dramatically improved conditions on the Island, the Supreme Court ruled that warders had no right to arbitrarily deprive prisoners of meals or to put them in solitary confinement without a hearing (Buntman, 16; Alexander, 57, 67, 112).

Notwithstanding the improvements, the prisoners were still vulnerable to petty acts of spite by their jailers, and their battle to assert their rights, especially in relation to correspondence and visits, continued. On 1 September 1976, Walter wrote to the Commanding Officer, complaining that Albertina had informed him that she had sent him a telegram for his birthday. He had not received this telegram or her special Christmas letter. Neither had he received the Christmas cards she had sent. "I was given other Christmas cards, but I informed the officers that I would rather have Christmas cards from my wife. This has never been done."

In 1973, the prison bureaucracy ruled that prisoners would only be allowed visits from "first-degree" relatives – in other words, only the immediate family. Uncles, aunts, nephews, nieces, cousins and in-laws were now excluded. The ruling was particularly harsh on those prisoners whose immediate family did not reside in Cape Town and could not afford to make the journey to Robben Island more than a few times a year. Many prisoners relied on their "second-" or "third-degree" relatives in Cape Town for regular visits. Unmarried prisoners like Kathrada also suffered because they did not have any so-called first-degree relatives. Kathrada complained that if he had known that he would be subjected to such a law he would have made sure he married before he went to prison! (Letter to Dasoo Iyer, April 1978.)

Walter felt deeply aggrieved by this ruling. He felt it was an unfair attack on people who came from an extended family system in which the concept of "first-" or "second-degree" relative was meaningless. Walter had formed a strong bond with his daughter-in-law Sheila and when her application to visit him was turned down on the grounds that she was not related to him "in the first degree", he wrote a strong letter of protest. He pointed out that Sheila had visited him on a number of occasions, and challenged the first-degree rule:

With respect, I contend that a husband and wife, legally married, cannot, by civilised standards, be regarded as constituting two separate entities. They on the contrary, and by virtue of the existing marital tie alone, make up an inseparable unit. This is the standard recognised and adopted world-wide in the arena of human relations. In fact, even a union by customary rites is accorded not only legal status, but is also socially recognised as a valid association between a man and a woman.

Because Sheila is married to Anthony by civil rites, she assumes the status of her husband and as a consequence of that reason, she becomes my relative in the first degree.

Walter told the Commander that he felt the authorities had taken "a narrow and mechanical interpretation of the rule, which even if it were accepted from a sociological and anthropological point of view, would be repugnant to and against human relations standards that are of universal application".

Lungi is now my eldest son living at home and is, together with his wife, Sheila, my daughter-in-law, responsible for attending to all my matters and family problems. My wife's age is advancing and her health is not the best. Consequently, I need to discuss with Anthony and Sheila jointly and separately, numerous family matters.

I should be obliged if you could reconsider the matter. If, however, you cannot be persuaded, I shall be very much pleased to make further representations in this regard to the Commissioner of Prisons (Letter to Commanding Officer, Robben Island, 3/2/76).

The Commanding Officer referred Walter's letter to the warders in the censorship office and the terse reply gives an insight into the real reason that Sheila was not allowed to visit.

In my opinion there are no special circumstances that necessitate a visit from his daughter-in-law, Sheila. In the past two months the prisoner has had four visits from family members. For your information I am also attaching hereto a letter from the local security branch in which she is described as a security risk.

His request is not approved and his motivation also does not justify further reference to the Commissioner.

Prisoner informed on 12 February 1976.

Walter refused to let the matter rest and continued his angry protests to the authorities. When the Commissioner of Prisons, General Roux, visited the Island on 15 November 1977, Walter took the opportunity to raise the matter again. He followed this up with another letter to the Officer Commanding. Added to his complaint about Sheila being denied permission to visit, he protested that he had been forbidden to write to some of his relatives:

> Mr Nelson Mandela's first wife is my cousin. She lived with me until she got married. Her two children are now married. One of Nelson Mandela's daughters is engaged. I consider it my duty to congratulate them in the important step they have taken in life. I accordingly seek permission to write to them.
>
> Mr Caleb Mase is my first cousin. He also lived with me until he got married. We lived not only as cousins but also as members of one family. I therefore play a very important part in their family affairs. I myself am vitally interested in their affairs as my close relatives. Recently Mr Mase lost his wife and it is my desire to write to him on this matter and many other matters of the family (Letter to Commanding Officer, 2/5/77).

There was no response, and in November 1977, Sheila appealed to Jimmy Kruger, the then Minister of Justice. She pointed out that she had started visiting her father-in-law in 1970 (before her marriage to Lungi), but from 1973 her requests for visits had been turned down. She explained that Walter was entitled to a monthly visit by two people: "However, most of the members of his family live in Johannesburg, and it is difficult for them to travel to Cape Town more than once a year. As a result, my father-in-law receives approximately five of the twelve visits to which he is entitled each year. If I were permitted to visit him, this would go some way towards increasing the portion of his entitlement that he actually receives" (Letter to Minister of Justice, 4/11/77).

Jimmy Kruger referred Sheila's letter to the Commissioner of Prisons, who in turn referred it to the security police, who reiterated that they considered Sheila a security risk and recommended that the request be turned down. In December 1977, Sheila received a letter from the office of the Minister of Justice informing her that her request to visit Walter Sisulu had been turned down. No reasons were given for the decision (Ministry of Justice to Sheila Sisulu, 7/12/77, Prison Files).

The composition of the prison population on Robben Island had changed in the early 1970s. The numbers of common-law prisoners had declined, while many of the political prisoners serving short sentences had been released. In 1974 the B section said goodbye to Neville Alexander, Fikile Bam and Don Davis, who had completed their 10-year sentences.

During the course of a discussion in the courtyard one day towards the end of 1975, Walter and Kathrada suggested to Mandela that he write his memoirs. They were concerned about the need to preserve history and to counter the government efforts to wipe the name of Mandela off the pages of the country's history. Walter was always concerned about transmitting knowledge to the next generation and he believed that Mandela's biography would be especially important for young freedom fighters. The pending release of Mac Maharaj would provide an ideal opportunity to smuggle out the manuscript. Mac would then arrange to have it published on the occasion of Mandela's 60th birthday, just three years away.

It was practice to transfer prisoners scheduled for release from Robben Island several weeks or sometimes months before their actual release date. The prisoners suspected that this was to prevent them smuggling letters and messages out. Although Maharaj was due for release in December 1976, Mandela's biography had to be completed well before that date just in case Mac was removed much earlier. Mandela started writing in January 1976, working every night, throughout the night, writing completely from memory without reference to notes. He then passed sections to Walter and Kathrada for comments. They then passed it to Mac and Laloo Chiba, who transcribed Mandela's handwriting into microscopic writing that would considerably reduce the bulk of the original. They followed this assembly-line arrangement until the manuscript was completed in April 1976, well ahead of their anticipated deadline.

With some time to spare, and being someone who always had some scheme up his sleeve, Mac suggested another project involving essays by several contributors. Mac proved to be a very competent commissioning editor, who persuaded even the notoriously difficult John Pokela to contribute. He proposed the theme "Problems of the Liberation Movement in Southern Africa". Nelson Mandela, Walter Sisulu, Ahmed Kathrada, Govan Mbeki, Billy Nair, John Pokela, Eddie Daniels and Andimba Toivo ja Toivo all contributed. The theme had been deliberately broadened to southern Africa so that Toivo ja Toivo could be included.

In his article, Walter outlined the history of colonial and imperialist exploitation and what it had done to African people:

> ... the common history of our people is imprinted with a particularly traumatic experience, which colonialism seems to have earmarked for our people – the wholesale slave trade that ripped open and destroyed the fabric of African societies. Slave-owning societies have existed before in many parts of the world and are related to a particular stage in the historical evolution of human society. But the slave trade that transported millions of our people into slavery in North and South America in particular, and killed many more in the process, was associated with developing capitalism and was practised on a scale that has never been equalled.
>
> In Africa, imperialism completely denied our cultural past and history and applied the theory of race superiority so as to stamp our peoples with the mark of permanent inferiority (Maharaj, 74).

In his view, the real aim of the Cold War was "not only to destroy the socialist countries, but also to halt the progress of the anti-colonial revolutions and to keep those countries that had gained political independence within the imperialist fold ... It is no longer open to doubt that the imperialists have long used the cloak of anti-communism to impede the struggles of the colonial and former colonial peoples" (Maharaj, 81).

Walter went on to analyse the particular difficulties faced by the liberation movement. He analysed the complexity of devising a strategy to deal with the Bantustans and the need to draw the people in the Bantustans into the battle against apartheid. Like Mandela he stressed the need for the liberation movement to analyse its own errors and weaknesses in dealing with the Bantustans. He argued that the boycott strategy had failed: "The boycott was ineffective because we were never really in a position to effect it."

He echoed Mandela's argument for the need for political mobilisation and the urgency of building an efficient political organisation. He ended his analysis on an optimistic note:

> In the course of a liberation war there are many long and dark days. The tiny nation of Vietnam, in a war that stretched over more than 30 years, faced many such bleak moments. But a people who want freedom, who are prepared to fight for it, are capable of superhuman efforts. We face a powerful enemy, but never can it match the strength of the enemy the Vietnamese fought and vanquished. The hatred of our people towards apartheid is deep and enduring. The people are our strength. In their service we shall face and conquer those who live on the backs of our people (Maharaj, 81).

# nine

The arrival of a new baby in the Sisulu family was always greeted with celebration, so Albertina was delighted when Beryl announced in 1975 that she was expecting a second child. She was not so pleased when she received word that Lindi was expecting a baby, and looked to Walter for advice:

> My dear Walter,
> How are you darling? I know you are fed up with me (for not writing). Sorry dear, it is not my intention to hurt you at all Walter, you know that very well … I once mentioned to you that children are a pleasure when they are still young, but as soon as they grow old, they are a headache.
> Dear Walter, I hope you have by now received a letter from Lindi. I asked her to write to you and tell you that she is expecting a baby by Xolile Guma of Swaziland. That is the blow we got from Lindi. Guma came to see me in connection with this but we did not come to any conclusion until you give advice … Please darling tell us what to do about Lindi's problem. We are very upset about it (Letter, 30/9/75).

Walter was naturally disappointed but as always he looked on the bright side of things. The young man in question came from a highly respected family and his father, Professor Sam Guma, had been in the ANC Youth League in the 1940s. The Guma family had later settled in Swaziland, where Professor Guma had a distinguished academic career with the University of Swaziland. In the ensuing discussions between the two families, it was resolved that the two young people should complete their education before thinking about marriage.

By the time Lindi's baby, Xoliswa Ayanda, was born in December 1975, all was forgiven and Albertina was thrilled to have a baby in the house once more. Lungi and Sheila had long since moved out to their own house in another part of Soweto, taking Ginyi, Thulane and Ntsiki with them and although the children attended the crèche opposite, it was not quite the same as having them live in the house. Beryl's baby Zama was born in the same month, but Beryl was living in Cape Town, so Leonard's mother, MaNdzimande, became the main grandmother in Zama's life. Ayanda, as she became known, filled an important gap in Albertina's life and was a major topic in the correspondence of her grandparents. Lindi had been home on holiday when the baby was born and when she returned to university at the beginning of 1976, Ayanda remained with Albertina.

The Lesotho campus of UBLS, where Lindi was studying, was openly political in 1975. In the wake of Mozambican independence, the struggle for Zimbabwean independence had intensified and, together with students from other African countries, the Zimbabwean students started the Lumumba Society, a Marxist group formed to give ideological preparation to students in Zimbabwe and Namibia. This society laid the foundation for later large-scale ANC activity in Roma. At that time Chris Hani, the fiery and highly respected MK leader, was engaged in building underground structures from his base in Lesotho (Shubin, 162). Lindi met Hani when he was invited to speak to the students, and she became increasingly drawn into ANC activities.

By the mid-1970s, the ANC was having more success in its efforts to build an efficient underground machinery. The re-entry of released Robben Island activists contributed to the rejuvenated underground. The former prisoners were invariably restricted, banished, generally harassed and closely monitored after their release, but this did not deter them from engaging in clandestine political work. After their release in 1973, Jacob Zuma and Harry Gwala were instrumental in the revival of the Natal underground, while Martin Ramakgade and Joe Gqabi strengthened underground structures in the Johannesburg area (Buntman, 39). The friendship between Walter and Joe Gqabi extended to their families. Joe's wife maintained contact with Albertina and for years she never failed to send Walter birthday and Christmas cards. After his release, Joe worked closely with Lungi. One of the projects they worked on was to get money to enable prisoners on the Island to study. The prison authorities refused to allow donors to cover the study costs of prisoners; such money was only permitted to come from prisoners' own families. Joe and Lungi would receive money from unknown sources (probably IDAF) and send it to the families of the prisoners, who would then send it on to their loved ones.

In May 1976, Clifford Sisulu died. He had never fully recovered from his amputation and his health had deteriorated steadily over the years. In the absence of his father, Lungi took the lead in organising the funeral, and Albertina successfully applied to the Chief Magistrate for permission to attend the burial. Clifford's death was not entirely unexpected, but there was a feeling of especial sadness nonetheless. He was the last surviving sibling in Walter's mother's family, so his death marked the end of an era for the Sisulu family.

Desmond Tutu, the recently appointed Dean of Johannesburg (the first black cleric to hold the post), made his first public stand against apartheid when he wrote to the Prime Minister on 6 May 1976. This was an impassioned plea for the government to abandon the Bantustan policy and accept urban blacks as permanent inhabitants of South Africa, to scrap the pass laws and to call a National Convention of recognised leaders. His letter contained a prophetic warning. "I have a growing and nightmarish fear that unless something drastic is done very soon then bloodshed and violence are going to happen in South Africa almost inevitably" (Du Boulay, 106). At the same time, Winnie Mandela also warned that there would be an upsurge of anger among black youth if nothing was done to address their grievances. But the warnings fell on deaf ears. In May 1976, Manie Mulder, Chairperson of the West Rand Administration Board (WRAB), made a statement that reflected the arrogance and ignorance of the white administration: "The broad masses of Soweto are perfectly content, perfectly happy. Black-White relationships at present are as healthy as can be. There is no danger whatever of a blow-up in Soweto" (Bonner and Segal, 78).

Nothing could have been further from the truth. The pot of resentment and despair was close to the boil in Soweto. Bantu education had brought about a dramatic drop in the standards of black education. From the 1960s onwards, overcrowded classrooms, often with only one teacher to 50 or more pupils (and untrained teachers at that), were the order of the day. However, industry's demands for skilled black labour increased as a result of the economic boom of the early 1970s, and the government was pressured to invest more in black education in the urban areas. As a result, 40 new high schools were built in Soweto between 1971 and 1974 and the number of children in secondary school increased almost three-fold. The dramatic increase in secondary school enrolment was not, however, matched by improved conditions (Bonner and Segal, 79).

With remarkable lack of foresight, the Department of Bantu Education (DBE) decided in 1976 to drop the Standard Six (final) year of primary school. Previously, only a small percentage of students with good passes in Standard Six were permitted to proceed to secondary school. With the dropping of Standard Six, almost all Standard Five students were able to enter high school. Consequently, a quarter of a million students entered high school in 1976, while schools were equipped to cater for an intake of only 38 000 (Bonner and Segal, 79). It was this group of students, already suffering the strain of arguably one of the most chaotic learning environments anywhere in the world, that was most affected by the DBE directive on Afrikaans.

The government's 1958 ruling that half the subjects in secondary school should be taught in English and the other in Afrikaans had never been enforced because of the practical difficulties involved. In 1974, however, the DBE decided to enforce the directive, beginning with Form One and Form Two (roughly Grades Nine and Ten today). Soweto had, and still has, probably the most linguistically diverse population in South Africa. All of South Africa's dozen or more languages are represented but unlike some black communities in regions such as the Cape and the Free State, few Sowetans spoke Afrikaans. "The ruling on Afrikaans was a blow to us. To do biology or history in Afrikaans was impossible. We felt as if the government did not want us to go to school," recalled Jongi Sisulu, who was a Form Four student at Daliwonga High in Soweto at the time.

The Afrikaans ruling was first enforced at Phefeni Junior Secondary, near the Sisulu home. "It was a major problem," said Nkuli, who was then in Form Four at Morris Isaacson High. "The pupils there were being forced to accept Afrikaans as their medium of instruction and as a result many pupils failed because they did not even understand Afrikaans when it was taken as a subject, let alone all other subjects being taught in Afrikaans." The majority of Soweto's schoolchildren spoke two or more languages and English was often their third or even fourth language.

Albertina shared the anger of black parents against the Afrikaans community, who insisted on mother-tongue education for their own children, yet expected black children to learn through the medium of their third or even fourth language. To make matters worse, most teachers in Soweto could barely speak Afrikaans, let alone teach in it. Parents, teachers and the community in general protested against the insane ruling that would bring learning to a grinding halt. Even the more conservative school boards resisted the idea and some resigned en masse in protest against the controversial directive. As the June examinations approached, panic set in among the pupils in the schools in which the decree was in force. The Form Ones and Twos at Phefeni Junior Secondary School initiated a strike, which quickly spread to several other schools (Bonner and Segal, 82).

On 14 June, Nkuli Sisulu was among the Morris Isaacson students who received a report-back from Tsietsi Mashinini, the head of their SRC. Mashinini told them that 400 SRC representatives of Soweto's secondary schools had met on Sunday 13 June and had agreed with his proposal that they hold a mass demonstration on Wednesday, 16 June. The students welcomed the announcement. They felt that parents and teachers had failed to get the DBE to rescind the hated Afrikaans ruling, so it was time they took matters into their own hands. "Though our school was not yet affected, we thought we had to take action before it was enforced in our school," recalled Nkuli. By the time she got back home on 14 June 1976, she had already written out her placards. "We had also been warned not to tell anybody about this planned action, we were not even to tell our parents. We had to go home and pretend that nothing was about to happen."

Albertina had also noticed that Nkuli and Jongi were up to something. "They were so secretive, those two. They would go to meetings in the afternoon and come back very late and I would fight with them. 'No Mama, we are from a students' meeting,' they would say. I just wondered what these meetings were all about." Zwelakhe, who was working for the *Rand Daily Mail* at the time, would ask Jongi and Nkuli what was happening at school, but they gave him little information. Lindi, who was spending the university vacation at home, noticed Nkuli's air of suppressed excitement. When she asked what was going on, Nkuli responded: "Just wait until Wednesday." Little did they know that by Wednesday Lindi would be in a cell in the dreaded John Vorster Square.

On Monday 14 June, Lindi was at home enjoying the company of two-year-old Ntsiki and six-month-old Ayanda. Albertina and Zwelakhe were at work, Jongi and Nkuli at school and Aunt Flora and her boys had gone out, so Lindi was alone when the security police arrived to take her into custody. Lindi begged them not to take her because she could not leave two infants alone. The police said they could take the children to prison as well. Lindi decided to take the children to Gogo Mantongomane next door. Gogo would not only take care of the children, she would also tell the rest of the family what had happened when they returned. When Albertina got home she found her household up in arms about Lindi's arrest. She knew that it was crucial to locate Lindi as soon as possible. People taken by the security police sometimes disappeared without trace. Families enquiring about loved ones would simply be met with police denials that such and such person was in their custody. She packed a case for Lindi, and the next day Zwelakhe and Sheila went to look for her at the most obvious place, John Vorster Square, the main destination for most detainees. They handed in the suitcase at the reception, but the police would not confirm that Lindi was there. They then went to a spot outside the prison and called out until Lindi heard them and responded. Every day after that one of them would communicate with her through the prison window.

Sick with worry about Lindi, Albertina did not imagine that things could get worse, but they did. By the end of the week she felt as if she had been plunged into an abyss.

On the morning of 16 June 1976, Nkuli and Jongi Sisulu went to school carrying their books as if it was a normal day. On arrival at school, however, all semblance of normality ended. At Morris Isaacson, Nkuli and her schoolmates collected their placards and left the school en masse. Nkuli recalled how they moved through Soweto, as if to the tune of some invisible pied piper:

> We asked our teachers to stay away and not to interfere. We followed our instructions very care-fully. We were told that when we got to the junior primary schools, we were to tell the young ones to pack their books and go straight home. We were to help the young ones to cross the roads so that they could get home safely. We would then pass on to the next school. The next school we got to was a high school, where they were busy writing exams. We asked the pupils to join us. Some joined us but others refused, and some of their teachers tried to resist, but we simply asked them to step aside and the students who were writing had their exam papers taken away and torn.
>
> On the way to the next school, we heard that the Principal of that school had heard we were moving towards his school and that he was planning on calling the police. It was then suggested that the boys were to cut the telephone ... The girls were told that they were to go into the class-rooms to collect all the pupils there to join us, and they were to instruct the little ones to go home.
>
> We found the response amazing, there was very little resistance among the pupils, and by now the crowds were swelling. Pupils were joining the crowds voluntarily, once they were told what the march was about. There was no violence, nobody was threatened, and nobody refused to join.
>
> By now crowds were growing bigger and bigger as we marched ... The people in the township were all surprised, because they had never seen a thing like that before. So everybody in the neigh-bourhood was standing outside watching us as we were marching and singing songs. I remember one of the favourites was "Senzeni Na?" meaning, "What have we done?"

By the time Nkuli and her group approached Phefeni Junior Secondary School, they were con-fronted by a phalanx of police cars, as well as mounted police. Students from other schools were also converging on Phefeni Junior Secondary. Suddenly, without any warning, they heard shooting and students started to scream and run in all directions. Bullets whizzed past Nkuli and she saw that Philip, one of her schoolmates, had been shot.

> When he got shot, we were all puzzled. It was the first time for many of us to experience this ... A friend simply grabbed him and pulled him along. By now the police were coming down the road and they were just shooting wildly. We tried to find somewhere where we could hide. Everyone was running for shelter, some were hiding against walls and peeping where the police were (this, I did not see at the time, was not offering much protection). I was standing with a friend of mine against the wall when she exclaimed "Auw, I didn't know that a revolution could start so simply!"

Nkuli was not aware that Jongi was marching a few hundred metres ahead. Jongi had been at his school, Daliwonga High, when they saw the column of marching children singing freedom songs:

> As they approached we simply left the school to join them. When we saw cars along the road, we would tell them to drive carefully. When we got near Holy Cross, we were stopped by a huge group

of police who were in front of Uncle Tom's Hall. They gave us orders to disperse in five minutes or they would shoot. We were still waiting for orders from those leading the march when the police started to shoot. Hector Petersen dropped. I saw him falling. I saw Mbuyisa picking him up.

From that moment there was chaos. Helicopters hovered overhead. Students were running all over the place. It was the first time I experienced teargas. I saw the other students run for buckets of water, wet their shirts and put them over their noses. We started throwing stones at the police. We tried to regroup after the teargas had been thrown. I felt terribly angry and the only thing I wanted to do was to fight the police.

Albertina was at work at the clinic when she heard that the children were marching. She was not unduly concerned. She did not imagine they would be in any danger. But during the course of the day, she became increasingly disturbed:

The reports we were getting from our patients were becoming more and more frightening. We heard that the children are in trouble, the police are shooting the children. We then heard that the children had retaliated and had killed a police dog and hung it over a fence.

Wednesday was the day I had to report to the police station according to my banning orders. I went straight there from work and from the police station I took a taxi home, but as we got nearer to Uncle Tom's Hall the taxi had to stop because the children were throwing stones at the police who were encamped in front of Uncle Tom's. It was like rain. The taxi had to deviate and go around so that we could get to my house from the Dube side, but it was worse there. We heard that the children had assaulted a man and were preventing the ambulance from coming to collect that man. The children were on the railway line throwing stones at the police to prevent them from coming to intervene. The taxi driver said "Mama, I cannot go any further." He dropped me at a house next to the Methodist Church and I had to walk down the main road from the bridge, past Phomolong Station to my house. That is how I got home that day.

And when I got home, Nkuli and Jongi were not there. We did not know what to do. I had to see to Flora because once she is worried she gets an epilepsy attack. I could hear the shooting and I did not know where to look for my children. Nobody cooked, nobody ate in our house that day.

When Nkuli and Jongi eventually returned home, they found Albertina waiting at the gate. She spent a few more anxious hours waiting for Zwelakhe, who turned up after 8pm. He had spent the day in Germiston covering the trial of two trade unionists who were ultimately sentenced to Robben Island. When he got off the train at Phomolong Station that evening, he saw cars burning and fire everywhere: "I just knew South Africa would never be the same again."

The next day the whole neighbourhood was in mourning and the Sisulus shared in the feeling of outrage and loss over young Hector Petersen's death. Albertina did not know Hector personally, but she knew his family. Mbuyisa Makhubu, too, was a friend of her children, and his mother was one of the neighbours who had been extremely supportive of the Sisulu family in difficult times.

The Soweto story made international headlines and newspapers around the world were splashed with the now-famous image captured by photographer Sam Nzima: an anguished Mbuyisa Makhubu cradling the limp body of Hector Petersen, running for help with Hector's distraught sister sprinting alongside. It was the picture that would come to symbolise the tragic events of Soweto and bring home the horror of apartheid to the world. The June 16 tragedy was initially likened to Sharpeville, but it soon became clear that the apartheid regime was dealing with an unprecedented rebellion that made Sharpeville seem tame by comparison. Within days the unrest had spread like wildfire to the University of Zululand at Ngoye, townships in Krugersdorp, Nelspruit, Pretoria, Port Elizabeth, Cape Town and many other parts of the country in a series of protests that changed the face of South African politics forever. By February 1977, the official death toll was 575 but the number of people who had actually died was much higher.

In what he described as "the worst day of my life", Zwelakhe personally witnessed the extent of the carnage when he was assigned to stake out the Orlando police station:

> Throughout the night there were these vans coming in, off-loading some stuff in the yard. Then, about midnight, a group of youngsters, children, 9, 10, 11 and 13, some of them still in their school uniforms, were taken from their cells [and] taken to this heap.
>
> Then a van came, and they were asked to load these things ... for the first time, we realised that that heap was in fact corpses. And these kids were told to take these corpses and throw them onto the truck ... whilst doing this, one could hear the groans from that heap. There were people still groaning there, who were not dead, most were just frozen by the shock, they were just scared.

Zwelakhe's editors at the *Rand Daily Mail* found it difficult to believe his eyewitness account and they published a toned-down version of his story, "so watered down as to be unrecognisable".

Inflamed rather than deterred by police shootings, the youth of Soweto continued to confront the police with a courage that stunned their parents. The older generation found that they could neither control nor protect their children. "There was no way you could prevent children taking part in the campaign," recalled Albertina. "Even if you wanted them not to join they will ask you: 'Mama, other children are dying. Should we be sitting here and watching them die?'" One day Nkuli came home with deep bruises on her stomach. She had been injured when the police opened fire on the premises of Morris Isaacson School. The girl in front of her was shot and fell. Nkuli jumped over her and ran. Police were surrounding the school and the students tried to climb the fence. The fence collapsed and the children toppled onto each other. On another occasion, she was burnt by teargas. "Her mouth and the nose were just a sheet of blisters," recalled Albertina. "I ran to the clinic to get her some medication but when I returned, I found her gone."

As the body count mounted, funerals became the new arena of political protest and students would hijack buses to attend the mass burials that were taking place around Soweto (Bonner and Segal, 90). Albertina recounted the agony of Soweto parents who could not prevent their children from participating in the funerals:

> In the morning you will see all the buses lined up alongside the railway line from Phomolong right up to Phefeni. Where they got the buses, nobody knows. They would go to the funeral and eventually they will come back home hungry, like hungry dogs with red eyes from the teargas. Then you will start making pap for them to eat. Mothers were in the street looking for their children. It's difficult to describe how those moments were.
>
> One day the nurses called me saying they saw Jongi and Nkuli running past the clinic. I didn't know what to do because the police were shooting. And I just thought even if they are killed, I must see their corpses. Because in most cases people didn't know what had happened to their children. We believed they were being dumped at night by the helicopters in the swamps of Mofolo, and that the area was smelling because of the bodies of the children that were there.

Like many other Soweto parents, Albertina was deeply disturbed by the orgy of looting and burning that was becoming a feature of the protests. One day a group of youths looted a butcher's delivery van as it was approaching Makgetha's store just around the corner from their home. Jongi decided to join in and helped himself to a piece of meat. When Albertina heard where the meat had come from, she was furious with Jongi. "Mama scolded me badly and told me to take the meat back and never to bring looted goods home again. I had to hide the meat and cook it secretly when she was out of the house." Albertina was even more disturbed by the rabid anti-white feeling among the youth. "Children were impossible in those days. You could not say anything to defend a white person." Her worst fears were realised when Dr Marvin Edelstein, a man she respected and admired, was killed by a group of students:

Dr Edelstein was working in Orlando East clinic when I met him before I moved to Shanty Clinic. This day he was visiting one of the clinics in deep Soweto. The children were so anti-white. They did not know who he was. They stopped the van between Phefeni station and our home and they killed him. People who knew him made it known immediately. It was terrible, just terrible. We were heartbroken. He was one of the best doctors ... because of his love of his work and the love of the people, he was known to all the clinics right up to Noordgesig. Some of the children knew him ... They felt sore, very very sore, but it was too late, there was nothing they could do.

The student leadership shared the concern of Soweto parents that the place was descending into anarchy, with the criminal element exploiting the situation. The Action Committee that had organised the 16 June march broadened its representation under the guidance of SASM and reconstituted itself into an umbrella body known as the Soweto Students Representative Council (SSRC). The SSRC, chaired by Tsietsi Mashinini, tried to provide political direction to the uprising. It organised a campaign calling for the release of all schoolchildren in detention, stay-aways in August and September, and a boycott of end of year examinations. Some SSRC members informally approached older ANC activists for advice on strategy. Lungi was one of those consulted by the students: "The uprising was too big. The students found themselves dealing with something they could not handle and increasingly they turned to us, especially people like Joe Gqabi, to give them direction."

However, it was virtually impossible for the SSRC to develop a coherent political programme and maintain the momentum of the uprising, given that they were unmercifully persecuted by the police and either detained or forced to flee the country. Even members of the innocuous Black Parents Association, formed on 21 June 1976 to give material assistance to people injured in the shootings and to assist the families of victims to arrange funerals, were harassed and some of them detained. Dr Nthato Motlana and Winnie Mandela were among those detained for their role in the BPA. By August 1976, Tsietsi Mashinini was forced into exile and his successor as chair of the SSRC, Khosto Seathlolo, followed in January 1977.

From the day his image was broadcast around the world, Mbuyisa Makhubu was unable to sleep at his home because the police were after him. He was pursued so relentlessly that he was eventually forced into exile. He found his way to Nigeria where he corresponded with his family for a couple of years, before disappearing without trace.

During this period, Lungi was working overtime helping people to leave the country. Mr Mathabathe, the principal of Morris Isaacson School, asked Lungi if he could help some students who were being hounded by the police. One of them, Tutu Booy, told Lungi that the police had asked him to inform on his fellow students and that he was terrified about what the police might do to him. Lungi responded to Mathabathe's pleas and took Tuku Booy and ten other SASM students out of the country. Around the same time, Lungi received an urgent instruction from the ANC to take JV Nkondo, the brother of Curtis Nkondo, out of the country:

His case was coming up on the following Monday. On Sunday afternoon I took him across Oshoek. Because it was a last-minute thing I had to take my own car. We left the car about 4km from the border post. I took him behind the border post, into a stream and across into Swaziland. He spoke no Zulu and no Siswati. I therefore had to direct him on a route that would ensure that he would not bump into any people. The route was well away from the main road. He walked all night, covering the 40-odd miles to Manzini where he contacted Stanley Mabizela.

In July 1976, Lungi was arrested and intensively interrogated about an activist called Sibusiso Ndebele, whom he did not even know. He gathered that the police had confiscated a package from Ndebele that contained information about Phindile Mfethi, an activist who was in the same ANC cell as Lindi. Lungi felt sure that the main purpose of this interrogation was to build a case against Lindi, who was undergoing a lonely ordeal that was to last almost a year.

*t e n*

Throughout the upheavals of June and July 1976, Albertina was consumed by anxiety about her children. Apart from her fears that Nkuli and Jongi could at any time join the growing list of young people who were shot or maimed by the police, she was almost out of her mind with worry about Lindi. The news filtering back from those in detention was not reassuring. Stories of torture by electric shock and brutal beatings abounded. And at the back of any parent's mind would be the history of detainees who had died in police custody – Looksmart Ngudle, Babla Saloojee, Ahmed Timol. The police were brutal enough to ordinary prisoners and memories were fresh in Albertina's mind of the horrific injuries on the body of Lindi's own cousin, Kenneth Sisulu, who had died in police custody. When Lungi was detained, she was distraught. In a moment of deep despondency she confessed to Sheila: "The Boers can do what they like to your father and I, but when they take my children they break me at the knees."

Fortunately, Lungi was released after three weeks. During his questioning, however, he was deeply disturbed to see a pile of parcels in the corner of the room bearing Lindi's name. He recognised them as the parcels the family had been sending Lindi since her detention. He was sure his interrogators had deliberately placed the parcels there to plant thoughts that Lindi might not be alive. These anxieties deepened when, on his release, he found that from the first week of August, Lindi had stopped responding from her usual window at John Vorster Square. The family had heard that she had been moved and was desperately trying to locate her.

Zwelakhe and Sheila went from prison to prison looking for Lindi. When they heard that she might be in Pretoria Prison, Zwelakhe stood shouting her name in the street alongside and was arrested in the process. He was released after some hours and had to return home without any news. Sheila finally managed to track Lindi down to a police station near Hartbeespoort Dam. "Detainees are not normally kept at police stations, so she was the only prisoner in the middle of nowhere," recalled Sheila. "When I saw her she was very agitated but then she relaxed and I was able to go home and reassure Mama that she was in good health." The family had heard from Pat Mamoepa, who had been detained at John Vorster Square at the same time as Lindi and subsequently released, that Lindi had been assaulted and tortured. Albertina was therefore greatly relieved by Sheila's report.

Lindi had been badly beaten shortly after her arrival at John Vorster Square. One policeman who had been particularly nasty to the family said, "I will fix her up. When we used to go to her home she was so arrogant. Now she is in our hands." She sustained a dislocated shoulder and damage to her lungs during the assault. She was taken to a district surgeon, who said her dislocated shoulder was the result of having slept in an awkward position and that the black marks on her body "could have come from sleeping on the concrete floor if you are not used to it". He concluded that her injuries were not consistent with beatings, and the abuse continued.

At first, Lindi imagined she would be out of prison in a few days. Shortly after her arrival, she received a parcel of toothpaste, soap and other necessities from her mother. With all her experience of prison, Albertina knew exactly what to pack. Lindi found the parcel amusing and thought, "She is packing as if I will be away for the whole month." She sensed that something dramatic had happened, and her suspicions were confirmed by incoming detainees, who told her about the Soweto eruptions. When she was transferred first to Pretoria, then to Hartbeespoort police cells, she realised she would not be going home anytime soon.

Just after she arrived at Hartbeespoort, the police told Lindi that Albertina had been arrested. They later told her that her mother had died. Lindi felt deranged with grief, but at the same time she felt there was something suspicious about the news. She repeatedly asked the police if it was true that her mother was dead, but they would not confirm or deny this.

Relief came when Sheila visited her and confirmed that the story about Albertina was not true. After Sheila left she demanded to see the magistrate and lodged a complaint. The following day Lindi was transferred to Pretoria, and then to Nylstroom, where the security police started their interrogation. She was questioned about Sibusiso Ndebele. Among the things he had been carrying when he was arrested was a parcel he had to deliver to Lindi. They grilled Lindi on the contents of the parcel, her contacts and the work they were doing. The police believed she was part of a group who had received training in the handling of explosives in Swaziland. They were also trying to prepare a case against Phindile Mfethi and wanted to get Lindi to be a state witness. She constantly asked the police why she was being held for so long without charges. "Sometimes I would be told they wanted to use me as a state witness against someone, they would not say who. Sometimes they would say they were holding me for interrogation."

At Nylstroom, she was subjected to further physical and mental torture. The police arranged for her to have a physical examination to see if she could stand trial. The doctor prescribed some tablets for her, and two hours later she had some kind of seizure: "By the end of the day my mouth was on one side of my face. It was such a traumatic experience. The only thing I knew of that could cause such a disfigurement of the face was a stroke and I could not understand how at that age I was having a stroke. I was scared out of my wits." Lindi refused to take the tablets again. They tied her hands behind her back and forced her to swallow them. After that, she refused to eat because she was convinced the police were trying to poison her.

The only respite she had in Nylstroom was a visit from Lungi and another from Nkuli and Sheila. To her great delight, Nkuli and Sheila brought Ayanda along with them. She marvelled at how her baby had grown, and what beautiful eyes she had.

According to the law, detainees had to be visited by a magistrate who then had to give a report to the Ministry of Justice. This was presumably to ensure that detainees were properly treated. Lindi was first visited by a magistrate on 28 June in John Vorster Square, shortly after she was assaulted. The report from the Magistrate's Office in Johannesburg to the Secretary of Justice said of this visit:

> I wish to inform you that the Magistrate Mr TC Henderson went to the police cells at John Vorster Square on 28 June 1976 to visit detainee Lindiwe Sisulu. He interviewed her. The magistrate reported that the detainee had no "complaints but requests that she be taken for X-rays for her lung". She was going for this when she was held for detention. Appears to be in good health.

Another report indicated that Lindi had demanded to see her baby and complained about being held indefinitely. On another occasion, she was reported to have requested a copy of the section under which she was detained. The other 15 or so reports record that she had no complaints. Reading these reports over two decades later, Lindi would note that they were mostly false, giving no indication of the pain and trauma she suffered, or her protests against her continued detention.

Initially, Albertina had not informed Walter about Lindi's detention because she was reluctant to upset him. After four months had passed without any sign that Lindi would be released, Albertina decided that she had to let Walter know what was happening:

> Lindi was arrested on 14 June. [Rest of sentence blacked out. One can only assume that it referred to the Soweto uprising.] She was taken to John Vorster Square in town. She was there only for two months. Beginning of August she was removed to Pretoria. She is now at Brits, still in Pretoria District on the way to Ermelo.

We understand she is arrested under Section 6 [the Terrorism Act]. She has not appeared in court as yet but defence has been arranged. We have not yet heard when she is going to appear in court. In these four months she has been seen once by Sheila and she says she is looking well, only worried about her baby. Though we are allowed to give her clothes to change we are not allowed to see her (Letter to Walter 7/10/76).

On Robben Island, the first indication of the drama of 16 June and its aftermath was a sudden deterioration in conditions. As always, the prison staff took out their anger about external political developments on the prisoners. There was a complete ban on news, pads of letters were blacked out, and if the uprising was even hinted at visits were arbitrarily curtailed.

Walter, in the meanwhile, was eagerly looking forward to a visit from Zwelakhe, scheduled for 6/11/76. After receiving Albertina's letter, he was anxious for further news about Lindi. When Zwelakhe arrived and greeted his father in Xhosa, the warder on duty ordered them to conduct their conversation in English because he could not understand Xhosa. Walter asked Zwelakhe how he was enjoying his work as a journalist. He then asked if there was any news about Lindi. Zwelakhe said there were no new developments. Walter then referred to the so-called independence of Transkei in a roundabout way by asking if a cousin in the Transkei who worked for SA Railway and Harbours would still be entitled to get free tickets now that he lived in a separate state. At this stage, the warder cut short the visit on the grounds that they were discussing a political issue.

Walter wrote an angry letter of complaint about the warder's conduct to the Commanding Officer. In the letter he defended their right to talk about the Transkei: "Both my wife and I were born and grew up in that area and despite my views on separate development, which are well known, I am interested to know my position and that of my family under the existing laws. It is my considered opinion that Warrant Officer Steenkamp acted arbitrarily and cancelled my visit while we were discussing a family matter. This was after I had spoken to my son for only about 20–25 minutes. I had last seen my son in 1972." He complained that it was not the first time Steenkamp had subjected him to that kind of treatment. "As you know I am serving a sentence of life imprisonment and have already served 15 years. It has been difficult to meet members of my family and my family is fairly large. They have to travel about a thousand miles at great expense to see me. I take a serious view of this matter and I place it before you in the hope that you will give this matter your urgent and prompt attention."

Mac Maharaj was part of the team responsible for smuggling newspapers and distributing news to fellow prisoners. One day he came across a report stating that Lindi Sisulu had been arrested, detained and severely tortured. Mac showed Walter the article:

I can never forget his reaction. I thought I had gone to console him with this bad news. His reaction was to say he was proud of his child. This was proof to him that she had grown up and developed a social consciousness that would necessarily keep her in the mainstream of struggle. What he had done was to shift from his mind the pain of the event and pull out of it something that would sustain him. That is how he approached all our problems. From the welter of painful incidents that belonged to a particular web, he would pull out a strand that would help you hold together (Talent Consortium Interview, Mac Maharaj).

Walter's brave reaction masked his anguish about Lindi's detention. He had never felt so helpless in his life. He took action by writing a long and powerful letter to the then Minister of Justice, Jimmy Kruger. Relentless in its argument and exhaustive in its detail, it was much more than a plea by a concerned parent; it was also a classic indictment of the practice of detention without trial in South Africa.

After setting out all the material facts of Lindi's situation, he launched into his analysis:

My concern, fear and anxiety about my daughter's wellbeing has been growing over the passage of time, weeks and months since her detention and there being no apparent end of her detention, I have reached the point where I am compelled to write this letter.

My fears and anxiety flow from what I believe to be the arbitrary action on the part of the security police which amounts to blatant abuses of power granted them under the Act 83 of 1967. It is necessary that I acquaint you with some detail of what I regard as abuse of power by the Security Police.

Although the Act purports to repose in the Commissioner of Police the power to release a Detainee if the latter answers questions to the satisfaction of the former or that no further purpose would be served in continuing the detention, it is generally known that in reality those powers vest in the security police alone ...

The increasing number of detainees who have died in detention, through causes other than normal, leaves me in no doubt that this shocking state of affairs is built in the entire system of detention and interrogation.

There have been allegations of torture or mistreatment ranging from crude physical assaults to highly sophisticated techniques and in many cases a combination of both. I may add at this stage that I have been actively engaged in politics for 40 years. My experience in the business of reporting, analysing and interpreting reports of various types has sufficiently equipped me to detect untruth, halftruths, exaggeration, etc.

Since my imprisonment I have interviewed a number of prisoners and received reports from many of them who have been through this machinery of arrest, detention, interrogation and conviction and sentence. I am satisfied that in general the security police do not hesitate to employ vicious methods both physical and psychological in order to extract confession from detainees.

It is not unknown that prisoners after months of detention are released unconditionally and without being charged or called as witnesses. It is equally not unknown that detainees who were charged were acquitted by the courts. In view of this, I am unable to pin my faith in this much-vaunted integrity or efficiency of the security police or on the assurance that innocent persons need not fear because of the provisions of the Act in question. As I believe from information by my fellow prisoners, persons are often kept in detention under this Act for purposes not contemplated by the Act nor authorised by it.

After extensive description of the illegal and heinous true purposes of detention without trial, both under apartheid and elsewhere under illegitimate regimes, Walter continued:

There is nothing in the Act or under Common Law that entitles the security police to behave as they do ... A detainee is both completely helpless and beyond any assistance. The fortnightly visits by a magistrate [were] apparently provided for to allay fears of maltreatment and purported to act as a check on the powers of the police. Most persons I have interviewed regard this visit as a farce. They found this official hostile ... and quite incapable of doing anything to alleviate their misery and wretched plight under detention.

I have gone to some length in setting out my belief in respect of abuses by the Security police not in order to condemn, but with a view to establishing the basis of my fear and anxiety. It matters little in the end if I am proved to be wrong. It is the present and the immediate future of the fate and wellbeing of my daughter, that I am concerned about.

Were I not a prisoner, I would have sought the support of my fellow citizens who cherish the Rule of Law and with a view of putting an end to this cruel state of affairs. As this is not open to me, I can turn only to you in your capacity as a Minister of Police and Justice to right the wrong and let the course of justice take its normal course as it would in any civilised society.

I fear for my daughter's wellbeing. Prolonged detention, especially in solitary confinement is bound to cause severe mental injury and as Lindiwe is only 23 years old, the damage may well be irreparable. Lindiwe and I have exchanged one letter each. Despite her attempt to be light-hearted, she nonetheless admitted experiencing acute depression over her daughter's plight. I place little reliance on her assurance that she is well or information from her visitors that she appears to be in high spirits. She and my family could do everything in their power to conceal any distressing news from me. As a prisoner of some 13 years I realise only too well how prisoners by tremendous effort present relaxed and smiling appearances to spare their loved ones pain.

In the event, I am without information about her treatment at the hands of the Security Police and I therefore fear and imagine the worst. Deaths have occurred through unnatural causes. Whether it was suicide or not matters little – what matters is that detainees here died through causes which are not natural. Should this ever happen to my daughter Lindiwe, I will lay her death at the doorstep of the Security Police and therefore, at yours, and in the last analysis blame the existing social system which has generated a conflict which is yet to claim many more lives on both sides.

I do not for a moment claim Lindiwe's innocence in terms of the law. Indeed, I have no information whatever in this respect and am therefore reduced to plain speculation. Perhaps she was involved in recent student demonstrations or with the African National Congress. Whatever her involvement, I ask that she be tried by the courts of the land if she has contravened any law. If she is a reluctant witness, the state has its remedies. If on the other hand she is innocent or if there is insufficient evidence to justify a prosecution, then let her be free to go to her mother and her child.

There are times when I believe that the sins of her parents are being visited on her head. The security police are not free from malice and improper motives.

Powerless as I am at present to come to my daughter's assistance in these trying days, I would be failing in my duty as a father to a daughter as one voteless and voiceless non-citizen to another and as one human being to another if I were to remain silent and not use my voice in protest at this outrage committed on my child.

I am in prison for only one reason – to do the utmost, my share in the process of releasing the nameless millions from this bondage. I have done this for over 40 years for people most of whom were unknown to me. By the same token, it is only natural that I do this for my own child.

I hope you will give this matter the urgent attention it deserves.

This passionate, yet reasoned communication was in many ways typical of the letters the Rivonia men were to write to the highest in the land. The tone was formal, dignified, upbraiding when necessary, and always logical. The rational intelligence and moral certitude of the author precluded any pleading, and the proper courtesies were always observed. Walter's legal arguments alone would have impressed Jimmy Kruger, a lawyer himself. Letters like these must have been unnerving reminders to the apartheid government that the "terrorists" they had jailed considered themselves the equal of anyone.

# Part Four

*1978–1989*

## Riding Out the Darkness

## FROM SIRENS KNUCKLES BOOTS AND OTHER EARLY POEMS

Somehow we survive
and tenderness, frustrated, does not wither.

Investigating searchlights rake
our naked unprotected contours;

over our heads the monolithic decalogue
of fascist prohibition glowers
and teeters for a catastrophic fall;

boots club the peeling door.

But somehow we survive
severance, deprivation, loss.

Patrols uncoil along the asphalt dark
hissing their menace to our lives,

most cruel, all our land is scarred with terror,
rendered unlovely and unlovable;
sundered are we and all our passionate surrender

but somehow tenderness survives.

DENNIS BRUTUS

*A Simple Lust. Collected Poems of South African Jail and Exile.*
Heinemann 1989, p4.

# *one*

The bureaucrats in the Department of Prisons took a dim view of Walter's letter concerning Lindi's detention, which was forwarded to them by the Commanding Officer of Robben Island. One of them wrote a comment on the covering note: "This is nothing more than an outcry against the security police and not worth the paper it has been written on" (Walter Sisulu, Prison Files). They decided not to pass the letter on to the Minister of Justice. Instead, it was handed to the security police and placed in Walter's file. It is difficult to say whether Walter's protest had any effect or whether a decision had already been taken to release Lindi. Whatever the case, on 13 May 1977 Lindi was taken from Nylstroom to Pretoria. She was given the pile of parcels that had been sent to her by her family and never passed on to her. Shortly after her arrival in Pretoria, to her great surprise, she was taken home – almost 11 months to the day after she had been detained.

There was great rejoicing at No. 7372 over Lindi's return. Albertina was relieved to have Lindi back, but was shocked by her physical condition: "She had lost so much weight and she looked pale and ill. I could see that she had been through a terrible experience." Albertina immediately arranged for Lindi to have a medical examination and set about nursing her back to health. She had the same concerns about Lindi that she had had about Max 14 years earlier. She knew that in the eyes of the security police, Lindi was a marked person and the chances of her being re-detained were high. The ANC was also concerned that the security police were still trying to build a case against her, and Lindi was advised to leave the country. Albertina agreed that this was the best course of action, even though the thought of losing another child to exile grieved her.

One of the first things Lindi did after her release was to apply to visit her father. The prison authorities forwarded her application to the security police with a note: "This office is aware that, because of her political activities, Sisulu was until recently still a detainee. This office is eager to know if, in view of this, your office has any objection to her visiting her father at this stage" (Walter Sisulu, Prison Files). The police replied that they had no objection to the visit. Lindi received her permit in June and made the trip to the Island to say goodbye. She managed to let Walter know in a roundabout way that she would be leaving soon. He was very encouraging and told her that he was thrilled to see his children engaging in struggle.

In June 1977, Lindi went to Mozambique via Swaziland. In Maputo she stayed with Ruth First, who was teaching at the Centre for African Studies at Eduardo Mondlane University. "Staying with Ruth was the best thing for me at the time," recalled Lindi. "Probably because of her own experience of torture and detention, Ruth knew exactly how to treat me. She never over fussed, but at the same time she was empathetic." Lindi's experiences in detention had strengthened her resolve to devote her life to the struggle, and from here she went to the Soviet Union for military training.

Lindi Sisulu was one of thousands of young people who went into exile in the wake of the 1976 upheavals. Most of them ended up in the ranks of the ANC. While new recruits injected the ANC with much-needed new blood, the influx created enormous logistical problems (Karis and Gerhart, 300). The ANC administration could scarcely keep up with ever-increasing numbers of recruits, most of whom were eager for military training. The camps in Zambia and Tanzania did not have the capacity to absorb large numbers of new recruits, so from 1977 onwards, military recruits were sent to the camps in Angola. Those who opted for academic training were sent to study in other African countries, as well as Cuba, the Soviet Union and East Germany. Max Sisulu was one of the members of the external ANC responsible for organising education and training for the new arrivals.

Inside South Africa, Albertina was actively involved in facilitating the departure of many young people. The post-1976 period offered new opportunities for mobilisation not only among the youth, but among women as well. Albertina experienced a change in the attitude of many women who had previously shunned her: "Some women, especially the church women, were so afraid of me, except those who were my own personal friends. There were women who used to call me a jail-bird and were afraid to be in my company because they were afraid to go to jail. After 1976, all that changed because now they knew what had happened to their children and who the enemy was. They would come to me and say 'Mama, what must we do now?' Our organisation of women became very strong after 1976."

Sowetans commemorated the first anniversary of the June 16 uprising at Regina Mundi Church in Rockville, Soweto. Speakers mourned those who had died and lamented the fact that despite their sacrifice, little had changed.

The government had dropped the controversial ruling on teaching in Afrikaans, but it had been too little, too late. From now on, black youth (and a small but significant section of white youth) would be satisfied with nothing less than the removal of apartheid. The power of the South African state was still unshaken, but the events of 16 June had dramatically altered the political landscape. The genesis of youth-based resistance and the concomitant political unrest had shaken black society to its foundation (Steve Mokwena, Unpublished notes).

Robben Island also felt the impact of the new generation when a flood of new prisoners poured in towards the end of 1976. A couple of months after the uprising, the Robben Island prisoners still had no clear idea of what had happened and dismissed some of the reports coming through to them as wild rumour. One of the more fanciful stories doing the rounds was that Soweto students had caused SADF soldiers to drop their guns and run (Mandela, 574). Eric Molobi, a Black Consciousness activist who had been severely tortured during a long prison spell, gave the Islanders a more accurate account of events when he arrived in August 1976 (Sampson 2000, 273). Molobi was followed by an influx of new prisoners, many of them Black Consciousness activists. Others were young MK cadres who had left the country for military training and had been captured on their return. There were also high-school students who knew plenty about street demonstrations, but little about politics.

The large majority of the new prisoners were sent to the general section, but some of them were placed in the cells adjoining the B section, in what came to be known as the A section. The whole isolation section complex was blocked off around 1977 and a wall was built outside to create a new section. A wall also blocked a passage that linked the two buildings. These walls prevented the isolation section prisoners from making contact with the new arrivals in "A section". The "SASO Nine", who included Saths Cooper, Strini Moodley, Patrick "Terror" Lekota, Pandelani Nefolovhodwe and Rubin Hare, were placed in this section after they arrived on the Island in December 1976. Later in 1977 they were joined by Tokyo Sexwale and Naledi Tsiki, two young MK cadres who had trained in the Soviet Union. They had been captured on their return to South Africa and tried with ANC veterans Joe Gqabi, Peter Nchabeleng, Martin Ramokgadi and student leaders Super Moloi, Murphy Morobe and Billy Masethla in what was known as the trial of the "Pretoria 12". Gqabi and Nchabeleng were acquitted, and the others were sentenced to terms on Robben Island. It was Ramokgadi's second spell of imprisonment on the Island. Harry Gwala also returned to the Island to serve a second sentence after he was tried and convicted in Pietermaritzburg for his role in reviving the ANC underground in Natal. Black Consciousness activists Khehla Shubane, Eric Molobi and Amos Masondo were also placed in this section.

For many of the new prisoners, like Soweto activist Sifiso Buthelezi, Robben Island was a place where their heroes were kept: "We really equated Robben Island with freedom" (Sampson 2000, 276). But not everybody revered the Robben Island veterans in this way. In fact, some of the new prisoners looked down at the "old guard" for what they perceived to be their cooperation with the prison authorities. As Kathrada recalled: "A lot of these chaps were not too friendly to us. They came with all sorts of perceptions. Some of them had the attitude that we knew nothing. In fact, they had the same attitude that the Unity Movement group had when they came in – that we were just stooges of the white man." Under the influence of Mandela, Sisulu and the Rivonia prisoners, Neville Alexander and his group had come round to the view that constant confrontation was unproductive and "negotiations, patient discussions and persuasion" were often more effective ways of dealing with the authorities. This did not mean accepting ill-treatment: "No semblance of servility [was] tolerated. Rudeness [was] rebutted as firmly as possible" (Sampson 2000, 277).

The new prisoners interpreted this approach as collaboration with the enemy. According to Saths Cooper, the SASO leaders were surprised by the amicable relations between prisoners and warders. "Our attitude was that we would have no truck with the enemy. Because we came from a background which meant not compromising with the enemy, we expected that the others should have the same attitude." The SASO leaders totally refused to cooperate with the prison authorities, and would greet other prisoners with a clenched fist. They also challenged a basic prison practice of keeping the lights on and got away with it. As Saths Cooper explained:

When we got to the section in 77/78, they had these fluorescent tubes and they were very bright. We would put our hand through the window and switch the light off. The night warder would then switch it on again. We would switch it off and so on. The head of the prison came to see us because he started getting complaints. We told him it was affecting our eyes. Eventually he agreed to allow us to have the lights off.

When they were put to work in the quarry, they downed tools when one of their number was injured. The warders set dogs onto them, there was a skirmish and Saths Cooper, Strini Moodley and Aubrey Mokoape were put into isolation for several months (Interview, Saths Cooper). Confrontation between the young prisoners and warders became a daily occurrence. The young men would refuse to raise their caps to the warders, and if the warders touched them, they would punch them back.

The veterans were bemused by the belligerent young radicals and disturbed to discover that they were regarded as old and conservative. Mandela said "To be perceived as a moderate was a novel and not altogether pleasant feeling". Mosibudi Mangena wrote: "Although some of us were young, we suddenly found ourselves looking old and moderate. Even the firebrand Harry Gwala felt that the behaviour of the young prisoners was sometimes anarchic" (Sampson 2000, 277).

The older prisoners also felt that some of the Black Consciousness leaders were arrogant. "One of them tried to tell us that they have a card-holding membership of two million!" recalled Kathrada. "Now even though we were in jail we wouldn't believe that type of nonsense. Secondly, he tried to tell us that the *amandla* salute originated with them. This was a lot of nonsense because when we were sentenced we were already saluting people with *amandla*." To their credit, the older leaders were philosophical about this behaviour and did not take offence. In his 1978 analysis of the Black Consciousness movement, Mandela wrote: "It is the prerogative of youth to exaggerate the importance of their organisation and to flex their muscles for everything under the sun just as we did in our younger days. They will probably mellow with time" (Maharaj, 38). There was a sense of admiration in his description of the trial of the SASO Nine:

It was a show trial full of fireworks. In the tradition of all freedom fighters, the accused carried the fight to the enemy, even inside his own den. They entered the awe-inspiring court packed with police, singing freedom songs, showing the fist, shouting "Amandla", even exchanging blows with the police. At one stage they dispensed with their lawyers, conducted their own defence and asked the presiding judge to recuse himself. They used the court as a platform from which to explain their views to the people of South Africa (Maharaj, 33).

Despite the efforts made to keep them separate, the two groups started interacting with each other. At first, this was through smuggled notes and messages. They also had some contact through Kathrada. The new prisoners did not have a library in their section, so Kathrada (who was the librarian for the isolation section) was allowed to take books to them until they were given their own library. (Khehla Shubane eventually became the librarian in A section.)

In October 1977, Aubrey Mokoape, Strini Moodley and Saths Cooper succeeded in bringing a court action before the Supreme Court, which forced the prison authorities to release them from isolation. At this point, they were put into the isolation section with the older prisoners. According to Saths Cooper's account, the interaction was mutually beneficial:

> When we got there we were inundated with non-stop questions, all manner of questions. Appointments were made to discuss issues. Madiba and I had an appointment to discuss why Coloureds, Indians and Africans should be in one organisation. There was also a socialisation period when Madiba was at pains to point out the customs, such as how people are addressed in a traditional Xhosa background. He used the example of a prisoner who did not understand these customs and upset some of the peasants from Transkei by calling them by their first names. All of us addressed them using terms of respect such as "Ntate". We also used nicknames as an endearment. In the case of Walter it was Nokwindla or Tyhopo.

Whatever upheavals they caused in prison life, Walter enjoyed the company of the young people. He felt that they brought fresh and interesting perspectives and their views had to be taken seriously. He was not the only one. Mandela invited Saths Cooper and Strini Moodley to give lectures to the older prisoners about Black Consciousness. Kathrada also enjoyed the discussions they had with the younger prisoners. "Strini and them were very good in their ability to understand and analyse things like films, much better than [us]. These were very enjoyable discussions and we learned a lot from them." One day they watched the film *The Wild One*, featuring Marlon Brando. The older prisoners apparently condemned the bikers, while Strini Moodley identified with their rebellious spirit, likening it to the spirit of the Soweto uprising (Sampson 2000, 285). For men of their generation, the ANC prisoners remained remarkably open to the views of their young compatriots, even on issues that shocked them. An example of this open-mindedness was described by Ahmed Kathrada:

> In 1972 or so came a young chap, called Salim Essop, a fourth-year medical student who worked with Ahmed Timol, who had been killed by the police. Essop was a very bright young fellow who spoke intellectually about homosexuality. It was the first time Madiba and Tyhopo were ever confronted with a political argument on homosexuality. Madiba asked Salim to write a document on homosexuality that we also sent to the general cells.

The willingness of the senior prisoners to listen to the younger ones paid dividends, and the former slowly began to exert their influence over the new arrivals by demonstrating that confrontation and retaliation were not always the most effective forms of action. Most warders relished using a full range of obscenities to address the prisoners. There was one particular warder who would always swear at Eric Molobi and laugh when Molobi responded. One day, Walter pointed out to him that by swearing back, he was lowering himself to the warder's level. "Why do you think he laughs at you? It's because warders are the vermin of the Afrikaners, and like to see you come down to their level. Why don't you try not swearing back?" Molobi followed Walter's advice, and the warder stopped provoking him (Sampson 2000, 279).

Gradually the dignity and commitment of the veterans had a sobering effect on the young lions. They came to see that persuasion and negotiation with the enemy did not mean selling out, and that the battles fought by the older prisoners made life easier for everyone. While some of the young people did not always see eye-to-eye with the old guard, they grew to respect and admire them. As with earlier groups of prisoners, Walter was regarded with particular affection by the younger prisoners. Saths Cooper sums up the assessment of Walter's character expressed by past prisoners:

> Of that group – the Rivonia Trialists – he was the one who was able to cross divides between groups and to relate to younger people in their own medium. There was no paternalistic relationship. He was also very affable and never really took exception. He ended up being, in my opinion, the one who was always called upon to mediate, to intercede, to reduce tensions and tempers, not only between political organisations but also within the ANC ranks. It was clear that he was the one who was always creating bridges so that whatever schisms existed, they were not given the opportunity to erupt. When things got tough, his intercession was crucial. He was the person who poured oil on troubled waters.

It is interesting to compare this with how the prison management regarded Walter. In 1967, the Prisons' Board reported: "This man appears at long last to have become more tolerant and understanding. He will never change his political views, but he seems to at last have realised that no one is persecuting him. He is one of the die-hards, but at least an intelligent one." In 1969 they thought his behaviour was "satisfactory", but in 1971, during Badenhorst's reign of terror (when Walter was one of those at the forefront of resistance by the prisoners), it was reported that his behaviour was poor: "Under no conditions will he submit to discipline. He is rebellious and a bad influence on fellow prisoners." A report in March 1973 described him as having "a cunning disposition", but went on to add "acts courteously towards members and gives no problems at all". In August 1973, he was reported to be a "good worker who can be trusted". In 1975 he was described as: "Quite elderly, quiet disposition – a poor worker and will not tire himself much. He still firmly believes in the activities of the ANC and believes in a communist government." The 1976 report said: "He is one of the prisoners who is very underhanded – appears to be quiet. Asks why his daughter-in-law doesn't visit him anymore. Asks for permission to appeal to Commissioner i.r.o. studies that were not approved. He is a consummate communist who will never alter his view." It was also reported that "all meetings are usually held in his cell" (Prisons' Board reports; Walter Sisulu, Prison Files). Although the attitudes to Walter varied over the years, depending on the different Commanding Officers and warders, he was respected (albeit grudgingly) for two things: his consistency and his influence over the other prisoners.

In apartheid South Africa, it was not uncommon for detained political activists to die while in police custody. After the death of Looksmart Ngudle (the first political detainee to die in custody) in 1964, detainees died with a sickening regularity: Suliman "Babla" Saloojee in September 1964; Solomon Modipane in February 1969; Ahmed Timol in October 1971; George Botha in December 1976; Phakamile Mabija in June 1977 – the list goes on and on. If the security police were to be believed, detainees in South Africa had a remarkable propensity for throwing themselves out of windows of high-rise buildings (especially Room 1026 of John Vorster Square), slipping in showers and banging their heads against walls or falling down flights of stairs.

The death of Steve Bantu Biko at the hands of the security police on 12 September 1977 was one of the most sinister examples of this pattern. The then Minister of Justice, Jimmy Kruger, at first claimed that Biko had died as a result of a hunger strike. However, this was belied by the shocking photographs illicitly taken of Biko's battered body, and the police had to find another explanation. They subsequently resorted to one of their standard explanations: that Biko had died after banging his head against a wall while police were trying to subdue him during a scuffle. Despite the weight of evidence suggesting police brutality, the verdict reached at the inquest was no different from those given in other inquests into the deaths of detainees – no one was to blame. But Biko's death was different. He was the most prominent South African leader to die in detention, and his inquest was carried out in the full glare of international publicity. It was in effect "a trial of the South African system in the court of world opinion" (Karis and Gerhart, 315).

Biko's death was followed on 19 October 1977 by the banning of 18 more Black Consciousness and related organisations. These included SASO, BCM, the SSRC, SASM, the National Youth Organisation (NAYO) and various provincial youth organisations, the Christian Institute and other cultural organisations. Reverend Beyers Naudé (an anti-apartheid Afrikaner and head of the Christian Institute) and East London-based editor Donald Woods (who was responsible for the pictures of Biko's body that had horrified the world) were banned, and over 50 leaders of the banned organisations were detained (Karis and Gerhart, 316). Among these were all the members of the Soweto Committee of Ten, which, since its formation in June 1977, was regarded as the legitimate local government of the people of Soweto (Karis and Gerhart, 332).

While black South Africans mourned the loss of a great son of Africa, and the international community expressed outrage at the new wave of repression, the white electorate returned the National Party to power by the largest majority ever in the all-white elections of November 1977.

The Black Consciousness activists, Soweto community leaders and student leaders detained in the October crackdown were all held at Modderbee prison in the East Rand. The fact that they were not put into solitary confinement but held in large communal cells housing about 20 prisoners each, gave them the opportunity to debate the key political questions of the day. Most Modderbee "graduates" felt fortified and enriched by this period of enforced reflection and analysis. The apartheid state had once again closed down all avenues of political activity (as it had done after Sharpeville) and activists had to ask themselves, "where to next?"

Meanwhile Black Consciousness activists who had not been arrested in the October crackdown were busy forming the Azanian People's Organisation (AZAPO). This new organisation, launched in Roodepoort in April 1978, departed slightly from its Black Consciousness roots in that it "defined apartheid as not merely a form of racial oppression but also as a form of class domination". Black workers were considered to be the vanguard of the revolution because of their position at the intersection of racial and class domination (Frederickson, 310). The establishment of the new organisation was disrupted when most of its leaders were detained within weeks of its formation. After their release, they regrouped and together with colleagues who had by then been released from Modderbee, they relaunched AZAPO in September 1979 (Karis and Gerhart, 325).

Two broad camps had emerged from the lengthy debates on future political strategy. Both groups acknowledged the need for a new organisational and strategic response to increasing state repression and both felt the need to incorporate class analysis into this response. However, they differed on whether the response should be an organisation in the Black Consciousness tradition or one that had a national democratic approach (Seekings, 35; Marx, 96; Karis and Gerhart, 317–8). Those who wanted to continue in the Black Consciousness tradition joined AZAPO. Others favoured a democratic and nonracial approach based on the Freedom Charter. This approach was eventually to find organisational expression in the United Democratic Front (UDF). Curtis Nkondo, a former Soweto school principal and chair of the Soweto Teachers' Action Committee, has been quoted as saying the preparations for the formation of the UDF began at Modderbee (Seekings, 35). Although he was no strong adherent of the Black Consciousness movement, Nkondo was invited by founder members of AZAPO to become its first president – no doubt because of his influence among teachers and students in Soweto. His tenure as president lasted only a few months, his obvious ANC sympathies making his position untenable, and he was suspended in 1980. His suspension widened the rift between Black Consciousness and pro-ANC activists (Karis and Gerhart, 324).

Similar ideological and organisational tensions between Black Consciousness and ANC camps were playing out on Robben Island. The ANC leadership was anxious to avoid conflict and to promote unity, so it did not encourage recruitment of prisoners from other ideological camps. Nevertheless, some of the young Black Consciousness prisoners were attracted to the ANC. Terror Lekota was one of them: "He took a great interest in me and we communicated through smuggled notes. He had great respect for me but he was almost impossible to control," recalled Walter (Houser and Shore, 168). After an exchange of correspondence with Mandela and Sisulu, Lekota decided to join the ANC. They both tried to discourage him, with Walter telling him the time was not ripe, but he was adamant. As they had predicted, Lekota's move did create tension. His BC colleagues ostracised him and some of them, angered by what they saw as his desertion from the ranks, staged an assault on him. One of them hit him over the head with a garden fork, and his attackers were charged with assault by the prison authorities. On the advice of Mandela, Lekota refused to testify, so the charges had to be dropped (Houser and Shore, 168; Sampson 2000, 280; Karis and Gerhart, 298).

Ironically, Lekota's assailant was one of a significant number of Black Consciousness prisoners who followed Lekota into the ANC. According to one study, out of the 31 arrivals in 1976, 25 joined the ANC, five remained aligned with the Black Consciousness movement, and one joined the PAC. "That such a dramatic transfer of allegiances did not involve more open conflict among these groups can be attributed to the mutual respect among these prisoners, united by their common opposition to the regime despite their own ideological differences. But the overriding effect of imprisonment on Robben Island, as at Modderbee, was to achieve a resurgence of support for the ANC and a rededication to continued opposition among the generation of activist leaders who had earlier launched the BC movement" (Marx, 98).

The ANC veterans were shocked at how little the young prisoners knew of the history of black resistance, and the informal political education courses, especially those on the history of the ANC, assumed a new importance. Many of the young prisoners were especially interested in Walter's life story, and he received many enquiries about various aspects of his political career. Perhaps it was this interest that prompted the commissioning of Walter's memoirs by Mandela, Kathrada and Laloo Chiba. Mac Maharaj had smuggled out Mandela's biography when he had been released in 1976. Mandela, Kathrada and Chiba felt that it was a matter of historical urgency and necessity that Walter's memoirs should also be written, given the crucial role he played in the struggle. Mike Dingake's imminent release would provide the opportunity to smuggle out the document. Because of Walter's problems with his eyesight and his famously illegible handwriting, it was decided that Walter should tell his story to Mike Dingake and Chiba.

Walter was happy about the decision and Dingake and Chiba spent every minute of their free time interviewing him. "Walter's memory was very sharp," recalled Chiba. "He had one of the most excellent memories of anyone I knew. He answered the questions with no hesitation, completely off the cuff. We drew a family tree ... as a first step towards writing his life history." They worked mainly over weekends and when work was cancelled because of bad weather. Dingake and Chiba would make their own notes during each interview; later, they would compare and combine these into one set of notes. They would then circulate these notes to Walter, Mandela and Kathrada for corrections and suggestions. Next they would revise the notes, incorporating the comments and suggestions. Just as he had done with Mandela's memoir, Chiba would then rewrite the final copy in tiny handwriting, about 2 000 words on a single sheet of paper slightly larger than an A5 page. Every evening, Chiba would hide the day's notes in a cupboard in the recreation hall. By removing one of its panels, and creating a hollow, they were able to remove the panel, insert the pages, and seal the panel again. The hiding-place proved to be secure and the manuscript remained safely tucked away until Mike Dingake smuggled it out in a photo album when he was released in May 1981 (Interview, Laloo Chiba).

Once Mac Maharaj had successfully smuggled out Mandela's biography on his release at the end of 1976, his colleagues had had to dispose of the original text. Mandela, Walter, Kathrada and Eddie Daniels divided the bulky manuscript into three sections, wrapped them in plastic, put them into three plastic containers and buried them in three separate places in the courtyard (Mandela, 568–72; Meredith, 320; Sampson 2000, 242). One day, Mandela woke up to find a work crew digging up the courtyard – it had been decided to build a wall in front of the isolation section. He alerted his colleagues, and they managed to retrieve two of the containers, but the third was discovered.

Unbeknown to Walter and his comrades, the prison authorities had also stumbled across a copy of one of the earlier drafts of his memoir, possibly while it was circulating among the prisoners. The discovery of the Sisulu and Mandela manuscripts kept the prison bureaucrats busy for a while. The "undesirable documents", as they were referred to by the prison authorities, were sent to the police graphologists in Cape Town who confirmed that the authors were Mandela and Sisulu. The documents were then summarised and analysed, then sent to the Commissioner of Prisons. In a Memorandum to the Minister of Prisons dated 7 November 1977, the Commissioner wrote:

> Subsequent to my memorandum in which the memoirs of Nelson Mandela were submitted to you, similar memoirs of Walter Sisulu are attached hereto also for your information ...
>
> The document is relatively disconnected and one gets the impression that it is not altogether complete ... The first page thereof deals with the founding of the refreshment station at the Cape in 1652 and the ensuing trek into the interior. Sisulu sees this trek ... as a deliberate attempt of the authorities to oppress and to dominate the native population.
>
> The rest of document deals with the establishment of the ANC, the early history thereof and the attempts that were made to co-ordinate the different black national movements under one organisation. The role of the South African Communist Party is also mentioned. Naturally Sisulu's role is also described. In fact, the whole document can be seen as a "memoir" of Walter Sisulu.
>
> As in Mandela's case, I do not believe that it will serve any purpose to prosecute him for this. In any case he is serving a life sentence for the same offences and nothing can be added to his sentence. I am however considering to also withdraw his study privileges permanently as he used study material for the composition of the memoirs.
>
> I am eager to know if you agree with my intended action. (Walter Sisulu, Prison Files)

The minister did agree, and at the end of 1977, Walter, Mandela and Kathrada (whose writing had also been identified on the manuscripts) were summoned before General Roux, the Deputy Commissioner of Prisons. He travelled all the way to Robben Island to inform them personally of their punishment: their study privileges had been suspended indefinitely (Mandela, 571).

The irony was that after all this, neither Walter nor Mandela's memoirs were published as planned. Once Dingake had handed Walter's story over to Tambo in Lusaka, it was given to Mac Maharaj, who embarked on the laborious task of rewriting Laloo's miniscule notes and having these typed up. Unfortunately, he was deployed before finishing the job, and the project was shelved, at first temporarily and then indefinitely. The truth was that ANC members in Lusaka were soldiers and politicans, not writers and researchers. Unlike their compatriots on the Island, they had no periods of enforced inactivity, and were always busy. They underestimated the time (and costs) any publishing project involves; they were also concerned about the repercussions publication might bring to the imprisoned authors.

Zwelakhe Sisulu would always remember June 1976 as one of the most dreadful periods of his life, yet it also marked a great leap forward in his professional development. He had started his newspaper career in August 1975 as one of the first black trainee journalists for South African Associated Newspapers. He had been seconded to the *Rand Daily Mail* from January to July 1976, which meant that he covered the Soweto uprisings. His next assignment was with the

*Eastern Province Herald* from August to December 1976; he arrived in Port Elizabeth just as the unrest started in that city.

For Zwelakhe and for many other black journalists, 1976 was a turning point in their careers. Zwelakhe recalls that before 1976, the black media was dominated by sports and sex: "Black journalists were known as people who did not focus on the real concerns of black people ... But [events in 1976] gave black journalists the opportunity to take stock of themselves and this they did" (Article 19 pamphlet). White journalists could not venture into the turbulent townships, so it was the black journalists who had to cover the violent confrontations between the police and students.

Black journalists and photographers shot into the limelight for their often courageous coverage of events, but they paid a heavy price for their new-found fame. Sam Nzima, the photographer who took the famous June 16 picture of Hector Petersen, was so badly harassed by the security police that he was forced to give up his promising photographic career and retire into obscurity. It was not uncommon for photographers to have their jaws and noses broken and their cameras confiscated by the police. In 1976 alone, 16 journalists were detained, more than in any previous year. Most of those detained were black journalists from the *World*, South Africa's second-largest newspaper with a circulation of 140 000. Percy Qoboza, editor of the *World*, was detained until March 1978. Joe Thloloe, a feature writer for the *World* and president of the Union of Black Journalists (UBJ), was detained for 547 days (Carolyn Dempster, "Tight Shackles on SA's Black Press", *The Star*, 21/2/83). In the October 1977 crackdown, the *World* and *Weekend World*, both owned by the Argus Group, were closed down and the UBJ was among the organisations that were banned.

Zwelakhe shared the resentment felt by many of his journalist colleagues: that after risking life and limb to do their jobs, they continued to be discriminated against by most newspapers. Freelance photographers used their own equipment. Their employers only supplied transport, so they suffered severe setbacks when the police confiscated or smashed their cameras. "Even at the *Rand Daily Mail* with all its liberal tradition, most black journalists were freelancers who were paid on the basis of the length of their story. Another area of resentment was that most newspapers continued to treat black journalists as legmen – people who would go out and get the information for the white journalist sitting in the newsroom to put together. In writing these stories, the white journalist would want to lead with the police version of events, which was almost always complete fabrication" (Interview, Zwelakhe Sisulu).

The *Rand Daily Mail* management faced a predicament: should they tell the truth at the risk of being closed down, or strike a middle path and try not to antagonise the security establishment? In order to survive, they chose the latter. Zwelakhe understood this at an intellectual level, but had difficulty accepting it. For black journalists, it was a very emotional issue. They were observing police brutality first-hand, so it was difficult for them to accept publishing watered-down versions of the truth. Black journalists also resented the practice of publishing stories under block bylines. They were disturbed at having their names put to stories that were distorted or toned down because they risked becoming targets of anger within their communities for not writing the truth.

Journalists felt it imperative to have their own organisation to address these and other grievances, so after the October 1977 banning of UBJ, they immediately replaced it with another organisation: the Writers' Association of South Africa (WASA). On 30 November 1977, WASA organised a march to protest against the arrest of a number of black journalists. Zwelakhe was arrested and charged with participating in an unlawful procession. He was found guilty and fined R100 or 50 days' imprisonment.

In July 1978, Zwelakhe was elected president of WASA, a position that would place him at the forefront of resistance against apartheid repression of the media and mark his emergence as a national political figure. In the same year, he was offered the position of news editor at the *Sunday Post*, the new Argus-owned paper that, together with *The Post*, replaced the banned *Weekend World* and *World*. He hesitated about leaving the *Rand Daily Mail*. Despite his criticisms of the liberal

establishment, he loved working there and believed it was the best possible professional environment for a journalist. When he had started working there, he had felt for the first time in his life
that he was in a truly intellectual environment. "I had the benefit of working with exceptionally talented people like the editor Raymond Louw, who was outstanding as a white editor in the context
of his times, and people like Peter Wellman and Chris Day. The photographer Peter Magubane was
also a source of great inspiration to us. It was a marvel to see him do his work in very dangerous
situations without much care for his safety."

Zwelakhe consulted his colleagues at the *Rand Daily Mail* about *The Sunday Post* offer. Their
view was that it was an opportunity not to be missed; for a black person to be given the opportunity to be a news editor at the age of 28 was quite unusual. Zwelakhe also felt that he would have
more opportunities for political engagement at *The Sunday Post*.

The year 1978 was a turning point for Zwelakhe not only professionally, but personally as well.
In December of that year, he married Zodwa Mdladlamba. Zodwa's family lived in the same neighbourhood as the Sisulus, and Zwelakhe had met her in 1969 while she was house-sitting for a friend
of his who was in detention. Albertina applied for permission to attend their wedding but received
no response from the magistrate, so she remained at home while the rest of the family attended the
reception at the YMCA in Dube. As had been the case with Lungi and Sheila's wedding, a letter
found in the Ministry of Justice files many years later gave Albertina permission to attend the wedding provided she did not make any speeches and adhered to her restriction orders. One can only
speculate as to why these letters were not passed on – malice, indifference or inefficiency could all
have played a role.

In its attempts to reverse African urbanisation, the Department of Bantu Administration stopped
building houses in Soweto in 1967. As a result, there was a critical shortage of housing in Soweto
throughout the 1970s (Bonner and Segal, 70). It became increasingly difficult for young married
couples to get houses of their own, so they usually had to live with their parents. After their marriage, Zwelakhe and Zodwa lived with Albertina while looking for a place of their own.

Albertina and Walter always saw marriage as proof of maturity and stability, so they were approv-
ing of Zwelakhe's marriage. Albertina was fond of Zodwa's family and Walter knew Zodwa's uncle,
the veteran PAC leader Selby Mdladlamba.

They were further delighted to learn that Lindi and her fiancé Xolile had set a date for their wedding, which took place in May 1979. Since she had completed her training abroad and returned to
Swaziland, Lindi was able to call home regularly. Around the time Lindi started phoning her family, they noticed strange sounds in the background whenever she rang and her calls were often cut
in mid-conversation. One day while spring cleaning, Nkuli noticed a strange device on the telephone plug. She called Lungi to look at it and they recalled that a group of telephone technicians
had recently come to the house to "fix" the phone. They concluded that the so-called technicians
were probably security police who had bugged the telephone. They gave the device to the family
lawyer, Priscilla Jana (Interview, Lungi Sisulu).

Zodwa had her first taste of harassment at the hands of the security police when they raided the
house one night looking for Lindi. "We wondered why 12 huge aggressive policemen had to come
looking for one slightly built woman and we shuddered to think of what would have happened if
she had been at home." Security police harassment aside, the family proceeded with wedding
arrangements and those members who could travel made the journey to Swaziland. From Robben
Island, Walter wrote to congratulate Lindi on her marriage and expressed excitement about seeing
pictures of his son-in-law for the first time.

Albertina's happiness about the marriage was tinged with sadness because it meant that her
granddaughter Ayanda had to leave to live with her parents in Swaziland. Walter understood how
difficult it was for Albertina to part with the grandchild she had taken care of since birth, and tried
to console her. On their wedding anniversary in July 1979, he wrote to express his appreciation of
her success in raising their children and keeping the family together:

Darling
I think this is the date on which we got married 35 years ago. I was certain of this date until I slid my pen on the paper when I began to have some doubt whether it was the 15 or 17 July. All these years I was sure but now?

Your welcome and most moving letter has had the desired effects ... It was not the volume that mattered, it was the quality, deep emotion and sincere expression of love which left an everlasting impression and kindled the fondest memories. I shall forever treasure it. I shall always imagine you in that excellent and fine spirit which it so vividly depicted ...

Concerning the progress you have made with regard to family matters and the manner in which you have handled them, I can only repeat what I have said in the past – absolutely superb. I have never felt as comfortable as I am. I am really happy about all the children. It is true I would have wanted the highest possible education but I think they will certainly make up for it. I was happy when there was a reunion of the children four years ago and now with Lakhe and Lindi all seems to be very well.

Now darling let me have the photos of the two girls at least. You know in fact that I want the photos of all of you including my bakhozi. Your last photo was taken by Mthetwa or Cuthbert Mawana 12 years ago. Can you believe that? Have you any photo of Max there? Please send me a duplicate of it. I know you would not want to part with it.

What are your plans about Nkuli? ... Let her not miss the chance of a university while she is still interested. By the way Tini, she needs your attention and guidance on her love affairs. I know you think she has no boyfriends. She has told me that she has one. We ought to know what kind of boy he is even if there is nothing serious at this stage; at least it is a way of educating them.

With love to you and the children and a million kisses to my beloved Ntsiki.
Ever loving Walter.

Albertina's third banning order expired two weeks after their wedding anniversary. Like clockwork, the security police turned up on 1 August 1979 with a new set of restrictions. Albertina was resigned to her banning orders being constantly renewed and she supposed that she should be thankful for small mercies because this time she was restricted for only two years, instead of the customary five-year ban. In a letter to the Director-General of Justice, the security police gave their motivations for the new set of restrictions:

Compol now reports that she is not drawing too much attention to herself presently, but recommends that she should be prohibited from attending any gathering for a further period of two years. Compol makes this suggestion in view of her previous activities and informs that she continues her contact with ANC suspects and has the potential to once again bring about a link between the ANC here and abroad which can bring about a revival of the organisation.

Although her activities have decreased in the past five years, she remains in contact with ANC suspects, and it is assumed that she will continue her activities if she should be unrestricted. Before being restricted she was extremely active in addressing and attending meetings. As a preventative measure it is recommended that she should be forbidden to attend any gathering in terms of Section 9 (1) of the Act on Internal Security 1950. She is a good speaker and has the potential of having a large following among the Blacks. A ban in terms of Section 9 (1) of the Act on Internal Security will prevent her from attending any gathering including social gatherings which should, in large measure, restrict her liberty ... She will nevertheless have to be watched closely with a view to stricter restrictions should she abuse the opportunity and intensify her undermining activities (Compol memo, Ministry of Justice files on Albertina Sisulu).

Albertina was not the only Sisulu under scrutiny. Once he became president of WASA, the security police showed an increasing interest in Zwelakhe. In July 1979 he was subpoenaed to give evidence against fellow journalist Thami Mkhwanazi, who had been charged under the Terrorism Act. The evidence he was supposed to give centred on two telephone conversations he had had with Mkhwanazi that had obviously been tapped.

Zwelakhe decided to consult Priscilla Jana, a Black Consciousness activist who had just set up a practice. "He was one of my first clients," Jana recalled. "The subpoena had put him into a very difficult position because there was no way he was going to testify against his friend, but ... it meant he would probably have to go to jail for five years from something quite peripheral. We agonised over it terribly for days, weeks. Zwelakhe was extremely concerned about the effect that a long prison sentence would have on his mother and on Zodwa. Eventually we got Ismail Mohamed, who was then an advocate, to represent him. As everybody knows, Mohamed was a brilliant advocate and he did a very good job of Zwelakhe's defence" (Interview, Priscilla Jana, 5/9/96).

When he appeared in court, Zwelakhe refused to answer questions about the telephone conversations, firstly on the grounds that this might incriminate him. Secondly, he argued that he had participated in the conversations in his capacity as a journalist and it was contrary to journalistic ethics for him to reveal details of the conversations. The prosecutor dismissed these arguments and sentenced Zwelakhe to nine months in prison. He was released on bail pending his appeal, and on 5 May 1980 the sentence was set aside. The appeal judge ruled that the magistrate who had imposed the sentence had erred in his findings, and the case was referred back to the same magistrate. Zwelakhe went back to court on 14 November 1980 on which date the magistrate accepted that his evidence was no longer necessary or valid. Meanwhile Thami Mkhwanazi had been found guilty and sentenced to imprisonment on Robben Island.

During the 1950s, when Joe Gqabi was a young journalist for *New Age*, he was a frequent visitor at the Sisulu home and his interaction with Walter continued on Robben Island. After his release from prison in 1976, Gqabi became a powerful influence on young Soweto activists. Zwelakhe was one of those who came under his influence. He had recollections of Gqabi visiting their home in the 1950s. "Joe was one of those people among adults who always had time for us kids, so when he came out, I certainly felt 'Here is a person to whom I can relate'. A lot of the people who came out of Robben Island before Joe were very cautious and in the initial stages of their release they wanted to avoid political activity. Many of us young people found that extremely frustrating, because we were desperate for authentic ANC leadership. When Joe was released, he attracted the young activists like moths to a flame because he was a brilliant tactician. In 1976 the Soweto student leaders seldom made a move without consulting him."

After he was acquitted in the trial of the Pretoria 12 in 1978, Gqabi revived his contacts with young activists and was at the centre of a network that included Zwelakhe, Jabu Ngwenya, Popo Molefe, Oupa Monareng, Eric Molobi, Murphy Morobe and Amos Masondo. In June 1978, Gqabi decided to go into exile. After he crossed the border into Botswana, he telephoned Zwelakhe. This was the signal for Zwelakhe to write an article about his flight into exile. The article not only served to alert people in Joe's network; it was also a blow to the regime when such a prominent activist escaped into exile. Zwelakhe saw Joe's departure as significant "because it meant for the first time, we had our own direct link – our own network that we would fit into outside the country".

Operating from Botswana, Gqabi was instrumental in the formation of the Congress of South African Students (COSAS) in 1979 and exerted a strong influence over key activists in AZAPO and AZASO. He emphasised that military struggle alone could not succeed without political struggle and he encouraged his protégés to participate in Black Consciousness organisations in the interests of broader unity. Zwelakhe shared this view that loyalty to the ANC and participation in a Black Consciousness organisation were not mutually exclusive. When he was re-elected President of WASA at the organisation's third annual congress held at Wilgespruit in September 1979, his speech – one of the most politically significant at the time – was an assertion of Black Consciousness ideals, combined with echoes of Mandela's watershed speech and the Freedom Charter (Karis and Gerhart, 323).

Zwelakhe's speeches and articles reflected the angry mood of the post-1976 period. At a memorial service in Orlando, he said, "They ban, stifle, gag, detain and even kill us, but when Biko falls another one just as strong will emerge. The death of a messenger does not destroy the message. No matter how or what means the government uses, they will never stop us. Sooner or later time will catch up with the makers of this evil system and history will be reversed. We shall hit back harder." Writing in *The Sunday Post* on 30 December 1979, he described the 1970s as a decade of intense political activity, a time when the lists of deaths in detention, bannings and banishments and political trials had grown far too long. "The bloody decade had drawn to an end and for black people and their organisations, it is a matter of looking back in anger."

Walter, meanwhile, was studying another revolution, seeing what lessons could be gleaned. In prison, he devoured any literature he could get about Vietnam, where the protracted war had finally come to an end. He wrote in 1976:

> We face a powerful enemy and a long war for freedom and we would do well to draw lessons from the heroic struggle of the Vietnamese people. They have faced the power of France and the power of the almighty US and triumphed. One of the lessons of the Vietnamese struggle was that their victory was as much a political as an organisational one, achieved by building and maintaining a mass movement. One of the ways in which they succeeded in building up this political machinery was by setting up a structure of interlocking self-help organisations throughout South Vietnam. Without efficient political machinery in the country our armed struggle will always be walking on one leg (Maharaj, 86).

In the post-1976 period, there was an ongoing debate in the ANC on how to build a political base inside South Africa. It was largely due to the absence of such a base that the ANC was unable to exploit the rise of Black Consciousness adequately, the re-emergence of the trade unions and the revolutionary fervour of the Soweto generation (Karis and Gerhart, 302). The Strategy and Tactics document of 1969 was based on the assumption that the armed struggle would be conducted mostly in the rural areas. The 1976 uprising, however, demonstrated that revolt in the urban areas had much more impact on the enemy. To control such an insurrection, the ANC needed to establish itself as a mass political organisation (Karis and Gerhart, 302).

To address the need for the re-organisation and reconstruction of the political underground machinery in the country, the ANC set up its Internal Political Reconstruction department in 1977. Mac Maharaj, newly released from Robben Island, was the secretary of the new department. He felt that the ANC placed too much emphasis on military incursions, at the expense of political mobilisation (Karis and Gerhart, 302). Soon after he left South Africa, Joe Gqabi submitted a detailed report to the ANC abroad on the operations and problems within the internal underground networks (Shubin, 202). The criticisms of Maharaj, Gqabi and many others pointed to the urgent need for the ANC to review its strategy and tactics. To this end, a delegation of ANC, SACP and MK leaders visited Vietnam in 1978. Oliver Tambo led the delegation, which included Thabo Mbeki, Joe Slovo, Mzwai Piliso, Cassius Make and Joe Modise. They were impressed by the Vietnamese Workers' Party strategy of creating a broad national front to unite all classes and strata of society, creating new organisations and working within and influencing existing ones (Karis and Gerhart, 302; Shubin, 194; Mbeki, 41–2; Seekings, 33).

A report on the visit was presented to a meeting of the ANC NEC at the end of 1978 and a Politico-Military Strategic Commission was set up to assess the relevance of the Vietnamese experience to the South African struggle. This was the first review of ANC strategy and tactics since Morogoro, and the membership of the Commission reflected the importance the ANC attached to the exercise. Oliver Tambo was chair, with Thabo Mbeki, Joe Slovo, Moses Mabhida, Joe Gqabi and Joe Modise forming the rest of the Commission (Shubin, 194; Mbeki, 41–2; Seekings, 33). The Commission consulted within the ANC, both inside and outside the country, but was unable to involve leaders on Robben Island at the time.

The feedback from activists inside the country confirmed what Gqabi had reported to the NEC – that many believed the ANC had emphasised military strategy at the expense of political organisation (Shubin, 203). The Commission's report was presented to the ANC in 1979, and summarised in a document known as *The Green Book*. The ANC accepted the proposal that its main focus should be on political mobilisation and organisation. Inside the country, this would involve building a front of popular organisations linked to a strong underground movement (Seekings, 34; Mbeki, 44).

While the ANC shifted its emphasis from military incursions to political mobilisation, the apartheid state redefined its own strategy and tactics. In 1977, apartheid's military supremos had outlined a new security ideology that came to be known as the "Total Strategy". This new strategy was based on the premise that South Africa was the target of a "Total Onslaught" directed from the Soviet Union. This was being waged at many levels – psychological, political, economic, diplomatic, social, religious and military. It was therefore necessary to respond to the "Total Onslaught" with a "Total Strategy" to defeat the enemies of apartheid.

The "Total Strategy" favoured by the Minister of Defence at that time, PW Botha, might not have been adopted by the government if the then Prime Minister, John Vorster, had remained in power. Under Vorster, policy on state security was determined by the powerful Bureau of State Security (BOSS), under the sinister General van den Bergh. BOSS was a rival of the military establishment and consequently had no interest in adopting its policies. As it turned out, the government was embarrassed by the Information Scandal of 1978, which uncovered a wide range of secret projects to counter the anti-apartheid campaign. The *Rand Daily Mail* and *Sunday Express* revealed that these projects were being illegally financed by the government with the knowledge and approval of the Prime Minister. The level of corruption was such that Vorster was forced to resign in 1979, and with him went General van den Bergh and the Bureau of State Security.

Their departure made way for PW Botha and his securocrats. Magnus Malan became Minister of Defence and Constand Viljoen the new Chief of the Defence Force. The "Total Strategy" became official government policy. This was a "carrot-and-stick" programme, a curious mixture of reform and brutal repression. On the "reform" side, the government tried to foster a black middle class by measures that included the lifting of trade restrictions on black businesses in the townships, electrifying the townships and reintroducing the 99-year leaseholds that had been abolished 20 years earlier. Soweto was a particular target of these reforms and Sowetans were once again allowed to buy newly built houses and to renovate their homes (Bonner and Segal, 104). The business community had already seen the need to improve conditions for African communities in urban areas if they wanted to avoid a repeat of the 1976 riots, and Afrikaner and English business tycoons set up the privately funded Urban Foundation in late 1976 to finance urban initiatives aimed at improving the quality of life in the townships (Lodge, 336; Bienert, 228).

According to *The Sowetan*, "The government hoped that this class of black people would have too much to lose to help the masses in the struggle for liberation" (Peter Magubane). They were partially successful because "a new class of residents, concerned with the safety and value of their property began to emerge" (Bonner and Segal, 104). In his address to the annual congress of WASA in 1979, Zwelakhe warned black people not to be fooled by these reforms: "We know that this government is making strained efforts to drive Black people into the laager with them, not as part of the laager but as part of the buffer – this is their total strategy. We have seen how this strategy tries to delay the inevitable by claiming to move away from discrimination". (Karis and Gerhart, 760).

The threat posed by the burgeoning trade union movement was also addressed in the government reforms. The government set up the Riekert and Wiehahn Commissions in 1979 to investigate labour relations – in effect to find ways to pacify the black working class. The Riekert Commission recommended improvements in the legal status of Africans with "Section 10" rights. The Wiehahn Commission recognised the need to draw African trade unions into the official collective bargaining system. This would give African trade unions the same rights as those of other racial groups, but it would also mean greater control of their activities in the political arena. The government adopted some of these recommendations in the new Industrial Conciliation Amendment Act of 1979. For the first time, African trade unions were recognised and able to enter into collective bargaining (Lodge, 338; Bienert, 228; Mbeki, 18).

In his speech to the WASA congress, Zwelakhe voiced the reservations many black trade unionists had about the new labour reforms: "Under the pretext of a more liberal dispensation, the white government tries to use the workers to police its racist thinking, and consolidate its policies. This is geared to stop the Black worker from responding to the universal cry: 'Workers of the World unite.' This government seeks to place Black people in carefully selected pockets where their movements can be monitored and kept in check" (Karis and Gerhart, 760).

While the government tried to seduce the black populace with the "carrot" of reforms, it used the "stick" of brutal repression in the form of detention, banning, assassinations and a whole array of dirty tricks to beat its opponents into submission. The adoption of the "Total Strategy" policy marked, in the words of writer and political analyst Allister Sparks, "the start of a massive militarization of the South African government, indeed of the whole country ... More and more the locus of decision-making moved from the [National Party] to the military-security establishment" (Sparks 1990, 108). The year 1979 saw the establishment of the notorious Vlakplaas Unit, which would play a prominent role in the torture, kidnapping and murder of political activists during the 1980s.

On a regional level, the Pretoria government tried to woo its neighbours into a "constellation of states" to fight against the supposed communist onslaught by not allowing the liberation movements to operate from their territories. The Botha regime offered the carrot of economic assistance to the countries that cooperated and used the stick of destabilisation against those that did not (Sparks 1990, 108). In 1979, the newly established State Security Council (SSC) adopted guidelines for cross-border raids, and a new counter-insurgency unit called Koevoet was established to deal with SWAPO in Northern Namibia. SWAPO had already experienced the sting of Pretoria's increased aggression in 1978 when approximately 1 000 Namibians were killed in SADF raids on SWAPO refugee camps at Kassinga and Chetequera in Southern Angola.

In pursuing its new strategy, the apartheid regime was boosted by the falling-out between the ANC and Mangosuthu Buthelezi in 1979. Buthelezi had revived the Zulu-based cultural movement Inkatha in 1975 with the encouragement of the ANC. The ANC had wanted Buthelezi to use the legal opportunities provided by the Bantustan programme to establish a mass organisation, which the ANC could use to prepare the ground for the intensification of its armed operations. However, things did not work out as planned ... As Oliver Tambo explained:

Unfortunately we failed to mobilise our own people to take on the task of resurrecting Inkatha as the kind of organisation we wanted, owing to the understandable antipathy of many of our comrades towards what they considered as working within the bantustan system. The task of reconstituting Inkatha therefore fell on Gatsha Buthelezi himself, who then built Inkatha as a personal power base far removed from the kind of organisation we had visualised, as an instrument for the mobilisation of our people in the countryside into an active and conscious force for revolutionary change (Greg Houston, Unpublished notes).

When Inkatha was first formed Buthelezi portrayed it as the reincarnation of the ANC after 15 years of quiescence. Inkatha adopted ANC colours and symbols and Buthelezi cast himself as a leader in the tradition of Chief Luthuli and Professor ZK Matthews (Sithole and Mkhize). Because he stopped short of accepting independence for the KwaZulu Bantustan and was critical of some aspects of the South African government, including the continued imprisonment of Nelson Mandela, Buthelezi was able with some success to cast himself in a different mould to other Bantustan leaders. The Black Consciousness movement, however, always identified him as part of the "system". At the funeral of Robert Sobukwe in 1978, militant youths reduced him to tears of rage and humiliation when they drove him away from the funeral on the grounds that they would not tolerate the presence of a quisling.

The banning of the Black Consciousness organisations had removed Buthelezi's main competitors as far as above-ground black political opposition was concerned. Inkatha had grown from strength to strength and Buthelezi was building his reputation in the Western world, especially in more conservative quarters, as a credible alternative to the ANC. His relationship with the ANC became increasingly strained and the final break took place after his meeting with the leadership of the ANC in 1979. His comments after the meeting alienated the ANC, and a few months later they publicly denounced him. Buthelezi's break with the ANC dovetailed with PW Botha's policy of wooing conservative black leaders. Throughout the next decade, the apartheid regime would skilfully manipulate the hostility between Buthelezi and the ANC, with devastating consequences for the people of South Africa.

# t w o

The year 1980 began on a sad note for Albertina, with the death of her friend and mentor, Lilian Ngoyi. Lilian was the most significant woman leader in the struggle of her generation, and a shining example to many. Although she spent the last years of her life under a banning order, she and Albertina had contrived to meet on occasion. Lilian lived in Mzimhlope, close to the clinic where Albertina worked, and sometimes slipped in pretending to be a patient. The two leaders were thus able to communicate this way. When Lilian died, Helen Joseph and Albertina, both of whose banning orders forbade their presence even at such solemn occasions, applied for special permission to be allowed to attend the funeral; Helen was granted leave to attend, but not Albertina.

The new decade, however, opened on a positive note for the liberation movements in southern Africa. Zimbabwe's independence in April 1980 was a huge boost, both psychologically and practically. It swung the geo-political balance in the region in their favour and provided new possibilities for the prosecution of the armed struggle. It was a big setback to the apartheid government's attempts to set up a "constellation of states" to fight against a "communist onslaught". Instead, the independent states of the region established the Southern African Development Coordination Community (SADCC), which had the central objective of reducing the economic dependence of member states on South Africa. These regional developments helped South Africans and Namibians to pursue their struggles with increased confidence.

In March 1980, *The Sunday Post* launched the Release Mandela campaign and its colourful editor Percy Qoboza became the campaign's public champion. As news editor of *The Sunday Post*, Zwelakhe worked well with Qoboza although they had sharp political differences. "We had our problems," Zwelakhe recalls. "He was aligned with the Progressive Federal Party, and we had a lot of encounters with each other, but I remember him with fondness. He was a typical Soweto character who thrived doing the rounds of the shebeens. He was a great inspirational speaker, he could get a crowd going."

Zwelakhe was in touch with Siphiwe Nyanda and other senior ANC operatives in Lusaka about the idea of a campaign to release Mandela. When Zwelakhe suggested the idea to his editor, he was pleasantly surprised to find that Qoboza had been thinking along the same lines, but was not too sure about how to package the idea. They decided that *The Sunday Post* would print a form calling for Nelson Mandela's release. Readers would sign these and send them back to the newspaper. Eventually, all the signatures would be handed to the government to show that a significant proportion, in fact the majority, of people in South Africa wanted Mandela's release. ANC activists in Durban joined the calls for Mandela's release by forming a Release Mandela committee (Seekings, 37).

There was criticism from some quarters within the organisation at the singling out of an individual, but it turned out to be a tactically brilliant move. People identified more easily with an individual than an organisation, especially someone as charismatic as Mandela, who was already attracting considerable international attention. In 1979, he was awarded the Jawaharlal Nehru Prize for International Understanding, and from 1980 onwards, he would receive an increasing number of awards from all corners of the globe. In South Africa it was illegal to support the ANC, but it was not a crime to call for the release of an individual political leader. For ANC members and sympathisers, Mandela's name was inseparable from that of the ANC, so the Release Mandela initiative was the first major political campaign that allowed them to identify openly with the ANC. The campaign also appealed to those who did not necessarily support the ANC, but opposed apartheid on humanitarian grounds. Many white liberals who would not dream of supporting the ANC were quite happy to display "Free Mandela" stickers on their cars. The campaign turned out to be a huge success that drew international attention, with the UN Security Council also joining in calls for Mandela's release (Sampson 2000, 319).

The Release Mandela campaign started as a newspaper campaign, but it also turned out to be an important tool for political mass mobilisation, as well as a source of valuable recruiting information that Zwelakhe passed on to MK. "Because the Release Mandela forms included home addresses, we were able to assemble a good demographic profile of ANC support. Large numbers of forms returned from the same section of a particular township would indicate to us that there was a significant pocket of ANC supporters there. We could therefore conclude that the place would provide fertile ground for recruitment for MK. Personally I was surprised at how strong the support was, particularly in Natal." Zwelakhe would send the forms indicating the areas where there were high levels of support to Siphiwe Nyanda, a senior MK operative in Swaziland.

In 1977, the Soweto generation that had gone for military training with MK began returning to South Africa as trained cadres in MK's first military operations since the 1960s. Their attacks focused on sabotage of railway communications, industrial installations, government offices and police stations. In 1977, police confronted two ANC fighters, Monty Motloung and Solomon Mahlangu, in Johannesburg. In the ensuing gun battle, an elderly white couple was killed and the two guerrillas were captured. Motloung, who fired the fatal shots, was beaten so badly by the police that he sustained brain damage and was unable to testify in court. Mahlangu was tried and sentenced to death.

When he was executed on 6 April 1979, Mahlangu became the first of a new generation of martyrs. Albertina Sisulu was one of thousands who rallied around Mahlangu's family in the days leading up to the execution. The experience had a profound impact on her and more than two decades after the event her face still crumples in agony at the recollection: "We, the women, went to Mamelodi to console his mother. For the government to kill your child like that! A healthy living person to be deliberately killed – that is one of the worst things a mother can experience. That is why I will never, ever support the death sentence, not even for the worst crimes." Albertina was among the people who kept vigil all night before the execution in solidarity with Martha Mahlangu, hoping against hope that the government would be swayed by international protests. But the government remained unmoved by the appeals for clemency that poured in from all over the world, including one from US President Jimmy Carter (Karis and Gerhart, 282).

In retaliation for Mahlangu's execution, an MK unit attacked Moroka Police Station in May, killing one policeman and injuring several others. In October, Orlando Police Station came under attack. In January 1980, police stations at Soekmekaar in the Northern Transvaal and Booysens near Soweto were also attacked (Mbeki, 40). The attacks on these police stations, where so many young people had been tortured during the Soweto uprising, greatly enhanced the reputation of MK.

The ANC plan to link military tactics to a wider political strategy started off on a successful note in 1980. Encouraged by the ANC, Popo Molefe and other Soweto activists organised a highly publicised protest campaign against the 20th anniversary of the Republic of South Africa (Seekings, 37). As part of the nationwide protest against the official Republic Day celebrations, MK launched a series of military operations, the most spectacular of which was a limpet mine attack on the oil storage tanks and refinery of the South African Coal, Oil and Gas Corporation (SASOL) in Secunda. The fires caused by the attacks raged uncontrollably for several days and the smoke could be seen as far away as Soweto, kilometres away. Damage was estimated in tens of millions of rands, and caused the government real concern at a time when South Africa was facing a reduction in oil supplies in the wake of the Iranian revolution (Ellis and Sechaba, 105).

In his annual address to the ANC, Oliver Tambo had declared 1980 the "Year of the Freedom Charter". On 26 June 1980 (the 25th anniversary of the Kliptown Congress), Zwelakhe oversaw the publication of the full text of the Freedom Charter in *The Sunday Post*. As part of a nationwide campaign to publicise the Charter, the student organisations COSAS and NUSAS distributed Freedom Charter leaflets on university campuses, in schools and throughout communities across the country. The Charter was popularised and debated as never before. Andrew Boraine, the 1980/1 NUSAS president, spoke at the Durban-Westville campus in 1981, something that would not have been possible in the 1970s. NUSAS worked hard at developing non-racial alliances and succeeded in getting University of Cape Town students to boycott for a week in solidarity with the black schools boycott (Frederikse, 173).

The student boycotts had started in April 1980 in the Western Cape. They quickly spread across the country and by the last week in May, the campaign had widened its scope from a protest concerning coloured education to a protest against the whole system of apartheid education (*Sechaba*, November 1980). Police attempts to break up meetings and marches by students led to widespread violence and several deaths in the Western Cape. In Ciskei, Bantustan leader Lennox Sebe's police detained large numbers of school children and students. The arrests were followed by a blackout on news of the detentions (*Sechaba*, November 1980).

Nkuli Sisulu had registered as a student at Fort Hare in 1979 and was arrested when Sebe's police raided Fort Hare, detaining many students. She was locked up for three days and beaten thoroughly. "She returned home black and blue," says Albertina. As anxious as she was for Nkuli to get a university education, she agreed that it was not a good idea for Nkuli to return to Fort Hare. Much to Albertina's concern Nkuli's education was once again disturbed (as it had been in 1976) by student unrest. Student groups began to link up with workers' organisations, especially with the emerging "community unions" who forged links within communities to support workers' struggles (Lodge et al., 39). The legal recognition of black trade unions in 1979 created a dramatic growth in union membership. This increased membership, coupled with the economic recession of the early 1980s, led to a huge increase in strike activity from 1979 onwards (Lodge et al., 38).

At its annual congress in October 1980, the WASA decided to extend its membership (which had so far been confined to journalists and writers alone) to all black workers employed in the media industry. The union was accordingly renamed Media Workers Association of South Africa (MWASA) and Zwelakhe was elected president. Later in the same month, MWASA embarked on strike action at *The Cape Herald*, the *The Post*, *The Sunday Post* and *The Star*. The two-month strike ended with a number of concessions from management, including formal recognition of MWASA as a trade union. Zwelakhe considered the strike a major success and his colleagues attributed its success to his strong negotiating skills (Article 19 pamphlet).

While the strike was still in progress, the security police decided to act against MWASA. In a memo to the Secretary of Justice dated 20 November 1980, the security police argued that WASA had "expanded and infiltrated practically all the English-speaking newspapers with the result that papers such as *The Post*, *The Sunday Post*, *The Voice* and the *Rand Daily Mail Extra* are considered mouthpieces of WASA and are used to propagate Black Consciousness ideology". The police wanted to restrict those involved in the strike but decided to wait until it had ended, as they did not want to give the "unfavourable impression" that the government was taking sides in the dispute. They also felt that there would be international repercussions from unions and the press if the journalists were banned, but concluded: "Taking everything into consideration it is however the opinion of the South African Police that these persons are using their careers as journalists, working for newspapers to further their political objectives to undermine the authority of the government and notwithstanding the result, their restriction has become necessary" (Security police memo to Secretary of Justice, 20/11/80).

On 29 December 1980, Zwelakhe was served with a three-year banning order. This restricted him to his home from 7pm till 6am, confined him to the magisterial district of Johannesburg, and banned him from being within any black, coloured or Asian area, any factory, political gathering or gathering of pupils, or any educational institutions. It also prohibited him from being involved in preparing, compiling, printing, publishing, disseminating or transmitting any publication as defined in the Internal Security Act. This effectively meant that Zwelakhe could no longer work as a journalist.

Writing in *The Sowetan* on 7 January 1981, Jon Qwelane commented that: "The black community felt outrage because here was a man who should be listened to instead of being silenced. It was felt the banning was a continuation of government harassment of a family already having to contend with living without a head of the household. [Zwelakhe] is easily the most formidable strategist to emerge in recent years. Like father like son, the saying goes, and Zwelakhe is trudging the Sisulu path to the past. He cannot be quoted now, because the banning order effectively sees to that. Yet a voice like Sisulu's should be heard, not silenced."

Piroshaw Camay, the General Secretary of the Council of Unions of South Africa (CUSA), requested an interview with the Ministers of Justice and Manpower Utilisation to discuss the reasons for Zwelakhe's restriction. At the same time, the Argus Company engaged Johannesburg law firm Weber Wentzel to make an application for exceptions to the restrictions to enable Zwelakhe to carry out his duties as a journalist. They also requested reasons for the restrictions. The Minister of Justice refused to vary the restriction orders because he had been advised by Compol that, "Mr Sisulu has described himself as a 'revolutionary propagandist.' The main purpose of the notices was to prevent him from influencing the masses through newspapers. To permit him to continue his employment as a journalist will negate his restriction notices. The application in question is therefore not recommended." The Justice Ministry also rejected Camay's request for a meeting (Department of Justice memo, 24/2/81). The president of the Africa Division of the International Confederation of Free Trade Unions (ICFTU) and veteran Tanzanian trade unionist Andrew Kailembu also lodged an appeal for the lifting of restrictions on Zwelakhe Sisulu and MWASA's Natal regional secretary Marimuthu Subramoney, who had been banned at the same time as Zwelakhe. He argued that such restrictions damaged the image of South Africa abroad. The security police advised the Department of Justice to reject the appeal: "it is inconceivable that Mr Kailembu is concerned about South Africa's image abroad. His organisation is one of the main international donors of funds for local organisations hostile to the government. Compol therefore strongly opposes any relaxation of their restrictions" (Department of Justice Memo, 3/6/81).

Zwelakhe's restrictions were part of a general crackdown on the media. The government forced the Argus company to close the *Post* and *Sunday Post* and banned many more MWASA office-bearers and *Post* reporters, including Phil Mthimkulu, Joe Thloloe, Mathatha Tsedu and Charles Nqakula. They all suffered the double blow of being both banned from political activity and effectively prevented from doing their work. "When you suddenly switch off, the effect can be quite devastating," according to Zwelakhe. "Suddenly you are removed from participating and that has been your life ... It was difficult for me to come to terms with that" (Article 19 Interview, 8).

It was not just Zwelakhe's life that was thrown into disarray. Journalist Peta Thornycroft made the following telling comments on the impact of Zwelakhe's new status as a banned person on his wife Zodwa:

> She has already learned to handle being the daughter-in-law of one of South Africa's most important prisoners, Robben Island lifer Walter Sisulu. Now she must cope with living with a husband who has been officially declared a "non-person" ... Already she is feeling the effects. First there was the shock, the resignation, then the incessant calls of concern and outrage from many parts of the

world for days and nights on end. Now she is starting that difficult period, the quiet after the almost heady storm, settling down to a life so dramatically changed that nobody who has not been banned can appreciate just how different this Government-prescribed lifestyle is from one's own (*Sunday Express*, 4/1/80).

A reserved person by nature, Zodwa found herself thrust into the public eye. "Yes, it is going to be hard to adjust," she admitted, "but not as difficult as it might be for some people. My mother-in-law has set me an impressive example. I have learned much from her. And after all, as a family, we are used to this sort of thing ... I admire my mother-in-law enormously. She has always been someone to look up to. She will help me to handle all this."

Despite Zodwa's brave face, Zwelakhe's banning created enormous complications in their living arrangements. Since the birth of their son Moyikwa in January 1980, Zodwa and Zwelakhe had redoubled their efforts to get a place of their own, without success. They were still living with Albertina. Strictly speaking, it was illegal for Albertina and Zwelakhe to communicate with each other or be in the same room together. It was of course impossible for them to observe such a restriction in their own home, but they had to be constantly alert to security police raids. Having two banned people in one small crowded house made for a very tense household.

Priscilla Jana was always amazed at how Zwelakhe, who clearly had deep ANC loyalties, managed to lead an organisation that had a strong Black Consciousness orientation. "He wanted MWASA to be like a parliament where people of different ideologies and different organisational commitments could come together and work." Jana believed he was able to have good working relationships with people from different political persuasions because of his mother's influence. "She was the mother in Soweto. It didn't matter whether you were Black Consciousness or PAC or anything, their home was an open home. And I think Zwelakhe inherited that streak of his personality from MaSisulu because she had this tremendous ability to bring people together. When people had any problems, be they political or nonpolitical, they could feel free to call at the Sisulu home" (Interview, Priscilla Jana). This "open-door" policy proved to be Zwelakhe's undoing when, one morning in June 1981, a young girl came to see him. She told him that some students from Botswana wanted to meet him. The following morning, two young men arrived and told Zwelakhe they wanted to meet the MWASA executive. Zwelakhe obliged by setting up a meeting with Thami Mazwai, the secretary of MWASA. The "students from Botswana" turned out to be members of the South African Youth Revolutionary Council (SAYRCO), which had been formed by former members of the SSRC who had fled the country to Botswana in the wake of the 1976 uprising. The first chair of the SSRC, Tsietsi Mashinini, and his successor, Khosto Seathlolo, were among the handful of Soweto students who had resisted incorporation into either the ANC or the PAC. After leaving Botswana, they had both found their way to Nigeria where they tried to set up SAYRCO as a military wing of the SSRC (Karis and Gerhart, 5: 282). Seathlolo had come back to South Africa to drum up support and recruit people for SAYRCO.

Mazwai went to meet the "students" at a house in Orlando East on 18 June. While their discussion was in progress, the security police swooped on them and Seathlolo and Mazwai were arrested. Masabatha Loate was arrested a few hours later. On Saturday 20 June, in the early hours of the morning, Zwelakhe was arrested. The police made much of Khotso Seathlolo's capture, and the news of his arrest was splashed across the papers. Brigadier du Preez, the Deputy Chief of the security police, announced that Zwelakhe was being held for questioning in connection with SAYRCO. Security police also confirmed the arrest of Thami Mazwai ("Police probe Sisulu 'link' with exiles", *Rand Daily Mail*, 23/6/81).

Zwelakhe's arrest cast a pall of gloom over the Sisulu household where memories of Lindi's detention were still fresh in everyone's minds. Like Lindi, Zwelakhe was being held under the Terrorism Act, which allowed for indefinite detention without charge. Albertina knew this meant that his detention was likely to be lengthy. She was distressed that her young daughter-in-law had to go through the same anguish she had experienced during Lindi's detention and that her grandson Moyikwa should suffer a separation from his father at such a tender age.

Albertina knew without a doubt that Zwelakhe had no links with SAYRCO exiles. The ANC had frowned upon the formation of SAYRCO and had expressed concern that the Nigerian government was funding the organisation. She knew that Zwelakhe would never have got involved with such an organisation and suspected that the security police knew it too, but were just looking for an opportunity to arrest him.

Ironically, Zwelakhe's detention came at a time when Albertina was herself enjoying freedom for the first time since 1964. Her restrictions ended in July and, much to her surprise, they were not renewed. She had been banned for 18 years, longer than any other person in South Africa. But she barely had time to celebrate her newfound freedom before she was inundated with requests to speak at meetings.

Albertina was already actively involved in trying to rebuild women's organisations, and the lifting of her restrictions allowed her to work more openly. She worked closely with veteran activists like Greta Ncapayi, June Mlangeni and Sister Bernard Ncube. She also recruited a number of young female activists to organise women in the ANC underground. One of these was young Soweto teacher O'Hara Diseko. O'Hara recalls that Albertina was deeply angered by the killing of children in the June 16 uprisings. "MaSisulu would always say that adults had to take the responsibility of facing the enemy and not children" (Joyce Sikhakhane-Rankin Interview, O'Hara Diseko). Together with other women, they formed a cell called *Thusang Basadi* ("Wake up women"). Albertina sent O'Hara to Botswana to discuss their plans with Florence Mapthsho, then head of the ANC women's section. She also guided O'Hara in sensitive work such as liaising with MK cadres, providing them with safe hiding places and coordinating their communication and supply systems.

*Thusang Basadi* organised women to support detainees and the families of political prisoners, and to help with organising funerals, with tracing missing members of ANC families and with the education of political prisoners. It also planned and staged protest marches outside municipal offices, calling for the dismantling of the dummy municipal structures and non-elected councils.

Albertina also worked closely with women from other communities. In 1979 she met Jessie Duarte, a young woman who was active in the student movement in the coloured communities. Jessie's political mentor, Bill Jardine, advised those students who wanted to take up education issues from a national liberation perspective to talk to Albertina, because of her experience in organising in Soweto and nationally. Jessie was part of a delegation led by Vesta Smith, a community leader from Noordgesig, that went to meet with Albertina, Greta Ncapayi and others in Orlando West. It was the beginning of a long and close political relationship between Albertina and Jessie, who acknowledges Albertina's influence on her political development:

We worked together almost on a daily basis. I became virtually her secretary over a period of 12 years. At that time we young women did not have a political home. We knew that there was FEDSAW, but it was not functioning. During the 1970s, we kept in touch with veterans from a Congress background like Amina Cachalia, but it was a vague contact. It had nothing to do with an organisational base. MaSisulu was like a one-woman political education course. She took me and a number of other young women through 1979 and the 1980s. They included Sicily Palmer, Feroza Adams, Benny Manama, Baby Tyawa and Susan Shabangu. We were called "MaSisulu's girls". MaSisulu was our political mentor who could tell us more about the policies of the ANC than anyone we knew. Her crusade was to develop what she termed a "petticoat" layer of women leaders that would take over when the older women were not there.

Albertina was also drawn into another campaign. In 1981, the government had decided to hold elections for the South African Indian Council (SAIC), an advisory body to the government that enjoyed little respect from progressive Indian organisations. The Natal Indian Congress, which had been undergoing a period of revival since 1978, responded by campaigning for a boycott of the SAIC elections. The Transvaal anti-SAIC Committee (TASC), which was formed in June 1981, met with an enthusiastic response from the Indian community, with one public meeting in August 1981 attracting over 3 000 people, making it the largest Indian political rally since the 1950s (Lodge et al., 42).

The anti-SAIC campaigners were keen to re-assert the Freedom Charter and the non-racial traditions of the Congress Alliance; and Albertina Sisulu was a veteran activist who was regarded as the embodiment of these traditions. At the national anti-SAIC conference in Durban on 10 November 1981, Albertina and stalwart Archie Gumede were among the main speakers. The next day, she flew to Cape Town where she addressed another anti-SAIC meeting in Athlone. At both meetings, she condemned the SAIC and urged her audiences to believe in and fight for the Freedom Charter.

In November 1981, she condemned detentions without trial when she spoke at a meeting of the Detainees Parents' Support Committee. In mid-December, she spoke at a Heroes Day function in Soweto at which she praised the heroes of the struggle and attacked the Bantustan policy.

Sadly, many of the gatherings that she addressed were funerals and memorial services for slain activists, as the government responded with increasing ferocity to the resurgence of the ANC. In January, the SADF killed 20 people in the Matola attack, the first cross-border raid into Mozambique. In June, a COSAS activist, Sizwe Kondile of Port Elizabeth, was abducted and killed by police. The following month, Joe Gqabi, by then the ANC representative in Zimbabwe, was assassinated by security police outside his home in Harare. Albertina attended his memorial service in Soweto.

On 19 November, the security police assassinated Griffiths Mxenge, the Durban lawyer who had played a key role in the ANC's underground, both before and after his stint on Robben Island. Albertina travelled to King William's Town, the Mxenges' place of origin, for the funeral. Both she and Walter had known the Mxenges for many years and it grieved her to see Victoria Mxenge widowed with young children to raise. Albertina delivered an angry speech at the funeral, condemning the policies of the apartheid regime.

The rest of the year would see the detention of increasing numbers of activists. Many of those detained were trade unionists. On 5 February 1982, Neil Aggett, a trade unionist and medical doctor, was found hanging in his cell. Aggett was the 54th political prisoner to die in detention and the first white political prisoner to die in police custody (Frederikse, 212, 225). With her own son in detention, Albertina empathised with Neil Aggett's parents. She was actively involved in the funeral arrangements and attended the service.

Neil's death heightened Albertina's fears about Zwelakhe's continued detention. She would have been even more concerned if she had known about the conditions under which he was being held. His prison cell was so small that he could touch all four walls without standing up. The bare light bulb in his cell shone continuously so that he could not tell whether it was day or night: "When it was hot, they would open the heaters so you would sweat and couldn't possibly sleep ... the only water was in the toilet basin and ... you have no other way but to go there, drink the water ... you don't wash for weeks on end" (Article 19 Interview).

After three months in John Vorster Square, Zwelakhe was transferred to Sandton Police Cells, where he was interrogated by the security police:

> They said I must tell them why I was detained. I said I didn't know ... so they sent me to this room called the "House of Truth," and there, the stock methods of torture used on detainees in South Africa were used on me. Some of them I find difficult to talk about ... being electrocuted, having your hands and feet cuffed and they put a broom through and you are swung by that for hours on end. Very humiliating things.

The purpose of the torture was to get Zwelakhe to implicate himself in the activities of SAYRCO, so that he could be charged. When the security police failed to get any proof of his involvement with SAYRCO beyond one brief encounter, they "released" him. The "release" was a technicality; they immediately redetained him as a state witness in the case against Khotso Seathlolo and Masabatha Loate. The police had already tried to force Thami Mazwai to be a state witness, but he had refused and been sentenced to 18 months' imprisonment.

George Bizos, who was defending Loate, was afraid that Zwelakhe, who had also made it clear that he would not testify, would also be imprisoned. He confronted Swanepoel, the prosecutor in the case, pointing out that since Loate had not denied the charges, Zwelakhe's evidence would make no material difference. The prosecutor agreed that Zwelakhe's testimony would have no bearing whatsoever on the outcome of the case, but admitted that he was under pressure from the security police, who wanted Zwelakhe in jail at all costs. Bizos told Swanepoel that he would not be true to his office if he insisted on a witness giving evidence that was not required, simply so that police demands to get the witness convicted could be satisfied (Interview, George Bizos). Swanepoel listened to his conscience and, resisting police pressure, put it to the court that Zwelakhe's evidence was not necessary. Zwelakhe was released on 25 February 1982 and Loate and Seathlolo were sentenced to 10 years in prison.

An article in *The Cape Times* commented critically on the government's increasing use of indefinite detention without trial to silence its more outspoken opponents against whom no legal case could be made. The cases of Mitchell's Plain community leader Johnny Issel and Zwelakhe Sisulu were given as examples of arbitrary detention as a form of punishment. At the time, Issel had been in detention for four months under "preventative detention" laws and had not been allowed to attend his mother's funeral, not even under police guard. The report commented that Zwelakhe was released after 251 days in detention:

> Yet Mr Sisulu was charged with no crime. There is no doubt that had he been the slightest bit guilty of anything in law, such a charge would have been laid. So those 251 days, with all the interrogation that presumably accompanied them, constitute officially sanctioned persecution of an innocent man. He has no redress against the state for this deprivation of his personal freedom or for mental pain and suffering, or for loss of earnings. He has no guarantee it won't happen all over again (*The Cape Times*, 1/3/82).

# *t h r e e*

"A man can get used to anything, and I had grown used to Robben Island," wrote Nelson Mandela in his autobiography (Mandela, 608). After more than a decade and a half on the Island, the Rivonia prisoners had become accustomed to life there. They were the permanent fixtures who had seen prisoners come and go over the years, and conditions change until Robben Island was a far cry from the miserable place it had been in the 1960s.

Conditions on Robben Island continued to improve in the post-1976 period. The year 1977 saw the end of hard labour on the quarries and prisoners no longer went out to work. "So weekends have lost their meaning, and every day is like any other," wrote Kathrada in 1978. "One has got all the time to play, to study, to talk, to read, or just laze away" (Letter to Dasoo Iyer, 88). From 1980 onwards, sections A and B were allowed to meet for organised events. Prisoners could play tennis on the full-sized all-weather tennis court that they had built in section B. There were also outdoor facilities for volleyball and tenniquoit. Prisoners were also allowed to play soccer and go for walks (Ismail Ayob and Associates, Memorandum re conditions on Robben Island, 9). Those who preferred more sedentary pursuits played chess, ludo, draughts and scrabble. Walter was "an avid player of scrabble," wrote Thami Mkhwanazi in his recollections of his days on Robben Island. "Inmates treasured their dictionaries, but Sisulu made his available for all to use during the games. Most of the pages were loose and one could find him trying to paste them together after games" (*Weekly Mail*, 15 July 1988).

Reading was a favourite occupation of prisoners and, by 1978, there was a depot stocked by the Cape Provincial Library on the Island, which boasted about 2 500 books. "From a quick look at them I must say they look promising," reported Kathrada to his niece Zohra. "At least a good start has been made. Unfortunately, so far there are no novels. We hope this will soon be remedied" (Kathrada, 95). By 1978, all the prisoners had beds, they were allowed half a dozen letters and visits a month and an unlimited number of photographs.

There was great excitement on 27 February 1978 when, for the first time on Robben Island, prisoners were officially allowed news. The prison management taped the Radio SA news service in the morning and afternoon and played it in the cells every evening. No one welcomed the change more than Walter, who had always been passionate about news. He was amused by Kathrada's tongue-in-cheek observation that reports of kidnappings, earthquakes, road accidents, oil spills, pollution and economic problems around the world made him almost glad he was in jail! (Kathrada, 89). Over the years, the prisoners had fought long and hard for the right to newspapers but despite their efforts (reinforced by pressure from the International Red Cross), the prison authorities would not relent. Finally, during a visit to the Island in 1978, the Minister of Prisons told the inmates that he was seriously considering giving them two daily newspapers. It was another two years before they got their wish.

By the beginning of 1980, prisoners were allowed magazines. The prison management also installed a new rediffusion system for transmitting to the cells. "We get two SABC news broadcasts daily," wrote Kathrada, "plus radio plays, quizzes, and radio and recorded music. This plus *Time* magazine has made a tremendous difference to our prison life. It's not only the political news that is important. Sports, drama, anthropology, book reviews – all this contributes to make us feel part of the world" (Kathrada, 119). By October 1980, the long-promised newspapers finally materialised and they were allowed *The Sunday Post, Sunday Express, Tribune* and the

*Rand Daily Mail*. For Walter, the arrival of newspapers marked a significant change in the quality of his life on the Island. Even the removal of certain articles by the censors could not diminish the pleasure he took in reading newspapers. Like Kathrada, he felt that with the advent of newspapers, they were suddenly short of time. They had a lot of catching up to do. "With the aid of letters, newspapers, magazines, radio programmes and visits," wrote Kathrada in 1981, "slowly but surely we are catching up with things. Naturally these cannot completely make up for almost two decades of deprivations but they certainly go a long way. If ever I get out of jail at least I won't feel like Rip van Winkle" (Kathrada, 139).

By the 1980s, Robben Island had become a symbol of the triumph of the human spirit over adversity. The Rivonia prisoners had played a central role in the struggles on the Island and their influence was felt far beyond the prison walls. The international campaign for the release of Nelson Mandela had ensured that Mandela was the most famous political prisoner in the world, and Robben Island the most famous prison. To counter this, the government considered removing the Rivonia prisoners from the Island in the hope that this would draw attention away from Robben Island. They also felt that the Rivonia prisoners exerted too great an influence on the younger prisoners, and that the ANC had become too powerful on the Island. These considerations led to the decision to remove Mandela and some of his colleagues from the Island (Mandela, 612; Interviews, Christo Brand and Isak Volschenk).

On the night of 31 March 1982, the Commanding Officer of Robben Island made a dramatic entrance into the B section, accompanied by a bevy of warders. He ordered Mandela, Sisulu, Mhlaba and Mlangeni to get ready for immediate transfer – he would not say where to. Kathrada was also let out of his cell because he was responsible for the "storerooms" – the cells in which the prisoners' belongings, accumulated over the long years of incarceration, were kept. Kathrada identified the belongings of his four colleagues while they hastily packed the contents of their cells into large cardboard boxes (Interview, Ahmed Kathrada). There was a general hubbub as other prisoners tried to find out what was going on. Within the hour, Walter, Mandela, Mhlaba and Mlangeni were on the boat to Cape Town, while their bewildered colleagues speculated long into the night as to where they might be going.

When they disembarked at the deserted dock, Walter and his colleagues were transferred to a truck. Because it had no windows, they had no sense of the direction in which they were travelling. After what seemed like an interminable drive with numerous stops (probably security checkpoints), they arrived at Pollsmoor Prison, a huge prison facility on the outskirts of the scenic Cape Town suburb of Tokai. They were ushered quickly through the eerily quiet reception area, and up three flights of stairs to their new living quarters. Their "prison penthouse", as Mandela called it, consisted of a large rectangular room with adjoining bathroom facilities and a small study for Mandela. The four comfortable beds, fresh linen and towels, luxuries they had not enjoyed for over two decades, made Walter feel as if they were "in a hotel rather than a prison". The following morning they discovered that they had a whole roof terrace "half as long as a soccer field" to themselves. Unfortunately, they could not get a sense of their new surroundings, as 12-foot-high concrete walls blocked the view (Mandela, 612).

The food at Pollsmoor was infinitely superior to that of Robben Island. They enjoyed breakfasts of porridge, jam, peanut butter and coffee. At lunchtime they were treated to huge helpings of meat and vegetables, while dinners consisted of thick vegetable or chicken soup with a daily helping of fruit. They were allowed more newspapers and periodicals such as *Time* and the *Weekly Mail & Guardian*, as well as their own FM radio. They were also permitted to write more letters and their correspondence was not so strictly censored.

Despite these improvements, Walter, like his colleagues, felt unsettled by the move. They missed the fresh sea air and natural environs of Robben Island, but most of all they missed the camaraderie. On the Island they had been at the heart of a vibrant prison community, while at Pollsmoor they were four political prisoners stuck in one corner of a huge prison complex that housed 6 000 common-law prisoners with whom they had no contact. They regretted their hasty departure from the Island, which had meant that they were unable to say goodbye to their colleagues. They were pleasantly surprised when Kathrada was also transferred to Pollsmoor in October. For reasons they could not fathom, the prison authorities also placed a young ANC activist, Patrick Maqubela, with them. Maqubela, who was serving a 20-year sentence for treason, was a young lawyer from the Eastern Cape who had been articled to the late Griffiths Mxenge (Mandela, 613).

Soon after their arrival at Pollsmoor, Walter and his colleagues were taken for a medical check-up, which revealed that Walter had a cyst on his right kidney. He was admitted to a Woodstock hospital on Wednesday, 28 April. Albertina flew to Cape Town the night before and visited him on Wednesday morning. When she walked into the hospital ward she was overwhelmed to find she was in the same room as Walter without a glass barrier between them – the first time in 18 years. "Am I allowed to kiss him?" she asked the police guards. It was a momentous occasion, and Albertina's anxiety over Walter's health was overshadowed by her joy at being able to embrace her husband. "Mama told me about your little love affair in the hospital," Lindi would write to Walter later. "She was so very excited about being able to hold your hand. I wish I could have been there to see you together."

Walter told Albertina not to visit him the following day, when he was scheduled for surgery to remove the cyst. He was afraid he might be in too much pain to enjoy the visit, and asked her to visit him the day after the operation instead. After he was discharged from hospital, the local papers reported that the prison authorities had issued a statement claiming that Walter Sisulu did not want his wife to visit him in hospital. Walter was furious and vented his anger in a letter, dated 4 May, to the Commanding Officer of Pollsmoor Prison, complaining bitterly that the conversation between him and his wife had been distorted and made public:

> … No one was authorised to make [this conversation] public. I therefore consider the action of the prison authorities grossly irregular to say the least. I should like to have a proper explanation as to why this was ever done.
>
> I should like to state further that despite my current circumstances as a prisoner, my relations with members of your department are based on mutual acceptance of each other's integrity and I always want to work in this spirit. Incidents like this are not compatible with this spirit.

Despite assurances that his surgery was minor, Walter's hospital stay caused considerable concern within the family, especially among those who were far away.

Their sentiments were perhaps best expressed by Lindi, who wrote: "I hope you are completely recovered by now. I would like to hear that you are fit once more. I'm in a terrible state of depression and anxiety when you are not well. For all our sakes you just have to keep well. You represent everything we are living for."

On 8 January 1982, the ANC celebrated its 70th year of existence. The ANC organised a special jubilee programme for ANC communities around the world, from Luanda to London and Tanzania to Moscow (Shubin, 230).

Four months later, Walter celebrated his 70th birthday. His most important birthday present was a visit from Zwelakhe, Zodwa and two-year-old Moyikwa. There was some controversy surrounding the visit, firstly because the prison authorities waited until the last minute before granting Zwelakhe permission to visit. Secondly, they refused to allow him to travel by train. The *Rand Daily Mail* editorial made a caustic comment on the saga:

It's a commentary in itself that Mr Zwelakhe Sisulu needs official permission to travel to Cape Town to see his father Walter, who has just celebrated his 70th birthday while a prisoner at Pollsmoor jail. Mr Sisulu has to do this because he is banned and confined to the Johannesburg area.

In any event, in response to Mr Sisulu's application a magistrate has relaxed his banning: he can travel provided he flies to and from Cape Town within the space of a day. That means he can have one visit of 30 minutes with his father, instead of the two 30-minute visits he would have enjoyed had he gone (more cheaply) by train as planned. No doubt the magistrate who has restricted the concession in this way has good reason for doing so. He must surely have information about the sinister activities which Mr Sisulu would have engaged in during the 30-hour train journey, and the extent to which the security of the State would have been jeopardised.

These irritations aside, Walter enjoyed Zwelakhe's half-hour visit immensely and he also had two more visits with Zodwa and Moyikwa – a treat, as he always relished getting to know his grand-children and daughters-in-law.

As well as good wishes from family and friends, Walter also received birthday greetings from all over the world. Messages of solidarity came from West German parliamentarians, the Greek, French and Canadian Communist Parties, the Soviet Women's Committee, solidarity commit-tees from Finland, Canada, Mexico, Panama, Mozambique and Ethiopia, the People's Progressive Party of Guyana, Women for Racial and Economic Equality in New York and trade union organisations in Italy, Afghanistan and Jamaica. The Aberdeen Peace Council marked his birthday by writing to PW Botha, demanding Walter's immediate release. Walter also heard from many old friends, including Father Trevor Huddleston, who was by then Archbishop of the Province of the Indian Ocean. "I only wish I could greet you personally," wrote Huddleston. "but as you know, I am one of those who is honoured by not being allowed to visit SA. I do assure you that you and Nelson are never forgotten in my prayers and I hope that you realise what a great inspiration you are to many across the world. We shall not rest until that great day when you and all other South African patriots are free" (Walter Sisulu, Prison Files).

The ANC marked Walter's 70th birthday by awarding him *Isithwalandwe-Seaparankoe*, the high-est award the ANC gives for meritorious service to the liberation movement. Walter was extremely honoured to follow in the illustrious footsteps of previous award winners, among them Chief Luthuli, Yusuf Dadoo and Trevor Huddleston. (*Isithwalandwe*, a title given to traditional heroes, were warriors given royal dispensation to wear the feathers of the rare Indwe bird. *Seaparankoe* is the Sotho and Tswana equivalent, meaning "He who wears the leopard's skin".)

One tribute that Walter did not come to know of until many years later was that given by his old and dear friend, Ruth First. At a special ANC gathering to mark the occasion, Ruth paid moving tribute to her comrade. She pointed to the famous photograph of Mandela and Sisulu standing in the courtyard on Robben Island, saying she thought that of all the photographs that existed of Walter Sisulu, this was the one that was most characteristic of the man: "It shows him as he is, attentive, with the power to listen and the power to understand. Sometimes a little slow to make up his mind but when he has heard the case and he is convinced, he is effective, he is enduring and he is a thinking man." Her tribute encapsulates Walter's character in a way few others have done:

He has committed all his life to the struggle for liberation – in the legal days, in the days of the underground and now in prison on Robben Island and in Pollsmoor. And in his person he is com-mitted to the practice of liberation because he is committed to the liberation of his people, of our people, but he is a liberated man in himself. He uses no devices to overwhelm others. He has pride, but no false pride. He has no arrogance, he has no malice. He is a plain and a straightforward man, he is a soft-spoken man, but he is a committed man, a man who makes no concessions when ques-tions of principles are at stake. He is a decisive man but he is not an authoritarian leader. Politics is his life and he believes in people.

He is committed to the liberation of all people. He is committed to the liberation of the African women. In his family Albertina Sisulu is a fine leader in her own right, but her capacity to lead and her political strength is also the product of a good marriage, a good political marriage that is based on genuine equality and on shared commitment. And this is why though Walter Sisulu is absent, when people need to refer back to the history of Walter Sisulu, they can find a living reference point in Albertina Sisulu and in Walter's children. One of the tributes to Walter Sisulu as a revolutionary is in the sacrifice and commitment which his entire family of children have made to the cause. In his children, we have the second generation of Sisulus deep in the struggle of our movement.

It is one of the crimes of this government of South Africa that it has held a man like Walter Sisulu behind bars for so many unbroken years ... but although this is a time for mourning his absence, for wishing that he were here among us, that we could have a birthday celebration in his presence, despite his absence this is a day of celebration and it is today that we should celebrate Walter Sisulu's life, Walter Sisulu's commitment, Walter Sisulu's political achievements.

Her tribute to Walter Sisulu was one of Ruth First's last public statements. On 17 August 1982, she was killed when she opened a parcel bomb sent by an apartheid death squad. The blast also injured Pallo Jordan, who was in her office at Eduardo Mondlane University in Maputo (Shubin, 232). Ruth First's death sent shock waves through the ANC, and Walter and Albertina were deeply saddened by the loss of their old friend.

*f o u r*

After the murder of Joe Gqabi in August 1981, Randall Robinson, executive director of the American organisation Trans-Africa, said they had evidence that classified United States Defence Department documents revealed that the Botha regime in South Africa had assembled an assassination squad to kill ANC leaders operating in the frontline states. He alleged that top-secret intelligence reports proved that US Defence Department officials knew of South Africa's assassination plans long before Gqabi was murdered. "Yet the US did nothing to dissuade its new ally from pursuing its plans. This renders the United States an accomplice in the killing of Mr Gqabi and others that may follow," commented Robinson (Greg Houston, Unpublished notes).

Throughout 1982, the apartheid government waged covert war on the ANC through intensified pressure on the frontline states, sabotage and murder. Pressure on the Botswana government resulted in the arrest of MK commander Joe Modise and ANC Revolutionary Council secretary Cassius Make in Botswana, where they served a year in prison for illegal possession of arms. Pretoria also warned the Swazi government to expel ANC representatives from Swaziland (Shubin, 229–31). On 4 June 1982, Petrus Nzima, the ANC's deputy representative and SACTU's representative in Swaziland, and his wife Jabu were assassinated in a car bomb in the Swazi town of Manzini.

As Petrus and Jabu Nzima came from Soweto, the grieving community organised a memorial service at the YMCA in Dube on 14 June 1982. The service also commemorated Joseph Mavi, the president of the Black Municipality Workers' Union, who had recently died in a car accident. Mavi, a bus driver, had successfully led 10 000 municipal workers in a strike in July 1980. As Albertina arrived at the YMCA, she noticed a strong, but not unusual, police presence, but thought nothing of it. Earlier, the police had told *Sowetan* reporter Len Kalane to leave as there would be no service. Once the service was under way, police surrounded the building. At 4.30pm they broke up the service and arrested all 250 mourners (*The Sowetan*, 14/6/82; the *Rand Daily Mail*, 14/6/82).

Albertina was among those arrested. Dr Nthato Motlana, Chairman of the Committee of Ten, and Ellen Kuzwayo, a member of the Committee, were also arrested, as were activist and former Robben Islander Eric Molobi, COSAS executive member Pat Lepunya and three reporters from *The Sowetan*, Len Kalane, Len Khumalo and Nhlanhla Mbatha. The mourners were crammed into five large police vans and driven to Protea Police Headquarters for "screening". "We were surprised by the arrests and had no idea what would happen," recalled Albertina, "but to keep our spirits up we sang while we waited." No one was charged, but police took everyone's fingerprints and photographed them. They were finally released after midnight.

Bishop Tutu and Khehla Mthembu, the president of AZAPO, both condemned the arrests as ill timed. The next day, *The Sowetan* noted that the timing of the crackdown, just two days before 16 June, was inflammatory, and commented angrily on the actions of the police:

> It is difficult to imagine why the chiefs of the police should focus so glaringly on this fateful day by their abysmal timing. It is almost as if some people have the death wish.
>
> There is of course talk that the net was thrown around the Dube Y to get some suspects the police had been after for some time. Even if that is the case it is most indelicate to do this kind of thing at a service such as this. This was after all a mourning service for a man who had died in a car accident. The way in which those who were at the meeting were roped in was just as unfortunate. There were women present with babies on their back, it is said.

ABOVE: *Zwelakhe and Zodwa Sisulu, wedding party, December 1978.* (Sisulu Family Collection)

RIGHT: *Albertina, Helen Joseph and Amina Cachalia, circa 1980s.* (Private Collection: Amina Cachalia)

RIGHT: *Albertina and Sheila Sisulu set off for Pollsmoor Prison to show Walter grandchild Tumi, the latest addition to the Sisulu family, February 1986. Behind is young Ntsiki Sisulu.* (Sisulu Family Collection)

ABOVE: *Albertina celebrating the one-year anniversary of the UDF with Father Smangaliso Mkhatshwa and Dorothy Nyembe, August 1984.* (Paul Weinberg)

LEFT: *Mewa Ramgobin consults with Ismail Mohamed during the Pietermaritzburg Treason Trial, 1985.* (Sisulu Family Collection)

LEFT: *Albertina dines with Azhar Cachalia and former American First Lady Jackie Kennedy-Onassis on the UDF trip to the USA, July 1989.* (Sisulu Family Collection)

ABOVE: *Walter, Archbishop Desmond Tutu and Albertina celebrate Walter's release from prison, 15 October 1989.* (Mayibuye Centre)

ABOVE: *Walter greets neighbours and friends on his return home after his release from prison in October 1989.* (Alf Kumalo)

ABOVE: *Leaders of the ANC are reunited in Stockholm in February 1990. Standing (from left) are Thabo Mbeki, Joe Nhlanhla, Govan Mbeki, Raymond Mhlaba, Oliver Tambo, Andrew Mlangeni, Walter, Wilton Mkwayi, Joe Slovo and Henry Makgothi. Seated are (from left) Alfred Nzo, Albertina and Elias Motsoaledi.* (ANC Commemorative Card No. 2)

ABOVE: *Old friends Walter and Nelson Mandela share a private moment in a public arena, 1990s.* (unknown)

ABOVE: *Walter and Albertina are joined by Andrew and June Mlangeni on a return visit to Robben Island, 1992.* (Jürgen Schadeberg)

ABOVE: *Walter reflects on his years at Robben Island during a return visit to the prison, 1992.* (Jürgen Schadeberg)

ABOVE: *Beryl Simelane, Max Sisulu, former US President Jimmy Carter and Lindiwe Sisulu, Carter-Meril Award presentation, December 1988.* (Sisulu Family Collection)

ABOVE: *Walter and Sam Nujoma, Lusaka, 1990.* (Sisulu Family Collection)

ABOVE: *Walter and Yehudi Menuhin, Cape Town, 1995.* (The Cape Times)

ABOVE: *Albertina addresses guests on the occasion of Walter's 80th birthday, 18 May 1992. Looking on are Oliver and Adelaide Tambo.* (Private Collection: Rica Hodgson)

RIGHT: *Albertina and and her son Zwelakhe are reunited after his release from prison, December 1988.* (Mayibuye Centre)

RIGHT: *The Sisulus gather together on a family holiday to the Transkei coast, December 1993.* (Sisulu Family Collection)

LEFT: *Hlakula/Sisulu family home, Qutubeni, Transkei.* (Beata Lipman)

ABOVE: *The Sisulu family reunited after the release of Jongi, Orlando West, March 1990. Front, from left: Jacqueline (Bibi) with Tshepang, Zwelethu, Walter, Vuyelwa, Albertina, Zodwa with baby Ziyeka; middle: unknown, Tumi, Moyikwa, Thulane, Zoya; back: Jongi, Sheila, Lungi Snr, Lungi Jnr, ANC bodyguard.* (Giselle Wolfsohn)

To add to the blunder, those arrested included well-known people like Dr Motlana, Mrs Sisulu and Mrs Kuzwayo. These people are not only household names in South Africa but are known the world over. South Africa should not be surprised that this story has reached world audiences by now.

One has stopped hoping to see the day when the security police show a little more respect for our people, particularly on such solemn occasions. Black people have, alas, almost become used to this serious affront to their culture and human dignity. Such services have been disrupted regularly and sometimes even with people getting themselves injured. In the meantime, all this is not doing any good to the other sectors of the police who seem to want to normalise relationships between themselves and the communities they serve (*The Sowetan*, 15/6/82).

On the evening of 15 June, Albertina's year-long respite from state-imposed restrictions ended when two security policemen delivered her fifth banning order. Since the beginning of 1982, the security police had been itching to slap Albertina with a stringent banning order.

On 25 March the Director-General of Justice wrote to the Commissioner of Police saying the Minister would not be prepared to act against Albertina on the strength of unconfirmed newspaper reports. The Commissioner replied that the newspaper reports had been confirmed by security reports.

The security police continued to argue that "Her conduct endangers public order and security of the state and it is recommended that her activities should be curtailed". While the Ministry of Justice agreed with this view, it did not agree on the banning order: "Her activities are restricted to meetings. It is therefore suggested that she should be forbidden to attend meetings for a period of two years. That will remove the platform from where she expounds her ideological views" (Ministry of Justice documents).

According to the new two-year banning order, Albertina was banned from any social or political gathering or place where students were being instructed. Unlike her earlier restrictions, she was not confined to a particular magisterial district.

A sullen and simmering Soweto marked the sixth anniversary of the June 16 uprising. The *Rand Daily Mail* editorial of 18 June 1982 captured the tension of the day:

A sigh of relief is appropriate: June 16 was observed with only little violence and a merciful absence of death. With the scars of 1976 still fresh for many, the day is rightly of deep significance to vast numbers of South Africans. It is because of this intensity of feeling that June 16 lends itself to emotional escalation, whether on the part of the people or the police ...

Attacks on buses or on commercial vehicles as occurred at the University of the North cannot but cause the police to move in, thus serving to contribute still more to angry feelings and leading to a spiralling of violence in which only armed force becomes the final victor. No doubt it was recognition of this which caused Bishop Desmond Tutu to put his own life at risk by going to the crowds outside Regina Mundi Cathedral and persuading them to cease throwing stones.

There must be comment on the behaviour of the authorities. The mass arrests which took place on Sunday in Soweto provided a distressing and ominous prelude. Certainly the police were engaging in that old South African official pastime of seeking out "agitators". When, on the eve of June 16, banning orders were served on Mrs Albertina Sisulu – as always, without benefit of trial or reason given – it seemed to serve as additional notice of a lack of tolerance by the government of any dissidents.

As it turned out the general lack of violence gave the police little reason to have to act toughly. But what the police did do was to make no bones about their attempt to prevent the media from properly reporting what was happening in Soweto.

Grabbing dozens of local and foreign journalists and keeping them at gunpoint inside the grounds of Protea Police Station was a startling assault on the public's right to know, capped by the peremptory removal from white journalists of permits allowing entry into Soweto, and capped in turn by efforts to give incorrect and misleading information.

The subsequent claim by the Commissioner of Police, General Mike Geldenhuys, that the banning of journalists from Soweto had contributed to the relative quietness of the day, is an appalling commentary from the head of the South African police force. The problem of cameras notwithstanding, journalists do not make events. They report them. Gen. Mike Geldenhuys' argument would lead us inexorably towards wide-ranging restrictions on media access to public events. It takes no account of the public's need to know, nor of the fact that such episodes do great damage to South Africa's name.

The lives of the majority of people under apartheid were so circumscribed by repressive laws that for many people, the services of a lawyer were as essential as those of a family doctor. Priscilla Jana, who represented hundreds of political activists from the late 1970s onwards, described human rights lawyers as people who had to be social workers, counsellors and a host of other things: "You had to go beyond the ambit and scope of your legal functions. When you took on political trials, they would not only harass the activist member. They would harass the whole family" (Interview, Priscilla Jana, 5/9/96).

After she had represented Zwelakhe in the Thami Mkhwanazi case in 1979, Jana had developed a close bond with Albertina: "We developed a strong and wonderful relationship," recalled Jana. "I represented every member of the Sisulu family, either through a court trial or some confrontation with the police. In the end I became a combination of her family lawyer, friend and child." When she first visited the Sisulus, Jana had been amazed at how so many people managed to live in one house. "In the early days I used to find it quite difficult to work out who was part of the actual Sisulu family and who wasn't. For many years I did not really know how many children MaSisulu had and I was too embarrassed to ask!"

Walter and Albertina celebrated the birth of a new grandchild on 24 November 1982 when Zwelakhe and Zodwa had their second child. As was customary, Walter chose the name, settling on Zoya (after the female Russian astronaut, Zoyenka) for his new granddaughter. He was greatly taken with the notion of women in space, as he firmly believed that no limits should be set on women's ambitions and capabilities. As welcome as the new arrival was, her birth brought to a head the need for her parents to move into their own house.

At the time, in addition to Zwelakhe, Zodwa and their children, Nkuli and Jongi were still staying with Albertina, as were Flora, her husband and two sons. Nanziwe Thethiwe, the daughter of Albertina's brother Rushman, had come to Johannesburg to pursue her studies and was also staying at the Sisulu home.

Zwelakhe and Zodwa had managed to buy a new house in Dobsonville a few months earlier, but could not move because of Zwelakhe's banning order. Priscilla Jana lodged a petition to have his banning order amended so he could move. In the petition, she emphasised the housing shortages in Soweto and pointed out that Zwelakhe had been on a waiting list since 1979. Since his new house was in Dobsonville, which fell under the magisterial district of Roodepoort, while Zwelakhe's restrictions confined him to Soweto, the petition requested that his restriction be amended to allow him to live in his new home.

The Director of Security Legislation came up with a rather strange response: "Compol has no objection to the request ... Sisulu is at present unemployed but is seeking employment. As there are better prospects of obtaining employment in Johannesburg, Compol recommends that Sisulu be permitted to be in the magisterial districts of Johannesburg and Roodepoort" (Ministry of Justice files). Since the security police were the ones responsible for the banning order that prevented Zwelakhe from working as a journalist in the first place, it seemed ironic that they should express concern about his employment prospects.

The effects of the government's total onslaught strategy were felt throughout 1982. Apart from the assassinations of Ruth First and Petrus and Jabu Nzima, the ANC London offices were bombed in April by a South African security police team headed by the notorious spy Craig Williamson. Youth activists were especially targeted by the apartheid murder squads. In April, COSAS activists Siphiwe Mthimkulu and Topsy Madaka were abducted from Port Elizabeth and killed by security police. Mthimkulu was in the process of suing the police for poisoning him with thalium while he was in detention. Later in the year, *askaris* – black counter-insurgency agents – masquerading as MK operatives falsely promised to take three COSAS activists for military training. Instead, the activists were taken to a mine bunker near Krugersdorp where they were killed and their bodies blown up. This was to become a favourite method of trapping young activists in the mid- and late-1980s. The deadliest government attack took place on 9 December when a South African raid killed 42 people in Maseru: 30 South Africans and 12 Lesotho citizens. The dead included the ANC chief representative in Lesotho, Zola Nqini, a former Robben Islander, several teenagers and a four-year-old child. The SADF death squad missed their main target, Chris Hani. Walter's old friend Phyllis Naidoo, who was living in Lesotho at the time, also escaped the slaughter. She would later write a heart-rending account of the attack entitled *Le Rona Re Batho*. Lesotho was rocked by the massacre, and 35 000 of its citizens attended the funeral, including the king and prime minister, as well as members of the diplomatic and UN community, who could not find words strong enough to condemn the attack. Putting aside all thoughts of his own personal safety and going against the advice of Mozambican President Samora Machel, a deeply distressed Oliver Tambo insisted on flying to Lesotho to mourn the dead and offer what comfort he could to the living.

On the day of the funeral of the victims of the Maseru massacre, MK carried out a retaliatory attack on the Koeberg atomic power station just outside Cape Town. The war of attrition escalated with MK's deadliest attack taking place in March 1983, with the explosion of a car bomb in front of the headquarters of the SADF in Church Street in Pretoria that killed 20 people and wounded over 200. While the military might of the apartheid state was hardly threatened by such attacks, an explosion in the heart of Pretoria and the fear of similar blasts increased the vulnerability and sense of insecurity of the white community.

Even as its death squads dealt out murder and mayhem in the region, the government continued to pursue its policy of reforms. In 1980, it had set up the President's Council, consisting of 60 government-nominated individuals from white, coloured and Indian communities, with a brief to advise on a new constitution. In May 1982, the President's Council submitted its proposals for a new constitution, the centrepiece of which was to be a "tricameral parliament" – the existing all-white parliament and two new parliaments, one for coloureds and one for Indians. The three parliaments would sit separately, but their executives would be part of the President's Council.

Africans were to be excluded from the new dispensation. According to apartheid logic, the majority of Africans were in any case citizens of the Bantustans. Also in 1982, Piet Koornhof, the ironically titled Minister of Cooperation and Development, introduced what came to be known as the "Koornhof Bills". These were the Orderly Movement and Settlement of Black Persons Bill, the Black Community Development Bill and the Black Local Authorities Act (Mbeki, 57). The Bills gave a small handful of blacks the right of permanent domicile in the urban areas while subjecting the vast majority to stricter influx controls.

The policy underlying these "reforms" clearly aimed to woo coloured and Indian communities away from the rising tide of popular mobilisation, but far from driving a wedge between these communities and the African majority, it united them. In fact, the call to oppose the government's constitutional proposals provided a powerful rallying point to the plethora of organisations that had been formed in the preceding few years.

On 23 January 1983, Reverend Alan Boesak addressed the Transvaal anti-SAIC Committee congress in Johannesburg. A rising political star, Boesak had just months previously been elected president of the World Alliance of Reformed Churches and had succeeded in getting that body to condemn apartheid as a theological heresy (Bredekamp, 315). At the meeting, Boesak used his oratory skills to persuade his audience to reject the government's constitutional proposals. He urged people to use "the politics of refusal" to say "no" to apartheid. In a departure from his prepared speech, he called for the formation of a "united front" of "churches, civic and student organisations, trade unions and sports bodies to organise joint opposition to the constitutional reforms" (Seekings, 49).

Boesak's call was a seed that found fertile ground. Many present had attended the conference with an agenda that went beyond the stated objectives of winding up the anti-SAIC campaign. The burning issue at the time was how to respond to the proposed tricameral parliament. Virtually all the major activists from the Charterist tradition were in attendance, and the delegates represented a cross-section of the nascent extra-parliamentary opposition (Mbeki, 57). Many had heard Oliver Tambo's annual January 8th address to the ANC on Radio Freedom. Tambo had declared 1983 "the year of united action" and called for "the organisation of all democratic forces into one front for national liberation". Those in the ANC underground had been involved in discussions with Lusaka about the need for some kind of coordinating structure. Others were familiar with Neville Alexander's call in 1982 for a united front against the Koornhof Bills. In the words of UDF biographer Jeremy Seekings: "Boesak's call fell on ground that was not just fertile but already prepared … Although Charterist leaders in different parts of the country may not have agreed over what such a body entailed, or precisely when it should be formed, by the end of 1982 most of them supported the idea of a nationwide front" (Seekings, 47).

Not surprisingly, the conference responded enthusiastically to Boesak's proposal and a national steering committee was set up to take the proposal forward. There was a flurry of meetings and consultations in the ensuing months as the steering committee actively canvassed for support for the proposed front in their respective regions. They also approached prominent individuals. Albertina, who had not attended the January meeting because of her restrictions, was approached by Moses Chikane and Jabu Ngwenya. "We wanted MaSisulu's participation because we needed the reflection of the ANC in the movement we were going to form," explained Chikane. "She was also important because she was one of the leading lights in the revival of FEDSAW" (Interview, Moses Chikane).

Albertina expressed her wholehearted support for the proposed front.

Selling the idea of a united front to the various regions was not a smooth or easy process. Overtures to get AZAPO to join the proposed front were firmly rejected. AZAPO instead joined forces with groups from the Black Consciousness and Unity Movement traditions that formed a National Forum Committee to act as a united front against the constitutional proposals. Members of the Committee included Neville Alexander, AZAPO leaders Lybon Mabasa and Saths Cooper, Bishop Tutu, Piroshaw Camay (the General Secretary of CUSA) and Emma Mashinini, veteran trade unionist and founder of the CAWUSA union. It also included Boesak, RAM Saloojee and Dr Nthato Motlana, who would all later be drawn into the UDF camp (Marx, 117, 295). At the National Forum committee launch in June 1983, attended by over 800 people representing 164 organisations, Neville Alexander criticised the proposed Charterist initiative, contemptuously dismissing what he called "national" or "ethnic" group approaches to politics. The National Forum's commitment to ideological purity was diametrically opposed to the UDF's broad inclusive approach, and at first it seemed unlikely that the two organisations might cooperate.

Nevertheless, several months of intensive lobbying to counter fears of ethnic domination and to overcome regional sensitivities finally yielded results. In May 1983, the Natal UDF Region was launched with Archie Gumede as its president. This was followed by the launch of the UDF in the Transvaal in May and the Western Cape in July. Veteran trade unionist Oscar Mpetha was elected president of the Western Cape regional executive. Elections for the Transvaal regional executive were postponed until August. Activists elected to the newly formed UDF regional executives were incorporated into the national steering committee, which then became known as the Interim

National Committee. When this held a two-day planning meeting at the end of July, Albertina was able to attend because her banning orders had just expired.

Although only three UDF regions had been organised, the Interim Committee decided that the national launch of the UDF had to take place in August. The establishing of the National Forum in June put the fledgling UDF under pressure to take the initiative in resistance politics; more importantly, the government was scheduled to table the constitutional proposals in parliament in August. With the launch just three weeks away, those at the meeting had to get through an enormous amount of business.

The energy and drive of the young activists impressed Albertina, and she returned home feeling that all the years of political work were finally paying dividends: that they were at last on the brink of something truly momentous.

With the introduction of the new Internal Security Act of 1982, the restrictions of a number of political activists came to an unscheduled end in July 1983. Zwelakhe, whose restrictions were supposed to have ended in December 1983, and Albertina, whose restrictions were to have ended on 31 May 1984, suddenly found themselves unrestricted. Compol immediately started lobbying for a new banning order for Albertina: "Sisulu has a long history of undermining activities. Although she is 63 years old, it has to be accepted that as she is the wife of Walter Sisulu, the blacks consider her to be a leading figure for as long as Walter Sisulu is in prison. That possibly explains her presence at meetings of those who are hostile towards the order in the republic ... if she is not further restricted, she will again start attending and addressing meetings."

The Ministry of Justice was not in favour of issuing another banning order at first:

The problem in her case is that, although Compol maintains that she is propagating violence, there is no reliable information to bear out this allegation. Compol relies on newspaper reports for confirmation of its allegations, but their reportage of Sisulu's remarks differs from that of Compol's sources. If she is not further restricted, and she continues to address meetings where what she says can be construed as advocating violence, and it can be proved as such, she should then be charged ...

The Minister ordered that Albertina's activities should be monitored, "and if information is received of her participation in activities that will endanger the maintenance of the security of the state or the maintenance of law and order, the matter must be referred to me for the necessary attention."

One can only assume that the Minister considered Albertina's participation in the UDF as a threat to law and order because on 5 August, two security police walked into the clinic where Albertina was working and arrested her. As she was led to the police car, women in the vicinity gathered around and shouted abuse at the police. They drove away with the words of the women ringing in their ears: "MaSisulu, ubuye nayo inkululeko." ("MaSisulu, come back with Freedom.")

Also arrested at his place of work was 25-year-old Soweto teacher, Thami Mali. The families immediately contacted Priscilla Jana, who established that the two had been charged under the Suppression of Communism Act for allegedly furthering the aims of the ANC through their activities at the funeral of ANC Women's League veteran Rose Mbele on 16 January 1983.

Albertina's arrest forced her to miss a crucial UDF meeting at which elections were held for the UDF Regional Executive Committee of the Transvaal region. Five vice-presidents were elected: Rev. Frank Chikane; Curtis Nkondo; Dr RAM Salojee, a vice-president of the Transvaal Indian Congress; Elliot Shabangu, a trade unionist; and Hans Hlalethwa of the Winterveld Action Committee. Mohammed Valli Moosa and Popo Molefe were elected joint secretaries and Rita Ndzanga and Eric Molobi were elected joint treasurers. Other members included Dr Nthato Motlana of the Soweto Committee of Ten and Rev. Cecil Begbie of the Witwatersrand Council of Churches. Albertina was elected President in absentia.

In an article on her election, journalist Anton Harber wrote:

The Transvaal regional council of the UDF elected her unopposed "as a great homage and as a warning to the State" at a meeting in Johannesburg. Mrs Sisulu replaced Dr RAM. Saloojee who headed the interim committee that established the UDF. Dr Saloojee announced the arrest of the "mother of the nation" with "bitter resentment". "At a time when there seems to be a belief that the State is softening up, we find the heavy hand of oppression being brought down on us once again," he said. Mrs Sisulu will now lead the Transvaal delegation to the national launching of the UDF in Cape Town in two weeks' time – provided she is no longer in custody (The *Rand Daily Mail*, 8/8/83).

The election of the Regional Executive marked the beginning of the Transvaal UDF's mass publicity drive in the townships. To coincide with the meeting, it distributed 250 000 copies of the *UDF News,* mainly in the Reef area. The newsletter made a call "to form one united force for freedom, marching under one banner with tried and tested leaders" (*The Star*, 8/8/83). The front page carried a powerful full-length image of Albertina.

Meanwhile, their lawyers had managed to establish that Albertina and Thami Mali would appear at the Krugersdorp Magistrates' Court. Family members and dozens of activists travelled to Krugersdorp, only to find that the hearing had suddenly been switched to Johannesburg. Albertina and Mali were told that they were alleged to have engaged in activities on behalf of the banned ANC. They were not asked to plead and the magistrate, Ms HS van Heerden, postponed their hearing to August 17 for the setting of a date for trial. The Attorney-General opposed the granting of bail and the two were remanded in custody (*The Sowetan*, 8/8/83).

At the hearing on 17 August, Albertina and Thami Mali heard that the charges against them arose from the funeral of Albertina's old friend Rose Mbele on 16 January 1983 at the Holy Cross Church in Orlando West. The State alleged that the two had sung songs praising the aims of the ANC, its activities and its leaders, distributed pamphlets, displayed ANC flags, draped the coffin of the deceased with an ANC flag, and praised the deceased for furthering the aims and objectives of the ANC, thereby creating sympathy and support for the organisation. The date for the trial was set for 17 October, and Albertina and Mali were remanded in custody in Diepkloof Prison.

The international Anti-Apartheid Movement (AAM) did much to publicise Albertina's detention abroad. They wrote to Foreign Secretary Sir Geoffrey Howe asking him to take action on Albertina's behalf. Although the Foreign Office responded that since Albertina was not a British subject it had no formal diplomatic or consular standing to intervene in her case, it did pay more attention than usual to the matter. Foreign Office spokesman, Ray Whitney, in a response of "unusual and considerable length", said they would follow developments in Mrs Sisulu's case closely. "We view with concern the system of banning, detention and imprisonment of people for their political beliefs in South Africa. The South African authorities are no doubt aware of the strong feelings of repugnance which these practices arouse in this country," he wrote (*The Sowetan*, 23/8/83).

For the apartheid government, the international chorus of disapproval brought about by Albertina's arrest had to be weighed against its determination to quell the fledgling UDF. The actions of Thami Mali and Albertina at Rose Mbele's funeral were not really the issue, as is evidenced by the fact that they were arrested a full eight months after the funeral. The real objective was to weaken the new movement by removing major activists from circulation. The imprisonment of Albertina and Mali was a sign of things to come.

# five

While Albertina Sisulu sat in solitary confinement in Diepkloof Prison, tens of thousands of people at the UDF national launch in Cape Town on 20 August 1983 cheered her election as one of the three UDF co-presidents. Frazzled activists had worked around the clock on the organisational and logistical arrangements to get representatives from over 400 organisations throughout the country to Cape Town. They had to deal with many last-minute crises, not least those created by the security police, who tried to put a spoke in the wheel by distributing bogus pamphlets giving false details about the launch. Finally, three weeks of frenzied preparations resulted in a resoundingly successful launch. Nkuli and Sheila Sisulu were among the hundreds of people from Johannesburg who travelled through the night to Cape Town in buses hired by the UDF, enjoying the party atmosphere: "We did not sleep at all. We sang freedom songs throughout the night."

The choice of venue – Rocklands Centre in Mitchell's Plain in Cape Town – was significant. The organisation opposing the divisive constitutional proposals was being launched right in the coloured heartland. The launch consisted of a conference for the delegates, followed by a mass rally. The public response was beyond all expectations, with between 12 000 and 15 000 people attending the rally. The conference hall and huge marquee were bursting at the seams while thousands of people who could not be accommodated braved the bitter cold outside. Zwelakhe Sisulu was one of the journalists who covered the event. In an article headlined "The herald of a new era", he wrote:

> The launching of the UDF in Cape Town at the weekend introduces a new phase in the struggle for liberation in SA. The number and character of the 400 organisations that constitute the UDF make it comparable to the Congress of the People held in Kliptown in 1955. The more than 12 000 people who streamed to the Rocklands Civic Centre in Mitchell's Plain turned the meeting into an emotional occasion, reminiscent of a revival meeting. Indeed, it called to mind the days of the Congress Alliance and some of the stalwarts of that era were there to be seen; there was Frances Baard, Helen Joseph, Archie Gumede, RD Naidoo and a host of others.
>
> Whether the UDF is going to be able to sustain the high note on which it started will depend on its programme of action which is now being finalised. Prior to its national launching, the organisation concentrated on establishing regional structures, and it is on these structures that its success will depend. The organisation's declaration which was adopted at the conference reads in part: "We, the freedom-loving people of South Africa say with one voice to the whole world that we cherish the vision of a united, democratic South Africa based on the will of the people. We will strive for the unity of all our people and the end of apartheid, economic and all other forms of exploitation."
>
> There were many highlights of the congress, but perhaps none as touching as the short address given by the ten-year old daughter of the banned journalist Johnny Issel. Her simple statement summed up the feeling of the crowd: 'My father cannot be here today. My father supports the UDF and he wants to be free" (*The Sowetan*, 24/8/83).

In the opening speech of the Conference, ANC veteran Frances Baard invoked the spirit of the 1960s when she quoted Macmillan's famed "Winds of Change" speech of 20 years before, saying she could now smell "the freedom air" sweeping through Africa (Sampson 2000, 330). Among the patrons of the UDF were Helen Joseph, Dennis Goldberg and Beyers Naudé. The nomination of Nelson Mandela and Walter Sisulu, such powerful symbols of the ANC, as patrons received a standing ovation, and the crowd responded enthusiastically when a message from Mandela was read out. It was announced that Mandela and his cell-mates in Pollsmoor had given their blessings to the gathering.

There was a joyous response to the announcement that the UDF would be headed by three presidents – Albertina Sisulu, Oscar Mpetha and Archie Gumede. Mpetha was in hospital with diabetes at the time. Archie Gumede, the only president in attendance, was carried shoulder-high by jubilant supporters. Not many people knew that the presidency had been a contentious issue during the lead up to the launch. The Natal and Transvaal regions had favoured Albertina Sisulu, but the Western Cape objected; they wanted Oscar Mpetha instead. Popo Molefe felt the differences stemmed from lack of trust between the regions: "We did not really know one another that well. And people were very sentimental about leadership coming from their own region."

By the eve of the launch, the matter had still not been resolved and the planning committee was up until the early hours of the morning locked in debate. Moses Chikane said he was taken aback when he arrived in Cape Town on the eve of the launch to find a crisis over the presidency: "I had serious problems with it. As far as I was concerned the matter had long been settled and we had already sent a message to MaSisulu that she had been nominated president. We had also told the Transvaal delegates, so we had 36 buses coming from the Transvaal full of people singing MaSisulu's name. How were we going to explain to them why we had backtracked?" (Interview, Moses Chikane.) The possibility of putting the matter to the vote was rejected, said Popo Molefe, "because it was clear that it might have left gaping wounds". A compromise was finally reached when the three regions agreed to have three co-presidents (Seekings, 55).

The UDF launch closed with a speech by Alan Boesak, an inspired choice, as (in the words of one commentator), Boesak was a consummate orator who could play his audience "like a violin virtuoso on a Stradivarius" (Seekings, 58). "We want all our rights, we want them here and we want them now," Boesak said to his mesmerised audience. No one doubted him when he said "I believe we are standing at the birth of what could become the greatest and most significant people's movement in more than a quarter of a century" (UDF files; *The Argus*, 20/5/83).

After the UDF launch, Zwelakhe was able to visit his father in Pollsmoor. He was in Cape Town in the first place because his restrictions had ended earlier than expected. Walter was delighted to get a first-hand account of the launch. The Pollsmoor prisoners had been following the unfolding of the new organisation with great interest. As far back as 1976, Walter had advocated the bringing together of "the widest and most diverse forces among all population groups" to destroy apartheid (Maharaj, 80). His concern over Albertina's imprisonment was mixed with pride at her election to the UDF presidency. Zwelakhe briefed him about Albertina's case and how the family was coping in her absence. Walter was encouraged to learn that his old friend George Bizos would be defending his wife. He also felt confidence in her ability to cope with her ordeal: "I knew she was strong, she would not weaken."

Albertina celebrated her 64th birthday on 21 October, a few days after the start of her trial. Walter felt pained that she was in prison on her birthday and he tried to keep up her spirits (and his own) in the only way he could – by writing a letter.

Darling Tini,

Last night I finished my last paper of this year's examinations. I will comment on this later. For the moment, remember it is the 21st of October – your birthday. We got up in a very good mood for the day. Even the SABC was in agreement with us as if they knew. They rendered one of the first pieces of Margaret Mcingana. We were in full swing back to the days of the Bantu Men's Social Centre. Though breakfast was served it was not possible to settle down to the meal while Margie's piece was still playing. We ended the day with a game of casino, but of course I was the loser because my mind was a thousand miles away in Diepkloof.

Beryl tried to set Walter's mind at rest by writing to him in detail about the progress of Albertina's trial, as well as more general family matters. He was glad to hear that Lungi and Sheila were looking after the house in Albertina's absence. In November 1983, Walter wrote back to thank her for her efforts: "Firstly I must thank you for the manner in which your letters make me feel a real part of the family. Secondly I am grateful that you went to Mama's case as I can imagine how she felt your presence. It must have consoled her. The fact that all of you can handle the affairs of the home jointly gives her great relief" (6/11/83). He also expressed his gratitude to Lungi:

> She [Beryl] has been lately so good in her letters. They give so much pleasure because they are very informative about members of the family who are in different parts of the world ... I must express my thanks to all of you for the manner you have looked after the home, in the absence of Tini. Do convey my sentiments to Sheila, Lakhe and Zodwa, to Nkuli and Aunt Flora and her family, as well as other members of the family. I must say that Tini's case does not look too good, however she has the best possible defence counsel. I am however happy about the way she is taking it ... Tell Sheila that I am grateful for her letter and will not reply to her now. I have very few letters left in my quota and I must keep regular correspondence with Mama – my girlfriend (6/12/83).

The first day of the Rose Mbele trial, as it came to be called, started in an atmosphere of tight security, in the Krugersdorp Magistrates' Court. The main state witness, Warrant Officer Johann Steyn of the Soweto Security Police, told the court he and a Major Schoeman were on duty at the Holy Cross Church on the day of Rose Mbele's funeral on 16 January 1983. Steyn said he used a video camera to film activities before and after the service at the church and later at the graveyard. Court proceedings were adjourned so that counsel and court officials could view the videotape. When proceedings resumed, the magistrate said the video clearly showed a woman in front of the church holding a plastic bag and distributing something to people entering the church. Next to her stood a man with a raised, clenched fist. When the procession left the church, a flag of black and green was seen at the head of the procession and the coffin, carried in relays to the graveyard, was draped with a flag of black, green and gold.

George Bizos, for the defence, said the two admitted to having been on a horse-drawn cart that carried Mrs Mbele's coffin. He also said it was obvious from the film that someone had handed out papers to people arriving at the church, but that they had not been handed out indiscriminately (*The Sowetan*, 18/10/83).

Albertina made no bones about what she had done and why: "Rose Mbele was a good friend of the family and an old veteran ... She used to take care of my children when we were in jail. She had been sick for a long time. We helped look after her. It was Zwelakhe's task to take her to the hospital whenever she was sick. I had to help with the funeral arrangements. I handed out copies of the programme and the obituary. They were in ANC colours. The ANC had to help the family. In my speech I acknowledged and praised her role in the ANC."

Barbara Hogan was in prison with Albertina at Diepkloof, although they did not see each other. "We were not allowed to meet or speak to each other. They made sure we never came into contact." Albertina remembers: "The prison staff told me that Barbara was giving them a hard time. She would demand to know whether I was being kept under the same conditions. She would say: 'Is MaSisulu being given this food? If she is not, then I don't want it. Take it away.'"

The family was worried about Albertina's health, but she herself was not concerned: "My diabetes did not trouble me too much because I had my treatment. I was taken to the doctor. They took me in handcuffs surrounded by these big white policemen. I sat in the back seat with one on either side of me and another car at the back. The doctor I saw was very sympathetic, but was careful just to treat me. He clearly did not want to talk about anything else."

On 24 February 1983, Albertina was sentenced in the Krugersdorp Regional Court to four years in prison, two of which were suspended for five years. She was released on bail of R1 000, pending appeal.

Albertina describes the events of that day with wry understatement:

I had spent seven months in solitary confinement. After I was sentenced, I was taken to Pretoria Prison in handcuffs in a convoy of three cars. As I walked through the corridors of Diepkloof Prison, the women prisoners who were cleaning were made to face the wall because they were not allowed to look at me. [This was standard procedure for preventing contact between criminal and political prisoners.] On arrival at Pretoria Prison, I was given the prisoners' uniform because I was now a convicted prisoner.

Priscilla came late at night to fetch me. She had managed to arrange for bail. I was surprised to be woken up at that time. She took me straight to her house where her husband had cooked a delicious curry for me. There we were eating curry in the early hours of the morning!

Priscilla Jana describes the frantic behind-the-scenes activity that lay behind Albertina's release:

When she was convicted and sentenced, I was so distressed, I forgot my family, my home, everything. I cracked up completely, I had to do something. She was granted bail and I was determined to get her out of jail on the same night. I had to beg counsel who wanted to go home at the end of the trial, that there was no way we were going home without taking Mama with us. And we had to lodge a bail application at about 7pm. It was a great deal of effort because we had to find a judge and I had to get counsel to argue it. It must have been about 8.30pm by the time we were granted bail.

And then we had to raise the bail money ... And to raise that kind of money in those days was virtually impossible. But I wouldn't rest. I had even forgotten to phone my husband to tell him I was delayed ... In those days we did not have cellphones. I literally went to everyone I knew and we collected little sums and finally at about midnight we had all the cash and we went to Pretoria Central Prison and we knocked on the doors.

I wouldn't move. I said we want MaSisulu – we've got the bail order and the money and we want her out. And poor Mama was fast asleep. They had to go and wake her. I don't know whether she was pleased to see me or not. She looked at me as though to say "What the hell was I doing there at that time of the night, waking her up?" ... We went straight to my house and by that time someone had told my husband what was happening, and he had cooked food and we all sat down at 3am to have this meal. It was quite amazing eating curry and rice at three in the morning before we took Mama home (Interview, Priscilla Jana, 5/9/96).

Meanwhile, Albertina's sentence had attracted attention at the highest international levels. In a statement issued by the United Nations Special Committee against Apartheid, Acting Chair Vladimir A Kraves said:

It is with deep indignation that I have learned on 24 February 1984 of the sentencing by the apartheid regime of Albertina Sisulu, an executive member of the Federation of South African Women, to four years in prison for singing freedom songs and supporting the ANC at funerals of ANC and trade union activists ...

The sentence was passed at a time when the international community is observing the Year of the Women of South Africa in tribute to the heroic struggle of South African women against apartheid. It also demonstrated the cruelty and determination of the apartheid government to silence and crush any peaceful opposition to its institutionalised system of racial discrimination, oppression and exploitation.

On behalf of the Special Committee against Apartheid, I strongly denounce the sentencing of Mrs Sisulu for her opposition to apartheid (United Nations Press Release, Department of Public Information, Press section, 29/2/84).

Gertrude Shope, the leader of the women's section of the ANC, weighed in as well: "The sentencing of Albertina Sisulu, president of the Federation of South African Women and joint president of the United Democratic Front to two years in the apartheid jails … is an act that must not and will not go unchallenged. Mrs Sisulu is one of the greatest leaders and a veteran activist of our liberation struggle. This trial must not be seen in isolation. It is part of a countrywide offensive by the regime in a desperate effort to stop militancy of the people" (Statement, 20/3/84).

In March 1984, Albertina travelled to Cape Town for three visits with Walter. By that time, contact visits were allowed and Walter was permitted to hold his newest grandchild, Zoya. Walter Sisulu praised his wife for her prominence in the UDF and the ANC, and they caught up on all the family news. Lindi was in the UK completing her MA at Sussex and Nkuli had enrolled for a BA at University of Western Cape. The constant interruptions in Nkuli's studies had long been a matter of concern and at one stage Albertina felt that it might be better for Nkuli to go abroad to study. She explored the possibility of a scholarship, but when she discussed the matter with Walter, he baulked at the idea of yet another child going into exile. Max was in Bulgaria, and Lindi and Zwelakhe were overseas, the latter having been awarded a prestigious fellowship to Harvard.

Walter described this celebratory visit in a letter, dated 5 April 1984, to Lindi:

I am not sure if I told you of Tini's visit after she was released on bail. I will not now go into details except to say it was more than exciting and to crown it all, she came with her amazing granddaughter Zoya, a really bright thing. I wish I had space and time to go into all that. There was also Nkuli, who remembered: "It is my first time to see you together."
Now my dear child how can I show you that I am very, very anxious to hear from you.
Give my love to all members of your family and one thousand kisses to Ayanda.
Your ever loving Tata.

Sometime in 1983 Albertina had met a young doctor called Abu Baker Asvat who invited her to work as his nurse in his surgery in Rockville, Soweto. Albertina knew Abu's family, in particular his aunt Dr Zainub Asvat, the sister of Albertina's friend Amina Cachalia. Abu Asvat had grown up in Vrededorp in Johannesburg. As a result of the Extension of University Education Act of 1959, he and his brother Ebrahim had been unable to get into medical school in South Africa, so their father had sent them to what was then East Pakistan (now Bangladesh) to study medicine. Abu was shocked by the poverty he saw there and his experience marked the beginning of a lifelong commitment to working to improve the plight of the poor. After completing his degree, he returned to South Africa to work at Coronation Hospital in Johannesburg. His constant objections to the discriminatory treatment of black doctors led to his dismissal. He then took over his brother's practice on the Old Potchefstroom Road in Soweto, where he started a crèche for the local children. When his surgery was ransacked during the 1976 uprising, he moved his practice to Rockville where he continued his community work in Soweto.

As part of his efforts to take medical services to the poor, Abu used a caravan as a mobile clinic. He would park in areas where people had no access to medical care and organise volunteer doctors and nurses to help provide care. From time to time, medical representatives would provide him with some samples, but he purchased most of the medication he gave out himself. One day, Abu accompanied Professor Joe Veriava on a visit to Winnie Mandela, who had been banished to the Free State town of Brandfort in 1977. Abu admired Winnie's efforts to improve the conditions in her poverty-stricken neighbourhood, and soon he was driving his caravan to Brandfort at least once a month to provide medical services to the community there.

Abu's deep hatred of injustice and oppression kindled his interest in resistance politics. No doubt his politically active aunt, Zainub Asvat, was an influence, but it was the Black Consciousness movement that was the driving force in his political development. It was these consciousness connections that led to his joining AZAPO in 1978. When Albertina retired from the Council in 1984, she decided to take up Abu Asvat's job offer. From the outset, she enjoyed her new job immensely. She and Abu were kindred spirits. Both felt deeply about the plight of the homeless. Both were committed to the overthrow of apartheid, which they understood to be the root cause of many of the health problems they treated. There were a few raised eyebrows about the president of the UDF working for the health secretary of AZAPO, but, like Albertina, Abu's political outlook enabled him to work alongside people of different political persuasions, provided they were committed to the overthrow of apartheid. Albertina and Abu developed a particularly close bond, which was never affected by their political differences. Dr Asvat understood that his nurse might be jailed at any time, and was flexible and understanding about the red tape generated by her various banning orders. He also gave generous time off for her visits to the Cape to see Walter and other family members in prison, and for her political work. It was a huge relief to Albertina to have an employer who empathised with her political activism, because after seven months in prison, she felt that she had a lot of catching up to do. She was amazed and delighted by the amount of work that had been done in her absence. In September 1983, the UDF executive had held its first meeting in Durban to work out its strategy and programme of action. Here it was decided to target the whites-only referendum on the new constitution on 2 November 1984 for UDF action. UDF-organised protest meetings around the country culminated in a "People's Weekend" on 29–30 October, with over 30 000 people participating in protest meetings, political rallies and rock concerts around the country. While it was a significant statement of protest, it had little impact on the outcome of the referendum. The white electorate turned out in large numbers, with 65 per cent voting in favour of the tricameral parliament.

The UDF was more successful in its campaign calling for the boycott of the municipal elections in the second half of November 1983. The Black Local Authorities Act of 1982 (one of the Koornhof Bills) had reorganised local government structures for urban blacks, with municipal councils being given greater powers and responsibilities. The institutions set up under this act were bitterly resented by township residents, and viewed as a poor substitute for the representation of Africans in central government. The black councils were not autonomous and, elections notwithstanding, councillors who did not toe the government line could simply be removed or replaced. To add insult to injury, the townships had to become self-financing, and it was up to the councillors to find ways of raising revenue. The only way they could do this was by raising rent, which further raised the ire of township communities (Sparks 1995, 332). The UDF therefore found a receptive audience for its boycott campaign, which took the form of open-air meetings, house-to-house visits, and distribution of leaflets and newsletters. The success of the campaign was evident in low voter turnout. In Soweto, a mere 10 per cent of the electorate voted and the mayor was elected by just over a thousand votes in a population of over one and a half million people (Lodge et al., 58).

At its National General Conference, the UDF decided to embark on a "Million Signatures" campaign against the tricameral elections, in the tradition of the petition for signatures that followed the drawing up of the Freedom Charter in 1955. (When youth activists in the Northern Transvaal approached older people for signatures, they were told that they had signed the petition already – in 1955! Lodge et al., 62; Seekings, 105).

The campaign helped publicise and generate further support for the UDF, but never really took off, especially in African townships where the more militant youth saw the signing of petitions as a moderate and "bourgeois" tactic. The Million Signatures campaign petered out with around 400 000 signatures collected, less than half the target. While this could not be considered a success, the UDF learned important lessons about organisation, strategy and tactics in the process (Seekings, 107).

The UDF's campaign to boycott the tricameral elections kicked off in earnest in July 1984. Its leaders travelled the length and breadth of the country, speaking at endless rallies and mass meetings. The campaign was described as "roadshow-style mobilisation" revolving around "high-profile leadership" (Seekings, 108). UDF orators like Alan Boesak and the articulate and linguistically gifted Terror Lekota made their mark on audiences around the country. Speakers from different racial groups and religious persuasions regularly shared the same platform. Veteran leaders of the 1950s were also great drawcards, and the songs, slogans and speeches at the meetings invoked the spirit of the 1950s (Lodge et al., 61).

Albertina was in great demand as a speaker and she was swept into a whirl of meetings and rallies both for FEDSAW and the UDF. The ANC had declared 1984 as the Year of the Woman and Albertina was part of a team of activists who worked intensively to resuscitate FEDSAW. The proposed revival of FEDSAW sparked a lot of debate and there were sharp differences of approach between Albertina and her young protégés.

Albertina's view was that FEDSAW had simply been lying dormant and needed to be revived to draw together South African women of all classes and races. She felt that they should proceed by going to every province and finding women who had been part of FEDSAW. However, the younger women took the view that they were building an organisation that would go beyond the old FEDSAW structures. Rather than start FEDSAW branches all over again, they wanted to encourage autonomous local organisations (such as church and cultural groups and civic structures) to affiliate to a national federation (Interview, Jessie Duarte).

The younger activists also wanted to proceed on a province by province basis before forming a national structure. They argued that if there were several independent provincial organisations, the government would find it more difficult to repress them. Jessie Duarte recalls Albertina's response:

> She threw quite a fit. She lambasted us no end because she felt we did not want to accept the centrality of FEDSAW. But MaSisulu is a strategist. She finally conceded ... that we might find it difficult to attract women into something called FEDSAW because of the threat of it being banned by the regime. When she was finally convinced that the route of organising via independent provincial organisations was the best route, she became the biggest champion of that perspective. This is where I saw her true strength.

Albertina's change of heart put her in direct conflict with Helen Joseph. Jessie described Helen as a "friendly adversary of Albertina". Helen loved to commit everything to writing, and she was very particular about records of meetings and minutes of discussions:

> Now in the Eighties if you organised on paper, you were killing your organisations because as soon as the Boers get hold of your minutes, you would land up in court. Helen and Albertina often disagreed on this issue. The two of them loved each other but they were equally stubborn.
>
> Helen wanted to see the rapid development of FEDSAW and did not see the value of organising on a provincial basis. At a meeting in Cape Town she complained: "I am looking around this room and I see all these women's congresses. Women's Congress of this and Women's Congress of that. What I want to see is the Federation of South African Women and that is the end of it." MaSisulu then got up and dressed Helen down.
>
> Now one of MaSisulu's faults, if you could call it that, was that she did dress people down. I cannot tell you the number of times I got dressed down. But it did not matter. You would go into a corner and cry a little bit, but you would come back and do the work because you would realise that the scolding was not meant personally. It was a zealousness to achieve an objective (Interview, Jessie Duarte).

Albertina set Sister Bernard Ncube and Jessie Duarte the task of drawing veteran activists into the process of building a national women's organisation. Jessie remembers that there were many women "who were reluctant to come out of their comfort zones because of their traumatic experiences in the 1960s but Albertina would insist on their participation". Jessie herself had first-hand experience of just how stubborn Albertina could be:

> She would not take no for an answer. There would be six or seven of us sitting there and she would say, 'Look, my girls, we are going to do this thing in this manner and there is not going to be another way because I've done this before and it has worked.' Perhaps one could regard that as negative now but at the time ... we needed somebody who could provide the kind of firm leadership MaSisulu was able to give.

Jessie also recalled that Albertina was very firm about the need to consult with the women in exile. They communicated often with Gertrude Shope and Ray Simons in Lusaka. ANC activist Ester Maleka was the go-between who would travel to Lusaka to canvass the views of the women in exile. In her public statements during this period, Albertina combined her recounting of the history of women in the political struggle with the campaign against the tricameral elections. A typical example was a speech she made at the Women's Meeting of AZASO Annual Congress in Orlando in June 1984. Sharing a platform with veteran leaders Kate Mboweni, Benedicta Monama, Amanda Kwadi and Dorothy Nyembe, Albertina outlined the history of FEDSAW and the role of women in the campaigns of the 1950s, then went on to attack the new constitution:

> All these years the women had been fighting side by side with men ... and I dare say without women in every struggle there is no progress. Today we are being divided. Our own children, which are Indians and coloureds, are taken away from us. Our own children are going to be called up as soldiers to fight against their own brothers. We as women are the only people who can stop that. The children are ours. They don't belong to the government ... they don't belong to anybody but the mothers of this country. We must stand up and say no to this new constitution of the government!

Albertina echoed this message in a speech at a UDF Don't Vote Rally in Kimberley in July 1984. She also attacked government quislings and called for the release of Mandela and Sisulu, saying there could be no negotiations without the genuine leaders of the people. Undeterred by her age or the fact that she had a jail sentence hanging over her head, Albertina continued her speeches at venues around the country, pulling no punches in her scathing denunciation of the apartheid regime's bogus constitution. She was particularly vocal in her disgust at the plans to conscript young male coloureds and Indians into the apartheid army.

On the first anniversary of the UDF, Albertina made what was perhaps her most evocative speech at the UDF rally at Selbourne Hall, Johannesburg. She was the final speaker on a platform that she shared with a number of UDF leaders, among them Cassim Saloojee, Tsepo Mbane, Smangaliso Mkhatshwa, Frank Chikane, Dorothy Nyembe, Jessica Sherman, Laloo Chiba, Aubrey Mokoena, Ebrahim Patel, Andrew Mogotsi and Jerry Ekandjo. In her lyrical address, she drew on the rhetorical legacy of the Freedom Charter, and invoked the powerful metaphor of motherhood to convey her feelings about the UDF:

> Sons and daughters of Africa
> To me today I'm a great big mother
> For today our multiracial baby is born
> For today our baby that will rule this South Africa in future is born
> The multiracial baby, the United Democratic Front
> Which is uniting the people to speak with one voice.

Which is uniting the people to tell the truth
Which is uniting the people to say no to the Koornhof Laws
Which is uniting the people to say away with the New Constitution, because it doesn't give us freedom
We are here today to celebrate a baby that was born on this date last year when one of their mothers was in jail. I knew I had a new baby in the crib although I was in jail. I was very happy to have this baby, but unfortunately for me, it was taken away from me before I could see it. But I'm happy to say today, all those people have come to witness that that baby was born and is kicking and ... it's marching the people to freedom.

She repeatedly stressed the multiracial nature and composition of the UDF, and countered the government's "divide and rule" policy by embracing those communities it had sought to privilege over the black African majority: "The government of this country is trying to tear our children away from us. Coloureds and Indians are not whites. They're our children; they're classified as non-whites. Since when are they whites? (applause from the audience) Why are they taking our children away from us? Because it [the government] is frightened of the resistance of the people against unjust laws of this country. Does it want our children to join apartheid?"

She had harsh words for those who had "sold out" to PW Botha's constitutional farrago – the Bantustan leaders Mangope, Sebe and Matanzima, as well as Rev. Alan Hendrikse and Amichand Rajbansi (respectively, the leaders of the small coloured and Indian groups who had agreed to the new constitutional proposals). Albertina's warnings to the apartheid government were as uncompromising as ever:

Are we going to say yes to apartheid? (Audience: NO!)
Are we going to allow our children to join apartheid? (Audience: NO!)
Are we going to allow our children to be called up for the army to fight against their brothers and sisters? (Audience: NO!)
You say NO, I'm with you.
No amount of intimidation, gaol, banishment, house arrest will stop the people from marching to freedom today.

She urged mothers to resist the government's plans to conscript their children: "It can have many armies, but the time is up, the patience of the people has been exhausted now. We have mothers here, black and white, mothers who know what it is to bring a child into this world, mothers who know what hardships they have endured. Are we as mothers going to allow a government to plunge our country into a bloodbath?"

She wound up with words of encouragement and praise for the UDF, once again stressing its role in uniting the struggle at a time when the government most hoped to split the opposition into warring factions.

I'm very happy to be one of those in the UDF, because in all these 17 years I've been banned it has been my wish that one day, I would get to such a gathering, a multiracial gathering, a gathering that gives me hope that this South Africa, one day, will be a just South Africa for everybody.

Albertina could well afford to be proud of the UDF. Its boycott campaign, described as the "most vigorous and sustained political campaign that black South Africans had ever been able to run", was a dramatic success (Sparks 1990, 333). Voter turnout in the election for the coloured parliament was around 30 per cent, while only 19 per cent of registered Indian voters turned out for their poll (Van Kessel, 25; Lodge et al., 61). Moreover, the UDF had achieved something more profound than dismal voter turnout. It had built a formidable network of organisations, from local to regional to national level (Sparks 1990, 333). By August 1984, the UDF had over 600 affiliates. Its campaigns had heightened political awareness and expectations in communities suffering the effects of the economic recession of the early 1980s, the poor administration and police occupation of black schools, and rent hikes imposed by corrupt and unpopular councillors.

On 3 September 1984, the very day the tricameral parliament was opening with overblown pomp and ceremony in Cape Town, residents of Sharpeville marched to the local council offices to protest against a steep rent hike. En route, protestors threw stones at the house of Kuzwayo Dlamini, the deputy mayor of Sharpeville. Shots fired from the house injured a member of the crowd. Infuriated, the protestors set the house alight and attacked and killed the fleeing deputy mayor (Van Kessel, 26). The incident was like a match to dry tinder. The angry crowd went on the rampage and the riot spread swiftly to the neighbouring Vaal Triangle townships of Sebokeng, Evaton, Boipatong and Lekoa. Within hours two more councillors were dead, their homes burned and council administration offices, beer halls, schools, shopping centres and gas stations destroyed. Army and police units were rapidly deployed and fired tear gas and rubber bullets at the rioters and onlookers alike. By the end of the day, 30 people were dead and over 300 injured (Van Kessel, 26–7; Lodge et al., 67; Sparks 1990, 336). In the ensuing week, the revolt spread with the speed of a veld fire to the East Rand townships of Tembisa, Wattville, Vosloorus and Daveyton, then to Soweto and other parts of the country (Gorodnov, 244). Despite massive deployment of troops and police units, the townships continued to burn.

The explosion of rage in the black townships pushed the tricameral parliament into the background. The dramatic occupation of the British Consulate on 13 September by six UDF leaders fleeing detention completely eclipsed it. UDF president Archie Gumede, Mewa Ramgobin, Billy Nair and Paul David occupied the Consulate to protest against detention without trial and draw international attention to the UDF. The British were obliged to deal with their unwanted guests and, as a result, UDF leaders were able to meet with both a minister of the British government and the Secretary-General of the United Nations (Seekings, 118). Even as they paraded like buffoons in Homburg hats and morning coats at the September opening of the tricameral parliament, the new coloured and Indian parliamentarians were already relics of a bygone era. By now, it was the UDF that occupied centre stage in South Africa's political drama.

# s i x

The UDF's achievements during the first year of its existence were not matched by success on the military front for the ANC. Boredom and frustration in the ANC camps at Viana and Pango in Angola resulted in mutinies in early 1984. Seven mutineers were executed and several others imprisoned at Quattro camp. The unthinkable happened when both Angola and Mozambique succumbed to the relentless pressure of South African destabilisation and agreed to withdraw support for the ANC. Angola and South Africa signed the Lusaka agreement in February, in terms of which SADF troops would leave Angola. However, the agreement failed because South Africa never withdrew from Angola. Mozambique and South Africa signed the Nkomati Accord in March. This forced Samora Machel to expel the ANC from Mozambique in exchange for a cessation of cross-border raids and aid to the Mozambican rebels, RENAMO. Unfortunately, the Botha regime did not keep to its side of the agreement and continued to support RENAMO. The removal of Mozambique as a forward base placed considerable pressure on the ANC to realise its objective of moving from "armed propaganda" (which relied on spectacular attacks) to "people's war", which placed more emphasis on locally planned operations. Around 1982, MK had already started establishing internal units. (This had been prompted by the 1982 deal in which the South African government transferred Ingwavuma in the north of the KwaZulu homeland to Swaziland. In return, the Swazi government signed a non-aggression pact and stepped up harassment of ANC exiles.)

Jongumzi Sisulu was one of the new breed of MK fighters who had been recruited and given military training inside the country. He had been deeply angered by the events of 1976 and the continuous police harassment his family experienced:

> The police would come and raid the house and we would be instructed to wake up and be pushed into a corner, naked as we were with no privacy. They would search the house and throw our books on the floor. We would have to pick up those books and go to school the next morning. Some of our family were in exile, some in jail and the police would still come and take another person. These things made me feel that violence was the only alternative, because our fathers had tried to negotiate with these people without any achievement. These were the things which influenced me to join MK.

Jongi had tried to leave the country to join MK on several occasions, but each time his plans were thwarted. On one occasion, a few days before he was due to leave, Albertina insisted he go to Cape Town. Jongi suspected that she knew his plans and did not want him to leave. He was sent to Cape Town and Beryl arranged for him to go to school there. He spent a year attending a high school in Guguletu before returning to Johannesburg.

Around 1983, Jongi met James Mncedisi Dubase, an MK cadre who had come back into the country after training outside. Dubase, whose MK name was Mahamba, was aware of Jongi's desire to leave the country and suggested that he train internally instead. Under Dubase alias Mahamba's tutelage, he learned the basics of sabotage and handling of firearms. He was joined in his lessons by Donald Modise, an underground operative who had been infiltrated into the country with Dubase. The three young men formed a unit and used Lungi's shop as their base. This was done in absolute secrecy without a hint to their closest family and friends, with the exception of Lungi.

After several months of training, they were ready for action. They were part of a unit of young men from Soweto, all in their mid-twenties. In March 1984, they tried to sabotage a railway bridge in Vereeniging. Jongi used his own car because "we were under pressure from outside [Lusaka]. We received word that there were complaints that it was too quiet in the country and we were supposed to be in action". While they were installing the explosive under the bridge, they were accosted by the police. In the ensuing fracas, Jongi and Donald Modise fled into the nearby farmlands in a hail of bullets. Donald was badly wounded. Jongi, who was also injured, managed to escape and made his way back to Soweto.

The following morning, a police patrol accosted the injured Donald Modise. According to the police report, Modise had pulled out a hand grenade and then threw it at the police, who shot and killed him. The confrontation and Modise's death were reported on the SABC news that morning. When Albertina saw the television report, she recognised Jongi's car with a sinking heart and thought that the police must have killed him. Meanwhile, Jongi had made it to a safe house in Soweto, and sent a message (via a third party) to Albertina to meet him. She examined Jongi's wound and told him to go straight to a doctor. He went to Dr Chivo in Meadowlands and told him a rather implausible tale about running away from the police because a friend was driving without a driver's licence. "The doctor just looked at me and shook his head. From there he gave me an injection and cleaned my wounds. After that, Mama would treat my wound in Dr Asvat's surgery. I would go there very early before the other patients and the doctor came in. No one knew that Mama was treating me. Even the doctor did not know."

Albertina was consumed with anxiety about Jongi. She knew that it was useless to try to turn him from his chosen path, but she was only too aware that he would soon have to face the choice between exile and prison. She was also concerned about his fiancée Jacqueline, their three-year-old son Thulane, and the second child they were expecting.

Even as his wounds were healing, Jongi continued with his MK activities and his unit carried out a number of operations. These included the sabotage of electricity pylons, the bombing of police vehicles and attacks on police. They also planned attacks on other targets, one of which was the SADF Witwatersrand Command Headquarters in Joubert Park. They attempted to establish more internal MK units by recruiting some young men from the South African Student's Movement. They trained the *laaities* (young boys), as they called them, to use AK47s and hand-grenades. Through Jongi's cousin, Mandisa Sisulu, they met a man who let them use a house he had rented in Magaliesburg. They used this house as a base and some of the *laaities* they recruited stayed there. Unfortunately, the same man was an informer. After receiving information from him, the security police set up a road-block between Randfontein and Magaliesburg on 31 July 1984. Dubase, Jongi and Cecil Kandia were intercepted on the way to the Magaliesburg house and arrested. Arms were found in the car. Police went to the farmhouse and arrested the other two people who were staying there. They also found explosives and sketches of targets in the house.

Jongi and his comrades were blindfolded and thrown into some police bakkies. Jongi describes the worst ride of his life: "There was an Alsatian dog in the bakkie into which they had thrown me. They drove this bakkie very roughly so that I was thrown all over the place and this dog was biting me. I got hold of an iron bar, it must have been by the window, and held on to it so I would not be thrown all over. I was then taken to Magaliesburg Police Station, then I was transferred the same night to Protea in Soweto. Then they started torturing me."

Two days after Jongi was arrested, Lungi and Mandisa were arrested and detained for three weeks. Meanwhile, Jongi was interrogated about Mahamba. "They kept saying to me 'You are not the big fish we are looking for'. They wanted to know where Mahamba was and I kept telling them I didn't even know Mahamba. One day, one of the MK people who had been arrested came and identified Mahamba. That day, I tell you we were tortured because they realised that Mncedisi was the Mahamba they had been looking for all along."

During that period there was a sharp increase in the numbers of MK cadres arrested. Most of them had been forced out of Mozambique into Swaziland as a result of the Nkomati Accord. They were met by a Swazi regime that had become even more hostile to the ANC since the death of King Sobhuza in 1983. South African agents were given free rein to track down MK operatives in Swaziland. A number of MK cadres were murdered, and those who did manage to get into South Africa were almost immediately arrested. Some of those arrested were put with Jongi's group. The State was obviously trying to link their activities as it built a case against them. Two months after his arrest, while Jongi was being interrogated and tortured by the police, his second son Tsepang was born. It was only after his group was charged early in 1986, making him an awaiting trial prisoner, that he would be able to see the new baby.

Amidst all the drama of Jongi's arrest and the subsequent detention of Lungi and Mandisa, Zwelakhe and Zodwa were preparing for their departure to the United States. In 1983 Zwelakhe had been awarded the Nieman Fellowship. This prestigious award brought selected mid-career journalists together for a year's study at Harvard. At the time, he was working as a senior reporter for *The Sowetan*, a position he enjoyed, but did not find particularly challenging. He also needed a break from the stress of political organisation. Despite his efforts, tensions between the Black Consciousness and Charterist tendencies in MWASA had come to a head early in 1984, when MWASA split over the question of whether or not to admit whites and affiliate with the UDF. Zwelakhe had long wanted to resign as MWASA president and did so after the split (Karis, 1987). Albertina and Walter were extremely proud that their son had received such a prestigious award; they were also happy to see him go to the United States because at least he would be safe from the threat of arrest or imprisonment while there. Albertina was correct in her suspicions that it was simply a matter of time before Zwelakhe was arrested or banned again. When his restrictions expired in July 1983, the security police had immediately argued that they be extended: "Compol reports that Sisulu can be regarded as a leading figure. The lifting or easing of his restriction orders will give new stimulus to the Black Power organisations which presently are experiencing a lack of dynamic leadership. As a result Compol advises that Sisulu should be further restricted."

The same memo shows that the Ministry of Justice bureaucrats could not, however, find any reasons to further restrict Zwelakhe:

> When looking at the remaining information which is available about Sisulu and which is largely based on reports that have not been signed, the information is of such a nature that it is not possible to bring a case against him with any measure of conviction for participating in activities which will endanger the security of the state or the maintenance of law and order. Subsequently it is recommended that he should not be further restricted but that Compol should carefully monitor his movements. If further information should come to light, actual steps can be taken against him. Sisulu is a slippery customer who goes to work in such a way that it is not possible to catch him out (Ministry of Justice memo, 13/6/83).

Fortunately, Zwelakhe was given a passport and he, Zodwa, Moyikwa and Zoya travelled to Boston at the end of August in time for Zwelakhe to take up the fellowship at the beginning of the semester in September.

In the meantime, the Vaal uprising had continued to rage unabated. The police were unable to quell the new spirit of defiance. Veteran trade unionist Petrus Tom recalled how, at the start of the uprising, the young people of Sharpeville had refused to heed the warnings of their elders that the police would shoot them, as they had done in 1960: "No, this is not 1960, this is 1984. You can't talk about what happened in 1960. What we are doing now is different from that" (Lodge et al., 68). The youth were right. The 1984 disturbance in Sharpeville was no one-day affair, but the beginning of a period of widespread and sustained resistance against the apartheid state. Just as the level of resistance was unprecedented, so was the response of the State. SADF troops were deployed in Soweto on 2 October and three weeks later, South African police and army units invaded the East Rand township of Sebokeng in a massive operation involving 7 000 soldiers (Lodge et al., 67).

The army occupation of the townships sparked off further protests, which culminated in a massive labour stayaway on 2 November when over 600 000 workers stayed away from work and 400 000 students boycotted classes. According to the Labour Monitoring Group, this represented "a new phase in the history of united action amongst organised labour, students and community groups".

The State blamed the UDF for the unrest and there was talk within government circles of banning the UDF (*Beeld*, 11/10/84). However, the government was aware of the adverse publicity that would result from banning an organisation that was the focus of international attention as a result of the occupation of the British Consulate in Durban. World media focus on South Africa sharpened when Bishop Desmond Tutu won the Nobel Peace Prize on 15 October 1984. The Commissioner of Police at the time, General Johan Coetzee, also argued against banning the UDF, as this would simply force it underground, making it more difficult for the State to monitor. Coetzee advocated a policy of containment by removing the leadership and exploiting divisions within the organisation (Sarakinsky, 157).

In the closing months of 1984, the continued occupation of the British Consulate continued to attract much interest both locally and internationally. When Mewa Ramgobin, MJ Naidoo and George Sewpersadh decided to leave the Consulate on 6 October, they were greeted by thousands. The British had to put up with their three remaining uninvited guests, Archie Gumede, Paul David and Billy Nair, until they decided to emerge from the Consulate on 13 December. The crowd of 6 000 that had gathered to welcome them did not get to see Archie Gumede and Paul David because they were arrested before they could leave the building, but Billy Nair was carried out shoulder high by the enthusiastic crowd.

On 11 December, Mewa Ramgobin, MJ Naidoo and George Sewpersadh, who had been detained in Pietermaritzburg after leaving the Consulate, were charged with treason along with Transvaal UDF leaders Aubrey Mokoena, Curtis Nkondo and Essop Jassat, who had been arrested in Johannesburg. Gumede and David were also included in the treason charges.

The treason charges were partly the result of international pressure to either release the detainees or charge them. It was probably this pressure that saved Albertina from being detained in the same period. A memo dated 21 August 1984 showed that the security police had ordered that she be detained for a period of six months in the new Johannesburg prison. Among the reasons given for her proposed detention were her presidency of FEDSAW and the Transvaal UDF, as well as the fact that "during March 1984 she visited her husband three times in the Pollsmoor prison. During these visits Walter Sisulu praised her inter alia as a prominent figure in the UDF and the ANC. Sisulu and her husband Walter are prominent figures and both enjoy world recognition as martyrs fighting for the so-called 'freeing of the black man in the RSA'". The security police emphasised her "long history of undermining activities": "She is regarded as a leading figure who declares her presence at meetings where an attack is made on the constitutional system. She has close links with leftist persons while she maintains her bond with the ANC. She advocates the overthrow of the present government while she is actively involved with the politicising of scholars and students" (Sisulu, Prison Files).

Rather than detain Albertina, the government decided to include her in the treason charges, a repetition of the events of 1956. On 19 February 1985, she was arrested in the early hours of the morning. Also arrested in the same police swoop were Frank Chikane (UDF Transvaal vice-president), Cassim Saloojee (UDF National Treasurer), Professor Ismail Mohamed and SAAWU trade unionists Isaac Ngcobo, Sam Kikine and Sisa Njikelana. They were taken to Durban, where they appeared in front of the Regional Magistrate on 21 February. Thozamile Gqweta was also arrested and charged a week later, bringing the number of accused to 16. Mewa Ramgobin was the first accused, and Albertina (the only woman in the group) was accused number nine. Sociologist Fatima Meer noted that it was the second time in 28 years that the State was seeking to convict its extra-parliamentary opponents of treason. It had failed to do so in the Treason Trial of the 1950s, when the judges had ruled that there was no evidence that, by adopting the Freedom Charter, the accused had plotted to violently overthrow the State. "The State however had remained unconvinced and in 1984 it brought more or less the same charge against a new generation of accused" (Meer, 10).

The families of the accused were well aware that their loved ones were likely to be in prison for a long time. Sheila describes the impact on the Sisulu family: "We felt as if Mama was going into a black hole. Nkuli was particularly affected. She was absolutely distraught."

It was a particularly difficult period for Nkuli. Her studies at UWC had been disrupted by the continuous class boycotts. She had also fallen in love and was engaged to Mthuthuzeli Mavumbe, a young man from Cape Town. At the time of her mother's arrest, she was expecting her first baby and she needed her mother's support more than ever, especially in the absence of Jongi and Zwelakhe and Zodwa. If past experience was anything to go by, Albertina would be in jail when the baby was born.

Even as the security police were planning to throw Albertina into prison, the possibility of Walter's release was being discussed at the highest levels of government. So successful was the Free Mandela campaign that even the most conservative Western governments had come to accept that Mandela's release was essential to any political solution in South Africa. Even right-wing German politicians, including the Bavarian leader and apartheid apologist Franz-Josef Strauss, advised Botha that he could no longer afford to ignore the demand to release Mandela. Under pressure, Botha announced on 31 January 1985 that he was prepared to release Mandela, the Rivonia Trialists and other political prisoners – but with conditions attached. The most notable of these was that they should unconditionally renounce violence as a means of furthering their political aims. "It is therefore not the South African government that stands in the way of Mandela's freedom. It is himself," Botha grandly declared (Meredith, 355; Sampson 2000, 335; Kathrada, 168; Mandela, 620).

The Pollsmoor authorities gave Mandela a copy of the President's announcement. He was not impressed and neither were his colleagues. Mandela saw the offer as a public challenge and decided that it deserved a public response. A UDF-organised mass rally at Soweto's Orlando Stadium (to celebrate Bishop Tutu's Nobel award) provided him with the perfect opportunity. At the rally (on 10 February 1985), Zindzi Mandela read out her father's message praising the work of the UDF and congratulating Bishop Tutu. It went on to explain that the ANC had turned to violence only after all other avenues of resistance had been closed and argued that it was Botha who should renounce violence. In his message, Mandela challenged Botha to dismantle apartheid, unban the ANC, free those who had been imprisoned and banished, allow the exiles to return and guarantee free political activity. He closed on a poignant but proud note: "I am not less life-loving than you are. But I cannot sell my birthright, nor am I prepared to sell the birthright of the people to be free" (Meredith, 356; Sampson 2000, 336; Kathrada, 168; Mandela, 623).

This uncompromising message was met with rapturous applause by tens of thousands of people, many of whom had not been born when the Rivonia Trialists went to prison. It was Mandela's first public message in 20 years, and it had a huge impact both at home and abroad, giving further impetus to the campaign for his release. Botha had tried to paint Mandela into a corner by linking his release to the renunciation of violence. Instead, it was the government that found itself in a corner. By 1985, Mandela was the world's most famous political prisoner and both Walter Sisulu and Govan Mbeki were approaching their 75th birthdays. The government had to find a way of releasing them without antagonising its right wing, or face the possibility that one of them might die in prison; the consequences, given the context of black anger and resistance and increasing international abhorrence of apartheid, would be too ghastly to contemplate.

Rumours about the possible release of the Rivonia prisoners dated as far back as 1966, when they were given official forms on which they were required to give details of where they would reside after their release. In 1971, friends sent Walter a set of clothes to wear when he was released, and in 1974 there was a rumour that Mandela had been seen in Lusaka (Kathrada, 202). Government attempts to find an acceptable formula for releasing the Rivonia group dated back to the 1970s. In 1976, Jimmy Kruger, then Minister of Prisons, visited Mandela twice to try to persuade him to accept retirement to the Transkei in exchange for a dramatic reduction of his sentence. His offer extended to Mbeki and Sisulu, who both shared Mandela's view that "it was an offer only a turncoat could accept" (Dingake, 221; Karis and Gerhart, 298; Mandela, 573).

The government tried another approach and enlisted the help of Mandela's nephew Kaizer Matanzima, hoping he would have more success in convincing Mandela to accept the Transkei offer. Matanzima played an active role in the release discussions, possibly out of concern for the wellbeing of his uncle, but more likely because Mandela's retirement to the Transkei would have boosted the credibility of his own illegitimate regime. Mandela made it clear to Matanzima that he would not allow him to use their familial relationship to draw the ANC into Bantustan politics and in fact refused to allow him to visit him in Pollsmoor (Sampson 2000, 337).

On 5 April 1984, Walter described the Matanzima machinations in a letter to Lindi, who was then in Swaziland:

My dearest Lindi

I wish to give you just a brief report about some attempts at our release, that is Nel, Govan and myself. I am sure your mother has given you some hints but I have a duty to report to you and Xolile directly.

A few years ago we were told by prison authorities that the president of Transkei, Chief KD Matanzima wanted to see the three of us ...

Last month a similar request was made ... By this time Winnie was already having discussions with KD who then informed her that he had wanted to discuss the whole matter with us, so as to give us details of the whole proposition ...

Briefly, he told her that for years he had been discussing the question of our release. Finally, the matter was discussed by him and the State President of the Republic. It was him who then encouraged him to make the necessary arrangements. All he wanted to know was whether we would be prepared to settle in Transkei ...

They had bought three plots of land at a place called Ezibeleni near Queenstown, which is also not far from KD's own place at Qamata. All provision had been made to take care of all our needs. He told her there is no question of Bantustans involved, whatever he meant by that ...

We naturally rejected this proposal as a condition not acceptable to us. It is as you may observe a violation of fundamental principles because it means an acceptance of Bantustan policies ... The government as you would expect denies that there was any plan or talk of releasing us. Of course, we are not so naïve nor do we think KD is off his head. It is quite inconceivable that we could accept such humiliating conditions. This, however, does not mean that we are happy to remain in prison indefinitely but it also does not mean that we should welcome release under any conditions.

The Rivonia prisoners were encouraged by the 1984 transfer of their old comrade Andimba Toivo ja Toivo from Robben Island to a Namibian prison, and his release shortly thereafter. By releasing Toivo, the Pretoria regime wanted to show its willingness to make concessions. It also hoped that Toivo would compete with Sam Nujoma for leadership of SWAPO, thereby creating a split within the organisation. Soviet historian Vladimir Shubin speculated "that this action was a kind of rehearsal for the freeing of ANC leaders. Their continued stay in prison was becoming more and more embarrassing for Pretoria" (Shubin, 267).

In a letter of consummate dignity, dated 13 February 1985, Mandela, Sisulu, Raymond Mhlaba, Ahmed Kathrada and Andrew Mlangeni rejected Botha's offer of freedom in what was a remarkably astute analysis of its implications, and the status of the struggle against apartheid. Many have commented on the political significance of their refusal, and for vast numbers of South Africans anxiously awaiting the response, the letter was a reassuring reiteration of the position of the ANC's leadership.

However, few have remarked on its sophisticated tone or its brilliant articulation of the current delicate political climate. The tone goes beyond that of equals addressing an equal; the register, even the vocabulary is that of senior statesmen and elders critiquing the blunders – of logic, analysis and ethics – of a callow junior politician. Each false assumption is exposed and deconstructed with relentless logic. For example, they write: "Note that on p.312 of Hansard you say that … you are not prepared to lead the whites to abdication. By making this statement you again … reaffirmed that you remain obsessed with the preservation of domination by the white minority. You should not be surprised, therefore, if in spite of the supposed good intentions of the government, the vast masses … continue to regard you as a mere broker of the interests of the white tribe, and consequently unfit to handle national affairs" (Kathrada, 170).

There is a measured and magisterial near-arrogance to the rhetoric used: it is the language not just of leaders, but of intellectuals and political savants. One could be forgiven for thinking that it was composed in a research library by authors with every tool for political observation and analysis at their fingertips. The influence of the authors' legal training is heard in paragraphs such as "Taking into account the … practice of the Dept. of Prisons, we must reject the view that a life sentence means that one should die in prison. By applying to security prisoners the principle that life is life, you are using double standards, since Common Law prisoners with clean prison records serve about 15 years of a life sentence … As far as we are concerned, we have long ago completed our life sentences. We are now being kept in preventative detention without enjoying the rights attached to that category of prisoners" (Kathrada, 172).

It is amusing to speculate about the effect this courteous, but stingingly worded missive must have had on the famously peppery "Groot Krokodil", a man increasingly unable to brook disagreement, much less contradiction, towards the end of his political career. Not only would this have dashed his hopes that Mandela and Sisulu would take the bait, buying him glory in the eyes of the increasingly critical international community, with the added bonus of compromising the ANC leadership and throwing it into internal division; for a deeply insecure man, this letter would have at some level confirmed his worst nightmare: that these terrorist criminals – mere prisoners, blacks and therefore inferior, ignorant beings – were possessed of an integrity that would make them the immovable force upon which his ship might actually founder. Their calm and unwavering commitment was to be more than a match for his intransigence. And for a man from a humble background, who never finished his university degree, the authority in their letter must have stung intolerably.

Govan Mbeki and Elias Motsoaledi, the two Rivonia prisoners still on Robben Island, rejected the President's offer just as emphatically. Dennis Goldberg, the only white prisoner in the Rivonia group, and isolated in Pretoria Prison, accepted the offer and was released soon afterwards. Commenting on the release offer, Kathrada wrote to a friend:

> To many it may have seemed as if we were a hair's breadth away from freedom. But in fact, from the very moment that the announcement was made, it was already a non-starter … It was so patently designed to humiliate us that there just could be no other decision for me but to reject it. But please understand that I'm not for a moment holding it against anybody who has accepted the offer. In matters such as these, it is unwise to ignore individual cases; … there may in fact be differing circumstances which may lead individuals to take another approach. So it is not advisable to point fingers and condemn without taking into account all the factors involved (Letter to Navi Joseph, 179).

Walter had exactly the same view concerning Dennis Goldberg's release. He had always felt that although Goldberg enjoyed better conditions in a "whites-only" prison, his incarceration was more difficult because he was cut off from the companionship of his comrades and unable to confer with them on important political decisions.

Walter was, however, far more concerned about the progress of the bail applications in the Pietermaritzburg trial than the possibility of his own release. He read the press reports avidly and received regular reports from Beryl. The news was not good. Efforts to secure bail for Albertina and her co-accused had been fruitless. In March 1985, Michael Imber, the Attorney-General, invoked Section 30 of the Internal Security Act to prohibit the court from granting bail to the 16 accused. The defence team, led by the brilliant advocate Ismail Mohamed, made an impassioned argument for bail, but to no avail, and the accused were remanded in custody.

Priscilla Jana tells a story that highlights the fact that Albertina's incarceration during this period was much more onerous than that of her co-accused. This was because as the only woman accused, she was effectively held in solitary confinement, while the men had each other for company and support. One day, Priscilla visited her clients, first stopping off at the men's prison. Here she found the trialists relaxing and playing chess in an atmosphere of camaraderie. Next she proceeded to the women's prison, where Albertina was being held alone. To her fury, she found Albertina on her knees, scrubbing the floor. In Priscilla's own words, she "hit the roof", and immediately took the matter up with the authorities. But nothing could change the fact that Albertina had to endure this ordeal alone.

The UDF organised mass protest meetings throughout the country. Over 5 000 people gathered in Durban to hear Alan Boesak and other UDF leaders challenge the government to arrest them as well, as their actions were no different from those of the arrested leaders (Meer, 5). The anti-apartheid movement around the world lobbied governments and non-governmental organisations to put pressure on the South African government concerning the denial of bail. The Bishops of England and Wales specifically called for bail for the Pietermaritzburg 16 and for international standards to be observed by the South African judiciary. Edward Kennedy was among 27 US senators who sent a letter to President Botha protesting against the treason arrests and charges.

In April, the French ambassador sparked off a flurry of correspondence between the Justice Department, the police and the Security Branch when he applied to visit Albertina in jail. A memo from the Security Branch to the head of the Pietermaritzburg prison outlined "the handling procedure" to be followed should the ambassador arrive:

> The Ambassador must be informed, tactfully, by yourself, that it is not convenient at this time, to permit such a visit. He must be invited to your office and this department must immediately be informed telephonically of the Ambassador's reaction. It will then be carried through to the Commissioner's office in Cape Town, who will then indicate what the next step is in the course of action (Ministry of Justice files).

In April, the defence appealed against the Attorney-General's refusal of bail in the Natal Supreme Court. Justice Friedman commented that should bail not be granted, the appellants faced the prospect of several years in custody before the conclusion of their trial. He said all possible solutions should be explored when dealing with a subject as important as the liberty of an individual who faced a lengthy awaiting-trial period. The bail decision was batted backwards and forwards between the Supreme Court and the Durban Magistrates' Court.

The proceedings were tedious and boring but there were moments of high drama, such as the events of 24 April. According to Fatima Meer, the courtroom was packed, and the accused were greeted with cheering and singing, until the magistrate insisted on order. The prosecutor, Gey van Pittius and Ismail Mohamed, for the defence, squared up, and the defence was soon protesting that the authority the prosecutor was quoting "was nonexistent in Heimstra or Butterworth" (Meer, 6). Mewa Ramgobin takes up the story:

> The prosecutor held hard onto his desk, white and swaying. I shouted "He is going to faint ... we have a doctor among us." [In the disarray,] the security police and court orderlies surrounded us ..., but one of the accused, Dr Jassat, did reach [the prosecutor] to administer the caring that was part of his life and training – he confirmed his pulse was there!

When we were being taken back to our cells, Mama's parting words were "I am so proud of you, that you can care for even those that oppress you" (Mewa Ramgobin, Unpublished notes).

The Natal Supreme Court finally granted bail on 3 May 1985. The Judge President of Natal, Justice Milne, called for the repeal of the section of the Internal Security Act that gave the Attorney-General power to prevent courts granting bail. Justice Milne said it was the function of the courts and not the Attorney-General to grant bail, and he could not understand why the authorities had considered it necessary to bypass the courts: "The Attorney-General hears only one side. He cannot test the information he is given. The accused must be given a chance to test the information."

Bail of R170 000 was granted on condition that each accused reported twice daily to a police station and refrained from leaving his or her magisterial district except with the permission of the Attorney-General or the investigating officer. At first there was a moment of anxiety, as it seemed that bail would not be given to Ramgobin, as he "might run to India", where he allegedly had "many contacts". Albertina's response was instantaneous: "If they keep Mewa, they must keep me too. I can understand their motive; they want to divide us. We must all refuse bail" (Mewa Ramgobin, Unpublished notes). Fortunately, bail was granted to all the accused, but they did have to surrender their passports and travel documents, which was not a problem for Albertina since she had never been allowed to possess a passport.

The accused also had to refrain from communicating with any state witness and to refrain from being active in any organisation mentioned in the indictment. As these included the UDF and the ANC Women's League, this meant that Albertina was once again effectively under banning orders and could no longer continue her political work. Nevertheless, the families and friends of the accused celebrated, and the brilliant work of the legal team was applauded.

Just as she had done after her 1984 stint in prison, Albertina immediately arranged to visit Walter. Despite the spectre of the trial hanging over their heads, they had a pleasant visit as they had plenty to catch up on their favourite topic – their grandchildren. The year 1985 was a bumper one in this respect. They happily anticipated Nkuli's baby in June and Lungi and Sheila's third child in December. Lindi, who had completed her MA in the UK and had returned to Swaziland at the end of 1984, gave birth to her second daughter, Nomvuyo, in March 1985.

They rejoiced at news of her arrival, although because Lindi was in exile, they had no idea when they would see the new baby. Another grandchild Walter had never seen was Max's second son, Shaka, born to Makhosazana Msimang, the daughter of Mendi and Agnes Msimang, who had been studying in East Germany. The Sisulus had been glad to learn of Shaka's birth in 1979. They were disappointed, however, that this was not followed by news of a marriage, but they continued to live in hope.

Meanwhile, the unrest that had flared in 1984 continued to burn throughout the country. The State blamed the UDF for instigating and directing the escalating violence, but the insurrection had a momentum of its own. At the UDF National General Council (NGC) meeting held in Azaadville, Krugersdorp in April 1985, general secretary Popo Molefe said in his report: "In many areas, organisations trail behind the masses, thus making it more difficult for a disciplined mass action to take place. More often there is spontaneity of actions in the township" (Seekings, 139; Lodge et al., 76). In the words of Jeremy Seekings: "The UDF's contribution to the revolt was more indirect than direct: its formation and initial campaigns inspired and informed local political mobilisation, and its structures facilitated contact between activists from different areas, but it rarely provided direct co-ordination or instigation" (Seekings, 180).

The UDF, originally formed to oppose the tricameral elections, now had to redefine itself in a new political context. The NGC provided the organisation with an opportunity for reflection. The Working Principles of the UDF were reformulated and the organisation streamlined for purposes of improved decision-making. The need to strengthen leadership was also emphasised (Seekings, 139). However, the latter was not easy to implement given that so many UDF leaders were in prison or in hiding. On 23 April 1985, Popo Molefe and Terror Lekota, who had respectively been re-elected general secretary and publicity secretary, were detained with Moses Chikane. On 11 June, they appeared in court in the small town of Delmas, near Pretoria, with 19 other activists, most of them from the Vaal Civic Association, on charges of terrorism, subversion and murder.

The indictment for what came to be known as the Delmas Trial was similar to that of the Pietermaritzburg Treason Trial, with the State alleging that the UDF (and indirectly, the ANC) had inspired the Vaal uprising (Moss, 150; Van Kessel, 27). George Bizos, who was part of the defence team for the Delmas accused, said the charges were so wide-ranging that office-bearers of the UDF were considered responsible for everything that happened in the country, even during the periods they were in detention (Moss, 6). The government's strategy of removing leaders by tying them down in lengthy court cases did weaken the UDF; but these court cases also provided a rallying point for UDF supporters.

Meanwhile, UDF affiliates proliferated in the Eastern Cape, largely through the efforts of strong regional leaders like Matthew Goniwe, a former political prisoner and teacher, and Fort Calata, named after the Johannesburg Fort where his grandfather, the veteran ANC leader James Calata, had been imprisoned during the Treason Trial. Goniwe and Calata lived in the tiny Eastern Cape town of Cradock, where they formed pioneering street and area committees (Seekings, 169). These new grassroots organisations, formed to fill the vacuum left by the break-down of local administration, were the basis of the tightly coordinated community movements that sprang up throughout the Eastern Cape (Lodge et al., 75). A high level of political organisation combined with rampant unemployment, economic recession and police harassment fuelled popular anger, so that by November 1984, the countrywide unrest had shifted to the Eastern Cape, where residents responded to state repression with a spate of consumer boycotts against white businesses.

The State responded with increased brutality. On 21 March 1985, police killed 21 people when they fired into a crowd of mourners on their way to a funeral in the Uitenhage township of Langa. Unbelievably, they picked the 25th anniversary of the Sharpeville massacre to do so. At the same time, more and more key political activists were being abducted and murdered by the State. On 8 May 1985, three UDF and Port Elizabeth Black Civic Organisation (PEBCO) activists – Sipho Hashe, Champion Galela and Qaqawuli Godolozi – disappeared after a UDF meeting. Their bodies were found a few weeks later. On 27 June, Matthew Goniwe, Fort Calata and fellow UDF activists Sparrow Mkhonto and Sicelo Mhlawuli were abducted and murdered in similar fashion. Their families, communities and organisations blamed the police. The Truth and Reconciliation Commission would later confirm that the security police were indeed responsible for the murders of the PEBCO Three and the Cradock Four, as they came to be known (Seekings, 145).

As a result of repressive laws that proscribed virtually all forms of political assembly, funerals had always carried a special significance for the oppressed communities of South Africa. They provided an opportunity for political expression and mobilisation and a therapeutic outlet for collective rage. The depth of outrage generated by the death of Matthew Goniwe and his comrades found expression in the funeral of the Cradock Four. Held on 20 July 1985, it was the largest funeral ever held in the region. Over 40 000 people from all over the country congregated at Lingelihle Stadium. Messages poured in from all over the world and several diplomatic missions were present. Mourners were electrified when a massive SACP flag was unfurled. It was the first time in decades that the banners of the ANC and the SACP were shown openly and defiantly on a public occasion (Mbeki, 65). The mood of anger increased when Rev. Beyers Naudé announced during the funeral that the President had declared a State of Emergency in 36 magisterial districts of the country.

But the newly declared Emergency regulations did not deter UDF supporters from converging in their hundreds at the Pietermaritzburg Supreme Court on July 22 when the Treason Trial resumed. The crowd sang freedom songs and shouted slogans while a huge international media contingent haggled with the police over their right to enter the courtroom. By this time, the state had submitted a 587-page indictment. If this was anything to go by, it was clear that the government aimed to keep the UDF leaders in court for months, if not years.

This year, 1985, was also the one in which my own personal journey would intertwine my life irrevocably with the Sisulu clan. In those days, I had only the vaguest glimmerings of what involvement with this illustrious family would entail, but it must be said that those who fall in love can be excused for not thinking too clearly.

This was the year Max Sisulu was awarded the Govan Mbeki Fellowship to further his studies. He was grateful for the opportunity to spend a year at the University of Amsterdam working on the research topic of his choice, a study of the micro-electronics industry in South Africa. From 1977 to 1981, he had been based in Budapest serving as ANC representative to the World Federation of Democratic Youth. By the time he returned to Lusaka in 1982, he felt he needed a change. On 28 August 1983 he had written to Alfred Nzo, the Secretary-General, to complain about an NEC decision that "despite being no longer a youth, I should remain in the youth section i.e. to become by decree a perpetual youth". Apart from the age factor, he said he felt the need for fresh challenges, "having served the Youth Section for over a decade and in various capacities, including that of being one of the founder members of the Youth Secretariat in Lusaka" (28/8/83).

I met Max when he came to address a meeting on South Africa at the Institute of Social Studies (ISS) in The Hague. At the time I was studying for a Master's degree in development studies at the ISS, having taken study leave from Zimbabwe's Ministry of Labour, where I had been working since the end of 1980. With participants from all corners of the globe, the ISS was a vibrant centre for political debate and discussion. Paul Daphne, a South African trade unionist and member of the ANC, invited Max to speak at the ISS. Before the meeting, Paul introduced us. We had a number of common friends and acquaintances within the southern African community in the Netherlands, and shared many interests. By April 1985, our friendship had developed into a much deeper relationship. Eventually, we were to marry, but that step (which was certainly made more adventurous, if not downright complicated by the Sisulu family's political history) would not take place until late in 1986.

The year 1985 marked not only the beginning of my relationship with Max, it also heralded the beginning of the United Nations Decade of Women. In June 1985, women from all around the world descended on the Kenyan capital of Nairobi for the World Conference that marked the beginning of the Decade. As a participant in the Women and Development Programme at the ISS, I was fortunate enough to get sponsorship to attend the NGO forum of the Conference. Before I left the Netherlands, Max asked me to buy a gift for his mother and give it to one of the South African delegates. In Nairobi, I met a group of women who agreed to deliver the gift. They expressed deep concern that Albertina Sisulu would be imprisoned, either as a result of conviction in the Pietermaritzburg trial or through the failure of her appeal in the Rose Mbele case.

Walter's old friend Ellen Kuzwayo had done much to draw international attention to the struggles of South African women through her biography *Call Me Woman*, published in 1985 to critical acclaim. A young white doctor, Wendy Orr, also made waves when she applied for a court order restraining the police from assaulting detainees. Orr, a medical officer for the Department of Health, was the first doctor to speak out about the treatment of detainees in prison (*The Sowetan*, 29/12/1985). Not surprisingly, the plight of women under apartheid came under the spotlight at both the government conference and the NGO forum. Gertrude Shope, the head of the ANC women's delegation, made a moving presentation. She pointed out that Albertina Sisulu and Winnie Mandela would have been present at the conference if it had not been for apartheid repression.

While I was in Nairobi, Max travelled to the Zambian city of Kabwe to attend the ANC's Second Consultative Conference. Taking place on the 30th anniversary of the Freedom Charter, the conference was the most significant gathering of the ANC since the Morogoro Conference in 1969. At Morogoro, the ANC had been in tatters; at Kabwe, the organisation was stronger than it had ever been before. The South African masses seemed to have heeded Oliver Tambo's New Year message, in which he called on them to "render South Africa ungovernable".

The buoyant mood of the conference was dampened by anger at the SADF raid on Botswana on the 14 June. Among those killed were a six-year-old child from Lesotho, two Botswana citizens, one Somali and eight South Africans. Five of these were ANC members, although none were members of MK. It was the third attack on South African refugees in a year. Journalist Nat Serache's home had been destroyed in a huge blast in February; and in May, ANC and SACTU activist Rogers Nkadimeng had been killed in a powerful car-bomb explosion. Rogers was the son of John Nkadimeng, Albertina's fellow underground activist, who had become the leader of SACTU in exile (Greg Houston, Unpublished notes, 173). The Kabwe conference decided that, in future, there would be no distinction between "hard" and "soft" targets. In a press conference two days after the Kabwe meeting, Oliver Tambo said: "When the regime sends its army across the borders to kill people in Botswana, including nationals of other countries, they are hitting soft targets – very soft and not even in their own country" (Greg Houston, Unpublished notes, 173).

In July 1985, Max travelled to London for a reunion with his brother Zwelakhe, the first since their meeting in Swaziland a decade earlier. Zwelakhe had completed his stint as a Nieman Fellow at Harvard and he and his family were en route back to South Africa. Their time in Cambridge, Massachusetts, had been a pleasant respite. Zwelakhe had had the opportunity to interact with fellow journalists from all over the world and to take political economy and law courses at Harvard. In addition to voluntary work at local hospitals, Zodwa, a radiologist by training, had also taken courses at Harvard. They enjoyed the proximity of the many libraries in sedate Cambridge, a far cry from Soweto, where six libraries served over two million people.

Max was excited about meeting his sister-in-law Zodwa, his five-year-old nephew Moyikwa and three-year-old niece Zoya for the first time. Since I was also in London at the time, he arranged for me to spend time with Zodwa. I wondered how someone who had just flown across the Atlantic with two young children could maintain such a calm demeanour. She seemed completely undaunted at the prospect of returning home to a country that seemed to be about to go up in flames.

Apart from catching up on family news, Max and Zwelakhe discussed the dramatic developments in South Africa that had caught the attention of the world. Testimony to this interest was the fact that Zwelakhe's visit to England was at the invitation of the British Foreign Office. During his short stay, he was taken on a tour of the country to visit major newspapers and BBC television studios. He also had several meetings with Members of Parliament and the House of Lords. Although Margaret Thatcher was insistent that the ANC was nothing more than a terrorist organisation, others in her government saw increased engagement with the ANC and internal anti-apartheid forces as central to any solution of the crisis in South Africa.

Contrasting British attitudes to the ANC and apartheid had been demonstrated when Walter Sisulu was awarded the Freedom of the City of Stoke-on-Trent in November 1984. Max, who had travelled to England to receive the award on his father's behalf, was amused by the controversy it had sparked off in the Stoke-on-Trent city council. Council members who had motivated for the award held Walter Sisulu up as "a shining example of patriotism and courage" and were deeply embarrassed that the Freedom of the City of Stoke-on-Trent had once been awarded to one of apartheid's architects, General James Hertzog. Councillor Bill Cawley had declared that "by honouring Walter Sisulu, the council was putting right a grievous wrong and removing an insult which cruelly and outrageously linked Stoke-on-Trent with apartheid in South Africa". Conservative councillors opposed the award, however, arguing that Walter Sisulu was a member of a Soviet-infiltrated organisation whose aims were rebellion and that he "had been indoctrinated by the Soviet Union into plotting violent revolution".

Zodwa and Zwelakhe returned to South Africa a few days before the declaration of the State of Emergency. While he was in the US, Zwelakhe had learned that the Southern African Catholic Bishops' Conference (SACBC) had decided to launch a weekly newspaper to be known as *New Nation* and that he was being considered for the position of editor. He took up this post of editor at the end of July 1985. One of his first tasks was to produce a trial edition of the paper to be tested around the country. In his editorial of this trial edition, entitled "The Year of the Fist", Zwelakhe wrote that local and international opposition to the State of Emergency had plunged the government into its worst political crisis. At least 10 European countries had recalled their ambassadors for consultations, the American ambassador Herman Nickel had not returned to his post since his recall, the US had cancelled any new investment, France had imposed sanctions and was spearheading a UN campaign to isolate South Africa. He quoted Father Smangaliso Mkhatshwa, then Secretary-General of the SACBC, who said the only option for the government was to dismantle apartheid and its institutions and to scrap the tricameral parliament in favour of a truly democratic parliament in a unitary state. Father Mkhatshwa urged the government to call off the Emergency, release all political prisoners and detainees unconditionally, stop all forced removals, withdraw the police from the townships and enter into meaningful negotiations with democratically elected leaders of the oppressed, including the leadership in exile. He also referred to an earlier statement of the bishops that warned: "It is clear that the black people of South Africa have reached a point of no return and no temporary suppression by violence, only a just sharing of citizenship, can give hope of any safety for the children, black and white, now growing up in the Republic, and prevent the horrors of civil war."

Another article in the same edition, headlined "Same song, new strength 1960–1985" analysed the difference between the two states of emergency:

> Although South Africa's two Nationalist Government states of emergency are 25 years apart, they have some striking similarities – and equally striking differences. The 1960 emergency – coming as it did in the era of Harold Macmillan's "Winds of Change" speech – ushered in a decade in which stringent security legislation became the order of the day, in a desperate effort to stem the tide of popular resistance to apartheid. That the legislation did not deter the momentum that had been building against apartheid is now history. And the current emergency is testimony to that. Some of the differences between the two periods become apparent when one considers that in 1960 the Nationalist government did not have to contend with an armed ANC, a strong labour movement and a network of community, church and youth organisations. Further, international concern about South Africa's policies was not at its peak. In 1960 the South African government was dealing with a subcontinent dominated by colonial powers.
>
> Witwatersrand University political analyst Mr Tom Lodge points out ... "Diplomatic isolation is a frightening prospect for South Africa. At present Pretoria is recognised as a legitimate government

and is unhappy to see itself downgraded to a banana republic." ... He argued that in 1960 the state had to cope with a less difficult situation: "Although there were popular people's organisations, they were not organised in a way that would render them indestructible, at least not in the short term. Now, there is a higher level of commitment among the youth, students, labour and community organisations. There exists a political culture that can be called revolutionary," Mr Lodge said.

A major difference between the crisis of 1960 and that of 1985 lay in the response of the international financial establishment. On 31 July 1985, 10 days after the declaration of the State of Emergency, the Chase Manhattan Bank of New York, under pressure from its investors and depositors, decided to call in its loans to South Africa. Other American and European banks quickly followed suit, plunging South Africa into its worst financial crisis ever. The Pollsmoor prisoners were both encouraged and surprised by this turn of events, remembering that in the financial turmoil following the Sharpeville massacre, the Chase Manhattan Bank had stepped in to provide large loans to the South African government when other banks had withdrawn. In an interview with Anthony Sampson, Walter Sisulu admitted that they had underestimated the power that bankers could wield to bring the South African government in line (Sampson 2000, 338). The South African government had its back to the wall and the reformists in Botha's cabinet knew that the only thing that would mollify the bankers was a promise of change. Chief among the reformers was the Foreign Minister, Pik Botha, who saw an opportunity for the President to make a dramatic announcement at the National Party Congress to be held in Durban in mid-August. Pik Botha drafted a speech in which PW Botha would supposedly announce "today we have crossed the Rubicon". In this case, it was expected that this metaphor referred to the dismantling of apartheid and the release of Mandela.

Expectations ran high after Pik Botha told senior Western diplomats to expect a momentous announcement from his President. The Pollsmoor prisoners waited in anticipation for the speech they expected to include a public statement on Mandela's release. Their hopes were dashed when President PW Botha stepped onto the podium in Durban City Hall on 15 August 1985 in front of the largest contingency of local and international press the country had ever seen – and basically told the world to go to hell. "Don't push us too far," he said with a characteristic wag of the finger. He made it clear that his government would not bow down to the "communist agitators" who were fomenting unrest. He said Mandela was a communist who would only be released when he renounced violence. Far from crossing the Rubicon as promised, PW Botha retreated into the laager. Rather than address internal and external demands for fundamental change, he chose to pander to his right-wing constituency. Pik Botha had obviously tried to push his President further than he was prepared to go (Sampson 2000, 339; Sparks 1990, 350; Harvey, 93).

Two weeks after the debacle of the Rubicon, the UDF organised a massive march to Pollsmoor Prison to demand the release of Nelson Mandela. Dramatic television footage broadcast around the world showed police firing tear gas and manhandling protestors. The incident sparked off widespread demonstrations and 31 people died in the ensuing clashes with the police (Sampson 2000, 341). The Johannesburg Stock Exchange was shaken to its foundations on what was described as "Black Tuesday" when the value of the rand plummeted and international investor confidence collapsed (Sampson 2000, 340). On 9 September, US President Ronald Reagan reluctantly imposed sanctions on South Africa to pre-empt stronger measures by Congress (Lodge et al., 391).

Amid mounting pressures from anti-apartheid lobbies around the world, the Botha government engaged the services of Fritz Leutwiler, the former head of the Swiss National Bank, to renegotiate South Africa's debt. The rabidly anti-communist Leutwiler was a close friend of Margaret Thatcher. Probably with her backing, Leutwiler managed to persuade the banks to roll over the beleaguered country's debt, but the international banking community's confidence in the apartheid government had been irreparably damaged (Sampson 2000, 341; Harvey, 101).

The unfolding crisis forced South Africa's business community to look beyond the government for solutions. On 13 September 1985, a delegation of white South African businessmen, headed by Gavin Relly, the newly appointed chairperson of Anglo-American, flew to Zambia to meet ANC leaders. Oliver Tambo headed the ANC delegation at the meeting, which was hosted by Zambian president Kenneth Kaunda. The businessmen were pleasantly surprised to discover that the ANC leaders were not the communist demons that apartheid propaganda made them out to be, and the meeting set the stage for future discussions between the ANC and South Africa's business leaders. The most significant outcome of the meeting was that the entrepreneurs agreed in principle that apartheid was unworkable and that the creation of a united and democratic state was the only way to ensure the economic survival of South Africa (Shubin, 296).

"Go well, peacemakers. Tell your great-grandfathers we are coming because we are prepared to die for Africa!" No doubt thoughts of the tragic death of her husband, Griffiths, were not far from Victoria Mxenge's mind as she uttered these words at the funeral of Matthew Goniwe and his comrades. She spoke as if she had a premonition. Barely two weeks later, Victoria Mxenge was felled by an assassin's bullet in front of her Umlazi home. George Bizos heard from reliable sources that her address had so angered the security police monitoring the funeral that they decided she should pay the ultimate price (Interview, George Bizos).

Albertina was deeply distressed by Victoria's murder and it grieved her that Victoria's three children were now among the growing numbers of children orphaned by apartheid. She admired Victoria, who after her husband's murder in 1981, had managed to bring up their children, keep their joint law practice going and continue Griffiths' political legacy. At the time of her death, Victoria was the treasurer of the UDF's Natal region and a leading figure in the Natal Organisation of Women (NOW). She was also one of the instructing attorneys in the Pietermaritzburg Treason Trial.

The Pietermaritzburg trial resumed on 5 August 1985 on a sombre note. Before their trial began, Albertina and her co-accused stood and bowed their heads, observing a minute's silence in sympathy for the victims of political violence. They were joined by the judge, lawyers for the defence and prosecution, and members of the public who were attending the trial. The judge, Justice John Milne, expressed regret that one of the most recent victims of the tragic violence afflicing the country was Mrs Victoria Mxenge, an attorney of the court, who was one of those representing the accused (*The Sowetan*, 6/8/85).

Victoria Mxenge's assassination angered the local students with whom she was very popular. Students in Durban and Pietermaritzburg decided on a week-long boycott of classes to mourn her death. Intermittent violence erupted into full-scale conflict when 300 axe-wielding Inkatha supporters stormed the Umlazi Cinema, where more than 5 000 people were attending a memorial service for Mxenge. Seventeen people were killed in the attack. In the orgy of violence that followed, almost all the shops in Inanda, Umlazi and KwaMashu were looted and burned. The looters targeted Indian-owned shops, and the Gandhi settlement at Phoenix was attacked and destroyed. Seventy people were killed in the violence (43 of them by the police) and over 200 were injured. Albertina was horrified by the violence and shocked to the core when a group of Inkatha supporters danced around Mxenge's house, threatening to burn it down and kill her orphaned children. State security documents produced years later would reveal that Inkatha's Central Committee had decided to make KwaZulu and Natal "no-go" areas for the UDF.

The Treason Trial proceeded against the backdrop of violent confrontation between Inkatha and the UDF in Natal, the unrest engulfing the rest of the country and the unfolding financial crisis. The UDF trials at both Pietermaritzburg and Delmas continued to attract intense international interest, and diplomatic representatives from the major Western countries were a constant presence in the visitors' gallery in the courtrooms. The Lawyers' Committee of Civil Rights in the US sent Judge Nathaniel Jones, a US circuit court judge, to attend, and the American Bar Association emphasised the importance of affording the accused a fair trial consistent with recognised international mores (*The Sowetan*, 6/8/85). Geoffrey Bindman, a British attorney, attended the Pietermaritzburg trial as a representative of the International Commission of Jurists. He described the trials as showpieces used by the government to keep the accused out of circulation (*The Natal Witness*, 25/10/85).

The first week of the trial was taken up with procedural arguments by the defence against the 587-page indictment that alleged that the UDF was a political front for the banned ANC and was spearheading a "revolutionary alliance" to overthrow the State. The specific charges were high treason, violations of the Terrorism Act and furthering the aims of the ANC.

The indictment did not charge the accused with violence. In fact, it specifically stated that they used non-violent forms of struggle such as strikes and boycotts. "However, the State alleged, non-violence was a subterfuge for violence and that when the accused acted non-violently, their intention was in fact violence" (Meer, 9). The State "alleged that the accused were guilty of treason and terrorism, not necessarily through their own actions, but through association and sympathy with organisations and persons who were engaged in such activities. It linked the 1985 treason trial to the abortive 1956 treason trial in that it traced the impulse for both to the 1955 Congress of the People. The plot for both treasons was enshrined in the Freedom Charter" (Meer, 10).

A direct historical link was provided by Archie Gumede, the co-president of the UDF, who had the distinction of being an accused in both the 1956 and 1985 trials. Another link with the past appeared in the person of Helen Joseph, also one of the 1956 Treason Trialists, who travelled to Pietermaritzburg to show solidarity, much to the delight of the UDF supporters who had filled the courtroom.

Ismail Mohamed argued that the judge should either quash the indictment or order the prosecutors to redraft it because the prosecution had improperly grouped all 16 defendants in one case and that the charges were too vague. He presented colour-coded charts showing that the different alleged offences occurred in various places from 1980–1985, and not all the defendants were involved in each of the purported crimes (*The Sowetan*, 6/8/85).

Fatima Meer gives the following account:

Ismail Mohamed said that treason was being confused with the individual's right of dissent and freedom of speech, and the problem did not lie in the fact that his clients were antagonistic to the State, but in the State's definition of treason ...

He said the State's allegation that the UDF had established underground structures was based on insufficient evidence, and to prepare his defence he needed details as to where, when and how each of the accused had become members and the basis on which the State assumed that they were aware that these structures were being used ... to overthrow the State by violent means.

He moved that three of the five alternative counts to the main count of treason, in the indictment, namely terrorism, furtherance of the objectives of an unlawful organisation, and furthering the objects of communism and/or the ANC be quashed.

The defence succeeded in a number of its objections. In a 73-page decision, Judge Milne ruled that certain technical objections to the indictment were correct and ordered the State to give the defence further information on certain charges. The judge also upheld the objection that no reasonable man could infer that Mewa Ramgobin, MJ Naidoo, Paul David and George Sewpersadh had joined a conspiracy ... simply because they had been responsible for [some] pamphlets [which paid] tribute to Nelson Mandela and Griffiths Mxenge. The judge's ruling was heralded by the jubilant gallery as the defence's second victory, the granting of bail being the first. The State modified its charge ... restricting it to treason, alternatively terrorism and pursuing the objects of a banned organisation. It withdrew charges of participating in terroristic activities against some (Meer, 9–13).

With the preliminary stages of the trial completed, the accused were able to go home for a short adjournment. Albertina looked forward to enjoying quality time with her new grandchild, Nkuli's daughter Vuyelwa, who was born in June, one month after her grandmother had been released on bail. When the trial resumed, Nkuli and the baby accompanied Albertina to Natal. They stayed with Beryl in Durban throughout the trial, driving daily to Pietermaritzburg. After the tedious and tiring days in court, Albertina found it a huge pleasure to go home to enjoy the company of Beryl's three-year-old daughter Pamela and baby Vuyelwa. It is telling and perhaps rather poignant that during the course of the trial, she completely reorganised Beryl's garden, filling it with plants and working in it almost daily.

Beryl was kept busy, too: every day that court was in session, she prepared breakfast and lunch for all 16 accused, as well as their lawyers and any well-wishers who were present. According to Mewa Ramgobin, "On arrival at the Supreme Court, Mama's first words were always: 'Are all of you OK? Come, eat before you are grilled in court'" (Mewa Ramgobin, Unpublished notes).

The trial proper started on the 21 October, the day Albertina celebrated her 67th birthday. Minutes before the trial began, all the accused and several members of the public stood up and sang "Happy Birthday" to her.

The accused formally admitted that they had made speeches expressing strong opposition to the "undesirable and unwise" system of apartheid but denied that their speeches or any other actions constituted treason, terrorism or the furtherance of the aims of an unlawful organisation. The prosecutor then introduced the State's case.

Fatima Meer once again takes up the story:

Counsel for the State, Gey van Pittius, contended that non-violence and mass mobilisation were essential congruents of war and struggle, and for the latter to succeed, "a revolutionary climate ... has to be created whereby the country and its people are made ungovernable". The state counsel emphasised the importance of revolutionary symbols in canvassing support for violent change in South Africa and listed songs, dances, slogans and poems in this context.

The state counsel further submitted that when the security of a State was very effective, revolutionary organisations were driven underground from where they continued their violent action, but used alternate, legal/legitimate organisations to pursue their ideological propaganda, justification of violence and mass mobilisation. The legal and illegal organisations in that situation complemented each other, there being a simultaneous propagation of violent and non-violent action. Building and mobilising support he contended, implied advocating violence (Meer, 16–17).

After the prosecutor's introduction, the State presented its key witness, ID de Vries, a lecturer at the Rand Afrikaans University, who was considered by the State to be an expert on the revolutionary movement in South Africa. However, the so-called "expert witness" turned out to be a disaster for the State. He knew nothing about the accused apart from information he had received from the police. His knowledge of the ANC, UDF or any of the other organisations he purported to have studied did not extend beyond the realm of theory. He tested the patience of the court with his confused and irrelevant theories, as well as his rambling manner of stating the obvious.

Due to his long-windedness, De Vries's evidence took up 344 pages of the court records. "He almost literally threw his doctoral thesis, much of it in its preparatory, undigested state, at the court," commented Fatima Meer. He exasperated not only the judge and the defence, but even the prosecutor, who eventually cut short his own witness, so he could move on to the presentation of video and audio evidence.

But this did not go well for the State either. Although they used inflammatory and highly select-ive clips taken from meetings and speeches, under cross-examination it was revealed that video footage had been edited, was shown out of context, that transcripts and translations did not match the actual words captured on recordings, and so on.

The remaining state witnesses were equally unhelpful. The defence revealed that documentary evidence collected by one of them had been tampered with to make dates match. Another wit-ness, a former detainee, admitted under cross-examination he had been offered freedom if he became a state witness.

The State's case finally crumbled when De Vries returned to the witness box for cross-examination. He put up such a poor show under Ismail Mohamed's incisive cross-examination that eventually the judge himself asked him whether he had "formed an opinion" that certain individ-uals and organisations were committed to violence. When he responded that he had not yet come to "a final opinion", Ismail Mohamed promptly interjected, "M'Lord, then I don't know the value of this whole evidence and of this witness." Justice Milne explained, "That's why I'm asking the question" (*Weekly Mail*, 13–19/12/85). After that, it was all over, bar the shouting. De Vries admitted that he was confused about his task and had made "fundamental mistakes" that could have misled the court and that he had no expertise to assess the correctness of statements or facts published in revolutionary literature (*The Natal Witness*, 5–6/12/85).

On 9 December, the Natal Attorney-General Michael Imber appeared in court for the first time and announced that the State was withdrawing charges against 12 of the 16 accused. The four SAAWU members would remain on trial. Judge Milne congratulated the defendants on their con-duct during the proceedings and appealed to them to restrain their celebrations until they had left the court (*The Natal Witness*, 9/12/85, 10/12/85).

Albertina would always remember the joyful crowd that greeted them with cheers and applause as they emerged from the courtroom into the arms of jubilant relatives and friends. There were wild scenes of celebration as the trialists proceeded to a city hotel where the festivities continued.

Local and international responses were positive. Mike Cowling, the Chairman of Lawyers for Human Rights, said: "Despite the fact that the laws are so widely phrased that virtually any crit-icism of the government could be construed as a criminal offence, the state has failed to make out even a basic case." US State Department spokesman Mr Charles Redman said the dropping of the charges demonstrated the importance of the role of South Africa's judiciary (*The Natal Witness*, 10/12/85).

The trialists and their families and friends were ecstatic. Though the State's case had not been strong, they had not expected such a speedy end to the trial, and considered themselves lucky. The Pietermaritzburg Trial demonstrated that even within the unjust apartheid judiciary, there were decent and fair judges. Judge Milne had earned the respect of the accused and his historic act of appointing two black assessors had made a significant difference. In contrast, Kees van Dijkhorst, the Delmas Trial judge, displayed his antagonism to the defendants and his political prejudices from the outset. The Delmas trialists remained in prison for much longer before they were granted bail and their case dragged on for more than three years, making it one of the longest trials in South Africa's legal history. The trial finally ended in November 1988 when Terror Lekota, Popo Molefe, Moses Chikane and some of the other defendants were found guilty of treason. Lekota was sentenced to 12 years in prison and found himself back on Robben Island. Molefe and Chikane received 10-year sentences. They all appealed successfully against the verdict and were finally released in December 1989.

The Pollsmoor prisoners, who had been following the proceedings closely, had their own little celebration, as did Albertina's family in Soweto. On International Human Rights Day, the six Transvaal UDF leaders made their first public appearance since their acquittal at a packed meeting in central Johannesburg. They shared a platform with Bishop Tutu, Sheena Duncan (President of the Black Sash) and Sidney Kentridge, the advocate who had been part of the defence team in the

1956 Treason Trial. When she got up to speak, Albertina had a defiant message for the jubilant chanting crowd. She said it was the beginning of the end of the apartheid system and black South Africans would not rest until the country was given back to them. "The leaders of our people may be jailed, detained, harassed and killed but their efforts will not stop till freedom has been won!"

The Sisulu family observed a "Black Christmas" at the end of 1985. This was the practice, begun after the 1976 uprising, of eschewing the luxuries associated with Christmas and keeping expenditure to a bare minimum. Blacks felt that they had nothing to celebrate, and saw no reason to swell the coffers of white-owned businesses. By 1985, there was almost a total observation of "Black Christmas" in communities around the country in what amounted to a massive boycott of white businesses. Some whites also observed this practice, restricting Christmas celebrations to religious observation only.

Despite the absence of conventional Christmas festivities, the Sisulu family had plenty to celebrate: Albertina's acquittal and a new baby in the family, Boitumelo (Tumi), the third child of Lungi and Sheila, born on 19 December. There was enormous excitement in the family when Lindi called from Swaziland to tell her mother that Max had completed his fellowship in the Netherlands, was back in Lusaka, and planning to marry a woman from Zimbabwe.

When Albertina travelled to Cape Town for her annual Christmas visit to Walter, she was able to give him a first-hand account of the dramatic end of the Pietermaritzburg Trial and tell him about the new baby. Most of the visit, however, was devoted to discussing Max's engagement. His unmarried status had long concerned his parents, and they were delighted that at last it would be coming to an end. They looked forward to meeting the new fiancée – myself – early in the New Year.

# *eight*

At the end of 1985, Walter and his comrades in Pollsmoor reflected on a remarkable year in which the prospects for their release had become brighter than in two decades in prison. They followed events closely, listening as they did to 20 news bulletins a day, from 5am to 11pm (Kathrada, 174). They relied heavily on the stimulation of the radio, newspapers, books and magazines to relieve the tedium of prison life. In a letter to young Leila Issel, Kathrada described a typical day in their lives:

> We get up early in the morning and do our exercises. This is very important to keep fit and healthy. Then we shave and shower and get dressed. After breakfast we clean our place. After that we are free to do what we want to. We read newspapers, books, or do our schoolwork. We have our own little FM radio so we listen to the news and other programmes. Or we can walk about in the yard until lunchtime. The afternoons are quite short. We are locked up again at 4 o'clock until the next morning. Once a week we see films, mostly from the Cape Provincial Library. Some of them are very interesting. We are only six so we cannot play many games. Two of my friends play tennis. On Robben Island I used to play Tenniquoits, but there is nobody to play with here. Every day in jail is the same. Jail is very boring and a waste of time (Kathrada, 167).

Walter was very diligent about his exercise, running around their small rooftop yard every morning and having two sessions daily on his exercise bicycle. He also sometimes helped Mandela with his "garden in the sky". The prison authorities had allowed Mandela to grow vegetables in 16 oil drums sliced in half lengthwise. Walter would often help him with the mixing of compost (Sampson 2000, 326; Interview, Christo Brand).

Looking back on his prison years, Walter would always maintain that it was the close companionship with his comrades that sustained him. They had been together so long that they had become a kind of extended family. They read each other's letters and shared information about family visits. Despite their close bonds, it could however be quite irksome to be in the company of the same people day in and day out, year after year. There was little new they could tell each other. The same anecdotes had been related over and over again, the same jokes laughed at countless times. At 56, Kathrada was the "baby" in the group, and he sometimes longed for company of his own age, especially as the *madalas* or "geezers", as he affectionately referred to them, were rather strait-laced as a result of their mission education. Conversation with them "absolutely prohibits the telling of 'rude' jokes as well as the use of four-letter expletives – even in anger!" (Kathrada to Sonia Bunting, 225).

In December 1985, Mandela was taken to hospital for surgery on an enlarged prostate gland. While in hospital he received a surprise visitor, Kobie Coetsee, the Minister of Justice. Mandela had previously written to Coetsee requesting a meeting to discuss talks between the ANC and the government, so he interpreted Coetsee's visit as "an olive branch", an indication that the government was coming round to the view that it had no choice but to talk to the ANC. The two men exchanged pleasantries, and the only sensitive issue discussed was Winnie's residence in Johannesburg. In August 1985, Winnie's house in Brandfort had been firebombed while she was in Johannesburg receiving medical treatment. She decided to defy her banning order and refused to go back to Brandfort, even after the security police ordered her to return. Mandela asked Coetsee to allow Winnie to remain in Johannesburg (Mandela, 513). Whether Coetsee intervened is not clear, but the security police never did force Winnie to return to Brandfort.

Mandela's hospitalisation sparked off new rumours of release. "I hope you were not among the gullible ones who are expecting his imminent release," wrote Kathrada to Shehnaaz Meer. "I was surprised that there have been crowds of people waiting outside the gates to see him! ... Obviously the media and the 'grapevine' have succeeded in persuading just about everyone that we are about to be released. The only people who remain unconvinced and thankfully unperturbed by all the excitement are ourselves" (Letter to Shehnaaz Meer, 201).

Far from being released, after his discharge from hospital, Mandela was taken to a new set of cells on the ground floor of Pollsmoor Prison. He was alone for the first time in 24 years:

> I was in splendid isolation. Though my colleagues were only three floors above me, they might as well have been in Johannesburg. In order to see them I had to put in a formal request for a visit, which had to be approved by the head office in Pretoria. If it was approved I would then meet them in the visiting area. This was a novel experience: my comrades and fellow prisoners were now official visitors. For years we had been able to talk for hours a day, now we had to make official requests and appointments and our conversations were monitored (Mandela, 514).

Walter, Kathrada and Mhlaba were unhappy about the separation and suspected (correctly, as it turned out) that the South African government was trying to pursue a policy of divide and rule by cutting Mandela off from his colleagues. Walter trusted Mandela's ability to handle the situation, but was nevertheless concerned about it. He and his colleagues were planning to register a strong protest with the authorities when Mandela requested a meeting with them. To their surprise, he asked them to desist from protesting. He indicated that if he was alone, it would be easier for the government to make an approach. His colleagues were not happy about the situation, but had no alternative but to accept it. Mandela believed that his isolation would give the ANC an excuse if things went wrong: "The old man was alone and completely cut off and his actions were taken by him as an individual, not as a representative of the ANC" (Mandela, 515).

Conscious that his actions might cause concern at ANC headquarters in Lusaka after his meeting with Kobie Coetsee, Mandela sent George Bizos to Lusaka to reassure Oliver Tambo that he would not do anything without his concurrence. Bizos suspected the government of trying to split the internal and external ANC, with the hope that Mandela would lead the internal wing. "I didn't think Nelson would fall for it, but he was unable to speak publicly for himself, and I was worried that they might be able to do things that would compromise him and cause confusion" (Harvey, 112).

The next visit Walter and his colleagues had with Mandela was on New Year's Day, a more relaxed affair in which they put political considerations aside. Kathrada wrote in one of his letters that they had enjoyed a surprise "party": "Tasty snacks were prepared in the mess and we even had tea in tea cups! When one is used to metal utensils for almost 23 years, it was not without nervousness that I handled a cup and saucer" (Letter to Shehnaaz Meer, 201).

Ever the optimist, Walter had great hopes for the new year, but he and his colleagues were not carried away by the belief held by many in the liberation movement, especially the youth, that the fall of the apartheid state was imminent.

Meanwhile, I was being confronted by the realities of life under apartheid for the Sisulus, even from a distance of several thousand miles. As I boarded a flight from Harare to Johannesburg on the first Saturday of March 1986, I gained some understanding of the pain of exile. The duration of the flight was a mere one and a half hours, but for my husband-to-be who had dropped me off at Harare airport, Johannesburg was more distant than the South Pole. I wondered how much longer it would be before he would be able to take a flight to the country of his birth.

Since we had returned from the Netherlands in December 1985, Max to Lusaka and myself to Harare, we had proceeded with our marriage preparations. Max had visited Zimbabwe to see my parents and it was now my turn to meet his parents in South Africa. I had been to South Africa twice before: once on a church trip and the second time on a visit to a close family friend. This time I was visiting as the fiancée of a man the apartheid government defined as an ANC terrorist, and I could not help feeling apprehensive as the flight landed; I did not realise just how nervous I was until I felt relief wash over me after passing successfully through the passport and customs controls. My future sister-in-law, Sheila Sisulu, whom I recognised from photographs, was waiting for me in the concourse. As we reached her car I was struck by the sight of a man I recognised as Lungi Sisulu changing the napkin of his three-month-old daughter. I commented that Max had vowed that as a South African man he would never change a baby's napkin. Lungi was highly amused. "Exile has confused him," he commented. "When he gets back home, we will soon put him straight."

As we drove through Soweto, I found the place both familiar and unfamiliar, repulsive and at the same time strangely beguiling. The monotonous rows of matchbox houses were not dissimilar to those in Zimbabwean townships, but the size of the place was mind-boggling. We finally reached Orlando West, where we found Albertina waiting impatiently at the front door of Number 7372. She embraced me as if I was a long-lost child returning home. "Welcome home, my baby, I am so glad to see you," she said as she hugged me. Inside the house, I met Zodwa once again. She showed me to a beautifully decorated room adorned with a big "Welcome" sign. As the afternoon progressed into the evening, I met other family members – Max's son Mlungisi, Albertina's sister Flora (called Aunt Flo by everyone), and her two sons Elliot and Sipho, Sheila and Lungi's teenaged son Ginyi and daughter Ntsiki, Zodwa's vivacious sister Nomvuyo and Nkuli's beautiful baby daughter, Vuyelwa. Sheila, Lungi and Zwelakhe later joined us for a family supper. The following day, we got up at the crack of dawn to visit Walter's mother's grave at Nancefield cemetery. Visiting the grave was a ritual that Albertina was insistent on observing whenever anything significant happened in the family. This time, the purpose of the visit was to introduce a new member of the family to Gogo.

As the week progressed, I was introduced to a bewildering array of relatives, friends and neighbours. During the day, Albertina went off to work at Dr Asvat's surgery and Zodwa did her radiography work at Baragwanath Hospital. Zwelakhe was working long hours at the *New Nation*, which in the few months of its existence was proving to be a great success. In their absence, Aunt Flo took it upon herself to show me around and introduce me to all the neighbours, starting with Gogo-next-door who, explained Aunt Flo, had been a pillar of support to the family during difficult times. "Shame, poor Ntsiki! Being separated from her child all these years. Man! These Boers are cruel!" she muttered, shaking her head. We then proceeded to Obert Ramorola, one of Max's childhood friends, who stared at me in disbelief. "You mean he is actually alive?" To my great embarrassment, she insisted on giving me five rand.

Another of Max's childhood friends, Simon Motaung, better known as Maye, was astonished and overjoyed to hear that his friend was alive and well. When Max called to find out how I was getting on, he in turn was astonished to learn that Maye's mother, Gogo Msana, a contemporary of Walter's mother, was still alive. Well into her nineties, Gogo Msana would pass by when she collected her grandchild from the crèche opposite the Sisulu home. It amused me to hear her calling 67-year-old Albertina "*mntanami*" ("my child"). In her presence, Albertina related the story of how Walter asked Gogo Msana to hide some books for him because he feared a raid by the security police. Gogo obliged, but she was so terrified of the police that she buried the books in her garden. Gogo took up the tale: "When we dug up those books months later, they were all destroyed," she recalled, cackling loudly at the memory.

I was deeply moved by the visit of Ma Molefe, a veteran of the 1950s, who limped along on her bad leg from her house some distance away. She was happy to learn that I had met her son Sipho, one of Max's friends also in exile in Lusaka. She was disappointed that I had never met Moses Mabhida, the 1950s SACTU veteran and ANC leader who had just died in exile in Mozambique.

I was taken to "Shop 7", Lungi's café and a favourite haunt of the young people in the family. It was also a centre where young activists and former Robben Islanders would gather. There I met Sammy Malapane, a young man who had spent six years on Robben Island after he had been arrested trying to leave the country for military training in 1977. On Robben Island, he became very attached to Walter and told he would like to become his son. Walter saw nothing unusual in this, as he was a father figure for many prisoners. The difference was that Sammy meant it literally, with the result that one day he presented himself to Albertina and announced that he had been sent by Walter to become part of the Sisulu family. Never one to turn anyone away, Albertina sent Sammy to Lungi, who gave him a job at Shop 7. Sammy's biological family assured the Sisulus that they had no objections to their adopting Sammy, and at the time Priscilla Jana was handling Sammy's application to change his name legally to Sisulu.

On the second weekend of my visit, the family held a traditional welcoming of the daughter-in-law – perhaps not so traditional, given that my family and Max were absent. Lungi bought a sheep and Jongi's father Dwelisa took charge of the traditional slaughtering. Beryl flew in from Durban for the occasion.

Albertina proudly introduced me to Priscilla Jana, whom she said had become more like a daughter to her than a lawyer. I also met Tina, Priscilla's lovely foster daughter, who was named after Albertina. Priscilla's name was always in the news for her work on one high-profile political case after another. I had admired her persistent but unsuccessful efforts to stave off the execution of the MK fighter Benjamin Moloise in September 1985. She also experienced her share of police harassment. She had been banned in 1983, and in December 1985 a firebomb was thrown into her house. Fortunately her husband Reggie had had the presence of mind to catch the device and throw it out into the street, where it exploded harmlessly.

Priscilla's office handled my application to visit Walter in Pollsmoor Prison. This meant handing in my passport to the police, something I did not enjoy doing. I was afraid that permission might be denied because of my connection with Max. Years later, I would come across a security police memo stating that "Elinor Batezat, the fiancé[sic] of Max Sisulu, a known ANC terrorist" had requested permission to visit Walter Sisulu. Fortunately, permission for the visit was granted, possibly because the police hoped to get information about Max.

A few days before I was due to leave for Cape Town for the Pollsmoor visit, Nkuli and her fiancé Mtuthuzeli (Teyi) phoned to ask if I could bring their baby, Vuyelwa with me, as they were missing her so badly. I readily agreed, but Albertina refused to entertain the idea. Since I was in the early stages of pregnancy, she did not think it was a good idea for me to travel all the way to Cape Town with an eight-month-old baby. When I tried to assure her that I would manage, she very firmly told me that she was a midwife, and she knew best when it came to the health of a pregnant woman. It took two days of phone calls from Vuyelwa's parents and the persuasive skills of Sheila to change Albertina's mind and allow the baby to travel with me. Fortunately, Vuyelwa was a delightful baby and gave me no problems on the flight. As we disembarked at Cape Town airport, a young white SADF officer took my hand luggage and carried it to the terminal. I wondered whether he would have been as eager to assist me if he had known the purpose of my visit.

Vuyelwa and I were met at the airport by her delighted parents. Teyi could scarcely drive his car for admiring his daughter, so much so that I became nervous that we might not reach our destination. However, we were safely delivered to the Cape Town suburb of Retreat, where Nkuli was staying with Beryl's friends, Mampie and Eugene Morgan.

Early the next morning, Mampie drove us through the verdant suburb of Tokai to Pollsmoor Prison for our 8.30am appointment. One of the warders obviously knew Nkuli well and could not conceal his delight at seeing little Vuyelwa. As we were led through the maze of corridors to the visiting room, he chatted amicably to Nkuli, asking after the wellbeing of other family members. He explained politely that because I was not yet officially a member of the Sisulu family, I was not entitled to the privilege of a "contact" visit with Walter Sisulu. Instead, we communicated through microphones on either side of the thick glass pane that divided us. Not that I could say much, as I was in tears for most of the visit. Walter had listed the questions he wanted to ask me in the little notebook he used for visits, but he tactfully turned his attention to Nkuli and Vuyelwa, and the 40 minutes was over all too soon.

The next day, I returned for my second visit. I knew what to expect and this time there were no tears. Walter wanted to know more about my family, my job, the wedding plans and the main item on the agenda – a name for the baby we were expecting. He was delighted when I told him we had chosen the name Vuyisile, Max's second name. It was a fortuitous coincidence, he said, because he had wanted to suggest the name Mini – after Vuyisile Mini, whom he had admired so much. I was amazed at how much ground we covered in our brief interview, and I left the prison feeling as if I had known Walter for a very long time.

Before Vuyelwa and I returned to Johannesburg, Nkuli took us to see Albertina's brother, Reverend Elliot Thethiwe and his wife Miriam, at their home at the Presbyterian Church in Langa. Uncle Elliot was recovering from having had his leg amputated as a result of complications caused by diabetes. He was nevertheless in high spirits. He wanted to know what Max was doing, what he had studied and what life was like in the exile community. He regaled me with stories of his experiences during the 1960 State of Emergency, and described how the Special Branch would park permanently outside their house whenever Albertina stayed with them during her visits to Cape Town. I cherished the memory of that visit because Uncle Elliot died a few months later.

While we were visiting Pollsmoor, Nkuli and I were unaware that another set of visitors, much more distinguished than ourselves, was paying a call that same day. The Commonwealth Eminent Persons Group (EPG) had been granted a visit to Nelson Mandela as part of its mission to assess the prospects for change and to explore ways to promote dialogue between the antagonists in the South African conflict. At the 1985 Commonwealth Heads of Government meeting in the Bahamas, British Prime Minister Margaret Thatcher had locked horns with the rest of the Commonwealth leaders, who were pressing for the imposition of comprehensive and mandatory sanctions against South Africa. In the face of Thatcher's intransigent opposition to sanctions, a compromise was found in the form of the appointment of a group of Eminent Persons to visit South Africa. Mandela had followed up Kobie Coetsee's hospital visit with two letters proposing talks on negotiations and was puzzled and frustrated by Coetsee's lack of response. He was therefore glad of the opportunity to raise the issue of negotiations with a group as influential as the EPG (Mandela, 517).

The reformist lobby within the South African government were well aware that a negative report from the EPG would make it difficult, if not impossible, to stave off sanctions against South Africa. This concern played a part in the conciliatory noises made by Pretoria in the first few months of 1986. An expensive government advertising campaign promised the dawn of a new era (Sparks 1990, 351) and in the first week of March the State of Emergency was lifted. The government seemed keen to accommodate the EPG's visit with Mandela, even to the point of organising a tailor to make a suit for Mandela to wear at the meeting (Mandela, 517).

Apart from the meeting with Mandela , the EPG consulted widely with a large number of South Africans from across the political spectrum. To their credit, the EPG looked beyond the deceptive calm and tranquillity of the major urban centres and were struck by the levels of violence in the country. They warned that "if a major conflagration was to be averted, time was running out" (Greg Houston, Unpublished notes, 192).

Some of the bloodiest clashes took place in Alexandra township in mid-February, in what the South African press dubbed the "Six-day War". Angry residents rioted after police attacked people returning from a funeral. Eighty people were killed and nearly 300 injured in six days of violent confrontations with police and riot squad units. General Obasanjo, the EPG co-chairman personally witnessed the violence when spending several days in Alexandra talking to residents

(Sparks 1990, 353). On 5 March 1986, 60 000 people converged on the stadium in Alexandra to bury 17 young victims of the violence. It was the first week of my visit to South Africa, and I had wanted to attend the funeral, especially as Albertina was one of the main speakers. Albertina, however, was adamant that it would not be advisable: "Not in your condition, my dear. Anything can happen at these funerals." Years later, I would read American author Adam Hoschchild's moving account of the event:

> I feel humbled at the majesty of the singing and the solemnity of the crowd, many of whom are weeping. Near a speaker's platform at one end of the field, the seventeen coffins lie in a row; each is covered with banners in the black, green, and gold colours of the African National Congress. Mothers and other relatives sit next to each coffin. An honour guard of teenage boys in brown berets and red armbands stands at attention next to them. For four hours under a broiling sun, speaker after speaker comes to the rostrum.
>
> One is Albertina Sisulu ... she is introduced, to much cheering, as "our mother, Comrade Mrs Sisulu."
>
> "This country is governed by frightened cockroaches!" she shouts.
>
> The crowd responds with a distinctive cheer: "OOOOahhh!" There are more OOOOahhs as she mentions Nelson Mandela and other African National Congress leaders.
>
> But in her talk, as in those of several other speakers, there is an undertone of anxiety. Since South Africa's latest wave of uprisings began in 1984, several hundred black collaborators, usually police informers, have been "necklaced" – burned to death with old gasoline-filled tires around their necks. Some of these revenge killings have been done by volatile, angry crowds just like this one. "Enough now!" Albertina Sisulu warns the young people. "There is no need for you to be fighting like dogs, man! The youth must be strong to say NO when something is wrong."
>
> Addressing the informers she adds, "We will deal with you when we are free" (Hochschild, 7).

Albertina also on this occasion made her oft-repeated appeal to mothers of white soldiers to stop the government from sending their sons to kill black children: "We as mothers – black and white – should be fighting together more and more. What happens to black children will happen to white children ... Today there is no peace in South Africa, but the government says there is. Why then are soldiers roaming the streets of the townships killing our children?" (Gorodnov, 261.) Her appeal to white mothers had a powerful impact, coming as it did at a time when increasing numbers of young white conscripts were traumatised by their experiences in the townships, and young white men were leaving the country in droves to avoid military service.

When I returned to Johannesburg after my visits to Pollsmoor, I found the family in a state of excitement about the start of Jongumzi Sisulu's trial. After his arrest in July 1984, Jongi had been detained under the notorious Section 29 of the Internal Security Act, which empowered security police to hold a detainee indefinitely for purposes of interrogation. Section 29 detainees were held in solitary confinement and allowed no visitors. After six months, Jongi was transferred to Diepkloof Prison together with 14 other MK prisoners. Shortly thereafter, they were transferred to Pretoria Central Prison. Jongi was charged with treason and terrorism together with four other MK cadres – James Mncedise Dubase, Lumkile Mkefa, David Matose and Joseph Maja. Dubase was the first accused and Jongi the second accused. There were long delays in getting the case in court, partly because Priscilla Jana had difficulty in getting counsel. The "struggle" advocates who normally took on such a case were tied up with other cases, and many advocates were simply too afraid to defend people the State had defined as terrorists.

The trial finally got under way in March 1986.

Priscilla Jana said they were the most boisterous group she had ever defended, representative of a generation that had no fear of white authority. "I remember the day I was telephoned by the security police to say my clients were appearing in court. I rushed off to the courtroom and from a long way off I could hear singing. There was no one around, not even a clerk of the court. They had all taken cover because they were terrified. Somebody came up to me in the passage and said 'The ANC is here!' and I said 'Oh God, those must be my clients!' At one stage they were angry about something and in protest all five of them stood up and in unison jumped onto the bench in front of them, which was quite a feat since they were handcuffed and chained together in leg irons. There was a mighty noise as they landed together on the bench, and the courtroom staff were simply terrified."

The family had seen very little of Jongi during the long awaiting-trial period, so his appearance in court provided an opportunity for a reunion. Jongi's father Dwelisa had come up from Engcobo for the trial. Albertina, Sheila and Zodwa took time off work to attend the first day of the trial. Together with Jongi's fiancée Jacqueline and their two sons and numerous family members and friends, we trooped off to the Supreme Court in Johannesburg. The families of the other accused had also turned out in full force, and tempers flared when the police tried to prevent people from entering the courtroom. Priscilla had to alert the judge inside the court and eventually people were allowed in. The accused, bound in handcuffs and leg irons and chained to each other, entered the court singing. There was pandemonium for a few minutes as greetings were shouted out to loved ones. The drama of their entry contrasted with the utterly boring proceedings, which began with a trial within a trial to test whether the statements of the accused were extracted through torture. I remember the State's counsel droning on and on in Afrikaans, which most of us could not understand. The only spark of interest was provided by the court interpreter who, with his eyes closed, chin in the air and hands clasped against his chest as if he was praying, translated the English and Afrikaans arguments into Zulu.

Once the case had been adjourned for the day, Priscilla arranged for some family members to go down to the holding cells to see the accused. Since I was visiting from outside the country, I was one of those given the privilege of 10 minutes with Jongi. He and his co-accused were extremely excited to talk to someone who was in contact with people in Lusaka. I was asked to pass on messages to dozens of people, most of whom I did not even know. Back in the courtroom foyer, I joined Albertina, who was surrounded by family members of the accused and some young activists. A young white policewoman told us very rudely to clear the area. I saw Albertina transform before my eyes from the smiling grandmother to the stern leader. She drew herself to full height, looked the young woman up and down and then gave her a severe scolding. "We are the mothers of these children on trial. We have a right to be here. You should be ashamed of yourself for talking to us in that way." The policewoman turned red with embarrassment and shock. It was obvious she was not used to a black person speaking to her in that way. Before she could formulate a reply, Albertina swept regally past her with the rest of us in tow. As we entered the large elevator, the young activists sang freedom songs and danced the *toyi toyi* with such vigour that the elevator shook with their rhythmic stomping.

Both Albertina and Lungi had been subpoenaed to give evidence for the State in Jongi's trial. They were both adamant that they would not comply, even though they were well aware that refusal to testify could result in a stiff jail sentence (*Weekly Mail*, 28/2–16/3). Priscilla Jana had argued strongly that Albertina and Lungi could give no information relevant to the case and the police did not pursue the matter, probably because they already had more than enough evidence to convict Jongi.

Jongi's trial lasted from March to May. On 14 May, Jongi and his comrades were convicted and sentenced to five years in prison and transferred to Robben Island.

A feature of the 1985–86 period were the "people's parks" that young activists created in the open spaces of Soweto and named after heroes of the liberation struggle. I was intrigued to see a "Mandela Park" and a "Sisulu Park" decorated with brightly coloured seats and sculptures made of scrap metal and other recycled material.

After the imposition of the 1985 State of Emergency, overt political organisation was impossible, so the focus shifted to mobilisation through street committees. In a process that started in 1985 and gained momentum in 1986, the Soweto Civic Association (SCA) formed street committees of between 40 and 50 households. Lungi Sisulu, who was active in the street committees, explained to me how they facilitated communication in the township and made it possible to organise clandestine meetings and events such as funerals at very short notice. In some townships of Soweto, as in other parts of the country, street committees carried out the functions of the collapsed local government administrations (Beck, 110). In the political lexicon of the UDF and ANC, the assumption of administrative, judicial, welfare, and cultural functions by local civic and youth organisations was referred to as "people's power" (Lodge et al., 135). It created a sense of euphoria among young activists, who imagined they had "rendered South Africa ungovernable and apartheid unworkable", and that freedom was just around the corner.

Like most senior UDF leaders, Albertina was only too aware that "ungovernability" was a double-edged sword. She was deeply concerned about the brutalisation of young activists and the emergence of the *"com-tsotsis"* who used political activism as a cover for violence and thuggery. She abhorred the murder of suspected political informers through brutal methods such as necklacing. I remember returning home with her one day to find a group of scruffy, hungry-looking adolescent boys at her front gate. The UDF driver told her that they were on the run from the police because they had necklaced someone in one of the East Rand townships. She shuddered with horror and lamented with agony written all over her face: "Why, oh why should they do such a thing? And they expect us to help them?" She believed that the criminal behaviour of some of the young comrades was a direct consequence of the intractable boycotts in township schools, and she was openly critical of the "Liberation before Education" slogan that was bandied about by militant student activists. She was deeply concerned that Max's son, Lungi, at the age of 20 had not yet completed high school as a result of disturbances in the education system throughout his school career.

Albertina believed the occupation of township schools by the army had exacerbated the problems in black education. There were widespread reports of soldiers humiliating teachers in front of children and administering corporal punishment to children (Webster, 153). "The government does not want our children to be educated," she complained in an interview. "The soldiers are even in the classrooms. Who can learn when the soldiers are pointing guns?" She cited the example of Matseke High School in Orlando West where soldiers had entered the classrooms and asked the students who the first man to come to South Africa had been. They went on to answer their own question: "Vasco da Gama! And where was your Mandela and your Tambo?" (*Africa Report*, Sept/Oct 1997).

Education was the burning issue of 1986. Sheila Sisulu, who worked for the South African Council for Higher Education (SACHED) Trust, explained to me the seriousness of the crisis. Teaching and learning in Soweto schools and many parts of the country had virtually come to a standstill towards the end of 1985. Pass rates were dismal and school principals had been forced to call off end of year examinations. The banning of COSAS in August 1985 and the arrests and detention of hundreds of student leaders had fuelled the anger of an already dissatisfied student population. Frustrated and hostile students tried to enforce the "Liberation before Education" slogan by attacking those who wanted to go to school. The result was empty schools and thousands of idle children wandering aimlessly around township streets. Around the country, more than one and a half million students were boycotting classes. Panicky parents tried to intervene without much success, until the SCA stepped into the fray. On 13 October 1985, the SCA organised a meeting of parents, scholars and teachers at which the Soweto Parents' Crisis Committee

(SPCC) was formed. The SPCC quickly organised a National Consultative Conference at the University of the Witwatersrand, which was attended by representatives of 145 organisations, including the ANC and AZAPO.

Parents, teachers and senior activists pushed for an end to the boycott and encouraged scholars to return to school and transform the education system from within. The ANC backed them up, and the slogan "Education for Liberation" was put forward to replace the "Liberation before Education" one that had caused parents so much anxiety. Pupils were persuaded to agree to a resolution in favour of a return to school conditional upon the government meeting a number of demands. These included the unbanning of COSAS, the release of detainees, and the recognition of student representative councils (Muller, 21).

Many pupils, however, were vehemently opposed to returning to school and felt that parents should first deal with the problem of securing the release of students in detention (Bonner and Segal, 121). In an article "Walter Sisulu arbitrates from afar", journalist Phil Mtimkulu reported on how Walter Sisulu unwittingly played a part in the schools boycott debate:

> Walter Sisulu has been in jail now for 21 years ... but last Sunday his name was dropped at a meeting and this resolved an impasse. This happened during a meeting organised by the Soweto Parents' Crisis Committee to try to solve the continuing education crisis in the townships.
>
> The pupils' representatives were against a return to school and called on children ... to abandon their desks and join the struggle against Bantu Education. Their slogan was *"Phambili Namzabalazo, phansi nemfundo"* ("Forward with the struggle, down with education").
>
> The pupils argued forcefully and appeared to be winning the day ... They were spread strategically throughout the hall. Their voices were heard here, there and everywhere.
>
> A former pupil leader from the 1976 era, who is now an activist, restored the balance ... when [he] stood up and dropped Walter Sisulu's name. He told the pupils what Sisulu had said to him about the importance of education while both of them were at Robben Island.
>
> Sisulu told him then that the country was highly industrialised and it would need equally skilled people to run it after independence. Nobody is sure if that is what Sisulu told him. But Sisulu, like Nelson Mandela, is revered by young activists.
>
> Though pupils continued arguing ... the wind had been taken out of their sails. They compromised and agreed pupils should return to school even if it was to continue fighting Bantu education.

One of the resolutions of the conference on the education crisis was the establishment of a National Education Crisis Committee (NECC), which convened a second national conference in Durban in March 1986. The choice of Durban as a venue angered Chief Buthelezi, who saw it as an invasion. The threat of violence forced the organisers to change the venue three times and the thousand-odd delegates had to be driven to the secret venue under cover of darkness. Even this did not prevent two busloads of Inkatha supporters from storming the delegates. In the ensuing clash, two Inkatha supporters were killed (*Sechaba*, May 1986; Beck, 104). In this highly charged and volatile atmosphere Zwelakhe Sisulu got up and gave the keynote address. In what amounted to a state-of-the-struggle address, he hailed the conference as a truly historic one, "in the tradition of earlier national meetings, such as the Congress of the People of 1955 and the 1961 All-in Africa Conference".

He went on to outline the crisis facing the South African regime and said the emergency had not crushed the resistance of the people. Instead, structures had been built that would survive the emergency and beyond. "Not only did our organisations grow in strength, they often took over the running of the townships. So we saw the emergence of zones of people's power in a number of townships." He also hailed the formation of COSATU and its strong stand in supporting trade union involvement in community and political issues, and noted that the ANC had emerged as the primary actor on the South African stage, not only among the black oppressed, but also among the white ruling class.

The gains that had been made notwithstanding, he disabused his audience of the notion that freedom was around the corner:

> We are not poised for the immediate transfer of power to the people. The belief that this is so could lead to serious errors and defeats. We are however poised to enter a phase which can lead to transfer of power. What we are seeking to do is to decisively shift the balance of forces in our favour. To do this we have to adopt the appropriate strategies and tactics, we have to understand our strengths and weaknesses, as well as that of the enemy.

By implication, he was criticising the "Liberation before Education" slogan. He voiced the concerns of UDF leaders about the tendency to violence among the youth, emphasising the need for the responsible exercise of power and making an important distinction between ungovernability and people's power.

> In a situation of ungovernability the government doesn't have control. But nor do the people. While they have broken the direct shackles of government rule the people haven't yet managed to control and direct the situation. There is a power vacuum. In a situation of people's power the people are starting to exercise control. An important difference between ungovernability and people's power is that no matter how ungovernable a township is, unless the people are organised, the gains made through ungovernability can be rolled back by State repression.
>
> Struggles over the past few months demonstrate that it is of absolute importance that we don't confuse coercion, the use of force against the community, with people's power, the collective strength of the community. For example, when bands of youth set up so-called "kangaroo courts" and give out punishments, under the control of no one, with no democratic mandate from the community, this is not people's power ... We know that this kind of undisciplined individual action can have very negative consequences.
>
> When disciplined, organised youth, together with other older people participate in the exercise of people's justice and the setting up of people's courts; when these structures are acting on a mandate from the community and are under the democratic control of the community, this is an example of people's power.

He stressed the important role of youth organisations "in trying to channel the militancy of unorganised youth into disciplined action, responsive and accountable to the whole community".

Zwelakhe's speech enhanced his reputation as one of the leading strategic thinkers in the democratic movement. Historian Tom Karis noted: "The UDF had not publicly formulated a fully defined strategy. Sisulu's address was a notable though short-range effort to do this." A leader in his own right, Zwelakhe was also backed by the weight of authority of his parents. As one commentator pointed out:

> The speech Zwelakhe Sisulu read was the product of a drafting committee but the choice of Sisulu as keynote speaker was rich in symbolism. Son of giants of the "struggle", Walter and Albertina Sisulu, Zwelakhe carried on to the stage ... the mantle of a family whose leading participation in the resistance encompasses several significant tendencies of post-World War II black politics ... The youth whom Zwelakhe hoped to influence could be counted on to know that the ideas he presented were those of the highest political authority of the resistance (Beck, 103).

Zwelakhe also warned that government would use increasingly vicious and illegal methods to suppress people's resistance. One of the most sinister and disturbing developments in the patterns of violence in 1985 was the emergence of state-sponsored vigilantes in communities around the country. UDF activists came under increasing attack from groups such as the "A-team" and the

"Phakatis" in the Orange Free State, the "Amasolomzi" in Ashton near Pietermaritzburg, the "Amadoda" in Cape Town and the "A-team" in Chesterville, Durban. In most of these areas, the State skilfully exploited inter-generational tension between older, more conservative workers and young UDF-supporting comrades. Crossroads near Cape Town was the scene of some of the worst vigilante-inspired violence. Johnson Ngxobongwana, the leader of a section of Crossroads, recruited a vigilante group, the "Witdoeke", named for the white head-cloths they wore to distinguish themselves from the young comrades (Lodge et al., 169). Violent confrontations between Witdoeke and comrades erupted into a full-scale war in May 1986 when the Witdoeke, aided and abetted by the police, attacked and destroyed UDF-aligned settlements around Crossroads. Seventy thousand people were driven from their homes and 60 were killed (TRC Report).

The Commonwealth's EPG, then shuttling between Lusaka, Pretoria and Cape Town, was appalled by the escalation of vigilante-related violence and warned that time was running out if a major conflagration was to be averted (Houston, Unpublished notes, 192).

Based on its wide-ranging consultations, the EPG had developed a "possible negotiating concept" that would involve the government releasing Nelson Mandela and other political prisoners and detainees, removing the military from the townships, allowing freedom of assembly, unbanning the ANC and PAC and allowing normal political activity (Sparks 1990, 353; Houston, Unpublished notes, 193).

The ANC's part of the bargain would be to suspend violence. Mandela was cautiously optimistic about the concept when the EPG met him on 16 May. When the ANC indicated that it would consider the idea, the ball was firmly in the court of the government. "For the government the moment of truth had come," wrote Allister Sparks. "The ANC seemed ready to accept the terms of the 'possible negotiating concept', and so the government would have to decide: did it really want to negotiate with them or not? There could be no more ducking and diving, no more doublethink and doublespeak, no more stalling even. The EPG was here and an answer had to be given" (Sparks 1990, 353).

The government gave its answer in dramatic fashion. On 19 May 1986, the day the EPG was to have met with a cabinet constitutional committee, the SADF carried out simultaneous bombing raids on Lusaka, Harare and Gaberone, all capitals of Commonwealth countries that the EPG had recently visited. The raids effectively ended the EPG mission, and Obasanjo and his colleagues flew out of South Africa the same night (Sparks 1990, 353; Mandela, 518; Sampson 2000, 350). Three weeks later, the EPG published a damning report of its mission, ending with the warning: "If the government finds itself unable to talk to men like Mandela and Tambo, then the future is bleak indeed" (Sampson 2000, 351; Seekings, 191).

When I left Johannesburg for Harare at the end of March 1986, members of the Sisulu family were eagerly planning to apply for passports to attend our wedding later in that year. Max was optimistically looking forward to another reunion with his siblings and my mother was preparing for an influx of South African visitors. The SADF raid on Harare dampened our spirits considerably. For my family, it was a worrying reminder of the risks of marrying a member of the ANC. The SADF was not selective in its deadly operations and it was not common for citizens of the frontline states to be among the victims of their raids. We were even more disheartened by PW Botha's declaration of a nationwide State of Emergency on 12 June.

The June 1986 Emergency was much more harsh and wide-ranging than that of the previous year. In the early hours of the morning of 12 June, police descended on sleeping townships around the country and arrested thousands of people. The largest number of arrests were in Soweto and Port Elizabeth. In the first few days of the Emergency, so many people were detained that the police had to use cold-storage facilities normally used for beer as holding centres (Lodge et al., 88).

In his comprehensive exposé of repression in the 1986–7 period, David Webster reported that 26 000 people had been detained by June 1987. "In eight months of this Emergency, security police detained as many people as the total held under previous Emergencies and security legislation for the past 26 years." This made South Africa second to none on the international index of repression, he wrote (Webster, 141).

PW Botha had clearly abandoned his flirtation with reform and the possibility of negotiations. Instead, he caved in to right-wing pressures to crack down hard on black resistance. The securocrats had been alarmed by the rising power of COSATU, dramatically demonstrated by the May Day stay-away of one and a half million workers, the largest ever. The government was aware of preparations for a massive commemoration of the tenth anniversary of the 1976 uprising, and this was no doubt also a consideration in the timing of the imposition of Emergency strictures.

The Emergency regulations involved an onslaught against the media. Several foreign correspondents were expelled from the country and a number of local journalists were detained under security legislation and emergency regulations (Webster, 167).

Around 3am on 26 June 1986, Zwelakhe and Zodwa were jolted awake by a thunderous banging on their doors, characteristic of the security police. But the four white men who forced their way into the house were not dressed in police uniform and their faces were hidden by the balaclavas they wore over their heads. They hauled Zwelakhe out of the house and bundled him into a car that sped away into the night. Alone with two small children, Zodwa immediately tried to call Albertina, but the telephone line was dead. It was sunrise before she finally managed to call and alert the family and Priscilla Jana. There were anxious moments for the family as they tried to establish that it was indeed the police who had taken Zwelakhe. Amid reports that he had been kidnapped by vigilantes, the government admitted that it was holding him.

Zwelakhe was taken to John Vorster Square where he was interrogated about the *New Nation*. He gave a full explanation of the paper's aims and how it had been set up. He was asked whether he supported violence, and questioned about the NECC. He told his interrogators he was not a member of the NECC, and had simply been invited to give the keynote address at its conference.

Zwelakhe was released three weeks later. His detention was part of the broader clampdown on the media; moreover, his address to the NECC had caused a stir in the security establishment and was a major factor prompting his detention. Later, a huge file of documents relating to this speech was found in the Ministry of Justice archives. The file contained Oliver Tambo's 1985 and 1986 addresses in which certain phrases and expressions were highlighted, especially the concept of "people's power" and "to consolidate, defend and advance the gains we have made". Apart from trying to show that the speech was ANC-inspired, Compol speculated on the Marxist influence: "In addition delicate information has come to light that Raymond Suttner, self-confessed Marxist and communist, had composed or helped to write Zwelakhe Sisulu's speech. This matter is being investigated." Compol's assessment of the speech provides an interesting insight into the security police understanding of political theory:

> On analysis of the "keynote address" there is no doubt that a direct effort was made to reconcile the powers of the revolutionaries. It was a message of resistance if not of revolt. Sisulu is well read in radical rhetoric and in that regard is affiliated to like revolutionary utterances by people like Tutu, Boesak, Winnie Mandela and others. It follows the same pattern of emotional, inflammatory speeches which are prescribed and give direction to the already highly politicised black youth.
>
> Given the present unrest situation, the militant youth find this kind of rhetoric fascinating and it further receives stature in the establishment of alternative authorities and education structures.
>
> The take-over of schools and "transforming them from institutions of oppression into zones of people's power" is directly linked to the alternative power structures. This radical Marxist terminology is the substructure of a Marxist recipe and has come a long way with the Paulo Freire awareness philosophy (Pedagogy of the Oppressed) of which Biko was a disciple.

These principles are a Marxist interpretation and can be ascribed to Black authors, anti-Afrikaner historians and exiles ...

This radical and revolutionary rhetoric is not the Black nationalism of pan-Africanism and African unity. It is a black racism with a Marxist substructure which is headed for confrontation and resistance.

Zwelakhe's three-week stint in detention was just a foretaste of what was to come.

On 19 July 1986, Max and I celebrated the birth of our son Vuyisile Mini Jeremy Sisulu. As the first grandchild in my immediate family, Vuyisile's birth was the occasion of great joy. Max sent a telegram to Pollsmoor and called his mother in Soweto. Albertina proudly boasted that she had lost track of how many grandchildren she had, and Walter conveyed his delight through a long congratulatory message. Ever since our meeting in Pollsmoor, we had corresponded regularly. In his first letter he said, "I wish we could have met each other under better conditions than was the case when you were here. I should however like to say I wish you to accept my conditions as they are. We naturally would like to live with all our loved ones, far from this abnormal life. We do look forward to such a day. Please do not upset yourself. It pains me greatly to see you disturbed." He said that he had passed our greetings to his colleagues, who had received them with great delight. He then included a message from Mandela, who had enjoyed reading my letter. Walter said he hoped I was not angry with him for letting his colleagues read my letters without my permission. "I hope Max will defend me because he has every reason to understand." In later letters he asked for a detailed account of my family and friends, my job and a description of the place where I lived. His letters conveyed the same sense of energy and optimism that I had felt in our two meetings. The only note of anxiety was about the postponing of our wedding date to September. Both he and Albertina made it clear that they wanted the wedding to take place as soon as possible.

They were delighted when Max informed them that Hector Nkula, an old ANC veteran who was exiled in Lusaka, would accompany Max to meet my father. Two years Walter's senior, Nkula was also born in the Transkei. He had trained as a teacher at Lovedale and joined the ANC and the SACP in the 1930s. Like Walter, he was involved in all the ANC campaigns in the 1950s and had joined MK in 1960 at the age of 50.

We picked up Hector Nkula at the home of Sylvia and Eddie Kwalo, the South African couple who accommodated him whenever he visited Harare. Eddie Kwalo had been the first person to come to Max's aid after he had been injured in the 1974 parcel bomb blast in Lusaka. They could now laugh at the memory of Max lying injured and Eddie shaking him and asking him: "Are you dead? Wake up, please wake up!"

Ntate Nkula took marriage discussions very seriously and I was amazed at the formal and extravagant language he used in our first meeting with my father. I had made it clear to him that as a 28-year-old woman I did not need to ask my parents for permission to get married, and I certainly would not entertain the idea of *lobola*. The meeting was therefore more of a courtesy call than a request for consent. Nkula either missed this point or perhaps chose to ignore it. He launched into an elaborate plea for my father to consider their humble request for the hand of his daughter. He even raised the question of *lobola*, saying that because they were in exile it might be difficult to meet the requirements, but they would certainly try to do what they could. I cringed and Max could barely conceal his amusement, but my father was impressed by the seriousness of Nkula's approach, and by the end of the evening they parted like old friends. When Max and I took Nkula back to the Kwalos, he entered triumphantly. "How did it go?" they asked eagerly. "Wonderful! Just wonderful!" enthused Nkula. Much to my dismay, he proceeded to give the Kwalos a detailed account of the discussion.

The next day, Max called Albertina to give her a full report about the meeting with his prospective father-in-law. He joked about how Nkula had mentioned his distant family connection with Albertina but as the evening wore on, the relationship became closer and closer until by the end, Nkula was Albertina's brother! I was glad to hear that Albertina approved of my stand on *lobola* and said she had not wanted *lobola* for any of her daughters.

As we prepared for our wedding, we came up against a major hurdle. Max did not have any document that identified him as Max Sisulu. Like many ANC members, Max travelled under a different identity. As part of their solidarity and support to the South African liberation movement, the governments of Ghana and Sierra Leone provided passports to the ANC, and Max had at various times assumed a Ghanaian or Sierra Leonian identity. At the time of our marriage, he was using a Ghanaian passport in the name of Dennis Maxwell. My cousin Terence Pike who worked at the Harare magistrate's court advised us that there was no way he could process our marriage documents without some official form of identification, such as a birth certificate. There was panic when the family in Soweto could not find Max's birth certificate, and the cost of calls to Johannesburg and to Lindi in Swaziland mounted as we tried to resolve the issue. I asked Lindi why the family simply didn't go to the Registrar's office and request a copy of the certificate. Lindi explained patiently that, for black South Africans, obtaining any document was a long and complicated process and that if we had to wait for a copy from the authorities, we would have to postpone the wedding indefinitely. It was also quite likely that the application would be referred to the security police.

In despair, Max went to consult with Walter's old friend Phyllis Naidoo, who at the time was based in Harare and lecturing in the law department at the University of Zimbabwe. Phyllis immediately organised an affidavit stating that she could confirm the identity of Max Sisulu as "the son of UDF leader Albertina Sisulu and ANC leader Walter Sisulu who has long been incarcerated on Robben Island". Fortunately for us, the court found the affidavit acceptable and we were able to proceed with our wedding on 5 September 1986.

We were disappointed that family members who had wanted to attend the wedding had been denied passports. Even Lindi in Swaziland was having difficulty renewing her expired Swazi passport. The denial of passports was one of the arsenal of repressive measures employed by Pretoria against political activists and their families. Sheila Sisulu was particularly frustrated by the State's persistent refusal to issue her with a passport. She had just been denied a passport to travel to Germany on a fact-finding tour on adult education. In 1987, she would once again be denied the opportunity to take up the prestigious Alan Pifer Award to go on a study tour of the US to examine alternative education for disadvantaged communities under the auspices of the US South Africa Leadership Project (USSALEP). Her requests for an explanation from the Department of Home Affairs were greeted by a wall of silence. When contacted by the media, their spokesman said, "it was not customary to furnish reasons for passport application refusals" and would not comment further (*The Sowetan*, 23/7/87). In a letter expressing his anger and disappointment, Walter wrote to Sheila: "I was at least confident this time, not because I thought the Nats had changed but because of many people who had gone through [received passports] even though they were leading political figures. Despite all this you have to put up a struggle and not be discouraged" (Letter to Sheila Sisulu, 22/8/87).

Beryl, who always had a passport under the surname Lockman, and her youngest daughter Pamela were the only family members in South Africa who were able to travel to Zimbabwe for the wedding. Her husband's cousin, Knowledge Simelane, and Mampie Morgan, who always accommodated family members when we visited Pollsmoor, accompanied her. Gerald's wife Jasu and their daughter Beryl Jnr travelled from Lusaka to attend the wedding. On her return, Beryl visited Walter to give him a full report. I also wrote him an account of the event. A month later, he replied with a long congratulatory letter expressing his delight that the marriage had taken place. He was especially interested to hear that Victoria Chitepo, then a cabinet minister in the Zimbabwe government, had been one of the guest speakers. He was aware that Victoria was the widow of Zimbabwean nationalist Herbert Chitepo who had been assassinated in a bomb blast in Lusaka in

1975, and was pleased to hear of my close friendship with their daughter Zine. He asked me to convey thanks on his and Albertina's behalf to Mrs Chitepo and members of my family, especially my father's relative Ibbo Mandaza, who had worked so hard to make the wedding a success. He enjoyed my account of how we were almost late for our own wedding because we got caught in a traffic jam near Harare magistrate's court. The congestion had been the result of roads being blocked off for the summit of the Non-Aligned Movement (NAM) at the nearby Sheraton Hotel. I was able to tell him that the ANC was strongly represented at the NAM summit, and that the South African crisis and Namibia's struggle for independence featured prominently on the agenda of the leaders of the 101 non-aligned countries.

A week after our wedding, Max returned to Lusaka and I continued my job at the Ministry of Labour. We were resigned to spending the first months of marriage apart because Max's ANC work made it impossible for him to move to Harare, while I could not move to Lusaka before I found some form of employment. Both sets of parents expressed their anxiety about the state of affairs. Albertina said she did not like the idea of a newly married couple living apart, but she could see that there was no alternative and also felt that her youngest grandchild would be safer in Harare because "the Boers are more likely to bomb Lusaka".

After the collapse of the Commonwealth EPG mission and the imposition of the June 1986 State of Emergency, it seemed that South Africa was at an impasse. In July 1986, Margaret Thatcher sent the British Foreign Secretary, Geoffrey Howe, to try to accomplish what the EPG had failed to achieve. His mission was spectacularly unsuccessful. Nelson Mandela and Bishop Tutu refused to meet him and PW Botha, in Howe's own words, "showed no willingness to comprehend, let alone accept, any world view but his own" (Harvey, 174; Sampson 2000, 359). In the light of the South African president's intransigence, Thatcher had no choice but to accede to a package of sanctions endorsed by the European Community (Harvey, 175; Sampson 2000, 359). In October, the US Congress overrode a presidential veto and passed the Comprehensive Anti-Apartheid Act, which imposed fiscal and financial sanctions on South Africa.

PW Botha and his government remained as belligerent as ever in the face of international pressure. The arrest and detention of students, teachers, youth activists, community workers and trade unionists continued unabated. Albertina's friend Sister Bernard Ncube and a number of other FEDTRAW leaders were among those detained. One of the most disturbing features of the 1986–87 Emergency was the detention of large numbers of children and adolescents. In 1982, eight people under the age of 18 were detained. That number went up to nine in 1984. In the wake of the 1985 Emergency, 2 875 children under the age of 18 were detained, some of them as young as 11 and 12. That number soared to 10 000 after June 1986 (Webster, 152). Members of the banned COSAS and local youth congresses were special targets of police repression.

Lungi Sisulu Jnr was one of the tens of thousands of young people drawn into the detention dragnet. As a member of COSAS, the chairman of the Dube branch of the Soweto Youth Congress (SOYCO) and a representative of his high-school SRC, he had little chance of escaping. In November 1986, SOYCO invited some Soweto entrepreneurs to a meeting at Daliwonga High School to talk about a consumer boycott that was to start on 1 December. SOYCO had found that during previous boycotts of white businesses, the local township retailers had taken advantage of the situation by increasing the prices of their products. SOYCO wanted to ask the businesspeople not to jeopardise the proposed boycott by raising their prices. But before the meeting could start, they were stormed by police and 15 youths were arrested, most of them members of the various SOYCO branches that had been tasked with coordinating the boycott. None of the businesspeople were interrogated or arrested, and the youths suspected that one of them had tipped off the security police about the meeting.

Lungi Jnr was among those who were arrested and taken to Protea Police Station, where they were fingerprinted and detained under the State of Emergency regulations. He was placed in solitary confinement for the whole of December. He was then moved to Diepkloof Prison, where he was placed in a communal cell with other detainees from SOYCO, COSAS and the UDF. He was shocked to find that children as young as 12 were in detention.

Journalists and media workers were also targeted for state repression. Journalists covering violence were tear-gassed and sjambokked. ITN cameraman George De'Ath was among those hacked and beaten to death by the Witdoeke in Crossroads confrontations. In 1986, 89 media workers were detained, many for lengthy periods (Webster, 159). Newspapers and publications, especially those of the alternative press, were threatened with closure. The success of the *New Nation* (indicated by a growth in circulation from 20 000 to 60 000 by the end of 1986) attracted the attention of the security establishment. In a meeting with the government in November 1986, the Southern African Catholic Bishops' Conference was warned that "the publication is dangerous and unworthy of the Catholic Church ... it publishes women's rights and liberation theology through the Kairos document" (Article 19 pamphlet, 13).

On 11 December 1986, the government passed especial State of Emergency regulations that amounted to a total news blackout on unrest incidents and any actions by the army and police. On 12 December, in the early hours of the morning, Zwelakhe was arrested. Six-year-old Moyikwa woke up to see his father being taken away by six plainclothes policemen.

Priscilla Jana immediately asked the Minister of Police, Adriaan Vlok, for the reasons for the detention of her client. The Minister's response was that Zwelakhe was an executive member of the NECC that had supported the Christmas Against Emergency Campaign. According to the Minister, his participation in the NECC was endangering and undermining the maintenance of public order (*Business Day*, 18/11/87). There was nothing the family could do but wait and hope for his early release.

I was very distressed when Albertina called to let us know about Lungi's detention, but she was quite philosophical about it, saying one could not expect anything else from such a government, and that he was just one of many thousands in prison. When the press reported Zwelakhe's detention a few days later, I remembered her attitude and received the news with some measure of equanimity. Walter's response to the detention of Zwelakhe and Lungi Jnr was similar to that of Albertina. He was disturbed, but not surprised. He was especially concerned about the impact the detention would have on Lungi Jnr's education, and he looked forward to getting a full report during Albertina's annual Christmas visit.

Christmas 1986 brought a pleasant surprise into the lives of the Pollsmoor prisoners, one that Kathrada referred to as "our gigantic leap into the 20th century". In November, the prison authorities had told them that they would be allowed to have television sets. As soon as he heard the good news, Kathrada's friend Enver Kharoochi quickly organised a set each for Kathrada and his Rivonia colleagues. Kathrada wrote to Enver to convey their thanks: "Please say that we are thoroughly enjoying the programmes; indeed a whole new world has suddenly been brought close to us and we are able to join with millions of people in laughter and joy – and also anger and frustration ... you spared no effort or time or energy to ensure that we got our sets as quickly as possible. My colleague, Walter Sisulu, criticised me for overburdening you. He just could not be convinced how impossible it was for me to persuade you not to overload yourself with the responsibility" (Kathrada, 219–20).

On Boxing Day, they enjoyed another treat when they were allowed, for the first time in their years in prison, to order a full meal from outside. They made the most of the opportunity and ordered a huge meal. Mandela was allowed to join them and they were able to enjoy a few pleasant hours together. "It was like eating at home," wrote Kathrada (Kathrada, 213).

*n i n e*

On 8 January 1987 the ANC celebrated its 75th year of existence. Max and I attended a huge meeting in Lusaka to mark the occasion. As speakers outlined the ANC's achievements and expounded on the state of the struggle, Jackie Selebi, then head of the ANC Youth League, commented wryly: "Seventy-five years! That is just too old for a liberation movement. How much older do we have to get before this freedom is won?" A few months later, as I read a moving 75th birthday tribute to Walter by former Assistant General-Secretary of the UN and head of the UN Centre against Apartheid, ES Reddy, I thought Jackie's remark applied to Walter's situation too. Seventy-five was too old to be a political prisoner. Surely freedom had to come soon?

ES Reddy also paid tribute to Zwelakhe and called for the observance of Walter Sisulu's birthday, commenting that although such gestures were relatively simple, they could have "great political impact". *The Star* newspaper in Johannesburg marked Walter's birthday with an article by Jo-Anne Collinge, who commented that on his birthday, "not the faintest echo of last year's furious rumours of his release can be heard". She said political prisoners released in recent years had described Walter Sisulu "as a warm person, deeply interested in new developments and a stranger to the notion of the generation gap". Her article also highlighted the situation of other members of the Sisulu family:

As Sisulu turns 75 today his son, *New Nation* editor Mr Zwelakhe Sisulu, sits in Sandton police cells detained under the State of Emergency. His wife, who is president of the UDF, faces the threat of eviction from their Soweto home as authorities crack down on the rent boycott. And the nephew who grew up in his home, Jongumzi Sisulu, is in jail, having been sentenced to 5 years for treason (*The Star*, 18 May 1987).

In his article "Jail birthday for Sisulu", Raymond Whitaker argued that the sharp swing to the right by white voters earlier that month "makes it less likely than ever that Mr Sisulu or Nelson Mandela, his friend and fellow ANC leader, will celebrate future birthdays in freedom ... Five years ago Johannesburg students celebrated Mr Sisulu's 70th birthday in public, but they may not risk doing so today".

In Pollsmoor Prison, Walter celebrated with a special birthday visit from his two youngest grandchildren. Vuyisile and I were to have visited in February, as both Walter and Albertina were keen to see their latest grandchild. They had been enchanted by the photographs I had sent, and according to Albertina, they spent a whole visit just staring at one photograph. Walter waxed lyrical about his grandson:

He is such a lovely baby with such big eyes. I think he has taken his grandmother's eyes. She had such wonderful eyes in her day. The chap has such a lovely smile ... How I wish to see him! Well, we shall watch the developments with patience in spite of our burning desire. In the world in which we live we have to take things calmly (Letter to Elinor Sisulu, 6/4/87).

We had some anxious moments when I was initially unable to get a visa. We did not put it past the regime to deny me a visa on the basis of my family connections. Fortunately, a second application was successful, so we timed our visit to coincide with Walter's birthday. We were joined by Sheila and 17-month-old Tumi. Since I was now officially a member of the Sisulu family, I was allowed a contact visit. Sheila and I and the two toddlers were led into a room near the reception area equipped with typical government-issue furniture. Seated in comfortable if somewhat threadbare armchairs, we awaited Walter's arrival. Our reunion was a poignant one and his joy at seeing the children was moving beyond words. Sheila laughingly reminded him of Tumi's first visit as an infant. Walter had been horrified to see Sheila carrying the baby in what looked to him like a basket, and she had had to explain that it was a carrycot, now in common use. He was not impressed by the new-fangled contraption. Even though we had a "double visit" – two 40-minute visits put together, time flew by and just as the children were warming to him, we had to part.

I remarked to Sheila that meeting in a relatively comfortable room with a warder sitting unobtrusively in a corner made the experience completely different from the previous visit. She agreed that it was a great improvement, but it was prison nonetheless. We were rudely reminded of this the following day when Sheila and I tried to give Walter a card that the older grandchildren had made for him. The warder stepped forward and told us that it was against the rules for us to hand anything to the prisoner directly. Every item had to be vetted by the prison authorities before it could be given to the prisoner. The incident upset Walter and he spoke sharply to the warder.

During the course of the visit, a new problem arose. Vuyisile, who had been uncharacteristically drowsy since our arrival in Cape Town, had a severe bout of vomiting and diarrhoea. After the visit, we left an extremely worried grandfather and headed back to Retreat where Mampie Morgan, our ever-gracious host, immediately arranged for us to see a local doctor. It turned out that Vuyisile had a middle-ear infection, common in children of that age, especially after a plane journey. My first instinct was to call Walter to reassure him that the child was fine. But to my shock, Sheila explained that it was not possible to call him at the prison, not even to leave a message. I had to content myself with writing him a letter and posting it in Tokai in the hope that it would reach him in the shortest possible time. His reply made all the tension and anxiety of the visit worthwhile:

My dearest Elinor and Vuyi
Your last visit positively left me with pleasant memories. It was our first meeting with our beloved Vuyi and the occasion was on my own birthday. To crown it all, Sheila and Tumi were there and the very coming together of you and Sheila with my youngest grandchildren did not only create a homely atmosphere, but left an indelible mark on my mind.

Let us face it, big boy, you were fast asleep – dog tired, but to hold you in my arms with your tremendous weight made me feel your presence sweetly and beyond imagination.

The boy was too good. He amused me when he dived for silver paper on the floor, which we were trying to hide from him. Well, the anxiety of waiting for you, not being sure what was finally going to happen was over … Tell Mama that I was thoroughly satisfied.

In response to my request to send him a copy of ES Reddy's 75th birthday tribute to him, he confirmed my suspicion that newspaper articles were discouraged: "But important articles like this may be sent, in spite of the general rules, because it gives me a chance to discuss matters with the authorities. The worst thing that can happen is that they can put it in my file" (8/6/87).

When we returned to Johannesburg after our Pollsmoor visit, Albertina fussed over Vuyisile and insisted that I take him for a further check-up with Dr Asvat. She gave us the last appointment of the day so we could get a lift in the car that Lungi sent to pick her up from work each day. The surgery was in a dilapidated old house in McDonald's Farm squatter camp, one of the more derelict parts of Soweto. As we waited for the doctor in the near-empty waiting room, Albertina explained that the place was normally crowded and sometimes they treated more than a hundred patients a day, most of them free of charge.

Abu Baker Asvat was the friendliest and most easy-going person one could hope to meet. His examination of the baby was a formality and he reiterated the instructions given by the Cape Town doctor. He was amused when I told him Mama would not be satisfied with the diagnosis of anyone but her own doctor. But his relaxed manner belied his fierceness when fighting for the rights of the poor and downtrodden; he wrote with passionate anger about the plight of the homeless:

> All people all over the world have certain rights, and the right to a home is one that no government can deny. Until such time that each and every one of us is adequately housed, we should not rest. A whole host of legislation, including the infamous Bantustans, contentious citizenship, the need to have a job before qualifying for a house and the long waiting period before a house becomes available makes the future of the homeless look very bleak.
>
> All the so-called squatter areas have common problems such as over-crowding, structures that become too hot in summer and too cold in winter, lack of clean water, extremely poor sanitation and no electricity. The trials and tribulations of these people are unimaginable ... It is a shame that a country that boasts the world's first heart transplant, and a second to none standard of living for its privileged class, is unable to look after its own people. Until and unless political rights are given to all on an equal basis, we will have a situation of inequality. Is it asking for too much for some projects to take a back seat, while the basic needs of the people are attended to after decades of neglect? (*City Press*, 20/9/87).

Abu Asvat and Albertina worked together to do what they could for the poor and deprived of McDonald's Farm and other communities. Abu had supplied medical care to numerous squatter camps (and had fought energetically on their behalf against the Soweto Council), and had almost single-handedly aided the community of Mochaeneng when it was threatened with forced removal.

As we left the surgery, Albertina pointed out the scrap-yard filled with abandoned cars. She explained that people lived in those cars. One morning, children in the area had directed her and Abu to one of the vehicles in which they found the corpse of an old woman. They suspected that she had died of hunger and cold. Abu had organised blankets and the building of 20 toilets to add to the three that were shared by 150 families. They then set aside a room in the surgery for a crèche. Albertina proudly pointed to children playing on the playground equipment they had provided, and to the soup kitchen that fed 70 to 80 children twice a week.

The partnership between Albertina and Abu Asvat was all the more remarkable in the light of the ongoing conflict between AZAPO and the UDF. Tension between the two organisations dated back to Curtis Nkondo's controversial presidency of AZAPO and continued over which organisation should convene the annual June 16 commemoration at Regina Mundi Cathedral. Things really soured when AZAPO picketed Senator Edward Kennedy's January 1985 tour, forcing him off a platform in Soweto, to the embarrassment of the UDF, which had organised the meeting (Marx, 174). The tensions between the two organisations erupted into bloody confrontation after 1985. By the end of 1986, hundreds of UDF and AZAPO supporters had been killed and houses of leaders bombed. The State played an active role in adding fuel to the fire. Fake UDF pamphlets were distributed in Soweto condemning AZAPO, and the police were said to be responsible for some of the bombings of leaders on both sides. In January 1987, the leadership of both AZAPO and UDF committed themselves to a peace process and agreed to halt further attacks on vigilantes (Marx, 174; Lodge et al., 280–82; Bonner and Segal, 127).

Albertina and Dr Asvat hated the conflict, which in their view played straight into the hands of the enemy. They did what they could to pour oil on troubled waters and made it clear that their working relationship was not in any way affected by the hostility between their respective organisations. "Both of us are mature politicians," said Albertina in an interview. "We know exactly what we stand for ... when it comes to work for the community we forget that. We are here as nurse and doctor. Our job is to save lives" (*Africa Report*, Sept/Oct 1987). Asvat called their relationship "a practical demonstration of unity in action". He agreed that their political differences did not hamper their working relationship and that they proved it was possible to work harmoniously together: "This should be a lesson that now, more than at any other time we need each other" (*City Press*, 6/3/88). Albertina appreciated having a boss who encouraged her political activity by giving her time off to go to meetings. "My doctor has been wonderful to me," she told me. "Do you know that throughout the months I was in jail in Pietermaritzburg and throughout my trial, he paid my salary? It must have been a strain for him, because he had to employ someone to take my place and he is not a wealthy man."

I never failed to be amazed by the way Albertina coped with a workload that would exhaust most people half her age. After a full day at the surgery, she would return home to find local activists waiting to see her. Most days of the week, she would face another three to four hours of meetings before going to bed. Her weekends were also mostly taken up with meetings and frequent interviews with local and overseas journalists, many of whom were interested in the mobilisation of women under apartheid.

In 1986 the UDF had undertaken to focus on the role of women as a key issue in its programme of action, while in August of that year the 30th anniversary of the famous 1956 Women's March to Pretoria was commemorated with special services around the country. The 1980s had witnessed a massive increase in women participating in existing organisations and the spread of women's organisations countrywide. Local struggles around rent, housing, transport and education had drawn women into grass-roots organisations, and women represented a large proportion of the rank and file membership in UDF affiliates (Houston, 238).

In May 1986, the UDF National Working Committee Conference resolved that new women's organisations be formed where none existed and existing ones be strengthened to pave the way for a strong national structure (Houston, 254). Albertina's big dream was the revival of FEDSAW and she saw the formation of the UDF Women's Congress in April 1987 as a step towards this goal. Because of the State of Emergency, the Cape Town launch of the Women's Congress was held secretly. It aimed to unite all women's organisations affiliated to the UDF, as well as to approach women's organisations outside the UDF to work towards the relaunching of FEDSAW. Albertina whole-heartedly shared the concern of the Women's Congress about the marked absence of women in regional and national leadership, and that discrimination against women at work, in the home and in political organisations was not challenged by UDF affiliates (Houston, 255–6).

One day while preparing the evening meal, we discovered that there was no electricity. We assumed that there was a power failure, as these were not uncommon in Soweto. However, we later noticed that only Number 7372 was without electricity. Albertina then remembered a letter she had received from the Soweto Council demanding that she pay for rent and other services within 30 days, failing which legal action would be taken. The electricity supply had obviously been disconnected. While we complained about the prospect of being without electricity in the chilly winter weather, Albertina calmly got out the candles and sent for someone to fire up the huge coal stove in her kitchen. We soon learned that the council had also disconnected the electricity supply to the homes of Winnie Mandela, Ellen Kuzwayo and Dr Nthato Motlana.

It was obvious that the Soweto Council, desperate to break the boycott of rent and service charges that had been started by the Soweto Civic Association (SCA) in June 1986, had decided to target prominent Soweto residents. The rent boycott and the growth of street committees had led to something of a political renaissance in Soweto at a time when widespread repression and detentions had crippled many organisations. The street committees facilitated consultation and co-operation within communities, thus ensuring the continued popularity of the campaign. They also successfully mobilised against evictions, making it almost impossible for the Soweto Council to break the boycott (Houston, 189; Lodge et al., 268; Bonner and Segal, 128). Far from breaking the boycott, the targeting of Soweto luminaries had the opposite effect. Amid much publicity, the leaders firmly stated their commitment to the boycott and the community expressed their solidarity. Albertina's lawyers took the matter up and early in June, the legal action notice against her was withdrawn for technical reasons (*The Star*, 10/6/87).

Among Albertina's admirable qualities was that she remained calm and unflappable in all situations. The inconvenience of living without electricity was no more than a pinprick to her and she made it clear that it would take much more than that for her to stop supporting the boycott. She responded to the harshness of life under apartheid through actions rather than words and went about her life with the minimum of complaint. She had little patience with whingeing or whining, as I learned when I moaned about how difficult things were for Zodwa and how depressed she had been when she had not been allowed to see Zwelakhe in detention. "You girls must learn that we can't expect any kind treatment from the Boers," she said sternly. She went on to deliver a sermon about how "we should remember that so many people are suffering under apartheid, that women have lost husbands and children and we cannot allow ourselves to be depressed and miserable because that is what the enemy wants". I was reminded of her reaction when I had told her how Walter had been upset during our visit. "I always tell him that he must never show them that he is upset." I could see why one journalist, after interviewing her, had referred to the "rock-like strength of Albertina Sisulu".

I also admired the strength of Zodwa who, I thought, was coping admirably with a difficult situation. In some ways, detention was worse than a prison sentence because it was so unpredictable. Zodwa had to contend with constant questions from her children about when their father was coming back. Moyikwa refused to celebrate his seventh birthday because he was waiting for his father. Zodwa kept Walter updated on their progress: "I visit Zwelakhe once every 14 days. In fact it should be a visit from any family member but I monopolise the visits (admission of guilt). The children are trying to be good, but the absence of their father is significant. Moyikwa works hard, but … his progress fluctuates, maybe because he takes time off to visit Lakhe, but the teacher thinks it is good for him and would rather let him work harder than not visit his father at all" (Letter to Walter Sisulu, April 1987).

Zodwa also had to deal with other practical problems. These included a summons from The Perm, the building society that had given them a mortgage. The summons, served in December 1986, ordered Zwelakhe to make immediate payment or risk losing his house. After their lawyers took up the matter and it was reported in the press, a Perm spokesperson announced that The Perm had halted the action when "it was realised that Sisulu's cheque was delayed from reaching its destination at The Perm" (*City Press* 15/1/87). The Sisulu family could not help wondering if there was not something sinister about a cheque getting "lost in the system".

Bob Tucker, the managing director of The Perm and one of the most progressive and enlightened people in corporate South Africa, moved quickly to rectify matters:

> Immediately we became aware we took the following action: All proceedings were stayed immediately. The attorneys were immediately instructed to withdraw the judgment and to arrange for publication of the withdrawal of the judgment in order to avoid damaging Mr Sisulu's credit standing. We did exactly what could be expected of us and in keeping with The Perm's attitude and responsibility to the community … We look forward to the day when we live in an undivided society and all staff are sensitive to the pressures exerted on all sections of the community" (*The Sowetan*, 20/1/87).

The Perm incident highlighted the practical problems faced by detainees and their families. Zodwa was conscious that she was in a relatively privileged position in that she was in full-time employment and had the support of her family. She emphasised that for many families in materially deprived circumstances, the consequences of the detention of a loved one were disastrous: "There are heads of families, breadwinners in detention. Some of the detainees supported elderly people. These old people face unbelievable hardship visiting their children in jail."

A couple of weeks after Vuyisile and I returned to Harare, Lungi Sisulu Jnr was released from detention. While in South Africa, we had been unable to visit him because he was using his mother's surname, and regulations permitted visits by immediate family members only. This meant that only his maternal grandmother, Greta Ncapayi, could visit him. Even Munemo, his younger brother, could not visit him because he was having difficulty getting an identity book. Immediately after his release, Lungi Jnr went to see his grandfather in Pollsmoor. As usual, the main topic was how he planned to proceed with his education. However, Lungi had only half his mind on this subject. He was excited by the launch of the South African Youth Congress (SAYCO) in March 1987. With 10 regional youth congresses comprising 1 200 affiliates and a support base of over two million, SAYCO was the biggest youth grouping of its kind in South African history (Seekings, 210). SAYCO's huge support base, its slogan "Freedom or death, victory is certain" and the militant and populist rhetoric of its first president Peter Mokaba sent shudders through the security establishment. At the same time, it provided a huge boost of confidence to young black activists like Lungi, and rekindled their determination to pursue their political activities regardless of the risks involved.

Lungi Jnr was fortunate not to have been tortured during his stint in detention. The police did question him about his family connections, and told him they were aware that his grandmother Greta visited Swaziland regularly. They wanted to know if any ANC people had ever tried to contact her while she was in Swaziland. It was not just idle curiosity that prompted the questions about Swaziland. At that time, the security police were intensifying their onslaught against ANC operatives in Swaziland and Mozambique. In April, ANC activist Gibson Ncube died after drinking poisoned beer brought to Maputo by an agent of the notorious Civil Cooperation Bureau (CCB). This was the shadowy and secret branch of the security forces responsible for kidnappings, torture, murder and the sinister "death squads". In the same month, ANC activist and poet Albie Sachs almost died of the horrific injuries incurred in a bomb blast in Maputo. Security police ambushes in Swaziland took the lives of the head of MK's Natal operation, Theophilus "Viva" Dlodlo, and two passengers in May, and MK operatives Cassius Make, Paul Dikeledi and Eliza Tsinini in July. Cassius was a member of the ANC NEC and the Revolutionary Council and a close friend of Max.

Walter and Albertina were alarmed by the reports coming out of Swaziland and guessed correctly that Lindi was in the thick of ANC activity there. People she worked closely with were being abducted or killed. Lindi herself was desperately trying to get her Swazi passport renewed so she could go to England to study for a PhD. She suspected that the reluctance of the Swazi authorities to renew her passport was related to the general clampdown on South African exiles. Walter and Albertina were eager for Lindi to leave and further her education (especially along the prestigious lines of a PhD), and were especially anxious about her safety and that of her children. Walter applied pressure on Lindi to leave by appealing to her maternal instincts: "I am really worried about your children, especially Ayanda. She is such a lovely intelligent child, sensitive and observant. Her personality is striking, even at this age. The uncertainty could be quite a great harm. This is a most decisive period in her life" (Letter to Lindi Sisulu, 4/3/87). Lindi finally managed to get her passport in time for her to get to York University for the start of the academic year. She and the children managed to spend a few days in Harare en route.

At the time, I was serving in my notice at the Ministry of Labour in Harare and preparing to take up a job with the International Labour Organisation (ILO) office in Lusaka. The ILO job came at the right time, just when Max and I were beginning to feel the strain of living apart. I would often remind myself, when I felt depressed about my husband's absence, of Zodwa and Albertina, who had to endure much longer separations from their spouses under far more difficult circumstances. I was delighted about moving to Lusaka although there was the feeling, especially on my side of the family, that it would probably be safer to remain in Harare. My argument was that all the front-line states were vulnerable to South African raids, and indeed the May 1986 SADF attacks on Harare supported my case.

Moving house and country with a one-year-old is never an easy experience and it was a wrench to leave my Zimbabwean colleagues with whom I had worked so long and come to value as personal friends as well as colleagues. I started my new job with a six-week briefing in Geneva where Judica Amri, my predecessor in the post, Bulelani Ngcuka, who was at the time on an internship at the ILO, and Bill Ratteree, my immediate superior in Geneva, took me under their wing and explained the politics involved in the post. Under the pretentious title "Associate Expert for ILO assistance to National Liberation Movements", I would be responsible for ILO projects and programmes for the ANC, PAC and SWAPO and the exiled trade union movements of SACTU, the PAC-aligned Azanian Trade Union Coordinating Congress (ATUCC) and the Namibian trade union organisation.

I was impressed by Bill Ratteree's encyclopaedic knowledge of the labour movement in South Africa. He had just finished working on a prize-winning film on COSATU and he made me appreciate what a privilege it was to have the opportunity to work with the trade unions in the most exciting period in South Africa's labour history. The power of the labour movement had just been demonstrated by the National Union of Mineworkers (NUM) strike in August, the most successful and longest legal strike in South African history.

I settled down very quickly in Lusaka, partly because Max had already done the hard work of moving into the apartment allocated to me by the UN, but mostly because of the warm welcome from the South African exile community in Lusaka. Max's circle of friends, especially Zeph Magketla and his wife Neva, Sindiso and Rita Mfenyana, Jacob and Kelibogile Chilwane, Pat Long and Nomvula Radebe, and "Castro" and Elizabeth Ramagkopa, were exceptionally welcoming, as was Ruth Mompati, who was virtually a surrogate mother to Max in his years of exile. Through Ruth and other associates of Walter and Albertina, like Tiny Nokwe, the widow of Duma Nokwe, Mark and Gertrude Shope, Agnes Msimang, John Nkadimeng, Sophie de Bruyn, Ray Simons and many others, I learned a lot more about the work of Albertina and Walter Sisulu in the pre-1960 period and understood why they were held in such high esteem in the liberation movement. In our correspondence, Walter showed a keen interest in hearing about old friends and comrades but I could not write about my work and generally avoided writing about ANC people. I was able to tell him that I had stayed at Brigalia Bam's apartment in Geneva, where I had met Ellen Kuzwayo who was attending a meeting there. He was delighted to hear how Ellen had smothered me with kisses when Brigalia had introduced me as Albertina's daughter-in-law. He replied to say how proud he was of Ellen's award-winning biography *Call Me Woman* and that he had written to congratulate her on her wonderful achievement.

On 11 June 1987, the State of Emergency was extended for another year. Zwelakhe Sisulu was "released" on 10 June 1987 and immediately redetained in terms of the new regulations. In reality, he remained in police custody throughout.

UDF operations were seriously hampered by the massive scale of detentions and repression and its regional structures severely disrupted. The entire full-time staff of the Transvaal region were in detention, and UDF activists had to develop a whole new culture of working underground. Many of those Albertina worked with were in detention or in hiding, but she somehow persisted with her work. Walter paid tribute to her efforts in a letter to Lindi: "Your mother is working very hard, plus a great deal of harassment, but she is very strong and amazingly calm about things in general. I wish I could see her more regularly because that means so much to both of us" (Letter to Lindi Sisulu, 4/3/87). In September, Albertina's four-year sentence in the Rose Mbele case was dismissed on appeal, partly because her co-accused, Thami Mali, had secretly left the country. It was a huge relief to the family and Walter wrote to congratulate her: "Darling, double congratulations for your birthday and winning your case. Thanks to Priscilla and George. Though uncertainties are part of our lives, this relief means a great deal. Hope some celebrations will be made this time. I will be with you in spirit."

Shortly after her birthday, Albertina travelled to Mbuzini, the site of the plane crash that had killed Samora Machel, to speak at a ceremony to mark the first anniversary of his death. She spoke about Samora's role as a liberator and the gains of the revolutions of Mozambique, Guinea Bissau and Angola:

> South Africa is what it is today because of the exploitation of workers from Mozambique by the huge mining companies such as Anglo, Gencor and Barlow. In addition thousands of Mozambican people are working in the farms where they are paid starvation wages. Against this background it is imperative that the people of Mozambique and South Africa fight jointly to end apartheid. The UDF calls on you, the workers, students, youth, women, chiefs and professionals in the eastern Transvaal to organise wherever you are, to form structures that will dent the apartheid machinery. Let each village be organised into meaningful structures of resistance against apartheid. In your day-to-day organising, be careful not to antagonise those who differ with you and those who do not understand the nature of our struggle. Let us try to educate and win as many people on our side as possible.

Despite Albertina's exhortations, it became increasingly difficult for the UDF to operate, and in February 1988 the UDF and 16 other organisations, among them key UDF affiliates, were restricted in terms of the Emergency regulations. The restrictions were so severe that they amounted to a de facto banning. Restrictions were also imposed on many UDF leaders. Albertina and the co-president of the UDF, Archie Gumede, were also restricted. (The third co-president Oscar Mpetha was already serving a five-year jail sentence.) (Seekings, 226–229).

Albertina maintained her optimism in the face of seemingly insurmountable problems of ferocious state repression. Asked in an interview in September 1987 whether she thought she would see freedom in her lifetime, she said she was optimistic because of the way the youth had taken up the struggle and were working to strengthen the UDF. "That unity and determination to fight for freedom gives me hope that I'll still be alive when we are free. While the government thinks killing our children has made us afraid, it has united us and made us more determined. It will take time to win. But it won't take more than five years" (*Africa Report*, Sept/Oct 1997).

Like Albertina, Nelson Mandela was also optimistic despite the bleak outlook. After the debacle of the Commonwealth EPG mission, it seemed there was no possibility for dialogue with the Botha regime, but Mandela felt that "the most discouraging moments are precisely the time to launch an initiative. At such times people are searching for a way out of the dilemma" (Mandela, 512). In June 1986, Mandela had requested an interview with General Willemse, the Commissioner of Prisons, "on a matter of national importance". When they met, he told Willemse he wanted to meet Kobie Coetsee, the Minister of Justice. It so happened that Coetsee was in Cape Town and Mandela was spirited to Savernake, Coetsee's official residence. They had a three-hour discussion in which Coetsee probed Mandela on whether he spoke for the ANC as a whole, under what circumstances the ANC would suspend armed struggle, and whether he would countenance constitutional guarantees for minorities in a new South Africa (Mandela, 519). For his part, Mandela asked for a meeting with the President and Foreign Minister.

Several months elapsed before Mandela heard from Coetsee again, but in the meantime, he was taken on excursions around the city and the Cape Peninsula. Mandela was careful not to get carried away by his increased freedom of movement: "I sensed that they wanted to acclimatise me to life in South Africa and perhaps at the same time, get me so used to the pleasures of small free-doms that I might be willing to compromise in order to have complete freedom" (Mandela, 521; Sampson 2000, 352; Sparks 1995, 36; Meredith, 369–70).

Kobie Coetsee had briefed PW Botha about the meeting with Mandela, but Botha had little interest in dialogue with the ANC. He was, however, keen to get himself out of the corner into which he had painted himself when he had demanded that Mandela first renounce violence before he could be released. He therefore mandated Coetsee to keep the channels of communication open with Mandela, with a view to finding a formula for releasing him without losing face (Meredith, 367; Sparks 1995, 48). Coetsee had several meetings with Mandela during the course of 1987, but they did not make much headway on the conditions of release. Mandela continued to demand a meeting with the State President, and he was adamant that his release had to be part of a package of measures that included unbanning the ANC. He pushed for the release of political prisoners, especially his elderly colleagues, Govan, Walter, and Oscar Mpetha (Interview, Nelson Mandela, 27/11/2001; Sampson 2000, 364; Meredith, 370). The government eventually agreed to release Mbeki on the grounds of his advanced age and declining health. Mbeki's release would avert the danger of his dying in jail and would also serve as a test-case to gauge the likely response of the general public to the release of Mandela (*New Nation*, 7–13 July 1987).

Once the decision was taken to release Mbeki, the prison authorities on Robben Island isolated him, a normal prelude to the release of a prisoner. When she heard about his isolation, Mbeki's lawyer Priscilla Jana applied to visit him. When her application was turned down, she did what any good struggle lawyer would do – she lodged an application for a court order to gain access to her client. The Commissioner of Prisons told Mandela that her action had jeopardised the whole deal for Mbeki's release. Mandela pointed out that the situation would have been averted if the prison authorities had taken the trouble to explain matters to Mbeki, and undertook to persuade Mbeki and his lawyer to drop the action. Again without explanation, Brigadier Munro, the Commander of Robben Island prison, walked into Mbeki's cell and told him to get dressed and come with him. Mbeki was bundled into an ambulance, then into a speedboat at the Prison Department Jetty, and then (accompanied by Brigadier Munro) taken by car to Pollsmoor Prison. On their arrival, he saw Walter coming down a flight of steps. Excited to see his old comrade for the first time in five years, he tried to catch his attention by opening the car window, but there were no handles on the inside. Walter unfortunately remained oblivious to his old friend banging on the car window and trying to signal to him (Sparks 1995, 60).

It was hardly an auspicious beginning for the meeting with Mandela, and the reunion was not a comfortable one. To get him to drop his court action, Mandela had to tell Mbeki that he was talk-ing to the government but he could not go into details because he had given an undertaking not to do so. Predictably, Mbeki was not impressed: "I was not very happy about the fact that he seemed either not to have sufficient confidence to tell me the full story, or, alternatively, that the other side might have come to some arrangement with him which he felt he could not break" (Sparks 1995, 59–60; Harvey, 134).

When PW Botha hinted in Parliament that Govan Mbeki might be released on humanitarian grounds, the media was abuzz with speculation. Asked what she thought about Mbeki's possible release, Albertina said she would be happy, but noted that the people demanded the release of all political prisoners. By saying it was releasing people on "humanitarian grounds", the government was "running away from the political issues they should be facing. Those people went to jail as ANC members. They must be released as ANC members" (*Africa Report*, Sept/Oct 1987).

On 4 November, Govan Mbeki was flown by military plane from Cape Town to Port Elizabeth. He was taken to the Holiday Inn hotel because he had no address to which to return – when he lived in Port Elizabeth in the early 1960s he had not been allowed to own a house. The prison authorities told him he could stay at the Holiday Inn for 48 hours while he made other arrangements for accommodation. On arrival at 5.30pm he was told to get ready to address a press conference in half an hour. "I had no idea what that meant. At the time I left this city there were only three newspapers. I thought at most there would be six people there – two representatives from each of the three papers." Instead, he was almost blinded by the flashes from hundreds of cameras and had questions fired at him from dozens of newspaper and television journalists (Schadeberg Interview, Govan Mbeki). He coped remarkably well with the ordeal and demonstrated that he was ready to get right back into the political fray.

His release was greeted by celebrations both locally and internationally. As soon as we heard the news, Max and I, who were on a visit to Harare at the time, rushed to the Sheraton Hotel to celebrate with Thabo Mbeki and other ANC members who were attending a meeting there. Albertina and other members of the Sisulu family were among the many people who flocked to the Johannesburg party organised for the newly released leader.

Ismail Omar, a member of the President's Council, claimed that Walter, Kathrada and Zeph Mothopeng would be released early in the New Year, even though PW Botha had dismissed media speculation about further releases of prisoners as "wild dreams". Their release, he said, depended on whether Mr Govan Mbeki was influential enough to restore calm to the strife-torn townships (*The Post*, 25/11/97, 2/12/87).

Mbeki certainly did not see his role this way and emphasised his unshaken allegiance to the ANC and the SACP. The white right wing were shaken by his statements and the militant rallies to welcome him, and began a letter-writing campaign calling on Botha not to release Mandela. Meanwhile, some National Party members complained about the "Mbeki experiment" (*New Nation*, 7–13 July 1987). The government responded to the right-wing backlash by placing Mbeki under house arrest less than three weeks after his release. He was also confined to the magisterial district of Port Elizabeth, and talk of any further releases faded away.

As the excitement over Govan Mbeki's release died down, South Africans counted the cost of another year under a State of Emergency. I received a letter from Sheila Sisulu reflecting on what a difficult and turbulent year it had been. The only positive event in 1987, she wrote, had been Oom Gov's release. At the forefront of the struggle for education, Sheila had been one of the parents who had spent countless hours protesting at the Department of Education and Training (DET) offices for textbooks and better facilities for black schools. The NECC, which had provided some hope of resolving the boycott crisis by mediating between boycotting students and education authorities, had been crippled by harassment and detention of its members. By the end of the year, Sheila felt quite despondent about the state of black education.

One of the justifications the State gave for the continued detention of Zwelakhe Sisulu was his membership of the NECC. In November 1987, Zwelakhe's lawyers presented an urgent application for his release. In their appeal, they pointed out that Zwelakhe had informed the police when first detained in June 1986 and again in December 1986 that he was not a member of the NECC executive, as the police had claimed. The appeal document noted that the police had not passed this information to the Minister of Justice: "Had this been the position, the Minister would have seen that Mr Sisulu had not actively participated in the activities of the NECC at all. That being the case there would have been no lawful basis to cause him to be further detained." The lawyers also argued that, in any event the NECC had become dormant: "That being so, it seems clear that even if, as is denied, Mr Sisulu had been a member or participant in the NECC's activities, that can no longer continue as the organisation is defunct. That being so, there is a material change which exists since the time of his detention. Once the basis for his detention no longer reasonably exists, there is no reasonable need for him to be further detained ... on these grounds."

Rand Supreme Court judge Justice Harms was not convinced by these arguments and dismissed Zwelakhe's appeal application with costs. He did, however, concede that the memo written by Zwelakhe in which he denied being a member of the executive of the NECC had not been handed to Minister of Law and Order, Adriaan Vlok. The memo had been withheld apparently on legal advice to the police that it was not relevant. Justice Harms said it could only be deduced that whoever advised the police had either not read the memo or chosen to ignore it. He also said it was clear from Sisulu's own keynote speech that some of the NECC's aims were indeed laudable, while others were, to say the least, legitimate. However, having regard to the speech as a whole, "it could be reasonably inferred that the NECC did evince an intention to overthrow the present structure of the State by using black children and exploiting the grievances surrounding black education" (*Business Day*, 18/11/87).

Zwelakhe's detention was kept at the forefront of the news by his journalist colleagues, his newspaper and the international awards he received. Shortly after his detention in December 1986, 11 leading journalists – all Nieman fellows – condemned Zwelakhe's detention. They included his former colleagues Richard Steyn, Ameen Akalwaya, Aggrey Klaaste, Percy Qoboza and Allister Sparks (*The Sowetan*, 18/12/86). While he was in detention, every *New Nation* editorial marked the number of days since he had been detained. On his 112th day of detention, the *New Nation* reported that Article 19, the London-based organisation committed to promoting freedom of expression, announced that Zwelakhe had been adopted as an honorary member of PEN, the worldwide body (*New Nation*, 2–8/4/87). His 126th day in detention was marked by the report that the Commissioner of the South African Police had just issued a new order preventing the press "from publishing any report which may incite or encourage members of the public to participate in campaigns, in South Africa or overseas, for the release of Sisulu and other detainees". The restrictions were patently ludicrous: they prohibited anyone from signing petitions, wearing T-shirts that called for the release of detainees, or sending telegrams or similar documents in which the government was called on to release a detainee. With the exception of "valid" church services, all gatherings protesting against the detention of, or honouring a detainee, or any symbolic token of solidarity were also declared illegal. Anyone found guilty of contravening these regulations could be fined R20 000 or sentenced to 10 years in prison (*New Nation*, 15–22/4/87). Max Coleman of the Detainees Parents' Support Committee (DPSC) said they would fight the new regulations in court. He said the DPSC refused to "give up our right to fight for an end to detention without trial" and would continue to render services such as legal aid, psychological counselling and medical assistance to detainees and their families (*New Nation*, 23–29/4/87).

In May 1987, Zwelakhe was selected by the Nieman Fellow Class of 1987 as winner of the prestigious Louis M Lyons Award for Conscience and Integrity in Journalism. Zwelakhe followed in the footsteps of fellow South African journalists Allister Sparks and Joe Thloloe in winning the award, named in honour of former Nieman Curator, Louis M Lyons. The citation of the award recognised Zwelakhe's courage and dedication in providing South African blacks with "an alternative voice amid the harsh efforts of the South African government to quell a dissenting press". In a letter nominating Sisulu, journalist Mike Pride praised the *New Nation* for "vibrant, aggressive reporting and a desire to be a voice of justice and reason in South Africa. This is a logical extension of Sisulu's efforts as a reporter, an editor, and a leading organiser of bright journalism". The letter praised Zwelakhe's courage and noted that: "Freedom of the press has yet to flourish elsewhere but in South Africa there is a government that claims a democratic Western tradition and then makes a mockery of it by putting editors in jail." In the same month Zwelakhe also won the 1987 SASJ Pringle Award for Press Freedom along with editors of the *Weekly Mail* Anton Harber and Irwin Manoim (*New Nation*, 14–20/5/87).

The *New Nation* editorial marked Zwelakhe's 140th day in detention by highlighting an article by well-known *New York Times* columnist Anthony Lewis. In his piece "To destroy a country – South Africa's tyranny in microcosm", Lewis wrote:

Mr Sisulu is one of the thousands being held under the emergency declared by state president PW Botha last June. I use him as an example because I know him, as do other American reporters and editors. Tyranny is easier to measure if you know one of its victims. Two years ago Mr Sisulu was a Nieman Fellow, one of the group of journalists chosen for a year of study at Harvard. He made a profound impression in two ways: as a professional, a newspaperman, and as a potential leader in his country, a person of understanding and dignity who could help South Africa move toward the politics of reason if he were allowed to do so. But he is not allowed to. That is the condition of being black in South Africa. It is the particular condition of Zwelakhe Sisulu and his family ... He is a symbol, but of course, the point is not only Zwelakhe Sisulu. Unofficial estimates are that 30 000 people have been detained since last June, including children as young as 11. The point is the weight of repression used by the government to crush the political yearnings of the majority of South Africans ( *New Nation*, 30/4–6/5/87).

In a memorandum dated 23 September 1987, Compol outlined the reasons for Zwelakhe's continued detention on the grounds that his views, expressed in the *New Nation* and in media interviews "are aimed at promoting the internal revolutionary onslaught. It also is closely related to the views expressed by the ANC and assists in subtly promoting the aims of the ANC and the UDF within RSA ... Sisulu tried to create a perception with the masses that the Government no longer has control over the situation in the RSA, that the ANC obtained the initiative via 'People's Power' and that 'victory' is in sight". The memorandum noted that the unrest situation in general, and the situation of coloured education in particular, forced drastic actions against prominent activists. Compol recommended that Zwelakhe "be detained for as long as the emergency situation exists under the emergency regulations, and if the emergency situation is lifted, his immediate further detainment in terms of article 28(1) of the Act on Internal Security, 1982 (Act 74 of 1982) be considered" (Ministry of Justice files).

On 4 February 1987, PW Botha read a document in Parliament that accused Zwelakhe and Geoff Budlender, the head of the Legal Resources Centre, of initiating a "White Coalition grouping" consisting of the Progressive Federal Party, the Black Sash, the End Conscription Campaign and the Johannesburg Democratic Action Committee. He claimed that the information came from a confidential ANC document and a "Programme of Action", which he said, revealed ANC plans to manipulate white organisations and to create a bloodbath in the country. Botha argued that it was security force action in South Africa and two neighbouring states that was mainly responsible for keeping the peace. He also claimed that the plan to organise whites to support the lifting of the emergency, the release of all detainees and the unbanning of all banned organisations was proof of "the cold-blooded way in which organisations can be drawn into the morass of SACP-ANC intrigues". He warned strongly against white involvement or sympathy with the ANC ( *Digest*, 13/2/87).

Despite PW Botha's rantings, the conviction that the ANC was central to any solution of the South African crisis continued to grow among whites. In February 1987, Frederick van Zyl Slabbert, the leader of the Progressive Federal Party, resigned from Parliament, citing frustration and unhappiness with the intransigence of white parliamentary politics. Van Zyl Slabbert's resignation was a blow to the Botha regime, and he rubbed salt into the wound when, in July 1987, he led a group of 61 white intellectuals, mostly Afrikaners, to Dakar, Senegal to meet with ANC leaders to discuss strategies for bringing about fundamental change and building national unity in South Africa (Houston, Unpublished notes, 197). While PW Botha pandered to his right-wing constituency by denouncing the intellectuals as "useful idiots" whose naiveté had "the ANC laughing up their sleeves", his own National Intelligence Service discreetly aided the meeting because it also saw the need for dialogue with the ANC (Sampson 2000, 363). Even members of the Broederbond, the very heart of the Afrikaner political elite, were surreptitiously making contact with the ANC. In June 1986, the Ford

Foundation brokered a meeting between prominent Afrikaners (including the chairman of the Broederbond) and Thabo Mbeki, Mac Maharaj and Seretse Choabe (Sampson 2000, 363).

The ANC was also enjoying growing international acceptance, especially in the US, Britain and other Western countries. Oliver Tambo worked tirelessly to raise the ANC's international profile. In January 1987, he met with the US Secretary of State, George Schultz, and he spent the better part of the year visiting the major Western countries (Rantete, 132). In the US, he met Henry Kissinger and the heads of General Motors and Citibank. The ANC also made considerable headway in Britain, despite Mrs Thatcher's antagonistic attitude (Harvey, 22). Robin Renwick, the High Commissioner sent by Thatcher to Pretoria in July 1987, recognised the crucial role of the ANC. During his four-year term, he maintained indirect contact with the ANC and played a role in promoting dialogue (Sampson 2000, 360). The British Foreign Secretary, Geoffrey Howe, and the Foreign Minister responsible for Africa, Lynda Chalker, both met with Oliver Tambo in defiance of Thatcher's ban on ministerial contact with the ANC (Harvey, 22).

Walter's old friend Anthony Sampson also played an active role in facilitating ANC contacts with the British business community. In October 1986, David Astor of *The Observer* organised a meeting at Sampson's house to introduce members of the ANC to some of the British corporate elite (Harvey, 21). One of the businessmen present at the meeting was Michael Young, Public Affairs Director for Consolidated Goldfields. Young subsequently persuaded his conservative chairman Rudolph Agnew to finance a series of secret meetings between members of the Afrikaner political elite and the ANC (Harvey, 20; Sparks 1995, 78). Meetings mostly took place at Mells Park, the secluded manor house in Somerset owned by Consolidated Goldfields. Thabo Mbeki led the ANC delegations at these meetings and more than 20 prominent Afrikaners, both church and business leaders, participated at various times (Sparks 1995, 87).

The first meeting took place in October 1987 between Thabo Mbeki, Harold Wolpe, and Tony Trew (on the ANC side) and Sampie Terblanche, Willie Esterhuyse, and Willy Breytenbach. South African intelligence chief Niel Barnard got wind of the meeting and approached Esterhuyse on his return to South Africa, explaining that the government wanted an informal contact with the ANC and asking him if he would be willing to report on future discussions. Esterhuyse agreed on condition he could tell Thabo Mbeki and Jacob Zuma that he was in communication with Barnard. Mbeki and Zuma had no objections, and Esterhuyse effectively became an informal channel between the Botha government and the ANC (Harvey, 130; Sparks 1995, 78).

While Niel Barnard was receiving regular reports on the Mells Park talks, he was also part of a committee of senior government officials engaged in discussions with Mandela. At the end of 1987, Coetsee had proposed that a committee of senior officials, including Niel Barnard, enter into discussions with Mandela (Mandela, 523; Sparks 1995, 36; Meredith, 371). Before meeting "The Team", as they came to be called, Mandela asked for permission to consult with his colleagues on the third floor. The prison management turned down his request, probably out of fear that Walter, Kathrada and company might put a spoke in the wheels by objecting to the idea. Mandela then took the matter up at a higher level, and his request was finally approved on condition he met his comrades individually. First, he met with Walter and told him that he had met with Kobie Coetsee to discuss the possibility of negotiations between the ANC and the apartheid government. Walter was not entirely surprised. He knew Mandela well enough to guess that something like this had been on his mind. Their warder Christo Brand had also spilled the beans about Mandela's meeting with Kobie Coetsee (Sampson 2000, 363; Interview, Ahmed Kathrada). Mandela recalled the conversations with Walter:

> I have been through thick and thin with Walter. He was a man of reason and wisdom, and no man knew me better than he did. There was no one whose opinion I trusted or valued more. Walter considered what I had told him. I could see he was uncomfortable and, at best, lukewarm (Mandela, 523).

Mandela could see that Walter did not like the idea, but "he put it in a very diplomatic way, saying he had nothing against negotiations in principle but he would have preferred the government to make the first approach". Mandela responded that if he had nothing against negotiations in principle, then it did not matter who started them. Walter nevertheless suspected the government of ulterior motives, and was also worried about the response of the liberation movement, both inside and outside the country. He knew that it would be futile to stop Mandela and told him he hoped he knew what he was doing (Interview, Nelson Mandela, 27/11/2001; Sampson 2000, 365). Mandela then spoke to Mhlaba, who asked him what he had been waiting for – if he had started five years earlier they would all now be out of jail! Mlangeni's response was much the same. Kathrada's attitude was similar to Walter's but he expressed his views more strongly. He did not like the idea because he felt that it might appear as if the ANC was giving in (Interviews, Ahmed Kathrada and Nelson Mandela). Years later, both Walter and Kathrada feel that Mandela was right. Walter acknowledged that if the decision to negotiate had been up to him, "I would have hesitated. I would have wanted certain things done. I might have lost the chance" (Meredith, 371).

Walter and Kathrada were not the only ones concerned about Mandela's decision. Mandela had asked Govan Mbeki, when they met just before Mbeki's release, to inform Tambo that he was having discussions with the government. "Govan did not do a good job," recalls Mandela. This was hardly surprising, considering that Govan resolutely opposed the idea. There followed a terse exchange of notes between Tambo and Mandela. Tambo wanted to know what Mandela was discussing with the government. "Oliver could not have believed that I was selling out, but he might have thought I was making an error in judgement. In fact the tenor of his note suggested that." Mandela responded that he was talking about one thing only – a meeting between the ANC National Executive Council and the government. He said the time had come to talk, and he assured Tambo that he would not compromise the organisation in any way (Mandela, 524).

Mandela's first formal meeting with "The Team" took place in May 1988 at the officers' club in Pollsmoor (Mandela, 525–7; Meredith, 372–3; Sampson 2000, 367). Subsequent meetings, usually called by the government, took place every week for a few months and then at irregular intervals, "sometimes not for a month, and then suddenly every week" (Mandela, 525). The government officials were surprised by Mandela's grasp of issues and knowledge of Afrikaner history. Mandela, on the other hand, was surprised at their ignorance of the ANC. He found that even Niel Barnard, who had studied ANC history, was somewhat misinformed because he "had received most of his information from police and intelligence files, which were in the main inaccurate and sullied by the prejudices of the men who had garnered them" (Mandela, 525).

Niel Barnard's brief was to sound out Mandela on the armed struggle, the ANC alliance with the SACP, nationalisation and the question of majority rule. Barnard told Mandela the ANC had to give up the armed struggle before he could be allowed to meet Botha. Mandela's response was that it was up to the government to renounce violence: "I decided to be firm and establish the principle that we don't go to them cap in hand. I told them the oppressor determines the methods used by the oppressed. If the oppressor uses negotiations, dialogue and persuasion – that is the method the oppressed will use. But where the oppressor tightens the screw of oppression and uses force to suppress legitimate aspirations, they invite the oppressed to do the same" (Interview, Nelson Mandela, 27/11/2001).

Mandela refused to countenance the suggestion that he cut ties with the SACP, arguing that the ANC had been working with the communists for the last 70 years: "If I dumped my allies on the advice of my enemy, you yourselves would never trust me because you would feel I would do exactly the same thing to you" (Interview, Nelson Mandela, 27/11/2001).

When he was Secretary-General of the ANC in the 1950s, Walter Sisulu was often asked the perennial question about whether the ANC was controlled by the Communist Party. One day, he replied impatiently: "Why should you always assume we will be controlled by the communists? Why do you never think that it might be we who are controlling the communists?" Mandela responded in much the same vein to "The Team's" obsession about communist control: "You gentlemen consider yourselves intelligent, do you not? You consider yourselves forceful and persuasive, do you not? Well, there are four of you and only one of me, and you cannot control me or get me to change my mind. What makes you think the communists can succeed where you have failed?" (Mandela, 527.) On the issue of minority rights under a government of the majority, he pointed Barnard and his compeers to the preamble of the Freedom Charter: "South Africa belongs to all who live in it," and assured them that whites had a place in a future South Africa (Mandela, 527). Mandela continued to press for a meeting with Botha to discuss the possibility of a negotiated settlement and the release of the Rivonia prisoners, especially Walter Sisulu (Sparks 1995, 49).

Mandela was aware that Niel Barnard was making approaches to the ANC because Barnard asked him whether he had any objections to the government talking to Thabo Mbeki. Mandela suggested he talk to Tambo instead. He had no idea of the Mells Park process. His position was like that of a chess player operating blindfolded. Anthony Sampson described Mandela's prison discussions with the government as "the loneliest stretch in Mandela's ordeal".

> It is common enough in world history for heads of government to maintain apparently intransigent attitudes to their enemies, while holding clandestine talks with them: as Nixon had done with the Vietnamese or as John Major would soon do with the IRA. But Mandela was in an especially exposed position. He was facing the government alone, knowing that they were trying to split him off from his colleagues, with whom he could not come clean. From his cell he was now caught up in intricate talks, interlocking with other talks in Pretoria, Lusaka and Britain, of which he could not properly be informed. One false move could destroy his leadership (Sampson 2000, 364).

Did Mandela ever worry about the risks involved in entering into dialogue with the hated apartheid regime? When I asked him this question, his response was that he relied on his reputation – anyone who knew anything about him would know that he could never be manipulated. His closest colleagues Walter and Kathrada certainly had every confidence in his ability to take on the regime, and once they heard that Oliver Tambo had given Mandela the go-ahead, their initial resistance to discussions with the government melted away. Walter also believed that Mandela's stature was such that his reputation would not be tarnished. In the words of his biographer, Anthony Sampson: "His generalised image seemed to transcend all the sectarian and national rivalries of Africa, and came to represent the universal black leader, the last great freedom fighter." Even a government-commissioned survey revealed that Mandela was overwhelmingly the choice of leader among all sections of the black population. Significantly, the findings of the survey were hidden in Pretoria's State archives and never made public (*New Nation*, 7–13/7/88).

Mandela's stature was growing both locally and internationally and with the approach of his 70th birthday, the clamour for his release reached a crescendo. *The Star* expressed the view of many in government circles who believed that Mandela the man would never live up to Mandela the myth: "Once he is freed, the Mandela myth would be cut down to size by political realities" (Sampson 2000, 369). In fact, the apartheid regime was dismayed as "Mandela-mania" gripped the world; the government even threatened to expel the BBC from South Africa for its live televising of the gigantic Wembley concert that was the climax of worldwide birthday celebrations. Seventy-two thousand spectators attended the celebrity-studded concert that was watched by an estimated 200 million television viewers in 60 countries worldwide (Sampson 2000, 368). The birthday celebrations were a powerful morale-booster for Mandela's Pollsmoor colleagues. Walter conveyed his excitement in a letter to Connie Njongwe, the widow of his old Congress Youth League colleague, Dr James Njongwe:

I have no words to describe it. To say it was a great success is no doubt an understatement. I have never heard or read of such a popular birthday. Great leaders of small and large countries throughout the world – east and west, sent their messages of greetings and solidarity. Church leaders including the Pope and the Archbishop of Canterbury did likewise, but the concert at Wembley was just tremendous to say the least. The world's superstars were there in full swing. Connie, can we wish for anything better? It is true we are still in the midst of a very dark forest, but the light on the horizon shines as the sun itself. Yes, that, perhaps, is pitched too high, but some element of truth, is it not?

What I am trying to say is that when the world takes such note of our humble efforts in South Africa, despite the difficulties, we are not only encouraged, but are deeply inspired with great confidence. The fact that we are still kept under these conditions no longer worries us, because there is one thing certain ... We shall overcome! (Letter to Connie Njongwe, 24/9/88.)

Sadly, the birthday celebrations were enjoyed by everyone except the prisoner himself. Mandela's health was suffering, partly as a result of the dampness of his cell, the pressure of the solitary discussions with his adversaries, but also because of the shocking news that on 28 July, his house in Orlando West had been burned to the ground. He mourned the loss of precious family memorabilia and was deeply disturbed about the circumstances of the arson attack, which was carried out by the neighbouring Daliwonga High School students, who had been embroiled in a violent feud with the Mandela Football Club. The feud was characteristic of the chaos prevailing in many townships in the mid-1980s.

Political and community leaders were being detained, jailed, tortured, banned and eliminated almost as fast as they were emerging, leaving a power vacuum in the townships in which hoodlums and gangs flourished. It was a time of mob justice, with angry young men forming loose groupings responsible for kangaroo courts, beatings and thuggery, often in response to other crimes or to punish police informers. Any grievance could result in the accusation of being an informer, and this then became a licence for abduction, torture and even killing. The boys who roamed the streets, intimidating residents, were often teenagers – many of them legally children. Some adults tried to organise the young people into constructive activities, and forming football teams in the name of political leaders became a trend of the time. One example was the Orlando-based Sisulu Football Club. It was against this background that Winnie collected together a band of young men, the Mandela Football Club, complete with coach Jerry Richardson. However, little soccer was played, and the members acted as her private bodyguards.

At first the Mandela Football Club was very popular within the Soweto community, and neighbours saw it as part of Winnie's social work endeavours. Unfortunately, the club members operated on the assumption that any young person who refused to join was a sell-out, and stories began to emerge of beatings and torture of so-called informers in the back rooms of the Mandela home. The uncontrolled activities of the club soon led to disquiet, then anger. The burning down of the Mandela home was a direct consequence of that anger. It was widely suspected that the police had a hand in the matter and that some members of the soccer club, the coach in particular, were agent provocateurs deliberately placed to foment conflict and confusion in the community. Significantly, the police and fire brigade stood by and watched while the Mandela house burned down.

Outraged by the lawless behaviour of the club, and Winnie's apparent refusal to curb their excesses, community leaders recognised that Winnie needed either help or discipline, or both. To address the house-burning debacle, SACC General-Secretary Frank Chikane brought together a group of prominent community leaders, among them Cyril Ramaphosa, Aubrey Mokoena of the Free Mandela Campaign, Sister Bernard Ncube and Reverend Beyers Naudé, forming what became known as the Mandela Crisis Committee (Sampson 2000, 375; Meredith, 378–9). Mandela instructed Winnie to disband the football club and told his lawyer, Ismail Ayob, that no charges should be laid against the Daliwonga students.

Walter was deeply disturbed by the press reports about the happenings in Soweto, and he and his colleagues looked forward to meeting Mandela on 4 August. It was the first time they had been allowed to see him since their December get-together. Walter gave an account of the meeting to Connie Njongwe:

> I was quite shocked to observe that he had lost so much weight, but [he gave] his usual answer "No, it is due to my exercises", but what was more shocking was the manner in which he was coughing. It was even difficult at first for him to talk. At that stage he was sure that it was ordinary flu and the doctors had also assured him so. Otherwise he was mentally and spiritually tip-top. We were really inspired by the manner in which he dealt with the problems that had emerged just at that time. By the way, when I speak of problems, I am referring to the burning of the house and football team affair. All this was extensively publicised (Letter to Connie Njongwe, 24/9/88).

Mandela's Pollsmoor colleagues were not surprised when they received news that Mandela had been admitted to Tygerberg Hospital on 12 August, where he was diagnosed with tuberculosis. Mandela's illness sparked off a new wave of speculation about his release and London's *Sunday Times* noted that from the point of view of the South African government, "the only thing worse than a free Mandela is a dead Mandela" (Sampson 2000, 370). The government ensured that Mandela was given the best medical treatment, and after several weeks at Tygerberg, he was transferred to Constantiaberg Clinic near Pollsmoor, becoming the first black patient to be admitted here (Mandela, 530–31; Sampson 2000, 371). At Constantiaberg, Mandela resumed his discussions with "The Team", and was visited by Kobie Coetsee, who told him that he wanted to put him in a situation halfway between confinement and freedom (Mandela, 530; Sampson 2000, 372).

On 9 December, Mandela learned the meaning of Kobie Coetsee's cryptic remark when he was discharged from Constantiaberg and driven to Paarl, the scenic Cape Dutch town 66 kilometres northeast of Cape Town. He was not surprised by the move. In Pollsmoor, his meetings with "The Team" would take place after lock-up time. He would be taken from his cell after 5pm and return only in the early hours of the morning. One day, as he was leaving his cell, he noticed some common-law prisoners peeping at him from the high windows opposite. They asked him where he was going to and if he was negotiating with the government: "I could not speak, I was so shocked. I then told the authorities that the prisoners were aware of what was happening and if they did not take me away from this prison there would be no secrecy" (Interview, Nelson Mandela, 27/11/2001). In Paarl, Mandela was installed in his new home, a warder's house in the grounds of Victor Verster prison. In the large secluded bungalow, with warders brought from Pollsmoor to attend his needs, Mandela adjusted to life in his gilded cage.

Three months after Nelson Mandela's birthday, the Sisulu family celebrated another birthday on a much smaller scale. When Albertina celebrated her 70th birthday on 21 October, family members and friends gathered in Soweto for a surprise party. On 5 August, Max and I had celebrated the birth of another son, Duma Walter, named after his grandfather and Duma Nokwe. As I was on maternity leave, I took the opportunity to travel to South Africa to take the new baby to see his grandparents and at the same time participate in the birthday festivities. My mother, Betty Quinche, decided to accompany me, which eased some of the strain of travelling with a very active two-year-old and a two-month-old baby.

Albertina was as always delighted to welcome yet another grandchild into the family and to meet her *mkhozi*. She instructed Lungi to show my mother around. Part of the sight-seeing tour included a visit to Abu Asvat's new surgery in Rockville. Asvat had finally lost his battle with the Soweto Council against the forced removal of the McDonald's Farm squatters. In January, the council police had arrived at McDonald's Farm and announced that the people had 15 minutes in which to pack their belongings and move. The shacks were then demolished by plainclothes men. The

McDonald's community was dispersed to the nearby townships of Dlamini and Tshiawelo. Asvat's surgery was the only building left intact among the ruins of the flattened squatter camp (*The Sowetan*, 31/1/88). It was the end of the crèche and feeding scheme that Albertina and Asvat had started. They had tried to stay on and serve the patients who continued coming to the surgery, but soon after the demolition of the squatter camp, the council broke down part of the building. The leaking roof finally forced them to move to new premises.

Abu Asvat was as easy-going and pleasant as ever, and Albertina repeatedly told my mother that he was like a son to her. With hindsight, I realise that Albertina was so attached to Abu because in some ways he was remarkably similar to her husband. Like Walter, he had absolutely no regard for private property and would literally take the clothes off his back to give to the poor. Like Walter, he had dedicated himself to a life of service, and saw the best in everybody. He also believed passionately in the equality of all human beings, regardless of colour, creed or social status.

While Albertina was at work, we made frenzied preparations for the surprise party. Beryl who had come up from Durban especially for the occasion, Sheila, Zodwa, Nkuli and I agreed that her birthday present should be a new wall-to-wall carpet in her bedroom. We had a long discussion about the colour of the carpet, with Sheila arguing against the peach colour we all favoured, saying Albertina's bedroom was already too feminine and we needed to prepare the room for Walter's return. We finally agreed on the colour, and on the morning of Albertina's birthday, Nkuli scrambled to get the carpet fitted and ready by the time her mother returned from work. Abu Asvat created some pretext for keeping Albertina at work late so that when she opened her front door, she was met with a long, drawn-out shout of "SURPR-I-I-I-SE!" from the dozens of people crammed into every corner of her small lounge. When she recovered from the shock, she turned to Abu and scolded him affectionately: "You knew about this all along! No wonder you insisted on driving me home!"

The party was a pleasant and informal gathering of family members, friends and neighbours. Dr Tim Wilson, the husband of Ilse Fischer, who had worked in Alexandra township at the height of violence, gave the only formal speech of the evening. He paid tribute to Albertina's commitment and perseverance in the face of enormous obstacles. He said the way she lived her life inspired people to face their struggles with courage and determination because they felt "if MaSisulu can cope, then so can we". The trio of singers led by Mary Mxadana provided the entertainment with their sublime rendition of "*If There is Love*". Zodwa and Zwelakhe's son Moyikwa contributed a slightly off-key version of "*You are my Sunshine*", which was greatly appreciated by the fond grandmother. I particularly enjoyed seeing Priscilla Jana again and meeting Albertina's colleagues from FEDTRAW, especially Amanda Kwadi. Professor Mohamed, one of the Pietermaritzburg Trialists, was also present with his charming wife and daughter. Mrs Mohamed confided that she knew how Albertina felt about Zwelakhe's continued detention because her daughter had also been in detention for some time, and like Albertina, they had no idea when their child would be released.

The "celebrity" guest of the evening was undoubtedly the UDF's Mohamed Valli Moosa, who had recently ended his dramatic occupation of the American Consulate. Valli Moosa, Murphy Morobe and Vusi Khanyile were among the many detainees at Diepkloof who had been "redetained" when the State of Emergency had been renewed in June 1988. Feeling that they would remain in detention indefinitely without any recourse to justice, Moosa, Morobe and Khanyile feigned illness and were taken to Johannesburg Hospital for treatment. They made a dramatic escape from the hospital and took refuge at the American Consulate at the Kine Centre in downtown Johannesburg. Despite the reluctance of their US hosts, the "Kine Three", as they came to be called, occupied the consulate for over a month, demanding nothing less than release without restriction or threat of redetention. Even after the government agreed to this demand, they continued their occupation in protest against the continuing detention of other activists (Seeking, 239). Like the occupation of the British Consulate in 1984, the occupation by the "Kine Three" was a massive publicity coup for the democratic movement, and Valli Moosa was subjected to much good-humoured teasing about how famous he had become.

During the course of the evening, Albertina insisted on a photograph with her *bakhozi* – my mother Betty, Zodwa's mother Mildred Mdladlamba, and Sheila's mother Mabasadi Mashile. Later she told my mother how much she appreciated the support and friendship of Mrs Mdladlamba and Mrs Mashile over the years. She expressed her admiration of these two women who, with no husbands by their sides, had managed to raise their children and keep their families together. She also acknowledged the moral support Zodwa had received from her mother and her sister Nomvuyo (Mamkhulu) during Zwelakhe's detention. "I am among my sisters, my dear," she concluded emotionally.

The day after the party Albertina received a birthday letter from Walter. Like a young girl who had just received her first love letter, she decided to read it alone in the quiet of her bedroom. Afterwards, she told us that she had never before received such a letter. Many years later, when I read it, I understood why she was so overwhelmed. It was a moving letter of tribute to her achievements over the years – her work as a leader, as the breadwinner of the family, and as a mother who had raised her children through difficult and trying times. Walter thanked her for her love and support during his incarceration and praised her for her strength and determination. He then went on to reminisce about their courting days. He reminded her that she was the only woman to attend the inaugural meeting of the ANC Youth League at the Bantu Men's Social Centre in April 1944, "but admit it, my dear, you only had eyes for your boyfriend".

Our visit to South Africa would not have been complete without a visit to Pollsmoor and Zodwa's sister Mamkhulu kindly organised flights for us to Cape Town. As we approached the prison, I fervently prayed that this would be our last visit to the place. A young man and a couple of warders were seated in very relaxed fashion on the steps at the entrance. The young man jumped up to greet us and asked who we wanted to see. His welcome became more enthusiastic when he heard the name Walter Sisulu. "Oh yes, come in, come this way! They will fetch Mr Sisulu for you. Mr Mandela used to stay here too until they took him to Victor Verster!" He waved us into the waiting room, and offered us drinks as if he were a society hostess. He fussed over Vuyisile and asked if we would like to buy him a teddy bear from the prison shop. As he went out to fetch the drinks, my mother commented: "What a friendly warder." She raised her brows in surprise at my response that the young man was in fact a prisoner, not a warder.

While we waited, we noticed a number of prisoners loitering in the passage and then came the buzz of excitement as Walter was led into the room. My mother and Walter got on like a house on fire. They both took out notebooks in which they had listed what they wanted to discuss. Walter held the baby for most of the visit, while trying to attract Vuyisile's attention. Vu was completely unimpressed with his famous grandfather and remained preoccupied with the toys we had brought with us. The atmosphere was far more relaxed than any of my previous visits, and one had the sense that Walter's continued presence in prison was a mere formality. Walter asked after Zodwa and the children and although he could not say much, he was obviously worried about Zwelakhe, whose most recent appeal against his continued detention had been turned down in June. *The Sunday Star* had reported that Zwelakhe's situation "again highlights the intolerable human costs imposed by the application of the country's security laws. Mr Sisulu, it is worth remembering, has been incarcerated for two years – without trial, charge or even coherent reason. If this is the way justice is served, the battle is long since lost" (*The Sunday Star*, 10/7/87).

Walter felt it would raise Zwelakhe's spirits if he could see his children, and suggested we ask Zodwa to make the necessary arrangements. Back in Johannesburg, Zodwa agreed, but said in view of the short time we had left in the country, a formal application would take too long and the best way to see Zwelakhe was to pretend we were visiting someone else. We decided that my mother should remain at home with Duma while Vuyisile and I accompanied Zodwa, Moyikwa and Zoya to the notorious Diepkloof Prison, better known as "Sun City". At the entrance, I gave the fictitious name of the person I was supposedly visiting. Although Zodwa had tried to reassure me that the checks were not as stringent as those at Pollsmoor, I was terrified that we would be caught out. As I tried to sit as inconspicuously as possible in the crowded waiting room, Vuyisile, who was enjoying the company of his cousins, ran riot around the place and resisted my attempts to restrain him. By the time we went in to see Zwelakhe, I was a nervous wreck. It was a complete contrast to visiting Pollsmoor. We were directed to a long line of booths, like counters in a bank. We squeezed into a booth where Zwelakhe sat on the other side of the thick glass partition. Everyone was speaking at the same time and we had to shout to make ourselves heard. I was shocked to see how much weight Zwelakhe had lost. He seemed to be in good spirits, and was happy to see Vuyisile for the first time. Moyikwa and Zoya were of course overjoyed to see their father and just watching them made the nerve-wracking experience of illegally entering Diepkloof Prison worthwhile.

Just before we left South Africa, my mother and I had an experience that gave us an inkling of what Albertina had gone through over the years. One morning at about 2am we were jolted awake by violent banging on the doors. We could not tell whether the banging was at the front or the back door – it seemed to be everywhere. Before we realised what was happening, we heard Albertina shouting: "Just stop that banging at once. Are you not ashamed of yourselves, waking decent people at this time of the morning? Do you not have anything better to do?" We heard her opening the back door, whereupon four powerfully built armed policemen entered and proceeded to search the house. My baby had been woken by the commotion and I was busy nursing him when they entered our bedroom. We had turned on the light, but they still found it necessary to shine their torches in our faces. My knees were weak with fear. It was not too far-fetched to imagine them shooting us and claiming afterwards that we were resisting arrest. Albertina, on the other hand, was not in the least bit intimidated and she continued to castigate the police as they searched the house and the back rooms. At the crack of dawn, she was out in her little garden, trying to repair the damage that heavy police boots had inflicted on her vegetables. When we commented on her fearlessness, she said she was used to police raids – they had been part of her life for over four decades.

A psychologist might be interested in speculating as to whether Albertina's passion for spring-cleaning and ordering her home and garden might be related to such raids – hostile strangers bursting into her home, fingering her possessions, throwing them casually onto the floor. Certainly her ceaseless quest for neatness was a feature of her generation; it was also part of her mission education, which taught that cleanliness was next to godliness, and her training as a nurse would also have contributed to her scrupulous sense of hygiene. But anyone watching Albertina scrub a room from top to bottom or ordering her dining-room drawers and polishing every implement the day after a raid might wonder whether she was not indeed re-establishing her boundaries, recreating order, and "cleansing" her space and possessions after the rough intrusions of the enemy.

By the end of 1988, the antagonists in the South African conflict had reached a stalemate, more appropriately described by Allister Sparks as a state of "violent equilibrium between a government that cannot be overthrown and a spirit of mass resistance that cannot be crushed" (Sparks 1990, 368). The State had pulled out all the stops in its attempts to crush black resistance, and had succeeded in inflicting considerable damage by actively fanning the flames of the violent conflict between Inkatha and the UDF. Despite the signing of an accord between Inkatha and the UDF/COSATU alliance, the violence raged on, claiming thousands of lives and causing massive social upheaval (TRC Report).

Shadowy elements of the security establishment had also continued their programme of "dirty tricks". Among the activists who fell victim to apartheid's assassins in 1988 was Dulcie September, the ANC representative in France, who was shot in Paris in March. In June, Stanza Bopape, a young activist who had worked closely with Albertina, disappeared after being detained. Police claimed that he had "escaped from custody". It was later revealed that he had been tortured and killed by the security police. In October, the End Conscription Campaign won a successful interdict against the SADF's "dirty tricks" campaign (TRC Report).

After the virtual banning of the UDF, the momentum of the struggle was maintained by COSATU, which had only been partially restricted and was therefore able to operate more freely than the UDF (Seekings, 229–231). The labour movement too suffered from the attentions of Pretoria's "dirty tricks" department. COSATU House was bombed in May 1987 by the security police. After the organisation moved its headquarters to Khotso House, which also housed the offices of the SACC and other nongovernmental organisations, it too was extensively damaged in a bomb blast. A month later, Khanya House, the office of the Southern African Catholic Bishops' Conference, was also destroyed in an arson and limpet-mine attack.

The widespread resistance to and massive boycott of the October 1988 municipal elections, despite the crippling restrictions on the UDF and the fact that it was illegal to campaign for a boycott, demonstrated that the State had failed in its bid to crush black resistance. As one analyst pointed out: "The government's 'total strategy' comprised a contradictory ragbag of counter-revolutionary policies and rhetoric imitated from French policies in Algeria and US policies in Vietnam. It failed in South Africa as it did in those countries" (Gottschalk, 195). Even in the iron grip of repression, there were encouraging indications that South Africa was on the brink of momentous change. Coups and unrest in the Transkei and Bophuthatswana pointed to the illegitimacy of the Bantustan system. Still more encouraging were the developments concerning Angola and Namibia. The battle in which SADF troops were forced by joint Cuban-Angolan forces to retreat at Cuito Carnavale in Southern Angola marked a shift in the balance of forces in the region, and put more pressure than ever before on South Africa to address the question of the independence of Namibia. The negotiations over Namibia's independence and the removal of Cuban troops from Angola, which began with the US as mediator and the Soviet Union as observer, culminated in the New York Accords signed in December 1988. Angola, Cuba and South Africa signed two interlocking accords providing for the independence of Namibia and the withdrawal of 50 000 Cuban troops from Angola. The accords opened the way for the installation of the UN Transitional Government (UNTAG) in Namibia to oversee democratic elections in 1989.

The effects of international pressure for the release of political prisoners began to be felt at the end of 1988. On 26 November, PAC president Zeph Mothopeng and ANC firebrand Harry Gwala were released from prison. Both men were in their seventies and in ill health.

Pressure for Zwelakhe's release from detention also began to have some impact in 1988. *The Star* cited a stinging US attack on South Africa's human rights record, which made special mention of the fact that Zwelakhe Sisulu and Raymond Suttner had been in detention since June 1986. In July, author Susan Sontag wrote to President Botha on behalf of the 2 100 members of PEN, the most distinguished literary organisation in the US, urging him to release Zwelakhe Sisulu "immediately and unconditionally" (*The Star*, 21/7/88). Norman Mailer, John Irving, Arthur Miller, Kurt Vonnegut, Wesley Brown, EL Doctorow and John Hersey were among the acclaimed writers who supported the call for his release. In November, Zwelakhe's plight was highlighted in a special BBC programme aimed at encouraging viewers to agitate for the release of "prisoners of conscience" throughout the world. The programme was one of a series of ten, each presented by a leading British public figure, to plead the cases of prisoners in various countries. Made in cooperation with Amnesty International, the series was the first of its kind in Britain, and commemorated the 40th anniversary of the Universal Declaration of Human Rights (*Business Day*, 28/11/88). In West Germany, anti-apartheid campaigners picketed a major bank doing business in South Africa, held up placards naming the suspended *Weekly Mail* freelance journalist Themba Khumalo (who had recently been convicted for activities associated with the banned ANC) and Zwelakhe Sisulu as examples of journalists suffering under apartheid (*New Nation*, 24–30/11/88).

In September 1988, a Compol memorandum on Eric Molobi and Zwelakhe stated that "the provisional release of Zwelakhe Sisulu" had to be viewed against the background of his political profile, which was enhanced by the establishment of the *New Nation*, and his involvement in the broader media situation in the country. His role in MWASA from 1977 to 1983, which according to Compol "indicated his dedication to the struggle", was also cited as a factor to be taken into consideration. "Furthermore, Sisulu's status as a member of the Sisulu family, a well-known and respected media personality and especially his role as a figure of martyrdom (as a result of his detention) in especially media circles is of primary importance in view of the publicity he already enjoys and probably will enjoy even more when he is released." The memorandum noted that the *New Nation* had flourished in Zwelakhe's absence, "which means that Sisulu's release won't necessarily enhance the newspaper's propaganda role. Yet the intensity of the scope and publicity surrounding his release would again enhance the credibility of the newspaper". Zwelakhe's involvement in the NECC, which Compol said was partly responsible for his detention, was no longer a factor, because under emergency regulations, it was a restricted organisation. Compol therefore recommended his release on condition that "he may not serve on the management of any organisation/movement (which by implication means present commitments have to be broken); that he may not have any alliance with the *New Nation*, which means he has to resign as editor; that he be registered as a listed person". The conditions were to be enforced for one year "after which Sisulu's position will be reconsidered" (Ministry of Justice files).

Zwelakhe was finally released on 2 December 1988, on the same day as his friend Eric Molobi, the national coordinator of the NECC and an executive committee member of the UDF. Molobi, who had been in detention for just over a year, was released on restrictions similar to those of Zwelakhe. Because Zwelakhe's restrictions prevented him from speaking to journalists, his lawyer Priscilla Jana addressed a press conference at the prison while he was kept in an office with family and a few close friends. As he was driven out of Diepkloof Prison, the car came to a sharp standstill as it was mobbed by local and international reporters. Priscilla had to ask reporters not to approach him.

The family was ecstatic about his release. "Until Friday, I had thought we were again going to spend another Christmas without him. As a family you are just kept in the dark. No one knew that the release was on the cards," Zodwa commented in a press interview (*Pretoria News*, 3/12/88). Speaking on behalf of Zwelakhe, UDF Acting Secretary Mohamed Valli Moosa reminded the press that the newly released Sisulu was concerned that he had left behind in Diepkloof Prison at least 180 other detainees, "the majority of whom are children".

The release of Zwelakhe and Eric Molobi was followed by a storm of protest over their restrictions. "Restricted to a twilight existence" (*Pretoria News*, 17/1/87) and "A prisoner in his own home," screamed newspaper headlines. The Southern African Catholic Bishops' Conference expressed disgust at the restrictions, saying the two men were among the leaders the government should be speaking to and "one day will have to speak to, so that the problems of our land may be resolved peacefully through negotiation rather than violence" (*Pretoria News*, 3/12/88). In letters to President Botha, journalists' associations from Sweden, Britain and Ireland called for the "immediate and total lifting" of Zwelakhe's restriction order (*The Star*, 5/1/89). The Association of Democratic Journalists (ADJ), of which Zwelakhe was a founder member, said the government's failure to charge Mr Sisulu after 721 days behind bars "leads to the unavoidable conclusion that the authorities have acted against him precisely because he is committed to telling the truth about South Africa and to fighting for a just and democratic society in which journalism is not a crime". ADJ national convenor Libby Lloyd concluded: "Zwelakhe Sisulu should be lauded for these actions, not punished."

The restrictions, which confined him to his house between dusk and dawn, and forced him to report twice daily to the nearest police station, were condemned as a new form of incarceration. Priscilla Jana said they were the harshest restriction orders she had ever come across. "We were in a series of negotiations about them but they [the security police] would not budge. In the end we had to agree to those stringent conditions. I still thought at that stage that perhaps we should go to court, but I think Zwelakhe had had enough by then. The conditions of his release were such that he might as well have stayed in prison" (Interview, Priscilla Jana, 5/7/96).

Journalists had to interview Zodwa in the study of their Dube home while Zwelakhe sat with his children in the lounge. "While it is great for the family to be reunited after such a long time, we live a life of insecurity and can never relax," she said in an interview. "We know the police are watching every move in the house. It is a nerve-racking experience. Theoretically, if the house caught fire after 6pm, he would be expected to stay in it. The order is so wide he can't drop his two young children off at ... school, a 'formal educational institution'." She said Zwelakhe spent most of his time reading. "His thinking, his mental energy is restricted. The biggest blow to him is being unable to resume his work as a journalist; it is like holding somebody's brain so that it cannot function. The uncertainty of his order – not knowing when it will cease so he can continue his work – is similar to detention, where one does not know when the person will be released. People released after long periods of detention are being made prisoners in their own home, shattering the hope of their families that they would be free to re-enter society" (*Pretoria News*, 17/1/89).

A spokesperson for the Detainees' Aid Centre in Johannesburg said that these restrictions affected every aspect of a person's lifestyle, causing an enormous amount of personal suffering. The Human Rights Commission estimated that at least 500 South Africans were living under such restrictions. Raymond Suttner, a senior law lecturer at the University of the Witwatersrand, who had been released in September after spending more than two years in detention, was similarly restricted. He was only allowed to go to his office under police escort. A member of the Suttner Support Committee said that the government was trying to perpetuate the anxiety experienced in detention by imposing all sorts of prohibitions on former detainees, forcing them to live under the constant threat of invasion by the police. He said ex-detainees often had to be treated for post-traumatic stress. Mature activists like Raymond Suttner and Zwelakhe Sisulu, who had both experienced imprisonment before, had better coping mechanisms than younger activists, who were often deeply traumatised (*Pretoria News*, 17/1/89).

Analysts believed that it was significant that Zwelakhe was released just a week before the international spotlight was due to fall on the Sisulu family in the form of the Carter-Menil Human Rights Award. A *New Nation* report of 20 October 1988 noted that:

> While the government is persistently keeping the Sisulu family out of the struggle against apartheid, the international community is continuously acknowledging their contribution. This was the clear message carried by the $100 000 Carter-Menil Human Rights Award announced in Atlanta, US this week. The prize was named after former American president Jimmy Carter and French industrialist Dominique de Menil. Carter said the award was for the "courage and dedication" of the Sisulu family, which symbolises the "invincibility of the human spirit in the face of inhuman cruelty." De Menil said the prize was given to the Sisulus as a demonstration of solidarity with all those – both inside and outside SA – who are opposed to apartheid.

Beryl was the only member of the family in South Africa who was able to travel, so she flew to London where she met Lindi, who was at the time still studying for her PhD in the UK. Max joined them from Lusaka and they proceeded together to Atlanta to receive the award on 10 December. They were besieged by the media, and a number of Zwelakhe's journalist colleagues interviewed them, including two former Nieman fellows who made a special trip from Boston to see them. They were interviewed by several international television crews and Max appeared on the Ted Koppel show with President Jimmy Carter. Beryl enjoyed the time spent with Max and Lindi – it had been many years since they had spent time together. She was also overwhelmed by the attention and hospitality of their American hosts.

Beryl of course wrote to Walter, describing the wonderful time they had all had. Walter found it difficult to describe his sense of elation at the combination of Zwelakhe's release and the Carter-Menil Award. He was so excited when Zwelakhe visited him shortly after his release and they had so much to talk about, that for once he did not pay much attention to his grandson Moyikwa, who had accompanied his father.

On 23 December, Walter was able to share his news with Mandela when he and his colleagues were taken to the cottage at Victor Verster. They were amazed by the luxury of Mandela's new accommodation and teased him about his "five-star accommodation complete with room service". Walter did not, however, envy Mandela's solitiude. He mentioned the seven-hour visit in a letter to Connie Njongwe: "We found him well though obviously lonely. How can it be otherwise when he only talks to prison warders? If we could be allowed to visit him more regularly it would make a bit of a difference" (Letter to Connie Njongwe, 1989).

Albertina's annual Christmas visit to Pollsmoor was a happy one and there was plenty of good news to share. Apart from the Carter-Menil Award, Walter was proud to hear that Albertina was the recipient of the William DuBois Award and a runner-up for the rectorship of the University of Edinburgh. They viewed the accolades heaped upon them as an indication of progress in the struggle for liberation and agreed that the international attention augured well for the New Year.

Walter's Christmas messages were also full of hope. His friends Sally and Daso wrote from London: "We may be thousands of miles apart, but our longings, years of comradeship and friendship have continued to cry out for yours and millions of our peoples' freedom. We long for that day to come swiftly! May you and Albertina be rejoined in happiness and peace." Shireen, Fuad, Irshad Basu and Bhaigora wrote: "Our fondest greetings for a 1989 that will fulfill many of the expectations and aspirations that are nearest to your heart and ours. We wish you health and happiness for the coming year and a reunion with family, friends and people." Walter's communications reflected the same optimism. To Zohra and Enver Kathrada, "We have reason to be optimistic on the basis of our own analysis." And in his New Year card to Ebrahim Mohamed, he said "We live in the most difficult times yet we have no doubt about the future. Everything has an end."

*t e n*

Walter's level of engagement with the world outside is perhaps best reflected in the letters he wrote from prison, and it is worth telling this part of the story largely through his own words.

The change Walter welcomed most in prison was when they were allowed to have visitors under the age of 16. He was beside himself with delight when his grandchildren were able to visit him. He looked forward to each visit with eager anticipation and after the visit would write to the child or parent concerned, reviewing every detail of their short time together. For example, after Zwelakhe and his family visited him shortly after Zwelakhe's release from detention, he wrote to Moyikwa: "I apologise to you and Zoya especially and Mama as well. I was unable to pay much attention to you when you were here because there was so much to talk to your father about. Remember I had not seen him for two years. Hope all will be well next time" (1989). This was typical: Walter was sensitive to the feelings of even his youngest grandchildren, and as unfailingly courteous to children as to adults.

When Lungi Jnr asked him if he knew how many grandchildren he had, he responded: "Yes, I think, I know not only the number but their dates of birth. I am, indeed, very proud of my children and my grandchildren and I am very grateful to have such a family, all dedicated to serve society" (8/9/89). He was happy to add to his biological grandchildren by "adopting" other grandchildren. When Albertina tried to arrange for Lungi Jnr to visit his grandfather, she was quite put out when his maternal grandmother Greta Ncapayi would only agree to such a visit on condition Lungi was accompanied by Munemo and Dumisani, his two half-brothers on his mother's side. Albertina had no choice but to agree, although this meant forking out two extra fares to Cape Town. Walter did not mind the two extra visitors, and after the visit he wrote to all three boys. He asked them about their school results and requested a report on the performance of their favourite soccer teams, Orlando Pirates and Moroka Swallows (8/6/83).

Walter had to urge Lungi Jnr to reply to his letters and preached to him about the benefits of letter-writing: "I am writing this letter in English, because I am much more used to writing English and also because I am quite confident that you boys can read and write English. After all you are now all in high school so writing in English should be a good practice." Munemo turned out to be a much better pen friend and responded: "Dear Grandfather, I am sorry for taking so long to write to you. We heard you are angry with us" (11/83). Walter replied: "Thanks so much for your letter. I was not really angry, but wanted to hear how you chaps are keeping. I am missing you boys. I am happy to notice that you are determined to pass at the end of the year. You, Lungi and Elliot should consider studying together next year. That will improve your standard greatly" (11/11/83).

When their grandmother Greta Ncapayi died in 1987, Walter wrote a long letter of sympathy to Lungi and his brothers. He had never let the tension over the custody of young Lungi interfere with his personal relationship with Greta, and they had continued to correspond with each other for over 20 years (Letter to Elinor Sisulu, 16/9/87). After their grandmother's death, their mother Mercy wanted the boys to return to Zimbabwe with her. Lungi was quite happy to go because he felt he would be better able to continue his studies in Zimbabwe, but Munemo resisted the idea. He wrote to inform Walter that he wanted to pursue a soccer career in South Africa; a soccer official had offered him a home and promised to act as his guardian. Walter advised: "I sympathise with your view and quite understand the basis for it. It will be necessary to give Mercy full particulars about the man who has given the offer to you ... You have given good reason for your views but we do not know who the man is and what his circumstances are. This aspect is very vital for us" (12/9/87). He wrote to Sheila to ask: "Do you know what is being done in the line of education for young Lungi and colleagues? I would be happy if you could give full particulars about their situation generally. How is my beloved grandbaby, Tumi? Did you apologise for me to her for calling her a boy?" (18/4/87).

He constantly praised and encouraged his grandchildren and expressed his adoration of them. When Lindi's daughter Ayanda wrote to him from England, he thanked her for "a beautiful, well-organised and neatly written letter ... I now have some idea of Manchester and your flat. It is a vivid and superb description. It pleases me to see you doing so well, baby" (14/9/89). To Lungi and Sheila's daughter Ntsiki, he wrote: "You have not written to me since your last visit. I hope you are well, my little angel. I am really missing you. This is a hurriedly written letter, just to say Grandpa thinks of you at all times and to wish you well in your schoolwork. I will write to you again. I love you, darling, greetings to all your friends" (18/5/87). When Ntsiki's brother Linda (Ginyi) promised to write every week, Walter replied: "Your letter was excellent ... but take it easy. Writing weekly will mean a lot of writing. The idea of a small workbook is a very good one. It will help you in many things" (18/9/87).

When she was concerned that Ginyi was not exerting himself in school, Sheila wrote to Walter for assistance: "Tata, I am appealing to you basically because he holds you in very high regard – I think a little talking from you about hard work and his future will be taken seriously if it comes from you. If possible you could rope in Uncle Nelson and others – it might do the trick. As you can gather, I am very worried about this boy" (6/5/87). Walter spoke to Mandela, who immediately wrote a letter to Ginyi, which Walter enclosed in his reply: "I must admit that I am not unduly worried. Ginyi is quite an intelligent boy. It is possible that something disturbed him during this period and remember he is a teenager. Nel, as you can see from this, has done more than I had expected. He has shown deep concern for the boy, for he loves him dearly" (29/5/87). Sheila responded gratefully: "You are just wonderful – always there for us, both in good and in not so good times. Thank you very, very much for responding so promptly to my request for help in motivating Ginyi to take his school work seriously" (10/6/87).

The grandchildren responded to Walter's attention and affection by confiding in him about things that were important in their lives. Walter was particularly pleased to receive this letter from Beryl's son, Thulane:

I have to apologise for not writing to you. I am really sorry. In order to make up I will write a long letter. It's really great being in Standard 9. It really makes you feel older even though I am 15 turning 16 on 5th May.

These December holidays while staying at Katie's house (Mom's friend), I had an encounter with everyone there, telling me to be proud of having you as a grandfather and that I should write to you. I didn't really find 1987 that nice. There were some good points like meeting a few girls here and there, although nothing happened. Somehow I have the feeling this year is going to be a good one.

The one thing I am looking forward to this year is the Matric Dance, in which us Standard IX's take part. I'm gonna have to get a date/girlfriend to go with me. I am certainly not going to miss it. I wonder what Dad's going to say about it for he objects to me seeing girls or going out to parties. Mom doesn't really mind about the Matric Dance ... Oh, by the way, Mom had an operation just at the beginning of this year ... After the operation she got sick and I was a little worried, but later I knew she would make it and she did. So I am very glad. I can't imagine how things would be without her (28/2/88).

Walter responded with characteristic warmth:

What a lovely letter you have written, big boy! ... I am particularly grateful to those people who have been constantly reminding you that you have a grandfather. It is true grandson that people in prison attach great importance to communication. In any case, letter writing is good for you because it is an important part of your schoolwork, especially in the level you have now reached.

I delayed my reply to yours because I wanted to write to you on the occasion of your 16th birthday. You have reached a very fascinating stage in your life when the whole world begins to unfold in front of your eyes. A great challenge is opening up. I must also congratulate you for the progress you are making at school. Here again, you have reached a vital stage in your studies – a preparatory stage to your final matric. I can well understand how exciting it must be for you to look forward to the matric dance ... I think it is reasonable for you to want a partner for the occasion. I am sure Len [Thulane's father] will understand. It is better that your friend should be known. That would have the effect of curbing any reckless choices. You may have told me the subjects you are taking, but I can no longer remember, yet I am keen to know. I know you take great interest in sports. What about films, music etc? We are all happy that Beryl pulled through. She is an inspiration – not only to you, but also to the whole of our family. She is too precious. As they say more precious than gold. Remember that always (23/4/88).

After he received the report of the matric dance, Walter replied: "At last I have your brilliant photo ... with a young beautiful lady. That clearly shows us how successful the whole occasion was. Unfortunately, you do not give the name of this lovely and lively child ... You are making progress at school. That is a good thing and we are proud. I therefore do not think you should even think of business. You should think only of the highest possible achievements in your academic career, nothing else" (6/88).

Though his quota of letters and cards had increased considerably over the years, it was still not enough to cover correspondence to his entire extended family. In December 1987, he wrote to Sammy, then working in Lungi's shop: "Son, I am not sending any Christmas cards for any of the family members. As you know, perhaps you do not; we are entitled to only 12 Christmas cards a year. I am going to rely on you to convey my Christmas messages to all at home and all my *bakhozi.*" He went on to congratulate Sammy on his work in the shop: "I am so delighted about your fine performance at home. All reports from every member of the family speak very highly of your work and great responsibilities. You and your brother Lungi quite clearly make a good team. Keep it up at all times." He also acknowledged the role of the famous shop in the life of the family: "Shop No. 7 is obviously popular or at least fascinates members of the family, especially the young ones. Every time I open my album they jump up with joy. 'Here is Shop No. 7!' I observed this at different times from young Lungi and Moyi. I am enclosing therefore a special Christmas card for Shop No. 7. Tell Lungi and Munemo I received their letter. I shall be making efforts to reply to them. I suspect that I have exhausted my quota for the year, but I will make a place because I consider their letters to be of great importance."

When Sammy's fiancé had a baby girl, he decided to call her Kathrada. Though he was honoured to have the child named after him, Kathrada felt that no little girl should have to grow up with the name "Kathrada" and he suggested she should rather be called "Kathy". Walter wrote to tell Sammy that Kathrada "wants all the particulars about the child as well as the mother of the child". Walter also wanted the date of birth, because: "We attach great importance to such matters."

He wrote to encourage his young friend Ruth in bringing up her young daughter Shanti:

I think you are doing well; no doubt you have got the necessary enthusiasm to carry through the task. The greatest pleasure to all parents is to nurse and develop a child, not only to manhood, but as near as possible to perfection. There are of course degrees of doing this, pleasant and tremendous tasks, depending on the stage of development of each society. In modern times, many parents try either directly or through assistance to read stories at night to their loved ones once they are capable of grasping what is being read to them. During our time and in the environment in which we grew up, we were fed on intsomi or fables by our parents/grandparents. I neither read nor narrated intsomi or stories to my own children, even though it was my desire to do so. These were largely due to our conditions, perhaps not very different to what they are now. However the upbringing of children fascinates me. I wish I had the opportunity, even at this stage. Yes, the first-born tends generally to engage more attention from the parents but not always, sometimes the last-born takes the cake (25/2/87).

Walter also paid a lot of attention to his family by marriage. He was especially appreciative of the moral support provided by Zodwa's family during Zwelakhe's detention, and wrote to Zodwa's sister Nomvuyo (Mamkhulu) to thank her for photographs of her daughter Nwabi with Zwelakhe's daughter Zoya: "They so amazed me – the way they posed, as if they were ladies from Hollywood." He also thanked her for supporting Zodwa: "I could not agree with you more that I have a strong daughter in Zodwa. She is indeed a strong girl and we are proud of her, but you must never forget that your own contribution has been one of the major factors. Your presence in that home, your attention and services will remain indelible to our minds. I am personally moved by all this. I do worry a lot about Zodwa, but her calmness is a source of comfort to us" (1/5/87).

In August 1987, he asked Zodwa to extend "not only my congratulations but also my high appreciation for Lakhe's achievements. This is shown by the high esteem in which he is held by people of standing in different walks of life not only in our beloved country, but in other parts of the world as signified by these awards and different comments in the media". He gave the example of David Astor, editor of the London newspaper *The Observer*, who was reported to have made some highly complimentary remarks about Zwelakhe. "It may appear to be perhaps immodest to speak thus about my own son, but it is difficult to hide one's feelings and appreciation on such matters." He also expressed his frustration at Zwelakhe's continued detention: "Though I try to be calm about Lakhe and his colleagues in detention I cannot contain my irritation" (29/8/87).

Walter and Albertina had a close relationship with Zodwa's mother, Mildred Mdladlamba, who wrote to Walter regularly. In a congratulatory letter on his 75th birthday, she wrote: "Spiritually, I have been with you since our last correspondence. Coincidentally yesterday you were all remembered (singly) at the Anglican Church 11am service. Isn't that good?" She gave him an account of how the family celebrated his birthday: "Tata, you are so loved by everybody – the whole affair is indescribable. We share your letters religiously over and over again. I wish I could write more often. The treat of Tatomkhulu's birthday cake left small, round, long and short little fingers on the icing. I'm sure you'd know the owners of all those fingers. Mntakwethu, that's just to show you how much you are remembered" (20/5/87).

Walter responded affectionately to his "dear Sister Mkhozi": "Your splendid and inspiring letter was just another clear evidence of how fortunate we are to have such a remarkable extended family, especially in times such as these. It has certainly given me a vivid picture of the happy relationship within our family. We could wish for nothing better. All in all, our dear Mkhozi, your letter for which I must sincerely thank you has delighted me greatly. You must also thank those who have constantly kept us in mind, over the years, by prayers and other material things." He ended the letter with an account of how their grandchildren, Moyikwa, Zoya and Mamkhulu's daughter Nwabi entertained him on their previous visit. Zoya and Moyikwa told him amusing tales about school. "To crown it all, Nwabi sang and danced for me. She was too good! I laughed heartily … What lovely things they are!" (20/7/1987.)

Walter was kept up to date not only on the doings of his grandchildren but also the children and grandchildren of his friends. Shireen Motala, the daughter of his old friend from Pietermaritzburg, Chota Motala, had informed him when she married a young man called Fuad Cassim. In his letter of congratulations, Walter wrote: "My mind goes back to the days when you were a child, you used to go in and out of the house in Boom Street, to the backyard full of toys of various kinds." He went on to reminisce about his longstanding relationship with her family: "Your home, Shireen, was my first Natal home." He also congratulated her economist husband: "I wish to give Fuad all my support and encouragement for his PhD. It seems to me that the greatest challenge to our social scientists in Africa is in the economics sphere. The correctness of Fuad's choice can therefore not be over-emphasised" (31/10/87). He was delighted to hear from her again after a long silence: "We are well and at present adjusting to life with a baby which is both extremely joyful and quite exhausting! Aalia is now experimenting with her first few words."

Walter was very particular about expressing gratitude to those who assisted his family in any way. He was especially thankful to Mampie and Eugene Morgan, Beryl's friends, whose home in Retreat was a convenient place to stay when visiting Pollsmoor. In a letter of thanks to the hospitable pair, he wrote: "Not only have you looked after Nkuli, our baby, for such a long time but you have attended to all my visitors with wonderful spirit." He expressed his regret that he had not ever met them and asked them to apply to visit him (29/11/87).

Much of his correspondence was devoted to exhortations about education and singing its praises. He told Jongi: "You must make sure that you will leave prison a better man. You must not be satisfied to understand human psychology [only], but you must acquire wider knowledge in general. Education is much more than getting college lectures and passing the subjects you have been studying. It means you must understand life and be useful in shaping society." He was always elated by the educational achievements of family and friends. In October 1987, he wrote to Xolile Guma: "We have heard the delightful news of your final success in obtaining your doctorate in economics. We are, indeed, proud of these achievements in spite of your many-sided problems that faced you and your family during this period" (22/10/87). When his sister-in-law Miriam Thethiwe, the widow of Albertina's brother Elliot, got her degree from UNISA, he sent a telegram: "Hearty congratulations, Dlamini. Well-deserved honours. We are proud and inspired. Rise ever more" (3/6/82). And when Miriam's son-in-law Thozie completed his doctorate, he too received a congratulatory note: "It is indeed a tremendous achievement, especially having regard to the conditions under which black men in this country struggle." His grandson Lungi spoke for many when he wrote to Walter: "You have encouraged many people to continue with education and they thank you for that; and so do I" (30/11/87).

Walter was especially interested in Lindi's PhD studies and was concerned that she might be sidetracked by her political work. "On what precisely is your dissertation?" he asked her in 1987. "You know I am vitally interested in history. There are for instance some new trends in South African history. New schools of thought seem to have emerged in which Harold [Wolpe] features. I have had very little material to read. Of course there are differences but if I know your field I may pursue the matter. This could help my own development. After many years of writing letters limited in scope and content one cannot but become too stereotyped."

Walter was glad to hear from Lindi that Harold Wolpe was her supervisor. He replied that she "could not have fallen in better hands". He said the topic of her thesis, "State and Women", "seems to me a very good choice, topical and fascinating in many ways. As far as I know, there is not much work that has been done in this field. In your earlier letters, you give a good outline from which it appears that your scope may be very wide. I assume that your period will be the beginning of the mining industry, at the close of the last century, to the beginning of the present century, but how far do you go? It seems to me that your thesis, though it may be specific, is in fact inextricably intertwined with the whole labour migratory system" (April/May 1989).

Towards the end of the 1980s, his letters took on an increasingly nostalgic tone. He wrote to a relative in the Transkei asking for a copy of his baptismal certificate from All Saints Mission, because the one he had was misplaced, and added: "Another thing, Nolita [our princess], one's place of birth is very important and deep rooted. I also always wanted to know about those mountain ranges that surrounded the deep valley of Amaqwati, from which the Xuba River rises from both sides, east and west. What is it called? When I research about my past, those forests, mountains and small rivers that I used to swim in those days – I must have a clear picture of them in my mind" (July/August 1988).

After a tussle with the prison authorities, Walter was given permission to correspond with Jongi on Robben Island. In June 1987, he wrote Jongi a long letter explaining the history of the Sisulu family. Jongi's response showed his deep appreciation: "I really wish our correspondence was not limited, for I enjoy every sentence of your letters. Whenever I read them I wish they can be endless. I thank you so much not only for the letter, but also and above all for caring so much about me. I am so grateful for the family background. It really makes me feel great. Tata, you must always update me with such information. I really need it" (July 1987).

Walter wrote a similar letter to Lungephi Lengisi, his other relative incarcerated on Robben Island. He updated him on news of the rest of the family in Johannesburg and in Engcobo. Lengisi's father had died at the end of 1985, and Walter had sent a telegram in time for the funeral. He told Lengisi that he had long wanted to give him a brief background on his mother's family: "Vina, your mother – she will forever remain a picture of what I consider to be the embodiment of humanity itself. She was deeply religious, full of love and understanding of people. I was and still am happy to have grown under her tender care." He described in detail the relationship between Lengisi's great-grandfather Vanqa Dyanti Hlakula and his own grandfather Abraham Moyikwa, the way the families lived and labour was organised. "In my next letter," he wrote, "I shall deal with other aspects. I believe this to be an important part of your education" (20/1/87).

Walter also reached out to friends from the past with whom he had lost contact. He remembered his friend Reverend Mooki who was part of family that had done community work in Orlando for two generations. In a nostalgic letter to "Our Dear Moruti" (*Moruti* being the Sotho term for Reverend), he said:

Old memories have been constant reminders that at least I should drop you these lines for the sake of old times. How can we ever forget all the fond memories of the 1940s ...? We vividly remember your tolerance, especially the warmth and kindness of your dear wife.

These forcefully come to mind when I see your pictures, your articles or your extracts of your poems. All these as you imagine kindle the nostalgic feeling about Johannesburg, particularly Soweto and surroundings.

History fascinates me, whether it be general or specific; thus some of your articles about our history evoked great interest in me ... Though my interest is largely in the general history of our country, especially the national liberation history, I am ... at the moment concerned with the history of the urban life of the African people in Johannesburg, in particular Soweto, but I neither have energy or ability to undertake such a project. I, as it were, am thinking aloud. The ideal person for it is Zeke Mphahlele [author of *Down Second Avenue* (1959) and considered by many to be the "father" of black South African literature]. He is however perhaps too busy, but you can find no better person for the job. There is the question of what aspect could one tackle in such a project since it is so vast. You may remember that Ray Phillips did some work on the African urbanization ... These of course are some of the ideas one should like to discuss one day.

Let me come to lighter things. As I am writing this letter, a picture unfolds of the old families of Soweto – the Radebes, Mvubasa, Mpanza etc. All these men have made a mark in history. One day, I saw a photo of Pitsane Kelly – the only son of the Motwala of No. 44 or 45 Orlando ... I am mentioning Pitsane, largely because he comes from an old respectable family. I knew his parents and all his sisters. His father was an agent of the *Bantu World* and Pitsane grew up selling the paper on behalf of his father. I was myself an agent of the *World* in the mid-30s ...

By the way coming back to Pitsane – from what I have heard from him, he is quite an interesting fellow. He is a socialite, one of the most well-travelled chaps and is a gold mine of information; if anybody deals with urban life, he could be very useful too.

What of the leading musicians of the township – both classical and jazz, Peter Rezant, Z Cele, W Sentso and B Ngakane. In my early days I took great interest in music and served in many singing groups. When I became the treasurer of the Youth League in 1944, I was able to organize social functions to raise funds – especially when some of our boys qualified as doctors – such as Nkomo, Njongwe, etc.

The Squatters Movement, of course, plays a vital part in dealing with urbanization. In fact, it is the central issue. By the way three years ago I wrote to Ellen Kuzwayo – not having in mind this issue, but mostly just to know about the old stalwarts of Pimville, including her father Merafe. I was surprised not so much [by] her swift reply, but by the wealth of information – even about people I had not enquired about ...

My dear old friend, I have registered this letter because I wanted to make sure that you get it. I do not have your address, hence my use of Dobsonville. Do let my family know when you get it. Give my love to your wife and all friends (9/5/86).

A year later, he wrote to veteran trade unionist leader Frances Baard to congratulate her on the publication of her biography, and noting that he hoped the prison library would get hold of it. He also enclosed a letter for her nephew Aggrey Klaaste, the editor of *The Sowetan* (4/4/87).

In his letter to Aggrey, Walter apologised for not writing to him directly and drew attention to his close association with Aggrey's relatives, the Baards and Molefes, and said he had read with sorrow about the untimely death of Reverend Molefe. "I hope other members of the family are keeping well. It is my duty, even at this stage to express my sympathy to the members of his family, and hope I am in no way opening up healing wounds." He encouraged Aggrey in the good work he was doing: "I have been reading some of your articles in *The Sowetan* – some of which have evoked great interest in me. I am particularly referring to your biographical notes or memoirs. I must confess some of these articles rather make me nostalgic." He asked Aggrey to send him a list of books on the development of the African in the urban areas. He said there would be a possibility that he might be allowed one or two of these books, but the list would in any case be helpful to the prison library. "Recently, I have been reading a number of biographies, Zeke's [Es'kia Mphahlele], Bloke Modisane, etc. I have not yet read Ellen Kuzwayo." He asked Aggrey to convey his regards to all his colleagues, especially Joe Thloloe, whose parents he was well acquainted with (4/4/87).

Aggrey responded: "When my aunt told me I had a letter from a Sisulu I immediately thought of Zwelakhe, who poor chap has been inside for a longish time right now. I was totally surprised and I must say honoured to read your name at the top of the very warm letter you wrote. Although the going tends to get rocky, we are keeping the faith. If you could perhaps also convey this to the other stalwarts with you there. The type of letter you wrote me was so nostalgically touching – almost as if my father was speaking from the grave."

Soon after Zeph Mothopeng's release, Walter wrote to Mothopeng's wife, Urbania. "Allow me to recall the past a little," he asked. "I think back to the 30s and early 40s long before we became good neighbours as we still are today. Apart from Zeph, I have a vivid picture of the Lonake sisters with their beautiful wonderful mother. It is a pleasure to think of those days and how the healthy friendship has developed since then." He recalled his prison days with Mothopeng: "Though circumstances were not of our own making you can well imagine what our coming together once more with Zeph meant. He was my immediate neighbour. We reminisced daily." He offered his congratulations for an award that had been bestowed on Mothopeng. "It was an honour, I believe, he long deserved. There are no two ways about it. I hope his health has improved."

He also wrote to his old friend Mary Benson in London and was delighted to receive an equally nostalgic reply:

It was wonderful to get a letter from you. I recognised your writing, way back you sent me a Christmas card – must have been 1961 or so ... I still recall first meeting you in 1951, in your small office in Commissioner St, when a few days later you called me up to join others on a platform and I was asked to say a few words. I was petrified, never having spoken in public and mumbled a few words ... I then sat down with a bump. The only trouble with your letter is that you don't say anything about yourself and your companions ... I often try to picture you all and wonder whether you have been able to keep Nelson's garden up, and I hear and read of Albertina with enormous admiration. Please ask her to give my address to your son-in-law and Lindi. I should love to meet them. I just missed meeting her some years ago and was very disappointed.

Much of last year, I was in New York and ... saw Thomas [Karis] quite often and had a glimpse of Gwen [Carter] too. She is now very old. Africa has a way of shaping people and inspiring. I hear you can now write poetry. I hope some epics will flow from your pens. Poems also can become songs. I wonder if any of you plays the guitar as Govan did. By the way, I was recently able to tell something of Molly [Fischer] and her family. Do you remember giving me a lift from her home one day in a very broken-down old car, and the time you and Duma [Nokwe] came to Frieda [Matthews] to ask me to help Chief with secretarial assistance when he won the [Nobel] prize.

How is your health? I chug along. I tell myself I should try to exercise just a bit with Nelson – the great example, but alas not very often. All the best to you and love to you and Albertina.

Walter never forgot Helen Joseph, especially at Christmas because she had established a tradition of arranging a Christmas gathering at her home. In December 1986, he thanked her for her Christmas card and recalled their days in the Treason Trial:

It seems as if it were only yesterday when we first appeared in the Drill Hall and thereafter travelled almost daily to Pretoria Synagogue. Time moves very fast and there is still so much to be done. Hearty congratulations for the Human Rights award. I am equally indignant and disgusted by the pettiness and vindictiveness of the Botha regime, especially to deprive you at your age [of the chance] to visit the USA and UK after so many years of confinement and hard times.

In 1987 he wrote: "Compliments of the season and good wishes for your speedy recovery. Helen, we are forever thinking of you – especially the days when your health seems to give much concern and anxiety. Your strong will to resist has continued to be a source of inspiration. What a wonderful faith! Keep it up!"

Via Lindi he sent 70th birthday congratulations to his age-mate Trevor Huddleston:

Your Grace

Firstly, I wish to acknowledge with thanks and appreciation your kind message of good wishes on my birthday last year. It kindled in me the fondest memories, which I shall forever cherish.

Now let me come to the main purpose of this short note. It has come to my attention that next June you will commemorate your seventieth birthday, and that at the same time you shall be retiring as Archbishop of the Indian Ocean Islands, perhaps also as an outstanding leading preacher of the Anglican Church. But I have no doubt that your glorious service not only to Christian faith but to mankind shall forever remain as a living example of the Christian principles. I do not profess to know much about Christianity, but from the little I know and from my reading of history, we are entitled to hold this as a shining example of a true Christian. Certainly this is how millions of humble people look at your service.

Please accept our humble congratulations and our very best wishes on the occasion of your seventieth birthday.

I say nothing about your retirement, since I know that your dedication and devotion to the cause of humanity has no end.

We are well in our circumstances and forever hopeful for a bright future.
Love and warm regards to all.
Your ever loving Walter (15/3/83).

On the same day, he wrote to the musician Wilson Silgu (via Zwelakhe):

You have no imagination how proud I was to learn that you have become an inspiration of our growing generation, of our musically-oriented Black youths. It is not just because of historical roles you have played as a pioneer of our jazz music, but also because you kept abreast with all the events in the musical world, particularly the events at home. You will perhaps wonder and even be surprised what has moved me after so many years ... the fact is that I have much more time to reflect on the past. My relationship with the Silgu family dates back to the early 30s when we all lived in Doornfontein and continued when we moved to Orlando East. I must however confess my guilty conscience, when I think of the way I neglected that family over the years because of no other reason than the fast life of our golden city. I recall with fondest memories your beloved mother and your sister Cherry. I recall the early beginnings of the jazz minstrels ...

This short note is intended mainly to compliment you on your good work and encourage you to keep the flags flying. Music is one of the greatest arts man has produced, if not the greatest. It is a remarkable contribution to society as a whole. Your beginnings were modest in a world of poverty yet it was a milestone in which our people have every reason to be proud. Keep it up, big boy! We are well in this little world of ours (15/3/83).

Through Raymond Mhlaba's son Joe, Walter sent a message to the artist George Pemba: "Tell George Pemba I was happy to read biographical comments in one of the papers – a very impressive record. I still remember the posters he used to make for meetings" (15/8/89).

In June 1985 he was thrilled to receive a telegram from Mendi Msimang, who was then heading the ANC office in London. It was his first communication from Mendi since the latter had gone into exile. "Your telegram was not only an inspiration to me but has also served to rekindle fondest memories," he wrote, taking the opportunity to convey his feelings about the progress of the ANC: "I believe it is appropriate on this occasion to express my own pleasure and a great feeling of satisfaction and pride at the remarkable progress you have made over the years. We cannot but be conscious of the fact that, we are, indeed, pressing through the most difficult times in our history. We have endured and will continue to endure in these conditions and even under worse ones." He reminded Mendi that he considered him part of his family. "It is therefore natural that to hear from you after so many years should be the cause for great excitement and joy, especially in view of our circumstances. Remember me to all friends. We are all well" (12/6/85).

Daso Moonsammy, an old friend and political associate, reminded him of his days as Secretary-General of the ANC when Daso's house was a place of refuge to which he retreated to work: "I can still recall when you spent many days and hours at [my] home ... working so hard. On one occasion my landlord asked me about you, I told him that you were a writer and that you were busy preparing for a writer's conference. He was so taken by you and the vast knowledge and experience that you have always possessed." Daso also commended him on his commitment to his exercise bicycle: "[We] were equally excited to learn that you are in good shape and still can perform so well in spite of the odds. When Kathy described you exercising, we formed a picture of you and recalled ... the tremendous energy you possessed which was an encouragement to all of us. Your calm and collected approach during moments of crisis and your ability to reflect so much warmth and love for the underdog – you showed so much affection for the neglected and uncared folks" (23/9/85).

In 1987, Walter received a letter from Ellen Kuzwayo asking if he had received the copy of her biography *Call Me Woman* that she had posted to him. He wrote back saying that the book had never arrived, but that he had watched a television programme on Ellen in which the book was mentioned. Ellen welcomed his letter: "[It was] like spring water to a traveller in the desert. I missed seeing that on TV. Now that I know you friends saw it, I am happy to do without having seen it. It compensates for the book you never received. The pity is that it never came back to me, with the inscription on it. I hope to come across it some day" (2/6/87).

Another old friend Sikosi Mjali had better fortune when she posted her health education book. "Do you still smoke?" she asked. "You will stop as soon as you read what the book has to say about cigarettes, Mzala."

Walter responded: "Thanks ever so much for your letter and the handbook which I read with great interest. I liked the simplicity and the style. It is of great value not only to children and teachers, but is particularly important to all adults. Its effect on me was immediate, one felt quite guilty. I have heard warnings from many people in the medical profession but they never made such a strong case as you made in your simple style." He went on to say that he had given up smoking in the early 1950s but if he had still been a smoker, her arguments would have definitely persuaded him to give it up (1/5/89).

Walter and Sikosi corresponded regularly and he constantly encouraged her writing endeavours: "I am happy with your decision ... provided the idea of writing a book is given the most serious consideration. On this I will continue to urge and encourage you." She in turn greatly appreciated his support: "Walter dearest Mzala, Am ashamed to receive your card as I plan and procrastinate sending yours ... You are the fixed Northern/Southern Cross star, so dependable, so TRUE. I am flattered that you've never failed to remember me, no matter what!" When Sikosi informed him that he shared a birthday with her granddaughter Masithathu Zanele, Walter sent her a card informing Masithathu that they shared a birthday and wishing her the best for her future as a young woman: "'Behind every male stands a woman.' Who says that? The 20th century is an era of women."

Early in 1989, Sikosi wrote to him about Alan Paton's death. Walter responded that he had known the famous novelist when he was the principal of Diepkloof Reformatory and as the chairman of the Liberal Party. "My last meeting with him was when he gave evidence in integration in the Rivonia Trial, which in itself was an act of bravery at that time." He also told Sikosi that he had been enjoying reports of the NAMDA Conference in Port Elizabeth, "in which your beloved first-born son – young Diliza, was playing a leading part. I read his opening address with great pleasure and pride. Siko my dear, can you wish for anything better?" He also responded to her account of the internecine violence in Natal. "The situation in Natal is indeed depressing. Some of us foresaw this type of situation developing, but were unable to prevent it. There are fundamental causes, plus other existing concrete conditions in the areas affected, but we cannot discuss these even superficially."

Another regular correspondent was Connie Njongwe, the widow of ANC leader James Njongwe. From his prison cell, Walter helped her to re-establish contact with Frieda Matthews. "You will be happy to hear that Sis Ricks i.e. Mrs ZK, has written me quite a sweet letter. Thank you for having given me her postal address. She says she is quite healthy in spite of her old age, as she will be 84 years old on 16 September 1989. She tells me that she paid Nelson a visit in November 1986, and was allowed only 40 minutes. After which she was very keen to meet you too, but unfortunately was told she could not! How very disappointed she was, after the very long, long trip of visiting Cape Town!" (24/8/89).

Walter had also been disappointed that Frieda had not been allowed to see him, especially since she had travelled all the way from her home in Botswana, but he received a detailed report of her visit from Mandela. In 1987, Frieda had written to him: "I have now prayed as often over the years for the joy we will all experience if we see you again some day. Strangely enough even though age is catching up with us, I still have hope" (28/5/87).

On the occasion of Frieda's 84th birthday, Walter wrote:

What amazes me about you is the tremendous energy you have, teaching piano, writing letters and memoirs. The only thing which was a near tragedy was the attack of pneumonia, but you survived *Ntombi ka Bokwe* [daughter of Bokwe]. This is a period I would never like to miss – the time of your birthday, when we think of the past with its ebbs, flows and its highly treasured experiences. I have had the pleasure of working with the members of your family, ZK, RT and Bokwe. The time and my situation do not permit me to reminisce about [these] events. I do not think I have ever met a man such as ZK, calm and dignified, no matter what the situation was like. When we have reached this stage in the history of our struggle, we cannot but think of such men (August 1989).

All too often, Walter had to send messages of condolence. In 1987 he was shocked to hear from Sikosi Mjali that her youngest son Xola had been killed in a car accident. "This untimely tragic death of Xola in the prime of his life has indeed shocked us. I am speechless and have no words to express my sorrow, nor words to console you at your moment of crisis. I have been wondering how your own health was in the light of such a profound silence. I wish you all the very best and all the strength in these circumstances" (1/9/87).

On the death of Albertina's brother Reverend Elliot Thethiwe in November 1986, he wrote to his sister-in-law Miriam (MaDlamini): "Accept our heartfelt sympathy on the tragic death of Elliot, your dear husband. Convey same to the rest of the family. His work is done. *Hamba Kahle Thole!*" (17/11/86). In 1983, he had paid tribute to his friend and comrade Yusuf Dadoo, writing to Albertina: "I am happy that you had the presence of mind to send a telex on the occasion of Yusuf Dadoo's death. He was a friend indeed, a part of us as a family in all respects. Though the European press said so little about so remarkable a man, the Black papers, especially in Natal, paid him a deserving tribute. I think I shall write to Winnie, his wife in London" (21/10/83). When Eli Weinberg died, Walter wrote to his daughter, Sheila, paying tribute to Eli's work as a photographer and his contribution to the struggle. "In spite of the lack of communication between us, I have never stopped think[ing] and enquir[ing] about you and Ilse [Bram Fischer's daughter] from all my visitors ... In this way, I have been able to follow your progress and I think you are doing well." However, the letter never reached Sheila because the security police decided that it would be undesirable for her to communicate with Walter.

Despite their differences, Walter paid generous tribute to James Moroka, the ANC's former President, when he died: "With Doctor Moroka's death, a rich and colourful life has ended. He will be remembered for his worthy contribution in various fields including medicine, politics, social welfare, education, farming, sports and business. During the years when we were privileged to work closely together, I found him to be a dedicated, loyal and caring colleague. With his death we bid farewell to the last of a highly honoured and inspiring generation."

In 1987, he wrote to Vuyo Mathole asking him to put him in touch with the sons of Reverend NB Tantsi: "I was very close to the old chap and feel very unhappy that I should be completely blank about the death of Reverend Tantsi" (26/3/87).

The result was the following letter from Reverend Tantsi's son, Dabulamanzi:

*Nkokheli* [leader]
I believe you are aware of the fact that my old man – Rev. NB Tantsi died more than 10 years ago. He held you in very high regard. He never ceased speaking about you and Mandela, in terms of spadefuls of superlatives.

I dreamt about you yesterday. I dreamt that you were telling me that the sun is about to rise. I am looking forward to seeing you before sunrise.

P.S. For want of knowing what one is permitted to write about I have censored myself.

Walter was delighted and gratified to receive Dabulamanzi's letter, and replied telling him how fond he was of his father: "We had a very close association dating far back to the early forties. I have a very high regard for him … He was one of the most important links between politics and religion. Some of the most important and historic gatherings were initiated by the Movement through him. NB was one of the most determined and dedicated leaders of our national movement … He has made a name in the AME church and in the Minister's Organisation and of course in the liberation movement. He was an all-rounder."

Walter also took time to respond to letters informing him of the various honours and awards that came his way. He was surprised and honoured in March 1989 when he received a letter informing him that he had been elected patron of the South African Cricket Board, the body governing cricket for black South Africans. "The Board wishes to pay a tribute to you as one of our brave leaders in the struggle," the letter said. "We also greet you as one who loves the game of cricket" (Letter from RA Feldman, on behalf of the South African Cricket Board, 17/3/89).

In August 1989, he wrote to Lindi, "You mentioned the fact that you were invited by students at Stoke-on-Trent to open their student union building which is named after us, and that the opening coincided with the arrival of the Mandela marchers and that they were welcomed by the Mayor on our behalf. We view all this with great enthusiasm. Kindly express our appreciation to the students and the Mayor of Stoke-on-Trent."

Through his exposure to various media, Walter kept up with what was going on in the world around him and often surprised family and friends with his knowledge of current trends. "I was amused (and astonished) by your apparent knowledge of trends in contemporary music," wrote Xolile Guma. "My informants tell me that you are reputed to be a great fan of one Whitney Houston, who I only got to know about through Ayanda. We agreed to collect some of the latest recordings for you" (9/12/88). My mother Betty shared Xolile's sentiments: "I had a good laugh when I read your letter. You mentioned the fact that Whitney Houston was Aretha Franklin's niece. I know both singers (not personally, of course) for their good voices, but I never knew that they were related you know. I was amazed at your knowledge of the outside world" (14/8/89). Walter responded that he was a fan not only of Whitney Houston but also Tracy Chapman, another talented young singer. We decided that this was proof that he would be no Rip van Winkle when he was finally released from prison.

# *eleven*

Over the years Albertina Sisulu's stature had risen considerably, not only in South Africa, but internationally, as evidenced by the increasing number of human rights awards that were coming her way. She was often described as "a symbol of courage, fortitude and calm endurance". Journalists, lawyers, political associates and even her enemies commented on her consistency of leadership. Many saw her as a rock of stability when the liberation movement seemed to be foundering in stormy weather (Interview, Allister Sparks, 1999). She was admired for her quiet, unassuming manner, her integrity and discretion, and the fact that she never sought media attention or public accolade. Women who worked closely with her described her as a source of strength and knowledge who taught them that the struggle for liberation was as much about patient building of organisation as it was about public displays of defiance (Interviews, Priscilla Jana, Jessie Duarte, Sister Bernard Ncube, Sheila Sisulu, Lindi Sisulu; Joyce Sikhakhane-Rankin, Interview, O'Hara Diseko). She had the best qualities of a generation that boasted women of the calibre of Ellen Kuzwayo, Winkie Direko, Frances Baard, Ruth Mompati, and many others. Theirs was a generation of women who demonstrated absolute commitment to the progress of their communities, the education of their people and the struggle against all forms of injustice and discrimination. At a time when young children were moving to the forefront of politics and the older generation was suffering loss of authority in the political domain, Albertina emerged as the archetypal matriarch, widely regarded as the "mother of the nation".

She was not, however, the only one. Winnie Mandela was also bestowed this mantle by an admiring press and adoring public. Her banishment to Brandfort elevated her to legendary status and her bravery and tenacity were undisputed. Like Albertina, she was an icon of strength and courage who endured terrible suffering and torment at the hands of the apartheid State (Meintjes, 220–225). But there the resemblance ended. Winnie eschewed Albertina's approach of painstaking organisation-building and teamwork in favour of dramatic acts of individual defiance. While consistency and reliability were hallmarks of Albertina's leadership, Winnie was given to bouts of unpredictability that confounded those around her. Her paradoxical nature was reflected in the diametrically different responses of those who knew her. To some she was a kind, loving, generous and loyal friend, while to others she was the devil incarnate. There is no doubt that Winnie was a valuable asset to the liberation movement. She was a hugely attractive figure whose breathtaking beauty was matched by a powerful charisma and sharp mind. Her feisty, impulsive personality appealed to a downtrodden people and even her severest critics could not help but admire her *chutzpah*. With Winnie around, there could never be a moment of boredom. One journalist described her as one of the most extraordinary women in history, comparable only to Helen of Troy and Cleopatra. In a literary sense she is certainly a fascinating character, and the contrast between her and Albertina brings to mind the flamboyant, dramatic Carmen and the dutiful, virtuous Michaela in Bizet's famous opera.

With their contrasting personalities and styles of leadership, Walter Sisulu and Nelson Mandela complemented each other to the benefit of their organisation. Unfortunately, this did not happen with Albertina and Winnie. The two women had never shared a warm relationship, despite the close friendship between their husbands. They had little in common other than the fact that their husbands were ANC leaders in jail for life; and for decades, the rigours of their respective banning orders meant that they rarely saw one another at a time during which they might have been expected to bond.

For the first 20 years of their husbands' imprisonment, both women stuck rigorously to the ANC strategy of presenting a united front and were scrupulously polite to each other. But whatever little relationship they had evaporated when Winnie returned to Soweto after her home in Brandfort was firebombed in 1985. Albertina had been absolutely horrified by Winnie's infamous Munsieville statement "Together, hand in hand, with our boxes of matches and our necklaces, we shall liberate this country" (Sampson 2000, 349), and she felt compelled to take immediate, but private action.

Winnie's speech had been made at a UDF meeting, so through the channels of the local convent, Albertina summoned Nomvula Makonyane, a Krugersdorp activist, whose husband Serge had translated Winnie's words. She made it crystal clear that "nothing of that nature must happen in and around Krugersdorp". Albertina believed that it was the duty of leaders of the liberation movement to curb the violent tendencies of its youthful constituency, not encourage them. Winnie, on the other hand, was the consummate populist who generally told the audience what they wanted to hear. Albertina objected to the statement not so much because it was politically unwise, but because she found it morally repugnant. She was not impressed by Winnie's subsequent claim that she had been misquoted. Meanwhile, the police promptly detained Serge Makonyane for three months, telling him he faced charges of incitement and instigation, simply for translating Winnie's speech. Winnie, however, was never arrested for making it, which perhaps points to the opportunism of the security police.

Albertina became increasingly concerned over reports about the Mandela Football Club soon after its formation in 1986. Anxious parents found their way to her doorstep to complain that their children were being coerced into joining the club. As reports of violent beatings and kidnapping mounted, Albertina passed on the reports, through carefully chosen emissaries, to the ANC in Lusaka. She was disappointed at the sense of disbelief in the responses from Lusaka, but she could also understand the reason for this. Some of the club's activities were so bizarre as to be unbelievable and to those far removed from the situation, the reports could easily be interpreted as an effort to discredit Winnie. Albertina eventually consulted Priscilla Jana, who advised her to refer complainants to the SACC.

UDF leader and fellow treason trialist Cas Saloojee commented about Albertina: "Mama didn't have the habit of intellectualising and philosophising. She always had the sense of what to do immediately and concretely." Almost without exception, Albertina's UDF colleagues and those who worked with her in women's organisations, remark on her practical approach to organisation and her almost instinctive sense of what to do in any given situation. Yet in the case of the football club, she was in a quandary. She was very clear on how to engage with her enemy, but locking horns with a comrade in the struggle was another matter altogether. She wanted to avoid a public spat with Winnie at all costs because of the damage it would do to the movement, and also to the morale of their husbands in prison. She could not seek Walter's advice because it was not possible to discuss such a sensitive issue in the presence of warders. She also knew that she had no influence whatsoever over Winnie. Albertina came to believe, as did many others in the community, that some members of the football club, especially its self-styled "coach" Jerry Richardson, were police agents planted there to cause mayhem in the community and division within the liberation movement.

Albertina had been relieved when the Mandela Crisis Committee was formed in response to the house-burning debacle. She was optimistic that the problems would be addressed, but the Crisis Committee soon found that matters were far more serious than they had anticipated. The violent activities of the football club continued unabated and, in November, Winnie and the club were implicated in the disappearance of two Orlando West youths, Lolo Sono and Siboniso Tshabalala. Nicodemus Sono reported that Winnie and some club members turned up at his house in a minibus, inside which was his bruised and badly beaten son, Lolo. Nicodemus pleaded with Winnie not to take his son away but she brushed aside his pleas and drove off. Lolo was never seen again. Winnie dismissed Nicodemus Sono's claims as complete fabrication, leaving it to an agonised community to decide who to believe.

Albertina returned from her Cape Town visit to find that the thuggery of the Mandela Football Club had spiralled out of control and several lives were at stake. On 29 December 1988, members of the club abducted four young boys from the Orlando West Methodist Church, on the strength of reports from Xoliswa Falati, the housekeeper at the manse, that the minister, Reverend Paul Verryn, was sexually abusing the boys. The accusation sent shock waves through a community that had deep respect for Reverend Verryn, and regarded the manse as a place of safety and refuge for homeless boys, many of whom were seeking refuge from political unrest in their home areas. Responding to reports that the abductees had been taken to the back rooms of Winnie's house where they were accused of being spies and savagely beaten, Crisis Committee members made several visits to Winnie to secure the release of the boys. At first, she denied that the youths were at her home but later claimed they were being held to protect them from the alleged homosexual advances of Verryn. One of the kidnap victims, Kenny Kgase, escaped and fled to the Methodist Church, where he reported that he and the other boys were being held against their will and that Stompie Seipei, one of their number, had disappeared.

By this time, the anti-apartheid alliance, the ANC in exile, and Mandela himself, were all frantic. Winnie and her soccer club had become a public relations triumph for the apartheid government, who were gleeful at her blunders; there was widespread community concern for the fate of the boys involved; and politically, Winnie was flagrantly defying the code of conduct that demanded that those in the struggle remain accountable to the community and loyal to their leadership. Mandela himself sent increasingly urgent instructions to disband the club, as did the Crisis Committee. Winnie only allowed the release of the remaining boys, Pelo Megwe and Thabiso Mono, after intervention from Oliver Tambo and Nelson Mandela themselves (Meredith, 380; Sampson 2000, 379). At a meeting called by the Crisis Committee, about 150 community and church leaders heard from the two released youths how they had been abducted and assaulted by Winnie and the club members. Another youth, Katiza Cebekhulu, who had days earlier defected from the football club, supported their account and claimed to have participated in the beatings himself. All three boys believed that Stompie was dead.

Amid the furore about the fate of Stompie, Albertina's life was convulsed by a tragedy that would cast a long shadow for many years to come. At about 4pm on Friday, 27 January 1989, two young men entered Dr Asvat's Rockville surgery. One of them approached Albertina, then handling reception duties, and said he needed medical attention. He gave his name as Mandla Nkwanyana, and went into the waiting room. However, he then left, apparently to buy cigarettes, before returning. A little later, he entered the consulting room. Albertina heard Abu ask: "Are you Mandla?" The reply was "Yes". Next she heard a shot, a scream, and another shot. She called out, but there was no response. She then ran to the back door and screamed for help. When she returned, she saw the men fleeing. She then found the doctor lying dead on the floor of the consulting room (*Business Day*, 19/10/99). Responding to Albertina's cries, Thandi Shabalala, a neighbour, arrived on the scene to find Abu Asvat on the floor and Albertina weeping. She called the police. The post-mortem later revealed that Abu Asvat had been shot twice in the chest at point-blank range with a 9-mm pistol.

How to describe the impact of Abu Asvat's murder? Devastation, disbelief, shock, grief. These words do not even begin to capture the feelings of his wife, Zohra, his daughter Hasina, his sons Sulaiiman and Aker, their family and friends, and the thousands of homeless people bereft of a man who had fought tirelessly for their rights. Albertina was absolutely shattered. Family members recall that they had never before seen her so distraught. She had never wept publicly, not through the years of detentions, trials, bannings and separation from her husband and children, but this time even she could not keep to her code of hiding her grief in public and *The Sowetan* published a rare photograph of her weeping at Abu's funeral. When Sheila Sisulu called Lusaka to inform Max and me of the tragedy, we felt enveloped by a cloud of grief and misery. Sheila said she would never forget Zohra's anguished lament – "my children are so young, my children are so young!" I recalled Abu's kindness to me when I had visited his surgery with my sick child and I wept at the terrible irony that this gentlest of souls had to meet his end in such a violent manner.

As news of the assassination spread, mourners from all walks of life flocked to the Asvat home in Lenasia in a massive outpouring of grief. Tributes poured in from a range of organisations, unions and political groupings. Abu Asvat was hailed as one of the few black political figures who had successfully straddled the divide between the Charterist and Black Consciousness political camps, and between the African and Indian communities. The "people's doctor", as he was fondly referred to, was buried at Avalon cemetery the day after his assassination, in one of the largest funerals ever held in Lenasia.

From the outset, the police implied that robbery was a motive for the crime because R135 had been taken from a drawer, but Albertina shared the widely held view that the murder was politically motivated. Political assassinations of anti-apartheid activists were not uncommon and there was certainly bad blood between Abu and the Soweto Council. Moreover there had been two previous attempts on Abu's life. At the height of the AZAPO/UDF conflict, two knife-wielding men had attacked Abu. The attackers fled when Albertina ran out and called for help (*City Press*, 6/3/88). Abu had hailed Albertina for saving his life and they had suspected that the "dirty tricks" department of the security police were behind the attempt.

In the light of previous attacks, the Asvat family may well have continued to suspect the security police if the inexplicable behaviour of Winnie Mandela had not turned their suspicions in an entirely new direction. The day after paying her respects at the Asvat home, she gave a press interview in which she claimed that Abu had been murdered because he was the only medical professional who would have been able to confirm that the boys in the kidnap drama had been sexually abused (*The Cape Times*, 30/1/89).

Winnie even implied in a television interview that there had been a cover-up by the Methodist Church (Meredith, 382). It emerged that Abu had indeed examined Cebekhulu at his surgery and Stompie at Winnie's house and had made it plain that he found no such evidence. Abu Asvat was clearly troubled and anxious in the days leading up to the murder, and the family received information that his state of agitation was linked to his refusal to confirm the claims of sexual abuse and his insistence that Stompie should be taken to hospital (Interviews, Zohra and Ebrahim Asvat).

Still traumatised by the death of Abu Asvat, Albertina was sickened by this turn of events and whatever little respect she had for Winnie evaporated completely. Privately she dissociated herself from anything to do with Winnie, and publicly she maintained a dignified silence – a silence she would pay a heavy price for years later. The estrangement of the two women was complete. Distance herself she might, but Albertina could not remain unaffected by the actions of the club.

On 15 February, the body of a teenage boy that had been lying in the mortuary since the first week of January was identified as that of Stompie Seipei. Jerry Richardson and other club members were arrested for the murder. On 16 February, the UDF and COSATU both cut their losses and formally disassociated themselves from Winnie and her activities. Murphy Morobe, speaking on behalf of the Mass Democratic Movement (the newly formed coalition of the UDF, COSATU and other anti-apartheid organisations), expressed outrage at Winnie's complicity in the abduction and assault of Stompie. The ANC censured her severely, but "offered a hand to her", urging her to "place herself under the discipline of the movement". A *New Nation* editorial demanded that "any structure that claims to represent our leaders MUST submit itself to the discipline of the people" (16/2/89).

In what was to be the next of many twists, Abu Asvat's murderers were swiftly apprehended. Twenty-one-year-old Zakhele Mbatha and 20-year-old Thulani Dlamini told a friend about the killing and admitted they were looking for a "hideout", as Johannesburg was now "too hot". The friend then contacted the police, and the pair were subsequently arrested. Both were found guilty and initially sentenced to death in the Rand Supreme Court. However, the Asvat family pleaded for clemency, claiming that neither they nor the murdered man believed in capital punishment. According to Dr Asvat's brother, Ebrahim, the entire family was satisfied that the perpetrators of the crime had been brought to book, but opposed the death sentence. "We do not believe anybody has the right to take another person's life, not the State or any other person. Capital punishment or taking another's life is a violation of basic human rights. And I know my late brother felt the same way ... But we still have our doubts that their motive was robbery. There must have been some other motive" (*Sunday Times*, 5/11/89).

Many remained equally puzzled. The perpetrators had been swiftly caught, tried and sentenced, an extremely unusual occurrence in cases of political assassination. Yet the State insisted that the motive for the murder had been petty theft. Police claimed to have investigated the alleged connection between the murder and the Mandela Football Club, with no substantive results. However, at the end of the trial, the State noted that it would continue this line of investigation.

AZAPO representatives rejected the finding of the court that the crime was simply a case of murder and robbery. The Asvat family was equally disbelieving. "Certain things just do not add up," said Dr Ebrahim Asvat. "If robbery was the motive, why did they leave more money than they took?" The perpetrators had taken R135 from a drawer in the surgery, but the police recovered R190 in notes in the doctor's wallet and R100 in coins strewn over the floor in the consulting room. Ebrahim Asvat also queried why the robbers had fired immediately – before taking any money from the consulting room.

Another perplexing feature of the murder and robbery theory was that if Mbatha and Dlamini wanted to "make money", as Mbatha's statement indicated, why had they chosen a doctor's surgery? There was a shop around the corner from the surgery – where Mbatha claimed he bought cigarettes after furnishing Albertina with his particulars. Both killers gave inconsistent alibis on the witness stand and the judge, Justice R Solomon, said they were "lying witnesses". According to AZAPO, "It was obvious that the two men were covering up something – it could be information related to individuals or organisations." Underlying this sentiment was the suspicion that Dlamini and Mbatha were hired killers. But even as the imposition of the ultimate sentence hung over them, Mbatha said: "I don't have anything to say because I don't know this offence I did not commit" (*Weekly Mail*, 10/11/89).

In September 1991, Dlamini was successful in his appeal against his death sentence. The Appeal Court in Bloemfontein substituted imprisonment of 20 years, plus eight years for another robbery. Mr Justice Nicholas, acting judge of appeal, said it was clearly proved that Dlamini had had the intention to kill Asvat, and that he had not established any extenuating circumstances. The trial judge – as he was obliged to do under the Criminal Procedure Act at the time – therefore sentenced him to death. However, under the 1990 Criminal Procedure Amendment Act, judges could impose the death sentence only if satisfied that the sentence of death was the "proper" sentence (*The Sowetan*, 25/9/91).

The police continued to investigate the Stompie case, but it would be years before a trial would take place, and by that time the political context would be completely different. Meanwhile all those affected by the traumatic events surrounding Dr Asvat's murder tried to pick up the pieces of their lives. Albertina had to adapt to the loss of her job and income, but most of all she missed the fellowship of her sympathetic employer.

Her first visit to Walter after the tragic event was a stressful one. It was impossible to tell him the whole story with a prison warder standing within earshot. Walter's normally buoyant spirits were considerably dampened; for him, the idea that Winnie could be implicated in the kidnapping and murder of children was too preposterous to imagine. He expressed his unhappiness in a letter to his friend Connie Njongwe:

Let me say your letter has been a source of comfort and inspiration especially in stormy days such as these. I am referring to a number of things that have suddenly sprung up during this period. As far as Ntsiki [Albertina] is concerned, she was lucky to escape. In that dangerous situation anything was possible. But she was simply devastated by the whole affair. As she said herself "It was like seeing my own son being murdered in front of my own eyes." Indeed she was very fond of the young Dr Asvat ... She saw me two weeks after the funeral and had not completely recovered from the shock.

I have spoken of storm in this period. I was really referring to great upheavals or convulsions in Soweto. I do not even have an appropriate description of these events but they are devastating to say the least. The media was too vicious ... It was an opportunity to attack the whole democratic movement to the bitterest end. It was more sickening than anything I can think of.

We can tell you no more than what we read in the press. It has been the most unfortunate incident of all. Well imagine what all this meant to Nelson. Our thoughts naturally go to him. Though he is more informed than us as he would be given both sides, but the fact that he is isolated aggravates his position. At least, we can share views with each other on various aspects of the problem. In the whole affair we are of course guided by the movement internally and externally in its statements (10/3/89).

To Sikosi Mjali he wrote:

The last few months were very strange to say the least. Firstly the media created an unprecedented excitement of expectations about our release and fixed even the date for such a release. Then secondly whilst this was dying out sudden great upheavals were sprung on us in Soweto. These affected not only us in prison but the whole movement, both here and abroad. The system which has long awaited such an opportunity left no stone unturned.... It was particularly hard on Winnie. We were really disturbed. Whatever the case, we are steeled. We have weathered the storms, even here, *Lududuma Ligqithe* — We shall overcome (10/3/1989).

From 23 January 1989, Walter spent 10 days in Tygerberg Hospital for an eye operation. The media got wind of the story and newspaper reports suggested he was going blind. An irritated Albertina denied the reports, saying he had had a cataract removed, a follow-up to a similar operation in the previous year (*The Sowetan*, 8/2/89; *City Press*, 5/2/89).

Media speculation that he would be released came to nothing, and he was taken back to Pollsmoor on his discharge. He informed his family that the operation had been successful, his vision had improved dramatically and that it would improve even more with new glasses. He commented that the treatment he received was very good, "from matrons to student nurses" (Letter to Beryl Simelane, 14/2/89).

Walter also received get-well wishes from Jongi on Robben Island:

I am very happy to learn that your eye operation was successful. Such operations are always disturbing and as they are very complicated, they always make me worried, moreover when I think of your age. Fortunately, you are quite a strong old man. People here always tell me how strong you used to be when you were still here, so that is one of the things which pushes me to the gymnasium, so as to keep me strong and fit. They should not look at me and say "Hey, you look very much unlike your old man." In any case Tata, please keep strong.

Jongi's account of the Easter festivities on Robben Island rekindled old memories for Walter: "On Saturday, B Section, E Section and F Section were packed in the hall listening to our own music. Our own musicians were playing various types of music. At that time, D Section was playing soccer against E Section. Then today, as it is an Easter Monday, our musicians were playing for D and E Sections, while F and G Sections were combined playing soccer. It was youth against the old ones, i.e. those who are above thirty are referred to as old ones. Everything was so beautiful" (April 1989).

Also in January, Walter, Kathrada, Mlangeni and Mhlaba had another visit with Mandela at Victor Verster where they discussed the memorandum that Mandela had drafted to send PW Botha. The memorandum repeated most of the points covered in discussions with "The Team", but Mandela wanted to drive the message home to the State President himself (Mandela, 535). Before the memorandum could be sent, PW Botha suffered a stroke, which put him out of action for several weeks. The stroke forced Botha to reduce his workload by resigning as head of the National Party. The Rivonia prisoners, who were watching the new developments with interest, were not particularly encouraged when Frederick Willem de Klerk, the Minister of Education and former Transvaal NP leader, became the new NP chief. While FW de Klerk was not part of PW Botha's inner circle of military and intelligence chiefs, he was known as a conservative who had actually opposed many of PW's reforms (Sampson 2000, 386).

In one of those fortuitous coincidences of history, FW de Klerk's brother Wimpie had joined the secret ANC-Afrikaner talks at Mells Park in August 1988. Wimpie de Klerk had a political outlook that was very different to his brother's and he became an ardent member of the Democratic Party when it was formed in April 1989 as a result of the amalgamation of the three white political parties – the Progressive Federal Party, the National Democratic Movement and the Independent Party – to the left of the NP. Their divergent political views did not mar their familial relation and Wimpie de Klerk kept his brother updated about the Mells Park process (Harvey, 164). Wimpie was an enthusiastic participant in the secret talks, which he saw as a major bridge-building exercise between the NP Afrikaners and the ANC, and his diary provides a succinct summary of the substance of the secret talks:

> Our agendas are very concrete and direct: on Mandela's release and ANC undertakings in that connection; on armed struggle and the possible suspension of it by the ANC; on the various steps that must be taken before pre-negotiation talks with the government can take place; on constitutional issues such as a transitional government; concrete stumbling blocks and the exploration of compromises to get out of deadlocks; on sanctions; on ANC thinking on all kinds of South African political issues and on government thinking on those self-same issues (Harvey, 159; Sparks 1995, 83).

Despite the positive spirit that prevailed at Mells Park, by the end of 1988 it had become clear that they were rehashing the same old arguments and the process was not going forward. It became obvious to the ANC leaders that the Afrikaners they were talking to were disaffected elements who did not have the power to move PW Botha from his entrenched position (Harvey, 155). The President was content to monitor the talks, but not prepared to concede to any of the basic demands that would create a climate conducive to negotiations. Mandela had not been released, and the hawks in the security establishment were continuing to call the shots. In South Africa, Mandela was experiencing the same frustration. His discussions with the government seemed to have reached a dead-end, and he had made little headway in his demands for the release of his colleagues and a meeting with the President.

There was, however, a brief flicker of hope regarding Walter's release. On the morning of 15 March, Walter was taking his morning exercise on his bicycle as usual when Kathrada joked "Beware the Ides of March" because "while we didn't expect a tragedy analogous to that of Julius Caesar, the day was nevertheless pregnant with possibilities" (Kathrada, 256). Barely half an hour later, Walter was taken to the Commanding Officer who told him that he was being taken to

Victor Verster to see Mandela. Walter told him that he welcomed the idea of visiting Mandela but would prefer to be accompanied by his colleagues. The Commanding Officer insisted that he go alone. On arrival at Victor Verster, Mandela explained that he had been asked by the Commissioner of Prisons, General Willemse, to inform Walter that he would be moved from the cells he shared with his colleagues to the ground-floor cells that Mandela had occupied before he had been transferred. Willemse had told Mandela that he was not at that stage in a position to give reasons for Walter's transfer. Willemse had wanted Mandela to reassure Walter that the move was not an attempt to isolate him. Walter told Mandela that he would not resist the move, but protested that he should at least be told the reasons.

When Walter did not return after a few hours, Kathrada noted that they "promptly resorted to the favourite prisoner's pastime; viz, speculation" (Kathrada, 256). When Walter did finally get back to Pollsmoor that afternoon, his belongings were moved to the quarters that had formerly been occupied by Mandela. The new quarters were very comfortable by prison standards, with one cell for exercise and one for studying, but Walter was not happy about the separation from his colleagues. In a letter to Lindi he wrote: "I however do not intend to make an issue out of this matter at this stage, but I will watch the developments. I am as it were trying to adjust myself. Your mother was so agitated about my separation from the others, I had to calm her down" (March 1989).

Albertina was especially upset about the separation from Kathrada, who monitored Walter's health, ensured he had the right medication, and read the Afrikaans papers to him. Kathrada was so concerned about Walter being locked up alone that he wrote a long letter of complaint to the prison authorities. who responded by deploying two warders to Walter's quarters at night. Kathrada was mortified: "By complaining I had actually made things worse for him. Now he was saddled with these two young chaps who hogged the television, and of course, Tata was too soft-hearted to tell them to change the channel when he wanted to watch the news or some other pro-gramme!" (Interview, Ahmed Kathrada). However, Walter appreciated the efforts of his comrade and in a letter to Kathrada's niece Zohra, he said: "You no doubt know by now that Kathy and I have been separated after 25 years. I am now where Nelson was before he went to Paarl. As far as reasons why, we can only guess or speculate. I am pleased to tell you that I am surprisingly well in my situation ... It is true that Kathy was particularly disturbed by my removal and told the authorities in so many words. He is one person who knows better than anyone about my health problems. Some of his representations to the authorities went a long way to ease my position" (2 July 1989). To Joe Mhlaba, the son of Raymond Mhlaba, he wrote: "The move threw me com-pletely out of gear and it took time before I regained my bearings. We are well and watching the developments with interest and confidence" (15/8/1989). To his granddaughter Zama, he said: "We are all confident that the question of coming home is on the cards, but as far as timing is con-cerned, we shall just have to have patience" (30/5/89).

When Mandela had been admitted to hospital the previous year, Kathrada had written to a friend about the "wave of speculation about his 'early' release which, theoretically at least, would have bearing on the position of the rest of us, especially my cellmate, Walter Sisulu, who is 76. My own view, however, is that there will be no releases – our adversaries still want their pound of flesh" (Kathrada, 243).

Kathrada was not far off the mark in his assessment. Prison files reveal that Walter was on the verge of being released in March. The Prisons Department had prepared psychological profiles on him, and his planned release had been approved by almost every government department, includ-ing Justice and Foreign Affairs. However, elements in the security establishment objected and the release was postponed to August or September ( *New Nation*, 20/10/89).

On 15 June 1989, Walter was allowed another visit to Mandela at Victor Verster. He was treated to a sumptuous meal prepared by Mandela's warder-cum-cook. Mandela gave him a glass of what he thought was the most delicious drink he had ever tasted in his life. As he sipped it, he felt he was becoming light-headed. "I was convinced that Madiba had given me champagne and I was getting drunk!" Mandela assured him that the drink was only a sparkling apple juice called Appletiser. Walter was not convinced, because the more he drank, the more light-headed he felt. He described the visit to Lindi, saying he found Mandela "quite fit and full of confidence as usual, but he says it is unlikely that they will release him this year. He was however concerned that I have not yet been released, but I am quite hopeful about the situation" (2/7/89).

PW Botha received Mandela's memorandum in March 1989. "Here for the first time since Verwoerd spurned Mandela's letter asking for a national convention 28 years before, was a concrete ANC offer to negotiate a peaceful settlement of South Africa's bitter conflict, reversing the organisation's commitment to the revolutionary overthrow of white minority rule" (Sparks 1995, 53). Soon after receiving the memorandum, Botha agreed to see Mandela. Botha's fear of unsettling his right-wing constituency dictated that the meeting be held in utmost secrecy. An apprehensive Mandela, immaculately turned out in a new suit provided by the Prisons Department, was smuggled into the President's office on 5 July. Aware of Botha's difficult temperament, which had apparently been exacerbated by his stroke, Mandela had resolved that "if he acted in that finger-wagging manner with me, I would inform him that I found such behaviour unacceptable, and I would stand up and adjourn the meeting" (Mandela, 529). Those present at the meeting – Niel Barnard, General Willemse and Kobie Coetsee – were spared the drama of such an occurrence, and the encounter between the two larger-than-life figures was a surprisingly cordial one. Perhaps Mandela's old-fashioned courtesy struck a chord with PW, and the two men chatted amicably about South African history and culture. The meeting was intended more as an ice-breaking exercise than a discussion of substantive issues (Mandela, 539; Sparks 1995, 56; Sampson 2000, 392; Meredith, 392).

The only tense moment came towards the end of the meeting when Mandela took advantage of the occasion to ask the President for the release of political prisoners. Botha said he could not oblige. Mandela then pressed for the release of Walter Sisulu on compassionate grounds. Botha ducked the issue by referring the matter to Niel Barnard. Mandela tried to follow up with Barnard on the drive back to the prison. He was furious when Barnard told him the political climate was not right for the release of Sisulu, and told him imperiously that he [Barnard] was "a civil servant who should carry out the President's instructions, not question them" (Sparks 1995, 56).

July was a month of reunions for Mandela. Winnie, his children and his grandchildren congregated at Victor Verster to celebrate his 71st birthday (Sampson 2000, 392). Four days earlier, he had had the opportunity to brief his colleagues about his meeting with PW Botha. Wilton Mkwayi came to Victor Verster with the Pollsmoor group. In March he had been hospitalised for a back operation, after which he had been transferred to Walter's old cell in Pollsmoor. Elias Motsoaledi was brought over from Robben Island. Walter called it a "marathon reunion" as all the Rivonia Trialists who had been imprisoned on Robben Island were present, with the exception of Govan Mbeki, who had visited two weeks earlier. Mandela was able to give them a full account of his discussions with the government and the events leading up to the Botha meeting (Letter to Zwelakhe Sisulu, 16/7/89; Letter to Elinor Sisulu, 16/7/89). It was also a unique occasion because for the first time they were all able to dispense with prison garb and wear brand-new suits of their choice.

In the same month, Walter also had a long-distance reunion with Gerald. At my first meeting with him in Pollsmoor, Walter had asked about Gerald and his family, and he mentioned him constantly in our correspondence. Eventually he sent me a letter for Gerald, which I forwarded to Kitwe. "I have written to Gerald through Elinor," he told Beryl. "I should have done so long ago. Though it was his duty to have taken the initiative because quite a lot happened to him over the years. He got married, had children who are much grown up now, yet there was never a direct communication between us. We are all guilty of negligence in this matter. Let us hope, however, this would mean a beginning" (29/5/89).

He was deeply moved by Gerald's response: "I must say that receiving your letter yesterday really overwhelmed me. We all broke down. The last time I read your letter was when you were in the 'Fort', when I was in Europe. I forwarded the letter to Max who was further north. That was about 27 years ago. I have since grown to be quite a responsible man. I am now 45 or will be on 26 December. I think a lot about you. You are always in my presence. Don't forget you brought me up. I'll always think about the old days – Kliptown, Makosa House, Tata Nel, Mama and Lungi." Gerald gave news of his wife Jasoda (Jasu), to whom he had been married for nearly 21 years, his eldest son Walden and his daughter Beryl. He also alluded to his departure from the ANC: "I would imagine that this is not the forum to discuss those matters ... There were many hurtful times during those periods, but that's life. You've got to keep on forging ahead. A 21-gun salute to you for your perseverance." Finally he wrote: "There is so much I'd like to say, but I'm so excited my mind goes blank. In my following letters I will calm down and write about other issues" (2/7/89).

"I must really thank you ever so much for your very excellent letter," responded Walter. "It has indeed proved to me that you have matured as you say. It has enabled me to peep through your windows satisfactorily. I must also thank you for your lively birthday message. We are pleased to get the photo of such a bright young chap, Walden. I hope and wish that both these kids are making some progress in whatever they do. Tell them Grandpa loves them very much, and hopes to see them someday soon."

In the first week of June 1989 Albertina received a visit from the police. They came bearing renewed restriction orders issued in conjunction with the renewal of the State of Emergency for the fourth year in succession (*New York Times*, 25/6/89). The emergency had however lost its bite in the face of unrelenting international pressure and a revival of popular protest at the beginning of 1989. In January, a hunger strike by female detainees in the Northern Transvaal spread like wildfire in prison and detention centres throughout the country. The strikers challenged the government to either release or charge them. On 9 February, the lawyers representing the detainees embarked on a 24-hour hunger strike in sympathy with their clients (Race Relations Survey, 1988). By April 1989, the strike action forced the Minister of Law and Order to release 900 detainees, many of them UDF leaders (Van Kessel, 43). The UDF and COSATU had meanwhile regrouped under the rubric of the Mass Democratic Movement (MDM). The MDM had no constitution, no policy guidelines, no elected leadership and no address (Van Kessel, 43). It was difficult for the State to take action against such a nebulous entity.

It was a sign of the changing times that the Soviet Union sent a diplomatic mission to South Africa for the first time since the two countries broke off diplomatic relations in 1956. Perestroika in the Soviet Union meant that the Pretoria regime could no longer invoke the Communist bogeyman, and in a move that would have been unimaginable just a decade earlier, the Soviet Union actively encouraged a negotiated settlement in South Africa. The long overdue winds of change were also beginning to blow for the Sisulu family. Despite his restrictions, Zwelakhe was issued with a passport to travel to the United States in May for a reunion of Nieman fellows in Cambridge. Asked about the changes in the southern African region, he said: "There is no question in my mind that what we're seeing in Angola and Namibia is due in large part to the flight of American capital from South Africa" (*New York Times*, 25/6/89). During his month-long trip, he also visited the Soviet Union and Cuba. Sheila was also finally given a passport. In May, Max and I met with her at the ILO-sponsored meeting organised by the ANC Department of Manpower Development, one of the many meetings held in Harare that brought together activists from "home" and exile to deliberate and plan for a New South Africa.

Meanwhile, the new US administration under George Bush was showing an interest in facilitating the move towards a negotiated settlement in South Africa. Herman Cohen, the new Secretary of State for Africa, who had described apartheid as a "human rights catastrophe", publicly committed himself to equal political rights for all South Africans. In May President Bush met with Archbishop Tutu, Reverend Beyers Naudé and Reverend Alan Boesak (Sampson 2000, 388). In the same month Edward Perkins, the US ambassador to Pretoria, delivered to Albertina a letter from President Bush in which the latter declared: "Your record of principled, nonviolent opposition to apartheid is an inspiration to many Americans who, like me, are deeply concerned about the future of South Africa. I would be grateful if you could come, at your convenience, to meet with me and ... members of my Administration to discuss the situation in your country." He added that the US Ambassador to South Africa would help her to get a passport and make travel arrangements, details that went some way to throwing down a gauntlet to the South African government (Letter from the White House, 11/5/89). The government, anxious to avoid further large-scale sanctions by the powerful Western nations, was faced with an awkward choice – did it keep an elderly grandmother under effective house arrest while the rest of the world fêted her, or did it allow her to travel abroad, knowing that if it did so, she would denounce apartheid at every step?

As soon as she received the invitation, Albertina wrote to tell Walter, who responded on 29 May:

I really thank you for your exciting letter with its surprising contents. Whatever reservations and criticism we have against the reactionary policies of the Republican Party, of which Bush is a symbol, an invitation from the President of the USA has great significance.

The impact of such an invitation is perhaps more than we could imagine.

I am confident they will find it difficult to refuse you a passport on an invitation from such a distinguished personality as President Bush, but with these people, anything is possible.

Albertina had already received another such invitation in February, in the form of a personal letter from Danielle Mitterrand (French President François Mitterrand's wife and a human rights activist in her own right). Mitterrand informed her that she had been chosen by the International Federation of Human Rights as one of 10 women to be honoured for their fight for human rights at a celebration on the occasion of the Bicentenary of the French Revolution. She was invited to Paris in June to address world delegates on the human rights scenario in South Africa (Letter from the Foundation Danielle Mitterrand, 20/2/89, translated by the French Embassy in South Africa).

So at the same time as the South African government was concerned at the very least to appear to be willing to negotiate and to project a reasonable, humane image in the global marketplace, international heads of state were requesting the privilege of an interview with Albertina, and organisations worldwide were clamouring to be allowed to honour her. The upshot was that having gained a special passport valid only for 31 days, Albertina set off on her first ever overseas trip on 16 June 1989, the 13th anniversary of the Soweto uprising. She was accompanied by her FEDSAW comrades, Sister Bernard Ncube and Jessie Duarte. Later, UDF leaders Curnick Ndlovu, Azar Cachalia and Titus Mafolo would join the party on the American leg of the trip.

The main objectives of the trip were to call for sanctions against the apartheid government; to draw global attention to human rights abuses, in particular, persecution of anti-apartheid activists in the form of assassinations, detentions, bombings and bannings; to fight for the legal right for democratic and peaceful organisations to operate; and to inform the West about the state of affairs in apartheid South Africa (Box AL2431: Records of the UDF 1983–1991, South African History Association Trust).

Albertina and her colleagues visited four countries: Sweden, France, the United Kingdom and the United States. In most of the meetings in all four countries, two issues kept cropping up: that of sanctions, and that of De Klerk's leadership. It was clear that the West was seeking internal anti-apartheid feedback on whether the demise of apartheid was imminent now that De Klerk was in the saddle. The delegation stuck to the party line, insisting that sanctions were an appropriate and necessary step, and that De Klerk was not necessarily interested in the welfare of the vast majority of South Africans, but in preserving the political and economic status of those in power.

In Sweden, Albertina met with the Prime Minister, Ingvar Carlson, and the Ministers for Foreign Affairs (Sten Anderson) and International Development (Lena Hjelm Wallen), as well as a host of other dignitaries and politicians. She also addressed the Socialist Women's International conference, where her speech was warmly received. The visit garnered a lot of media attention, and the delegation found that, in general, the Swedes were well informed about the situation in South Africa. There were no contentious political issues to be raised or thrashed out, as the Swedish government openly supported the ANC and UDF calls for comprehensive sanctions. The visit was pleasant and affirming, as was the trip to France. Here Albertina met with both the Mitterrands, and the delegation was able to address the President of the French Parliament. Here, there was perhaps a more dubious response to the call for sanctions, but the gala presentation to Albertina was a high point.

In the UK, the delegation spent time at the Anti-apartheid Movement's headquarters, meeting with Neil Kinnock and other members of the Labour Party (who committed themselves to sanctions should they gain power – in 1989, not a particularly immediate prospect), as well as religious organisations and leaders. Albertina addressed a rally held in London to protest against Thatcher's imminent meeting with De Klerk. She pulled no punches, stating that "[De Klerk] needs more money, he needs more loans from your banks, to keep apartheid going – to pay the army and buy arms. [He] … is asking Western countries to help the Nats stay in power" (20/6/1989).

Then it was on to meet the "big guns" across the Atlantic. If the pace had been hectic before, here it was a whirlwind. The delegation met a veritable Who's Who in American politics – leaders, ministers, civil rights activists, journalists and opinion-makers – from the President, George Bush, to former President Jimmy Carter, to Jesse Jackson, to Coretta Scott King, Martin Luther King's widow. On three successive days, the UDF group met with President Bush, James Baker (Secretary of State) and Robin Cohen, Under-Secretary of State for African Affairs, as well as Congressman Gray, leader of the majority in the house. All were noncommittal on the issue of sanctions, but it was clear that the Bush regime was interested in how the ANC and the UDF would approach the possibility of negotiations with the apartheid government – what their conditions and terms would be. Senior politicians were also keen to gauge how the black majority saw De Klerk, and whether he represented hope for an imminent end to conflict in the region.

At the White House meeting on 2 July, Albertina and her delegation appealed to President Bush to apply maximum pressure on the South African government to create conditions for free political activity, and reiterated the UDF's call for comprehensive and mandatory sanctions against South Africa. Bush listened intently to Albertina's account of repression in South Africa, and he seemed outraged by the detention of young children. He undertook to work with other major Western powers to develop programmes aimed at resolving the political impasse created by apartheid.

Albertina hailed the meeting as a milestone in the struggle against apartheid; it was the first time an internal anti-apartheid organisation had been invited to the White House. In a statement released by the White House, Bush said: "Sisulu personifies the struggle for human rights and human dignity. Her presence here is an inspiration to us all." A statement released by the United States Information Service in Pretoria said that after his meeting with Albertina Sisulu, Bush promised to step up assistance to black South Africans for education, community development, employment, housing and human rights. Bush was quoted as saying that "apartheid is wrong and must end" (*The Sowetan*, 4/7/89).

The UDF provided a graphic account of human rights abuses in South Africa, not just to influential politicians, but also to the UN, the Carter Foundation and the Ford Foundation, as well as the *Washington Post* and *New York Times*. The delegation also lobbied for support for the planned Conference for a Democratic South Africa scheduled to be held later that year.

After the meeting with President Bush, Margaret Thatcher, who had showed no interest in meeting Albertina and her delegation, decided that she would meet them after all on their return to London en route to South Africa. There was speculation that her decision may have been influenced by PW Botha's 5 July meeting with Mandela. The meeting, which took place at No. 10 Downing Street on 12 July, was historic in that it was the first time a British Prime Minister had met with internal representatives of the South African majority since Sol Plaatje and his ANC delegation had met Lloyd George in 1919 (Seekings, 245). It was also extremely significant that Thatcher, who had always leaned towards the "terrorist" judgement of the ANC, should meet with supporters and members of an opposition movement she had previously either ignored or opposed. The occasion signified the newly elevated status of the MDM and ANC (Seekings, 245).

While it was not to be expected that the Tories would give way on the issue of sanctions (which they strongly opposed), there were nevertheless some interesting implications. It was made clear to Thatcher – who had always taken the line that the ANC should renounce violence – that there could be no question of imposing conditions for negotiation on the ANC without establishing similar conditions on the apartheid regime. According to Azar Cachalia, the meeting with Thatcher differed from the one with the US president in that "Thatcher lectured while Bush had listened". Albertina did not warm to Margaret Thatcher at all, and she felt that the British Prime Minister was not open to understanding the suffering of black South Africans. For Albertina, the most positive feature of the meeting was Thatcher's statement that she expected Mandela, Sisulu and Oscar Mpetha to be released after South Africa's whites-only elections in September.

After the Thatcher meeting, the delegation briefed Sir Shridath Ramphal, Secretary-General of the Commonwealth – whose members often found themselves diametrically opposed to Thatcher on the question of South Africa. There was valuable consultation on the likely position Thatcher would take apropos de Klerk at the next Commonwealth conference in Kuala Lumpur. It was meetings like this that afforded the UDF – an organisation barely able to operate legitimately at home – the opportunity to make and plan strategy in an international environment.

The schedule, which ranged from meetings with heads of state to morale-boosting contacts with activists in exile, and included interviews, report-backs, press meetings and gala occasions, was gruelling. The delegation members had to remain diligent and entirely focused on their political mission. One of the poignant aspects of these first trips by activists who had previously been banned, restricted or jailed, was that little time was allowed for private personal reunions with family members who had spent years, sometimes decades, in exile. Lindi, who was still in England completing her PhD, was ecstatic at the thought of seeing her mother for the first time since she had gone into exile 12 years earlier. Yet she was to find that no accommodation had been made for her in Albertina's packed schedule. She had to follow her mother from meeting to meeting, snatching the odd moment together en route. Meanwhile Max was pacing around our Lusaka home, unable to understand why his mother didn't call him. He suffered a serious case of sibling rivalry, complaining that Lindi was "keeping Mama to herself!" But the truth was that Albertina barely had time to eat and sleep, much less indulge in the luxury of personal phone calls that, for once, would not be bugged.

Albertina finally managed to spend some time with Lindi towards the tail end of her visit and Lindi provided a detailed report to her father in Pollsmoor:

*Tata wam othandekayo [kakhulu]*, 'My dear father whom I love [very much]'
These days I'm never sure what your address is or will be. We've been hearing so many rumours out here. Anyway, whatever the outcome, I wish I could be there.
Mama is presently in the USA. Seeing her was quite beyond anything I can describe. I'm still pinching myself to make sure that I'm awake, that it is not all just a dream. She looks so young and healthy. It's remarkable! She is taking everything in her stride and is impressed with the friendship of the people she has met. So far she seems particularly impressed with the Swedish people she

met, which included the Prime Minister there. Hey, wethu Tata kutheni umkakho eswenka kangaka nje? Akasemhle! I think we have to start buying you clothes now otherwise you will look like *umatshingilane* next to her ... Anyway, mandingaziqibi, she'll have lots to tell you ...

Vuyo was so excited to see her granny, she kept asking me "Is that my granny?" and "Do the other people know she is my granny?"

PS. Mama returned from seeing Bush, Jesse Jackson, Carter etc. She came back on a Tuesday evening and had an appointment with Margaret Thatcher on the following day – Wednesday. She seems to have enjoyed her stay and reception in the States, but is not too sure she likes Britain. She had an appointment with Neil Kinnock the following day, and had lunch at the House of Commons. In the afternoon, she went to see the Archbishop of Canterbury, Robert Runcie. In the evening, she had another appointment. This time with Sonny Ramphal – Secretary of the Commonwealth. She was so busy; in fact the only person she did not see was the queen!! By the end of the week, she was really tired. Fortunately for me she was allowed to come and spend some time with me. She did not have the rest we had both hoped she would get. First, she had to get a little present for all the *bazukulwana* back home because these would not understand how Gogo can go abroad and not bring a present back. That took us the whole of Saturday, and even after that we still had not got a present for all of them. It's amazing how many *bakuzulwana* were on the list and I had never heard of even half of them, in fact it turned out to be the whole of Phomolong. I had to insist at some point that she couldn't get a present for the whole neighbourhood as she did not have enough money nor would she be able to carry them home.

She'll be back by the 1st of August and she will be with you the very next day. You'll need a whole week to cover all the news she has for you (10/7/89).

Lindi wrote to Walter again after Albertina's departure for Lusaka: "Mama has just left and already I feel such a loss. Many people keep asking me how I feel about seeing Mama after so long. I normally don't know how to respond. It's something you can only feel, but not describe. More than that, it's an acute combination of deep joy and equally deep sorrow. It was poignant. Now that she has gone, I realise just how alone I am" (1 August 1989).

What did Albertina make of this first international trip, the first direct accolades from the global community – the whirl of attention from some of the most powerful figures on the world stage, the glittering gala events, the hotels and limousines, the wall-to-wall media attention? Typically, she behaved as she always did. Whether she was in a township or the White House, her duty was the same: to advance the cause of the struggle and to support her family – in that order. She was not influenced by glamour and fame – or easily intimidated by the aura of power. There is something both cavalier and endearing in her indifference to rank and power.

In Lusaka, we looked forward to Albertina's visit with great anticipation. There were endless calls between Lusaka and Kitwe about Gerald's plan to travel with his wife Jasu and his children, Beryl and Walden, to join the big reunion. Family members and ANC leaders congregated in the VIP lounge of Lusaka airport to meet the UDF delegation. ANC NEC members Gertrude Shope, Ruth Mompati and Thomas Nkobi were as excited as we were to see their old friend for the first time since their departure from South Africa in the early 1960s. It was an uncharacteristically cold and overcast day, and there was an air of unreality as the plane landed. Albertina later told us that when she walked down the steps and saw Max in the distance she did not recognise him at once, and for a few seconds she wondered why Zwelakhe had followed her to Lusaka! To say that their reunion was an emotional one would be an understatement. "They [Max and Gerald] left as teenagers and now I am meeting them as adult men with their own families," Albertina said in an interview. She had a lot of catching up to do, especially with Gerald's family, none of whom she had ever seen before. She also met Shaka, Max's second son, for the first time, and was reunited with Lungi Jnr, who had come up from Zimbabwe for the occasion.

The Lusaka leg of the trip was no less gruelling than the others, and Albertina, Sister Bernard and Jessie were constantly occupied with interviews, report-backs to the ANC and meetings with women's organisations. Much of the time was taken up with briefings with the ANC, especially the Women's League. I accompanied them to a huge conference of African women from all over the continent at Lusaka's Mulungushi Hall. The women listened spellbound to Albertina's address about the abuse of young children under apartheid. At the end of the formal programme, Zanele Mbeki graciously organised and hosted a lunch for the three women. As we savoured Zanele's delicious *biryani* in the Mbeki's shady garden, people spoke about what the visit had meant to them. Albertina, Jessie and Sister Bernard, ever dutiful, spoke about the political significance of their trip and focused on what needed to be done in the future, while the exiles like Sindiso Mfenyana and Steve Tshwete spoke nostalgically about the past. Overcome by emotion at the reunion with her old friend Ntsiki, words failed Tiny Nokwe, and she burst into song. The mellifluous tones of her song expressed better than words the exiles' powerful longing for home.

After their formal programme ended, Albertina moved out of the hotel to spend a few days with us in our tiny Lusaka apartment. A few friends joined us for a family dinner, and Gerald was able to give Albertina a rundown on what had been happening in his life during their many years of separation. After the guests left, I wearily trudged into the kitchen, with 11-month-old Duma on my back, to wash the piles of dishes. I had barely started when Albertina protested: "Tyini, what are you doing washing dishes when you have a baby to attend to! And these young people are just sitting down!" She shooed me out of the kitchen and turned to a startled Lungi Jnr, young Beryl and Walden. "Into the kitchen all of you, at once!" She followed them into the kitchen and joined in the cleaning operation. By the time they were finished, the kitchen was sparkling. Gerald's wife Jasu watched in amazement. It was completely outside her experience for adolescent boys to be ordered into the kitchen to wash dishes. Coming from a culture in which daughters-in-law are expected to do all the work, I really appreciated my mother-in-law. Her principle of treating everyone as equals applied as much to the practical details of everyday life as to her politics.

Albertina's visit ended all too soon. We said fond goodbyes and she left with instructions to "make sure you write to your father and brief him about everything". The letter I wrote to Walter shortly thereafter invokes the spirit of the visit more than anything I can write now:

By now you have seen Mama and heard about the trip – the places she visited and the people she met. For us it was like a dream to actually have Mama right here in our house meeting with the children, who she has not seen for so many years and the grandchildren who she had never met.

We tried to follow the progress of the visits to Sweden, London, France and the US, but unfortunately the coverage here was not very good. There was also some confusion here about the exact dates when the group would arrive here. We spent quite a few weeks of suspense. I cannot tell you how excited Max was. Every day we received various sets of orders about what must be done in the house. I told Lindi that it was just as well that I had already met Mama and knew that her main concern would be seeing her children, and not the state of the house, otherwise I would have had a nervous breakdown. As it was, I just relaxed and waited for Mama to arrive.

It was wonderful that Gerald, Jasu and children were also able to travel from Kitwe to see Mama. It was their first time seeing Lungi and Shaka. It was also the first time Lungi and Shaka had ever met and that all four boys [Max's sons] were under one roof together, so it was a wonderful reunion all round (24/8/89).

Walter also received a brief but moving report from Lungi Jnr: "Grandmother's visit to Zambia was wonderful. Daddy was the happiest person in the world, when she [Grandma] touched down at the airport. I was extremely happy. I even wanted to reverse the days, as her departure day came closer and closer, but how do you work against nature?" (28/8/1989.)

# twelve

Albertina returned home on 30 July 1989 to a rousing welcome. More than 200 people, mostly women in FEDTRAW's green, gold and black garb, turned out at Johannesburg airport to welcome Albertina and Sister Bernard with a rousing rendition of *Nkosi Sikelel' iAfrika*. The two women returned in time to witness the first phase of the MDM's Defiance Campaign, launched on 2 August. Over the next few weeks, black patients in cities around the country presented themselves at white hospitals for treatment, students marched on white schools to demand that they open to all races, activists invaded whites-only beaches and boarded whites-only buses, and members of the National Union of Mineworkers defiantly used "whites-only" facilities at their workplaces. On 20 August, the sixth anniversary of its formation, the UDF declared itself unbanned. The End Conscription Campaign and other organisations followed suit. Individual activists broke their restriction orders. The mood of protest found expression in rallies, protests and marches around the country. The campaign also encompassed protest action against the new Labour Relations Act.

The government responded by detaining MDM activists. National leaders Valli Moosa, Trevor Manual and Titus Mafolo found themselves in the police dragnet as well as a number of regional leaders, but the MDM was not deterred (Seekings, 253). The dramatic resignation of PW Botha on 14 August encouraged the spirit of resistance. Furious that leader FW de Klerk had announced a meeting with Zambian leader Kenneth Kaunda without informing him, Botha threw one of his famous tantrums and accused De Klerk of betraying him "with a smile on your face and a dagger in your hand" (Sparks 1995, 88). Instead of bowing down to his blustering and bullying as they had done countless times before, Botha's cabinet ministers told him one by one that the time had come for him to go. That night, South Africans were treated to a confused, rambling speech on television by an angry President Botha, in which, to the delight of millions, he announced his resignation.

FW de Klerk again became the Acting President just as the Defiance Campaign was climaxing with nationwide protest against tricameral elections. Marches and demonstrations culminated in a national stayaway of three million workers, the largest in South African history, on 6 September, election day. The protests were met with vicious repression. On 2 September, police had dispersed crowds using water cannons with purple dye that marked the marchers, making them easy targets for arrest. Mitchell's Plain police officer Gregory Rockman broke ranks and denounced the police for behaving like "wild dogs". On election night, over 20 people died in the Western Cape (Seekings, 254).

On 14 September, De Klerk was elected President. As he took up the reins of power, he was in a delicate position. The eyes of the world were upon him and he was anxious to cultivate his image as a leader committed to reform. He was, however, faced with an ANC that had seized the moral high ground by setting out its formal proposals on how to move towards a negotiated settlement. Informed by the Mells Park talks, the ANC document set out five preconditions for negotiations: the release of all political prisoners; the lifting of bans on restricted organisations and individuals; the ending of the State of Emergency; the removal of all troops from the townships, and an end to political executions. The UDF and COSATU had declared their support for the document in July; the frontline states declared their support as well, and at a meeting in Harare on 21 August, the Organisation of African Unity formally endorsed the document, which became known as the "Harare Declaration". Though the Declaration committed the ANC to intensifying the armed struggle and internal resistance against apartheid, it was conciliatory in tone and stated that violence could be suspended while both sides agreed on constitutional principles and a mechanism for drafting a new, nonracial constitution. The Harare Declaration also won the support of the United Nations and the international community. It was a major diplomatic coup for the ANC, because it put the onus on the apartheid government to meet the conditions that would provide the necessary climate for negotiations (Sparks 1995, 87; Harvey, 187; Sampson 2000, 394; Mandela, 544).

In addition to pressure on the diplomatic front, the new President faced pressure on the financial front. The ANC, anti-apartheid groupings and development agencies from the US, Europe and Asia and members of the UN Special Committee for Apartheid had been campaigning to halt the rescheduling of South Africa's international debt (*Weekly Mail*, 21–27/7/89). With less than a year to go before South Africa's $11–13 billion external debt agreement expired, the pressure was on Pretoria to reach an early rescheduling of its debt in the face of Commonwealth pressure to link the rescheduling agreement with faster political reform. Commonwealth ministers had made it clear that the issue of South Africa's debt would be high on the agenda at the Commonwealth Heads of State Summit, scheduled to take place in Kuala Lumpur, Malaysia, on 18 October 1989. It was clear that the release of Walter Sisulu in time for the Kuala Lumpur summit would strengthen Margaret Thatcher's bid to stave off further Commonwealth sanctions against South Africa.

When the hawks in the security establishment had blocked Walter's release in March, the government had postponed the release to September, but concerns about the reaction of the white electorate had once again put a spoke in the wheel (*New Nation*, 20/10/89). In September, the government confirmed that the release of Mandela and others was on the cards, when Roelf Meyer, the South African Minister of Constitutional Development, said in an interview with the BBC that Mandela could be released within weeks. By the end of September, rumours were rife that Sisulu would be released within weeks to "test the waters" before releasing Mandela.

Walter wrote to Frieda Matthews: "The uncertainty of our position continues. For six months I have been staying where Nelson was before. It appeared that I was on my way out. Perhaps I am, but the situation could easily get worse. We will nevertheless watch all developments. But we do have more regular contact than before, not only with my other colleagues who are nearby, but Nelson as well. On such occasions we are allowed to use our own clothes. This is something new."

Mandela continued to apply pressure from his corner of the ring. A week after the elections, he advised De Klerk, through Kobie Coetsee, to show his bona fides by highlighting the release of 10 political prisoners, including Sisulu and Kathrada. When they met in September, Mandela urged Walter to take a "low-key" approach once he was released (Sampson 2000, 397). The ANC in Lusaka wanted the exact opposite of a low-key approach and, in Lusaka, Joe Slovo argued that increased political activity was needed to ensure the release of Mandela. On 9 October, the ANC in Lusaka put out their own plan of action, emphasising the need for the leaders to reaffirm their commitment and mobilise support for the Harare Declaration (Sampson 2000, 395).

On 8 October, Albertina had flown to Cape Town to visit Walter and to meet with Mandela, together with other leaders of the Mass Democratic Movement. Accompanied by Nkuli, she went for what was to be her last visit to Walter in Pollsmoor on Tuesday, 10 October. Nkuli described the visit: "There was a strange atmosphere and wild excitement when we arrived. We asked Tata what was up, but he only told us he could not spend much time with us that day." She noted that there were many visitors and "people from the government" mingling with senior prison officials.

The pieces of the puzzle fell into place that evening when Albertina and the other MDM leaders, Cyril Ramaphosa, Cas Saloojee and Murphy Morobe, were having their meeting with Mandela at Victor Verster prison. Mandela stopped the meeting so that they could watch the 8pm news. It turned out to be a historic broadcast. De Klerk announced that the government would soon release Walter Sisulu, Ahmed Kathrada, Raymond Mhlaba, Andrew Mlangeni, Elias Motsoaledi, Wilton Mkwayi, Oscar Mpetha and PAC leader Jafta Masemola. All the prisoners would be released unconditionally. Ramaphosa told journalists that the five MDM leaders were overwhelmed with emotion, but their feelings were mixed because of the omission of Mandela. Albertina told Mandela: "I am taking you home with me now." Embracing her, he said, "Yes, I do want to go home."

After the meeting with Mandela, the MDM party rushed to make arrangements to fly to Johannesburg before Walter arrived home. When they found the flights fully booked for the next two days, Cyril suggested to Albertina that she should receive Walter in Cape Town. "I will never forget her reply," says Cyril. "She was adamant that 'I must get back because he must find me at home where he left me'." After much effort, they managed to hire a car and drove through the night, a distance of 1 400 kilometres. They arrived in Johannesburg at 1pm on Wednesday. As they turned the corner into the street, the first thing they noticed were the huge tents outside the Sisulu home. They learned that since De Klerk's announcement that the prisoners would be released, journalists and groups of activists had set up camp around the house. They all wanted to be there for the moment when Walter Sisulu stepped through his gate after an absence of almost three decades.

Lungi Sisulu Snr remembers that even the children at the nursery school opposite the house were drawn into the excitement, fascinated by visitors and foreign journalists, many of whom were white. "Apart from the police, they had never seen so many white people in one place before." The children had also heard teachers talking about the imminent release of Ntate Sisulu, so they expected him to come round the corner at any minute. There were many false alarms, which brought them to the crèche fence shouting "Nangu Sisulu, Nangu Sisulu" (There is Sisulu, there is Sisulu).

Mlungisi Sisulu Snr, who usually undertakes the task of organising food supplies for any family gathering, describes the week preceding his father's release: "Like a wedding or a funeral, people came to stay. Meals had to be prepared for at least a hundred people a day." He had to order a couple of sheep from the local livestock dealer, who flatly refused to accept any payment.

Albertina stepped into her house to find that preparations for the welcome were well under way. The people of Orlando West needed little encouragement to prepare a fitting welcome for their leader. Overlooked by stern-looking marshals, a constant stream of people flowed in and out of the Sisulu home – friends, relatives, members of the MDM and the Women's Federation. Women from the neighbourhood and the Orlando branch of FEDTRAW organised a roster system for cooking and baking. The women cooked in the backyard, using huge three-legged pots over open fires. Similar scenes were played out at the homes of other leaders who were to be released – Andrew Mlangeni and Elias Motsoaledi in Soweto, Oscar Mpetha in Cape Town and Raymond Mhlaba in Port Elizabeth. Wilton Mkwayi had no home to go to as his wife had died while he was in prison, so Winnie Mandela was making preparations to receive him at the Mandela home.

Friday 13 October brought goods news for Albertina – her restrictions had been lifted. She had been worried that she would not be able to participate effectively in her husband's release, since she was not allowed to be in the same room with more than 10 people. She had also heard that Walter was in Johannesburg and could walk through the door at any moment! She would have to wait a little longer, however. Walter did not return that night, nor the next. Each day he did not return she felt weighed down by disappointment. After waiting 26 years, she found the last stretch unbearable.

It was a taxing time, both physically and emotionally. Albertina recalls: "It was a very trying week. I had less privacy then than at any time in my life. Journalists followed me everywhere, even to the shops when I went to buy vegetables." For most of the week, she stayed at home, close to the telephone, and to keep herself occupied, she supervised the spring cleaning of the entire house. Renowned among family and friends for keeping a meticulously clean home, Albertina surpassed even herself on that occasion. The household was thrown into a frenzy of cooking, cleaning, sweeping, painting and polishing. Journalists asked Albertina whether Mr Sisulu would recognise the house when he arrived, since it had been transformed from a typical four-roomed Soweto match-box house to a big (by Soweto standards) three-bedroomed home. "Oh yes," she replied, "the house was designed according to his plan. We sent him pictures of the house at every stage of construction and he actually chose the room in which we are sitting as his study."

"Walter Sisulu! Akheko ofana naye! Walter Sisulu, there is no one else like him" chanted the crowd of young people, as they bobbed up and down in the rhythmic stomp of the *toyi-toyi* dance. Their exuberant dancing threw clouds of dust into the air and the ground vibrated under their feet. The dancing crowd in front of No. 7372 grew larger as the afternoon wore on into evening. Journalists, local and foreign, swarmed all over the place like locusts. There was an air of festive jubilation.

The police then arrived at the house they had raided countless times before. In a typically South African scene, and with spectacular lack of sensitivity, they fired tear gas into the crowd on the grounds that it was an "illegal gathering". The *toyi-toying* stopped abruptly. Coughing and spluttering, people dispersed into the night, only to come back barely an hour later in even larger numbers. Journalists and activists alike settled down to an all-night vigil.

Emotions, already kindled by the Defiance Campaign, had been aroused to the verge of hysteria by news of the releases. People flocked to the homes of the leaders to prepare for their return. The MDM hailed the news of the releases as a victory for the people of South Africa, the sanctions campaign and the international solidarity campaign to isolate the apartheid regime. The MDM had arranged "reception committees" with offices around the country to organise countrywide marches and rallies as part of massive celebrations to welcome the leaders. Speaking on behalf of a newly launched National Reception Committee, two days after the official announcement, MDM leader and chairperson of the reception committee, Cyril Ramaphosa, said the MDM would make sure the released leaders came home to a welcome "befitting their status in the struggle".

As part of the MDM's Defiance Campaign, the trade union movement had already planned marches against the Labour Relations Amendment Act for Saturday 14 October. These marches were partially transformed to "victory marches" to celebrate the release of the leaders. Throngs of activists who had taken part in the marches in Johannesburg that Saturday morning marched to Soweto. After doing the *toyi-toyi* in front of the Sisulu home amid shouts of "Long live the ANC!", they moved to the Mandela home, where preparations were under way for the welcome of Wilton Mkwayi. The crowds then moved on to Andrew Mlangeni's home in Dube. En route they brought traffic to a halt at Maponya Shopping Centre, one of the busiest thoroughfares in Soweto.

By this time, people were beginning to express concern about the delay in the releases. There were even fears that the government had changed its mind. Rumours and counter-rumours about the release flew back and forth through the township (*Weekly Mail*, 20/10/89). Two elderly tailors, the Sisulu's neighbours for the past 30 years, whose shop Walter had used as an escape route when he was on the run from the police all those decades ago, voiced their concern:

"Do you think they have taken him to a hotel?" asked one anxiously.

"No, no, no," said the other, "I am certain not."

A thought struck his friend: "If they *have* taken him to a hotel, d'you think he'd eat there?"

"Yes," came the worried reply, "what would happen to all the food Albertina has prepared?"

"Well, anyway, it would be nice to see Walter again," said the other philosophically.

By nightfall, there was still no sign of the leaders. The regime seemed reluctant to relinquish its hold on the men it had held captive for so long. Spirits were flagging as families, supporters and the press resigned themselves to another night-long vigil. Murphy Morobe, the publicity secretary of the UDF and member of the National Reception Committee, said the waiting game to which the government was subjecting the prisoners' families and communities would only worsen tension.

While family and friends were giving his house a rapid facelift in preparation for his return, Walter Sisulu was spending his last night behind bars in a Johannesburg prison, reminiscing with his co-prisoners. They discussed their last meeting with Nelson Mandela, which had taken place on 10 October. Walter, Kathrada, Mlangeni, Motsoaledi and Mkwayi had discussed their impending release and the fact that the government wanted them to give undertakings that they would not cause any trouble or unrest once they were out of prison. Mhlaba later told the press: "Our decision, together with Mandela, was that we refused to give any undertaking of that nature." They said an emotional goodbye to Mandela, who later wrote of his "unalloyed joy that Walter and others were free. It was a day we had yearned for and fought for over so many years" (Mandela, 542). At 5.30pm their visit to Mandela ended, apparently to make way for the visit of Albertina Sisulu and the other MDM leaders. They were taken to the warders' mess and given dinner. While watching television in the mess, they heard De Klerk's announcement that they would be released unconditionally. Walter was overjoyed that he would be released with his colleagues.

They left Cape Town on 13 October. Walter admits to some sadness. "The warders were ... happy that we were going home but at the same time sad to see us leave. When you are with people for so many years you develop good and personal relationships ... [It] was like parting from good friends."

They were flown on a regular South African Airways flight to Johannesburg. At Diepkloof Prison, they met Jafta Masemola, the PAC leader who was also to be released. They spent Saturday talking about their experiences on the Island. They had been told they would have to wake at 2am to be escorted home at 5am. Mkayi described the process: "On arrival at Sun City [Diepkloof Prison] reception at 4am, we saw a forest of plain-clothed men we concluded were policemen. The doors opened minutes after 5am and we were each escorted to a waiting car, and driven home in this manner: each one in a separate car, in front of which was another car occupied by several policemen. Behind was a van carrying our prison luggage of 26 years and right behind the van was another car. In other words, the six of us were escorted home in 24 vehicles, four vehicles for each of us."

Shortly before sunrise on Sunday 15 October 1989, 5.30am to be exact, a police convoy rounded the bend into Sisulu Street in Phomolong in Orlando West. Fearing a raid, some of the marshals scurried away. Journalists were confused too. Only one reporter took the sensible course. When a small grey-haired man emerged from the vehicle, the journalist asked "Are you Walter Sisulu?"

"Yes I am, and how are you?" came the prompt reply (BBC report). Walter signed for his belongings and said: "Let me see my wife." In an instant, the morning was filled with ecstatic and triumphant cries and ululation. "He is here! uTata has arrived!" Sisulu was thronged by enthusiastic supporters as he made his way towards his house. Inside, Albertina and daughters Nkuli and Beryl, exhausted by never-ending interviews, streams of visitors and *toyi-toying* comrades, were fast asleep. Nkuli was awakened by the cries, and rushed to wake her mother.

Albertina recalls the moment: "I was so confused. I stood there trembling from head to toe. I was nervous as a new bride. I had to be dressed like a child." She reached the living room in time to see her husband walk through the door. They embraced. That embrace marked the end of a long and painful era for the Sisulu family.

Pandemonium reigned outside the house as people sang and *toyi-toyied* with renewed energy. Similar eruptions of wild celebration were taking place at the Mandela home, where Wilton Mkayi had been dropped off by police, as well as at the homes of the Mlangenis, Motsoaledis and Kathradas in neighbouring Lenasia. The news spread through Soweto like wildfire. A *Weekly Mail* report captured the spirit of the day:

As news of the releases began to spread through Soweto, so did the carnival atmosphere. Disbelieving residents wanted to know whether journalists had "really, really seen them". Groups of hundreds of strong comrades did the *toyi-toyi* down the street. The roads were filled with noisy motorcades as youths, acting as self-appointed traffic wardens, unilaterally declared Soweto's main routes to be one-ways. The highly politicised "party" ebbed and flowed and crowds moved from house to house ...

Soweto was awash with black, green and gold. Makeshift ANC flags, fashioned from any material people could find, were everywhere. A huge black, green and gold ANC flag was draped across the walls of the Sisulu house. A smaller flag flew over the roof. Though still banned, the ANC had come out into the open, as was illustrated by the whispered exchange between two young activists holding up an ANC flag in front of the Sisulu home.

"You don't have to wear that" said the one youth, pointing to a scarf which – out of habit – his companion had wrapped around his face to hide his identity. "Our leaders are back – it's all changed." The other boy pulled the scarf away, revealing a broad smile.

In Cape Town, Lungephi Lengisi, who had been abroad on UDF business, had not heard the news. When he arrived on that Sunday at Pollsmoor for a scheduled visit with Walter, he was annoyed when warder Christo Brand told him he could not see his uncle. "Just look at those newspapers that are under your arm," said Brand in response to his protests. "The more I told him to look at his paper, the more annoyed he became. He did not understand what I was getting at" (Interview, Chriso Brand, August 2001; Interview, Lungephi Lengisi). When the truth finally dawned, Lengisi's irritation turned to joy and he rushed off. In Harare, Max, Sheila and I were attending one of the many meetings held in the Zimbabwean capital during that period, enabling activists from home and those in exile to plan for the new South Africa. That Sunday morning, Max and I were startled out of our sleep by Sheila banging at our door and shouting jubilantly: "Tata is home! Lungi has just called to say Tata is home!" She rushed off to book a flight back while Max tried to call home. Not surprisingly, the line was engaged, and he spent three hours calling before he finally got through and heard his father's voice again for the first time in 27 years. Shortly afterwards, Gerald also managed to get through to Walter and speak to him – after a gap of over 30 years.

Sheila failed to get a flight that Sunday and had to wait until the next day. That night, we had a celebratory dinner at the home of Jaya and Premmie Apelraju, an ANC couple based in Harare. Lungi Jnr joined us – like Sheila, he was busy arranging his travel to Johannesburg. Max looked rather pensive amid all the excited chatter. Although his father had been released, he was still in exile. It was a bittersweet time for us. I was also unable to travel because my own father was terminally ill at the time. It grieved me that my father, who since my marriage to Max, had followed so closely the developments in South Africa, could not share in the triumph of the moment.

In England, Lindi was also assailed by mixed emotions. She was not in an environment in which she could celebrate her father's release in the way she would have wanted and her joy was tempered by a sense of isolation. And in Soweto, Zwelakhe could not join the festivities at his parental home because his restrictions did not allow him to be in the company of more than one person at a time.

Inside his home, Walter was coping graciously with hundreds of hugs, handshakes and telephone calls. When he emerged just before noon, chants of "ANC! ANC!" rose from the crowd. Lungi had several moments of anxiety that his father would be crushed by the surging crowd: "As we tried to keep some space between Tata and the crowd, people shouted 'We want to see our leader! Why do you want to stop us?' They were quite hysterical. They had waited too long." The confusion was further complicated by a battle among journalists: "They had staked out their claims to particular vantage points the previous day. All hell broke loose when these arrangements went haywire."

Leaving fighting journalists in his wake, Walter proceeded to a meeting of the National Reception Committee. Later that evening, the seven released leaders addressed a special press conference at the Holy Cross Cathedral. Raymond Mhlaba and Oscar Mpetha had been specially flown from their homes in Port Elizabeth and Cape Town for the conference.

There was not an inch of space in the church. Benches broke under the weight of the people. Those who could not get in, watched through the windows. One of the journalists present commented that he had never in his whole life seen such a press conference. In the jam-packed church, adorned with ANC flags, the leaders restated their commitment to the ANC, dispelling government hopes that they might set up an "internal wing of the ANC" with a different agenda to that of the ANC in exile. The press conference ended with the singing of the African anthem *Nkosi Sikelel' iAfrika* (God Save Africa). As hundreds of voices sent the beautiful melody soaring into the Soweto night, Walter and Albertina Sisulu knew that it was just a matter of time before all their children would be home. For the people of South Africa, it was just a matter of time before Nelson Mandela would be free and the vision of a democratic future realised.

# Part Five

## *1990–2002*

## *The New Dawn*

## MTHANDI WESIZWE

Ngubani omabhongo ngelakhe ikamva?
Ngubani onegugu ziinto zakowabo,
Ohlala elinde ukubon'iintezintle,
Othemba linzulu, naxa kungkuhle?

Woba yinjinga kwizwe elikhoyo,
Lingalityalwa nelakhe igama.
Ngumthandi welizwe azalelwe kulo,
Ngumthandi wabantu belakhe ibala.

Zojinga phezu kwakhe iintsikelelo.
Lomana lincuma lakumkhangela
Iphakad'elikhoyo. Nezakhe intshaba –
Kulow'akaphumi mdintsi natyheneba.

Yimbunguzulu kwaneqhayiya,
Kwabakowabo nesakhe isizwe.
Zibongisela ngaye neentombi zakowabo.
Loba sisifungo negama lalowo.

Yincamisa-mxhelo, siyolo selizwe,
Zingapheli kulowo iziteketiswana.
Ngumthandi wentetho nesiko lakowabo,
Ngumlwi nezimbi zezwe lakowabo.

Luyol'olukhulu xa asinga ekhaya.
Milambo, mifula, ziinduli neentaba,
Ziziba, zingxangxasi, zithetha lukhulu
Kuloo ntliziyo iluthando lunzulu.

Mthandi wabantu, mthandi welizwe!
Ithamsanqa leNkosi malithontsele kuwe.
Mayikuwele imibethe yeZulu,
Zivuyiswe ngawe iinto zakowenu.
Ivumb'elimnandi lesafikane
Livale amaho, umlomo liwuqhole.

JOHN SOLILO

*(Last four stanzas omitted.)*
*Translated into English by*
*Ntombi Dwane.*

## THE PATRIOT

What person has high hopes for the future?
Who takes pride in matters affecting his home?
The one that spends all the time looking for
    the good;
The one holding firmly to hope against all odds?

That is the one who shall be champion in the Land;
Neither will his name ever get forgotten.
He is the true patriot of his Motherland;
He is the one who dotes on his countrymen.

Above that one shall boughs of blessings hang.
On him shall the smile of the Present world hearken,
His avowed foes also will pay him homage;
Boredom and loathsomeness know not such a one.

He indeed is the perfect beau and boastful pride
Of his kinsmen, and truly of all his countrymen.
The maidens of his country sing endless praises
    of him;
His name shall surely be the pride and honour to all.

He, indeed is the beloved, the thrill of the Land;
He is forever regaled with pretty names of
    endearment.
He is the ardent admirer of the language and culture
    of his people;
He can be trusted to stand in clear opposition to the
    evils of his land.

The greatest, the deepest joy wells up within him as
    he faces home;
Great rivers, flowing streams, and mountains,
Deep wells, waterfalls all resonate deeply with joy
In that heart of his that harbours such deep
    affection.

Lover of people, Great Patriot!
May the blessings of the Lord drip onto you!
May the soft dew of the firmament fall on you!
May all your countrymen derive great joy from you!
May the sweet fragrance of the goose-weed
Seal your nostrils, and may it flavour your lips with
    its sweetness!

*o n e*

If ever the entire global community had an *annus mirabilis*, a golden year, it was 1989. In that year, anything seemed possible, even world peace. It was a brief and unforgettable time of miracles, of new optimism, fuelled by more and more extraordinary symbolic moments of transformation. Almost overnight, with little warning, the Berlin Wall – that symbol of the total breach between two Northern empires – was dismantled. The media images were compelling – ordinary, everyday people chipping away at it with tools from garages and workboxes. This was final proof of the near-silent collapse of the Soviet empire, and the melting away of the Cold War.

The tip of the African continent was also undergoing an extraordinary transformation. Suddenly, it was possible that apartheid might die a tidy death at the negotiating table, instead of through civil combat on increasingly bloody streets. The frontline states, too, were faced with the amazing possibility that they no longer had to fear destabilisation, cross-border raids, bombs and assassinations. Apartheid's most heinous laws – the Immorality Act and the Mixed Marriages Act, the Separate Amenities Act, and the Population Registration Act – fell like dominoes. The optimism of 1989 was carried forward into the opening months of the new decade. On 2 February, FW de Klerk finally did what his predecessor PW Botha had been unable to bring himself to accomplish. De Klerk crossed the Rubicon when he announced to a stunned parliament the unbanning of the ANC, PAC and SACP and the imminent release of Nelson Mandela and hundreds of other political prisoners. Nine days later, Mandela's walk out of Victor Verster prison was televised to millions around the globe. On 21 March 1990, the 30th anniversary of the Sharpeville massacre, Namibia became independent under the leadership of a SWAPO government.

But these incredible developments were still a few months away as Walter Sisulu enjoyed his first weeks of freedom. As one of the protagonists in the drama of rapid political transformation, he had little time to bask in euphoria. He spent the first hectic days after his release giving press interviews and receiving the never-ending stream of well-wishers. When the welcoming celebrations outside the house showed no signs of abating after a week, he was visited by Major General Viktor, the SAP Divisional Commissioner for Soweto. By a strange quirk of fate, Viktor was the security policeman who had fingerprinted and charged Walter after the Rivonia arrests in 1963. He asked Walter to wind down the celebrations: "I think you've had your welcome now – and as far as I am concerned you are very welcome back in Soweto – but I think it's time we come to an agreement." Walter thanked him for his reasonable approach, but asked him to appreciate the amazing discipline of the people. "You must take the entire situation into consideration. People are moved. You don't want them to be bottled up." He pointed out that people were just coming in to shake hands and leave after a couple of minutes. "Now General, if that is not really an orderly deed, then what is?" ( *Weekly Mail*, 20–26/10/89; *New Nation*, 20–26/10/89.)

Walter also spent time responding to telephone calls and letters of congratulation that poured in from all over the world. These included letters from leaders both abroad, such as US President George Bush, and at home. Chief Buthelezi, in his capacity as President of Inkatha, wrote: "No group of people could ever have been released from jail to be received with greater joy in their country than you and your comrades." He mentioned that he had campaigned for many years for their release, and went on to acknowledge Walter's role in the Rivonia Trial and the Youth League: "You have a very distinctive place in the struggle. Together with Dr Nelson Mandela, Mr Oliver

Tambo and Mr Robert Sobukwe, you rose above the others in the Youth League to put your own personal mark on history" (Letter from Mangosuthu Buthelezi, 26/10/85).

Walter was particularly moved by the telephone calls he received from his old struggle comrades. He reports that even Joe Slovo, who was "not a chap to be easily excited", was very emotional when he spoke to him. Walter also received a call from Adelaide Tambo, telephoning on behalf of her husband, whose doctors had advised him against calling himself. Adelaide told Walter that "this one day has done for him [Tambo] what it would have taken the doctors six months to achieve".

Years later I asked Albertina how she and Walter had adapted to being together again after all the years of separation. Her face lit up at the memory. "No problem at all," she replied, laughing. "The only thing we would argue about was that your father had got used to sleeping with the lights on in prison. I would switch the lights off and he would switch them back on again. In the end I managed to get him out of that habit."

The only souls who were not thrilled to have Walter back home were Nkuli's little ones. They were accustomed to sleeping in their grandmother's bed and were not amused when they were moved out of the room. They were unimpressed by this old man who held everyone's attention, especially that of their grandmother. If Walter tried to chastise them, little Zwelethu would remind him: "This is our Gogo's house." Walter was highly amused when he overheard my son Duma referring to him as "that Grandpa who stays at Gogo's house".

Because the house was continuously overflowing with people, some interviews had to be conducted in the bedroom. Journalists Shaun Johnson and Thami Mkhwanazi spoke to Walter while he ate lunch perched on the edge of his bed. They were struck by his "mental agility, charisma and energy, which belied his 77 years". He told them how impressed he was by the discipline of the youth: "In the first group I addressed, you could hear a pin drop when I talked. When I was finished they went without any trouble. Senior people would have found it difficult to behave that way – I will never forget it. And what's more, they took the message home. Some of the parents came to tell me they were so happy because I had told the youth about education, that they must pay particular attention to it whatever else they do" (*Weekly Mail*, 20–26/10/89).

There had been speculation among those who had little knowledge of the ANC that "younger township activists [might] not be keen to see septuagenarians like Mr Sisulu giving them orders" (Patti Waldmeir, *Financial Times*, 11/10/89). Such speculation proved to be baseless. Walter's leadership was unquestioned, and the older and younger generation of leaders bonded effortlessly. Walter felt that the young MDM leaders were steady and balanced young men: "I am struck by their demeanour, their utterances, their planning. I think they are absolutely wonderful – more organised than we were at the same age, more systematic" (*Weekly Mail*, 20–26/10/89). The young leaders were equally impressed with the veterans. Commenting on the way Walter immediately and capably took up the reins of leadership, Cyril Ramaphosa said: "He was a reservoir of strength and experience. He was one of the most careful speakers. He weighed each word and each concept carefully. You always felt the weight of his experience and the depth of his political knowledge. His approach was always measured and diplomatic. He was a joy to work with."

Within days of the release, the leaders set up an ANC Internal Leadership Core headed by Walter, Mandela (still in prison at the time), Govan Mbeki, Raymond Mhlaba and Mac Maharaj. Walter was chair of the new structure, whose immediate task was to set up the internal machinery of the ANC. "We had to hit the ground running," recalls Cyril Ramaphosa. The ILC operated until the middle of 1990 (Rantete, 7). German businessman Ernest Kahle, who was the general manager of Munich Reinsurance, gave them a floor in his headquarters in Sauer Street in downtown Johannesburg, not very far from where Walter had had his offices in the 1950s. When Cyril took Walter to the new premises for the first time, he showed him to the largest office on the floor. Walter looked at the room, then silently turned and led Cyril to a smaller office. "'The big office must be reserved for Madiba,' he said. He spoke firmly and the matter was clearly not for debate," Cyril recalls. The MDM leaders had considerately set aside two private rooms complete with beds so that their elderly leaders could rest whenever they needed to. Walter looked into the rooms and told Cyril: "We will not be using these." "And he was right. They never ever used those rooms" (Interview, Cyril Ramaphosa). Walter said he had no intention of resting because "I am a man who is in a hurry for freedom" (*New Nation*, 20–26/10/89).

Though the ANC was still officially banned, the release of the Rivonia leaders amounted to a de facto unbanning of the organisation. On 29 October, a huge welcome home rally was held at the First National Bank Stadium near Soweto to celebrate the return of the leaders, the first ANC rally in four decades. Walter gave the main speech in which he saluted the people of South Africa, the rank and file membership of the ANC, the UDF and the women's, youth and civic organisations. He drew attention to those on death row: "We commit ourselves to sparing no effort to save them from the gallows." He thanked the international community for the role it had played in the struggle against apartheid and said that the OAU and the socialist countries "will be remembered by the people of South Africa forever". He also paid tribute to the frontline states, particularly the people of Zambia and President Kenneth Kaunda for housing the ANC headquarters. He called on the international community to intensify sanctions: "We are in no doubt that sanctions are to a very large extent responsible for making the government responsive to the demands of our people." He outlined the history of the ANC from the time of the Defiance Campaign, saying the ANC had consistently been committed to the politics of peace and negotiations. He said the ANC was pre-pared to discuss the suspension of hostilities, but there could be no question of it unilaterally abandoning the armed struggle (Address to National Welcome Back Rally, 29/10/89).

Walter was never a great orator. His was the kind of deliberate and thoughtful delivery that appealed to the intellect rather than the emotions, but this mattered little to the tens of thousands of young people who for most of their lives had heard the history of the ANC only in furtive whis-pers. To hear one of the founding fathers of the modern ANC recounting the history of the organ-isation at a mass rally was a thrilling experience for many in the 80 000-strong crowd.

On 9 December 1989, Walter gave the keynote address at the Conference for a Democratic Future, a gigantic gathering of almost 4 500 people representing over 2 000 organisations (Seekings, 255–6). The conference was significant in that it brought together the Charterist and the Black Consciousness camps. AZAPO and the BCM were both represented, and AZAPO leader Itumeleng Mosala also made a keynote speech. Walter was positive about negotiations, while Mosala was more cautious. Walter also drew attention to the historic significance of the conference: "Not since the Congress of the People in 1955 has so broad an assembly come together to chart the future of our beloved country." He emphasised the importance of unity, saying that "the tech-nique of divide and rule is the modus operandi of the apartheid state". He welcomed the partici-pation of those who had different visions of the future: "That is to be expected, even welcomed. We do not advocate that any group has a monopoly over all the answers. The democratic forces in this country recognise the need for the co-existence of diverse views. The only exception that we make is that we will not accept racism in any form. We argue that diversity is a wonderful resource from which new solutions to our problems will be found."

The aim of the conference was to thrash out how to make use of the political and legal space created by De Klerk, and once again start determining the agenda of political change (*Weekly Mail*, 8–14/12/89). Walter expressed the view that the strategic objectives of De Klerk's changes were "reform to the minimum extent … and the protection, as far as possible, of the privileges of the white minority. We are aware that De Klerk has no choice but to go further than his predecessors on these points. But we know that … he has limits beyond which he will not go. It is our historic purpose to take him there; or go without him." He drew attention to De Klerk's aim of creating "a negotiating forum convened on the basis of representation from the tricameral parliament, the Bantustans and other 'groups', such as the group described as 'urban blacks'. All of De Klerk's 'groups' will have the power of veto. In other words, the white minority 'group' will retain the power to prevent fundamental changes to the system" (keynote address at the Conference for a

Democratic Future, 9/12/89). It was resolved that a new constitution should be drawn up by a fully representative Constituent Assembly.

In all his speeches and interviews, Walter spoke consistently about the need to maintain and even intensify sanctions. Here he disagreed with Allan Boesak, who had told reporters at the Commonwealth Summit in Kuala Lumpur that perhaps De Klerk should be given six months' grace to make good on his promises of reform (*The Citizen*, 18/10/89). Walter argued that the pressure on the South African government had to be maintained: "There must be no chance for the government to retreat and reorganise its strategy of delay" (*Boston Globe*, 18/10/89). He said ever since John Vorster's regime, "we have been made endless promises ... all within that magic period of six months." However, Walter was as polite as ever regarding Boesak's remarks: "One must remember he is a churchman and they look at things differently" (*The Citizen*, 18/10/89).

There was no slackening in the pace of Walter and Albertina's work over the festive season. Nkuli recalls that the house "was like an ANC office". People continued to flock to the Sisulu home with their problems. When I asked Albertina how they spent their first Christmas together in decades, she laughed. "There was no such thing as Christmas for us. It was like any other day. We worked throughout that period."

It was a sign of the changing times that early in the new year, Walter and his colleagues were given passports to travel to Lusaka to meet with the ANC leadership in exile. Walter headed the delegation made up of the Rivonia Trialists, Govan Mbeki, Kathrada, Mkwayi, Mlangeni, Motsoaledi and Mhlaba. Accompanying them were Albertina, Epainette Mbeki, June Mlangeni, Caroline Motsoaledi and Dideka Mhlaba. The delegation also included a powerful contingent from the MDM, led by Cyril Ramaphosa of the National Union of Mineworkers (NUM) and Chris Dlamini of COSATU.

It is difficult to convey the sense of dazed euphoria we experienced as we welcomed them at Lusaka airport on 15 January 1990. There was a festive atmosphere as ANC Youth League members danced to the incessant beating of drums. The flight was expected at 2pm, but an hour later we were still waiting, when the rain came down. This dispersed some of the crowd, but 700 eager ANC cadres remained on the airport apron huddling under umbrellas until the flight eventually arrived (*The Star*, 16/1/90).

The NEC members had lined up in orderly queues on the airport apron, but as the leaders emerged from the aircraft, the ranks disintegrated as people surged forward to embrace them. Gerald's son Walden was the first to break the cordon behind which we were standing. He rushed forward and hugged Albertina. I was amazed at the speed with which Max, carrying our three-year old son Vuyisile, managed to reach Walter. As the three generations embraced each other, their joy was a sight to behold. Thabo Mbeki, who was more disciplined, waited in the line of 30-odd NEC members to greet his parents Govan and Epainette for the first time in three decades. The jubilation on Thabo Mbeki's face was mirrored in the faces of Alfred Nzo, Thomas Nkobi, Ruth Mompati and other NEC leaders. Decades melted away as parents and children, old comrades, friends, former prisoners, exiles and internal activists embraced each other.

At some stage I found myself next to Ahmed Kathrada. Before I had a chance to greet him, he said: "Hello Elinor, how are you!" I was surprised that he knew who I was, but when the same thing happened with Andrew Mlangeni, it dawned on me that of course they would be able to recognise me – they had seen photographs and read all my letters to Walter.

When we came back to earth after the first few glorious moments of reunion, Walter and his colleagues were formally received by Grey Zulu, the head of UNIP (the Zambian ruling party) and members of the diplomatic corps who were also present (*The Star*, 16/1/90). They were taken through the arrival formalities and ushered to the vehicles waiting to transport them to State House, where they would be guests of President Kaunda during their stay in Zambia. When Max asked those responsible for the delegation's itinerary when he could see his parents, he was told that there would be a state reception. Gerald, who had travelled from Kitwe to welcome Walter and Albertina, and Max were furious at being told that no provision had been made for the members of the delegation to spend time with their families. After all, a few words of greeting and a hug at the airport did not constitute a sufficient reunion for people who had been separated for nearly 30 years. I found it ironic that the ANC, which had always deplored the break-up of family life under apartheid, should place such little importance on the reunion of families. One had the sense that the political objectives were so overwhelmingly important that emotional needs had to take a back seat.

Max then made his own arrangements with Zambian officials for us to visit Walter and Albertina. By then Lindi had arrived in Lusaka, and we all made the trek to State House, where we were fortunate to bump into President Kaunda. He told us how happy he was to host the delegation, especially his personal friend and mentor Walter Sisulu, and said that we should feel free to visit whenever we wanted to. It was wonderful for Max, Gerald and Lindi to be able to spend a little time with their parents, but it had been a long day and they had an even more gruelling day ahead of them, so we did not stay long.

The next day saw the beginning of the historic three-day meeting that brought together for the first time the 35-member NEC, the seven released political prisoners, and representatives of the MDM. The meeting opened with a welcoming ceremony attended by about 700 ANC members. In his address, Walter reiterated an appeal he had made in the 1950s: a call to ANC members not to be afraid of subjecting themselves to constructive self-criticism: "The important thing is that when an organisation makes mistakes, it must learn to correct them. A political movement can only succeed if there is criticism, if there is honesty, discipline and order" (*Weekly Mail*, 20–26/1/90). The meeting had to grapple with the question of how to proceed with the negotiations and the status of the armed struggle, as well as questions of leadership raised by Tambo's illness, the release of the Rivonia veterans and Mandela's imminent release.

The NEC meeting was followed by an open meeting for all members of the ANC. Lindi and I were among the thousand who attended the meeting at Lusaka's Mulungushi Hall. Periods of transition are always unsettling and there was a lot of unhappiness within the ranks of the ANC. Many cadres, especially within MK, were uneasy about the secret talks that had been taking place with the South African government, and some of them associated negotiations with capitulation. Many were horrified by Alfred Nzo's public statement earlier that week that the ANC did not have the capacity to intensify the armed struggle in any meaningful way. Walter and his colleagues felt the full force of the dissatisfaction within the ranks at the increasingly stormy gathering. Walter could not mask his shock as person after person got up to voice their grievances. The members were somewhat mollified when he said that the ANC would work towards negotiations while at the same time intensifying the armed struggle to maintain pressure on the Pretoria regime. He said later that he was aware that there were problems, but that he had been taken aback by the level of anger among the rank and file. He felt that the absence of Oliver Tambo's leadership had been an unsettling factor, and that the issue of communication within the organisation had to be addressed urgently.

At the beginning of the visit, Max had asked the ANC if his parents could spend one evening with us in our home. He was told that it might be possible for members of the delegation to have one free evening to visit their families and friends in Lusaka. Every time he checked, he was told to ask again the next day. Finally, on Thursday evening he was told that his parents would be free the next evening, but for security reasons, the delegation could not be split up. If he wanted to invite his parents for supper, he would have to invite the whole delegation. If the entire delegation was invited, we could not leave out members of the NEC or the families and friends of the other leaders. Because the gathering was by now huge, we had to invite our neighbours, and the list grew and grew. I was preparing for an ILO seminar, so it was impossible for me to take the day off work. Fortunately our exile family rallied around and helped with the preparations. Lindi worked from the crack of dawn until the guests arrived that night. So with just one day's notice, we hosted dinner for over 200 people in our first-floor two-bedroomed flat. Every room was crammed with people, and guests overflowed down the staircase into the garden, with journalists and camera crews adding to the squeeze.

What with running to and fro serving food and entertaining guests, we counted ourselves lucky if we had five minutes with Walter and Albertina or anyone else present. I envied Moeletsi Mbeki and his father engaged in deep conversation, completely oblivious to those around them. I was hoping to talk to the women in the delegation, the elder Mrs Mbeki, Mrs Motsoaledi and Mrs Mlangeni, about how their lives had been changed by the release of their husbands, but there was no chance. I was not surprised when towards the end of the evening, Lindi broke down in tears, saying she had had more time with her father when she visited him in jail: "At least then I could have an uninterrupted half an hour with him."

However, one thing I could not miss, seeing Walter and Albertina together for the first time, was the moving tenderness and affection they shared. Everyone remarked that they were like a couple on honeymoon and how wonderful it was to see two people of that age so engrossed with one another. I remember Cyril Ramaphosa watching them in amazement. "Their body language is of two people in love," he remarked. "In the struggle you don't expect people to be so expressive. They stand out easily as the most loving couple in the struggle."

After a special summit of the frontline heads of state, Walter and his delegation left for Tanzania, where they received a heroes' welcome. They were delighted to be received by former president Julius Nyerere, and were glad of the opportunity to thank both him and President Hassan Mwinyi for Tanzania's significant contribution to the struggle against apartheid. They addressed a huge rally in Dar-es-Salaam and received a welcome from young people at Solomon Mahlangu Freedom College. From Tanzania they flew to Addis Ababa.

Next they proceeded to Sweden for an emotional reunion with Oliver Tambo. After his stroke (brought on through massive overwork) several months earlier, Tambo had gone to Sweden to recuperate at a private clinic, as he would not have been able to rest sufficiently in London. Arrangements were made through Billy Modise, the chief representative of the ANC in Sweden, and the delegation were eager to know whether they would be able to see their old comrade. Tambo's doctors had to decide whether or not the excitement would be too much for their patient, who had lost the faculty of speech and was still very frail. Once they gave the go-ahead for a private meeting with no press, a delighted Tambo redoubled his efforts at rehabilitation in anticipation of seeing his friends. The Swedish government bent over backwards to facilitate the historic reunion and offered unstinting hospitality.

The long-awaited meeting was profoundly moving – Tambo still could not speak, but words were not necessary. Many of those present were struggling not to shed tears. Billy Modise's one regret was that there were no cameras present to record the historic moment. Later, when asked, Walter could not find words to describe being reunited with his old friend; the feelings "ran too deep".

The delegation returned home at the end of January just in time to hear President de Klerk's dramatic speech unbanning the ANC, and to prepare for Mandela's release. Walter and Albertina joined Winnie and other ANC leaders in a chartered flight to Cape Town. Their flight was delayed, and they only arrived after 2pm, thus delaying the release, which was scheduled for 3p.m. They drove straight to Victor Verster Prison, where Winnie joined Mandela in his long-awaited walk to freedom. Their excitement about the release was dampened by anxiety about the arrangements. Walter was worried that the huge crowd that had congregated at the Grand Parade in the heart of Cape Town would become restless as a result of the delay in their heroes' arrival: "We were very concerned with keeping the situation under control." Walter relaxed only after Mandela's driver managed to get their car through the crowds by taking a back route (Mandela, 555). Walter and Albertina accompanied Mandela to his first press conference at Archbishop Tutu's official residence at Bishopscourt; next, they flew to Johannesburg for a rally at the First National Bank Stadium in Soweto. Here Walter introduced Mandela to the 120 000 people who had filled the stadium to overflowing (Sampson 2000, 410). Like Walter, Mandela was not the kind of orator who whipped up audience emotions. He shied away from populist rhetoric, and urged the youth to go back to school (Mandela, 560).

At the end of February, virtually the same delegation returned to Lusaka, this time with Mandela at the head. Once again, we went to receive them at Lusaka airport where we had our first experience of the phenomenon of "Mandela mania". Tens of thousands of people flocked to Lusaka airport to see their hero. I cannot remember Mandela's arrival or whether we even managed to get near the delegation. As we negotiated our way through the sea of humanity surrounding the airport, the streets lined with excited people all the way to the city, I could not help thinking of the burden of expectation and the weight of responsibility resting on the shoulders of Nelson Mandela and the ANC leadership.

The Mandela trip followed the pattern of the January one, with a closed consultation of the NEC followed by a report-back to the membership, and meetings with the East and southern African heads of state. This time, the atmosphere was more positive. There was greater certainty now that the ANC had been officially unbanned, and excitement about "going home" was beginning to mount within the exile community. There was a greater acceptance of negotiations and the opportunity for direct communication laid to rest lingering doubts about Mandela's prison consultations with the apartheid government. At the open meeting, Mandela had the audience of exiles eating out of his hand, especially when he announced that he was prepared to serve the ANC in any capacity whatsoever – if the ANC decided he should be a security guard, carrying a baton and wielding a whistle, he would do it. The announcement that Mandela had been formally welcomed into the NEC and given the official position of deputy-president was met with thunderous applause.

There was no question of inviting anyone for supper on this visit, but we did manage to spend time with Walter and Albertina at State House. Max had a moving reunion with Mandela, and I remember Walter and Albertina beaming with pride when Max introduced his family. Mandela wanted to know how Max and I had met, and asked me, "Who was the one who proposed, you or Max?" He then wanted to know how long I took to accept the proposal. I could see why people were bowled over by his charm and charisma.

Meanwhile contacts between the ANC's backroom team and Pretoria's intelligence services continued apace. In September 1989, Thabo Mbeki, Aziz Pahad and Jacob Zuma, the ANC's intelligence chief, met the deputy-head of South Africa's National Intelligence Services in Lucerne, Switzerland. They met three more times in Switzerland during February and March of 1990. At their final meeting, they set up a steering committee to prepare the ground both for the return of the exiles and for the first meeting between the government and the ANC's NEC. Although the ANC was no longer an illegal organisation, individual members had not been given indemnity and were therefore liable to prosecution for violation of security laws if they entered South Africa. The first task of the ANC's advance party into South Africa, headed by Jacob Zuma and Penuell Maduna, head of the ANC's legal department, was to negotiate an Indemnity Bill to enable the exiles to return (Sparks 1995, 122).

In Lusaka, the NEC appointed Jackie Selebi as head of the newly established repatriation office to prepare applications for indemnity and facilitate clearance for ANC cadres wishing to return to South Africa (Ngculu, Unpublished manuscript; Houston, Unpublished notes, 217). ANC NEC and

SACP leaders were thus able to travel to South Africa to attend the historic meeting of 2 May 1990 between the ANC and the government at Groote Schuur, the State President's official residence. Walter was part of the ANC's 11-person delegation that included two women, Ruth Mompati and Cheryl Carolus. They were the first black women ever to participate in an official meeting in that bastion of white male supremacy. The outcome of the three-day indaba was the Groote Schuur Minute, which allowed for the release of political prisoners, the return of exiles, and the amendment of security legislation. In the same month, the Indemnity Act was introduced. This provided for temporary or permanent indemnity against prosecution for returning exiles (TRC report).

These were welcome developments for the Sisulu family. Jongi Sisulu was one of five young ANC prisoners released from Robben Island on 30 March. Albertina immediately arranged for his flight home. Lungi and Sheila, who met him at the airport, told him that Walter and Mandela would be arriving on a flight from Durban within the hour. Jongi waited nervously for the father he had not seen since he was five years' old. Walter did not recognise the young man standing with Sheila and Lungi until Sheila said: "Tata, this is Jongi." With a cry of joy, he hugged Jongi, exclaiming in amazement: "I didn't recognise him, I just didn't recognise him!" (Pippa Green, *Leadership Magazine*, May 1990). Zwelakhe had once remarked that the police were not happy unless they had a Sisulu in jail, and indeed in the previous three decades there had always been at least one or more Sisulus in prison. Jongi's release marked the first time since the 1960s that not one single member of the family was incarcerated. Ten days after Jongi's release, Lindi returned home as part of Jacob Zuma's team, after 14 years in exile. She arrived at the airport just in time to spend a few minutes with Zwelakhe who, as Mandela's press aide, was accompanying Mandela to the UK to attend another Wembley Stadium concert in his honour. Jongi's release and Lindi's return provided the occasion for a big homecoming party. Albertina announced that it was only a matter of time before Max and Gerald returned home (Pippa Green, *Leadership Magazine*, May 1990).

Max ended his 27 years of exile on 1 June 1990, when we flew into South Africa for a 10-day visit. Vuyisile and Duma were too young to appreciate the significance of the occasion, and Max remarked that he felt nothing when we landed in Johannesburg. Perhaps he had already returned home in a figurative sense when he had been reunited with his parents in Lusaka. He also had little time to reflect on the emotional implications of homecoming. He had been besieged by requests for interviews and meetings even before we left Zambia. There was a lot of media interest in the ANC's first-ever policy statement on the environment, which Max and Stan Sangweme, a South African working at the United Nations Environment Programme, had drafted. The ANC's stand on nationalisation was a burning issue and corporate South Africa was keen to know more about the Moscow-trained economist heading the ANC's Department of Economic Policy.

Walter's driver Dominic Mncube brought Albertina to the airport to meet us. Our first stop was the ANC headquarters in Sauer Street, where we had to drop Max so he could attend a meeting. We saw little of him for the rest of the week as he was swallowed up into an endless round of meetings and interviews. He did manage to reunite with his childhood friend Maye, but had little time to see anyone else. Because of the hectic programme he and his parents followed, it was not possible to have a homecoming celebration for Max, which I thought was a great pity. Meanwhile, I felt I had returned to a very different home to the one I had visited on previous occasions. It was wonderful to have Walter at home, but we hardly saw him or Albertina. They were either at work or attending to the never-ending stream of visitors. Nkuli and I would later commiserate about the frustration of this period. For years, she had looked forward to cooking her father's favourite meal when he finally came home, but she never had the opportunity. Because of the large numbers of people visiting the Sisulu home each day, the ANC Women's League team (which had undertaken the large-scale cooking at the time of the release) continued to cook for the household for the next six months. I shuddered to think what the situation was like at the Mandela home, where the volume of visitors was much higher.

# t w o

Towards the end of 1990, Walter and Albertina were beginning to show the strain of overwork during what had been an extraordinary and hectic year. We became very concerned about their state of health, as did the ANC. They clearly needed a holiday, so their trip to the Soviet Union in November 1990 came at a most opportune moment.

Their invitation to visit the Soviet Union for "rest and treatment" came at a time of changing USSR-ANC relations. After decades of supporting the ANC, Gorbachev's government, battered by economic crises, was cosying up to the De Klerk regime, and its links with the ANC were deteriorating. Simon Makana, the ANC representative in Moscow, was worried that some Soviet diplomats might be relaying the information he gave them to Pretoria (Sampson 2000, 420). In this context, the Sisulu visit signalled the importance of maintaining links at the highest possible level. Walter and Albertina attended a military parade and reception in Moscow to mark the anniversary of the October Revolution, and Walter was able to speak briefly with Gorbachev. They also visited MK cadres at the training centre at Perevalnoye, which had by then been officially reorganised into a Ground Forces College. Commanders, instructors and cadets gave them a warm reception. This part of the trip was especially significant for Walter's bodyguard, Edward Mbundu. He had studied there 10 years earlier before being imprisoned on Robben Island (Shubin, 382).

After their official meetings, Walter and Albertina were taken to a sanatorium at the Crimea resort of Yalta, where they were finally able to relax and enjoy a holiday. Their stay, under the personal care of Dr Vyacheslav Tetyokin, made a huge difference (Correspondence, Vladimir Shubin, 19/8/2002). They came back rejuvenated. When I told Albertina they looked 10 years younger, she waxed lyrical about the treatments and exercise they had received. We teased them about looking like a couple just back from honeymoon, and Walter said the trip had indeed been a long-delayed honeymoon, as they did not have one when they had married all those years ago.

Meanwhile, the family was slowly reassembling in South Africa after decades of fragmentation. Max, myself and our sons left Zambia in December 1990 when my contract with the ILO ended. Max took up a four-month fellowship in the Department of Economics at the University of the Western Cape, where he greatly appreciated the welcome and moral support he received from Professor Loots, the head of the department, and colleagues like Pieter le Roux. Walter's friend Dullah Omar, who was at the time in the Law Faculty of the university, also provided a welcoming presence. Allister and the late Sue Sparks kindly gave us the use of their Cape Town apartment for the duration of our stay. After Max completed his stint at UWC, we moved to Johannesburg and lived with Walter and Albertina for a few months while looking for a house of our own. We finally found a house in Kensington, just a stone's throw from where activist and academic David Webster had been so brutally gunned down in 1989. Lindi returned for good at about the same time and was immediately immersed in the work of the ANC security department.

Those returning home from exile were by no means guaranteed safety. Political assassinations were not uncommon and returning exiles had to tread carefully. The upheavals of homecoming also proved difficult and unsettling for many people. We considered ourselves fortunate that we had a stable family to return to and a large network of supportive friends.

Walter and Albertina had little time to spare for family matters; they had their hands full with matters of national urgency. Soon after his release, Walter had been invited by King Goodwill Zwelithini to visit him in the KwaZulu capital of Ulundi. Walter was eager to accept, and was urged to do so by Mandela. The visit was tentatively approved by the ANC, provided the visit took place at the king's palace in Nongoma. This was because it was thought that going to Ulundi would suggest recognition of the homeland. As soon as Mandela returned from Lusaka, he telephoned Chief Mangosuthu Buthelezi to explain that Walter would be visiting the king in Nongoma, not Ulundi. This did not go down well, and Walter was later told by one of the Zulu princes that the royal family felt insulted because Walter had no right to tell the king where he wanted to meet him. Mandela tried to explain that the ANC membership did not want Walter to go to KwaZulu at all, and the Nongoma proposal was a compromise: "We managed to get this compromise approved. Surely you can bend as well?" But the king refused to see Walter. Looking back, Walter regretted the ANC stand because "we would have gained much by meeting him [the King], even in Ulundi" (Houser and Shore, 196).

Although Walter and Mandela were anxious to cultivate a relationship with the Zulu king, this was met with fierce resistance from Inkatha (Mandela, 566), and internecine violence in Natal increased dramatically. In the last week of March 1990, over 200 people were killed and 20 000 forced to flee the area in what came to be known as the "Seven Day War". Within months, the violence spread to the Reef, and continued to spiral over the next two years. In July, the first train attack took place, marking the start of a series of attacks on black commuters in the Witwatersrand. Between 1990 and 1993, at least 572 people were killed in 600 incidents of train violence (TRC report).

Walter and Albertina were naturally deeply distressed by the carnage and, like the vast majority of people in the country, they were convinced that a "third force" was orchestrating and directing the violence. As leaders, they were constantly receiving reports of violence. One Saturday afternoon, a man arrived at their home, covered in cement dust, in a state of shock. He told us that after an Inkatha rally, a stick-wielding mob had descended on a nearby row of houses and systematically destroyed them. His brother had been killed and he had barely escaped with his life. "The police just looked on and did nothing," he said over and over again.

"The police did nothing." This was the refrain in black communities throughout the country. The ANC leadership was constantly confronted with the question: "How can we continue to negotiate with these people when they are killing us?"

One of Walter's main roles in the ANC in the 1990s was that of conflict resolution. Like many other ANC leaders, he was prepared to risk his life in pursuit of peace, especially in strife-torn KwaZulu-Natal. Walter often travelled around the country with Kgalema Montlante, a former Robben Islander who would later become Secretary-General of the ANC. Drawing as little attention to themselves as possible, they visited flashpoints for violence around the country, mainly the youth structures of the ANC, calling for peace.

Trying to find peace in Natal meant dealing with Buthelezi, described by Walter as "a man who thought and worked in strange ways". Their task was also made harder by the ultra-militant attitude of some ANC leaders in Natal. Walter had many run-ins with the firebrand Harry Gwala. "He had been difficult on Robben Island," Walter remembers, "and he was difficult outside as well." Kgalema Montlante recalled how at one meeting in Natal, Walter had told the people that the ANC leadership wanted them to lay down their weapons and work for peace. Speaking after Walter, the wily Gwala said he agreed with the leadership, but it was difficult to meet their wishes because the people of KwaZulu had no weapons to lay down. He said perhaps the leadership should first supply them with weapons, then they could lay them down. This message, which was received with glee, completely undid Walter's good work (Interviews, Kgalema Montlante and Lucky Mabaso).

Meanwhile, the ANC leadership had to answer to the challenges and criticisms of the more militant youth. Walter was no exception, even in his own home. I remember evenings of debate when

Lungi Jnr would challenge his grandfather about what he saw as the inept response of the leadership to the attacks on defenceless communities. Walter would listen carefully, and respond gently but firmly to what were really strong criticisms.

The protracted process of negotiations between the government and the liberation movements suffered another breakdown after the massacre on 17 July 1992, when a column of migrant workers from KwaMadala hostel carried out a murderous attack on the sleeping inhabitants of the township of Boipatong. Thirty-eight men, women and children were hacked, stabbed to death or shot. A distraught and angry Albertina led a delegation of ANC women to Boipatong to console the women who had lost relatives and try to assist them. The message to the ANC leadership at the subsequent funerals was loud and clear. At a rally, Mandela was confronted by angry township residents shouting: "You are like lambs while the government is killing us." Something dramatic and drastic had to be done about the political violence.

In response, the ANC withdrew from negotiations listing 14 demands the government would have to meet before talks could resume. The main ones related to ending the violence: the implementation of earlier agreements to secure the migrant workers hostels and to halt the carrying of so-called "cultural" weapons by Inkatha members (Sparks 1995, 147).

Eric Mtshali, a veteran trade unionist who worked for the ANC intelligence in Natal, describes an incident that captures the quality of the relationship between Mandela and Walter during these tense and dangerous times. Mandela was due to speak at a rally in Nongoma when the ANC received information that members of Inkatha were planning to kill him. After checking that the threat was credible, they contacted Jacob Zuma, who went with Mtshali to advise Mandela against attending. Mandela held firm, saying, "My job is to go to Nongoma tomorrow. Yours is to protect the President of the ANC." When Zuma and Mtshali realised that they could not change his mind, they hastily left the room to call Walter in Johannesburg and beg him to intervene. As they returned, they heard the telephone ring and Mandela answer. Next, they heard him laughing: "Oh, they have reported me, they have reported me." Apparently Walter had immediately telephoned Mandela to order him not to go to Nongoma. Mandela complied with his old friend's instructions and did not go (Jabulani Sithole Interview, Eric Mtshali).

Internal political affairs also kept Walter and Albertina busy. It was with mixed feelings that they bade farewell to the UDF. The decision to disband this organisation was taken at its last conference in March 1991, at which Walter gave the keynote address. He paid tribute to the sterling work it had done, noting that its formation had "decisively turned the tide" against the PW Botha regime. He saluted the decision of the UDF's 1990 conference to assist in the building of legal branches of the ANC. Nevertheless, now that the ANC was a legal organisation with a registered mass membership, things had changed, and key UDF personnel had transferred wholesale to the ANC.

At the ANC's July 1991 conference, Mandela was confirmed as President. Cyril Ramaphosa became the new Secretary-General. To avoid a contest for the position of Deputy-President between Thabo Mbeki and Chris Hani, which might have proved divisive, Walter was persuaded to stand, and won easily.

By 1991, the dust of internal reorganisation had settled, and the ANC was ensconced in its new offices at Shell House in central Johannesburg. Together with his father, Max moved into Shell House, where he continued his work with the ANC's Department of Economic Planning.

Walter's old friend, Rica Hodgson, came in to work as his secretary. Rica had spent most of her days in exile working for the International Defence and Aid Fund. When she returned to South Africa after 1990, she had no plans to get another job, but when Barbara Masekela, Mandela's personal assistant, asked her to work for Walter, she could not refuse. Rica was a small, tough and efficient woman with a colourful and courageous history.

She ran Walter's office with an iron hand. I would tease her about the contrast between her and her boss. Walter seldom used strong words and had a tendency to talk in euphemisms, while Rica always called a spade a spade and could swear like a trooper. She was very protective of him and tried her best to prevent people taking advantage of his kind heart. "Hordes of people came into that office and as soft as he is, Walter would have attended to all of them and worked himself to the point of absolute exhaustion. I saw it as my job to keep him alive."

At Shell House, Walter continued in his role of backroom organiser and Mandela's principal confidante. "Madiba would consult him on everything," recalls Barbara Masekela. "He never made a major decision without speaking to him."

The "triumvirate" of the 1950s was at last restored when Oliver Tambo returned to South Africa. He had recovered sufficiently from his stroke to resume work, although nothing on the scale of the work he had done in his years in exile. "It was a wonderful day when OR came into the office," says Rica Hodgson.

Walter was overjoyed to have his old comrade just across the hall from him. On the few occasions I visited the office, I found it incredibly moving to observe the close companionship of these two veterans. They consulted each other constantly, and they very clearly savoured each other's company. Mandela relied heavily on them for advice. Well into their 70s, they were still the "engine" that drove the ANC. Rusty Bernstein provides an apt summary of how their skills complemented each other in the roles they played: "Mandela's endurance and charisma made him the symbol of our liberation struggle … Tambo's single-mindedness and diplomatic skills sponsored the worldwide campaign against apartheid … And Sisulu, the 'father of them all' set the strategic directions and the standards of humanity and comradeship which characterized the South African liberation movement … The interconnection of these three great men shaped our [nation's history] through the decades of struggle that led to a new South Africa" (Rusty Bernstein, 148).

Albertina was meanwhile coping with the complex issues surrounding the leadership and direction of the ANC Women's League. In brief, in May 1990, the women's section of the ANC convened a meeting in Lusaka, at which an interim leadership corps was formed. Although Winnie Mandela had never been part of the ANC Women's League structures, it was felt that they had to try to reach out and involve her. When the Mandelas had visited Lusaka, the Women's Section went out of their way to provide Winnie with a package of information and briefing notes and bent over backwards to try to integrate her into their activities. When the leadership of the Women's Section arrived back in South Africa in June, they enlisted Sister Bernard Ncube to make sure that Winnie was included at a high level. This courting of Winnie upset many of the FEDSAW women whom Winnie had always treated with contempt, but the Lusaka contingent insisted that Winnie be involved for the sake of unity. For the likes of Albertina, Sister Bernard, Nomvula Mokonyane and others who knew first-hand the difficulties of working with Winnie, and felt the pain that her actions had caused in her community, the Lusaka group's insistence on involving Winnie was a bitter pill to swallow.

At the first Women's League conference in Kimberley in April 1991, Winnie arrived late, and then stood against Gertrude Shope for election to office, even though some of the senior women present asked her not to. Albertina had already been nominated, but had declined to stand so that the field would be clear for Gertrude Shope, who won with a large majority. Both Albertina and Winnie were elected to the executive. The women from exile soon found out the truth of their colleagues' accounts of working with Winnie. They found that her main weakness was her inability to work in a collective. It was impossible to get her to come to meetings. She was never available and would not return messages. "When we telephoned her, she would not come to the phone. It seemed she was determined to dodge the collective. She turned it into an art form." She never took part in policy discussions or addressed problems within the organisation. Worse still, officials alerted Walter to the fact that Winnie had on one occasion organised some of the women in the PWV to demonstrate against the ANC leadership, which action caused significant conflict and confusion within the Women's League, as well as embarrassment to the organisation.

The December 1993 Women's League conference in Durban was described by Baleka Kgositsile as "a nightmarish experience". Winnie, supported by cheering hangers-on from outside the League, conducted an American-style drive for election. Albertina, on the other hand, was a reluctant candidate who was prevailed upon to stand for the sake of preserving unity. Gertrude, like Albertina and other veteran women, represented a somewhat staid, if dutiful and disciplined approach to serving on the executive. Winnie's populist approach won the day and she became president of the ANC Women's League. Among other things, this meant the end of any focus on gender issues in the League. The full history of this period of travail has yet to be recounted, and falls beyond the scope of this biography, except to say that for Albertina it was an experience she would prefer to forget.

These were also years of hectic international travel for Walter and Albertina. In August 1991, they travelled to Singapore and Australia at the invitation of the respective governments. They stopped over in Mauritius, where they were welcomed by the Mauritian foreign minister. In Singapore, they met with the Prime Minster Mr Goh Chok Tong. Next was a whirlwind tour of Australia's major cities, in the course of which they met Bob Hawke and Gareth Evans.

Walter took an immediate liking to Evans, Australia's dynamic and forthright foreign minister. They discussed Australia's financial assistance to the ANC and Walter was asked about the degree of threat posed by the right wing in South Africa. Walter urged the Australian government not to lift sanctions, as the time was not yet ripe. Albertina meanwhile attended numerous meetings with women's groups and organisations. The visits demonstrated the enormous support for the struggle to end apartheid.

Late in 1991, they headed to North America, where they visited seven major Canadian cities, before heading south to New York, Washington, Atlanta and Boston.

Derrick Z Jackson, who interviewed him, gave an accurate thumbnail sketch of Walter's tirelessness in *The Boston Globe*:

> If you ever think about being tired, think about Walter Sisulu. Sisulu is 79. His days and nights are spent driving and flying to meetings. His midnights and predawn hours are often spent hopping in a car to quell township disturbances. Too often, his destination is the funeral of a young person. His only admitted sources of relaxation are listening to choral music and visits with his grandchildren ... During his visit to Boston he said: "For the time being, destiny decides that I am one who is here to help the situation. When the situation changes I will perhaps relax."
>
> Sisulu moves around with almost none of the fanfare of Mandela ... Sisulu's visit to Boston, to raise money and remind people that the white government is still enforcing apartheid and encouraging violence among black people, was marked by a private visit and a reception with about 200 die-hard activists. That is how one 79-year-old person spends the autumn of his life.

Jackson's assessment was all too true. Since his release from prison, Walter had yet to spend an entire month at home. If he was not abroad, he was travelling extensively within South Africa, heading wherever he was needed or could be of use. In 1992, he was made Chancellor of the University of Venda, a duty he took very seriously and this meant frequent trips to Venda as well.

Back in South Africa, Walter managed to find time to celebrate his 80th birthday in May 1992. Together with a group of black businessmen, Rica Hodgson arranged a huge party. All Walter's old friends were there: Oliver Tambo, Joe Slovo, Ahmed Kathrada and Andrew Mlangeni. Joe Slovo jokingly reminded Walter of how he was among those who would try to break up Communist Party meetings during his Youth League Days. There was recognition of how far the ANC had come since then, but one of the speakers pointed out that although it was a victory that Walter Sisulu could celebrate his birthday as a free man, he still did not have the right to vote. Over two years had elapsed since his release from prison and we still did not have the nonracial democratic South Africa that he had gone to prison for.

Another guest remarked that Walter Sisulu was probably one of the most active octogenarians in the world; his schedule certainly made no concessions to advancing age.

Back on the international circuit, he addressed the 10th summit of the Non-Aligned States in Jakarta, Indonesia, in September 1992. He told the delegates that, although negotiations to bring about a democratic South Africa had started two and a half years previously, these were not as advanced as they should be. He appealed for pressure to be maintained against the regime.

A month later, Albertina attended the Labour Party conference in Blackpool in Britain at the invitation of the charity, One World Action, to talk about women in South Africa. In an interview with journalist Alice Thomson, she was able to expound her views on gender and transformation, noting that women were particularly affected by poverty, illiteracy and unemployment: "Our women are exploited three times over. They are oppressed by the traditions and customs of our society ... by the government and by the menfolk." She said she dreamed of a nonracist, nonsexist democratic South Africa with a government elected by all the people: "Whether the government elects a white president or a black president, it must be a government run for the people and voted for by the people – and that includes women" (*The Times*, 2/10/92).

Walter's next trip abroad, to China, Taiwan and South Korea, in October 1993, presented special challenges. Walter had received pressing invitations both from the People's Republic of China and the Republic of China (Taiwan), and decided that he should visit both countries. At the time South Africa had diplomatic relations with Taiwan, but not yet with the People's Republic of China. "When we were preparing for that visit, we were pressurized by the People's Republic to disentangle the two visits," recalls Lucky Mabaso, Walter's political assistant. "Walter was firm about his decision and told the representative of the People's Republic that he had made an undertaking to visit Taiwan and he would have to fulfil it. [He] felt that the ANC should not be held ransom to myopic ideological approaches ... He always emphasized the ANC's independent point of view" (Joyce Sikhakhane-Rankin Interview, Lucky Mabaso).

Walter and Albertina never failed to find pleasure in reuniting with family and friends whom they had not seen for years. They were both very particular about the hospitality that had to be accorded to visitors and the need to express gratitude for past kindnesses. When Father Charles Hooper sent word that he was coming to visit, Albertina called on her children to welcome him. Unfortunately, his visit took place when everyone was either out of the country or out of town. Albertina was annoyed by the family's lack of availability. I was the only one around and she lectured me about how good these Anglican priests had been towards her during the struggle, and how Charles Hooper had been a surrogate parent to her children while they were at school in Swaziland.

Father Trevor Huddleston also returned to South Africa in 1994. It was a poignant moment for the priest who described his days in "the Africa of Sophiatown, Orlando, Pimville" as "the honeymoon period of my life which had taught me the meaning of love in such a way that no other time or place could ever supplant it" (Huddleston 1991, 25). Walter was up at the crack of dawn to meet him at the airport. We prepared lunch for him at No. 7372, and the neighbourhood poured in to see "Father". Some knew him from the Sophiatown days and others from when he had worked at Holy Cross Church. Some had not yet been born during his service in South Africa, but had heard about him from their parents. Others just came to pay tribute to the man who was for so long at the helm of the anti-apartheid movement.

Robin Denniston, Huddleston's biographer, wrote of the reunion between veteran activists: "One warm winter in May 1994, two elderly men were sipping tea in Orlando West ... One reminded the other that fifty years earlier they had drunk tea together, looking across at the same great church of Christ the King. Simultaneously and spontaneously the two ancient revolutionaries raised their cups: 'Mission accomplished' they said, and laughed. The two men were Walter Sisulu and Trevor Huddleston" (Denniston, xv).

Sadly, Huddleston's attempt to come "home" to South Africa did not work out. Walter did all he could for his old friend, but was terribly distressed at being unable to spend as much time as he would have liked with his age-mate. The problem lay in the circumstances rather than the individuals; Huddleston was retired, while Walter was still working full-time and non-stop for the ANC. The choice of a whites-only old age home was also disastrous, as Huddleston had little in common with the other residents. After two months, Huddleston gave up and returned to the UK.

In August 1994, Walter had a reunion with Lazar Sidelsky, his lawyer of the 1950s. Sidelsky subsequently framed a letter he received from Walter after that visit: "When I saw you at my 50th anniversary party, I knew that you were familiar but I could not place you. Afterwards I remembered clearly. I'm sure that you also recall that day way back in 1941, when I brought you to a young man, Nelson Mandela, with the request that you'd take him to your firm as an articled clerk. You can now look back on that day as a truly historic occasion."

In September 1992, Max left for Cambridge, Massachusetts to study for an MA in Public Administration at the Kennedy School at Harvard University. I followed with our sons Vuyisile and Duma a few months later to take up a fellowship at the Bunting Institute at Radcliffe College to start work on this book. Albertina and Walter encouraged us to go, and were pleased that Max would be getting a degree from Harvard.

We left a country where violence was still raging. After so many years and months, it seemed that not much progress had been made regarding negotiations. The road to freedom was much longer and complicated than we had imagined, and many bitter blows remained to be endured.

One of these was a tragedy both for the nation and our family. On 10 April 1993, we received the terrible news that Chris Hani had been assassinated. We were plunged into despair. That a white right-wing extremist should have killed Chris Hani, the Umkhonto we Sizwe chief and senior SACP and ANC leader, was not in itself a surprise. A larger-than-life figure with a tremendous charisma and an intellect to match, a powerful and persuasive orator who inspired fierce loyalty in his followers, Chris Hani was the epitome of the romantic guerrilla leader. He had long been targeted by apartheid's assassins. It was the timing of his murder that was so shocking. The armed struggle had been suspended and despite his initial misgivings, Chris had committed himself to a process of peaceful change through negotiation. Even from the point of view of his enemies, there could be no justification for his death.

For the Sisulu family, as for many others in the liberation movement, Chris's death represented far more than the loss of a leader. It was the loss of a personal friend. Max and I found it difficult to cope with our feelings of bereavement. Max and Chris had been close friends since their early days of exile, when they lived in the same house in Lusaka with Oliver Tambo, who was effectively a surrogate father to them. Chris had personally welcomed me to Lusaka with a warmth I will never forget, enfolding and including me in the affection he held for Max. It was appallingly difficult for us being away from South Africa at such a time. I remember walking through the streets of Cambridge in shock on the morning we heard the news, unable to comprehend how everything around me could be normal when Chris had just been killed. At least at home we would have been part of a collective mourning process.

As was to be expected, there was little coverage of the assassination in the American press, except for one haunting image of Oliver Tambo, sitting disconsolately in the driveway of Chris's home, grief etched in every line of his body. Max and I were extremely worried about the toll the tragedy would take on OR's fragile health, and we were saddened but not surprised when we heard two weeks later that he had suffered another massive stroke, and had not survived. Both Nelson Mandela and Trevor Huddleston said that when they buried Oliver Tambo, they were burying a part of themselves. Walter felt the same way, and his staff remember how despondent he was, and how gloomy the atmosphere in the office was in the days after Tambo's funeral. The nation mourned for another great leader who had seen the promised land, but not reached it.

The assassination of Chris Hani shook South Africa to its foundations and jeopardised the prospect of peaceful negotiations. Mandela had to appeal for calm on national television, and ANC leaders had to work frantically to calm their enraged constituency. The country was on the brink of a civil war once more, and only the ANC leadership had the capacity to pull it back (Sparks 1995, 188; Johnson, 275). Ironically, Chris's murder led directly to the speeding up of negotiations (Sparks 1995, 189). Even the National Party recognised how dangerous it would be to drag out the negotiations any longer. In other words, it took Chris Hani's assassination in the driveway of his home to drag the negotiation process out of the limbo in which it had stalled. A new sense of urgency was felt at the World Trade Centre in Kempton Park, scene of the negotiations, and even the thuggish invasion by the AWB lunatic fringe in June 1993 could not derail the process.

In July 1993, just as we were preparing to return to South Africa, we had another shock. An acquaintance asked, "Did you hear that your parents-in-law were involved in a shooting incident with the South African police?" The person was at least able to assure me that, although lives had been lost, Walter and Albertina were unhurt. Full of dread, we called home to find out that a shootout on the Soweto highway between police and Walter's bodyguards had left one man dead and three injured.

According to *The Star*, "ANC PWV chairman Tokyo Sexwale ... said the Sisulus were travelling in convoy with two other cars [when] Sisulu's security men realised they were being followed. The unidentified car sped past the security men and positioned itself alongside the car the Sisulus were travelling in. The car was 'unmarked, white, had no blue lights and the occupants were not wearing police uniforms.' The security men took 'defensive' action, he said, but it was not yet clear where the shooting came from. The security men's car rolled ... One of the bodyguards was in Baragwanath Hospital's intensive care unit yesterday morning [and] the driver died in hospital" (*The Star*, 19/7/93).

There was a great deal of anger at what looked suspiciously like an attempted assassination. Meanwhile, counter-accusations were made by the police, and the bodyguards were accused of carrying unlicensed weapons. The ANC insisted on a full investigation and requested that an attempted murder docket be opened. Walter and Albertina themselves maintained a dignified silence, and confined their attentions to the injured security men, visiting them in hospital to wish them well. Confronted with reiterated reports that the police car in question was unmarked, Witwatersrand SAP liaison officer Major Eugene Opperman said: "I don't care what the ANC says, the car had a blue light switched on, it had police registration plates and all the policemen were in uniform."

However, the police found themselves with egg on their faces when it turned out that by sheer coincidence, the second police car called to the scene was being trailed by a German television crew which was filming a documentary on crime in Johannesburg. Their footage of the scene provided clear evidence that the police car in question had no blue light, no registration number and the men in it were not in uniform. This confirmed our suspicions that the police had a sinister agenda, and it was chilling to be reminded so close to home that the "third force" was not merely an academic issue. Walter and Albertina were lucky; we could not help thinking about the many occasions activists had experienced harassment at the hands of police or security forces when there had been no German television crew to confirm their stories.

According to Senior Counsel Ishmael Semenya, the inquest into the matter found that the police were liable for the killing of the Sisulus' bodyguard. However, it is not clear whether the state subsequently prosecuted those responsible or not.

After all the danger, grief and loss of 1993, it was with relief that we could finally anticipate and celebrate South Africa's first democratic elections in April 1994.

Looking back on this landmark event, Walter mused, "The remarkable thing that happened there which makes our revolution one of the greatest was the fact that while there was tension throughout the country and many powerful forces were talking about civil war, on the day of the election the masses of people were determined only on one thing, to make their cross, to make the election a success. They started early in the morning, five o'clock. They were patient, they tolerated even the weakness and the mistakes that emerged. It was a remarkable moment I can never forget. A situation I am unable to describe properly, where the masses gave us all leadership in an amazing way" (Houser and Shore, 205).

I accompanied Walter when he voted for the first time in his life, a few weeks short of his 82nd birthday, at a polling booth in Diepkloof. When I commented that it was a pity he and Mama could not vote together, he said he did not mind – it was important for the leadership to be spread out so that they could cover as many polling booths as possible. He was scheduled to vote at 10am When the media had not arrived as expected by then, I suggested to him that we wait for a few minutes, as I felt that such an historic event should receive media coverage. The archivist in me was anxious for a photographic record, but he demurred: "I was told to vote at 10am and that is what I am going to do." So one of the figures who had done most to bring about this extraordinary day voted quietly, with little fuss and ceremony.

Albertina meanwhile voted in Orlando West near Phomolong Station. While Walter's approach to voting was one of duty and sober satisfaction, Albertina bubbled over when asked how she felt voting for the first time: "The excitement was unbelievable – going to jail, being forced to leave my children – it was all worth it to live to see this day."

The press caught up with Walter later in the day and journalist Steven Laufer was one of those who interviewed him. In an article entitled "Tata moves off centre stage" (*Weekly Mail & Guardian*, 29 April – 5 May, 1994), Laufer summed up Walter's character in a description that applies equally to Albertina: "For Sisulu life has been and will continue to be about service to the people, although characteristically, he never uses the words. There is no cant, no self-delusion, no hyperbole. Just the quiet pleasure of being able to sit back and allow the history of which he has been an active participant to pass review."

# *t h r e e*

For Walter and Albertina Sisulu, the tumultuous and euphoric weeks following South Africa's first democratic elections were marked for them by milestones of immense significance, both personal and political.

On 17 July 1994, Albertina and Walter celebrated their 50th wedding anniversary. This was no ordinary golden wedding celebration. More than 1 000 people converged on the Vista University Hall in Soweto. The guests included community leaders, writers, artists, MPs and Thabo Mbeki, then the Deputy-President of the country. Nobel laureate Archbishop Desmond Tutu presided over the couple's renewal of their marriage vows. Following closely on the heels of the ANC's political triumph in South Africa's first democratic elections, this celebration marked a pinnacle of personal triumph for Albertina and Walter Sisulu. As one of the guests remarked: "Fifty years of marriage under any circumstances is a remarkable achievement. Fifty years of marriage under a system which deliberately set out to tear families apart is a miracle."

As guest of honour at the celebration, Nelson Mandela, the newly elected President of South Africa, paid tribute to these two icons of the struggle. He credited Walter as a major influence in his own political development and acknowledged Albertina's role in keeping the embers of struggle burning during their long years of imprisonment.

On a lighter note, Mandela had the guests in gales of laughter with his version of how the couple came to marry: "As young men we used to visit the nurses' home in the 1940s. When Walter saw Albertina, he said to me 'ndiyayithanda le'ntombazana' (I like that young lady). But you see, Walter was very shy. He was too shy to approach Albertina, so she proposed instead."

"Nelson is so naughty," was Albertina's response, amidst much hilarity. Fortunately for her, most of her family and friends knew the real story of the proposal.

Marriage for Walter and Albertina has been an empowering and fulfilling experience because they supported each other in their political careers and did not allow themselves to be constrained by prevailing stereotypes about the roles men and women should play in the family.

In an interview, Albertina once proclaimed, "I got my freedom the day I married." In her case, this startling statement was literally true: from the very beginning, Walter broadened her horizons and applauded her development. There was never any element of competition in their relationship, and each has always taken pride in deferring to the other. After Walter's release, Albertina immediately accepted his political seniority. Meanwhile, Walter had nearly burst with pride when Albertina headed a UDF delegation that met with the American and British premiers in 1989. When they toured the US together in 1990, some of the groups they met harked back to Albertina's previous visit. "Your mother is well known in the States," Walter proudly reported back to his children. "At most places I was introduced as Mrs Sisulu's husband!"

But no matter how egalitarian and mutually supportive the guiding principles of their marriage, it still does not explain how it has endured for over 50 years, especially when the bulk of those years were spent thousands of miles apart, with one of them in prison and the other banned. The secret is without doubt their great and abiding love for each other, as their prison letters have shown.

In a typical birthday message, written after Walter had been in prison for nearly 20 years, she wrote: "I never thought for a moment that I could do without you Walter, but because of your wise and repeated words of courage here I am today. A man like you is not yet born. Perhaps with the coming generation there will be a lucky woman who will give birth to a child of your qualities.

To me you are everything. You know that very well. All this, my dear husband, is to wish you happy birthday. May your health be good so that we can celebrate your next birthday at home."

Needless to say, Walter and Albertina attach great value to marriage – and welcome news of impending matrimony with great joy. To them, it is one of life's finest and greatest blessings, and they are often hurt and bewildered when the marriages of those dearest to them fall apart. The early 1990s were years of shock, dislocation and stress for families returning from exile and activists emerging from long periods of detention. Many relationships could not survive the trauma of reunion after long periods of separation, or relocation, that the return from exile entailed. Albertina and Walter's own marriage is so strong that it survived not only the decades of separation, but also the period of reunion – ironically, a time when a great many relationships and families came adrift.

Walter and Albertina may have sailed through these stormy seas without distress, but their children were not so fortunate. Every one of them experienced relationship challenges in the turbulent years of the 1990s, causing Albertina to snap in exasperation: "It seems as if you children waited for your father to come out of jail to present him with all these problems!" There was an element of truth in this; as a natural mediator and peace-maker, Walter was approached by family members and friends for advice on personal and domestic matters as well as matters of state, and his counsel and advice soothed many of us. It was during this period that the marriages of Lindi and Nkuli broke down. There was no doubt that the elder Sisulus mourned the dissolution of their daughters' marriages, but their support for their children and grandchildren was as unstinting as always.

A few weeks before their golden wedding anniversary, Walter and Albertina had taken their places in another momentous ceremony, this time of international historical significance, when on 10 May 1994, Nelson Mandela was formally sworn in as the President of the Republic of South Africa, with appropriate pomp and dignity. Walter felt quiet satisfaction at this final ritual that confirmed that the long years of struggle, sacrifice and martyrdom had come to fruition. Almost exactly 50 years before, he had picked out the young country greenhorn who had entered his office, and had groomed him for political leadership, even then seeing him as a future leader of his nation. It was a sweet vindication.

His family were also well to the fore of the new dispensation: Albertina, Lindi and Max were among the 450-odd new parliamentarians sworn in to the country's first democratic parliament, prompting Mandela to joke that he was considering legislation to limit the number of Sisulus in parliament. Zwelakhe was the first black person to head the South African Broadcasting Corporation. Max would eventually become the ANC Chief Whip in Parliament, and Lindi would later become one of the few female Ministers of Intelligence in the world.

As I sat in the public gallery with Walter at the opening of the first democratic Parliament in 1994, we overheard two women conversing about how remarkable it was that so many of the parliamentarians were women, mostly black, in what used to be a predominantly white male Afrikaner preserve. This was no accident, but the result of concerted efforts by the ANC Women's League in the run-up to the elections to ensure greater inclusion of women in the political process. Under pressure from the League, the ANC NEC had announced in December 1993 that at least one-third of the candidates it submitted for election would be women. Albertina had been the highest-placed woman on the list of candidates.

Parliament was nevertheless a very unfriendly environment, especially at first, recalled Thenjiwe Mtintso, herself a member of Parliament at the time, who later became Deputy Secretary-General of the ANC: "With all the rushing around, taking care of business, looking at all those piles and piles of documents, trying to make sense of the struggle in that particular terrain" (Joyce Sikhakhane-Rankin Interview, Thenjiwe Mtintso).

Life in parliament was particularly demanding for veterans like Albertina, Adelaide Tambo, Ellen Kuzwayo, the late Dorothy Nyembe, Ruth Mompati, Lydia Kompe and others. In a democratic dispensation, these women would have been members of parliament 20 years earlier. Because of apartheid, they became parliamentarians only well after the age of retirement. No concessions were made to their age and seniority, and like everyone else, they had to cope with the heavy demands of parliamentary committee work and commuting between Cape Town and their respective constituencies. The burden of work took a heavy toll, and Ellen Kuzwayo collapsed more than once in Parliament itself. This particular group was very alert to criticisms of "getting on the gravy train", and often went without the administrative and logistical support they were entitled to.

Like her other veteran colleagues, Albertina was extremely diligent about her parliamentary work, reading all the required documents, and attending every meeting. She made herself available to everyone who wanted a minute of her time, and all this without a personal assistant or secretary to brief her, keep an appointment book or screen her visitors. Thenjiwe Mtintso was among those who admired Albertina's perseverance and ability to cope with the stress of Parliament. "She was able to analyse the challenges that faced us in a simple, practical, down-to-earth manner. When we formed the Women's Caucus, MaSisulu and MaNjobe [Makho Njobe] were the ones who were always there." She and others deeply appreciated the guidance of these women, who never pulled rank or used their seniority in their dealings with younger women. Thenjiwe goes on to point out that this was true of both Sisulus: "Tata and Mama Sisulu are one couple that have the right to make a lot of demands of the ANC but they do not feel they are entitled. At their age they continue to give. They are an embodiment of the kind of leadership that we want to build for the ANC. I wish we could immortalise them" (Joyce Sikhakhane-Rankin Interview, Thenjiwe Mtintso).

Albertina had to deal with other public obligations as well as her parliamentary duties. In 1994, she was elected President of the World Peace Council, and in 1995, she hosted the assembly of the World Peace Council. Because of the end of the Cold War, the Council had changed its emphasis; instead of focusing on the ending of the arms race, it now concerned itself with ending regional wars, especially in Africa, which made the choice of a South African icon as President a logical one.

Walter retired from the post of ANC Deputy-President in 1994, but his workload did not decrease. As thrilled as he was about the new ANC government, he was deeply concerned about the wholesale redeployment of experienced cadres to Parliament and government. His political aide, Lucky Mabaso, recalls that Walter was worried that this would weaken the ANC and that he felt that the leadership should have applied its collective mind to work out a more effective deployment policy. Mabaso believed that Walter's experience as the first full time Secretary-General of the ANC tasked with building the structures of the movement in the 1950s had given him insight into the importance of organisation-building. On the other hand, Walter was equally aware of the importance of placing within government and parliament legislators and civil servants with the capacity to translate ANC policy into tangible goals (Joyce Sikhakhane-Rankin Interview, Lucky Mabaso).

Stepping down as Deputy-President of the ANC did not mean that Walter slowed down his pace. For the next two years, he continued with organisational work, much of which entailed smoothing over sticky problems. "Wherever there were fires, Walter would be called upon to go and put them out," recalled Rica Hodgson. "The ANC still needed his diplomacy and mediating skills."

On his 85th birthday, Walter made a statement that epitomised his attitude to service: "I'm grateful I've lived this long, but I don't want to live indefinitely. I want to however continue to be active in politics and work for the improvement of our people. I have spent my whole life as an activist and as long as there is blood in my veins I'll continue to work."

Towards the end of 1996, Walter and Albertina travelled to the US on a fundraising trip on behalf of an organisation, Education Africa, which had started a Walter Sisulu Scholarship Fund. In November, they made a journey to Ireland with a similar purpose, this time to raise funds for the

Albertina Sisulu Trust. At Rica Hodgson's suggestion, they included Stoke-on-Trent in the UK on their itinerary. This was where Walter had been given the Freedom of the City 10 years earlier. The Stoke-on-Trent Council greatly appreciated Walter personally coming to express his gratitude. "It was a very moving occasion," says Rica. "When Walter entered the Council chamber, some of the councillors were so moved by his presence, they were in tears." It was a fitting conclusion to what was to be their last international trip.

With Albertina based mainly in Cape Town, Walter and Albertina spent a lot of time apart, and after a while they began to feel the strain. In the latter half of the 1990s, Walter's health began to deteriorate. He began to experience weakness in his right leg and shaking of the right hand. In 1996, he was diagnosed as having Parkinson's disease, a degenerative neurological disorder. It was clear that he could no longer maintain his punishing schedule, and would have to slow down. He began to spend more time in Cape Town with Albertina.

In 1998, there was a significant decline in his vitality, as he experienced progressive heart failure. His doctor is of the opinion that he suffered a "silent" heart attack round about this time. In August 2000, he had a pacemaker put in, which was upgraded shortly after his 90th birthday in May 2002. Walter himself insists it is the devoted attention of Albertina that helps him to cope with his failing health.

One sad outcome of Walter's health problems was that he and Albertina finally had to wrench themselves away from No. 7372, with all its memories, good and bad, and move to Linden in Johannesburg proper, so as to be closer to the necessary medical facilities. Both Lesedi Clinic in Soweto and Milpark Hospital in Johannesburg have offered him the best possible care. Walter is a huge favourite at the hospital, and whenever he is admitted, dozens of staff, from the doctors and nurses to the drivers, cooks and cleaners, make their way to his ward to see him. Walter's doctor, Nalin Patel, explains the reason for his popularity: "He is always the first to extend his hand in greeting." Dr Patel also remarks, "He is amazingly sharp mentally, given his age and condition of health."

After Walter's ill-health forced him to retire, and while Albertina was still serving in Parliament, I was able to spend a lot of time with Walter, both at the parliamentary residences in Acacia Park, and in Johannesburg. Many leaders and celebrities came to visit us, including household names such as Jesse Jackson and Danny Glover, but the meeting that stands out in my mind was with Yehudi Menuhin. Menuhin had asked to see Walter, and the latter was very keen to thank Menuhin in person for his patronage of Kutlwane Masote, the grandson of Zeph Mothopeng and an extremely gifted young cellist. Menuhin had offered the young musician a chance to study at his school for musically gifted children. It was a great privilege to see the two elderly men, born in the same year, each a world leader in his own field, chatting away.

Throughout her political career, Albertina Sisulu had always maintained a good relationship with the press. Being a spokesperson for her movement was an integral part of her job and she never turned journalists away. She did not think twice when one day in 1987 she was told that a British journalist called Fred Bridgland wanted to speak to her. In a hasty interview between meetings, the British journalist showed her a card from Dr Asvat's surgery and asked her to confirm whether the writing on the card was hers and whether she would have stamped the date on the card. With a quick glance at the card she confirmed that it was her writing and that it was part of her job, as Dr Asvat's nurse, to have stamped the date on the card.

Albertina did not realise it at the time, but she had made a grave error. If she had thought about it more closely, she would have realised that on the date in question, 30 December 1989, she had not been in Dr Asvat's surgery but visiting Walter in Pollsmoor, as was her normal practice at that time of the year. Such an error was perfectly understandable. Not many people can remember at a moment's notice where they were on a particular day eight years previously, without consulting a diary or some kind of record, much less an overburdened and distracted 79-year-old. Albertina did not ponder on the reasons for Bridgland's line of questioning, or his emphasis on the date stamped on the card. She therefore did not realise that she had been wrong about the writing on the card and the date. It was a mistake for which she would pay dearly.

Bridgland used the video-taped interview with Albertina in a subsequent television documentary on the experiences of Katiza Cebekhulu, the former member of the football club who made a number of sensational claims about Winnie Mandela, including the accusation that she was personally involved in the murder of Stompie Seipei. Bridgland hammered the point of the date home, for a very good reason; it was the day Cebekhulu claimed to have been taken to Dr Asvat's surgery by Winnie. In her evidence in the Seipei kidnapping case, Winnie's alibi was that she was in Brandfort at that time, which was borne out by Jerry Richardson and others during the trial for Stompie's murder. However, Cebekhulu had insisted that Winnie had herself taken him to Dr Asvat's surgery for examination on the same day, placing her in Soweto at the time of Stompie's death. Richardson and his co-trialists subsequently made the same claims, alleging that they had lied under oath during the Stompie trial to protect Winnie. However, Cebekhulu, Richardson and other soccer team members were unreliable witnesses. It was clear that Bridgland was hoping that Albertina – a woman of unimpeachable rectitude – could break Winnie's alibi.

The interview was subsequently shown on television, and those watching it certainly picked up on the dramatic significance of Albertina's answers, even if she herself had not. None of the Sisulus watch much television, and Albertina herself never saw the broadcast of the interview, but I did, and I realised that Albertina must have made a mistake because from my research for this book I knew that she was in Cape Town during that period. Even Walter's prison records confirmed Albertina's visits to Pollsmoor during that period. To my eternal regret, I did not pursue the matter more aggressively immediately after watching the unfortunate Bridgland interview, and consequently Albertina's error went uncorrected.

The Truth and Reconciliation Commission (TRC), under the leadership of Archbishop Desmond Tutu, was set up to uncover human rights abuses in the apartheid era. The TRC also investigated human rights abuses from quarters other than the apartheid government. Among these were the activities of the Mandela Football Club during the 1980s. For nine days in November 1987, the TRC hearings focused on the sordid and tragic events of the unhappy period that saw the disappearance and murder of Stompie Seipei and the assassination of Dr Abu Asvat.

To Albertina's dismay, she was one of the people called to give evidence before the TRC on that period. Her appearance before the TRC was a deeply painful process, not only for her but also for Walter, who accompanied her to the hearings. Her evidence started off on a bad footing. Hanif Vally, the TRC counsel, confidently presented Albertina with Katiza Cebekhulu's card, expecting her to confirm that she had been present in the surgery that day, and was extremely shocked and dismayed when she stated that she did not recognise the handwriting on it. After stating "I'm sorry, I wasn't expecting this" (to which Archbishop Tutu interjected "None of us were!"), he went on to question Albertina closely about the Bridgland interview. The contradictions between the two were glaring, and Albertina was hardly forthcoming with explanations – mainly because she and Vally were talking at complete cross-purposes. She did not recall who Bridgland was, let alone remember his interview, and she could not work out why she would have said the card was in her handwriting. She was not in Dr Asvat's surgery on that day and was therefore not in a position to confirm or break Winnie's alibi.

Unfortunately, it was all too easy – especially in the context of other evidence heard, in which it was clear that many were terrified of Winnie, or blindly loyal to her – to interpret Albertina's stance as that of a rigidly loyal ANC stalwart who jibbed at implicating Winnie Mandela in a serious crime, or who was afraid to tell the truth. This view was articulated by Commissioner Dumisa Ntsebeza who said that his impression was that Albertina was trying to say as little as possible to avoid implicating Mrs Mandela because of the close relationship between the Mandelas and the Sisulus (Orr, 319; Boraine, 246).

Albertina strenuously denied this, but the damage was done. Ironically, it was the Asvat family's lawyer, Mr Kades, who then hastily undertook some basic investigation and checked the card in question against a sample of Albertina's handwriting (taken from the card she had filled out on the day of Dr Asvat's murder, which was on public record as being in her handwriting). This showed that the writing on the two cards differed markedly – in Kades' words, "one doesn't have to be a handwriting expert to determine that these two documents are not in the handwriting of the same person." Upon examining the cards, Zohra Asvat also confirmed that the handwriting was that of a woman who used to work in the surgery whenever Albertina took time off. Zohra also recalled that her husband usually gave Albertina leave during that week between Christmas and New Year, so it was unlikely Albertina would have been in the surgery on that day (Interview, Zohra Asvat, January 1998).

On behalf of the Asvat family, Kades said "we find it perfectly acceptable that a person of the age of Mrs Sisulu when making the video, might well have assumed that … because it was a card that emanated from Dr Asvat's office, that it was obviously completed in her hand" (Orr, 320).

Albertina herself asked to be recalled so that she could explain the contradiction, which had gained a great deal of prominence in the media. However, she did not offer any real explanation, simply reiterating that her testimony before the Commission was the truth, and that she had been mistaken in the video. This was not enough for the media, neither was Mr Kades' claim of being satisfied that Katiza's card had not been filled out by Albertina. Doubts lingered, and for the first time in her life, Albertina had the unhappy experience of having her integrity questioned.

Albertina was deeply hurt at being suspected of withholding information about Abu Asvat's murder. After all, it was she who had identified the murderers after they had been arrested, and during their court case she gave evidence that helped to convict them. Her son Lungi pointed out the painful irony that Albertina should be accused of trying to protect Winnie: "She was the one person who condemned the soccer team activities from the outset and tried to do everything possible to address the problem within the structures."

Lindi Sisulu felt that the whole process had been a flawed one in that Albertina was subjected to questioning, in the full glare of the public, about a video she had never even viewed, prepared by a right-wing journalist who may even have manipulated information for his own ends. If the necessary cross-checking and confirmation of dates had been done before the public interview, it would have prevented a great deal of confusion and saved Albertina and her family a lot of humiliation and heartache.

The Truth Commission experience was the only time in Albertina Sisulu's life that her integrity had been questioned and the whole ordeal traumatised her. She simply could not believe that she could be dragged against her will into something she found so utterly abhorrent. When Winnie tried to embrace her during the proceedings, Albertina gave her the cold shoulder, one of the few times in her life that she snubbed anyone. She was not, however, prepared to make public her strained relationship with Winnie. Throughout the years of political struggle, she had maintained her code of behaviour – that one did not take comrades to task in public, as this simply provided the real enemy with ammunition and she stuck rigidly to this position.

The year 1999 marked the beginning of a new dispensation and real retirement at last for Walter and Albertina. The day after the inauguration of Thabo Mbeki as President of South Africa in 1999, and the farewell dinner to the former President, Mandela and Graca Machel came to visit Walter and Albertina at their home in Linden. Mandela visited his old friend whenever he could, especially when Walter was ill. Usually his visits were quite rushed, but that occasion was different. It was a beautiful day, and Mandela said he preferred to sit outside. I had never seen Mandela look so happy and relaxed. The conversation centred mainly on the inauguration. I told Mandela how moved I had been when, after making his inaugural address in Parliament, Mbeki had wanted to go back to the Vice-President's seat, but Mandela had stopped him and insisted that he take the President's seat. Walter congratulated Mandela on his departure from office: "It is a wonderful thing you have done, Diba! Others should follow your example!" I did not think it possible that I could admire these two men any more than I already did, but on that day they rose even higher in my esteem. In a continent in which too many leaders have clung to power at all costs, it is profoundly moving to be in the presence of a leader who, while as popular as ever, is prepared to let go the reins of power.

Both Albertina and Max left Parliament at the end of 1999. Parliament bid farewell to its Chief Whip in a moving final session. Albertina had the satisfaction of listening to ANC MPs and opposition parties alike praising Max for a job well done.

Albertina now relishes the time spent with her husband and family. She continues to be passionately committed to the wellbeing of children in her community and devotes much of her time to the Albertina Sisulu Foundation, which is building a multi-purpose community centre in Orlando West, Soweto. She and Walter love listening to choral music and watching soccer. Walter supports Kaizer Chiefs while Albertina supports Orlando Pirates, and it is a delight to witness their affectionate rivalry during soccer matches. They often reminisce about their days of courtship. Particularly amusing is the story of the missing tennis racquet. Albertina was an avid tennis player until she asked Walter to take her racquet for repairs. "Your father was so jealous of me playing tennis that he never brought my racquet back." A slightly discomfited but amused Walter insists that he genuinely misplaced the racquet!

The family enjoys spending the Christmas holidays together, and when Walter's health permitted, we took the opportunity to visit some of the national parks. One Christmas we went to Knysna and the Tsitsikamma Forest. At the end of the holiday, Max and I had to drive to Cape Town, and Walter and Albertina to George, from where they would catch a flight back to Johannesburg. John and Mara Limboropoulos, friends of Mlungisi Snr, insisted that we spend an hour at their holiday apartment in Plettenberg Bay before proceeding on our journey. After ten minutes, John's domestic worker asked if her friend could come and greet Ntate Sisulu and MaSisulu. The friend then asked if *her* friend could come, and in no time, word had spread throughout the complex and beyond. A steady stream of workers arrived to pay their respects. Hours after Walter and Albertina had left for George airport, people continued to show up, and I will never forget the disappointment on their faces when they learned they were too late. John was completely bemused. "I thought I was bringing them here to enjoy an hour of peace and quiet," he said. The incident was just one of many that illustrates that as much as Walter and Albertina have been fêted by the famous and the powerful, it is among ordinary people that they are most respected and revered.

Walter and Albertina have also experienced their fair share of a tragedy shared by all too many African families. They too have lost young relatives to the scourge of AIDS. They feel that people should know that no family is immune, and that they too had felt first-hand the impact of AIDS. They are forthright in their support of HIV/AIDS education campaigns, and take the view that the disease is the "next apartheid" – an enemy to be fought with all available resources.

# EPILOGUE

On a perfect autumn day in May 2002, caterers rushed purposefully in and out of the Walter Sisulu Sports Stadium in Randburg, putting the last touches to the cheerfully decorated hall that was to serve as the venue for over 400 guests at Walter's 90th birthday luncheon. Children dressed in ANC T-shirts ran squealing, but were hushed for the arrival of former President Nelson Mandela and Graca Machel. Next came the impeccably suited President of South Africa, Thabo Mbeki. At last, a car drew up to one of the side entrances, and a frail, silver-haired man was helped out, accompanied by a woman whose dignified bearing made no concession to advancing years. Side-by-side, they advanced to the seats of honour. The man wore a dark, sober suit; his wife wore the white she favoured for celebratory occasions. Cyril Ramaphosa and Tokyo Sexwale began the song, and it was taken up all around the hall: "Walter Sisulu, there is no one like him."

Walter was born in the same year as the organisation he had spent a lifetime building, so his 90th birthday provided the perfect opportunity for the ANC, friends and family formally to acknowledge his role and thank him for his efforts. There was a certain irony to the gift they chose for him, which was unveiled with great fanfare: a luxurious reclining chair for a man who had never rested in the service of his country, people or organisation.

The event was a fitting blend of honour and intimacy; speeches were made by both the highest dignitaries in the land and members of the family, while the live music Walter and Albertina enjoy so much was provided by the Imilonji Kantu Choir and the Buskaid String Ensemble. Cyril Ramaphosa brought his own personal brand of charm and humour to his role as Master of Ceremonies.

Helen Moffett, the editor of this book, who sat directly behind the guests of honour, commented: "Two things struck me about Mama and Tata. One was that during a long afternoon of music, poetry and a great many speeches, they sat in rapt attention throughout. Their interest never wavered, even though Walter was visibly tired by the time the festivities wound down. The other deeply moving thing to witness was the physical closeness and warmth between the Sisulus. It wasn't overt, but they were always touching. Either they would hold hands under the table, like teenagers, or you would see Mama constantly stroking her husband's knee. What stood out was the tenderness between them."

Nelson Mandela rose to salute his dear friend and comrade once more:

Walter Sisulu has lived through and witnessed the major events of the last century that shaped South Africa. What is more important, is that he was a major participant in decisively shaping and making that history ... There can be no greater and more inspiring example in the history of our organisation, and hence of our country, than Walter Sisulu: a man whose every deed speaks of leadership ... which brought us to where we are today as a country and a people.

He also stressed Walter's role in setting an example:

The absolute selflessness with which he gave his life to the struggle is especially important to remember and hold dear as the new conditions create the temptations of self-interest and personal enrichment. Corruption, opportunism and self-serving careerism have no place in the organisation Walter Sisulu led and helped build. ... He was a unifier, not a divider. Where others of us would speak a hasty word or act in anger, he was the patient one, seeking to heal and bring together.

We congratulate him on his birthday and thank him for having given so entirely of his life to the struggle and to our organisation. And when we talk about how entirely he has done that we cannot forget to mention Albertina who was such an integral part of that giving in entirety.

Mandela spiced the solemnity of his words with gentle teasing, as he spoke affectionately of their long and close friendship, and reminisced about the days when he and Walter were "young and foolish". He closed with words he has often repeated about Walter Sisulu: "Many of us have received awards and accolades and have held high office in the organisation, but even without holding a formal position in the ANC, Walter Sisulu has always been senior to all of us."

President Thabo Mbeki followed with a moving and lyrical address that borrowed from traditional Xhosa praise poetry, Shakespeare and the Bible. His speech articulated the way in which Walter Sisulu is valued by his family, his community and the political organisation to which he devoted most of his life:

> In our company sits a son of our people, a husband, a father, a grandfather in his own family, an uncle, a cousin ...
>
> Every space in this place that he dignifies by his presence, is occupied by a material force of joy, of celebration, of triumph, of a people reborn. Together we sit in wonder ... that we could have one with us with whom we feel an intimate companionship, but whose life and being gives us the entitlement to say to the peoples of the world, that we are precious ...
>
> We must, like him, be loyal to our people and their cause, honest in our purposes, humble in our conduct, constant in our good humour, devoted to the imperative for human solidarity, truly African, and principled, without counting the cost.
>
> We are met here today to celebrate 90 years of one who has been and is all these things ...
>
> Mama, thank you very much for what you are and who you are. Thank you very much for what you have done to lead us, in your own name, and what you have done to enable your dear husband to lead our people.

Most apt of all was the poem with which he began his speech, *An African Elegy* by Nigerian writer Ben Okri. To some, it might have seemed valedictory; yet it encapsulates so much of the spirit in which Walter and Albertina worked, struggled and finally triumphed, without bitterness, and with infinite patience and hope – their capacity for "bless[ing] things even in pain":

> We are the miracles that God made
> To taste the bitter fruit of Time.
> We are precious.
> And one day our suffering
> Will turn into the wonders of the earth.
>
> There are things that burn me now
> Which turn golden when I am happy.
> Do you see the mystery of our pain?
> That we bear poverty
> And are able to sing and dream sweet things
>
> And that we never curse the air when it is warm
> Or the fruit when it tastes so good
> Or the lights that bounce gently on the waters?
> We bless things even in our pain.
> We bless them in silence.

That is why our music is so sweet.
It makes the air remember.
There are secret miracles at work
That only Time will bring forth.
I too have heard the dead singing.

And they tell me that
This life is good
They tell me to live it gently
With fire, and always with hope.
There is wonder here

And there is surprise
In everything the unseen moves.
The ocean is full of songs.
The sky is not an enemy.
Destiny is our friend.

Thankfully, in the case of Walter and Albertina Sisulu, destiny has indeed been their friend. They have been blessed with the gift of longevity, and have had several years together to make up for lost time, to connect with family and friends, to look back together at the extraordinary events in which they played such integral roles. Listening to them reminiscing with friends and family is the best history lesson one could hope for. Part of why their story is so important is because in being at the centre of one of the most extraordinary movements of the twentieth century, they provide a living link with the giants of the South African struggle – Lembede, Luthuli, ZK Matthews, JB Marks, Kotane, Dadoo, Govan Mbeki, Ruth First, Bram Fischer, Joe Slovo, Lilian Ngoyi and many others. Walter and Albertina Sisulu were indeed part of the proverbial cast of thousands – whom they remember and honour.

They continue to enjoy their grandchildren and savour their time together. They suffered greatly in the past, but in all the years of the struggle, they were miraculously spared the particular tragedy of losing a child. They know how fortunate they are that they and their children were spared to see the fruits of their sacrifices: in the words of Ben Okri, they are "the miracles that God made". As Charles Villa-Vicencio has pointed out: "By virtue of their steadfast stand against injustice and oppression, Walter and Albertina Sisulu stand out as moral beacons for their contemporaries as well as for future generations."

Their relationship continues to be a source of inspiration to all those who meet them, as they continue to radiate the respect, loyalty, love and devotion that has characterised their 58 years together.

Indeed, their suffering has turned into one of the wonders of the earth.

# WALTER SISULU
*Ancestor Chart*

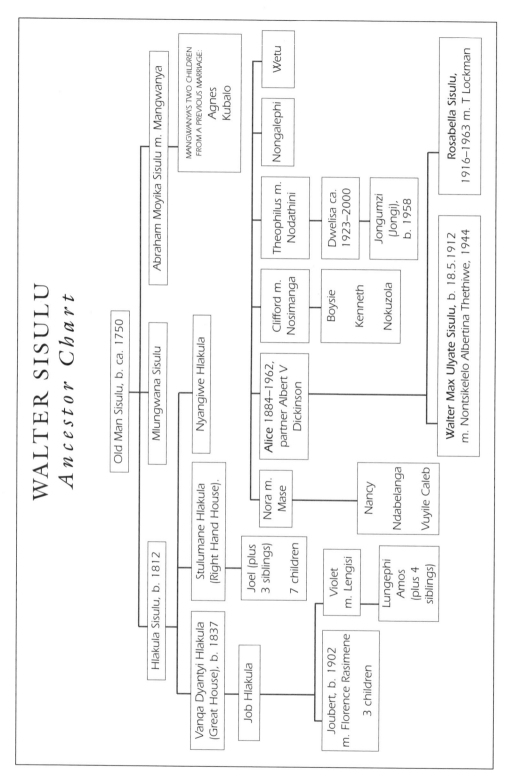

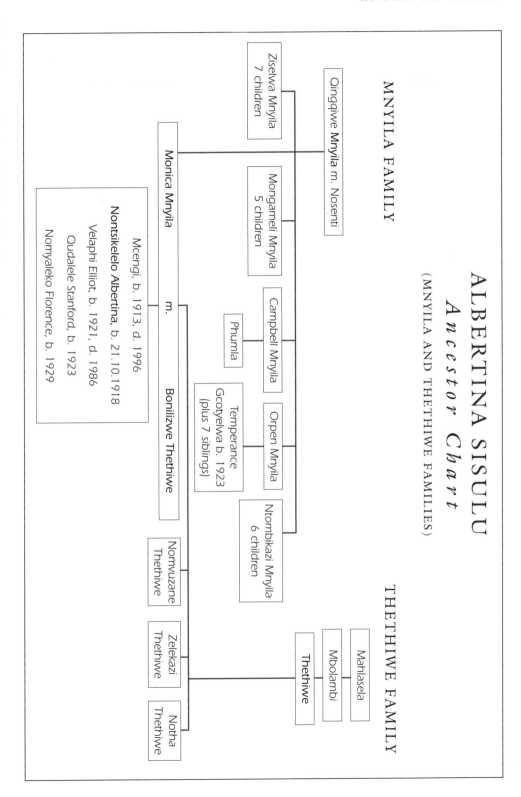

# ALBERTINA SISULU
## *Ancestor Chart*
(MNYILA AND THETHIWE FAMILIES)

**MNYILA FAMILY**

Qingqiwe Mnyila m. Nosenti

Ziselwa Mnyila
7 children

Mongameli Mnyila
5 children

Campbell Mnyila

Phumla

Orpen Mnyila

Temperance
Gcotyelwa b. 1923
(plus 7 siblings)

Ntombikazi Mnyila
6 children

Monica Mnyila

m.

Mcengi, b. 1913, d. 1996
**Nontsikelelo Albertina, b. 21.10.1918**
Velaphi Elliot, b. 1921, d. 1986
Oudalele Stanford, b. 1923
Nomyaleko Florence, b. 1929

Bonilizwe Thethiwe

**THETHIWE FAMILY**

Thethiwe

Mahlasela

Mbolambi

Nomvuzane
Thethiwe

Zelekazi
Thethiwe

Notha
Thethiwe

# BIBLIOGRAPHY *&* FURTHER READING

*Author's note*

Nelson Mandela's biography *Long Walk to Freedom* has been one of the major sources of this biography. I have used both the Abacus edition (for the period covering 1960–77) and the MacDonald Purnell edition (for the remainder of the book). I apologise for any confusion this may cause.


## UNPUBLISHED SOURCES

### A. PUBLIC RECORDS

Department of Correctional Services, Pretoria: Prison records of Walter Sisulu
Department of Justice, Pretoria: Department of Justice files on Albertina Sisulu, Jongumzi
    Sisulu, Lindiwe Sisulu, Mandisa Sisulu, Mlungisi Sisulu, Walter Sisulu, Zwelakhe Sisulu
National Archives of South Africa, Pretoria: Municipality of Johannesburg – Health
    Department files on Albertina Sisulu
    Witwatersrand Local Division criminal case files on Walter Sisulu
*South African Who's Who* (1950)

### B. NON-PUBLIC RECORDS

Africa Fund archives, New York
Centre for African Studies Library, University of Cape Town
    *Rivonia Trial Record, Extract of Walter Sisulu's evidence*
Cory Library for Historical Research, Rhodes University, Grahamstown:
    *Cape of Good Hope Civil Service List, 1910*
    *Coulter, Jean. They live in Africa, 1988*
    *Donaldson and Braby's Cape Province Directory, 1919*
    *East London Frontier Red Book, 1907–1912*
    *The General Directory and Guide-Book to the Cape of Good Hope and its Dependencies, as well*
    *as Natal, Free State and the Transvaal, 1882–1884*
Henry Schomberg Library New York
    *Alphaeus Hunton Papers*
Mayibuye Centre, University of the Western Cape, Bellville:
    *International Defence and Aid Fund (IDAF) Papers*
Newspapers:
    *Advance*
    *African Communist*
    *The African Record*
    *The Guardian*
    *New Age*
    *Spark*
South African History Archive, University of the Witwatersrand, Braamfontein:
    *United Democratic Front (UDF) Papers*
South African History Association Trust:
    Box AL2431

### C. ORAL INTERVIEWS, CONDUCTED BY:

**The Author, Elinor Sisulu, 1992–2002:** Albertina Sisulu, Jongumuzi Sisulu, Lindiwe Sisulu, Mlungisi Sisulu Jnr, Mlungisi Sisulu Snr, Nonkululeko Sisulu, Sammy Sisulu, Sheila Sisulu, Walter Sisulu, Zodwa Sisulu, Zwelakhe Sisulu; Neville Alexander, Ebrahim Asvat, Zohra Asvat, George Bizos, Christo Brand, Dennis Brutus, Amina Cachalia, Azhar Cachalia, Laloo Chiba, Moses Chikane, Saths Cooper, Michael Dingake, Ilse Fischer, Rica Hodgson, Barbara Hogan, Trevor Huddleston, Temperance Gcotyelwa, Priscilla Jana, Ahmed Kathrada, Archie Khayingane, Metty Hluphekile Khubeka, Wolfie Kodesh, Lungephi Amos Lengisi, Gerald

Lockman, Henry Makgothi, Makaziwe Mandela, Nelson Rolihlahla Mandela, Sam Mase, Govan Mbeki, Rose Mda, Murphy Morobe, Chota Motala, Sister Bernard Ncube, Sindiswa Ndita, Lionel Ngakane, John Nkadimeng, Curtis Nkondo, Leila Patel, Evelyn Rakeepile, Cyril Ramaphosa, Mewa Ramgobin, Cassim Saloojee, Anthony Sampson, Lazar Sidelsky, Joyce Sikhakhane-Rankin, Beryl Simelane, Allister Sparks, Toni Strasburg, Miriam Matsha Thethiwe, Daisy Titus, McDonald Titus, Isak Volschenk.

**Luli Callinicos, 1990–1994:** Walter Sisulu.

**Barry Feinberg, 2002:** Wolfie Kodesh, Ben Turok.

**George Houser and Herbert Shore, 1995–1997:** Walter Sisulu.

**Helen Moffett, 2002:** Elinor Sisulu.

**Thembeka Mufamadi, 2002:** Raymond Mhlaba, Wilton Mkwayi.

**Nhlanhla Ndebele, 2002:** Frene Ginwala.

**Joyce Sikhakhane-Rankin, 1998–2002:** O'Hara Diseko, Jessie Duarte, Bertha Gxowa, Lucky Mabaso, Thami Mali, Nomvula Mokonyane, Kgalema Motlanthe, Thenjiwe Mtintso, Jongumuzi Sisulu, Max Sisulu, Mlungisi Sisulu Jnr, Zwelakhe Sisulu.

**Zama-Swazi Simelane, 1998:** Toni Bowes.

**Jabulani Sithole, 2002:** Eric Mtshali.

**Nanziwe Thethiwe, 1997:** Bhuqindlela Mahlasela, Ngubomhlaba Mahlasela, Nopamethe Matshezi Mahlasela, Mafa Maphila, Novulile MaQhinebe, Pumla Mnyila, Zwelidumile Mnyila, Nozamile Thethiwe, Stanford Thethiwe, Hanjiwe Nongodlwana Thsatshele, Makuthiweni Zamliza.

**Charles Villa-Vicencio, 1992:** *Albertina Sisulu: A Woman of the Soil* (extended oral interview).

**Babylon Xeketwane and Mlungisi Sisulu, 1992:** Dabulamanzi Gcanga, Nolusapho Hlakula, Archie Khayingane, Bhabane McAllister Khayingane, McDonald Malungela Lwane, Sindiswa Ndita, Dwelisa Sisulu.

## D. CONFERENCE PAPERS, SEMINAR PAPERS, THESES, PUBLIC LECTURES, BROADCASTS

Ajulu, Rok. *Engcobo: Economic and Social Setting to c. 1915.* Unpublished manuscript. Undated.

Alexander, Neville. "Robben Island: A Site of Struggle". Conference paper delivered at a Robben Island Museum conference, Cape Town. 1992.

ANC Video Unit: Ongoing Interviews with Walter Sisulu.

BBC Interviews with Walter Sisulu, 1989.

Benson, Mary. Transcript of a dramatised documentary on Robben Island based on historical records and oral testimonies and recollections of prisoners. Broadcast 16 November 1992.

Bouch, RJ. "The Colonisation of Queenstown (Eastern Cape) and Its Hinterland, 1852–1886". Unpublished doctoral thesis. Institute of Commonwealth Studies, University of London. 1990.

Buntman, Fran. "Continuing and extending resistance and struggle: The role of Robben Island, 1488–1805". Seminar paper presented at the University of the Witwatersrand, Johannesburg. 1994.

Callinicos, Luli. *Biography of Oliver Tambo.* Unpublished manuscript.

Deacon, Harriet. "Place of Banishment: Convicts and 20th century political imprisonment". Conference paper delivered at a Robben Island Museum conference, Cape Town. 1992.

Deacon, Harriet. *Place of Tobacco Trees: 19th century institutions.* Conference paper delivered at a Robben Island Museum conference, Cape Town. 1992.

Fester, Gertrude. *Merely Motherhood Perpetuating Patriarchy? Women's organisations in the Western Cape, South Africa.* Seminar paper presented for the Centre for African Studies, Cape Town. 1998.

Heeten, Kalan. "Cracking the Apartheid Monolith". Unpublished research paper.

Herbstein, Denis. *IDAF: The History.* Unpublished manuscript. 1988.

Houser, George and Shore, Herbert. *I Will Go Singing: Walter Sisulu speaks of his life and the Struggle for Freedom in South Africa,* Robben Island Museum. 2000.

Houston, Gregory. "Road to Democracy 1960–1990". Unpublished notes.

Karis, Thomas. *Issue: A Journal of Opinion,* Volume XV. African Studies Association. 1987.

Mokwena Steve. "Marginalised Youth in South Africa". Paper presented at Joint Enrichment Programme Conference on Marginalised Youth, 7–9 June 1991.

Ngculu, James. *The Honour to Serve: Recollections of an MK Soldier.* Unpublished.

Odendaal, André. "Robben Island – Bridgehead for Democracy". Paper presented at the Mayibuye Centre Winter School, Bellville. 1994.

Pamphlet. *Pietermaritzburg Trial, 1985.* Source unknown. 1985.

Penn, Nigel. "From Penguins to Prisoners: Robben Island, 1488–1805". Conference paper delivered at a Robben Island Museum conference, Cape Town. 1992.

Ramgobin, Mewa. "Pietermaritzburg Treason Trial". Unpublished notes. 2002.

Sikhakhane-Rankin, Joyce. "Post Rivonia Stress". Unpublished notes.

Sisulu, Elinor. "Walter Sisulu and the ANC". A public lecture delivered at the University of the Witwatersrand, Johannesburg. 2002.

Sisulu, Walter. "Brief Notes in the Event of a Death Sentence". Unpublished notes, Rivonia Trial. 1964.

Sisulu, Walter. (As narrated to Michael Dingake and Laloo Chiba.) *Prison Memoir: Walter Sisulu, 1975–1976.* Unpublished manuscript.

Sisulu, Walter. "Visit to Australia by ANC Deputy President Comrade Walter Sisulu (7–22 August 1991)". Unpublished report.

Sisulu, Walter and Evans, Gareth. Transcript of a Press Conference with Mr Walter Sisulu, Deputy President of the ANC and Senator Gareth Evans, Parliament House. 13 August 1991.

Udit, P. "Engendering the National Liberation Struggle in South Africa (1945–1995)". Thesis. Department of Sociology. University of Essex, Colchester. 1997.

Wagenaar, EJC. "A History of the Thembu and their Relationship to the Cape, 1850–1900". Unpublished doctoral thesis. Rhodes University, Grahamstown. 1988.

## PUBLISHED SOURCES

### A. Newspapers and periodicals

*African Communist*
*African Report*
*Business Day*
*City Press*
*Die Beeld*
*Digest*
*Drum*
*Fighting Talk*
*Liberation*
*Pretoria News*
*Rand Daily Mail*
*SASPU National*
*Sechaba*
*The Argus*
*The Boston Globe* (USA)
*The Cape Herald*
*The Cape Times*
*The Daily Telegraph*
*The Evening Sentinel* (UK)
*The Natal Witness*
*The New Age*
*The New Nation*
*The New York Times (Special Report)*
*The Observer* (UK)
*The Rock*
*The Sowetan*
*The Star*
*The Sunday Express*

*The Sunday Post*
*The Sunday Times*
*The Transvaler*
*The Voice*
*The Washington Post* (USA*)*
*The Weekly Mail*
*Vrye Weekblad*

## B. Articles and pamphlets

Article 19. "An editor in prison". Zwelakhe Sisulu. The International Centre on Censorship, London. 1988.

Beck, Karl S. "Democratising the United Democratic Front: The Muddy Slope", in *Apartheid unravels*. Hunt-Davis, R. (ed.) University of Florida Press. 1991.

Bredekamp, Henry. "Alan Boesak", in *They Shaped Our Century. The Most Influential South Africans of the Twentieth Century*. Human and Rousseau, Cape Town. 1999.

Gottschalk, K. "State Strategy and the Limits of Counter Revolution", in G Moss and I Obery (eds). *South African Review 4*. Ravan Press, Johannesburg. 1987.

Gottschalk, K. "United Democratic Front: 1983–1991 – Rise, Impact and Consequences", in Liebenberg, Ian; Lortan, F; Nel, B; Van der Westhuizen, G (eds.). *The Long March: The Story of the Liberation Struggle in South Africa*. Haum-de Jager, Pretoria. 1994.

Green, Pippa. "The Sisulu Family", *Leadership Magazine*. May 1990.

Green, Pippa. "No Man's Island". *Cosmopolitan*. May 1991.

Jordaan, Pallo. "Book Review: Moses Kotane: South African Revolutionary. A Political Biography by Brian Bunting", in *Sechaba*. 1976.

Meintjes, Sheila. "Winnie Madikizela Mandela", in *They Shaped Our Century. The Most Influential South Africans of the Twentieth Century*. Human and Rousseau, Cape Town. 1999.

Muller, Johan. "People's Education". *South African Review 4*. Ravan Press, Johannesburg. 1987.

Sarakinsky, Ivor. "State, Strategy and the Extra-Parliamentary Opposition in South Africa, 1983–1988", in *Politikon*, Vol. 16 (1). 1989.

Seekings, Jeremy. "Trailing behind the Masses: The United Democratic Front and Township Politics in the Pretoria-Witwatersrand-Vaal Region 1983–1984", in *Journal of South African Studies*, Vol. 18 (1). 1991.

Sisulu, Walter. "Challenges for Africa". First annual lecture delivered by Walter Sisulu in honour of the 25th anniversary of the Africa Fund. 1991.

Sisulu, Zwelakhe. "People's Education for People's Power", in *Issue: A Journal of Opinion*, Vol. XV. 1987.

Sithole, Jabulani and Mkhize, Sibongiseni. "Truth or Lies? Selective Memories, Imaginings and Representations of Chief Albert Luthuli in Recent Political Discourses, in History and Theory". *Theme*, Issue 39. December 2000.

Southern Africa – The Imprisoned Society, in cooperation with the UN Centre against Apartheid. "Walter Max Ulyate Sisulu, Leader of the African National Congress and Man of the People". 1982.

Supplement '89. "Political Prisoners; Releasing the People's Leaders". Issued by SA Pressclips, Cape Town. 1989.

Webster, David. "Repression and the State of Emergency". *South African Review*. 1987.

## C. Books

Akbar, MJ. *Nehru. The Making of India*. Penguin Books, London. 1989.

Alexander, Neville. *Robben Island Prison Dossier, 1964–1974*. UCT Press, Cape Town. 1994.

Babenia, Natoo as told to Edwards, Iain. *Memoirs of a Saboteur. Reflections on my Political Activity in India and South Africa*. Mayibuye Books, Bellville. 1995.

Backscheider, Paula R. *Reflections on Biography*. Oxford University Press, Oxford. 2001.

Basner, Miriam. *Am I an African? The Political Memoirs of HM Basner*. Witwatersrand University Press, Johannesburg. 1993.

Batezat, Elinor and Mwalo, Margaret. *Women in Zimbabwe*. Sapes, Harare. 1989.

Beinert, William. *Twentieth-century South Africa*. Oxford University Press, Cape Town. 1994.

Benson, Mary (ed.). *The Sun will Rise. Statements from the Dock by Southern African Political Prisoners.* IDAF, London. 1981.

Benson, Mary. *A Far Cry. The Making of a South African.* Penguin Books, London. 1990.

Bernstein, Hilda. *For their Triumphs and their Tears: Women in Apartheid South Africa.* IDAF, London. 1985.

Bernstein, Hilda. *The World that was Ours. The Story of the Rivonia Trial.* SA Writers, London. 1989.

Bernstein, Hilda. *The Rift: The Exile Experience of South Africans.* Jonathan Cape, London, 1994.

Bernstein, Rusty. *Memory Against Forgetting. Memoirs of a Life in South African Politics. 1938–1964.* Viking, London. 1999.

Bizos, George. *No one to Blame? In Pursuit of Justice in South Africa.* David Philip Publishers. Cape Town. 1998.

Bok, Sissela. *Alva Myrdal. A Daughter's Memoir.* Addison-Wesley Publishing Company, Cambridge, MA. 1991.

Bonner, Philip and Segal, Lauren. *Soweto: A History.* Maskew Miller Longman, Cape Town. 1998.

Boraine, Alex. *A Country Unmasked. Inside South Africa's Truth and Reconciliation Commission.* Oxford University Press, Oxford. 2000.

Brutus, Dennis. *A Simple Lust: Collected Poems of South African Jail and Exile*, including "Letters to Martha". Heinemann Educational Books, London, and Hill & Wang, New York. 1973.

Bunting, Brian. *The Rise of the South African Reich.* IDAF, London. 1986.

Bunting, Brian. *Moses Kotane: South African Revolutionary. A Political Biography.* Mayibuye Books, Bellville. 1998.

Callinicos, Luli. *A Place in the City.* Ravan Press, Johannesburg, and Maskew Miller Longman, Johannesburg and Cape Town. 1993.

Callinicos, Luli. *Gold and Workers 1886–1924.* Ravan Press, Johannesburg. 1994.

Callinicos, Luli. *The World That Made Mandela: A Heritage Trail of 70 Sites of Significance.* STE Publishers, Johannesburg. 2001.

Carter, Gwendolen M; Karis, Thomas and Stultz, Newell, M. *South Africa's Transkei. The Politics of Domestic Colonialism.* Heinemann, London. 1967.

Chikane, Frank. *No Life of My Own. An Autobiography by Frank Chikane.* Skotaville Publishers, Johannesburg. 1988.

Clingman, Steven. *Bram Fischer: Afrikaner Revolutionary.* David Philip Publishers, Cape Town. 1998.

Cobbet, William and Cohen, Robin (eds). *Popular Struggles in South Africa.* James Currey, London. 1988.

Collins, Diana. *Partners in Protest. Life with Canon Collins.* Victor Gollancz Ltd, London. 1992.

Daniels, Eddie. *There and Back. Robben Island 1964–1979.* Mayibuye Books, Bellville. 1998.

Davenport, TRH. *South Africa – A Modern History.* University of Toronto, Buffalo. 1987.

Deacon, Harriet; Penn, Nigel; Odendaal, André and Davidson, Patricia (compilers). *The Robben Island Exhibition EsiQithini.* Mayibuye Books, Bellville. 1996.

De Gruchy, John W. *The Church Struggle in South Africa.* David Philip Publishers, Cape Town. 1990.

Denniston, Robin. *Trevor Huddleston. A Life.* Macmillan, London. 1999.

De Villiers, Simon A. *Robben Island: Out of Reach. Out of Mind.* C. Struik, Cape Town. 1971.

Dingake, Michael. *My Fight against Apartheid.* Kliptown Books, London. 1987.

Dlamini, Moses. *Hell Hole Robben Island. Reminiscences of a Political Prisoner.* Spokesman Books, Nottingham. 1984.

Du Boulay, Shirley. *Tutu: Voice of the Voiceless.* Penguin Books, London. 1989.

Edgar, Robert R and ka Msumza, Luyanda. *Freedom in our Lifetime. The Collected Writings of Anton Muziwakhe Lembede.* Ohio University Press, Athens, Ohio, and Skotaville Publishers, Johannesburg, with Mayibuye Books, Cape Town. 1996.

Ellis, Stephen and Sechaba, Tsepo. *Comrades against Apartheid. The ANC and the South African Communist Party in Exile.* London: James Currey and Bloomington and Indianapolis: Indiana University Press. 1992.

Feit, Edward. *Urban Revolt in South Africa, 1960–1964.* Northwestern University Press, Chicago. 1993.

First, Ruth. *117 Days: An account of Confinement and Interrogation under the South African 90-day Detention Law.* Penguin Books, Harmondsworth. 1982.

Forman, Sadie and Odendaal, André. *A Trumpet from the Housetops. The Selected Writings of Lionel Forman.* David Philip Publishers, Cape Town, Zed Press, London and Ohio University Press, Athens, Ohio. 1992.

Frederikse, Julie. *The Unbreakable Thread. Non-Racialism in South Africa.* Zed Books Ltd, London. 1990.

Fredrickson, George M. *Black Liberation: A Comparative History of Black Ideologies in the United States and South Africa.* Oxford University Press, Oxford. 1996.

Gerhart, Gail M. *Black Power in South Africa. The Evolution of an Ideology.* University of California Press, Berkeley and Los Angeles. 1979.

Gish, Steven D. *Alfred B. Xuma. African, American, South African.* New York University Press, New York. 2000.

Gorodnov, Valentin. *SOWETO: Life and Struggles of a South African Township.* Progress Publishers, Moscow. 1988.

Harber, Anton and Ludman, Barbara (eds). *A–Z of South African Politics. The Essential Handbook.* Penguin Books, London. 1994.

Harrison, Nancy. *Winnie Mandela: Mother of a Nation.* Victor Gollancz Ltd, London. 1985.

Harvey, Robert. *The Fall of Apartheid. The Inside Story from Smuts to Mbeki.* Palgrave, London. 2001.

Henderson, Ian (ed.). *Man of Christian Action. Canon John Collins – The Man and his Work.* Lutterworth Press, Guildford and London. 1976.

Hochschild, Adam. *The Mirror at Midnight. A South African Journey.* Viking Penguin, New York. 1990.

Holland, Heidi. *The Struggle: A History of the African National Congress.* Grafton Books, London. 1989.

Hooper, Charles. *Brief Authority.* Collins, London. 1960.

Houston, Gregory F. *The National Liberation Struggle in South Africa. A Case Study of the United Democratic Front, 1983–1987.* Ashgate Publishing Company, Hants. 1999.

Huddleston, Trevor. *Naught for Your Comfort.* Collins, London. 1977.

Huddleston, Trevor. *Return to South Africa: The Ecstasy and the Agony.* Fount (an Imprint of HarperCollins Publishers), London. 1991.

International Commission of Jurists, Geneva. *The Trial of Beyers Naudé.* Search Press Limited, London and Ravan Press, Johannesburg. 1974, 1975.

Jabavu, Noni. *The Ochre People.* John Murray, London. 1963.

Joffe, Joel. *The Rivonia Story.* Mayibuye Books – UWC, Bellville. 1995.

Johns, Sheridan and Hunt Davids, R. Jnr (eds). *Mandela, Tambo and the African National Congress: The Struggle against Apartheid, 1948–1990. A Documentary Survey.* Oxford University Press. 1990.

Johnson, RW and Schlemmer, Lawrence (eds). *Launching Democracy in South Africa: The First Open Election, April 1994.* Yale University Press, New Haven and London. 1996.

Johnson, Shaun. *Strange Days Indeed: South Africa from Insurrection to Post-Election.* Bantam Press, Johannesburg. 1994.

Joseph, Helen. *If this be Treason.* André Deutsch, London. 1963.

Joseph, Helen. *Side by Side.* Zed Books, London. 1986.

Kantor, James. *A Healthy Grave.* Hamish Hamilton, London. 1967.

Karis, Thomas and Carter, Gwendolen M (eds). *From Protest to Challenge: A Documentary History of African Politics in South Africa, 1882–1964.* Hoover Institution Press, Stanford. 1977.
    Volume 1: Sheridan Johns. *Protest and Hope, 1882–1934.*
    Volume 2: Thomas Karis. *Hope and Challenge, 1935–1952.*
    Volume 3: Karis, Thomas and Gerhart, Gail. *Challenge and Violence, 1953–1964.*
    Volume 4: Karis, Thomas. And Gerhart, Gail. *Political Profiles, 1882–1964.*

Karis, Thomas and Gerhart, Gail (eds). *From Protest to Challenge: A Documentary History of African Politics in South Africa, 1882–1990.*
   Volume 5: Karis, Thomas and Gerhart, Gail. *Nadir and Resurgence, 1964–1979*, UNISA Press, Pretoria. 1997.

Kasrils, Ronnie. *Armed and Dangerous: My Undercover Struggle Against Apartheid.* Heinemann, London. 1993.

Kathrada, Ahmed. *Letters From Robben Island.* Mayibuye Books in association with Robben Island Museum, Cape Town. 1999.

Kgosana, Philip Ata. *Lest We Forget. An Autobiography.* Skotaville Publishers, Johannesburg. 1990.

Kuzwayo, Ellen. *Call Me Woman.* Ravan Press, Johannesburg. 1996.

Lawrence-Lightfoot, Sara. *Balm in Gilead: Journey of a Healer.* Addison-Wesley Publishing Company, Reading MA. 1989.

Lazerson, Joshua N. *Against the Tide: Whites in the Struggle Against Apartheid.* Westview Press, Boulder and Mayibuye Books, Bellville. 1994.

Lekota, Mosiuoa Patrick (Terror). *Prison Letters to a Daughter.* Taurus, Pretoria. 1991.

Lelyveld, Joseph. *Move Your Shadow.* Times Books, New York. 1985.

Lerumo, A (Michael Harmel). *Fifty Fighting Years. The Communist Party of South Africa, 1921–1971.* Inkululeko Publications, London. 1971.

Levine, Janet. *Inside Apartheid. One Woman's Struggle in South Africa.* Contemporary Books, Chicago. 1989.

Lewin, Hugh. *Bandiet. Seven Years in a South African Prison.* Heinemann, London. 1974.

Lobban, Michael. *White Man's Justice. South African Political Trials in the Black Consciousness Era.* Clarendon Press, Oxford. 1996.

Lodge, Tom. *Black Politics in South Africa since 1945.* Longman, London and New York. 1983.

Lodge, Tom; Nasson, Bill; Mufson, Steven; Shubane, Khehla and Sithole, Kokwanda. *All, Here, and Now: Black Politics in South Africa in the 1980s.* Ford Foundation-David Philip Publishers, Cape Town. 1991.

Luthuli, Albert. *Let My People Go. An Autobiography.* Collins Fount Paperbacks, London. 1989.

Magubane, Bernard Makhosezwe. *The Making of a Racist State: British Imperialism and the Union of South Africa 1875–1910, Africa.* World Press. 1996.

Magubane, Peter. *Portrait of a City.* New Holland Publishers, London. 1990.

Maharaj, Mac. *Reflections in Prison.* Zebra Press and Robben Island Museum, Cape Town. 2001.

Mandaza, Ibbo. *Race, Colour and Class in Southern Africa.* Sapes Books, Harare. 1997.

Mandela, Nelson. *Long Walk to Freedom.* Macdonald Purnell, Randburg. 1994.

Mandela, Nelson. *Long Walk to Freedom.* Abacus, London. 1995.

Marks, Shula. *Divided Sisterhood: Race, Class and Gender in the South African Nursing Profession.* Witwatersrand University Press, Johannesburg. 1994.

Martin, Tony. *The Pan-African Connection. From Slavery to Garvey and Beyond.* Majority Press, Dover. 1983.

Marx, Anthony W. *Lessons of Struggle. South African Internal Opposition, 1960–1990.* Oxford University Press, Oxford. 1992.

Mattera, Don. *Memory is the Weapon.* Ravan Press, Johannesburg. 1987.

Matthews, Frieda Bokwe. *Remembrances.* Mayibuye Books, Cape Town. 1995.

Matthews, ZK. *Freedom for my People.* David Philip Publishers, Cape Town. 1991.

Mbeki, Govan. *The Peasant Revolt.* International Defence and Aid Fund. 1984.

Mbeki, Govan. *Learning from Robben Island. The Prison Writings of Govan Mbeki.* James Currey, London; Ohio University Press, Athens, Ohio; David Philip Publishers, Cape Town. 1991.

Mbeki, Govan. *Sunset at Midday: Latshon'ilang'emini.* Nolwazi Educational Publishers, Braamfontein. 1996.

McCord, Margaret. *The Calling of Katie Makanya.* David Philip Publishers, Cape Town and Johannesburg. 2000.

Meer, Fatima. *Treason Trial 1985. The Arrest and Charge for Treason.* Madiba Publications, Durban. 1989.

436

Meer, Fatima. *Higher than Hope.* Hamish Hamilton, London. 1990.

Meli, Francis. *South Africa Belongs to Us: A History of the ANC.* Zimbabwe Publishing House, Harare. 1988.

Meredith, Martin. *Nelson Mandela. A Biography.* Hamish Hamilton, London. 1997.

Mhlaba, Raymond. *Personal Memoirs – As Narrated to Thembeka Mufamadi.* Human Sciences and Research Council (HSRC) and Robben Island Museum, Cape Town. 2001.

Moss, Glenn and Obery, Ingrid (eds). *South African Review 4.* Ravan Press, Johannesburg. 1987.

Moss, Rose. *Shouting at the Crocodile.* Beacon Press, Boston. 1990.

Mostert, Noël. *Frontiers. The Epic of South Africa's Creation and the Tragedy of the Xhosa People.* Jonathan Cape, London. 1992.

Mqhayi. *The Making of a Servant and Other Poems.* Ophir, Pretoria. 1972.

Mtolo, Bruno. *The Road to the Left.* Drakensberg Press, Durban. 1966.

Naidoo, Indres and Sachs, Albie. *Prisoner 885/63: Island in Chains: Ten Years on Robben Island.* Penguin Books, London. 1982.

Naidoo, Phyllis. *Le Rona Re Batho. An Account of the 1982 Maseru Massacre.* Phyllis Naidoo, Verulam. 1992.

Ndlovu, Sifiso Mxolisi. *The Soweto Uprisings: Counter-memories of June 1976.* Ravan Press, Johannesburg. 1998.

Ntantala, Phyllis. *A Life's Mosaic.* David Philip Publishers, Cape Town. 1992.

Orr, Wendy. *From Biko to Basson.* Contra Press, Saxonwold. 2000.

Peires, JB. *The House of Phalo.* Ravan Press, Johannesburg. 1981.

Phillips, Howard. *"Black October": The Impact of the Spanish Influenza Epidemic of 1918 on South Africa.* Government Printer, Pretoria. 1990.

Plaatjie, Sol. *Native Life in South Africa: Before and Since the European War and the Boer Rebellion.* Ravan Press, Johannesburg. 1982.

Pogrund, Benjamin. *Sobukwe and Apartheid.* Jonathan Ball Publishers, Johannesburg. 1990.

Rantete, Johannes. *The African National Congress and the Negotiated Settlement in South Africa.* J.L. van Schaik, Pretoria. 1998.

Reddy, ES (ed.). *South Africa's freedom struggle: Statements, speeches and articles including correspondence with Mahatma Gandhi of Yusuf Mohamed Dadoo.* Sterling, New Delhi. 1990.

Resha, Maggie. *My Life in the Struggle: Mangoana Tsoata Thipa Ka Bohaleng.* Congress of South African Writers, Johannesburg. 1991.

Roux, Edward. *Time Longer than Rope. The Black Man's Struggle for Freedom in South Africa.* University of Wisconsin Press, Madison. 1964.

Roux, Edward. *S.P. Bunting: A Political Biography.* Mayibuye Books, Bellville. 1993.

Russell, Diana EH. *Lives of Courage: Women for a New South Africa.* Basic Books Inc., New York. 1989.

Sachs, Albie. *The Jail Diary of Albie Sachs.* Paladin Grafton Books, London. 1990.

Sampson, Anthony. *The Treason Cage.* Heinemann, London. 1958.

Sampson, Anthony. *Drum: An African Adventure and Afterwards.* Hodder and Stoughton, London. 1983.

Sampson, Anthony. *Black and Gold. Tycoons, Revolutionaries and Apartheid.* Coronet Books, Hodder and Stoughton, London. 1987.

Sampson, Anthony. *Mandela. The Authorised Biography.* HarperCollins *Publishers*, London. 2000.

Schadeberg, Jürgen (ed.). *Nelson Mandela and the Rise of the ANC.* Jonathan Ball Publishers and Ad Donker, Parklands. 1990.

Schadeberg, Jürgen. *Voices from Robben Island.* Ravan Press, Johannesburg. 1994.

Seekings, Jeremy. *The UDF. A History of the United Democratic Front in South Africa, 1983–1991.* David Philip Publishers, Cape Town; James Currey, Oxford and Ohio University Press, Athens, Ohio. 2000.

Shubin, Vladimir. *ANC: A View from Moscow.* Mayibuye Books, Bellville. 1999.

Sikhakhane, Joyce. *A Window on Soweto.* IDAF, London. 1977.

Simons, HJ and Simons, RE. *Class and Colour in South Africa 1850–1950.* Penguin African Library, Harmondsworth. 1969.

Slovo, Joe. *The Unfinished Autobiography*. Ravan Press, Randburg and Hodder and Stoughton, London. 1995.

Smith, Charlene. *Robben Island*. Struik Publishers, Cape Town. 1997.

South African Institute of Race Relations. *Race Relations Survey*. Johannesburg. 1960–1990.

Sparks, Allister. *The Mind of South Africa*. Heinemann, London. 1990.

Sparks, Allister. *Tomorrow is Another Country. The Inside Story of South Africa's Negotiated Revolution*. Struik, Cape Town. 1995.

Suttner, Raymond and Cronin, Jeremy. *30 years of the Freedom Charter*. Ravan Press, Johannesburg. 1986.

Suzman, Helen. *In No Uncertain Terms. Memoirs*. Jonathan Ball Publishers, Johannesburg. 1994.

Truth and Reconciliation Commission. *Truth and Reconciliation Commission Report*, Vol. 3. Juta Publishers, Cape Town. 1998.

Unterhalter, Elaine. *Forced Removal. The Division, Segregation and Control of the People of South Africa*. IDAF, London. 1987.

Unterhalter, Elaine et al. (ed.). *Apartheid Education and Popular Struggles*. Ravan Press, Johannesburg. 1991.

Vadi, Ismail. *The Congress of the People and the Freedom Charter Campaign*. Sterling Publishers Private Limited, New Delhi. 1995.

Van Kessel, Ineke. *Beyond Our Wildest Dreams: The United Democratic Front and the Transformation of South Africa*. University Press of Virginia, Charlottesville. 2000.

Van Onselen, Charles. *The Seed Is Mine. The Life of Kas Maine, a South African Sharecropper, 1894–1985*. David Philip Publishers, Cape Town. 1997.

Villa-Vicencio, Charles and Niehaus, Carl (eds). *Many Cultures, One Nation. Festschrift for Beyers Naudé*. Human and Rousseau, Cape Town. 1995.

Waldmeir, Patti. *Anatomy of a Miracle: The End of Apartheid and the Birth of the New South Africa*. Viking, London. 1997.

Walker, Cheryl. *Women and Resistance in South Africa*. Onyx Press, London. 1982.

Walshe, Peter. *Black Nationalism in South Africa: A Short History*. Spro-Cas Publication: Ravan Press. 1973.

Wells, Julia C. *We Now Demand! The History of Women's Resistance to Pass Laws in South Africa*. Witwatersrand University Press, Johannesburg. 1993.

Welsh, Frank. *A History of South Africa*. HarperCollins*Publishers*, London. 1998.

Willan, Brian. *Sol Plaatjie: A Biography*. Ravan Press, Johannesburg. 1984.

Wolpe, Annmarie. *A Long Way From Home*. David Philip Publishers, Cape Town. 1994.

Woods, Donald. *Biko*. Paddington Press, London. 1978.

Wright, Richard. *Black Boy (American Hunger)*. HarperPerennial, New York. 1993.

Zwelonke, DM. *Robben Island*. Heinemann African Writers Series, London. 1973.

**D. WEBSITES**

http://www.anc.org.za
http://www.truth.org.za
http://www.sahistory.org.za

**E. DOCUMENTARY FILMS**

Lipman, Beata (Producer and director) for SABC1. *Walter Sisulu – Father of the Nation*. 1996.

Schadeberg Film Company. *Robben Island*. 1992.

Talent Consortium. Patsanza, Miriam (producer) and Matshikiza, John (director). *Walter Sisulu*. 1993.

# INDEX